D1564594

Bellini

Life, Times, Music

1801 – 1835

Printed in the United Kingdom by Biddles Ltd, Surrey

Published by Sanctuary Publishing Limited, Sanctuary House, 45-53 Sinclair Road, London W14 0NS, United Kingdom

www.sanctuarypublishing.com

Photographs courtesy of Museo Civico Belliniano, Catania; Museo Teatrale alla Scala (and Biblioteca Livia Simoni); Teatro alla Scala/Erio Piccagliani; Museo Correr, Venice; Conservatorio di Musica, Naples; Teatro Carlo Felice, Genoa; Biblioteca Comunale, Palermo; Dr RL Copeman; Victoria and Albert Theatre Museum; Teatro Massimo, Palermo; Teatro Massimo Bellini, Catania/Consoli; Teatro Comunale, Florence/Locchi; Teatro La Fenice, Venice/Giacomelli. Music examples reproduced here courtesy of Ricordi

ISBN: 1-86074-405-2

Bellini
Life, Times, Music
1801 – 1835

STELIOS GALATOPOULOS

"Vincenzo Bellini". Oil portrait by Carlo Arienti.
(Before April 1827)

To all my family and friends
&
For Maria Callas and Tullio Serafin

Contents

Preface and Acknowledgements

My earliest conscious encounter with Bellini's music was his last opera, *I Puritani*, at La Fenice, Venice. I was then in my teens and previously I had seen only *La traviata* at the theatre, a concert performance of *Aïda*, a few operettas, some operatic cinema film and heard a few 78rpm opera records.

Although Bellini's music cast a certain spell on me from the beginning, I was unable to hear more of his music for the next few years because his operas were then seldom performed. Not only was there a shortage of suitable singers but Bellini's music, as well as Donizetti's, was at that period rather generally regarded as almost disreputable. Nevertheless, this unjustified attitude was at the same time redeemed by some veiled, abiding feeling that the appreciation and value of this type of music was not really heard in a fair perspective.

This fair perspective was fortunately to come about before too long. The advent of Maria Callas – an artist of genius who understood the highly individual Bellinian style (different to Rossini's or Donizetti's), which she adapted to contemporary sensibilities, together with the eminent conductor Tullio Serafin – brought a renaissance of this music and, in turn, of other music of this period, the Ottocento. The repertoire was expanded and several singers and conductors followed the way in which Callas and Serafin so auspiciously opened.

After my experience with *I Puritani*, my interest turned to Verdi, Puccini and other composers. At the same time, I began to educate myself in opera and classical music and attend performances and listen to recordings whenever my university studies permitted.

It was a performance of *Norma* at Covent Garden, London, in 1952 (with Callas in the title role) that brought Bellini back to my life. Bellini emerged as a lyrico-dramatic composer of stature. His music, deceptively simple on paper, is bound with the words, enhancing them with an abstract dimension that raises opera to high art. Subsequently, with performances of *La sonnambula*,

I Capuleti e i Montecchi, *La Straniera* and *Beatrice di Tenda*, the continuing efforts of eminent scholars, conductors, singers and producers and the availability of several recordings, Bellini's canon was rebuilt.

By the late 1960s, I became a music critic and also began to write articles and books. Except for *Adelson e Salvini*, Bellini's student work, I saw all his operas in the theatre. However, my interest went beyond the enjoyment of his works and the writing of articles and reviews about them. I embarked on serious research for a biography of the composer. This research took me to Catania (Bellini's birthplace), several other places in Italy, London and Paris, where Bellini wrote his final opera, *I Puritani*.

At some fairly advanced stage in my labours, a lecturer's transitory statement that a biographer should capture and amalgamate the life and work of his subject remained in my mind. When Richard Ellmann's celebrated biography *Oscar Wilde* dealt with both the life and the work of his subject, I was convinced that this was the right course to take. Further considerations also persuaded me to cover the period as well, if I had any aspirations of producing a definitive work.

Bellini: Life, Times, Music has been long in gestation, perhaps too long, but apart from crucial new material that sometimes would alter substantially the conception of the work, I needed time to reflect on my subject and accept objectively his shortcomings as well as his achievements. However, before this book was completed, I produced another biography, *Maria Callas: Sacred Monster*, in which the life and work of the subject are viewed as inseparable aspects. Both books were written with the same dedicated quest.

The people who have helped with the long preparation of this book are many. Professore Francesco Pastura, long-time director of the Museo Belliniano in Catania and a pioneer in researching Bellini's life, helped me with important information and made it possible for me to acquire appropriate illustrations for my as-yet-unwritten book. Of even greater importance was Pastura's enthusiasm and ability to inspire one as young and inexperienced as I was at the time. Unfortunately, my acquaintanceship with him was rather short; I was able to go to Catania only two more times before he died, in 1969. However, the Museo remained helpful under Pastura's successor, Padre Don Giusúe Chisari, who died in 2001. My appreciation also extends to signor Giovanni Pappalardo.

I was fortunate in knowing Callas and Serafin personally. In addition to Callas's performances – always a unique experience – I benefited greatly from musical discussions with her. It was amazing how well versed she was, musicologically, and with perception she demonstrated vocally and on the piano many facets of Bellini's style. Her psychological analysis of Bellini's heroines, especially those that she had portrayed – Norma, Amina, Elvira, Imogene – was equally enlightening and fascinating. With Serafin, it was rather different; like a patient grandfather, he always answered concisely my numerous questions.

Afterwards, when I began to put information together, professoressa Anna Mondolfi and professore Terenzio Gargiulo of the Naples Conservatorio (where Bellini studied) gave me their undivided attention and guided me to sources of essential information, even providing me with unpublished letters and some music.

Following the Naples Conservatorio, I sought help from the illustrious Casa Ricordi of Milan. From the beginning, signora Luciana Pestalozza went out of her way to help me with important information, some of which is only to be found in the unique Ricordi Archivio. Moreover, not only could I quote some music examples from their published scores, but also signora Pestalozza corrected and completed in her own writing my compilation of the list of Bellini's works. My thanks also extend to signorina Renata Vercesi of Ricordi, who was always ready to offer her help. I feel permanently placed in Ricordi's debt, as I do towards the Museo Teatrale alla Scala (and the Biblioteca Livia Simoni) and to La Scala itself.

My association with the Museo Teatrale began many years ago. The wealth of documentary information and the exceptional and rare illustrations that I bought from them, which included Sanquirico's stage designs and also pictures of singers who created roles in Bellini's operas, have enhanced my book considerably. I am forever grateful to Maestro Tintori, the director of the Museo, and to his right-hand man, signor Lorenzo Siliotto, who often gave a great deal of his time in tracing appropriate material for this book. Alas, both of these gentlemen are now dead.

I am equally thankful to the Museo Correr, Venice, where I discovered Bagnara's original, hitherto-unknown, stage designs for *I Capuleti e i Montecchi* and *Beatrice di Tenda* and bought copies to include for the first time here.

Dottore Pierluigi Pizzocaro of Milan has been of particular assistance for many years. He ran useful, often crucial errands for me and also helped constructively in translating Bellini's difficult letters, documents and reviews and maintaining something of their individual flavour.

The late Dr Roy Jesson, a fine musician and scholar, also helped me with my translations and kept a vigilant eye on the progress of my manuscript, rescuing me on occasion from exaggeration. Similarly, the late Harold Rosenthal, founder editor of *Opera* magazine and an excellent chronicler with an amazing filing system, put me on course a few times.

A long telephone conversation with Andrew Porter sometime in the 1970s enabled me to put things in a better perspective and convinced me that there were also other ways to analyse the music of an opera. Nevertheless, it was his scholarly yet succinct reviews that taught me a great deal about the style of the Ottocento. So, too, in a different approach, did the enlightened writings of Dr Friedrich Lippmann. Also, my lengthy conversations with professore Massimo Bogianckino, ex-director of the Spoletto Festival and later of La Scala and other theatres, undoubtedly widened my horizons.

Walter Talevi of Rome, art historian and translator, spent many fruitful hours with me in Italian libraries and theatres. Frank Ellement of New York, R Ralphs of Wimbledon, London, and Daisy Lilley and Sandra Cipriani, both of London, also helped with translations.

From Erio Piccagliani, for many years the photographer of La Scala, I was able to buy excellent photographs for this book. Sadly, he died several years ago and his photographs are no longer available. My thanks also extend to Nino Costa.

Among librarians – that special breed of people so necessary to a writer – who helped me, A Sopher, ex-head of Music Services, Westminster City Libraries, provided me with basic material at the beginning of my research. So too did Dr MA Baird, ex-music librarian of London University, who obtained rare Bellini scores and useful books for me, and patiently discussed several aspects of my manuscript. I owe even a greater debt to R Howard Wright, former music librarian, Borough of Richmond-upon-Thames. His enormous help over many years ended with his premature death in 2001. In addition to his extraordinary ability in tracing rare publications, he had exceptional editorial aptitude and I was fortunate to have known him. My debt also extends to Vivian Liff and George Stuart, who most generously let me use their unique record collection and library, the *Stuart-Liff*.

Both Dr Stanley Sadie (editor of *Grove New Dictionary of Music and Musicians*) and Nicolas Slonimsky (editor of the American publication *Baker's Dictionary of Musicians*) read the manuscript of *Bellini*. Their reports encouraged me greatly. My gratitude is inestimable.

Without the enormous help, encouragement and friendship that I was so fortunate to receive from so many people, I might never have completed the book that became so great a part of my life.

Stelios Galatopoulos
Richmond, Surrey, 2002

1

Beginnings – Catania (1801-19)

Anecdotal biographies do not usually command much trust when unsupported by documentary evidence – a reasonable observation, provided it is not taken to extremes, as there are rarely sufficient documents to illuminate all phases of a great man's life, particularly his early years. Under such circumstances, even legends are useful, as long as account is taken of the number of documents and the quality of the legends. There are many anecdotes and legends about Vincenzo Bellini's early years but only one document. In the Museo Belliniano in Catania – which is in fact the house in which he was born – there is the only known source, a short manuscript amounting to twelve handwritten pages which give details of Bellini's childhood. The manuscript is anonymous and undated. Grammatical mistakes, together with immature sentence construction, suggest that the author was someone young and not fully educated but yet who had been an eyewitness to at least some of the events described. It could easily have been a younger brother or sister, or a close friend of the family, who felt compelled to keep a record of the earliest years of a much-admired and promising brother, possibly after Bellini had left Catania at the age of 17 and a half to further his studies at the Conservatorio di San Sebastiano in Naples.

The possibility that this manuscript was expressly prepared for the instruction of some biographer is remote. Filippo Gerardi, who published his 24-page *Biografia di Vincenzo Bellini* in 1835, a few weeks after the composer's death, seemed not to have been aware of the anonymous manuscript and, in fact, wrongly gives his subject's date of birth as 28 November 1804 – out by three years. Other early biographers[1] – Filippo Cicconetti (1859), Coco Zanghi (1876), Michele Scherillo (1880s) – not only used the anonymous manuscript (albeit much too late for the manuscript to have been expressly prepared for them) but also added their own uncorroborated contributions to these documented fables so that, in time, they became more or less accepted as fact. Most of the stories obviously emanated from the imagination of the Catanese, who in later years, when Bellini became the most celebrated Italian operatic composer of his time, effortlessly added to the legend of their illustrious compatriot.

It will therefore be prudent to recount the information as given in the manuscript, ignoring as far as possible unsupported embroidery. But before quoting the anonymous author, the origins of the family must be traced.

Vincenzo Tobia Nicola Bellini, the composer's grandfather, was not a Catanese. He was born on 12 May 1744 in the mountain village of Torricella Peligna in the Abruzzi, central Italy. It was at Torricella that the family was first registered in as far back as 1660,[2] when Tobia, the composer's great-great-great-grandfather, and his wife, Anna Pacifico, settled there. Their son Rosario had three sons: Carlo, Rosario and Falco. Carlo became a priest and Falco a cleric; Rosario married Francesca Mancini, also of Torricella, and became the father of Vincenzo Tobia Nicola (1744-1829) and Anna Maria. Nothing is known of Rosario's occupation or of any musical talents that he may have had, save for a reputation that he could play the violin. However, it is known that his son, at a very early age, showed a definite inclination towards sacred music – at the age of eleven he entered the Conservatorio di Sant' Onofrio a Capuana in Naples, where he studied under Carlo Cotumacci and Giuseppe Dol[3] and also under Antonio Porpora between 1760 and 1761. During his last year at the conservatorio, in 1765, Vincenzo Tobia became a *maestrino* – an instructor to younger students.

Of Vincenzo Tobia's work at the conservatorio, we know little, except that his oratorio *Isacco figura del Redentore*, with verses by Metastasio, was performed by his fellow students at his graduation. This, like all the music that he may have composed, is lost.[4] In 1767, he moved to Catania, a pleasant, quiet, seaside Sicilian town with a population of about 26,000. The volcanic eruption of Mount Etna in 1669 and the severe earthquake on 11 January 1693, when over 16,000 people perished, practically demolished the Greco-Roman and mediaeval town of Catania, but the Catanese soon rebuilt it and erected the magnificent Benedictine monastery of San Nicolò.[5]

No reason for Vincenzo Tobia's decision to settle in Catania can be found, except that there were many churches, convents and monasteries and several families there, providing work for church musicians. It was the illustrious Biscari family who employed Vincenzo Tobia as *maestro di cappella*. The head of the family was Ignazio Paterno Castello, an intellectual and highly cultured man who housed in his palace a noteworthy museum of ancient art, as well as a little theatre for his young nephew, whose musical education was entrusted to Vincenzo Tobia.

Before long, Vincenzo Tobia established himself as a musician of considerable merit. Of course, he had to work hard for, in addition to his employment with the Biscaris, he was the organist of several churches and gave lessons in music academies and to private students. In whatever spare time he may have had, he devoted himself to composition – his first work in Catania, a drama in the form of an oratorio, *Giosuè vittorioso sopra i cinque re di Canarea*, was first performed in August 1772 during the feast of Sant' Agata.

Seven years after he settled in Catania, Vincenzo Tobia married Michela Burzio, a widow, and two years later they had their first child, a son, whom they named Rosario, after his late grandfather. Four other children followed – Carlo, Pasquale, Anna and Agata[6] – but only Rosario showed an interest in music and took up his father's profession, becoming an organist and music teacher. He, too, composed music for the church, but nothing is known of his works save for a list which has survived accidentally in the local records,[7] although it is known that he was a kind and generous man. In short, Rosario Bellini seems to have made little impact, perhaps because he was overshadowed by his father, a much more dynamic personality. According to Policastro,[8] Rosario was lame in one leg and had to use crutches – a disability that obviously had no effect on his professional life but may have given him a certain inferiority complex.

On 17 January 1791, Rosario Bellini married Agata Ferlito, the daughter of Carmelo Ferlito, a book-keeper, and Giuseppa Cristaldi of Catania. The 23-year-old Agata was beautiful in a way atypical for a Sicilian – she had an abundance of blonde hair, fair skin and very blue eyes.[9] Furthermore, she was cultivated, well read and, although she did not play any instrument, she greatly appreciated music. Like the Bellinis, Agata was not rich, but she had connections with some of the wealthiest and most influential families of Catania. She had two brothers, Francesco and Vincenzo Ferlito.[10]

During the night of 2/3 November 1801, the Bellinis' first child, a boy, was born in their apartment at the Palazzo dei Gravina Cruylas (now the Museo Belliniano) in Via della Corsa, Catania, to which they had moved on their wedding day. On 4 November, the child was christened at the Church of San Francesco Borgia in Catania and given the name of his grandfather, Vincenzo. His other names were Salvatore (the name of the priest who had baptised him), Carmelo and Francesco (the names of his maternal grandfather and uncle, who was also his godfather).

According to the anonymous author of the manuscript, the Bellinis' first-born was breast-fed by a wet-nurse who, however, returned to her lover after six months. For more than three months thereafter, "the infant was fed on fish, as he refused any other wet-nurse's milk".

Apart from such charming irrelevancies, the manuscript mainly concentrates on the child's talent for music, which was apparently evident from a very early age. At first, he showed this by responding greatly to rhythm in music and indicating by his expression the effect that music had on him. "When he was hardly one year old, the child, using music paper for a baton, tried to imitate his father conducting." Also, if he heard any music, he would immediately leave off whatever he was doing, even his food, and insist on being taken to where the music was being performed. Then, "at the age of 18 months, and accompanied by his father, he sang beautifully an aria by Fioravanti".[11] This event may have taken place during a family celebration for the birth of his parents' second child, Carmelo.[12]

Because of this extraordinary accomplishment and the musical precocity that Vincenzo (at home he was called by the nickname Nzudduzzu, a diminutive of the Sicilian dialectical Nzuddu, for Vincenzullo) appeared to possess, Rosario decided to commence his education, both scholastic and musical, at the age of two. The delicately beautiful child was ardent and full of vitality but also, on occasion, unexpectedly aggressive. However, he got on well "with his first teacher, the priest Antonio Neri,[13] who apparently tried to teach him to read and write, while his father gave him practical instruction in the theory of music". We are further informed that, at the age of four, Vincenzo began to understand the technique of musical instruments and to show that his memory – for music, at least – was remarkable. His impetuous character became more pronounced and he was hardly ever absent from the side of his grandfather when he conducted music (usually his own) in churches.

Recording Bellini's first public appearance, the anonymous author says that "one evening (probably in 1805) when Vincenzo Tobia was conducting a large orchestra at the Church of the Cappuccini (the Capuchin Fathers often organised such manifestations in which dilettantes also took part without remuneration), little Vincenzo – who was by his side, having worked himself up to such enthusiasm – began to cry, demanding to be allowed to conduct the orchestra himself. To please him, the grandfather gave in and let him have the paper that had the measures on and his baton. The child at once began to conduct so expertly that everybody was amazed – particularly the Capuchin Father Luigi Monte, who was moved to tears."

Moreover, the anonymous author asserts that "Bellini (who was little more than five years old) had acquired admirable powers of execution on the piano" and follows with details of the performance of the child's first example of his talent, at about the age of six – his musical composition on the words "gallus cantavit"[14] (relating how St Peter would deny Christ thrice before the cock crew), which were explained to him. The little piece (not a proper motet) "for soprano voice, and dedicated to his Italian-language teacher, the canon Francesco Furci", was in all probability incorporated by Furci either into the service of Palm Sunday or the Thursday of the Holy Week.

Within a year of this event, at the age of seven, Bellini began to take lessons in Latin from the canon of the cathedral, Don Francesco Strano, who was also the librarian of the University of Studies in Catania. After two or three months of studying Latin, "Bellini composed two *Tantum ergo*s, one for tenor voice with clarinet obbligato – played by a dilettante, Giuseppe Pizzarelli – performed in the Church of San Michele, belonging to the Minorite Fathers, which made a great impression; the other was performed at the Church of the Monastero della Trinità."[15]

A little later, "Bellini produced a third composition [unspecified] which so amazed his grandfather that he told him, 'If you study, I will give you lessons three times a week.'"

At this stage, the anonymous author again shifts his attention to young Bellini's scholastic studies by giving a list of the subjects that he apparently read: "When he was ten, he took up philosophy with Don Giuseppe La Rosa, a canon of the cathedral; French with Don Francesco Furci; Greek with Don Sebastiano Castonrina; and English with Don Carmelo Platania, a doctor of medicine and lecturer at the University of Catania."

The author then returns to music, obviously referring to the period between 1808 and 1814, when, at the age of seven, Bellini began to take lessons from his grandfather. He "composed masses, three *salve* (*regina*) and some ariette with both Italian and Sicilian words".

Other accounts given by the author about Bellini's early years include the occasion when he played a famous organ: "One day [probably at the age of ten], accompanied by his schoolfriends, Bellini went to play the organ at the Church of the Benedettini. His friends declared that he was incapable of it. He answered, 'I bet you some sweets that I can play it.' They then went into the church and asked a brother to allow him to play the organ. Bellini climbed up onto the organ, but he was too small to manage the pedals. The organ had five banks of keys and he asked his friends to play on the keyboards from the sides, under his direction. When some of the church fathers (a few of whom were pupils of Rosario) enquired who was playing, the brothers told them that it was a stranger. On discovering the little Bellini, the fathers were amazed and offered to give him musical instruction."

The nine *Versetti da cantarsi il Venerdi Santo* for two tenors and organ, composed by Bellini when he was 14, have been described by Pastura,[16] who discovered the autograph manuscript: "Eight of the *versetti* are to texts by Metastasio, while the ninth is written to a Biblical text in Latin containing the phrase, 'Jesus autem emissa voce magna expirabit' – typical 18th-century ariette demonstrating the influence of Vincenzo Tobia, who remained true to the teachings of the Naples Conservatorio half a century earlier."

The sensitivity of young Bellini's character is displayed in various undocumented anecdotes. We know from his brother[17] that he was superstitious, hypersensitive, impulsive and no doubt lived on his nerves a great deal. His great sensitivity was evident from a very early age. Once, when he saw a woman in tears being led by two guards to the police station, his immediate reaction was to start shouting and crying at the guards in defence of the woman, asking them to set her free. We also know, from Bellini's youngest sister, Maria,[18] of the touching episode when one day the young Vincenzo saw from the window of his house two little boys standing outside in the rain. He brought them into the house and gave them his food. Eventually, when his parents took command of the situation and found out that the two boys were orphans whose only relative was a poor grandmother somewhere in Catania, Vincenzo's first thought was that the two boys should stay and live permanently with him and share his belongings. In the end, when his grandfather had taken the boys to the local orphanage and, with a certain relief, declared that he was glad to have had them taken off his hands, Vincenzo said, "But you feel much happier now, after what you have done."

Another composition appeared when Bellini was twelve. This was a song for mezzo-soprano and piano, "La farfalletta", which, according to Agostino Gallo,[19] was performed at Palermo during the visit of the Russian royal family in 1845-6. This is Bellini's first song to have survived, but its authenticity is questionable. Writing in *L'Olivuzza* (Palermo, 1846), Gallo related how the song came to be composed:

> Even at so tender an age as twelve years old, Bellini was a "little" man, somewhat thin but tall and well formed. There was nothing boyish about him except for the enormous charm of his pink-and-white complexion, sparsely lined with very fine veins, and the blond hair which, like golden curly threads, fell in waves to his cheeks and shoulders...
>
> One of their neighbours, Marietta Politi [at the time about eight years old], the daughter of a respectable gentleman, was receiving musical instruction from Vincenzo's father... He took his son to Marietta's home so that her parents could see his progress in music ... The children fell in love and, in response to Bellini's suggestion, Marietta's father had a little puppet theatre made for her while her brother wrote a little farce, with a song and an intermezzo for her girl doll. The brother, being aware of his sister's fondness for the boy, and more as a joke than otherwise, alluded to her infatuation in the verses he provided for her doll... Vincenzo wrote melodies...

One of the songs that Bellini wrote for Marietta was "La farfalletta" and Gallo published it,[20] claiming that he had acquired the manuscript from the heirs in Catania.

1812 saw the beginning of a period of economic crises and, as with the majority of the Catanese, the consequent depression seriously affected the Bellini family. Rosario had to work hard to keep his large family of six children, which became even larger with the birth of Maria in 1813. Bellini's grandfather lived alone on the money from the music lessons that he gave and a pension provided by the Biscari family. During the following year, the Bellini family decided to move to a more economical house near that of the grandfather, and as Vincenzo was the favourite grandson, he went to live with him. Vincenzo was still studying music with his grandfather, and by moving in with him he could also help with the private music lessons. In this way, Vincenzo Tobia helped his son financially, as Rosario thus had one less child to keep.

Again, this is a rather obscure period in the affairs of the family. The little we know is that, before Bellini moved to his grandfather's house, he composed another mass, which was performed on a feast day in the monastery of San Benedetto. A year later, he followed it with a group of eight verses, which were sung after the sermon on Good Friday at the Church of San Nicolò l'Arena. Only some fragments of this music have survived, and from them we can see that it was written for two tenors with organ accompaniment. There is intensity in the melody and a moving melancholy in the vocal parts that rises to a dramatic *crescendo*, expressing anguish and fatalism.

Thus far, Bellini had been considered merely a precocious child, but now his ability to achieve dramatic expression in his music, along with his constantly developing technique, caused his grandfather and father to look upon him with great hope and expectation.

At one point in 1816, the anonymous author recorded an isolated statement: "Bellini enrolled at the university for a three-year course in medicine. To his parents' remark, 'Why waste this time?' he answered, 'To take up a profession.'" Commenting on this far-fetched statement, Weinstock[21] wrote, "Confusion almost certainly entered the mind of the anonymous writer because Carmelo Platania, who was said to have taught the child English, was a professor of medicine." But Bellini never learned English. Writing to Florimo[22] in 1833 from London, Bellini said that he did not understand even a syllable of the English language.

Nothing else is known about the three-year course in medicine except that years later, in letters to Florimo and Giuditta Turina, his lover, Bellini proffered certain medicinal remedies. The most probable explanation, however, was given by Pastura,[23] who pointed out that Platania was a family friend of the Bellinis and young Vincenzo may have attended some of his lectures as a listener rather than as a regular student. It must also be mentioned that, at the generally critical age of 16, Bellini may have worried about his future. Undoubtedly, he loved music more than anything else and wanted to be a composer, but at the time the uncertainties and insecurity of this profession, which were evident to him from the examples of his father and grandfather, made him think of adopting safeguards. In this frame of mind, the young man may well have declared on the spur of the moment that he would study medicine.

It is also interesting to quote Pastura's observations about Bellini's general education:[24] "The adult had no knowledge of the English language, spoke

French badly... He did not seem to have profited much from Furci's classes in the Italian language and the whole Bellini *epistolario* shows no sign of any Greek... Of philosophy, he had only that of common sense, an atavistic inheritance from the millenary experience of the Sicilian people... In literary matters, Bellini was not uncultivated; his culture – disorderly, perhaps, but his own – was acquired more by intuition than by study, assimilated more through his sensibility than through his intellect." Nevertheless, whatever else Bellini may have done, the anonymous author claims that in Catania he even enjoyed a certain fame, as he had impressed the community from a very early age with his musical compositions.

No doubt it was all true in the eyes of the anonymous author, albeit in an exaggerated way. One must be mindful of the way in which parents, relatives and family friends – particularly in Mediterranean countries – are eager to accord a touch of genius to the actions and general behaviour of their children, practically from early infancy. In such a climate, the exaggerations of this author are by and large not particularly extraordinary, but in this case we have to take note of them because the child in question grew up to become a very important operatic composer. The infant may well have sung an aria by Fioravanti, a technically difficult piece of music, but what happened in all probability was that he sang the tune of the aria that he had memorised – a common enough accomplishment, even among very young children. The same applies to the assertion that, when little more than five years old, he played the piano admirably, an accomplishment further enlarged upon by Filippo Cicconetti.[25] In fact, Bellini never really became proficient as a pianist.

The truth of the matter is that his infant compositions and those of his teens undoubtedly prove that he was endowed with musical talent. However, what is not proved is that he was an infant prodigy, which was an accolade bestowed upon him first by his adoring compatriots and then carried forward in more authoritative form by early biographers of this famous romantic composer. One fact that we do know about the young Bellini is that, although well over the required age of admission at the Naples Conservatorio, and as a result of an entrance examination and assessment of his compositions brought from Catania, he was placed in the beginners' class. That he subsequently did well at the conservatorio and, on graduation, also produced a relatively remarkable opera (*Adelson e Salvini*) does not necessarily substantiate claims that he was a prodigy.

During 1816 and 1817, the Bourbon government made radical reforms in the administration of the Kingdom of the Two Sicilies and they appointed Don Stefano Notarbartolo, Duke of Sammartino and Montalbo, as the Intendant of Catania. The Duke arrived in Catania in 1818 with his wife, Donna Eleonora Stradella, and to welcome them the Catanese offered musical performances featuring Bellini as musician, composer and director. It would seem that Bellini immediately made a good impression on the Duchess Eleonora, as he was subsequently often received at her house and also taught her young brother to play the flute.

Vincenzo, who was 17 in that year, already appeared grown up, and his slender appearance, with blond hair and blue eyes (uncommon for a Sicilian), inherited from his mother, lent him a romantic look that was extremely appealing. Although he dressed simply, as the family could not afford much, Vincenzo always appeared elegant, so that people noticed and liked him – a fact of which he was well aware and in which he took pride, sometimes to the point of vanity. He was, however, seized by sudden moods of depression, more often than not without visible reason, just as he had been as a child.

His music – especially a *Scena ed aria di Cerere* for soprano and orchestra; *E nello stringerti a questo core*, an *allegro* in the form of a cabaletta for soprano and orchestra; and *Ombre pacifiche*, a trio for soprano and two tenors accompanied by piano, all of which were written between 1817 and 1818 – was considered beautiful by the aristocratic ladies and dilettantes of Catania, who often invited him to perform his works in their homes. As at that period Catania had no public theatre[26] at which opera or other musical plays could be presented, some secular musical performances were given in the private theatres of wealthy families.

By the beginning of 1819, Bellini had progressed musically to the extent that he found the environment of Catania confining, and his musical studies under his grandfather had reached a point beyond which they could go no further. In the previous year, he had received lessons in counterpoint and his piano technique had improved. His grandfather had taught him all he knew, and there was at that time no music school in Catania. Moreover, his grandfather and father, aware of his talent, became convinced that, if he were to develop further, he would have to leave Catania. The obvious place was Naples, as Vincenzo Tobia already knew.

Naples possessed the most famous conservatorio in Italy and, possibly, the world, but the Bellinis simply could not afford to send Vincenzo there.

After discussing the problem, they concluded that Vincenzo should apply to the City Council (the Decurionato) for a scholarship. Vincenzo prepared his application to the Intendant dell Vallo di Catania and, with the help of the Duchess Eleonora, the application was eventually submitted with a covering letter from the Duke. The date of application is not recorded, but it could well have been 3 May 1819, as it is unlikely that the Duke would have delayed in forwarding it. In his covering letter, he wrote, "Sir, you will present for the Council's decision the enclosed application of Vincenzo Bellini Ferlito, whose request shows praiseworthy inclinations which are not far removed from the City Council's view of the arts."[27]

The manuscript of Bellini's application, which was written in the third person, is not in his handwriting, and Pastura says in his book[28] that it was probably copied neatly for him by his uncle Vincenzo Ferlito, who often helped the family with their letter-writing. The signature on the application, however, is that of Bellini:[29]

Vincenzo Bellini Ferlito, encouraged by his genius and by the example and education he has received from his own people, his grandfather and father, has produced even at his early age some compositions, the merits of which have been applauded by his friends, tolerated by the indifferent and have not been rejected by his competitors.

He wishes to satisfy that desire which he cannot extinguish to go to higher schools so that he will be enlightened by those things that he admires but are beyond his grasp as he does not yet possess the necessary principles of learning.

As his father is without salary or any other regular income and has to support a large family, and his grandfather is in a similar situation, the boy cannot hope to have any help, not even the smallest, of which he has particular need in order to take himself to Naples... As this need is publicly known, and the applicant is grateful for the interest that his own country will be taking in him, he promises to do his utmost to prove [himself] worthy of the public's expectation of him.

Vincenzo Bellini Ferlito.

Two days later, on 5 May 1819, the Council met to discuss Bellini's application. The Prince of Pardo, the Patrician of the City of Catania, was the chairman.

Not everyone in the Council was an admirer of the young composer, and the application provoked much discussion, but as the Patrician read Bellini's application aloud, and as it had been submitted to the Council by no less a person than the Duke himself, their decision was, in the end unanimously in the affirmative, notwithstanding certain reasonable conditions.

The Council replied:

> Today, 5 May 1819, the council met in the town hall… It was agreed to assign to Don Vincenzo Bellini one annual grant to enable him to go to Naples in order to study music.
>
> The council, who recognise the merits of his grandfather and the hard work of his father towards the science of music and also the disposition and brightness of the applicant himself, declared that it was an honour for the community to grant this praiseworthy pupil, Bellini, the requests that he made in his application to start on the third of this month. It was also approved unanimously that 36 onzes[30] were to be given him annually for four years, with the understanding that, after the first year and every six months, a certificate must be obtained from his tutor stating that he has attended his music classes satisfactorily. If he abandons his studies for any reason, he will have to refund the money he has hitherto received. Signed by all present and sealed.

The family was overjoyed at the wonderful news, although they were all upset at having to part from their beloved Vincenzo, especially his mother, as Naples was a long way from Catania, considering the methods of transport then available.

As the grant was effective immediately, Bellini decided to leave for Naples on 5 June, allowing a month to arrange the journey. His mother prepared his clothes while his grandfather spent most of the time available in giving him further musical instruction and helping him to select those ten of his compositions (written between 1817 and 1819) most suited to impress the examiners at the conservatorio. These included masses, *Tantum ergo*s and vocal music for soprano and other voices.[31] Also, the Duke of Sammartino gave two letters of introduction, one addressed to Giovanni Carafa, Duke of Noja, the Intendant of the Naples Conservatorio; the other to General Naselli, the general administrator of the Naples Ministry of the Interior.

Bellini left Catania by mail-coach for Messina, where he spent six pleasant days with his paternal aunt Anna and her husband, Filippo Guerrera. On 14 June, he sailed for Naples, where, after a rough journey, he arrived on 18 June 1819 to commence his life's mission.

2

Naples – *Adelson e Salvini* (1819-25)

In 1806, during the French occupation of Naples, King Giuseppe Napoleone consolidated the two music schools there – the Santa Maria di Loreto and the Pietà dei Turchini – into the Real Collegio di Musica. Two years later, the college was renamed the Conservatorio di San Sebastiano, and at this time it was moved to a more spacious building, formerly the magnificent monastery for the nuns of San Sebastiano. In its new status, the conservatorio ceased to be ecclesiastical and partly charitable; it became a government institution, and its students wore semi-military uniform. Further changes followed in 1826, when the college becoming the Conservatorio di San Pietro a Maiella (the name of the convent to which it was finally moved).

When Bellini became a student at the Conservatorio di San Sebastiano, in 1819, a deeply rooted conservatism infiltrated both the musical curriculum and the method of teaching, generally. All the teachers were former students, rather old and, as self-perpetuating musicians, followed closely the 18th-century musical tradition, specifically that of the Neapolitan School. They were also autonomous in the practical running of their classes, as long as they followed the principles of Nicolò Zingarelli, the musical director. The administrator of the conservatorio was the Duke of Noja, who was also the superintendent of all the royal theatres in Naples.

The education department and, to some extent, the disciplinary jurisdiction of the students was managed by the Reverend Don Gennaro Lambiasi. With the possible exception of the Paris Conservatoire, no other musical institution has produced a more distinguished list of students or professors than the San Pietro a Maiella and the colleges that were united under its name – Alessandro Scarlatti, Francesco Durante, Nicola Porpora, Tommaso Traetta, Niccolò Jommelli, Nicola Piccinni, Giovanni Paisiello, Carlo Coccia and many others were all connected with it at one time or another. In 1819, Saverio Mercadante was a *maestrino* there. (Many years later, he would become the musical director.)

The timetable of lessons was as follows: Monday, Wednesday and Friday for principal subjects and Tuesday and Thursday for singing and instrumental coaching. On Saturday, singers and instrumentalists had lessons together. Five afternoons each week, the students received lessons in basic education. In the hours left free – presumably one afternoon a week – the students participated in the building of a small theatre inside the conservatorio where the best composers could, on graduating, have their works performed. A typical day's work began at 4.45am. At 5.15am, the students were expected to attend early-morning mass before breakfast. Between 6am and 9am, they studied and prepared for lessons, which lasted until noon, when there would be a break for lunch and recreation. An afternoon sleep followed, during the summer months. Then lessons continued from 4pm until 6pm, and again from 8pm until 10pm, when the students would study in their rooms, helped by their *maestrini*. Their days would finish with evening prayers in chapel and then supper.

This was a completely new life for Bellini, as he had never before been in such a big city (Catania had at that time around 36,000 inhabitants, compared to Naples' half a million), and the conservatorio was full of strangers. Although Bellini naturally missed his family, he felt neither uncomfortable nor particularly lonely during his first days in Naples, as his mind was fully occupied by the fact that he still had to qualify for an entrance examination to the conservatorio. In addition, he had to continue to work hard so that the first six-month report to his sponsors in Catania would be satisfactory.

There were technical faults and shortcomings in the ten compositions that Bellini had brought with him as part of the entrance examination, but the board of the conservatorio was sufficiently impressed to accept him – in the beginners' class, rather than in the advanced section, as has often been stated. Even so, the board's decision was quite exceptional because, at the age of 17 and a half, Bellini was well above the customary admission age that the regulations of the conservatorio required. However, he was billeted with the older students.

At the conservatorio, Bellini quickly made several friends with whom he would always remain popular. He struck up an extraordinarily close lifelong friendship with Francesco Florimo. A Calabrian, Florimo came from San Giorgio di Murgetto in the district of Reggio, the neighbouring province of Catania, from which it is separated by the Straits of Messina. At the time that

Bellini arrived, Florimo had already been at the conservatorio for two years. What possibly helped to bring Bellini and Florimo together at the beginning was that they both spoke more or less the same dialect. And if there was little in common in their characters, their differences were complementary and blended well. Florimo, who was a year younger but looked much older than Bellini, was calm and somewhat passive in nature, his outlook neutral without being negative. He used these qualities in such a way that he won Bellini's affection, and even though Florimo's intelligence was little above average and his only ambition was to become the archivist at the library of the conservatorio, he was not a dull person.

Bellini reacted towards Florimo with complete devotion, and their friendship – which was mutually frank and honest – never seriously wavered. Several years later, when Bellini had become famous, he wrote to Florimo, telling him that he was the only friend in whom he could find comfort. If ever they had a disagreement during their years at the conservatorio, it was always Bellini who took the first step in breaking the ice to resume the friendship. On the other hand, Florimo was not insensitive in such cases and would respond with all the warmth and understanding expected of a good friend. Perhaps the most significant quality that Bellini found in Florimo – at the beginning of their friendship, at least – was a certain security that stabilised any conflicting impulses that he found in himself.

Thus Bellini soon established himself as a student and settled down happily to life at the conservatorio. The money that he was receiving from Catania was just adequate for his needs, but as he was unused to having many expenses, this did not particularly bother him. Naturally, there were things that he would have liked but, like most students, he simply learned to go without. In a letter to his uncle Guerrera in Messina, dated 31 July 1819, he wrote:[1]

Dearest uncle, my wishes are completely satisfied. You tell me that your family is in the best of health... I thank God that this terrible illness has left you. Only one thing makes me sad and sorry: the fact that Donna Cristina has given up her music. She has a piano that she doesn't use while I would so love to have one here to alleviate my soul. I wanted to buy a cembalo but I couldn't even find one. They make small pianos but they want a most awful price for them, and that cousin of mine has this wonderful instrument for nothing. God sends bread to those who have no mouth. Please tell my aunt that I don't yet know which French "muslins" will be fashionable...

I kiss yours and Aunt Anna's hands affectionately... Remaining now and ever your loving nephew.

Young Bellini's rather artless letter was not without veiled connotations. Anyway, his hope that his uncle might send him the idle instrument remained unfulfilled.

The first six months at the conservatorio went by smoothly. In January 1820, Bellini passed his examinations – in advanced harmony, theory and elements of *partimento* – so successfully that he won an annual scholarship. The Council in Catania was not only satisfied with his success, which confirmed their expectations, but also decided that, as he had won a scholarship, they would give the 36 onzes that they would otherwise have sent to him to his family instead.

In 1820, under the guidance of the secret society known as the Carbonari, the Neapolitans revolted against their Austrian monarch, King Ferdinand I of the Two Sicilies. After a small-scale civil war, the Carbonari demanded a constitution from Ferdinand, who had no choice but to grant it. This came into force on 9 July. The Holy Alliance intervened, determined to restore Ferdinand to his royal powers, and after some fighting the imperial troops entered Naples on 23 March 1821. Ferdinand, who had left Naples a few months earlier, returned to his throne on 15 May.

With the status quo restored, many revolutionaries were arrested, and it was reported to Lambiasi that two of his students, Francesco Florimo and Vincenzo Bellini, were believed to have been involved with the Carbonari. The Minister of Police, at the time busy convicting other dangerous revolutionaries, left the matter with the school authorities. Lambiasi decided to act like a priest rather than as the rector of the college. No doubt he did not consider the activities of the two students serious, as there was strict discipline at the conservatorio. The students had a full day of study and slept in a dormitory, so they could not have gone very far in their political adventures. Lambiasi closed the case after a confession in which absolution was granted, on the condition that Florimo and Bellini publicly proclaimed (and made sure that they were heard and seen to proclaim), "Long live our King Ferdinand, consecrated by God and by Right," which they did on 30 May, at a celebration of the

King's name-day in the San Carlo Theatre. The case may seem to have been unimportant, but if it had been dealt with by the police, rather than left with the far-sighted Lambiasi, it could have meant imprisonment for the young revolutionaries,[2] however superficial and trivial their association with the Carbonari.

Although the effect that incident had on Bellini is unknown, it certainly did not affect his work at the conservatorio. Apart from the excellent results that he produced in his January examination, he sent to Catania a *Messa di gloria* that he had undertaken to write. This composition – for four voices, chorus and orchestra – was performed at the Church of San Francesco d'Assisi in Catania on 14 October 1821, the name-day of the Austrian Emperor. The work impressed the Catanese and confirmed to the council that their scholar was not wasting his time in Naples. Among Bellini's early teachers was Giovanni Furno, who taught harmony and accompaniment. His *maestrino* and tutor was Carlo Conti,[3] but it seems that, at about this time, Bellini moved to the class of Giacomo Tritto.[4] (A *capriccio ossia sinfonia* composed by Bellini during this period bears Tritto's signature.)

In the following May, in 1822, Bellini had an opportunity to meet Gaetano Donizetti (1797-1848), when his opera *La zingara* was performed at the Teatro Nuovo in Naples. Donizetti's first opera, *Enrico di Borgogna*, had been performed in Venice on 14 November 1818 with enough success to launch his career.[5] However, his second opera, *Le nozze in villa* (Mantua, 1820), was such a failure that he retired from the theatre for a year of further study. In January 1822, he scored his first great success with *Zoraide di Granata* at the Teatro Argentina, Rome, which established him – in Italy, at least – as a composer of considerable merit. The success of *La zingara* (with libretto by the Neapolitan Andrea Leone Tottola) created great excitement amongst the students of the conservatorio, as well as their teachers, who were interested to hear the work of an ex-student of the renowned Giovanni Simone Mayr. The manner in which Bellini came to hear *La zingara* and subsequently meet Donizetti is best told in Florimo's words, written more than half a century later:[6]

> Carlo Conti, who had been Bellini's tutor at the conservatorio, said to Bellini and me, "Go and hear Donizetti's *La zingara*, for which my admiration increases with every performance. In that opera, one can

find such musical dialogue and a septet finale of act one that only a pupil of Mayr could have written."

We soon went, and the recitatives, an important part of the opera, captured the imagination of Bellini, who immediately obtained a copy of the score and studied it and played the septet every day – so much so that he remained fixed to the seat of his piano. A short time later, he begged Conti to introduce him to Donizetti. When Bellini returned from the meeting, still full of enthusiasm, he told me, "Apart from the great talent that this Lombard has, he is also a truly beautiful, big man, and his noble countenance – sweet, but at the same time majestic – arouses affection as well as respect."

The meeting with Donizetti was for Bellini a most exciting event. So too was another meeting of a different nature. At one point during December of the same year, Florimo introduced him to a young lady by the name of Maddalena Fumaroli. Apparently, Bellini first saw her accidentally one day, when he was strolling in the town, through a small telescope that he carried with him. He was obviously very much taken by the appearance of the girl and could not believe his luck when Florimo so conveniently happened to know her family. Twenty-year-old Maddalena was the daughter of Francesco Saverio Fumaroli, a well-to-do and much-respected Neapolitan judge. Fumaroli denied nothing to his daughter that would improve her education. The scholar Don Raimondo Guarini, who particularly excelled in poetry, was her teacher in literature, and although she was young, Maddalena was also well versed in other subjects, including music and the art of sketching.

Bellini's courteous manners and likeable disposition soon endeared him to the Fumaroli family. Furthermore, from the beginning, there was a mutual attraction between him and Maddalena. As she was so musical, he offered to give her lessons in singing. The young lady was delighted and Bellini visited the Fumarolis as much as his free time from the conservatorio would permit. It did not take long for what had begun as flirtation between the two young people to blossom into a secret love, primarily expressed during their singing lessons – Bellini through his music, Maddalena through the verses that she wrote.

Apart from his visits to the Fumarolis and an occasional visit to the theatre, Bellini spent the whole of 1823 immersed in his studies. By this time, he had been admitted to the classes of Zingarelli, the director of the conservatorio, and he had to work even harder. Nicolò Zingarelli (1752-1837), a Neapolitan, had studied at the Conservatorio di Santa Maria di Loreto. A contemporary of Cimarosa, he had been a successful composer of both church and operatic music, which was performed all over Italy and widely in most European cities.[7] In 1813, he returned to Naples and took up the directorship of the Conservatorio di San Sebastiano.

Zingarelli was a great teacher. From his experiences in both Italy and abroad, he tried to bring out the best in all his students. From them, he expected discipline and hard work. His philosophy was that they should study theory of music thoroughly and the works of the Classical composers at this stage of their training in order to acquire sound musical background before devoting themselves to composition. He treated Bellini like a son, taking a special interest in his studies, always ready to correct his work and give him valuable advice:[8] "If your compositions 'sing', your music will most certainly please. If, instead, you amass harmonies, double counterpoints, fugues, canons, notes, counternotes, etc, the musicologists may or may not approve of you after half a century. The public, however, will disapprove of you. Therefore, if you train your heart to give you melody and then you set it forth as simply as possible, your success will be assured. You will become a composer. Otherwise, you will end up being a good organist in some village."

Mainly through Zingarelli's encouragement, Bellini discovered Haydn and Mozart, whose music he began to study avidly, particularly the scoring of their respective quartets and quintets. With all this hard work, it is not surprising that, as far as we know, he produced only two compositions during his first year with Zingarelli – a sinfonia and four settings of *Tantum ergo*.

Bellini's musical appreciation was by no means confined to the Classical composers but also extended – even more passionately – to the Neapolitan School. Jomelli and Paisiello were great favourites of his, but most of all he admired Pergolesi. An episode that Florimo was to relate many years later describes the effect that Pergolesi's music had on Bellini.[9] One day, Florimo found Bellini playing the piano in his room, his eyes red from weeping. "It's marvellous," Florimo exclaimed, "but why are you crying?"

"How can I not cry," Bellini replied, "when I contemplate this sublime poem of sorrow [Pergolesi's *Stabat Mater*]? I shall be so happy if, in my life, I have the good fortune to create a melody as tender and passionate as this one. I would like that very much. Then I would be happy to die as young as Pergolesi[10] did."

1824 began auspiciously for Bellini. He did well in his annual examination, and on the strength of this he was made a *primo maestrino*, a position that also meant that he could visit the theatre twice a week.

During the carnival season of 1824, Bellini heard a Rossini opera in the theatre for the first time. After its great success at the Teatro La Fenice, Venice, in the previous winter, *Semiramide* was now having its first performance at the San Carlo, Naples, with Joséphine Fodor-Mainvielle and Luigi Lablache – two of the best singers of the time – as Semiramide and Assur respectively. Apparently, Bellini was unusually quiet during the evening, so impressed was he by the music that he seemed, for once, lost for words. On his way back to the conservatorio, he suddenly exclaimed to Florimo and their companions, "Do you know what I think? After *Semiramide*, it's futile for us to try and achieve anything."[11]

Like most Italians, especially of the younger generation, Bellini was clearly captivated by the music of Rossini. He still liked Donizetti's music, but he put Rossini on a pedestal, referring to him as the greatest composer of the day – the *maestro di maestri*. This was very much against the canon of Zingarelli, who belonged to the previous generation and strongly disapproved of Rossini's music. There were others, to be sure, who shared Zingarelli's opinions, not only in Naples but also in other parts of Italy. As with most innovators, Rossini also had detractors who readily accused him of overloading the vocal line with redundant embellishments and all but destroying the purity of Italian song with Germanic orchestration. They justified their argument by harking back to the Camerata, who based the principles of opera on the musical side of the ancient Greek tragedies. Even so, Rossini, triumphed over all before him (notwithstanding a few inevitable setbacks). By 1822, he became unequivocally the most famous composer in Europe.

Meanwhile, Bellini certainly knew how to deal with his teacher's objections (which were, in any case, short-lived), by often giving in diplomatically, only to repeat the same thing later. Zingarelli also exploded at others, usually his best students, such as Mercadante and the brothers Luigi and Federico Ricci, for he felt that, by imitating Rossini, they were not only harming themselves but, by example, the other students as well. In reality, Zingarelli held Rossini himself responsible for the "ruination" of his students, as he used to say, and once created the opportunity to tell him so to his face. Rossini was invited to a musical function at the conservatorio on the pretext that he would act as one of the adjudicators of the students' works.[12] After showing that he was impressed with what he had heard, Rossini congratulated the young composers and then spoke words of high praise and esteem for Zingarelli, who was, after all, the great teacher of these illustrious students. "My dear maestro," Zingarelli commented in his usual severe manner, "do not try to ruin all my students who imitate you and only you." To this, Rossini promptly answered, "Your dear young musicians, reverent maestro, would not be ruined at all, if they were to imitate you and only you." Having received his answer from the invulnerable Rossini, Zingarelli nodded and said nothing more about it.

Meanwhile, the happy state of Bellini's affair with Maddalena was not to last much longer. Even though most of the friends of the Fumarolis – and certainly Guarini, her tutor – knew of the love affair, Maddalena's parents were completely in the dark. When they did find out, they disapproved and immediately asked Bellini to stop giving their daughter singing lessons, gradually cut down his visits to their house and eventually not to see Maddalena at all. Both Bellini and Maddalena were heartbroken at the Fumarolis' unexpected and cruel decision, but, having no choice in the matter, they pretended to have accepted their plight while privately they swore eternal love and hoped that one day they would overcome all obstacles and marry. For the moment, they contented themselves by writing to each other secretly every day.

It was most probably during this period, when the young lovers were clandestinely communicating with one another, that Bellini composed the aria "Dolente immagine di Fille mia" and the *scena ed aria* "Quando incise su quel marmo" to Maddalena's verses. Her poetry reveals the purity of her soul and the intensity of her passion for Bellini. He in turn expressed the words tenderly through his music, which enjoyed great success with the aristocratic society of Naples. This success pleased Bellini, but he really wanted to compose music that would elevate him from the status of a student to that of a professional composer. Apart from the fact that this was his vocation, he believed that, once he was established, Maddalena's parents would accept him.

An incident later described by Florimo[13] may have helped give Bellini the final incentive to make a name for himself. During the early part of the evening of 4 August 1824, he was in town with Florimo when a carriage passed them by. Realising that the carriage belonged to the Fumarolis, Bellini left Florimo behind and ran after it, finally catching up with it at the Teatro Nuovo, where the carriage stopped. The Fumarolis and their daughter entered the theatre, where Mercadante's *Elisa e Claudio* was to be performed that evening. Bellini only just managed to see Maddalena, but he was seen by her father, who took exception to his daughter being followed by the young man he particularly wanted to prevent her from seeing. The following day, Fumaroli complained about Bellini's behaviour to Lambiasi, who scolded the young man and told him that such undisciplined actions must never be repeated. This must have been hurtful, but Bellini certainly was not going to stop loving Maddalena. On the contrary, more than ever before, he was determined to make a name for himself and win over her father, whom he believed to be his only obstacle.

By the late autumn of 1824, Bellini was hard at work on his first opera. Before that, he had composed a number of *sinfonie* (one in 1823 and the others between 1824 and 1825), which later formed a group of six, and also the cantata *Ismene*, which was performed in 1824 at the wedding of Antonio Naclerio, a friend of Bellini's in Naples.

When Bellini decided to write an opera, he chose the libretto *Adelson e Salvini* by Andrea Leone Tottola.[14] Tottola was not a particularly good librettist; Bellini may have chosen him because he had been the librettist of Donizetti's *La zingara*. Although Zingarelli knew of Bellini's project, he did not help during the composition of the opera in order to ensure that his student would be free to reveal his own personality, but when he heard the work at the last two rehearsals, he did make several suggestions to tidy up the score. The all-male cast was selected from Crescentini's[15] class at the conservatorio. The work, written in three acts with spoken dialogue using the Neapolitan dialect, is a *semi-seria* opera. The comic element is mainly provided by the character of Bonifacio, a *basso buffo*. Not surprisingly, it shows much Rossinian influence, even though Zingarelli did not approve.

It has often been stated that *Adelson e Salvini* was given its first performance in the little theatre at the Conservatorio of San Sebastiano on 12 January 1825.[16] This date seems unlikely, however, according to Pastura.[17] On the night of 4/5 January, King Ferdinand I of the Bourbons died. On 5 January, the *Giornale delle Due Sicilie* published an order that all theatres and places of entertainment should be closed for the next ten days, due to national mourning. The Teatro Nuovo reopened on 15 January and the San Carlo the next day. Bellini's *Adelson e Salvini* was therefore performed at some point between 15 January and 15 March. (We also know this from the movements of Donizetti, who had left Naples for Palermo on 15 March and who was, according to Florimo,[18] present at the first performance.)

Adelson e Salvini was a great success, both with the public and with the teachers at the conservatorio, so much so that it was performed every Sunday for the rest of the year. To crown Bellini's happiness, "At the end of the performance, Donizetti went on to the stage and embraced him and, with tears in his eyes, told him how wonderful he thought the opera was. Full of emotion, Bellini found himself unable to utter a single word. Eventually, he offered his hand to Donizetti, who embraced him again and kissed him." Bellini could hardly contain himself as now, with his present accomplishment, Maddalena would not be refused him, and by this time he was more in love with her than ever. He already saw himself a double victor – once in his first opera and again in his first love – and at only 23 years of age. Feeling quite confident of his decision to ask Maddalena to be his wife, Bellini discussed the matter with Florimo, who did not agree with the proposal. Unlike Bellini, he saw things in their true perspective and tried to prevent his friend from taking such a step, believing that the outcome could only be disappointment and further humiliation.

The young composer may have had success, even triumph, with his first opera, but this was still a student effort and as yet his future was by no means established. Florimo could see clearly that Bellini's success was nowhere near enough to persuade Maddalena's parents to consent to this marriage. It was no use, however, trying to explain this to Bellini. His friend Giuseppe Marsigli, who was Maddalena's teacher in painting and a good friend of her family, acted as his go-between. The Fumarolis saw no fresh grounds for discussion. Their refusal of Bellini still stood.

Florimo's words came true. Bellini chose not to risk further disappointment over his pursuit of Maddalena. His thoughts turned to Catania, his home, and he was overcome with a great longing to see his family. On the day after he learned of the Fumarolis' refusal, he sailed for Sicily.

ADELSON E SALVINI

I *Dramma semi-serio* in three acts. Libretto with spoken dialogue (Bonifacio's lines in Neapolitan dialect) by Andrea Leone Tottola. First performed with an all-male cast (students) at the theatre of the Conservatorio di San Sebastiano, Naples, sometime between 15 January and 15 March 1825.

II *Dramma semi-serio* in two acts. Libretto in Italian (with *recitativo secco* replacing the original spoken dialogue), almost certainly revised by Felice Romani from the first version. First performed (in Domenico De Meo's realisation) at the Teatro Massimo, Catania, in September 1992. Petrika Ionesco designed the stage sets and costumes.

CHARACTERS AND ORIGINAL CASTS		I	II
Nelly, an orphan, Struley's niece	Soprano	Giacinto Marras	Alicia Nafè
Salvini, an Italian painter, Adelson's protégé and close friend	Tenor	Leonardo Perugini	Bradley William
Lord Adelson	Baritone	Antonio Manzi	Fabio Previsti
Fanny, Adelson's ward	Contralto	Unknown	Lucia Rizzi
Struley, a proscript nobleman	Bass	Talamo	Roberto Coviello
Bonifacio, Salvini's Neapolitan servant	Basso comico	Giuseppe Ruggiero	Aurio Tomicich
Geronio, Struley's confidant	Bass	Ciotala	Giancarlo Tosi
Madame Rivers, Adelson's housekeeper and Fanny's governess	Mezzo-soprano	Luigi Rotellini	Eleonora Jankovic

The action takes place on an island castle in Ireland during the 17th century. Nelly is engaged to be married to Lord Adelson. Salvini is staying (together with Bonifacio) as a house-guest at Lord Adelson's island castle, off the coast of Ireland.

ACT I

Fanny is sitting in the park of Adelson's castle, painting a picture, and through art expresses her love for Salvini, her teacher. Madame Rivers and Geronio are awaiting Lord Adelson's return to the island for his marriage to Nelly. Meanwhile, Colonel Struley, banished by the Adelson family (probably for political reasons), has returned to the island, secretly intending to take Nelly from Adelson by whatever method necessary. While Struley is planning his line of action, Bonifacio appears. He does not feel particularly elated, as his brother-in-law in Naples has just warned him by letter to watch out for his enraged creditors, who may catch up with him, even abroad. Bonifacio's extrovert comments on his problem are interrupted by the arrival of Salvini, his master. The young painter is hopelessly in love with Nelly, and whenever he approaches the girl she immediately rejects him. He tells Bonifacio of his grief.

Struley, who has overheard the conversation, uses this knowledge to his own end. He shows Salvini a forged letter, purportedly from Adelson, in which it is claimed that an uncle has forced him to marry a rich girl of noble birth in London. All Salvini has to do is expose Adelson to Nelly. Then he can persuade her to run away with him in a boat already prepared by Struley.

Nelly, alone, muses about her love for Adelson and her joy at his imminent return to marry her. Presently, Salvini appears and, to her surprise, informs her of Adelson's supposed falseness. However, as he is in love with her, he offers himself as a substitute. Horrified, Nelly runs away while Salvini, hearing in the distance Adelson's return, becomes very upset and rushes off.

The scene changes to the courtyard of the castle, where Madame Rivers, Fanny, Geronio, Nelly and the people from the estate greet Adelson, who is very happy to be with his fiancée again.

ACT II

While preparations for the wedding are being made in the grounds of the castle, Struley learns from Geronio of Salvini's hapless confrontation with Nelly. Wasting no time, he orders Geronio to set Nelly's house on fire so that, in the confusion, they can abduct her, together with Salvini, if need be. As they depart, Bonifacio and Nelly appear, discussing Salvini. Bonifacio tells her that it is her great beauty that has caused the susceptible young man to fall in love with her.

Just then, Salvini is seen walking in the park with Adelson, and the pair are engaged in serious conversation. After having unsuccessfully attempted suicide, Salvini now confides his plight to his friend. However, when Adelson hears that Salvini is desperately in love, he assumes that his passion is directed towards Fanny and readily consents to the marriage. Similarly, Salvini is overjoyed, taking it for granted that Adelson means Nelly. But his happiness is soon diminished when, in a meeting with Struley, Geronio and Bonifacio, he is fraudulently led to believe that, although Adelson had married "Milady Arthur", he is nonetheless determined to seduce Nelly. Salvini's unhappiness turns to anger when Adelson subsequently makes it clear that the girl offered to him in marriage is Fanny.

Set on revenge, Salvini tells Nelly that Adelson is already married and urges her to elope with him. She refuses. Having seen Struley back on the island, Nelly strongly suspects that he is behind these machinations to separate her from Adelson.

Wasting no time, Struley and Geronio set fire to Nelly's house. As they are about to carry her off by force, Salvini, realising that Struley has misled him, dashes into the flames to rescue Nelly.

In the ensuing scene (which takes place offstage), Struley fires a pistol at Nelly, while Salvini wounds him and also kills Geronio. At this, Nelly faints and Salvini thinks that he has killed her, too.

Eventually, the inconsolable Salvini appears and begs Adelson to punish him as he deserves. Adelson, who has learned that Nelly is safe and hiding, makes definite arrangements for Salvini's marriage to Fanny. Salvini is too upset to listen, but, when Nelly appears, he begs for forgiveness. He then says that he will be delighted to marry Fanny but that first he must spend a year with his mother in Italy.

Adelson, Salvini, Nelly and Fanny – later joined by Bonifacio and the people from the estate – express their joy and happiness. Only Struley and Geronio (who has not died after all) abstain from the rejoicing.

Tottola's libretto suffers from inept continuity, ill motivation and haphazard plot construction – defects present in many plays of the period. Bellini revised the opera between 1827 and 1829, reducing it from three acts to two, replacing the original spoken dialogue (in Neapolitan dialect) with recitatives in Italian and reallocating the roles (originally taken by male students) to a mixed cast.

According to L Orrey in *Bellini* (London, 1969), Tottola found his source in the three-act drama *Adelson e Salvini* by Prospere Delamare (Théâtre Gaieté, Paris), published in 1803, which itself was an adaptation of François-Thomas de Baculard d'Arnaud's[19] (1718-1805) novella *Adelson et Salvini, Anecdote Anglaise* (Paris, 1772). Tottola's characters Fanny and Bonifacio do not appear in either d'Arnaud's or Delamare's works. In the opera, Fanny provides some vocal balance while the *basso buffo* Bonifacio represents an essential character in Neapolitan works of the period.

The overture, in D major, is in two sections. The first, an *andante maestoso*, is short and repetitive, and if it has no particular individuality and the conception is rather artless, there is a certainty about it that raises it above the level of an experiment by a student-composer – which is precisely what Bellini was at the time. This is even more evident in the longer second section, an *allegro*, which has two contrasting themes. The first is light and lively, Rossinian in structure but not in melody, while the second has more than a touch of melancholy, with its final section (again Rossinian) recalling the overture to *L'Italiana in Algeri*. Although the overture to *Adelson e Salvini* is not, on the whole, very accomplished, its musical structure is nevertheless regular and assured.

The introduction – an ensemble for Fanny, Geronio and Madame Rivers – includes Fanny's short aria "Immagine gradita del ben" ("Beautiful image of my beloved") and very short orchestral and choral passages. It is not a brilliant introduction, but it contains interesting points, such as the descending chromatic passage of the opening and the zest and certain charm of "Immagine gradita", which is in the style of the 18th-century short aria.

The chromatic scale (presumably used to express a particularly sad feeling) is most successful, especially when interrupted by two vigorous chords in the instrumental prelude to "Immagine gradita", creating an effective contrast:

It seems, however, that this use of chromaticism was more by coincidence than intention since, although it occurs again in the opera, it is completely abandoned at the saddest moments, when its use would have been obvious. The student-composer employed this formula because he had heard it rather than because he needed it. The least successful part of the introduction is Geronio's vocal line. Here, the lack of variety in the *tessitura* produces a monotonous effect.

Only three recitatives are with orchestral accompaniment. The rest are in *recitativo secco* style and tend to be rather dull. Even though Bellini never used this style again, he shows that he had at least mastered the art of writing this essentially Italian form of musical speech.

Struley, the noble exile, is a melancholy character, and in his recitative "Geronio ancor non viene!" ("Geronio has not yet arrived!") he expresses his fury and longing for revenge with considerable dramatic force. It is all the more a pity that his ensuing aria, "Io provo un palpito" ("I feel my heart beating"), misfires. There is no trace of bitterness, veiled or otherwise, in this aria, in 6/8 metre, and such disparity between words and music betrays Bellini's lack of experience.

The next scene introduces Bonifacio, Bellini's first and only *buffo* character. His aria "Bonifacio, beccheria qui presente" ("Bonifacio was loitering here") is bright and lively, if not particularly comic. Here, the most comic effect is achieved not through the vocal line, as might be expected, but by clever use of the orchestra. The orchestral movement that accompanies the first half of the aria is based on one short *buffo* motif, but the masterful way in which it is varied gives it great charm and even elegance:

Then suddenly the orchestra introduces another short *buffo* motif, and at once the aria gains further liveliness and interest, so that the vocal line (actually a monotone) appears to be comical of its own accord:

Bellini was content to give his *basso buffo* little more than *parlando* passages throughout the opera. While depriving him of *cantabile* expressive singing, this provides him with many opportunities to comment audibly on the passions of others, as in the next duet, which he sings with Salvini.

A duet from the stage point of view only, musically this amounts to a big aria and cabaletta, with florid development for the tenor and quasi-*parlando* comments from the bass. Salvini's extravagant and rather ridiculous outbursts are punctuated by cynical asides from Bonifacio, to good dramatic effect. The composer was clearly striving for effect in the florid music, much of which remains in a very high *tessitura* and includes high Es and Ds, together with frequent octave leaps to high Cs.

Nelly's romanza "Dopo l'oscuro nembo" ("After the dark cloud"), in F minor, is outstanding. This is the first aria of many in which Bellini expresses simply and movingly the emotions of tender love. It is in two verses, with the vocal line subtly varied in the second, but without virtuosity:

(Second verse with Bellini's own ornamentation)

Every note follows simply and logically, conveying the inward rapture of the character. Even in the final cadenza, on the word "oggetto", Bellini refuses to succumb to rhetorical virtuosity.

In the duet "Felice istante" ("Instantly happy"), there is a touch of the true Bellini in Salvini's elegant opening phrases, with their delicate accompaniment in thirds:

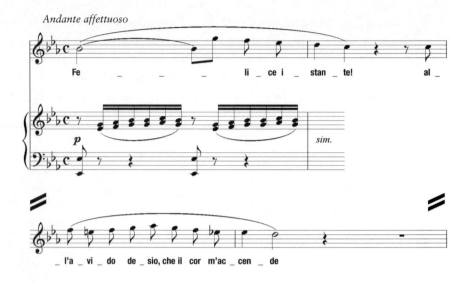

This style is not maintained, however, in the jaunty *allegro giusto* that concludes the duet. Its tub-thumping energy is merely superficially stirring, rather than passionate or moving in any true musical sense. But in the trio "Signorina... Oh, Dio! Vien grate" ("Miss... Oh, God! You are welcome"), when Nelly and Salvini are joined by Bonifacio, the melodies are worthy of Paisiello at his best and foreshadow some of Donizetti's most charming moments (ie *L'elisir d'amore*). The interlocking soprano and tenor lines are combined with typical *parlando* comments from Bonifacio. Both Salvini and Nelly express their feelings in passionate phrases; he pours out his tormented love for her while she is distressed that she cannot respond because of her pledge to Adelson. Bonifacio, who is also worried about his master, Salvini, contributes musically in a completely different style.

The finale to the first act consists of a short pastoral chorus, which is agreeable enough but of no particular interest. Adelson's aria "Obbliarti! Abbandonarti!" ("Forget you! Leave you!"), a short solo, is typically Rossinian but rather monotonous. It leads directly into the duet with Nelly, "Cari accar che mancar" ("A happy opportunity missed"), in thirds. The concerted passage that ends this act is lively and well orchestrated.

Struley's aria with chorus "Ehi! Geronio", which opens the second act, is somewhat austere and much more in keeping with his character than his first-act aria. The chorus merely acts as accompaniment and the text gives information. Only with "La presenza del nemico" ("The presence of an enemy") do the text and the music introduce emotion, and at once Struley's characterisation becomes more important.

If the duet "Poni l'essa a contanto del fuoco" ("Put your bait near the fire") for Nelly and Bonifacio is effective rather than distinguished, that which follows for Adelson and Salvini, "Torna, o caro, questo seno" ("Return, my love, to my breast"), at least begins with an expressive melody of elegant purity, which is taken up in a slightly more decorated form by the tenor. Unfortunately, the totally inappropriate appearance of a chirpy little Rossinian motif puts an end to this moment of elevation, and the final *allegro assai* is in the vulgar and blatant style into which Bellini was, at times, apt to lapse in his duets for male voices.

Bonifacio's second aria, "Taci, attendi, e allor vedrai" ("Silence, wait, and then you will see"), is mostly *parlando*, with the orchestra leading the vocal line. Apart from a *buffo* motif in thirds, the orchestra plays two related vocal themes which Bonifacio partly accompanies. The themes alternate and give the aria a certain lightness (and a shape similar to that of a rondo) which is very much in keeping with Bonifacio's character.

The grand finale brings the work to a very lively finish. Salvini's *moderato assai* "Ecco, signor, la sposa" ("There, sir, is the bride") is the most distinguished number – an essential part of the musical unity, as well as complete in itself. Melodically, it is related to Fanny's "Imagine gradita" in the introduction of the opera. Its text, telling of resolution, is very long, extending to 16 lines – one of the longest ever set to music. Without repeating one word, Bellini set it in the extraordinarily small space of 32 bars.

Far from being a masterpiece, even as a student work, *Adelson e Salvini* was a most auspicious first attempt. Even so, its shortcomings are not difficult to note. The orchestration, although careful and at times remarkable, has occasional lapses, often sounding thin, even for Bellini's type of melodic line. The same applies to the harmony, which is largely unenterprising and occasionally downright crude. Moreover, the majority of the numbers – which are linked either with accompanied recitative or *recitativo secco* – still remain isolated pieces and do not form part of larger complexity. However, as far as melodic invention, simple and well-measured musical construction and theatrical sense are concerned, the opera was a revelation, and where there are larger structures – as in the introduction and the finales, etc – these are very successful.

Apart from his melodic invention, probably Bellini's greatest achievement in his first opera is the way in which his scenes – uneven though they may sometimes be – do not misfire, a common enough fault with many first operas. He evidently had an instinct for music that was suitable for the theatre.

There may be no real originality in *Adelson e Salvini*, but the evidence of a distinct and fairly well-formed individuality cannot be denied. If a great deal of this work belongs to the past, it is not because the composer was unacquainted with the modern trends of opera in his time but because of the demands of Tottola's libretto, which, written in 1815 (and not revised for Bellini), did not allow for complex arias or the substantial use of the chorus. What belongs to the future is the way in which Bellini balanced the arias with an equal number of ensembles. His later revisions were wisely confined to skilful cuts rather than any drastic alteration of the style of the work.

As with many first works, there is in *Adelson e Salvini* a strong influence of personal involvement, more than in any other of Bellini's works. Remembering his unsuccessful love affair with Maddalena Fumaroli at the time, it is not difficult to see why he wrote his heartfelt music for Nelly and Salvini, the love-stricken and unhappy artist, with his generosity and enthusiasm.

The opera is described as a *dramma semi-serio*. This is mainly due to the lightening of the *melodramma* by the *basso buffo* character of Bonifacio. Bellini may not have created a unique character here, but much in Bonifacio's music achieves artless merriment. Strangely, he is not suggestive of the Rossinian *buffo* character but of the 18th-century type, particularly da Ponte's Leporello, Massetto and perhaps Titta in Martin y Soler's *Una cosa rara*.

3

Bianca e Gernando
at the San Carlo (1826)

The journey from Naples to Sicily could not have been a pleasant one. We can only guess what went through Bellini's mind during the few days that this journey required. Most probably, a disappointed and unhappy, even bitter young man was returning home. As far as his career was concerned, he had nothing to be disappointed about, of course. Not only had he graduated with honours from the conservatorio but he had also – and this was of great significance – produced a promising work in *Adelson e Salvini*. However, he had failed in his first adult love affair and the disillusionment permeated his thoughts.

Bellini was obviously in a highly pessimistic frame of mind when he broke his journey in Messina to stay for a few days with his uncle Guerrera. Hearing that the post of choirmaster at the cathedral was vacant, Bellini declared that he would very much like to apply for it and promptly went to see the Duke of Sammartino, who at that time was the Intendant of the town of Messina. The Duke, however, brought him to his senses by reminding him that the community of Catania had made it possible for him to study in Naples and that he was not, after so many years of good work, going to finish up as a choirmaster, a position that was nothing less than suicide for a promising composer.

The matter may not have gone much further. In *Omaggio a Bellini* (1901) Arenaprimo mentions this incident, but the 1908 earthquake in Messina destroyed the city records that would have provided documentary evidence about the filling of the choirmaster's post. In any event, Bellini was not appointed, nor did he ever refer to it again. But in 1828, in a letter to his uncle,[1] he mentions the visit: "Who knows? Probably, in a few years, just like four years ago, I will see my dear uncle, my affectionate aunt and my lovable Cristina again. I live with this hope and I will try to fulfil it on the first convenient occasion."

After a few days in Messina, Bellini went on to Catania to see his parents.

Florimo ignored this visit to Sicily when he later wrote about the events of his friend's life. However, no documentary evidence is needed to imagine the joy and happiness of Bellini's parents in seeing their son after six years. He had left Catania as a promising young musician and he was now returning after having graduated from the most famous conservatorio they knew. Moreover, he had composed an opera that had been successfully performed.

Even more importantly, he was hardly home when wonderful news reached him from Naples that Zingarelli, who had been very impressed with *Adelson e Salvini*, had decided to go all the way towards providing his best student with every scope for advancement. The Teatro San Carlo had in its charter a clause whereby exceptionally promising students could be commissioned to write a cantata or a one-act opera to be performed on a gala evening. Securing the support of the Duke of Noja, who was still governor of the conservatorio and also superintendent of the Neapolitan theatres, Zingarelli determined to make use of the clause for Bellini's benefit. For that year, 1826, the offer stipulated that the work should be ready for performance on 12 January, the day on which Prince Ferdinand's birthday was to be celebrated.

Undoubtedly, Bellini's dormant ambition to write operas must have been reawakened. He accepted the offer at once. Consequently, having stayed with his parents for only six days, he left Catania. A different young man was returning to Naples than the one who had left only a fortnight earlier. On his arrival, he asked to be granted permission to write a two-act *opera seria* for the theatre instead of a cantata or a one-act opera. He felt that this would give him the best chance of employing all of his creative powers. Then, if he was successful, he would have the chance of making a name for himself. Behind all this was still the challenge of winning Maddalena's hand.

With tremendous enthusiasm, Bellini immediately began to think of the opera that he would write, and this time he felt more confident that even Fumaroli would be impressed. He was, after all, commissioned as a professional composer to provide an *opera seria* for the Teatro San Carlo, one of the most famous opera houses in the world – in Italy, second only to La Scala in Milan. Besides, after writing for the San Carlo, he would stand a greater chance of other doors opening for him. This time, Florimo did not disagree with Bellini's renewed hopes and expectations, as far as Maddalena was concerned. In fact, he was quick to foresee that Maddalena could well be a great inspiration in the composition of the opera and sincerely wished to act in any way that would help his friend succeed. Bellini's determination to do his best is further shown in his refusal to accept Tottola – the official poet of the San Carlo at the time – as his librettist. Tottola had been the librettist for *Adelson e Salvini* and Bellini obviously had not been fully satisfied with him as later, in Milan, he made revisions to both the libretto and the music.

Meanwhile, Bellini suggested as librettist Domenico Gilardoni, a young and then unknown poet. Surprisingly, the management of the San Carlo accepted Gilardoni, even though he does not seem to have produced any work of consequence before this time. Nothing very much is known about him either except that he lived in Naples, was about the same age as Bellini and wrote libretti. Although he would never provide Bellini with another libretto, Gilardoni later provided Donizetti with eleven,[2] the most successful of which was for *Il paria*. He died in 1832, with a brief career of only five years behind him.

Gilardoni's talent seems to have been uneven. On occasion, he could be brilliant, especially in his verses, which at their best develop character relations in convincing detail. However, at other times, as in the first scene of Donizetti's *L'esule di Roma*, his verses are ugly and disjointed. His weakest point, however, was plot construction. It is not known how Bellini came to know of Gilardoni or his work, but he must have been impressed by his writing and no doubt felt that he could do better with this new librettist than he did with the rather uninspired (although perhaps more consistent) Tottola.

The libretto that they decided upon was *Bianca e Fernando*, and Bellini may well have chosen it, as it was very popular at the time and it dealt (although in a romanticised fashion) with Sicilian history.[3] It was based on Carlo Roti's[4] play *Bianca e Fernando alla tomba di Carlo IV, duca di Agrigento*, which had been produced with success at the Teatro dei Fiorentini, Naples, and in several other theatres. Even though Gilardoni's libretto deals with events that involved the people's revolution against Filippo, their tyrannical usurper, the Neapolitan censor did not object and asked only that the name Fernando be changed. The name of the reigning King was Francesco, but both the late King and the heir apparent were Ferdinandos. According to Florimo, the censor did not want to risk a comparison with them. Whether or not the censor made other objections, Florimo does not say; by the time he wrote about this, in 1871, he may have forgotten, remembering only the fussiness of the censor, who appeared satisfied with a change from Fernando to Gernando. The opera was consequently announced as *Bianca e Gernando*.

Bellini almost certainly began the composition of *Bianca e Fernando* at some point during the first week of September. He still lived at the conservatorio, and an event that Florimo related later to Michele Scherillo (who mentions it in his book)[5] reveals that the music of *Bianca* was being composed at around this time: "For some days, Bellini was trying very hard to find the motif for Bianca's cabaletta 'Godrà l'alma dolce calma' when one day Mozart's symphony in G minor [K550] was performed at the conservatorio. After Bellini had heard the symphony, he said that he had found the motif and now he must put it on paper; the idea came from the first phrase of the Mozart symphony."

The opera was written expressly for Adelaide Tosi, Giovanni David and Luigi Lablache, three of the best singers of the day. Tosi, the daughter of a well-known lawyer in Milan, had studied with Crescentini. She first made a name for herself in 1822, when she successfully replaced the indisposed Isabella Colbran in the premiere of Rossini's cantata *Il vero omaggio in Verona*. As it turned out, Tosi did not sing in *Bianca e Fernando* at its Neapolitan premiere, although she did appear in the revised version in Genoa in 1828.

David, the son of a very famous tenor from Bergamo, Giacomo David, was primarily a Rossinian tenor possessing an extraordinary range, which extended from the C below the staff to high G. He also did not sing in the Neapolitan *Bianca* but, like Tosi, he did in the second version. From the original cast, only the bass Lablache – then at the beginning of his remarkable career – sang at the premiere.

Lablache, son of a French father and an Irish mother, was born in Naples in 1794. His musical studies at the Naples Conservatorio included singing, piano, violin and violoncello, and it was said that he could have made a successful career in any of these. Endowed with a huge voice and an equally huge but fine physique, he possessed genius and eventually became one of the finest singing actors in the history of opera. Although he was supreme in the tragic roles with which he is generally associated, Lablache was also extremely successful in comic parts – his Dr Bartolo (*Il barbiere di Siviglia*), Dulcamara (*L'elisir d'amore*) and Mozart's Figaro were interpretations of the first rank. Above all, however, his greatest comic portrayal was that of the title role in *Don Pasquale*. Lablache was to create roles in two more Bellini operas, *Zaira* and *I Puritani*. He died in Naples on 23 January 1858.

By the middle of December, Bellini had finished his opera and rehearsals began at the San Carlo. Everything was going smoothly until 9 January, only three days before the gala premiere, when it was officially announced in the *Giornale delle Due Sicilie* that the performance was postponed, by order of the King. The gala evening had been arranged in honour of Prince Ferdinando, whose birthday was on 12 January, but eventually the King felt that there should be no celebration in that year, as it was the first anniversary of his father's death. In fact, the entire royal family left Naples on 10 January for the nearby Demanio di Calvi, where they stayed until 17 March. This unexpected postponement disappointed Bellini, but there was nothing he could do except wait out the five months until his opera was performed, rescheduled now for 30 May, this time on the occasion of the Prince's name-day.

A revival of Rossini's *La donna del lago* filled the evening of 12 January at the San Carlo. For Bellini, the postponement meant more than having to wait. As Tosi and David had been contracted to appear in other theatres during the time of the postponed premiere, they were replaced by Enrichetta Méric-Lalande and Giovanni Battista Rubini. Consequently, the composer had to modify the roles to suit the voices of the newcomers and, of course, conduct full rehearsals again. However, more trials and anxieties were in store for him, practically up until the day of the premiere. On 9 March, the King of Portugal died in Lisbon and King Francesco ordered Court mourning in Naples for two months. This period of mourning had hardly ended when, on 5 May, the royal Princess Gunegonda Dorotea di Sassonia died and a new mourning was ordered – for three weeks, ending on 26 May. In the meantime, during the early part of May, the King suffered attacks of rheumatic fever, and it was only known on 29 May – the day before the announced premiere of *Bianca e Gernando* – that the performance would definitely take place.

During the rehearsals for the opera at the beginning of May, Bellini met the composer Giovanni Pacini, who was at that time the artistic director of the San Carlo, an office that he invariably used for his own ends. On most gala evenings, whether they were at the San Carlo, the Fondo or the Nuovo, an opera by Pacini would more often than not be performed. The son of a couple of travelling singers, Pacini was born in Catania in 1796. After studying, like Rossini and Donizetti, with Padre Stanislao Mattei at the Bologna Liceo, Pacini produced his first opera, *Annetta e Lucinda*, in Vienna in 1813 at the age of 17. Around 80 operas followed.

For reasons unknown, it seems that Bellini did not like Pacini much from the beginning. Maybe he saw through his jealousy and slyness – Bellini was not one to ignore such matters. Pacini, who obviously tried (perhaps too cleverly) to appear generous and helpful to the young composer, even 40 years later, wrote in his *Memorie Artistiche*, "After my *Margherita d'Inghilterra*, I helped with the rehearsals of *Bianca e Gernando*, the second work of dear Bellini."

This cannot be true, as Pacini's *Margherita* was produced six months after *Bianca e Gernando*. He may have made a mistake, of course, confusing *Margherita* with his *Gli ultimi giorni di Pompei*, which was produced in the previous October, seven months before *Bianca*. However, not long after the premiere of Bianca, Pacini showed his ill feelings towards Bellini rather more openly.

Those who helped with the rehearsals of *Bianca e Gernando* were Florimo; Cottrau, a music publisher and a friend of the composer; and Donizetti. As with *Adelson e Salvini*, only during the last rehearsals did Zingarelli come to assist. Donizetti was in Naples at the time, also preparing a new opera, *Elvida*, for another gala performance at the San Carlo on 6 July, as well as staging a revised version of his *L'ajo nell' imbarazzo*, to be given under the title *Don Gregorio* at the Teatro Nuovo. Reporting his impressions of *Bianca e Gernando* to his teacher Simone Mayr, Donizetti wrote that "Our Bellini's *Bianca e Gernando*[6] (not *Fernando*, which is naughty) will be performed this evening at the San Carlo. It is beautiful, beautiful, beautiful, especially as it is his first opera. Unfortunately, it's too beautiful, as I shall find out with my opera in 15 days' time."

Bianca e Gernando was successfully produced on 30 May 1826 before the royal family and the Neapolitan public. The ballet *Sofronimo e Caritea* was also performed, as it was the custom of the period to present a ballet between acts of an opera. The approval of the King no doubt helped the success of the opera, but this success continued with the general public at subsequent performances. Florimo later described the reaction of the King and the public:[7]

The Court of Naples followed the same custom as the Spanish Court, whereby the public was not expected to applaud in the theatre when royalty was present, unless the royal person first gave the signal for applause. At gala evenings, the etiquette was pushed to the point at which new operas or ballets were never applauded. The public had to wait for the second performance, when the Court would not be present, to express their opinion and pass their judgement. In 1819, when Mercadante gave his *Apoteosi d'Ercole* at the San Carlo, Ferdinand I, breaking the old custom, gave the signal for applause in the trio beginning with the words "Non sempre ride amore". In 1826, Francesco I, following the example of his father, did the same with Bellini in the duet between Bianca and Gernando beginning with the words "Deh! fa' che io possa intendere". The public in both cases followed the King's example enthusiastically and both operas enjoyed the most brilliant success.

On 13 June, the *Giornale delle Due Sicilie* published a favourable review of *Bianca*: "Although sometimes the slightly immoderate vivacity of modern music is felt in this score, it is the austere laws of the old music that control Bellini's style. He never sacrifices feeling to meaning, and in our opinion this is a composer's chief virtue. At this stage, we shall not try to compare with other well-known composers. We will merely say that Lablache's aria; the trio of Lablache, Rubini and Manzocchi; the *largo* of the quintet in act one; and the duet between Rubini and Lalande in act two are some of the most laudable pieces of new music heard in recent times at the Teatro Real di San Carlo."

The success of *Bianca e Gernando* extended to 25 performances in its first season. That there were flaws in the work is certain, as Bellini later revised it for presentation in Genoa, but it scored a spectacular success with the Neapolitan public and it was not difficult to foresee that Bellini had a promising future.

However, Pacini,[8] writing many years later, minimises the success of the opera: "*Bianca e Gernando*, the first work of dear Bellini, was a success and, although without enthusiasm, at least it was a happy event, inasmuch as I proposed to Barbaja – and I am not boasting about it – to engage Bellini as the composer for the opera *d'obbligo* at La Scala. Bellini, my well-known fellow citizen, composed *Il pirata*, which was a resounding success, as everybody knows."

Whether Pacini did speak to Barbaja about Bellini is doubtful. Apart from what he wrote, there is no evidence to support the claim, and his subsequent behaviour after Bellini had left Naples reveals a very different Pacini. Whatever the case, Barbaja did eventually engage Bellini for La Scala, but that wasn't until nine months after the advent of *Bianca e Gernando*.

Very little is known of Bellini's professional activities during these nine months, except that he was still staying at the conservatorio, where he may also have continued his duties as a *maestrino* and, no doubt, cherished high hopes of writing his next opera for La Scala or for one of the Neapolitan theatres. It is strange, however, that he does not seem to have composed any music during this rather long period. No evidence exists that he had, and Florimo, who always knew his friend's every move, has nothing to say about this. Admittedly, Florimo was then extremely busy, as at some time in May he had been appointed archivist of the Conservatorio di San Sebastiano, yet he did find time to make a transcription of the score of *Bianca e Gernando* for voice and piano, two copies of which were sent to Bellini's family.

Of course, there is also the question of Maddalena. With the success of *Bianca e Gernando* at the San Carlo, Bellini naturally felt that he was to some extent established as a composer, at least in Naples, and that he would have the chance to compose operas for other theatres. So, more confident than ever, he made another move to approach Maddalena's father. Again, he asked Marsigli to act as his ambassador to the Fumarolis. However, not only was he completely rejected but Fumaroli also returned all the letters that his daughter had received from him, saying finally, "My daughter will never marry a poor piano-banger [*suonatore di cembalo*]." Florimo wrote of this incident:[9] "I remember that Bellini was waiting with me for the answer to his message to the Fumarolis, and one can imagine how anxious he was. He read immediately in his friend's face the terrible answer, even though Marsigli put on a different expression. At the words of his friend, confirming the bad news, I saw him becoming pale and shaking. He recovered his strength, however, and, holding my hand, he assured me that he would try again and win."

The whole affair must have been a great blow to the persistent young man, and it is possible that he fell ill during this period. This would account for his inactivity for at least some of the time. Bellini would never again approach the Fumarolis. On the contrary, a move later came from the Fumarolis themselves.

A letter that Bellini wrote on 19 July 1826 to his cousin Cristina Guerrera[10] throws little light on his plans. In fact, it makes things more puzzling: "You may have heard from the newspapers that, thanks to God, my opera fared well and the public was very pleased with my modest first effort. Through a good friend of mine, my uncle Don Filippo will receive a parcel from me containing material for a dress for my aunt in Catania and three excerpts of music from my opera for you... I don't know whether we will see each other this year, but I believe that it will be difficult for me to leave Naples. For the moment, be satisfied with those excerpts that I've sent you and pray to God that my other *semi-seria* opera – which I will be presenting at the Teatro del Fondo – will be a success. I will send you the most successful excerpts."

It is impossible to know from the letter which opera Bellini had hoped to produce at the Fondo. He could have been referring either to a new work that never materialised or, more likely, to a revised version of *Adelson e Salvini*, with recitatives instead of dialogue. (Manuscripts at the Naples Conservatorio indicate that this score was modified for singers of the Fondo.) In any event, whatever the project was, it proved abortive. The reason why Bellini would not go to Catania during the summer is easier to see – he had hopes of further engagements and he wanted to be on the spot in Naples. None came, however – at least, none that he accepted during that year. But Bellini continued to stay at the conservatorio, which had moved its premises to the more spacious nearby convent of San Pietro a Maiella by September.

Sometime during the end of February or the beginning of March 1827, Barbaja at last made up his mind and offered Bellini a commission to write an opera for La Scala, to be performed in the following autumn. The offer included a monthly salary for the period in which Bellini would be composing the opera, with the stipulation that he would move to Milan.

Domenico Barbaja (1778-1841) was then one of the most incredible and interesting figures in the world of Italian opera and one of the most remarkable impresarios of all time. Although he had practically no education (it was rumoured that he could only write his name), he was extremely intelligent and possessed a shrewdness that more than made up for his illiteracy. He began his career as a cafe waiter in Milan. Fame first came to him through his invention of a mixture of whipped cream with coffee or chocolate known as *barbajata* (today known as *granita di caffè*).

From his invention, Barbaja accumulated his first capital, which, although modest, was sufficient in the hands of an enterprising man to form the foundation of a successful future. This was to come first from speculation in army contracts during the Napoleonic wars and then from the exploitation of the gaming rooms at La Scala, which were used by the audience during the intervals of performances. Before long, his fortune reached huge proportions, enabling him eventually to become the impresario of La Scala. Barbaja knew nothing about music, but what he did know was how to combine a natural flair for business with considerable good taste.

In October 1809, he went to Naples, where he not only managed to obtain a licence from the Bourbon government to operate theatre gaming rooms but was also granted a subsidy. Before long, he became an impresario, and for the next 30 years he controlled the San Carlo and, at various periods, the Fondo and the Nuovo in Naples. During the period 1821-32, he was at the same time impresario of the San Carlo, La Scala[11] and both the Kärntnertortheater and the Theater an der Wien in Vienna.

Several writers have described Barbaja as gross and lacking even the rudiments of decency and honesty. Judging by his portrait, this does not appear to have been the case, and Pacini, whose career benefited considerably from Barbaja's influence, wrote in his memoirs, "With Barbaja, his word was as good as a contract. Where are these honest, solvent impresarios today?" Apart from Bellini and Pacini, other composers wrote operas that were commissioned by Barbaja,[12] including Rossini, Mercadante, Donizetti, Conti, the brothers Ricci and Carl Maria von Weber.

Barbaja's interest in Bellini was explained by Florimo:[13] "It was [Barbaja's] *modus operandi* to commission all promising young graduates of the conservatorio to write operas for the royal theatres, the San Carlo and the Fondo. Barbaja always maintained that, with a small investment, he found among his young recruits the one who would bring him large profits."

Once Bellini was given the contract for an opera at La Scala, he became anxious to go there and left Naples by coach on 5 April. No doubt he thought that, when his opera was over, he would be returning to Naples, as he left all the belongings that he would not need in Milan with Florimo. However, the future had other plans in store for him.

4

Success in Milan, Felice Romani
and *Il pirata* at La Scala (1827)

The coach journey from Naples to Milan took seven days. Equipped with letters of introduction from Zingarelli and in the company of Giovanni Rubini, who was travelling part of the way, Bellini set off full of ambition and hope for his career, if disillusioned over his failure to be accepted by the parents of his beloved Maddalena.

Artistically, conditions in Milan were not much different from those in Naples, except that in Milan – and this meant La Scala – the standards were higher. La Scala represented the Italian art of the theatre at its best and Milan was the centre of theatrical business in Italy. The Milanese public was reputed to be the most critical and the most demanding, expecting always to have the best singers, the most talented composers and, generally, the best of everything. The leading singers seem to have been even more demanding. It was not uncommon for some of them to decide how many arias should be provided by the composer and even where they should occur, regardless of the necessity or dramatic requirement of the plot.

From the time that Bellini arrived in Milan, on 12 April 1827, until the production of his opera *Il pirata* on 27 October, little documentary evidence exists pointing to his activities.[1] One of the letters of introduction that Zingarelli gave to Bellini was addressed to the composer Saverio Mercadante, who was at that time occupied with rehearsals of his opera *Il montanaro*, scheduled to be presented at La Scala on 16 April. Bellini had known of Mercadante's operas in Naples and may even have met him. He certainly met him soon after he arrived in Milan and, probably on his recommendation, took lodgings in Contrada Santa Margherita, which was only a few metres away from La Scala and a place in which artists usually stayed, including Mercadante.

In Milan, through Zingarelli and Mercadante, Bellini presently made two good friends, the elderly couple Francesco and Marianna Pollini. Francesco (1763-1843), born in Ljubljana, had been a student of Mozart in Vienna and, later, of Zingarelli in Milan. An accomplished pianist and small-scale composer, Pollini became the first professor of piano at the Milan Conservatorio, in 1809.[2] In Milan, he married the very musical Marianna, who, although not a professional musician, played the harp and sang well. The Pollinis were old friends of Zingarelli and often introduced his graduates into the musical circles of Milan. Bellini captivated the Pollinis at once and they took him to their hearts like a son. The young composer, a stranger in Milan, found in the Pollinis a second family whose friendship was to last throughout his lifetime.

The librettist of Mercadante's *Il montanaro* was the Genoese Felice Romani (1788-1865). Romani had received a Classical education and had also studied law, but before long he devoted himself to poetry and to writing for the operatic theatre, for which he had a natural talent. His greatest strength lay in the poetic skill with which he was able to create characters; the verses of his libretti always lent themselves to musical treatment, making it possible for the words and the music to form a genuine marriage. Undoubtedly a transitional figure, Romani linked the age of Pietro Metastasio (1698-1782) and Carlo Goldoni (1707-93) with the fully developed Romanticism of Salvatore Cammarano (1801-52) and Francesco Maria Piave (1810-76). Even though he was very attached to the 18th-century poets and Italian Mediaeval and Renaissance literature, he was by nature, temperament and outlook on life a Romantic. In his book *Felice Romani* (Rome, 1965), Mario Rinaldi described Romani as "a Classical writer who became a Romantic without knowing it".

Although his contemporary Jacopo Ferretti (1784-1852) also wrote libretti[3] distinguished for their literary taste and sharp social comment, it is Romani who represents the early-19th-century libretto, when Classicism and Romanticism met face to face in Italy. Thus he contributed greatly to the desire of musical Italy, in the first half of the 19th century, to create operatic works more sincere than those of the preceding century.

The most concise summing up of Romani was provided by Guido Manzoni in his book *L'Ottocento* (Milan, 1913/1964). He wrote, "More than anyone else after Metastasio, [Romani] brought to the stage the richest and the most fluid and harmonious vein of actions and forms and adapted them exactly to musical expression; he appeared opportunely just when Italian melodies were being sung to the entire civilised world."

Romani's first works for the theatre were the libretti *La rosa rossa e la rosa bianca*[4] and *Medea in Corinto* for Simone Mayr in 1813. He went on to provide successive Italian composers with about 120 libretti[5] in a long career in which he established himself as the best Italian librettist of the 19th century before Arrigo Boito. Undoubtedly, Romani reached his peak during the years 1827-33, when he collaborated with Bellini (and perhaps, to a lesser extent, with Donizetti), for whom he wrote *Il pirata*, *La Straniera*, *Zaira*, *I Capuleti e i Montecchi*, *La sonnambula*, *Norma*, *Beatrice di Tenda* and the revised version of *Bianca e Fernando*.

Carrying a letter of introduction from Zingarelli, Bellini was presented to Romani by Mercadante. The meeting in all probability took place during the rehearsals of *Il montanaro*, as Mercadante left Milan for Lisbon after his opera had been staged. On 2 June, Bellini wrote to him in Lisbon. The letter – the only letter extant from this period[6] – shows that there was a close friendship between them and that Bellini already knew Romani well:

> My dear maestro, what a dreadful thing you tell me. How could a woman bring herself to do such a thing? How were you able to bear such terrible grief without taking revenge on her and her seducer? Oh, God, when will the world see the end of all evil?…
>
> I'm told that Isabella was always of a very volatile nature and happy to be courted by crowds of *cicesbei*. While for years she pretended to be in love with you, she had two more men whom she used to entertain at different hours… My dear maestro, I beg you to set your mind at rest, as you've lost nothing by losing Isabella. Remember Fiesco in the great Schiller tragedy telling his wife of his infidelity and his preference of an extremely ill-famed woman. His wife wisely replies, "Either Fiesco is innocent or I didn't lose anything." And this scene is a good parallel to your case…
>
> Please write to me. I will always be available to give you any comfort that I can. Remember always that you have a true, sensitive and faithful friend in your loving Bellini.
>
> Romani sends his regards, and Florimo asks me to give you his compliments every time he writes to me from Naples.

As Romani's work was known in Naples, Bellini almost certainly studied some of his libretti of the operas performed there. However, it is doubtful that Romani had heard of Bellini, unless the success of *Bianca e Gernando* had reached his ears. When Romani and Bellini met, a great and intimate friendship was born between them. Even though Romani was 13 years Bellini's senior, he saw in the young composer qualities that he appreciated greatly. Bellini demanded from a libretto both quick action in the plot and harmonious verse, expressed with the kind of simplicity that could carry supercharged emotion. For his part, he proved in due course that, at his best, he was the first Italian composer to possess the ability and the temperament to realise these qualities through his music. "Give me good verses and I will give you good music," Bellini maintained. Taking into account his period and experience to date, this explains better than anything else the mutual understanding between the two men. Their close friendship would endure for six years, during which time they would produce seven operas together.

According to Florimo, the subject of *Il pirata* was proposed by Romani and readily accepted by Bellini. Since Romani hardly ever wrote original plots in his libretti, he found the source of *Il pirata* in the Irish clergyman Charles Maturin's play *Bertram, or the Castle of St Aldobrand*, first produced at Drury Lane, London, in 1816. (Romani was most likely acquainted with Isodore JS Taylor [known as Raimond] and Charles Nodier's published French translation of the play, which was performed in Paris in 1821.) Although Romani changed much of the action, the subject – especially the roles of the two protagonists – provided several passionate and dramatic situations. These were the merits that attracted Bellini, who realised that such Romantic characters were then an innovation on the operatic stage. (As a matter of fact, they would prove prototypes for several such characters.) Also, the fact that the action of *Il pirata*, like that of *Bianca e Gernando*, takes place in Sicily, was an added attraction.

The collaboration of poet and musician seems to have been complete from the beginning, as obviously they both tried to give each other their best. Emilia Branca (who became Romani's wife in 1845, nine years after Bellini's death) described this initial stage in the association between Bellini and Romani in her book about her husband,[7] published 17 years after his death:

Bellini was in those days still under the influence of his college upbringing and without any experience or personal involvement. He was timid, not used to living in an elegant environment, and full of that ardour that can only be found in a Sicilian. It was of great moment for him to meet a true and genial friend who was able to understand him and in whom he could confide with ease. Henceforth, they became inseparable, and it was obvious that the one was made for the other; they responded to a complexity of sentiments, impressions and affections with a similar artistic concept... "I alone read in him," wrote Romani, "that poetic soul, that passionate heart, that wonderful mind anxious to fly beyond the sphere in which he was restricted by school influences and by the servility of imitation. It was then that I wrote *Il pirata* for Bellini, a subject that I thought suitable and capable of touching the depths of his art, and I wasn't wrong. From that day, we understood each other and together we fought the spitefulness of the musical theatre little by little, with courage, perseverance and love."

Branca, who had spent many years courting Romani before he eventually married her, was very jealous of the mutual affection that existed between the two men. Later, in her superficial effort to glorify her husband, she is often unreliable in her handling of facts. Unfortunately, several writers have quoted her indiscriminately, with the lamentable result that important information that could throw light on Romani, as well as on Bellini and other composers who collaborated with him, has been seriously distorted. In the case quoted, Branca merely used a condensed and inexact version of the obituary notice on Bellini that Romani had written in the *Gazzetta Piedmontese* in October 1835, shortly after the composer's death.[8] But it was her own comments in this instance that slightly belittle, rather than distort, Bellini's personality.

The singers engaged by La Scala for *Il pirata* were Méric-Lalande and Rubini, both of whom had sung in *Bianca e Gernando* in Naples and whose capabilities were already known to Bellini. The third principal singer was Antonio Tamburini, one of the most distinguished artists of his time. Tamburini's baritone voice was even, accurate and forceful throughout its wide range. A master of florid singing, he too was an accomplished actor, like Lablache (who had the lower voice of the two), specialising in the early stages of his career in *opera buffa* and later in dramatic roles. After *Il pirata*, Tamburini created leading roles in Bellini's *Bianca e Fernando*, *La Straniera* and *I Puritani*. He was born in Faenza, Italy, on 28 March 1800, retired in 1859 and died in Nice on 8 November 1876.

Rubini[9] (1795-1854) was a very different singer. At first, his career was not particularly distinguished, perhaps because, at the beginning of the 19th century, when Rossini was producing his operas, Giovanni David, Manuel Garcia and Andrea Nozzari were the reigning tenors. They were all experienced singers of Rossini's music, which was all the rage at that time and some of which had been written expressly for them. Furthermore, Rubini's appearance then militated against him, as he had a pockmarked face and an awkward figure. Moreover, he had neither taste nor cared about his dress and was certainly no actor. He was, however, a perfect vocalist, inasmuch as he could ravish the ear with incredible beauty of sound. When Bellini and Donizetti began to write their operas and the Rossinian tenors had passed their peak, the world then discovered Rubini. He became the ideal tenor, surpassing all of his immediate predecessors and eventually becoming the first male singer (excepting the *castrati*) to achieve international fame corresponding to that previously reserved for prima donnas.

Chorley's[10] description of Rubini at the time when he was hailed as the greatest tenor in the world is the most apt: "There was never an artist who seemed so thoroughly and intensely to enjoy his own singing – a persuasion that cannot fail to communicate itself to audiences… As a singer and nothing but a singer, he is the only man of his class who deserves to be named an artist of genius."

By all contemporary accounts, Rubini's voice had immense power, purity and sweetness; it was a natural organ of prodigious range, to which his own skill added several highly effective notes. Fétis[11] says that his chest range covered two octaves, from C to G, carried up to F by "head notes". What made this remarkable was his ability to make the transition to falsetto with such consummate skill that it was impossible to detect the change in the vocal method.

On 12 August, three *opere serie* were announced for the autumn season at La Scala: Bellini's *Il pirata*, Pacini's *L'ultimo giorno di Pompei* and Rossini's *Mosè in Egitto*.

When rehearsals for *Il pirata* began, Rubini found Bellini's music difficult to sing. There was nothing technical in it that was beyond his skills, but he fell short of the composer's demand that singers should act with their voices as well as their bodies. Nevertheless, Bellini was determined to get the best out of him and, after hours of constant rehearsal, managed to make Rubini forget himself and become Gualtiero, the character that he was portraying in the opera. Furthermore, on no account would he allow Rubini to incorporate roulades and other embellishments that were not in the score. Florimo related an episode that took place in Bellini's house when Rubini was rehearsing his role, told to him by Conte Giacomo Barbò:[12]

> They started to rehearse the duet between Gualtiero and Imogene. But soon they met with the same difficulties as before and exclaimed, "You don't put half of the soul you've got into it! Here, where you could easily move the public, you're cold and languid. Put some passion into it. Have you never been in love?"
>
> Rubini didn't say a word to this, as he was very confused. Then the maestro said, using a rather sweeter voice, "Dear Rubini, do you think you're Rubini or Gualtiero? Don't you know that your voice is a goldmine not entirely discovered? Listen to me, I beg you, and one day you'll be grateful. You are one of the best artists. Nobody can be your equal in *bravura* singing. But this isn't enough!"
>
> "I understand what you mean, but I cannot despair or enrage myself just for the sake of make-believe," Rubini answered.
>
> "The truth is that my music doesn't please you because it doesn't give you the usual opportunities. But if I have in mind a new style and a music that can express completely the words and form a union of singing and drama, should I give it up because you don't want to [work] with me? In fact, you can co-operate with me, provided that you forget yourself and put yourself into the soul of the character that you represent. Look how it should be done."
>
> So Bellini started to sing. In spite of his undistinguished voice, inspired, he was moving to such an extent that he could have roused even the hardest of men. Deeply moved, Rubini followed with his outstanding voice.
>
> "Bravo, Rubini. There you are, you *have* understood me! I'm happy. I will expect you to do the same tomorrow. Above all, always remember to practise while standing and accompany yourself with gestures."

With Méric-Lalande and Tamburini, it was different, as Filippo Cicconetti wrote in his *Vita di Vincenzo Bellini*: "It was easier to make the soprano and Tamburini understand. In a short time, they realised what the young maestro wanted and they decided to help him with their goodwill."

Il pirata was produced at La Scala on 27 October 1827 to enthusiastic acclaim from both the public and the critics. The ballets *Eustichio della Castagna*[13] and *Alceste*[14] were also performed, between the acts. The opera achieved 15 performances to full houses, the last performance given on 2 December, to close the autumn season. The unqualified success of *Il pirata* enthused Bellini to the point of compelling him to describe the reception of his opera in detail to his uncle Vincenzo Ferlito. Two days after the first performance, before the Milan press had begun to review the opera, Bellini wrote:[15]

My dearest uncle, rejoice together with my parents and relations, as your nephew has had the good fortune to have made such an impact with his opera that he doesn't know how to describe it. Neither you nor the others – nor even I, myself – could have hoped for such an outcome.

On Saturday the 27th of this month, the opera was presented, but from the dress rehearsal word had already gone around that there was good music in it. The time came for me to be called to the pianoforte. I appeared and the public received me with great applause. The overture began and was very popular; the introduction – with only one chorus – was sung very well, but as it was performed in the middle of a thunderstorm, the public didn't appreciate it enough and consequently it received very little applause.

Rubini's entrance (after his *aria d'entrata*) created such a furore that it cannot be described. I got up as many as ten times to thank the public. The prima donna's cavatina was also applauded. The chorus of the pirates, which has echo effects, was very pleasing because of the novelty of having the echo thought out so well, and then, in the end, the voices go backstage, singing all the time with the other orchestra, which is on the stage and made up only of wind instruments. All this had such an effect, and I received so much applause, that I was overcome with joy to the point that I burst into convulsive tears for as long as five minutes... Therefore, these happy hours will give me the incentive to progress in my career with honour, and this I will do by studying.

You must give this news to my friends and then the papers will persuade my enemies, if I have any. In the meantime, it's not necessary for me to return to Naples. Not for the moment, anyway. I will first try out the opera in this part of Italy and I'll decide what to do depending on any offers that are made to me then. I will let you know what happens…

I can already see tears of happiness in the eyes of my parents and grandfather and those who, like all of my relations, love me so much…

Surprisingly, no description of *Il pirata* or of its success was sent to Florimo immediately after the premiere, but on 16 January 1828, when Bellini was sending music to Ricordi for publication, he discussed the opera with him:[16]

I like hearing your views on music and I find them sound. As you will see, the copy of the manuscript is full of mistakes… Lalande's exit is correct, as you say, but Mme Lalande made me shorten it because she is completely incapable of any delicate sentiment, having none herself, and therefore she cannot express this feeling in the cabaletta. The duet, my dear Florimo, was a complete success, the best thing of all, right up to the last note, and especially in the *largo*. You can't possibly imagine the effect it had. Everyone had tears in their eyes… I can't tell you enough about Rubini's scene, either, although it's so small that you would never imagine how striking it was and how divinely he sang it…

I hope that that scoundrel Ricordi will publish the score this month. That's what he promised me, anyway, when I saw him the day before yesterday.

Please give my regards to Donizetti with my best wishes.

Bellini's enthusiasm over *Il pirata* was amply justified by the press notices, all of which showed great appreciation of both the work and its performance. On 2 November, *I Teatri*, after praising nearly all the numbers of the opera (with a few minor reservations), concluded, "Despite the very few flaws that we have observed in this opera, we can confidently describe it as a work of absolute intelligence and excellent taste."

At the close of the season on 2 December, the *Gazzetta privilegiata* commented on Rubini's performance in *Il pirata*: "Sometimes Rubini indulged in stylish ornaments and proved that he has good taste. He also gave some passages in his aria brilliance and passion, in a way that both the poet and the composer expected of him. We have already mentioned that it was this opera that introduced us to Rubini's dual personality as a singer and actor, and it wasn't his fault if, in other operas, he was restricted merely to the conventional execution of an aria and it wasn't possible to hear more of his beautiful and delicate intonations."

The great success of *Il pirata* in Milan did not go unnoticed. The enterprising Barbaja decided to present it in Vienna, in his other important theatre. Not only would the singers go there but so would the sets and everything else, even the orchestral parts of the score, making the whole project financially more viable. So hardly had the last curtain fallen when, on 3 January 1828, Bellini was officially told by Antonio Villa, Barbaja's deputy in Milan, that the opera would be performed at the Kärntnertortheater in Vienna on 25 February 1828. There was to be a change in the cast, however, as Adelaide Comelli, Rubini's wife, would be singing the role of Imogene.

This upset Bellini greatly. Lalande, for whom he had expressly written the role, had been a great success and, above all, she had been able to express his intentions to a high degree. He could not expect anything like this from Comelli, whom he considered an indifferent singer.[17] It was also the first Bellini opera to be heard outside Italy and, moreover, it was to be heard in an important theatre in Vienna. On 4 January, Bellini wrote a diplomatic letter to Rubini[18] in which he stressed the artistic merit of his opera and the requirements for its success without direct mention of Comelli:

> My dear Rubini, I was very surprised yesterday when I heard that, with great haste, the management has asked for the score of *Il pirata* from Villa, who has sent it by coach to Vienna. So do what you can. Please tell me, who are the other singers in the cast? Remember, this opera belongs to you, because it's the only one that has been written expressly for the range of your voice... But what will become of my *Pirata* if you have already started to prostitute it with other singers who are wrong for it?...
>
> Remember that, at La Scala, your enemies had the opportunity to say that you triumphed only because you had an excellent partner, and that you yourself are capable of singing merely a cavatina. And all this because Lalande has been singing music that has been written for her and is suitable for her voice. Therefore, don't precipitate yourself into a performance that will be most advantageous to you when you are with Lalande... Consider that, if *Il pirata* is a failure in

some other country because of bad singers, our enemies will criticise the opera and it will therefore lose the high esteem that it now enjoys throughout Europe, especially in Paris, where they have asked for 1,000 printed copies from Ricordi and where they wish to engage you for at least three months... Please receive my embraces and also give them to your other half. Please answer me by return of post, if I am still worthy of your friendship. Goodbye, my dear Rubini. Your friend, Bellini.

Surprisingly, Bellini failed to mention the projected performance of *Il pirata* in Vienna or his letter to Rubini in the letters that he wrote to Florimo on 12 and 16 January.[19] He may well have waited for Rubini's reaction, because in his letter to Florimo[20] of 21 January he blames Comelli severely: "We think *Il pirata* is to be performed in Vienna and it is said that Comelli wants to sing the part of Imogene. You can see what a horror it's going to be, and this is why I've written to Rubini...for him to understand that Comelli would ruin this opera, which was his only joy in the world, both for the singing and the acting. I'm waiting for an answer to this letter to hear if he will have the courage to have the opera performed. That witch and ambitious ass of his wife may well persuade him to go ahead with the performance. Alas, patience."

After *Il pirata* had closed the season at La Scala, Bellini continued to live in Milan, where he occupied himself mainly with the preparation of the score of his opera for publication by Giovanni Ricordi. The score was dedicated to Duchessa Litta, whom Bellini had met through the Pollinis and who had showed great interest in his work. Even though Bellini had made several friends through Romani and the Pollinis in Milan, it is clear from his letters to Florimo that he often felt lonely. On 2 January,[21] he wrote:

I thought that yesterday I would have received your letter with the newspapers, as you had promised me the last time you wrote, but I was disappointed... I'm also waiting for Zingarelli's opinion and yours on the piece of music [*Il pirata*] that you have seen and your decision as to whether or not to show Zingarelli the entire score...

I thought that Ricordi wouldn't have made me pay for the transport, but everyone seems to be in one way or another either a thief or a "Jew".

I will now give you some theatre news. Donizetti's *Il borgomastro* [*di Saardam*] will be performed tonight. I haven't been to any rehearsals, but those who have been to the dress rehearsal have told me that in the first act there is nothing and that in the second there is a duet that might be quite pleasing, but all in all the opera won't be a success. Tonight we shall see, and in my next letter I will tell you.

Do write and tell me what Barbaja says about me and about other plans. Signor Pacini is satisfied in manoeuvring intrigues not only there but also here. He has already arranged for a letter to be received by Unger,[22] written perhaps by Winter, in which he tells of the enormous success that Pacini's *Margherita* had on its fourth night, and Unger has already sent this letter to the correspondent of the theatre, so that it should appear in the *Giornali di Teatri*. I have been told that this correspondent – who used to be not very keen on Pacini, as you probably realised from what he said about *Pompei* – changed his mind after Pacini sent him a small sum of money. You can deduce what a trap this is, and I wouldn't put it past him if he has told this correspondent something against me. Anyway, for good music, one doesn't need bribes.

Madame Pollini received a full letter of thanks from Zingarelli for taking care of me. As the days go on, this care increases and is performed with the greatest imaginable discretion and thoughtfulness, even [to the extent of] advising me of the smallest things. I see them every day and I usually have meals with them twice a week...

Love to all my friends and companions and finally embracing you, with all my heart and with the longing to embrace you personally and asking you to love me always. Believe me, I am beginning to feel rather lonely and depressed, as I have no ties here and I am far away from my dearest friends. Only the charming Pollinis have helped me to alleviate my boredom, and my love for my career helps me to suffer with resignation. Goodbye, my dear Florimo. Don't forget your friend Bellini, who loves you with all his heart. Goodbye.

In an undated letter to Florimo, Bellini further says,[23] "I've heard the gossip about Pacini. They're preparing to hiss and shout him out of the opera house for *La primavera*, which he wrote for Lalande. Incidentally, she will be staying here. They are sending Favelli to Vienna, and apparently she will be performing with Comelli in *Il pirata* on 26 February. And just think what a failure that will be. But enough – this is what happens to all operas that are revived. Oh, for the stars! Oh, for the stars!"

Contrary to Bellini's fears and predictions about the Viennese *Il pirata*, Comelli rose to the occasion (according to Rubini, his wife performed nothing less than a "miracle of San Gennaro") and did not let down either her fellow singers or the composer. In fact, *Il pirata* scored a success in Vienna comparable with that in Milan.

The main reason why Bellini continued to stay in Milan was that he was hoping for new contracts. On 12 January, he wrote to Florimo,[24] "I still believe that Barbaja will offer me something for the autumn or for the Milan Carnival. I would like to write for Genoa in the spring, but in the meantime all Milan will want me to write for them. Everyone here is telling me that I'm bound to be engaged. Some people are already claiming to know even what fee I will be offered.

"I haven't heard anything definite about the spring season in Genoa, so God only knows whether they will engage me or not. In the next few days, however, the Genoa theatre representatives will be coming to Milan and will most probably make me an offer."

The offer did come from Genoa, through Merelli, who, on 13 January 1828, asked Bellini if he would write an opera for the opening of the new Teatro Carlo Felice in the forthcoming April. Bellini hesitated at first for reasons that he mentions to Florimo on 16 January:[25]

The other day, the theatre correspondent Merelli[26] came to my house and made an official proposal from the impresarios in Genoa that I should write for the next carnival season in Genoa. However, as the company hadn't yet been assembled, I didn't want to commit myself and told them that they should first get all the singers together and then, if I felt like it, I would accept their offer. So we left the matter at that, and in the meantime I might be able to get a better offer from Venice or Turin.

Yesterday, Count Melzi told me in confidence that Villa might offer me a contract for the autumn season at La Scala as soon as he knows what the company is going to be like. I can't decide yet what I should do, as one has to be very careful and act according to circumstances and then decide what to accept. I don't think that it will be possible for a company to be formed for the autumn in [La Scala] but that, almost certainly, one will be available in August. It's also possible that David will be available, after Genoa. If I have Rubini in August, I will certainly accept the offer for here and another theatre for the carnival season, but I can't tell you anything final now. Think about it and tell me what you hear from your end...

Nothing else materialised, however, and by the middle of February Bellini accepted the offer from Genoa. There was no time to write a new opera, as the new theatre was due to open at the beginning of April and Bellini did not like to compose hurriedly, so he proposed that he should refurbish *Bianca e Gernando* instead. This was accepted and the singers engaged were Adelaide Tosi and Giovanni David, for whom Bellini had originally composed *Bianca e Gernando* in Naples. Lablache's role was to be taken by Tamburini. However, during the time in which Bellini was considering the offers, there was some intrigue taking place concerning who would get the contract for Genoa. Whereas Donizetti merely suggested that his *L'esule di Roma* – already a great success at the San Carlo – might be performed in Genoa, Pacini, according to Bellini, slyly tried to get the commission himself. In his letter to Florimo[27] on 16 February, Bellini says:

> Until you receive this letter, I don't know how much you'll have laughed about all the resolutions that have been made by Tosi, Barbaja, Donizetti and Pacini for Genoa... You may know that David has been engaged for Genoa and that Tosi asked Barbaja to produce [Pacini's] *Pompei*, but he refused; also, the same happened for the plan of producing [Nicolò Vaccai's] *Zadig e Astartea* for David.
>
> In the meantime, Pacini has been scheming and, as he says, he has succeeded. (I heard this from David, who was laughing at what I'm about to tell you.) According to Pacini, Merelli gave him a letter from the authorities of Genoa inviting him to write a new opera for the opening of the theatre. Imagine how happy Pacini was to be asked to do this. (Perhaps you didn't know that Pacini has already written a few pieces of music for his *Zaira*.) He then ran to David and asked him to write to Barbaja and persuade him to give his permission for [Pacini] to accept the commission for Genoa. David did, as it was also advantageous to Barbaja, who would have received a substantial share of Pacini's royalties.

Three days after David's letter was posted, [the authorities in] Genoa wrote to me. Imagine what a blow this must have been to Pacini. Believe me, I knew nothing about all this, and David told me that he was surprised at this news, too, as he thought it was certain that Pacini had got the contract. But Cavaliere Peluso, who has the ultimate authority to sign contracts, knew nothing of Pacini's case...

Once the contract was signed, Bellini immediately set to work. Not only did he re-adapt the music of *Bianca e Gernando* to suit the voices of his singers, but he also added four new pieces, including an overture in place of the original short introduction. Furthermore, the whole opera was reconstructed, helped by Romani, who also mentioned these changes to Florimo,[28] so that he would inform the Neapolitan publisher Cottrau, who had already issued the original score of *Bianca e Fernando*: "Tell Cottrau that, out of the whole of *Bianca*, the only pieces entirely unchanged are the big duet and the romanza; everything else is altered, and about half of it is new, so these two unchanged pieces are the only ones it will be any use sending to Genoa."

Sometime before mid March, when Bellini left Milan for Genoa, another development took place. Following the success of *Il pirata* at La Scala, which established Bellini as an operatic composer, the Fumarolis seem to have retracted their rejection of him as a son-in-law. Now, through Marsigli, who had been Bellini's unsuccessful ambassador in the past, they informed him of their favourable change of mind. In the past, such news would have given Bellini the greatest happiness, but now he received it with indifference. Since arriving in Milan, he had become so preoccupied with building up his career that his love for Maddalena – previously a great incentive – gradually but positively cooled. He was no longer interested in marrying her. In fact, he did not answer Marsigli or the Fumarolis; instead, he asked Florimo to reply for him, as he was too busy and could not spare the time. In his letter to Florimo of 16 January 1828,[29] Bellini wrote, "I hope all goes well with Fumaroli. I could never have given her a proper life, financially, because of my interest in my career."

Despite Bellini's rejection of her, Maddalena remained constant in her love. She wrote to Bellini twice herself, but the letters remained in Milan unanswered. When Bellini returned and found them, he went only as far as to mention it in a postscript in a letter to Florimo on 12 May 1828:[30] "I've received two letters from Fumaroli from an earlier date, as I was in Genoa at that time and they have arrived here. I'm thinking of not answering or of sending the answer through you."

Before long, Maddalena wrote a third letter. On 9 June 1828, almost casually, Bellini wrote to Florimo,[31] asking him to act for the third time as the go-between: "I enclose an answer to the three letters that I've received from the Fumarolis. She wants to marry me at all costs, but I have no intention of getting myself a wife. I don't have the money to keep her, either, and I've said so to her 1,000 times, and that, at her young age, she will be able to cure certain sentiments dictated by inexperience. Give her the page enclosed here in my letter via Donna Michellina and let's hope that this persuades her."

Maddalena never again tried to approach Bellini but accepted the loss of her only love, albeit with a broken heart. She never married, and her sad life came to an end six years later, when she was only 32.

Revealing his egocentricity, Bellini thought that he could justifiably act in this way. Once he felt that an affair had ended, he had little time for another's feelings. He had undoubtedly loved Maddalena, but his pride was deeply wounded by the way in which her parents had treated him and, as he was able to overcome his love for her, he decided that it was his prerogative to refuse her. Furthermore, it may have been that, having failed to marry at the time that he desired to (or thought that he did), he no longer wished to tie himself completely to one person. His subsequent celebrity as an operatic composer may also have spurred his desire for freedom. Moreover, there was Giuditta Turina, whom Bellini met in Genoa during the production of *Bianca e Fernando*. Giuditta was beautiful, young, rich and safely married. It was convenient for Bellini to fall under her spell, and although the love affair lasted for five years, when Giuditta was eventually free and marriage was possible, he shied away.

Some early biographers have made a great deal out of very little, as regards Bellini's love life, to the point of considering him little short of a philandering libertine. No documentary evidence exists to support this. Episodes referred to are of course plausible, and one would be surprised if they had not happened to Bellini just as they happen to most people. Gian Carlo Holst, in his *L'amante di Bellini* (Milan, 1924), says that, in 1840, he spoke to a woman called Ismena in Catania who told him that she had been Bellini's fiancée before he left to study in Naples. No other evidence to support this exists, however. There was also another Catanese girl, Marietta

Politi, for whom it is suggested that Bellini wrote the song "La farfalletta". No doubt there were more girls in Catania to whom the adolescent Bellini paid attention and also some who flirted with the handsome and elegant blond Catanese. However, these adolescent flirtations did not affect him, as he never again referred to them. Only Maddalena made her mark, and if he in some ways behaved badly towards her, he still retained some affection for her during the rest of his life.

Later, when Bellini became an international celebrity, others formed (perhaps romantic) attachments to him. There was the singer Giuditta Grisi – for whom he wrote the part of Romeo in *I Capuleti e i Montecchi* – and, more conspicuously, the fiery, irresistible Maria Malibran. It is unsurprising that a great deal of attraction between these fascinating ladies and Bellini existed, but the extent to which this attraction was mental, physical or both, we simply do not know. Whatever the case, these incidents in his life did not last for any appreciable length of time. These ladies were artists, too, and before long their commitments took them in other directions. With Giuditta Turina, however, it was different; documentary evidence proves the existence of her love affair with Bellini, which lasted for over five years – as long as the composer stayed in Italy.

Also, Florimo cannot be overlooked when considering Bellini's emotional life. Most writers have avoided commenting on Bellini's special friendship with Florimo (other than noting the latter's role as *fidus Achates*), who by and large deliberately removed and even altered parts from their correspondence that presumably would have shown his friend in a bad light. Others all but dismissed even the possibility of a homosexual relationship, justifying their adjudication on the terms that it is indeed difficult for many people – particularly Anglo-Saxons who are unfamiliar with early-19th-century Mediterranean society – to comprehend that a demonstratively passionate friendship has nothing to do with homosexuality. These same writers also reassure us that the "phenomenon" of homosexuality indeed existed even in the early 19th century, but that it was abhorred. Such statements are naïve, at best, if not ignorant. One wonders what evidence would have declared a relationship homosexual. Mediterranean passionate friendships sometimes are of a homosexual nature, sometimes not, although bisexuality is often a common occurrence.

In Bellini's case, his actions, his attitude towards marriage and, above all, his intense concern for Florimo's blatant jealousy of any liaison that even remotely implied sexual activity speak volumes. Whether Bellini's relationships were mentally and/or physically bisexual is not, in itself, crucial; what is significant is the extent to which their nature was a vital component in his life and, in turn, how the course of his work was affected. Nevertheless, in the final analysis, it must be left to the reader to draw his own conclusion.

Almost all of Bellini's letters to Florimo end with the tenderest expressions of love. One must also remember the conventions of the period, especially in the style of letter writing, but it was only to Florimo that Bellini wrote:

> Receive my embraces and believe that I am always your Bellini, who loves you.
>
> My love for you has become necessary for my very existence. Therefore, for my peace of mind, I don't want to have any doubts about this or about your love for me.
>
> Let's not forget the grief of our separation, but the desire to embrace each other again will console us. My dear Florimo, our friendship will make everybody envious, and when we die, what [other] people will remember about us will be all praise. This should be enough for you to know that our friendship could never be broken. Our friendship has already been tested, so no one can doubt its strength.

Furthermore, Bellini never stopped talking about Florimo. His friends and acquaintances heard so much about Florimo that they often felt that they knew him. It was said in Milan that Madame Pollini really had two sons, Bellini and his friend.

Although Bellini described in a letter to Florimo – gently and with considerable diplomacy – the time that he first had sexual intercourse with Giuditta Turina, the question of marriage may have been understood to be an act of disloyalty. In another letter, describing how well his affair was going with Giuditta (a married woman), he significantly adds, "This passion will protect me from marriage." In part, this may have been a reassurance of loyalty to his friend.

Florimo never married, either. He lived to be 86 and remained the archivist in the library of the Naples Conservatorio. In 1882, almost 50 years after Bellini's death, he published a book about his friend under the title

Memorie e Lettere.[32] Evidently, Florimo never overcame the loss of the only person that he had ever loved and continued to speak of him passionately. The book begins:

> Even when I write down the name of Vincenzo Bellini, enormous feelings are reawakened in me, to speak of the friend of my youth, of the most tender friend, whose friendship still has such a hold on me. This was the friend who didn't believe that his joys could be fulfilled unless he shared them with me and who felt that sorrows were less sad if he were able to confide in me. Even in the last moments of his life, when he was almost unconscious and immediately before death, he spoke my name with the name of his mother. I was deeply moved. I can't be an indifferent biographer for him, and no matter how I try to be guided only by reason, I'm incapable of keeping my heart silent. I've tried to keep my heart silent, but always, in the end, I was convinced that, by doing so, I was betraying the sacred friendship that has kept me tied to such a dear memory.

Not unexpectedly, Giuditta Turina felt jealous of Florimo. At one time, Bellini wrote to him:[33]

> She doesn't want me to write to you about our affair, because she fears that some of the letters may be lost, but as I speak to everybody about you, I can't help speaking to her about you as well. She has a great respect for you and is almost jealous of my affection for you. She wants to see your portrait and she often says, "Bellini, let's go to Naples to see your friend," and I say to her, "Let's go." This conversation is repeated again and again. She wants to read your letters and I tell her that this isn't possible, because your affairs don't permit me to do so, and she believes that you write to me about some other lovers of mine and that that's why I refuse to show her your letters. But apart from this, we're in perfect harmony, and as a lover I'm very happy and don't wander from one beautiful girl to another.

Again, Bellini's words express his invulnerable loyalty to Florimo and, in the end, tactfully justify his involvement with Giuditta. Florimo's jealousy of Giuditta was even stronger. The moment that he was convinced that his friend's affair was not merely a passing fancy, he reacted as a scorned lover. "I know that you've always been, and still are, strongly opposed (I don't think that I can change my nature) to any of my amorous passions," Bellini wrote to him.

Nevertheless, Giuditta did become friendly with Florimo and began to correspond with him after her separation from Bellini. Florimo tried to comfort her by assuring her that Bellini remembered her and had never really loved another woman.

It is difficult at the best of times to analyse sexual relationships between people, especially those who have been dead for a long time, because intimacies of such a nature are seldom committed to paper and information obtained from outsiders, when it does exist, is usually unreliable. The majority of Bellini's extant letters were written to Florimo, who later published them. On his own admission, however, he destroyed certain letters and parts of letters[34] that he considered would show his friend in an unfavourable light or were intimately private to themselves and of no concern to other people. Also, Florimo did not publish his own letters to Bellini, even though he had retrieved them (with Rossini's help) immediately after the composer's death.

The unpublished letters could have explained much of the development of Bellini's character, especially in the later stage of his brief life, and could have illuminated his relationship with Florimo. Bellini's rare comments on his own character in those letters to Florimo that were published – "You know that it's in my nature to look for sentiment as well as physical love"; "I change like the wind!"; "You know my weakness for falling desperately in love" – could apply to most people at certain times of their lives.

The possibility that, by destroying certain letters, Florimo was also concealing his own homosexuality cannot be ignored. Ultimately, of course, the outcome of his action did Bellini more harm than good. Several writers later assumed that the destroyed information was most uncomplimentary and that it made Bellini appear mercenary, ruthless with ambition and an intriguer who used his personal charm to conceal a calculating nature. True, Bellini wanted to succeed in his work and, as he was unable to write operas quickly, he wanted to be paid as much as possible. There is no doubt, either, that he was at times jealous of Donizetti, his competitor. A few months before he died, he wrote to his uncle Ferlito an amazing confession of this jealousy.[35] The point at issue on this occasion was the great success of *I Puritani* followed by Donizetti's unsuccessful *Marino Faliero*. Pastura, who admired Bellini greatly but who was also impartial in his judgement of him, summed up the situation well:[36] "For [Bellini], it was not a matter of the unlimited success of his *I Puritani* but of that definitive success – proclaiming him the victor in a contest between him and Donizetti – that placed him in the position that was his due – that is, first after Rossini."

Nor did Bellini try, through jealousy or spite, to take any action against Donizetti or any of his fellow composers, although others did, such as Pacini. Bellini alone suffered.

IL PIRATA

Opera seria in two acts. Libretto by Felice Romani. First performed at La Scala, Milan, on 27 October 1827 on a triple bill with the ballets *Merope* and *I pazzi per progetto*, both choreographed by Antonio Cortesi, the first to music by Luigi Viviani and Giacomo Panizza, the second by an unknown composer. Alessandro Sanquirico designed the stage sets.

CHARACTERS AND ORIGINAL CAST

Gualtiero, Count of Montalto, partisan of King Manfredi, now leader of the Aragonese pirates	Tenor	Giovanni Battista Rubini
Imogene, Ernesto's wife, previously in love with Gualtiero	Soprano	Enrichetta Méric-Lalande
Ernesto, Duke of Caldora, an Anjou partisan	Baritone	Antonio Tamburini
Goffredo, a hermit, former tutor of Gualtiero	Bass	Pietro Ansilioni
Adele, chief attendant to Imogene	Mezzo-soprano	Marietta Sacchi
Itulbo, companion of Gualtiero	Tenor	Lorenzo Lombardi

The action takes place in the Caldora Castle, Sicily, and its vicinity in around the 13th century. Ernesto, the Duke of Caldora, fell hopelessly in love with Imogene, but she was in love with Gualtiero, the Count of Montalto, who, like her elderly father, was a partisan of Manfred, the natural son of Frederick II, King of Sicily. In his plan to eliminate Gualtiero, Ernesto became a partisan of Charles of Anzou, the rival claimant to the throne, who defeated Manfred in 1266. When the Angevin Party came to power, Ernesto exiled Gualtiero, who fled to Aragon, where he armed a squadron of Aragonese pirates and for ten years waged war on the Angevins, always hoping to vindicate himself and win back Imogene. However, Gualtiero was unaware that, during his long exile, in order to save her father's life, Imogene had been forced to marry Ernesto and was living in the Caldora Castle. In the Straits of Messina, Gualtiero's pirate fleet was defeated by Ernesto's Angevin forces and forced to flee with a single vessel. Shortly afterwards, Gualtiero was overtaken by a storm and cast upon the coast of Sicily, near Caldora. The story begins at this point in time.

Act I

Scene 1: The seashore near the Caldora Castle. In the background stands the dilapidated watchtower of an ancient monastery, which is now a hermit's retreat.

Led by the hermit Goffredo, fishermen and their wives pray for the safety of a ship in distress in the raging storm. Presently, the storm subsides and, as the survivors land, the fishermen go to inform Imogene, Duchess of Caldora, of the shipwreck. The leader of the survivors is Gualtiero, erstwhile Count of Montalto, who is now a pirate. Only Goffredo, who had once been his tutor, recognises him. Gualtiero declares that, despite his adventures and hardship, he still loves Imogene. However, when he enquires about her, Goffredo hides him in his retreat before Imogene appears to offer hospitality to shipwrecked sailors in accordance with Caldoran custom. Itulbo, Gualtiero's companion, poses as the captain and, when Imogene asks whether the shipwrecked crew had encountered the pirates, hides the truth and says that their leader may have been captured or killed. Horrified by this information, Imogene relates to Adele, her attendant and friend, a nightmare that she has had which involved her beloved Gualtiero and her angry husband. At this moment, Gualtiero returns and cries out at the sight of Imogene. Itulbo promptly saves the situation by explaining that his companion is not quite himself, due to their recent hardship, while Goffredo leads Gualtiero away. Imogene, who has not recognised Gualtiero, is nevertheless disturbed by vague memories. Before she leaves, she promises to help the shipwrecked sailors.

SCENE 2: A terrace before the Caldora Castle. It is night.

After the pirates have paid their respects to Imogene, Gualtiero arrives. Imogene's sympathy has been so aroused by the stranger that she has sent for him. At first, he evades her searching questions, but eventually he reveals his identity. However, their joy at finding each other again soon vanishes when Adele arrives with a young boy, whom Gualtiero recognises to be the son of Imogene and Ernesto. Seized by grief and desire for revenge, Gualtiero attempts to stab the boy, but Imogene's anguished cry saves him. Gualtiero then tries to persuade her to fly with him, but she refuses and declares herself resigned to her miserable destiny. As he rushes out, swearing vengeance, Imogene thanks God for saving her son's life. Meanwhile, martial music announces the arrival of Ernesto.

SCENE 3: An illuminated part of the castle's grounds.

Ernesto happily boasts to his knights and soldiers of his decisive victory over the pirates. Presently, however, his celebratory mood changes when he senses his wife's lack of warmth in greeting him. He tells her that, although he defeated the pirates, their leader managed to escape. Then, hearing of the shipwrecked men that his wife has sheltered, Ernesto urgently orders that their leader should be brought to him for questioning.

Goffredo arrives with Gualtiero and Itulbo, still claiming to be leader. However, after questioning them, Ernesto is not satisfied and has them arrested as suspected pirates. Imogene pleads for them and Ernesto eventually agrees to let them go free, but commanding that they should leave by dawn. In the meantime, Gualtiero has difficulty in containing himself and is about to attack Ernesto when Imogene averts this by fainting. Although Ernesto's attention is distracted, his suspicions are further aroused by his wife's unusual behaviour. While he confers with his knights, the revived Imogene gives vent to her sorrow. Adele pleads with Imogene to hide her distress and Itulbo and Goffredo try to restrain Gualtiero, who is still bent on vengeance.

ACT II

SCENE 1: A salon leading to Imogene's apartments.

Imogene's ladies pray for her repose. When they depart, she comes in and Adele tells her that Gualtiero insists on seeing her once more. Presently, Ernesto enters and, after Adele leaves, reproaches Imogene for loving Gualtiero. She admits to his accusations but reminds him that, when he took her from her father, he was fully aware of this love and that he had no concern then for the way that she felt.

A messenger rushes in bringing Ernesto a letter that informs him of Gualtiero's presence within the palace. As he hurries out to confront his enemy, Imogene follows trying to stop him, lest he is killed and brings death to their son.

SCENE 2: A terrace before the castle, as in act one, scene two. It is almost daybreak.

Gualtiero orders Itulbo to prepare their ship for departure. As he goes, Imogene enters hurriedly and warns Gualtiero that he has been discovered, urging him to leave immediately. She refuses all entreaties to fly with him, but as they say a last farewell Ernesto surprises them and challenges Gualtiero to a duel. Imogene tries to separate them but is eventually led away by Adele.

SCENE 3: Ground-floor courtyard to the castle.

Having killed Ernesto in the duel, Gualtiero surrenders himself to be judged by the Council of Knights. He expresses his remorse for causing Imogene so much grief and hopes that one day she will forgive him. As he is taken away, Imogene, overcome by her husband's death, loses her reason. While waiting for the trial of her lover to finish, she imagines that she sees Ernesto calling for his son. She then asks her son to tell his father that it was she who saved his life when Gualtiero wanted to kill him and asks her dead husband to forgive her, as she is innocent.

When Gualtiero is found guilty and condemned to death, in Imogene's imagination she sees before her a scaffold for his execution and entreats the sun to hide from the horrible sight.

Charles Robert Maturin's five-act tragedy *Bertram*, on which Romani's libretto for *Il pirata* was based, is part Gothic and part Romantic and was a great success at the Theatre Royal in Drury Lane, London, in 1816, despite Coleridge's severe criticism that it was "rant and nonsense". In fact, the success of the play on the English stage was to last for several years.

Romani most probably used the French translation of the play by Taylor and Nodier, which was first performed in 1821 at the Théâtre du Panorama-Dramatique in Paris. It is also probable that there were other intermediary steps, as very little of the action in the play and nothing of the Gothic has remained in the libretto. Whatever the case, Romani kept only the general outline of the plot. Gualtiero was considerably tamed from the wild and hard hero to a more civilised one, although slightly less irrational, while Ernesto was transformed from a kindly warrior into a vindictive monster. (In the libretto, Bertram becomes Gualtiero, Imogine becomes Imogene, St Aldobrand becomes Ernesto and the Prior becomes Goffredo.) By curtailing and simplifying the drama, Romani improved on *Bertram* considerably, omitting some of the information embedded in the play that often made it tedious. There is, however, an important gap in Imogene's character and actions. Did she commit adultery?[37] Only her cryptic "corregere l'error di cui siam rei" ("to find absolution for the sin we have committed") in her duet with Gualtiero (act two, scene two) hints vaguely that something of this nature took place.

The Romantic characters of Gualtiero and Imogene were to have many successors, but in 1827 they were prototypes on the operatic stage. They must have appealed greatly to Romani, who had until then been a convinced Classicist. His libretto, although not one of his best, is full of Romantic colouring and contains excellent opportunities for dramatic situations, the last two scenes achieving some degree of poetic eloquence.

What makes the libretto remarkable, however, are the new elements that it brings to Italian opera. *Il pirata* marks a new stage in the evolution of opera from the 18th-century drama of situation to the 19th-century drama of action. But if the almost obligatory happy ending of the 18th-century drama changed to a tragic *dénouement* with the coming of Romanticism, the Classical tradition that confined all violence out of sight was still maintained.

The portrayal of emotions aroused by tragic happenings not actually seen could also be realised through music; in no other medium could the emotional response to action be more fully realised than in tragic opera. However, Romani was not quite happy that the libretto ended with

Imogene's mad scene while sentence was being passed on Gualtiero offstage, but for different reasons. Having already sacrificed much of the lucidity and development of the story in order to provide passionate and dramatic situations (at the beginning of the opera, Imogene and Gualtiero are forcibly kept apart), he felt that his libretto left Gualtiero's fate too much to the imagination. In fact, he provided another two short scenes in which Gualtiero commits suicide, as in the Maturin play. (The pirates rush in to save Gualtiero but he prefers to throw himself over a bridge.)[38] Bellini chose not to set these to music, however, as they would have diminished the effect of Imogene's mad scene, if not destroyed it altogether.

The overture to *Il pirata* (in D major, 3/4 time) is in three sections. The first two are very short. Attention is held in the first (*allegro con fuoco*) by the simple yet effective way in which the two sentiments – daring attack and moving gentleness – are depicted by alternating *forte* and *piano* phrases of irregular length separated by rests and pauses. The second section (*andante maestoso*) is partly new and partly an elaboration of the theme from the first movement of the overture to *Adelson e Salvini*, which here gains more weight. In the third section (*allegro agitato*), which is much longer, several passages borrowed from the second section of the overture to *Adelson* – here better worked out and linked together – succeed in sounding surprisingly original, lively and never uninteresting.

The grand and violent motif of the short but compact orchestral introduction to the opera proper splendidly suggests the bursts of storm, boiling waters and mingling of sea and sky. The ensuing chorus "Ciel! qual procella orribile" ("Heavens! What a terrible storm") leads into prayer as the storm's fury subsides. This semi-religious choral prayer is effectively joined by the fishermen and Goffredo's austere, solemn voice. Rossinian in structure, this chorus is basically an improved adaptation of a tender motif in Salvini's "Nelly, che pena, o Dio" (*Adelson e Salvini*) and indirectly recalls the choral parts in Rossini's *Mosè in Egitto*. The "shout" "Ahi, miseri" ("The wretched ones") after a long and sudden silence dramatically changes the atmosphere into one of horror and pity.

Gualtiero's aria "Nel furor delle tempeste" ("Beneath the raging storm") is preceded by the telling and eloquent recitative "Io vivo ancor" ("I still live"), a melodious declamation sustained by tremolos and chords in which Gualtiero soliloquises his love for Imogene:

This aria – unconventional with supporting dance-like rhythm and heroic accents alternating with elegant, melodic contours – is Bellini's first attempt of the kind for the male voice. Contrasting emotions are powerfully suggested by the stylishly constructed phrases. After the impetuous "Nel furor delle tempeste", feelings of love are evoked in "Come in angelo", and there is a touch of nostalgia at "Di virtude consiglier" where the *legato* melody and harmonies in the minor key convey the feeling of something recalled long ago – an exceptional blend of ardour and poignancy.

The experiment almost comes off. In its time, however, it was completely successful, because Rubini was able to give it all the dramatic accents it requires. (The part was, after all, written expressly for him, with his extraordinary vocal technique, his artistry and with the help of Bellini's forceful coaching.) That the qualities of this aria are not fully realised today is partly because there is no equivalent of Rubini.

Regrettably, the next scene lapses into banality, with little musical characterisation in the choral sections. (Similar music does duty for both pirates and fishermen.) Gualtiero's cabaletta "Per te di vane lagrime" ("For you on vain tears") is conventional and provides interest as well as excitement solely through its brilliance and a ringing top D.

Much more dramatic expression is to be found in Imogene's first scene. In her recitative "Sorgete; è in me dover quella pietade" ("Rise; compassion is my duty"), in which she questions Itulbo about the voyage, there is a unique combination of sweetness and dignity and even a certain grandeur.

Her aria "Lo sognai ferito esangue" ("I dreamed that he was lying in blood"), in two verses, achieves its purpose in a most novel way.

Each verse begins with broken, heavily accentuated declamation, becoming lyrical only towards the end. Bellini also implies a touch of uneasiness by using a melody of restricted compass, and the tragic atmosphere is underlined by simple yet moving choral interjections.

The pirates' chorus "Evviva! allegri!" ("Hurrah! Let's be merry!"), an F major tarantella in 6/8 time accompanied initially only by wind instruments, is first heard offstage. It is a trivial piece of music,[39] but this contrasting triviality gives greater weight to the following scene, in which Imogene questions Gualtiero, still not recognising him. Here, recitative and arioso alternate with such unusual invention that the actual changes are hardly noticeable.

The duet – particularly "Tu sciagurato! Ah! fuggi" ("You unhappy one! Ah, flee!") – is sustained with great charm and colour, but the blending of the two voices, although treated gracefully, merely sketches what the orchestra expounds harmonically – the use of the oboe on the word "dolore" in "Se un giorno fia che ti tragga degli altari al piede il tuo dolore" ("If one day your grief pushes you into marriage") and the short notes on the beat that build up a sense of agitation, passionately expressing the overwrought state of both characters. Nevertheless, in Gualtiero's "Pietosa al padre!" ("Pity for your father!"), an *andante sostenuto* in C minor, there is a remarkable fusion of the vocal line and the orchestra. However, in retrospect, the scene as a whole assumes great significance, inasmuch as here Bellini's striving to express words dramatically through his music begins to take shape, heralding his ultimate achievement in this respect in *La sonnambula* and *Norma*.

Ernesto is introduced by a march (in F major, 4/4 time), which is followed by the warriors' chorus "Più temuto, più splendido nome" ("A more feared and splendid name"), with a stage band. This is a very ordinary tune whose banality, if not its triviality, is unrelieved by its orchestration. Not that Ernesto's aria "Si vincemmo, e il pregio io sento" ("Yes, we conquered and are proud"), borrowed with minimal alteration from Adelson's "Obbliarti! Abbandonarti!", is an improvement. This is the least interesting part of the opera, possibly because Bellini found the character of Romani's Ernesto antipathetic. In actuality, it was the composer himself who miscalculated when he discarded some of Romani's lines which essentially build Ernesto's characterisation as well as the plot. Ernesto's words were to the effect that, although he had stained himself profusely with enemy blood, he was not satisfied, as Gualtiero fled unpunished. Even so, this baritone aria, despite its inadequacy, is a forerunner of Rodolfo's "Vi ravviso" (*La sonnambula*) and Riccardo's "Ah! per sempre io ti perdei" (*I Puritani*).

Bellini rises to the occasion in the exquisite sextet "Parlati ancor per poco" ("I want to speak to you again for a little longer") in the finale to act one. In declamatory style, he skilfully gives one motif to Gualtiero and his companion, Itulbo, heroic and forceful in character, and another to Imogene and her confidante, Adele, feminine and full of anxiety. Ernesto and Goffredo have distinct vocal lines of their own:

The first two motifs are like a duet for four voices, with Ernesto providing an effective contrast and Goffredo generally commenting, yet the different emotions saturate the music as the voices blend in a masterly way with the chorus and orchestra and with one another without losing their own individuality. The result is a perfect union of art and theatrical sense that arouses and stirs the listener. It does not resolve the action, but it is expansive and an outlet for suffering spirits.

The second act begins with the chorus "Che rechi tu?" ("What's new?"), in which Imogene's ladies comment sympathetically on her melancholy. It is not a noteworthy piece, its only merit being in focusing our attention on Imogene's problems, thus making the ensuing scene more effective.

In the duet "Tu m'apristi in cor ferita" ("You have opened a wound in my heart") between Ernesto and Imogene, the declamatory style gives way at the *larghetto* to more lyrical outpourings in conventional thirds and sixths, creating a tension in Ernesto's reproaches to Imogene. The duet "Vieni, cerchiam pè mari al nostro duol conforto" ("Come, let our grief find solace on the seas") for Imogene and Gualtiero (the scene is Romani's invention, so that the lovers may have a last embrace) is notable for its tenderness and melodious phrases and for preparing the ground for the powerful trio "Cedo al destin orribile" ("I surrender myself to the horrible destiny"), when Ernesto enters and only at the very end reveals himself to the two lovers. Although the greatest merit of this trio is the finely articulated, long-spun vocal line, the orchestral accompaniment also makes a subtly appropriate contribution.

The composer's genius is more evident in the last two scenes of the opera, when for the first time he penetrates deeply into human emotions. All his capabilities, melodic invention, originality, feeling for expressing words, orchestral colour and dramatic declamation are here made use of simultaneously. Gualtiero's "Tu vedrai la sventurata" ("If you should see the unhappy cause") reaches great depths of pathos through an essentially tender and delicate melody, enhanced by brilliant embellishments – expressly written for Rubini's extraordinary vocal capabilities. With less talent in the vocal delivery, the aria unavoidably becomes less memorable.[40]

The final scene begins with a prelude of wide scope – Bellini's first achievement in purely instrumental melody:

A long, intensely emotional cor anglais solo – accompanied by harp, violas, two *soli* violoncelli and two *soli* contrabassi – is a masterpiece of instrumental colouring, during which every movement and reaction of the mentally deranged Imogene is prescribed in the score. The cor anglais substitutes for the human voice while Imogene, in effect, mimes the physical action. She appears delirious and weeping holding her son by the hand. While she looks for something in the air, she momentarily rejoices before relapsing into gloom. In vain, her son tries to console her, but she can no longer hear him. He then runs into Adele's arms, begging her to help his mother. Adele, weeping, draws closer to Imogene but soon realises that she has lost her reason.

Imogene's recitative "Oh! s'io potessi dissipar le nubi" ("Oh, if only I could disperse the clouds"), a telling arioso not entirely abandoning the declamatory form, describes her madness realistically and with dignity, in musical terms. All her passionate grief is summed up in "E desso... Ernesto! Ei parla... Ei chiama il figlio" ("It is he... Ernesto! He speaks... He calls his son"). Her aria "Col sorriso d'innocenza" ("With an innocent smile"), a beautiful melody with long-drawn phrases and mood painting from the orchestra, gives an abstract dimension to the words, thereby deepening their meaning – a worthy forerunner of the best in *La sonnambula*.

Following a solemn brass fanfare and offstage male chorus announcing the condemnation of Gualtiero, Imogene's short recitative with female chorus changes the mood and atmosphere to prepare for the nadir of her despair as she imagines she sees a scaffold for Gualtiero's execution and her own purification.

The cabaletta "O sole, ti vela" ("Oh sun, quickly cast yourself in darkness") is in two verses, linked by a short recitative. The *fioriture* in the first are part of the melody and in the second they are further elaborated with perfectly integrated embellishments:

Allegro giusto

Even at the moment of final despair, the composer introduces subtle contrasts, as when the powerful phrase beginning "O sole" changes abruptly to the pathetic "Ma il sangue già gronda" ("But already the blood is flowing"). The construction and, to some extent, the melody of this cabaletta recalls, if only fleetingly, the musical style of Spontini and, indirectly, that of Rossini. What Bellini offers, in addition, is the longer span of melodic phrases which ultimately transform human emotions into completely musical terms. It is primarily this quality that has contributed to making this the first great mad scene in 19th-century Italian opera – undoubtedly the precursor of Donizetti's mad scenes in *Anna Bolena* and *Lucia di Lammermoor* and of some of Bellini's subsequent operas, namely *I Puritani*.

With *Il pirata*, his longest score to date, Bellini revealed his individual talent as an operatic composer, even though there is still evidence of Rossinian influence, especially in the parts that he borrowed from his own opera *Adelson e Salvini*. The highly evocative declamatory style, used throughout the score with musical invention and without dispensing with melody – in fact, lengthening the melodic phrases – began to restore dramatic expression to opera. True, Bellini was experimenting, and not surprisingly the opera is uneven – the relapses sound more ordinary than they would otherwise – but often the experiment is successful and the originality striking. When this is so, the composer does not merely sketch or delineate the leading characters of the drama but enters into their hearts. Above all, he has begun to free himself from convention, and if his musical phrases at their best are not yet better than those of his most eminent contemporaries, they are certainly quite individual.

The roles of Imogene and Gualtiero require singers who are able to overcome considerable vocal difficulties and still have enough power in reserve to act the characters that they are portraying. Imogene, like Norma, must be a dramatic *soprano d'agilità*, although the former is a far easier role in practically all aspects. Gualtiero must possess a tenor voice with dramatic as well as lyric qualities and must be capable of singing florid music and unusually high notes.

The original interpreters, Rubini and Méric-Lalande, were able to achieve all these qualities, although not without Bellini's persistent coaching. It was, after all, a new way of singing that he required. The role of Imogene assumed even greater dimension when Giuditta Pasta sang it, and Bellini considered it well suited to her voice. Wilhelmine Schröder-Devrient was also very successful as Imogene. Although vocally she may not have been as accomplished as Pasta or Méric-Lalande (she had to transpose the part down), with her extraordinary dramatic talents and exciting personality she was able to bring to life Imogene's tragic situation. (She would later sing Romeo in *I Capuleti e i Montecchi* and would win Wagner's admiration.)

The mantle of Gualtiero fell on Mario, who found the role very suitable for his talents. "We have never heard Mario to such advantage," wrote Chorley in 1845. After Pasta, Giulia Grisi (1811-69) took the role of Imogene, which she sang with Mario as Gualtiero. Chorley called her "superb, looking magnificent" and "singing with all her lustre of voice and more than her old volubility of execution". Strangely, both Mario and Grisi dropped *Il pirata* from their repertoires after having sung in it comparatively seldom – about 15 times – throughout three seasons. This may have been because, as Théophile Gautier wrote, Grisi found the role of Imogene a little high. The opera then fell into neglect for many years. This was most probably because, as in other Bellini operas, dramatic singers with coloratura technique were not easy to be found.

In the previous century, *Il pirata* was revived in Rome in 1935 for the centenary of Bellini's death, with Iva Pacetti and Beniamino Gigli, and in 1951 at Catania, with Lucy Kelston and Mirto Picchi. Neither of the Imogenes really possessed the requirements of the role; they merely helped to make the performances of *Il pirata* possible. The Gualtieros, on the other hand, were much better; Gigli offered a marvellous voice and Picchi had intelligence and not inconsiderable vocal technique.

The opera had to wait until 1958 to be magnificently revived at La Scala. Maria Callas, a dramatic *soprano d'agilità* in the true tradition of Pasta, found Imogene an ideal role for her extraordinary dramatic-vocal talents. The Gualtiero of the performance, Franco Corelli, was also able to do justice to the role and contributed considerably to this triumphant revival. Callas also sang Imogene (in concert) in 1959 at Carnegie Hall, New York, and in Philadelphia. Despite this, however, few revivals of *Il pirata* followed. Again, suitable singers simply were not available.

It was left to Montserrat Caballé to revive the opera with any success, first in concert at Carnegie Hall (1966), then at the Maggio Musicale Fiorentino (1967), in Philadelphia (1968) and in concert at Drury Lane, London (1969).

Lucia Aliberti's Imogene (Valle d'Itria Festival, 1987) captured the pathos of the role to a degree, her performance losing some of its impact for trying too often to imitate Callas's timbre and vocal inflections, thereby diminishing her individuality.

5

The Second *Bianca* in Genoa (1828)

For the first season of the new opera house in Genoa, the Teatro Carlo Felice, works of four Italian composers – Rossini, Donizetti, Bellini and Morlacchi – were chosen. With the exception of Rossini, who did not come to Genoa and in any case did not write a new work for the occasion but instead contributed his *Il barbiere di Siviglia* and *Otello*, all the other composers came to stage their works. Donizetti wrote *Alina, regina di Golconda*, Morlacchi wrote *Colombo* and Bellini offered his refurbished *Bianca e Fernando*. This was the second time that Bellini and Donizetti had produced operas for the same season, the first having been in Naples, where Bellini gave *Bianca e Gernando* and Donizetti staged *Elvida*.

Bellini arrived in Genoa with several letters of introduction given to him by friends in Milan. One such was to the Marchesa Lomellini, but apart from her he met few people at the beginning of his stay, because he had not yet finished the revisions of *Bianca e Fernando* and the rehearsals were scheduled to start on 24 March. However, everything went smoothly until the last rehearsal with the orchestra, when Tosi decided that she did not like her aria. Like Rubini in *Il pirata*, she too wanted the music to provide her with the opportunity to exhibit her vocal technique. But Bellini was just as firm with Tosi as he had been with Rubini. In his letter to Florimo of 5 April,[1] he described how he successfully handled the incident, acting according to his artistic beliefs:

Last night was the last full rehearsal and tonight will be the final rehearsal. The pieces on which I have my hopes set are the three cavatinas, the finale of the first act, the duet and the two scenes of the second act, especially Tosi's scene, which is indescribably effective. The first tempo is made up of a *largo*, the second is the *agitato* that you know about and the third is made up of a cabaletta which is brilliantly declaimed and transports the listener. We certainly won't have a failure.

In this case, however, as the theatre is new, and as there will be many foreigners about on the first night and too much light in the auditorium, I believe that the opera won't have much of an effect. But on Tuesday, the second night, the opera will make a greater impact and everyone will then be able to comment on it constructively. Yesterday, the duet made everyone there cry. David and Tosi sang it like angels and David, in particular, sang it better than ever…

I don't know who came up with the preposterous idea that Tosi has amorous designs on me. Neither she nor I have any thoughts of keeping each other company, and you can be quite certain that, even if I did want to get married, I wouldn't choose a wife from the theatre. It's absolutely true that we have a perfectly harmonious friendship, but this is perhaps because she needs me. As for me, I would be ashamed if I liked her only for what she could do for me. I feel real friendship towards her, and this has nothing to do with the fact that I'm a maestro. You must know that, having seen the piano version of my two new pieces, she wasn't satisfied with the first tempo of the cavatina, so I wrote another. She rehearsed the cavatina with the orchestra and, as she sang it like a crow and therefore didn't really make a good effect, she wanted yet another, but at the same time she didn't want the *stretta* of the scene because she said that it has no agility, that this is music for boys and that, if I hadn't changed it for her, she would have substituted another piece for it. So you can see I've been through a difficult period, but I didn't write to you about it earlier because I didn't have time. I told her that I wouldn't change one note – not because I wanted to annoy her but because I wanted her to perform my music with the tempi as I wrote them. This wasn't a whim on my part; I wanted to give the music the colour as I conceived it. She fought for two days but, seeing my obstinacy and self-confidence (I also kept telling her that she was capricious while I handled her with the utmost care) and because she couldn't find support in either David or the Marchesa Grimaldi, who is the director of the opera, she finally sang my music as I've written it. My dear Florimo, my music had such an effect that afterwards she came back to me to ask for my forgiveness.

David, however, told me that it was Donizetti's idea to make the changes in Tosi's music. I had already suspected as much, because Tosi herself told me that, when Donizetti went over the role with her, he said that the *stretta* of the aria was no good. I believe that what he said was his own honest opinion, without malice and because of his own concern about her. But then, his having gone over it, suggesting so many changes of tempo, all quite different from my own, confirms what I've always believed – that it's absolutely impossible to have friends in the same profession. And the fact that he's staging his own opera immediately after mine[2] doesn't inspire me to believe that he'll take kindly to my success...

I leave you now, Florimo. Receive my embraces and give my regards to Zingarelli and all my friends. Goodbye from your Bellini, who loves you.

The season at the Carlo Felice began on 7 April 1828. The first offering of the evening was an *Inno reale*[3] by Donizetti as a compliment to the royal family, who were all present. Bellini's *Bianca e Fernando* followed, with the new ballet *Gli adoratori del fuoco* by Giovanni Galzerani staged between the two acts of the opera. *Bianca* was a great success, even more than in Naples, and according to the official record it ran for 21 performances. After his success, Bellini wrote a glowing and lengthy letter to Florimo on 10 April:[4]

My fears are over. The opera has produced the desired effect. The first night in a new theatre – although floodlit, and with all the Court in attendance in the royal box, accompanied by the nobility in the other four boxes, and with all the beauties of Genoa and many from elsewhere in *grande toilette*, the music and the singers nevertheless triumphed. This wasn't confined only to a few numbers, either; the public was very happy with the entire opera, particularly with the second act. Also, the King sent one of his chamberlains to thank the maestro and the singers. He also sent a message to say that he was sorry that, as he was in the theatre in an official capacity, he was unable to applaud. Last night, he kept his word and reserved applause – according to the Court etiquette as laid down by the Teatro di Torino – for the duet of the second act, which is said to be absolutely beautiful, and he listened to the rest of the music without once taking his eyes off the singers, who were all very, very pleased. In this performance, Tosi sang 1,000 times better than on the first night, as did David and Tamburini. After the first night, my enemies started to speak badly of the opera, but after the applause from the King they had to eat their words and say that, in order to enjoy Bellini's music, it's necessary to listen to it more than once, as with *Il pirata* in Milan. But how many people have the common sense to understand that, even when one can't applaud, one can still enjoy something?...

All Genoa is very happy with the opera, except that they have to pay 28 francs for a seat and eight to stand...

I haven't sold the copyright of the score, and now I'll have the new pieces printed. My contribution will be a little more than a third of the expenses and I will share the profits with the publisher. I'll also reserve the right to dedicate the new pieces – the three cavatinas, the two scenes, the chorus and the overture – at my pleasure. Hopefully, I shall do well out of it. Ask Cottrau if he would let me sell some copies from a shop. If so, I'll send them to you and, if you agree, offer him the usual commission.

For the moment, I'll stay here, but in a fortnight I'll decide if I have to go back to Milan, because the air is better there than here. I will leave you now, because I have a million letters to write to Milan and home, etc. Let Mr Zingarelli and Crescentini, the rector, and the Andreani family and all our friends read this letter. I hope they will be pleased, and our enemies, too, so that they may die [with envy]. Goodbye, my dear Florimo. Love me and pray to God that my good fortune will continue. I don't know yet what contract I will have for the carnival season. I won't come to Naples, even if they cover me in gold. I would like to go to Venice, but I don't yet have an impresario. Enough – we will wait for what fortune brings us. Be happy, my dear, and stop worrying. Goodbye.

Your Bellini, who loves you.

Although *Bianca e Fernando* was a great success with the public, the critics had great reservations. On 11 April, *L'Eco di Milano* reported, "The music of *Bianca e Fernando* doesn't compare with the composer's music for *Il pirata* and is without themes throughout. The second act is a long bore."

On 12 April, the *Gazzetta di Genova* was more constructive: "At the new Teatro Carlo Felice, Bellini's opera *Bianca e Fernando* continues to be performed. The more we listen to the style of the music, the more we appreciate its merit. The better pieces are the duet of the second act, which is beautifully rendered and sung by David and Tosi; the charming romance; and the rondo, exquisitely executed by Tosi, with which she ended the performance. The public fully appreciated the opera."

For the inaugural season at the Carlo Felice, two overlapping companies were engaged, one for *opera seria* and the other for *opera buffa*. The second opera to be performed was *Il barbiere di Siviglia*. In a letter to Florimo[5] on 16 April, Bellini wrote, "Rossini's *Il barbiere* has been performed and it was an unbelievable failure. Even Tamburini didn't seem to be the same person that he was in Milan, because on this occasion he was partnered by a very bad prima donna and a mediocre tenor. Tosi continues to have trouble with her throat, but one hopes that she will sing tomorrow, as the King – who can no longer bear to hear this *Il barbiere* – yesterday ordered that *Bianca* should be given extra performances instead... So tonight *Bianca* will be performed and we shall see what happens..."

After the failure of *Il barbiere*, Rossini's *Otello* was produced with David and Tosi in the leading roles and with the mezzo-soprano Brigida Lorenjani in the tenor role of Rodrigo. With Rossini absent from Genoa, Bellini's services were required. He mentions this to Florimo on 21 April:[6] "Last night, the Marchese Grimaldi – the musical director – tried hard to persuade me to write a cavatina and *scena* for Lorenzani, who is singing Rodrigo in *Otello*, and as I couldn't refuse directly, I've done so by asking an inflated price for it. My price is 1,000 francs, and so far they've offered me 500, but I'm stubborn and I won't write for less than 1,000 francs."

If Bellini wrote this cavatina, it was unfavourably received by the press: "Mme Lorenzani would have been happier if she hadn't introduced the aria that became the 'war horse' 'Un bel giorno'; even the most beautiful songs don't fit the themes of every opera."

The new version of *Bianca e Fernando* was to be published by Ricordi. However, not forgetting Cottrau, who had published his first *Bianca*, Bellini promptly sent him the new soprano *scena* "Deh, non ferir! Ah, sentimi" through Florimo on 10 April:[7] "It was very hard work for me to copy all this so quickly. This is something I won't be able to do again. I've done it now in order to show my gratitude towards Cottrau, because he never asked for any money for printing the score..."

Quite satisfied with his success in Genoa, Bellini left for Milan on 29 April in the great hope of obtaining a contract for a new opera for La Scala. Shortly before he left Genoa, he received a proposal to write an opera for Turin, but he turned this down. In a letter to Florimo[8] on 19 April, he explains:

> In Milan, I'll start my studies again and begin preparations for my next opera, the subject of which I still don't know, nor where it will be performed. Conte Ferreri has invited me to write for Turin, but he won't pay me more than 3,500 lire. Pollini advised me not to accept less than 4,000.[9] I've told Ferreri this and also my condition that Romani writes the libretto. I haven't yet had an answer. My last condition will certainly stop all negotiations; all the libretti in Turin are written by Conte (I don't know his surname), who makes a *pasticcio* of Metastasio's libretti, as in *Didone e l'Ezio*, which Mercadante told me about. I won't write for this kind of libretto even if they give me the kingdom. I also have doubts about the company, which has Camporesi, who is good but 45 years old; Lorenzani, as you know; and Bonfigli, who they tell me has a nice voice but is a ham. On top of all this, they'll have a bad libretto, so it will be a complete failure. Really, my dear Florimo, I would rather not write at all than be hissed at, especially in these times, when I have made many enemies out of jealousy for my *Pirata*.

Another important event took place during Bellini's stay in Genoa. He had already heard much from Marianna Pollini about the young, beautiful Giuditta Turina, the rich wife of Ferdinando Turina. In Genoa, he was introduced to her by the Marchesa Lomellini, and the dedication "Gran scena di aria finale – 'Deh, non ferir! Ah sentime' – nella *Bianca e Fernando* – Cantata dalla Signora Adelaide Tosi – Composta e dedicata alla Signora Giuditta Turina – da Vincenzo Bellini" now turns our attention to this woman's association with the composer.

BIANCA E GERNANDO (I) AND BIANCA E FERNANDO (II)
I *Melodramma* in two acts. Libretto by Domenico Gilardoni. First performed at the Teatro San Carlo, Naples, on 30 May 1826.
II *Melodramma serio* in two acts. Revisions and additions in both the libretto and music by Felice Romani and Bellini respectively. First performed at the Teatro Carlo Felice, Genoa (at the theatre's inauguration), on 7 April 1828. The opera was preceded by an *Inno reale*

composed for the occasion by Donizetti and on a double bill with the ballet *Gli adorati del fuoco*, choreographed by Giovanni Galzerani. Alessandro Sanquirico designed the stage sets.

CHARACTERS AND ORIGINAL CASTS		I	II
Bianca, Carlo's daughter	Soprano	Enrichetta Méric-Lalande	Adelaide Tosi
Gernando, Carlo's son	Tenor	Giovanni Battista Rubini	—
Fernando, Carlo's son	Tenor	—	Giovanni David
Filippo, an adventurer	Bass	Luigi Lablache	Antonio Tamburini
Carlo, Duke of Agrigento	Bass	Umberto Berettoni	Giuseppe Rossi
Viscardo, Filippo's aide	Mezzo-soprano	Almerinda Manzocchi	Elisabetta Coda
Eloisa, Bianca's attendant	Mezzo-soprano	Eloisa Manzocchi	Marietta Riva
Clemente	Bass	Michele Benedetti	Agostino Rovere
Uggero	Tenor	Gaetano Chizzola	Antonio Crippa

The action takes place at Agrigento during an unspecified time.

Filippo, an adventurer, having deprived Carlo, Duke of Agrigento, of his territory, has kept him secretly in prison; Carlo has been reported dead to his people and his children. His daughter Bianca, a widow with a child, does not know of Filippo's treachery and believes him to be an honest and faithful man, so much so that she has entrusted the regency of her family's dominions to him. In his scheme to legalise his position, Filippo seeks to marry Bianca. She in turn means to accept him and give the people of Agrigento a legitimate lord and defender. At this point in the story, the opera begins.

ACT I
SCENE 1: The courtyard of the palace. In the background are the city and harbour of Agrigento.

Bianca's younger brother Fernando, who was banished from Agrigento by Filippo, is now a grown man. He returns from Britain with a band of mercenaries to avenge his father. His plan is to appear before Filippo as a soldier of fortune with the name of Adolfo and thus try to win his confidence. In his mission, Fernando soon finds a trustworthy ally in Clemente, a former soldier and the only person who has recognised him.

SCENE 2: Filippo's apartments in the palace.

Fernando is presented to Filippo as Adolfo with the pretext of having important information regarding the heir to the dukedom (ie himself). Filippo is happy to receive him, but when he hears that Adolfo saw Carlo's son killed in battle in Scotland, he has serious doubts about the authenticity of the story. Adolfo then produces a letter in Fernando's handwriting (supposedly taken from him after he fell in battle) and Filippo and his aide, Viscardo, are so delighted to have such strong evidence that, as a reward, the soldier is taken into official service. However, Fernando's joy at his success thus far is diminished when he hears of Filippo's impending marriage to Bianca. Without another thought, Fernando jumps to the conclusion that his sister has been a partner in Filippo's schemes.

SCENE 3: A square in Agrigento.

Bianca declares to the people of Agrigento her faith in Filippo – he will always defend their fortunes. She then speaks of her own new-found happiness, but when she hears the story of Fernando's death recounted by the soldier (having failed to recognise her brother) in such a stark, almost cruel way, she is so disturbed that she begins to feel uncertain about her decision to marry Filippo.

ACT II

SCENE 1: Courtyard of the palace in Agrigento.

After Filippo has informed Adolfo of his intention to marry Bianca, he entrusts him with the task of killing the imprisoned Duke Carlo. Filippo explains that, when the proud Carlo would not agree with his aspirations to marry his daughter, he managed to draw him into a dark prison, at the same time convincing everybody, including Bianca, that Carlo had died of natural causes. Viscardo, Filippo continues, will lead Adolfo to the secret prison where the old man lies. Adolfo is further instructed to make Carlo's suffering more painful by telling him that his son is dead and that his daughter has become Filippo's wife. Another soldier will then kill the old man, under Adolfo's supervision. Fernando thus discovers that his father is still alive, but his happiness is again marred by his belief that Bianca has been Filippo's accomplice.

SCENE 2: A room in Bianca's apartments.

While Bianca is preparing for her wedding to Filippo, she tells Eloisa, her lady-in-waiting, of her intense grief that the loss of her father has caused her. Still troubled by the news of her brother's death, Bianca asks to see the soldier again. Fernando reveals his true identity and accuses Bianca of complicity to Filippo's treachery. She denies any complicity and also does not believe that Filippo is guilty until Fernando tells her that their father is alive, indeed kept in a living tomb, and that he, Fernando, has been given instructions to supervise his killing. Bianca then agrees to dress up as a soldier herself and go with Fernando to their father. Before they go, Fernando muses on the forthcoming reunion with his father and accepts Bianca as his sister once more.

SCENE 3: The tombs of the dukes of Agrigento, where Carlo is kept prisoner.

Carlo feels that death is approaching; only Fernando can save him from his living tomb. He then asks God to banish Bianca from his mind, as he, too, believes that she has been Filippo's accomplice. Presently, Fernando and Bianca arrive. They are horrified to see their father in such circumstances and Bianca is convinced of Filippo's treachery. Father and son are reunited, but Carlo talks of vengeance on Filippo and Bianca, whom he curses on recognising her. Before long, however, Carlo becomes very understanding and forgives his heartbroken daughter.

While Fernando and Bianca are being reunited with their father, the populace of Agrigento, stirred into action by Fernando's partisans, revolt against Filippo. When Bianca and Fernando face Filippo, who has burst in on them, he threatens to kill Bianca's son. Bianca implores Filippo to spare the life of her son and in return his life will also be spared. Just then, however, Clemente disarms the unobserving Filippo and rescues the child.

SCENE 4: The great hall of the palace.

Amidst great rejoicing, Duke Carlo is hailed as the ruler of Agrigento. Bianca thanks Heaven for their present happiness.

Gilardoni based his libretto of *Bianca e Fernando* on Carlo Roti's play *Bianca e Fernando alla tomba di Carlo IV, duca di Agrigento*, which had been successfully produced at the Teatro dei Fiorentini in 1820.[10] The ballet *Bianca di Messina*, by Salvatore Taglioni, with music by Brambilla and much the same characters and plot, had been produced at La Scala in 1824.[11] Play, ballet and libretto are all very loosely based on historical fact. A Charles II of Anzou, who was at one time imprisoned, can be traced in Sicilian history. This Charles had a daughter called Bianca, but he had no son called Fernando, and nor was he connected in any way with Agrigento, where the action in Gilardoni's libretto is supposed to take place.

Unlike most opera plots of the period, that of *Bianca* is simple and unconfused. It has certain basic similarities with *Fidelio* in the way in which Fernando and Bianca rescue their imprisoned father. Another unusual aspect of the libretto is that there is no tangle of passions in it; the story is devoid of any sexual love. What Gilardoni tried to bring to it – and what Romani considerably improved upon, when he later made additions and tidied up generally – was a certain dignity to the problems of the father and his children.

Eleven declamatory bars, in restlessly changing tempo, introduce the *andante*, which forms the first, main part of the overture. Despite some originality in these first bars and beauty in the melody of the *andante*, the overture fails to rise far above banality. Repetition in the following *allegro* hinders full development, resulting in seemingly undue length and tediousness; although apparently outlined by a more experienced hand than that which wrote *Adelson e Salvini*, it is still less substantial in musical conception. Of the first four numbers of the opera, only one – Fernando's cavatina "A tanto duol" ("From such grief"), with short chorus – merits special mention for its limpid melody, already characteristically Bellinian:

The remainder of the music is weak and uninteresting until the fifth number, the trio "Di Fernando son le cifre" ("This is Fernando's monogram"), in which the composer rises to the dramatic possibilities of the situation. The bold nature of Fernando's deceit is well noted in the recitative, the asides and the virile description of the battle in which he is supposed to have been killed. The other two characters are also well differentiated. The orchestral accompaniment subtly suggests Filippo's doubts as he examines the letter in Fernando's handwriting. The pauses before the words "gode, esulta" in Fernando's "Di mia morte" create a dramatic effect while at the same time giving an opportunity for the entry of Viscardo into the trio.

The finale to the first act contains many well-varied episodes. Almost all the music is distinguished and is often beautiful. The chorus "Viva Bianca" ("Long live Bianca"), which begins with trumpets and drums, is in fine style and conveys a feeling of festivity and rejoicing, using a polonaise rhythm. It is also significant that Bellini was already able to use the simplest harmonies to great effect:

The vigorous recitative "La mia scelta a voi sia grata" ("May my choice be right") establishes Bianca almost at once as an imposing character – Bellini's first heroic female creation, a prototype of Norma and Beatrice. The aria "Contenta appien quest'alma" ("My soul is fully content") further delineates her character in infectiously lively melody. (With the elimination of the rests and different *fioriture*, which change the gaiety into desperate anxiety, this aria later became the cabaletta "Ah bello, a me ritorna", which follows "Casta Diva" in *Norma*.)

In the trio "Il lor duce?" ("To the leader?") for Bianca, Filippo and Fernando, the voices maintain a unified line without losing their individual character. This is followed by Fernando's melancholic *largo* "Ah che l'alma invade un gel!" ("I have a feeling that something dreadful is about to happen!"), which develops into a quintet with choral accompaniment. The opening, with its alternating *staccato* and *legato* phrases and elegantly used chromatic harmony, is both original and moving, and the ensemble is built with a sure hand. The voices are interestingly distributed: one soprano, two tenors and two basses. Although the score indicates two tenors, the second, Viscardo, was sung – in both the Naples (1826) and the Genoa (1828) premieres – by a mezzo-soprano, still producing a somewhat unusual ensemble.

The dialogue between Filippo and Bianca in "Qual da folgore colpita" ("I was struck by a thunderbolt") begins vigorously but soon loses most of its impact, ending somewhat tritely.

It is in the spirited concerted section "Lieto apparve questo giorno"

("How pleasant this day seems"), an *allegro con fuoco*, that the composer ingeniously uses Bianca's violent interruption of the ensemble with "Rode e lacera il mio petto" ("In the evening, those words of his grind my heart") to heighten the dramatic tension of the scene and conclude the act with much anticipation of what is to follow.

The second act is much more successful than the first. (In the original version, *Bianca e Gernando*, the second act lacked weight and importance, but this was remedied by four extra numbers that were added when Bellini revised the opera.) Filippo's sombre aims and Fernando's suppressed indignation are musically set in varied recitatives which are both dramatic and vigorous in their vocal stress. These recitatives are accompanied by a series of thrilling motifs and effective outbursts, such as "La vive!" ("He is alive!"), building up the dramatic atmosphere relevant to the characters of the two men. Filippo's aria "Allor che notte avanza" ("Night approaches"), although a little monotonous due to insufficiently varied accompaniment, nevertheless conveys much appropriate acrimony and gloom.

In the next scene, Bellini reveals himself as a true melodist. He also shows how well suited he was to write for the female voice. The fine romanza "Sorgi, o padre" ("Arise, Father") for Bianca and Eloisa is preceded by an instrumental introduction that sets the atmosphere:

The romanza is extremely well constructed, achieving a good balance between the voices. Solo parts alternate with duets in thirds and sixths, and the accompaniment, although simple (as if played by a "huge piano"), is subtly varied to enhance the vocal line. The duet has a beautiful cantilena and, if not as dramatically accomplished as some of the composer's later duets, is their legitimate forerunner.

A further duet, "No... Mia suora più non sei" ("No... No more, my lady") between Bianca and Fernando is powerful, particularly in the declamatory but melodious recitative "Don te chiamate, or dianzi!" ("Do not disturb me at this moment!"). The duet itself, with strong Rossinian influence in the orchestral accompaniment, is marred by commonplace cadenzas until remedied by a rise in dramatic tone in Fernando's revelation to Bianca "Inorridisci, nostro padre!" ("Horrified, our father!").

Fernando's aria "All'udir del padre afflitto" ("On hearing of the misfortunes of an afflicted father") has great similarity in texture, rhythm and motifs to the first movement of Beethoven's piano sonata opus 27, number two, in C-sharp minor ("the Moonlight"), although here these appear in the key of F major, modulating to A flat. It is well adapted, however, and the result is effective without giving the impression of parody.

Carlo's cavatina "Da gelido sudore" ("I feel myself shivering") is musically distinguished for the dramatic depth given to the character. The *andante maestoso* orchestral introduction suggests immediately, in a few skilful bars, the plight of the aged and infirm prisoner who has been buried in a living tomb. Here, the composer does not resort to undue emphasis but subtly conveys the character's state of mind through unhappy recollections of his distant children and the thought of approaching death. Minor harmonies and telling use of the Neapolitan sixth chord all contribute to the atmosphere of this cavatina.

The ensuing trio "Oh, Dio! qual voce" ("Oh, God! That voice"), for Bianca, Fernando and Carlo, begins with great simplicity in both the vocal and harmonic lines. During the anxious dialogue that takes place, the scene becomes dramatically effective with the return of the melody in Carlo's lament when he, astonished and ruffled, drives his daughter away.

Another powerful episode follows at the beginning of the finale, when Filippo threatens to kill Bianca's child. (In the original version, the child does not appear in the flesh. When Romani revised the libretto, he required the child's presence, as he had done in *Il pirata* – an anticipation of the infanticide theme that was to be used so strikingly later, in *Norma*.) The most noteworthy piece in this scene is Bianca's touching maternal invocation "Deh, non ferir!" ("Alas, do not strike!"), which is typical of Bellini's style, with limpid melody and simple yet appropriate accompaniment:

Bianca's aria finale, "Alla gioia ed al piacer" ("Such irresistible joy and pleasure"), does not have the bounding, forcible expression of "Ah! non giunge" in *La sonnambula*, nor is it as imaginatively composed. Nevertheless, it is unusually mature in context, working up to great animation and fully expressing Bianca's final joy:

Bianca e Fernando differs extensively from *Bianca e Gernando*. Four new numbers, added in the second act, include *coro, scena ed aria* "All'udir del padre afflitto" (Fernando); *recitativo* "Sai tu, Clemente" (Clemente-Uggero); *recitativo* "Da te chiamato, or dianzi" (Bianca-Fernando); and *recitativo ed aria finale* "Deh, non ferir" (Bianca). Also, the original short prelude to the opera was replaced by a full-length overture. Furthermore, Bellini introduced new material into recitatives, added instrumental passages and, with Romani (who provided the text for the new numbers), revised the libretto generally.[12]

In a letter to Florimo[13] on 27 February 1829, Bellini informs him that, "Of the whole of *Bianca* [*e Gernando*], only the big duet and the romanza have remained entirely unchanged; all the rest is altered, and about half is new."

Except for the overture, all the additions and changes proved to have been definite improvements. Nevertheless, the refashioned *Bianca e Fernando*, although not a beginner's effort, remains an uneven work, especially the first act, much of which is dull and uninspired. Perhaps because of the nature of its libretto, the opera is deprived of the winning charm of *Adelson e Salvini* but, to a certain extent, attains the appropriate dignity that is called for. Above all, the most positive gain is the build-up of Bianca as a more balanced and imposing character.

Bianca e Fernando also aspires far higher than *Adelson e Salvini*. Not only does it show a definite advance in its best numbers, but it also achieves a much more poignant dramatic expression; the orchestral accompaniment (the *recitativo secco* is completely abandoned) is more interesting, more melodious and richer in dramatic and psychological modulations and the various numbers are generally better knit.

With the possible exception of "Sorgi, o padre", the melodies in *Bianca e Fernando* are not as irresistibly memorable as later Bellini melodies were to be. More memorable is the way in which the culminating moments of the drama inspired Bellini to such powerful musical expression.

Although the opera was revised after *Il pirata*, *Bianca* remains the inferior work. But even at the time of its first production, its resounding success (obviously merited by the several good pieces in it, despite its inequality) demonstrated that Bellini was a new operatic composer to be reckoned with. It was this that gave him the chance to write *Il pirata*, begin his collaboration with Romani and carry his name outside his own country.

Incidentally, in the composition of *Bianca*, Bellini borrowed music from the trio (Nelly's part) in *Adelson* and used it in the trio "Il lor duce?" in the finale of the first act.

Since 1837, the opera has been staged only once, at the Teatro Margherita Genova in 1978, although it also had two concert performances, in 1976 (RAI, Torino) and 1981 (Queen Elizabeth Hall, London), yet none of these revivals did justice to the work. Neither Jasuko Hayashi nor Cristina Deutekom (the 1976 and 1978 Biancas, respectively) met the vocal or dramatic requirements of the role. The 1981 Bianca, Sandra Hahn, fell considerably short in expression and Bellinian cantilena, and consequently the role never really came to life. The same applies to the interpreters of the role of Fernando.

As with all Bellini's heroines, it is difficult to find the right interpreter for Bianca; neither Montserrat Caballé nor Joan Sutherland – two of the most eligible contemporary singers for the role – showed any interest in it.

6

Giuditta Turina and *La Straniera* (1828-29)

Giuditta Turina was the eldest child of a rich silk merchant from Pavia, Giuseppe Cantù, and Carolina Sopransi. The mother, who belonged to a noble family, was the daughter of Baron Luigi and Giuditta Appiani. The family lived in Milan, where Giuditta was born on 13 February 1803, while Gaetano, the only other child in the family, was born a few years later. Giuditta's beauty and graceful manners, her education in the fine arts and her wealth made her one of the most eligible young ladies in Milan. Her parents, however, made their own arrangements, and at the age of 16 Giuditta was married to Ferdinando Turina, then aged 24 and also a rich Milanese silk manufacturer. The Turina family came from Casalbuttano, a small village near Cremona, where they had their silk factory. They also owned vast areas of fertile land, which made them the richest family in Lombardy.

Ferdinando was handsome and basically good-natured, although boorish in some ways and certainly without Giuditta's good manners and elegance of living. The marriage went badly from the beginning – the two were unsuited, and certainly no love developed between them. They had no children. Ferdinand spent most of his time in his factory at Casalbuttano, while the little time that Giuditta spent there was in seclusion. She spent the greater part of her life at her parents' house in Milan and at their country estate at Moltrasio, on Lake Como. From time to time, she travelled with her brother. It was on one of these occasions that she met Bellini in Genoa, where like many other Milanese they had gone to attend the opening of the new theatre. Although Bellini and Giuditta probably fell in love at first sight, it was later, in Milan, that the affair developed.

Almost everything that we know about their relationship is to be found in Bellini's letters to Florimo and in some that Giuditta wrote to Florimo after Bellini's death. Very little is revealed in the 13 extant letters written by Bellini to Giuditta. Except for the compromising ones that he wrote to her from Paris (which caused her separation from her husband), Bellini's letters were tactfully formal, usually containing polite greetings and expressing good wishes to Giuditta's husband. Many vicious accusations have been levelled that Giuditta used Bellini merely to obtain a separation from her husband and that she caused the deterioration in the composer's health that led to his premature death. This scandal stemmed mainly from the insinuations of a Milanese society lady, which were transmitted to Michele Scherillo, one of Bellini's earlier biographers.[1] She said:

> Signora Turina was rich in patrimony, but she was poorly endowed morally and intellectually; she was generous in every way and spent money freely to satisfy her own caprices. Consequently, by becoming associated with her, Bellini's reputation as a man was diminished and shaken. The separation from her husband had to come about, owing to their incompatibility. Poor Bellini, along with other unfortunates, was trapped in the snare, and he too served only as a pretext.
>
> Giuditta Turina was not beautiful, but she was tall and had a good figure. Although her face was not in the slightest way expressive, it had something sinister about it. She was a great gossip, with a biting tongue that could damage the soundest reputation. Besides this, she was a shameless intriguer. She died old and full of afflictions, mourned by no one. Only one friend – if you can call him this – remained to her, ----R-, who always considered her one of the main causes of the ruin of poor Bellini's health.

None of these accusations – especially those pertaining to Bellini – are true. Indeed, documentary evidence shows rather the reverse. Giuditta was no doubt complex and at times highly strange and difficult, and the unhappy relationship with her husband could hardly have helped. In addition, she was often ill. Her ailments were possibly psychosomatic, to a degree, but more often than not, when Bellini was the centre of attraction amongst his theatre friends, Giuditta was excluded from the scene. As for the accusation that Giuditta was responsible for the ruination of Bellini's health (it was widely believed that he died of tuberculosis brought about by amorous excesses), documentary evidence disproves this. Before his death in Paris, Bellini had not seen her for over two years, and the post-mortem examination confirmed that there was no tuberculosis.

After their first meeting, Giuditta left Genoa for Casalbuttano and a week later Bellini returned to Milan. For some time, he refrained from writing anything about her to Florimo. Either he thought that the affair would be ephemeral or he wanted to reveal it gradually, hoping that in this way Florimo would accept it more easily.

The first veiled references to Giuditta appear several months after their meeting in Genoa. In a letter to Florimo on 30 June 1828,[2] Bellini wrote almost casually, "Now I'm involved with a pretty woman and don't know how it will end. I think that she's in love with me, but I must be on my guard. She is already married and I've found out that she is 25 years old – not from her but from Madama Pollini, who has been acquainted with her for a long time and is a close friend. Enough of this intrigue. I will tell you more about it if it progresses as fast as it has done during the first few days since it started."

There is no mention of Giuditta in his subsequent letters to Florimo until 24 September,[3] when Bellini writes, again casually, "My ladyfriend isn't well, and I'm sorry that I have nothing more of interest to tell you."

In his next letter to Florimo, on 27 September,[4] Bellini pours out the whole story of his love affair. After details about his projected opera, *La Straniera*, the subject changes abruptly. The story is better told in Bellini's own words:

When I arrived in Milan last year and got to know many people, I began to be well received in society and even had a few affairs, but they didn't last long for, as you know, I look for sentiment as well as physical love. Before long, however, I discovered that, with most of them, only the latter prevailed, and that was sufficient for me to give them up while still remaining friends. I continued to drop one and take up another until I went to Genoa, where I became acquainted with my present lover, of whom the Pollinis had often spoken to me... Whenever anyone mentioned her family, Madama Pollini used to say that Giuditta was the best of them all, and that she comes from a family who have millions. Her husband is head of one of the richest houses in Milan, owning a silk factory in a place called Casalbuttano, about 45 miles away, where they spend most of the year. Their name is Turina, and she is the person to whom I dedicated the rondo from *Bianca*.

She was introduced to me by Marchesa Lomellini, and she received me with such kindness that I was charmed on the spot. Moreover, she is affectionate and with a sweetness of manner that quite bowled me over. However, I first became really interested in her about a couple of days later, when I visited her for the first time at her apartment. She was with her brother, her only travelling companion (her husband being occupied with his business affairs). When she saw me, she blushed scarlet, and this unexpected phenomenon rather surprised and enchanted me and made me desire to make love to her.

The visits were kept up for the next few days, and then, when she had to take to her bed in great pain, I took advantage of her indisposition to show my loving concern by keeping her company the whole day. I was alone with her for several hours, and you know how the thoughts uppermost in one's mind can slip unintentionally into the conversation. We began to call ourselves lovers. She expressed grave doubts as to my constancy, because I had to travel about so much and she couldn't always be in Milan. We kept arguing these points, and all the time we were in Genoa the pleasures were confined to conversation, hour-long embraces, amorous kisses and sweet whisperings of love. Nevertheless, she continued to have doubts of my love, and for my part I secretly wondered if in fact it would be any different from my other Milanese affairs.

As she had to leave Genoa for Casalbuttano, she promised to write to me as soon as I returned to Milan, which I did about a week later. I wrote to her first but had no reply. I then wrote a second letter, rather formal, because I intended to provoke her and because I had to let her know about some commissions entrusted to me by friends in Genoa. This time she replied, complaining of my somewhat offhand tone. I wrote again, but no longer in the rapturous terms of my first letter, for I was beginning to see my suspicions confirmed. She did reply, but only after some time, saying that she would be in Milan the coming Wednesday and that she hoped to see me at the theatre.

By this time, I had decided to put her out of my mind, not wishing to appear as someone who runs around after women, and so, when Wednesday evening came, I went as usual to the theatre but didn't even glance towards her box. When I learned from some friends that she had been asking after me, I told them that I'd be going to see her that evening. Determined to stick to my resolution, however, and knowing that she would be leaving the next day at noon, I went to her only at the end of the performance and remained standing as I greeted her and wished her *bon voyage*.

She was fuming with rage, but the next day, at eight o'clock in the morning, her servant arrived with the message that his mistress wished to see me. I went along, and when she reproached me for my cold demeanour, I answered that in love one does not joke, and that I thanked God I hadn't lost my peace of mind. She then explained that she couldn't reply at once to my letters for fear of arousing her husband's suspicions, as well as for other reasons. Finally, I was persuaded, but I remained on my guard. She left but was back in Milan the following week. She went to the theatre very seldom, in order to be with me, and after a few evenings of amorous discourse, embraces and kisses, I gathered the flower of love almost in haste, because her father was at home and we had all the doors open. Swooning with love, she said to me, "Bellini, will you always love me? Will you love me still more?..." I replied to her, swearing that I would, if she deserved it. In fact, being a very rich, beautiful woman, with all the qualities that mark her out as being desirable company, she has always been invited everywhere, but now she has put all this behind her. She no longer goes to noisy parties, and her only pleasure is with me. When she does find herself in a crowd, she is afflicted with melancholy, and now that all the signs indicate that she truly loves me, my mind is tranquil. The affair seems to be serious, so I am now confiding our secret to you...

To Madama Pollini, who is a woman of the world, I have confided everything, and she sometimes corrects me, as she always does in other things, and perhaps in another letter I will tell you more. I've not told you anything before because I was afraid of alarming you unnecessarily, as the affair was likely to fizzle out. Now I think it will last, and this is the honest history of it. My dear Florimo, this affair will save me from marrying, and you, I believe, will understand my weakness in letting myself fall desperately in love.

Give my regards to all and receive my embraces. Signor Pollini sends his regards, and love me as I love you. Goodbye. Your Bellini.

Giuditta's initial apparent disinterest, when she failed to answer Bellini's letters, may have been her way of controlling herself. Her position as a married woman must have made her insecure when she realised that the affair was not mere flirtation but that she was genuinely falling in love. Consequently, she might have sought assurances of Bellini's love before she gave herself to him. She certainly went on loving him, even after he died.

When Bellini returned to Milan from Genoa, he had no contract for a new opera. However, because of his already considerable reputation as an opera composer – in Italy, at least – he hoped to write a new opera for the forthcoming carnival season at La Scala. In the meantime, *Il pirata* was being prepared for production at the Teatro San Carlo, an event that both pleased and infuriated him. As in Vienna, Rubini and his wife were to be the protagonists, and Bellini was again on the warpath against Comelli, especially since *Il pirata* was to be staged in a gala performance on 30 May, on the occasion of the King's name-day. Through Florimo, whom he appointed as his representative in Naples, Bellini tried hard to persuade Barbaja that Tosi should be substituted for Comelli. "Try anything to stop Comelli from singing in *Il pirata*, and do it in such a way that Rubini won't suspect what you're doing," he wrote to Florimo. Bellini also hoped that Zingarelli would exert his influence on Barbaja. "A Zingarelli miracle?" he asked. Whether or not Florimo and Zingarelli tried to get rid of Comelli, Barbaja paid no attention and, in fact, did not permit Florimo to help with the rehearsals.

Contrary to Bellini's fears, *Il pirata* was a success at the San Carlo, as it had been in Vienna. The Milanese *I Teatri* reported, "What enthusiasm this beautiful opera can incite when it's well produced... The enthusiasm reached its peak with the cavatinas and in the last recitative with Rubini's grand aria... Comelli-Rubini corrected a few faults in some of her arias and in some of her ensembles, for which she had been criticised, and *Il pirata* reached its zenith when these changes were made."

With *Il pirata* successfully launched in Naples, Barbaja went to Milan in June when Pacini's new opera, *I cavalieri di Valenza*, was in rehearsal at La Scala. He met Bellini on 10 June, and on the following day Bellini described the meeting in detail to Florimo:[5]

> Villa wanted me to go and see Barbaja, who wished to talk to me very urgently, and I said that I had no desire to be compromised with a madman, which he is. As we were talking, we saw Barbaja nearby, who, with a smile, shook my hand and in his usual way said, "Baron F, have you received my letter?"

I coolly responded, "No," and he, hiding his surprise, asked Villa, "Did you not send my letter?" I, in the same tone as before, answered that I was certain that his letter had never been addressed directly to me and that therefore I had ignored it. You can imagine that he was quite put out by my answer and, trying to hide his displeasure with a smile, said that he would like to give me a copy to frame... We finished off with Barbaja inviting me to lunch this morning, and as I was leaving he made several propositions to me, but I hinted at my preference to write for the carnival in Milan, even though I'm not yet quite sure of the cast.

Nobody knows whether the King of Naples will permit Lablache to leave Naples. In any case, Tamburini will come here and then I will have Lalande and Winter. Pollini tells me that, in a way, it will be for the better if Rubini doesn't come here, as it will then be impossible for me to produce another opera without it being compared to *Il pirata*. It might be easier to change the style and compose in a new spirit with different singers. Therefore, I will accept the contract for Milan in any case. Perhaps in the next few days, the difficulties of the fees and all other obstacles will be overcome and I can sign the contract.

Barbaja's offer was all that a composer could wish for, but to Bellini it posed problems. Despite Pollini's constructive advice, Bellini really preferred to write again for Rubini. However, Rubini was at the time under contract to the San Carlo and Bellini did not want to return there at this stage of his career. Nevertheless, he agonised for three days, wondering what to do. "The whole of Milan advises me not to abandon La Scala," he wrote to Florimo, "but all my real friends want me to be careful of the singers and the libretto, because it's impossible for either myself or Romani to produce another *Pirata*."

On 14 June, Bellini[6] finally decided to write for La Scala – "God help me," he declared. The opera would open the carnival season on 26 December with Lalande, the tenor Bernando Winter and Lablache or Tamburini, while Romani would be the librettist. Two days later, Bellini informed Florimo:[7]

This morning, I signed the contract to write for La Scala. After much bargaining, my fee has been arranged at 2,000 ducats. It may sound small, but I think you'll agree that it's not really such a bad fee, considering that for each of my last two operas I received only 500 ducats and for my first only 150. So it would seem now that there has been a little rise, don't you agree?

Right now, I'm also in the throes of producing *Il pirata* at Lucca during August and adjusting the part of Ernesto for [Brigida] Lorenzani, the part of Gualtiero for a certain tenor named Reina[8] and that of Imogene for [Giuditta] Grisi,[9] who they tell me should make a good job of it.

I have asked to be paid 340 ducats for my journeys to and fro, the equivalent of 1,500 francs, which will remain intact, as I have been offered free board and lodgings at Lorenzani's, who lives in Lucca with all her family... We'll see what kind of answer I get from the impresario, who probably won't pay me as much as she should for my labours. But enough of this.

If you by any chance have any marvellous ideas for a libretto, send it to me by post, because I may not find anything here.

My health is good, and I hope yours is too... Accept my warmest embraces and give my news and good wishes to Zingarelli, and believe me – I am always your Bellini, who loves you.

Nevertheless, even after signing the contract, Bellini's worries about the new opera were not over. Finding a suitable subject for a libretto was always a difficult task for him, but he was hopeful, as Romani, Florimo and his friends in Milan were also searching for one. Bellini felt more apprehensive at the prospect of having to write the tenor role for Winter, a singer whom he bluntly described as a "dog". Bernando Winter's voice was of poor quality and his Italian pronunciation apparently atrocious. Twice in the present season at La Scala, when he had sung in Pacini's *I cavalieri di Valenza* and in Donizetti's *L'esule di Roma*, the public had strongly disapproved of him.

This seriously concerned Bellini, who could not get Rubini and *Il pirata* out of his mind. Furthermore, all the operas produced at La Scala during that season without Rubini in the cast had failed, and even the music of *L'esule di Roma* – which Bellini considered to be good – could not save the work. Through Florimo, Cottrau and other influential people in Naples, Bellini tried to persuade Barbaja to release Rubini, so that he could be in Milan for as short a time as necessary to sing in the new opera. Permission was also required from the Bourbon Court, but it depended mainly on Barbaja, who completely ignored the request. However, through Florimo, Bellini went on trying to find a way to bring Rubini back to Milan while keeping Domenico Reina in reserve as an alternative to Winter. On 27 September, Bellini wrote to Florimo[10] that he had received good reports of this singer:

> I've written to the tenor Reina in Lucca. He answered me courteously and assured me that his voice has a virile timbre and is always in tune throughout its range, from B flat under the stave to A above at full volume and in the falsetto notes as far as E flat. He has flexibility of voice at full volume and considers his style suitable for my music. Furthermore, he is quite prepared to work like a dog and do everything the way I tell him; he realises that this is the only way to go about it. All this makes me believe that he is a humble young man who will go far. Everyone tells me that his voice is beautiful and that his personality and acting ability leave nothing to be desired. His only defect is that he is short, but for this there is no remedy.

Eventually, after great consideration, Bellini decided to use Arlincourt's romance *La Straniera* for his libretto. For a time, he had considered another Arlincourt romance, *Il solitario*, and one of Schiller's dramas. (The exact one is not known, as our only reference, in a letter to Florimo, does not give the title.) On 5 August, several weeks after he had signed the contract with Barbaja, he wrote at length to Florimo:[11]

> Both Romani and I, and even Pollini, favour Arlincourt's *La Straniera*, the idea with which you yourself have inspired me in one of your letters. Romani won't follow the comedy part in it but will more or less unite the best Romantic situations (don't tell anybody about this, in case another poet steals the idea), which are: the arrival of Arturo on the little island of Montolino; the meeting between Arturo and La Straniera at the fountain; the recognition scene of Valdeburgo with La Straniera, his sister, and the duel with Arturo; the judgement; the *dénouement*; and the death of Arturo. All these may possibly be divided into four little acts, to give the impression of time and place. This is all very promising, but Romani thinks that it will be very difficult to do well without a good tenor for the part of Arturo. The only alternative is to give the part of Arturo to Tamburini...and the

role of Valdeburgo – which is very interesting – to Reina or Tamburini (this all depending on Rubini coming)...

If Rubini has the part of Arturo, I'm almost certain that it will be a success, as he is a good character actor, and everything will be original and impressive. But without Rubini, I may be taking a risk...

I've never said anything about Tamburini, but you should hear what he says about me. Winter, too, is my enemy, because I was unable to defend him against the Milanese public... Therefore, one still has enemies whether one does good or ill, in spite of the fact that one tries hard not to give them any reason. In the meantime, they do the same and we shall all go to the devil...

Although Bellini was unwilling to write for Winter, who thereby became his enemy, he certainly approved of Tamburini and is therefore unlikely to have spoken against him. Tamburini, however, was displeased because the two roles written for him – Ernesto in *Il pirata* and Filippo in *Bianca e Fernando* – were short, and in Naples he denigrated Bellini and his music. Nevertheless, Bellini later wrote other parts for him.

Bellini's difficulties were not only in assembling a satisfactory company for his opera but also with Romani, who was not progressing with the preparation of the libretto. On 6 August, Bellini wrote to Florimo:[12]

I don't understand how you can tell me that I only write to you once a week. For a start, this is not true, as in the past few days I've been writing to you every other day instead of twice a week, and this was because I've had no news from you. I am also very worried about that blessed Romani, who has only given me a boatman's chorus so far and nothing else at all – and even this chorus may be discarded if I have to write a duet or an aria for Tamburini, because I must present the theme in the introduction, and this is very difficult. This evening, there is going to be a conference with the directors, as they want to have a talk with Romani and me in order to be reassured that the opera will be produced for the opening of the season. They really, really want this at any price, and if the second act isn't finished, they want the first act only to be produced. So tonight we shall see what resolutions are made for Romani, because if he doesn't give me the words, I can't write the music.

Notwithstanding Romani's apparent dilatoriness, it is evident from Bellini's letter to Florimo[13] on 23 August that Rubini was still the main worry. Hearing that the tenor David might not go to Paris, Bellini's hopes were raised that Barbaja might keep David in Naples and thus be able to send Rubini to Milan. There was also the question of whether Lablache or Tamburini would be singing in the new opera. In the letter, Bellini wrote:

> Barbaja ought to reply to my letter this week. At the same time, I shall know of the King's decision about Lablache, and so by the beginning of September I shall be able to start work. If I finish by 26 December, the opera will be performed. Otherwise, I shall have to find some good excuses. All in all, my dear friend, it is necessary for me to know for whom I have to write. If I start at the beginning of September, it leaves me three and a half months to write the opera. Barring any mishaps, I think that that should be enough...
>
> After discussing the matter with Pollini, we have decided that to give the part of Arturo in *La Straniera* to Tamburini would be a great risk, because he is cold and his voice, like all bass voices, is monotonous and incapable of sufficient variation. Therefore, as Tamburini may be available, I shall give him the part of Valdeburgo, La Straniera's brother, and perhaps I will give the part of Arturo to the tenor Reina. But enough of this. I will settle everything when I know.

The letter that Bellini anxiously awaited from Barbaja during the last week of August never arrived. However, Bellini heard from Cottrau, who, contrary to his expectation, tried to persuade Barbaja not to release Rubini. Cottrau's letter enraged Bellini but, at the same time, made him realise that there was no hope of Rubini coming to Milan, and at last he was able to make definite plans about the allocation of the roles. On 1 September, Bellini informed Florimo of his decisions:[14]

> You gave me some hope about Rubini because you told me that he is bound to come here and that he himself was going to present my letter to Barbaja. Cottrau, however, surprised me when he said, "Abandon all hope of having Rubini, because Brabaja definitely won't release him from Naples." Those were his words. In this case, I believe what Cottrau says rather than the hope that you still seem to have. Cottrau

is a good friend and he wouldn't have said such a mean thing unless it came from a reliable source. But we must also remember that it would be in Cottrau's interests to keep Rubini there, because he could easily sustain an opera, which couldn't be said for a David or a Winter. My dear Florimo, your soul is that of an angel, and don't judge others by yourself. Be careful, because everything is false and fraudulence has more resemblance to truth than truth itself. Don't forget my suspicious thoughts and don't exchange them with anybody whom you may think has come to help you. These saviours will have their personal motives...and their advice won't always be the best... Remember to be sceptical so that you aren't disappointed...

I've definitely decided to give the role of Valdeburgo to Tamburini, Arturo to Reina, La Straniera to Lalande, Isoletta to Unger and the part of the Abbot of St Irene (and, afterwards, that of the second bass Osburgo) to Biondini.

Once Bellini had decided on the allocation of the roles, he started work with renewed enthusiasm. The composition of *La Straniera* began on 9 September, when he received from Romani the first part of the introductory chorus. On the following day, he wrote to Florimo:[15]

Romani has promised me the rest of the introduction by tomorrow, and as soon as I receive it, I will transcribe it... In the meantime, this very morning I have written the music for the chorus and I like it very much, and if it is sung in tune it should be quite effective.

The situation in this scene is very new, and it should have a great success in Milan because it complies with the taste of the public there, who always like as much novelty as possible. I still tremble at the thought of having to create an opera in Milan after *Il pirata*. The cantilenas of my present songs are at the same time vague and clear, and I hope I can remember them all and orchestrate them harmoniously without any confusion.

Bellini had hardly started work on his new opera when another obstacle presented itself. In around the middle of September, Romani fell ill and further work on *La Straniera* was consequently suspended. The directors of La Scala suggested Rossi[16] as a substitute librettist, for Romani's illness was expected to last several days, but Bellini refused. He wrote to Florimo,[17] "Even though Rossi could write me a good libretto, he would certainly never be able to write such good verses as Romani, particularly for someone like me, who is very attached to beautiful-sounding words; as you saw in *Il pirata*, it was the verses and not the situations that inspired my genius. Romani is therefore necessary to me."

While Romani was ill, Bellini decided to spend a few days in the country. On 5 October, he went to Burgo Morgne (now Burago Molgora), a little village near Vimercate not far from Milan, in order to "breathe some fresh air", as he wrote to Florimo.[18] However, the real purpose of this letter was to tell Florimo – to whom he had already written eight days earlier, but from whom he had as yet received no reply – that he was very anxious to know what his reactions to the Turina affair were:

> I hope that my last letter, in which I told you about my love affair, hasn't upset you. I assure you that I'm more than calm and that nothing will come between me and my career, and that everything is secondary when it's a question of one's honour against fame. I've not received a letter from you in this post, nor in the previous one... My dear Florimo, I will leave you now, because I have no further news from this little village, which makes me feel that I have come here to enjoy the rain like a fish does the water. I hope that by tomorrow I will have received your letter from Milan, which should have arrived there this morning. In the meantime, I send you my warmest greetings and embraces and my regards to everyone. Goodbye.

On the following day, Florimo's letter arrived in Burago. He also sent a second portrait of himself, as Bellini had given the first to the Pollinis. Bellini answered on 17 October[19] from Milan:

> I've heard that you've sent me the portrait through a friend of Bruischi's. Thank the latter on my behalf, as I was unable to meet his friend. I have asked you for this portrait for the purpose of giving it to the person who now possesses it [Giuditta Turina]. However, I didn't deserve the irony (which is quite clear to me) of ending your letter with 40 full stops...
>
> Although you might think that I'm living a degenerate existence, I

would like to tell you that I'm 1,000 times fatter than I was at college, and if you happen to be travelling in this part of the world, you'll be able to see for yourself and be convinced. Therefore, for all your ironies, I can only blame myself, because I believed that my best and unique friend was ready to receive everything in confidence direct from my heart. After your insulting answer to my letter, I will know how to act in future and I will abandon all hope of believing that you are a friend in every sense of the word. Although I don't doubt that your feelings for me are truly sincere, it seems, however, that your behaviour is, without reason, too crude and unfriendly and is directed solely by caprice on your part.

Florimo had known about his friend's affair with Giuditta long before Bellini had written to him about it; gossip had reached him through Tamburini and Tosi, who had been performing in *Bianca e Fernando* in Genoa, where Bellini had met Giuditta the previous April. After Bellini's last letter, Florimo stopped his sarcastic remarks about the affair. His letters to Bellini are not extant, but it can be seen from Bellini's own letters that henceforth Florimo avoided any direct confrontation about this matter. However, Bellini still wanted to justify his love for Giuditta and, above all, to make Florimo – who obviously could not help showing some coldness in his letters – not only accept the situation but also give it his blessing. On 1 December, Bellini wrote to him:[20]

I'm very happy that you haven't been upset about my new relationship. But I know that deep down you have always been, and still are, opposed (I don't think that I can change my nature) to any of my amorous passions. This I tell you because it's clear from your letter that you have no regard for my friend because she is jealous of your friendship with me, as she thinks that there is something extraordinary about it – with which, of course, I agree.

Don't believe that I read all your letters to her. I thought that I would let her read your last letter and, although she didn't want to, I told her that I had confided in you our secret only in terms of it being a love affair, nothing else. But enough. I'm glad that the affair is also in harmony with you now and doesn't perplex you in any way.

She is ill at present, but I think that she will soon be better, because her illness is only a monthly affair and she is now undergoing a cure.

However, Giuditta's illness, which Bellini had first mentioned on 24 September, continued. "Signora Giuditta is in a pitiful state because her illness is getting worse," Bellini wrote to Florimo[21] on 27 December. "From Sunday until now, she has had five haemorrhages and 36 leeches on her stomach, and she's also had a very high temperature. All this upsets me very much. She read your kind letter and told me to send you her best regards."

Obviously not wanting to tell Bellini directly that he disapproved of his love for Giuditta, Florimo took a different stance by expressing doubt as to Bellini's affection for him. Bellini answered Florimo promptly on 4 March:[22]

> I'm so sorry, really very sorry, for the outrageous and unpleasant doubts that you have concerning my affection for you. You must understand that Giuditta's jealousy of you has been caused by my feelings for you, which are, after all, quite extraordinary. Now, the same Giuditta has tremendous esteem for you, because she is convinced that our friendship is like that of two brothers and is invulnerable. She loves you almost as much as I do, and yesterday I saw proof of this. When I read her your letter, she cried all the time, and I reread it to her several times. Do you understand? Yes or no? My love for you has become necessary for my very existence. Therefore, for my peace of mind, I don't want to have any doubts about this or about your love for me.

Evidently, Bellini was upset and disappointed with Florimo's reaction to Giuditta. His letter to Florimo[23] on 14 March 1829 makes it clear that the affair was, after all, his own business:

> I was telling you that Signora Giuditta is suffering the "tortures of Tantalus", because her convalescence and the bad weather have made it impossible for her to hear *La Straniera*, even though the theatre is close by. Do you understand? She wanted me to tell you this, and she also sends you her best regards and thanks you for the kind thoughts that you have for her.
>
> The opera will be dedicated to Signora Giuditta, as you will see in the note on the front of the score, in the same way that it was done for *Il pirata*. The name of Signora Giuditta Turina must be printed. Understand? Please see that this is done properly. You should know by now how much it means to me.

From the next five years, only five letters from Bellini to Florimo are extant: one from 20 January 1830, three between September and December 1831 and one from London in 1833. Only in one (19 September 1831) does Bellini mention Giuditta, merely writing, "Giuditta is well and sends her regards."

It is possible that Florimo withheld from publication many of Bellini's letters of this period. If there had been a rift in their friendship, it was obviously resolved by the time that Bellini and Giuditta went to Naples in early 1831, and yet it was in February 1834 that Bellini recommenced writing to Florimo regularly, by which time the affair with Giuditta was long over. The affair undoubtedly affected their friendship, more on Florimo's part, even though he was assured by Bellini that his affection for Florimo would not diminish. Whether it was rational or not, Florimo was just as jealous of Giuditta as she was of him, if not more so.

The composition of *La Straniera* was resumed on 17 October, when Romani was well again and writing more verses, although it was clear that it would have been impossible for the opera to have been ready for production on 26 December. On 12 November, it was announced in *I Teatri* that Rossini's *L'assedio di Corinto* would be performed instead.

Although Romani continued to be dilatory, an anecdote[24] from the time during the composition of *La Straniera* shows the great compatibility that existed between composer and librettist. One day, Bellini was sitting at the piano, alone and unable to write. The score of *La Straniera* was finished except for the final scene. Up until then, he had found the quality of Romani's verses excellent, but in the final scene – La Straniera's aria – he came to a standstill. The verses no longer appealed, being tender and melodious when what he needed was burning, passionate poetry. He asked Romani to visit him and told him of his difficulty.

"Well," said Romani, "I'll give you some verses within half an hour."

In fact, he took only a quarter of an hour to produce new verses for the aria finale. Bellini looked at it, speechless.

"You don't like this either?" Romani asked.

"Frankly, no!" Bellini answered.

"Well, I'll write you a third one. Then let's see if I can make you happy."

Neither the third nor the fourth pleased Bellini. The poet, shaking his head, began to doubt the maestro's inventiveness. "Now I've got to tell you that I don't understand what you want any more," he said wryly, folding up the paper and putting it into his pocket.

"What do I want?" Bellini exclaimed, his cheeks suddenly bursting with colour and his eyes lighting up. "I want something that is a prayer, a plea, a resignation and a protest. I want something that's both a threat and a lament, both moving and expressing suffering at the same time." Thrusting himself at the piano, full of inspiration, Bellini began to play and the amazed Romani began to write. "This is what I want," Bellini finally said. "I hope you understand."

"And here are the words," the poet answered, handing them to the composer with a smile. "Do you think I've interpreted well?"

Deeply moved, Bellini embraced his poet. They were both worthy of each other, and the aria finale of *La Straniera* was a masterpiece, even if it had been rewritten five times. No other obstacle seems to have stood in the way of the opera's composition.[25]

After *L'assedio di Corinto* had opened the season at La Scala, yet another Rossini opera followed: *Zelmyra*. Then, on 14 February 1829, *La Straniera* – performed with two ballets by Golzani, *Buondelmonte* and *L'avviso ai maritati* – scored a great success with both public and critics, establishing Bellini as a composer with something new to say.

L'Eco di Milano reviewed *La Straniera* on 16 February:

Bellini is in search of innovation and thus deserves praise. He has adopted a method which we don't really know whether to describe as sung declamation or declaimed song. The purpose of this effort seems to be to reunite the forces of declamation to the tenderness of song. The danger could be that of confusing declamation and song, thus producing monotony, dragging unevenness and uncertainty in the cantilenas, coupled with a lack of pleasant, memorable themes. Of course, this is only a generalisation. We shall soon find out when he has overcome this difficulty, which is by no means an easy task...

There is a beautiful melody in the quartet of act two which, surprisingly, was appreciated least of all. There are also beautiful choruses; one in particular, along with another cantilena, reminds us a little of *La donna del lago*. This is considered by some to be a reminiscence and not a plagiarism, a fact that we consider as proof of the study that Bellini has undertaken of good examples. But this is enough for now. Bellini should be happy with the applause that he received and with the way in which his music was performed.

Madame Lalande demonstrated the splendour of her talents while Tamburini distinguished himself in his mastery of singing and force of expression. Reina had a long role but not much to sing and Unger an aria with flute accompaniment about which we cannot say whether it was really beautiful or just unusual.

The sets were the usual Sanquirico ones that, if seen in any other country – where they wouldn't take Sanquirico for granted – or painted by another painter, one would have considered as outstanding. The costumes and all the other accessories were also good. The orchestra, on the whole, was marvellous.

Three days later, the *Gazzetta privilegiata di Milano* published an article on Bellini and *La Straniera*:

Following the eruption of Rossini's torrent (it is not long since the young master took his first footsteps in his career of attempting a genre that could be called new for that period), Bellini also showed courage in three successive works. Therefore we will not say, as others would, that he is the restorer of Italian music. We value his talents enough and his modesty in believing that he will accept this as a valid compliment. Nevertheless, Bellini is on the way to attaining this. Naturally, if he adheres to his potential, and if the public and the singers support him, it's certain that he will be classed as one of the first links in the chain joining the old music to the new.

What I mean by old music is that which was written before Cimarosa, Paisiello, Mozart, Zingarelli, Giuglielmi, Sarti, Anifossi, Piccinni, Traetta, Sacchini and others of that school. Their music enjoys eternal freshness. For a master who possesses the force and genius to divert himself as much as possible from pursuing a style that guarantees success in order to follow another one in which success is rarer and therefore more difficult, this deserves praise and encouragement. This quality is then justified when someone like Bellini possesses it, a young man of great taste and knowledge, achieving his aim without forcefully upsetting the still-dominant fashion. We go further in saying that also, in his third score, he sustained the correct balance between old and new music and that, above all, he avoided a terrible confusion of genre. In fact, the truly serious character is maintained in the score of *La Straniera*, both in the recitatives and in the main rhythms of the arias and other pieces...

On the day after the premiere of the opera, Bellini wrote to Romani[26] (then in Venice) that *La Straniera* had overtaken *Il pirata* to a great extent: "The way in which the opera was staged and the way in which the music was executed had such an unexpected effect on the public. However, no poet, no musician could have imagined that people in the theatre would rejoice so much or that all the women would wave their handkerchiefs about, particularly in such scenes as Valdeburgo's, when he intervenes in the Judgement. The same applies to the final scene, when La Straniera forces the man she cannot love to marry another woman."

At this point, as if suddenly aware of being too transported by his enthusiasm, Bellini adds, "Burn this letter, because it's not fitting to describe our own triumphs." Finally, he solemnly affirms his recognition of the poet, whom he asks to remain the same friend and collaborator always, because "together we will attain a greater career by far!".

On 16 February, Bellini informed his parents about his latest success through a letter that he wrote to his uncle Vincenzo Ferlito:[27]

All Milan is very enthusiastic, and I don't really know whether I'm coming or going, I'm so happy. I think you should have already received the libretto. Florimo will soon send you all the newspaper reports of *La Straniera*, so it's unnecessary for me to say more. You should be happy with this, and I could wish for nothing more, but nevertheless I shall not abandon my studies, so that I will progress further, and if God will help me I hope to impress my name on this generation...

When you receive the newspapers you can then tell everybody and, if possible, put an article in the Palermo newspaper.

In a letter to Florimo[28] written from Milan on 16 February, Tamburini, who had in the past spoken out against Bellini's music, more than makes amends: "Oh, what a success and what fanaticism our mutual friend's opera has created. Everybody is praising me, especially Bellini, in telling me that I'm like Rubini in *Il pirata*, and I can assure you that Bellini wrote a good score for me, and that he has compensated me for *Il pirata* and *Bianca e Fernando*.

Consequently, with great pleasure I withdraw what in a moment of great anger I said and which I particularly meant (although with reason). But let's forget that and proclaim, 'Long live Bellini!' and rejoice with me in his triumph – a triumph the likes of which I can't recall during the eleven years of my career."

The main reason for *La Straniera*'s success was the new way in which Bellini expressed drama through music, as described by Florimo in his *La Scuola Musicale di Napoli*: "In *La Straniera*, Bellini avoided flowery ornamentation and substituted melodies that weren't too syllabic." The opera was performed 26 times in its first season at La Scala, always to full houses and constant displays of enthusiasm.

Bellini had come a long way since his student work *Adelson e Salvini*. All the promise that he had then shown was starting to materialise. *Bianca e Fernando* had enjoyed great success and *Il pirata* even more. Now, with *La Straniera*, he was looked upon as the hope of Italian music. However, after his third success in a row (not counting the student work), things did not work out quite as expected. As soon as the performances of *La Straniera* were finished, Bellini left Milan on 17 March 1829 for Parma, where he was anxiously expected to write a new opera.

LA STRANIERA

Opera seria in two acts. Libretto by Felice Romani. First performed at La Scala, Milan, on 14 February 1829 on a triple bill with the ballets *Buondelmonte* and *L'avviso ai maritati*, the first choreographed by Giovanni Galzerani to music by Francesco Schira, the second by Serafini to unidentified music. Alessandro Sanquirico designed the stage sets.

CHARACTERS AND ORIGINAL CAST

Alaide (La Straniera)	Soprano	Enrichetta Méric-Lalande
Arturo, Count of Ravenstel	Tenor	Domenico Reina
Valdeburgo, the Baron (Alaide's brother)	Baritone	Antonio Tamburini
Isoletta, daughter of the Master of Montolino, betrothed to Arturo	Mezzo-soprano	Caroline Unger
Osburgo, Arturo's confidant	Tenor	Luigi Asti

The Prior of the Spedalieri	Bass	Domenico Spiaggi
The Master of Montolino	Bass	Stanislao Marcionni

The action takes place at Montolino Castle and its environs in Brittany in around 1300.

Romani preceded the libretto for *La Straniera* with an explanatory summary, necessary to understand what takes place in the opera. On his wedding night, King Philippe-August of France took a sudden aversion to his bride, Princess Isambour of Denmark, and deserted her. Philippe then fell in love with Agnès (Alaide, La Straniera, in the opera), daughter of the Duke of Pomerania, and married her despite the fact that he was still legally married to Isambour. It was impossible for Agnès to live in Paris with Philippe, who was threatened with excommunication unless he returned to Isambour. Consequently, Agnès was sent to Brittany to live in strict solitary splendour in the Château of Karency until a better solution could be found. Philippe ordered that Agnès should be treated like a queen and also secretly sent her brother Léopold, Prince of Merania, to watch over her safety. Léopold, under the assumed name of Baron Waldeburg (Valdeburgo in the opera), took up residence in the neighbourhood of the château. Before long, however, the unhappy Agnès escaped, leaving behind a friend to take her place, and went to live at a lonely spot on the shores of Lake Montolino, hoping to find peace in her solitude. Here, although the local inhabitants thought her strange and suspected her of being a witch, Count Arthur de Ravenstel (Arturo in the opera) fell desperately in love with her, not knowing her true identity and despite the fact that he was already betrothed to Isolette, the young daughter of the Master of Montolino. The consequences of Arthur's love for Agnès form the heart of the action of the opera, which begins at this stage.

ACT I

SCENE 1: Courtyard of Montolino Castle. At the back is a lake and beyond it the festive illuminations of the village are visible.

At first, the voices of people in boats on the lake are heard celebrating the anniversary of the restoration of Brittany to Philippe-Auguste by the English. The people are making merry because of the forthcoming marriage of Isoletta and Arturo.

The action then shifts to a meeting between Isoletta and Valdeburgo. It is revealed that Isoletta is very unhappy and worried about her fiancé, who has abandoned her on the eve of their marriage because of a mysterious foreign woman, La Straniera, with whom he is now in love. "I saw her yesterday on the lake," Isoletta explains. "By her actions and by her face, she didn't appear human, but she had a divine beauty. I heard her singing to herself, saying Arturo's name."

Valdeburgo, who naturally knows all about the mysterious woman, tries to console Isoletta by reassuring her that Arturo will eventually return to her. Just then, distant sounds are heard and La Straniera, heavily veiled, crosses the lake in a small, dark boat pursued by people in several other boats, uttering threats. Isoletta becomes more agitated, and when her father (the Master of Montolino) and Osburgo (Arturo's friend) appear she complains about Arturo's disposition towards La Straniera. Osburgo promises to try to bring Arturo to his senses.

SCENE 2: Interior of La Straniera's cottage by the lake.

In his effort to discover La Straniera's identity, Arturo steals into her cottage. While he is waiting, he looks at a portrait of her and declares his passionate love. La Straniera, Agnès (her name changed to Alaide in order to preserve her *incognito*) is heard coming; she expresses her sorrow for love's deception. When she meets Arturo, he professes his love, but even though she feels the same towards him, it is impossible for her to reciprocate, as there is an insuperable barrier of fate between them. Arturo's continued declarations of love and promises always to respect her secrets fail to persuade Alaide, who departs without giving any further explanation.

SCENE 3: A part of the forest near Montolino Castle. La Straniera's cottage is visible.

In vain, Valdeburgo tries to persuade Arturo to return to Isoletta. Although he values her purity of soul, Arturo confesses that he loves only La Straniera. As they approach her cottage, La Straniera suddenly appears out of the forest and Valdeburgo, who has recognised her, only just manages to stifle her real name. Alaide, feeling very happy at this unexpected meeting with Valdeburgo, her brother, embraces him, much to Arturo's consternation – he has no idea who either of them is, and he jealously accuses Valdeburgo of being his rival. Alaide and Valdeburgo urge Arturo not to make rash conclusions. Arturo's doubts are resolved, at least temporarily.

SCENE 4: A remote place outside La Straniera's cottage. Facing it, some rocks rise by the lake.

While a storm gathers, Osburgo and some hunters appear with Arturo, whose jealousy flares up again when he overhears Alaide and Valdeburgo planning to flee together. Convinced that Valdeburgo is his rival, Arturo challenges him to a duel. Valdeburgo is wounded and collapses into the lake. Both Alaide and Arturo think him dead. When Alaide, beside herself, reveals that Valdeburgo is her brother, Arturo jumps into the lake in an attempt to rescue him. Meanwhile, Alaide picks up the sword that has wounded her brother in order to defend herself against the approaching crowd. Finding a bloodstained Alaide, the crowd accuses her of murder. In a moment of self-incrimination, Alaide admits that she has caused her lover's death, whereupon Osburgo and his men take her away.

ACT II

SCENE 1: The Grand Salon, where the Tribunal for the province sits. At the back, a door.

The Prior interrogates Alaide, who denies having committed the murder but refuses to give any information about it. Even when Arturo appears and confesses that he is the killer of Valdeburgo and the Prior warns her that she may still be an accomplice, she remains non-committal. While the hostile crowd demands that both Arturo and Alaide be executed, Valdeburgo, who was only wounded, walks in and saves the situation. As he takes Alaide away, the people insist that her identity should be revealed first but she unveils her face only to the Prior, who lets her go.

SCENE 2: A part of the forest (as in act one, scene three).

Valdeburgo is reconciled with Arturo and persuades him to return to Isoletta and marry her. Arturo accepts, but only on the condition that Valdeburgo and Alaide attend his wedding.

SCENE 3: Isoletta's apartment in Montolino Castle.

The sad Isoletta is bemoaning her unhappiness when she is informed that

Arturo has returned and that the wedding ceremony will take place as originally planned.

SCENE 4: The porch of the Church of the Spedolieri.

The guests sing their praises for Arturo and Isoletta. At first, however, Arturo hesitates to enter the church, and when he sees Alaide, who has been concealed behind one of the monuments in the churchyard, he rushes to her instead. This distresses Isoletta, who tears the nuptial wreath from her head. However, Alaide intervenes, picks up the wreath, unveils her face and tells Isoletta that she is La Straniera. She then guides Arturo and Isoletta into the church. Valdeburgo follows them in, but presently Alaide comes out of the chapel. Very disturbed, she kneels and in her prayer asks heaven to accept her sacrifice. As she listens to the culmination of the chanting from inside the chapel, she realises that Arturo and Isoletta are now married.

At the last minute, however, Arturo is unable to give her up and rushes out to find her. The Prior, following him, meets La Straniera and hails her as their queen: Isambour, La Straniera's former rival, is dead. Agnès must now go back to take her rightful place by the side of Philippe. With the latest revelations, Arturo despairs and commits suicide while Agnès prays that she too may die.

In this libretto, there is much extravagance of plot. The character of Alaide, in particular, does not achieve reality, even if the verses in themselves are harmonious. Romani created several dramatic situations, but he also missed opportunities; in the recognition scene of Alaide and Valdeburgo, for instance, there is no intimate, dramatic echo in either the verses or the music. These lapses can only be explained by the fact that Romani had to prepare the libretto in a hurry.

In *La Straniera*, the independent overture is dispensed with in favour of an orchestral prelude (in A major, 6/8 time, *allegro assai*) in the style of a tarantella; this is followed by a very short *allegretto*, which leads into the chorus "Voga, voga, il vento tace" ("Row, row, the wind is low"), a quasi-barcarolle. At first, the tenors are heard – in unison, then divided – followed by sopranos and then basses, singing the gentle, lilting melody. The whole effect is charming and cheerful, even if the means employed seem a little naïve to modern ears, and one can quite understand the impression it made at the time, given the effective *mis-en-scène* provided.[29]

The first scene, the duet "Io la vidi" ("I saw her") between Isoletta and Valdeburgo, misfires. It is surprising that Bellini – who had already shown his concern for dramatic characterisation – should give both characters such unsuitable music. Their opening recitative hardly suggests Isoletta's state of mind and the graceful, pleasing duet would be more appropriate as a love duet. The simple-minded Isoletta, abandoned by Arturo on the eve of her marriage, is very unhappy and anxious about the mysterious stranger with whom Arturo is in love. Even the short consoling phrases that Valdeburgo sings are at odds with both character and situation. He is troubled by events of the gravest nature, yet the graceful harmony that surrounds his melodic phrases expresses anything but that. Nor does the chorus, which heralds the stranger assumed to be a witch, reflect any mass anxiety. The chorus begins well, with the crowd's "La Straniera!" and "l'iniqua fattuchiera" heard in the distance just before Alaide's first entrance, but the effect is not maintained. Even so, it is Romani's words that prove effective, rather than Bellini's music. Only the second part of the duet between Isoletta and Valdeburgo – beginning with her aria "O, tu che sai gli spasimi di questo cor piagato" ("You know the feelings of my wounded heart", in A-flat major, 4/4 time, *allegro animato*), later joined by Valdeburgo, their voices moving in parallel tenths – achieves a degree of characterisation and, with its sad undertones, to some extent saves the scene.

Nothing of exceptional musical interest happens in the following pages until Alaide's suave "Sventurato il cor che fida" ("Unhappy is the trusting heart"), in G minor, *andante*, more arioso than aria. Preceded by a noteworthy oboe solo, in which the instrument is treated as a human voice of wide range, it begins offstage and is introduced by a harp and brief, florid vocal cadenza on the syllable *ah*. It is an expressive outlet for Alaide's feelings, but it reflects little of her tragic situation. The composer uses this melody as La Straniera's (Alaide's) *leitmotif* but achieves only partial individualisation. Neither Alaide's and Arturo's recitative nor their passionate duet "Serba i tuoi segreti" ("Keep your secrets"), which follows, can be said to be entirely successful. There are exquisite passages, such as the gentle and refined "Deh, non punirlo" and "Serba i tuoi segreti", but although the melodies of these passages convey warmth, they are hardly appropriate and furthermore deteriorate finally into a very banal cadenza. Some touching moments, however, are achieved in the simple but revelatory duet "Un ultimo addio" ("A final farewell") – *allegro moderato*, in 3/4 time – and in the huntsmen's chorus "Campo ai veltri" ("Field of the greyhounds"), which are pleasing despite their partial triviality.

Bellini comes into his own in the succeeding dialogue, when the passions of Alaide, Arturo and Valdeburgo are in conflict. Here, Arturo's part is the most accomplished, especially in the passage leading up to "Un solo accento" ("A single word"), where the dramatic-heroic force of the music gives stature to the character. Valdeburgo's song "No, non ti son rivale" ("No, he is no rival") has an exuberance that provides a good beginning to the trio proper, in which the characters maintain their individuality within the overall musical unity.

The atmospheric introduction to the next scene, with its distant thunder and lightning, is achieved by the simplest orchestral means, foreshadowing to some extent the storm scene in Verdi's *Rigoletto*. The chorus "La Straniera a cui fè", although musically naïve, is also of great dramatic merit and originality, and the way the composer uses it is one of his greatest inspirations, at least in his earlier works. Whispering *staccato* and sudden *crescendi* graphically convey the evil that poisons Arturo's mind with suspicion and hate. This masterly treatment of the chorus is unequalled in any known opera of the period:

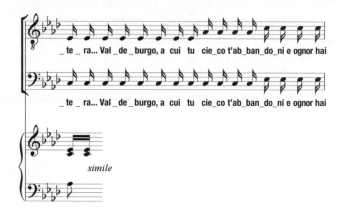

Most of the music of the first-act finale raises the opera to a higher musico-dramatic level. Arturo's recitative with Valdeburgo "O ciel! qual nome?" ("Heavens, what name?") is declamatory in style and dramatically convincing, Arturo being very impetuous and Valdeburgo resistant to him. The orchestral music is, however, somewhat thin during their eventual duel.

Alaide's "Un grido io sento" ("I heard a cry"), which is the main theme of the finale, has the particular kind of touching simplicity that we have come to associate with Bellini's music:

Moderato assai

Having picked up the sword that wounded her brother, Alaide faces the angry crowd accusing her of murder. With its apparently simple melody, made more effective by the contribution of the robust chorus, the scene becomes a "mad scene" (albeit of restricted compass), forming an exciting and dramatically interesting finale to the first act.

On the whole, the second act is fuller and certainly more intense. There are still weaknesses and lapses, but they do not diminish the dramatic tension. The Prior's interrogation of Alaide opens the act with expressive music. Here again, the contribution of the chorus, reminding Alaide that the penalty for murder is death, makes the scene both musically and dramatically convincing. Only a surprising lack of instrumental support in places prevents this scene from being wholly outstanding. Nevertheless, there are excellent passages, such as "Morte è sospesa" ("The death sentence is suspended"); the powerful dialogue "Oh! prodigio" between Arturo and Valdeburgo; and, above all, Valdeburgo's request to Alaide, "Meco tu vieni" ("Welcome"), which is the most expressive melody in the entire opera:

Allegro

(In his obituary of Bellini, Hector Berlioz, who was not a great admirer, described this passage as "a short air with practically no modulations, without developments or orchestral themes or any vocal display. It is, in a word, simple, and yet it expresses the meaning of the words with overwhelming truth.")

Two somewhat inferior scenes follow. The duet "Sì!... Sulla salma del fratello" ("Yes!... I swear by my dead brother") between Arturo and Valdeburgo suffers greatly from over-emphasis and an inappropriately buoyant rhythm, while Isoletta's aria "Ah! se non m'ami più" ("Ah, he no longer loves me") becomes musically static, after an ornate opening. This is despite the excellent orchestration (a flute obbligato accompanied by a small group of strings).

The chorus "E dolce la vergine" ("How sweet the bride is") and, even more, the quartet "Qual sarà dolor che uccide?" ("What sadness will kill me?") restore dramatic interest. The quartet, beginning unaccompanied, shows Mozartian influence, but Bellini does not sacrifice his own individuality.

The final scene of the opera is in many ways the most striking. Alaide's prayer "Ciel pietoso" ("Merciful Heaven"), the temple chorus in the background and her recitative "Sono all'ara" ("I am at the altar") are tender, moving and melodically fascinating – typical of what was later to be described as Bellinian (ie the use of beautiful, languid cantilena). The short recitative "Silenzio, succede" ("Quiet, something is happening") has a thrilling melody in declamatory style and effectively fades away in "Io moro" ("I shall die").

The ensuing cabaletta, "Or sei pago, o ciel tremendo" ("Now you are needed, tremendous Heaven") rises in vigour and vehemence to the level of "O sole, ti vela", the cabaletta that concludes *Il pirata* (see page 90). In this melody, there is freedom and dramatic intensity, as well as unusual grandeur, and this created a sensation at the time that it was written. In fact, it was the most dramatic cabaletta of the period, its inner vitality particularly heralding those of Verdi:

La Straniera may not be as appealing as *Il pirata* in its melodies, or as inspired or interesting, but it is more experimental, yet discreet – its forms are moderate and varied, and if the composer's evident determination to fuse his music with the words is only partially achieved, the music in itself has a sureness of touch – a definite advance over Bellini's previous works. For its period, it was an innovatory opera. At best, the composer was able to carry out his intention of declamation in dramatic dialogue, which for the first time in his operas predominates over extended musical numbers and assumes great vigour and vividness. The music generally is restricted not by conventional forms but by means of expressive simplicity. (Even Valdeburgo's "Meco tu vieni", which was borrowed from *Adelson e Salvini*, is much simpler here.) One of Bellini's greatest achievements is the dramatic use of the chorus (also an innovation in its period), which is no longer merely decorative but in this work often expresses the vindictiveness of the populace against La Straniera. Donizetti learned a great deal from the treatment of the chorus in *La Straniera*, which contributed to the success of his *Anna Bolena* a year later.

The greatest weakness of *La Straniera* (and it is a serious one) is inadequacy in the depiction of surroundings and a lack of stylistic unity. Alaide, for instance, remains an incomplete character. No one alludes to her mystery or her tragic existence, and she consequently fails to arouse the tension of curiosity. These weaknesses are not difficult to explain. Bellini was a composer who obtained perhaps his best musical thoughts by studying the verses of the libretto meticulously. In the composition of *La Straniera*, he did not have this facility. Due to Romani's great delay in preparing the libretto, he had to compose a great deal of the music without knowledge of the verses. "I am creating motifs daily," he wrote to Florimo. "I am trying to provide myself with motifs, and I'm producing some good ones which I hope I shall be able to place and develop effectively, when I have the libretto."

This, however, did not prove to be a complete success. Some of these haphazardly produced ideas were beautiful but only coincided approximately with the individual episodes of the opera for which they were adapted. Despite this, surprisingly, the opera does not suffer too much from patchiness or fragmentary construction. For the very successful final scene, the circumstances of composition were different. Although the dramatic quality of the verses originally provided for this scene was impressive enough, Bellini persuaded Romani to write fresh poetry. In the end, the magnificent new verses inspired by the composer's conception served in turn to be an inspiration for the composer.

La Straniera enjoyed a great success in Italy when it was first produced and achieved performances in Vienna (1831), Paris (1832), London (1832), New York (1834), Lisbon (1835), several German theatres and elsewhere. However, it soon fell into obscurity. Even in Italy, apart from a few performances after its presentation in Palermo in 1840, the opera had to wait until 1954 before being revived for a single performance in Catania. Only *Bianca e Fernando* and *Zaira* among Bellini's professional operas were to suffer a similar fate.

It would seem that *La Straniera*'s biggest drawback with modern audiences is the implausibility of its plot and, to some extent, the absence of memorable tunes. Also, in *La Straniera* the leading tenor role is an inferior one but the leading soprano role should have attracted several singers. However, neither Giuditta Pasta, Maria Malibran, Giulia Grisi, Maria Callas nor Joan Sutherland ever attempted it. Perhaps by the time that both Callas and Sutherland became involved with Bellini's music, other operas were more attractive to them. Callas, in fact, thought *La Straniera* to be a very uneven work.

Eventually, it was left to Renata Scotto to score one of her greatest successes as La Straniera, which she sang in Palermo in 1968 and in Rome in 1969. Despite occasional hardness on high notes, her ability to phrase Bellini's music stylistically, and often with great expression, enabled her to do justice to an unknown Bellinian heroine.

Montserrat Caballé was the next La Straniera. Although she sang the role in a concert version in New York in 1969, she too was able to make this heroine a revelation, with lovely vocal quality and often very expressive singing. However, until now, no major theatre has taken up the opera.

7

The Failure of *Zaira* in Parma (1829)

In as far back as 1821, Archduchess Marie Louise of Austria,[1] the ruler of Parma, had decided that a new theatre was necessary in the city, the old Teatro Ducale being too small and now obsolete. Marie Louise appointed Nicola Bettoli as architect for a theatre to be built on the site of the convent of Sant' Alessandro. Construction took seven years, and by the spring of 1828 arrangements had started for the commissioning of a new opera to open the theatre in the spring of the following year. The first composer to be approached was Rossini, who declined the offer, apparently on the grounds that he wanted 3,000 luis instead of the 1,000 offered. Rossini had been living in Paris for four years, and when the offer came he was recovering from the shock of his mother's death in the previous February. He was already expected to compose two operas for Paris,[2] and his intention to withdraw afterwards from the operatic field was already suspected in France. In April 1828, the Paris publication *La Revue musicale* reported, "Rossini has promised to write *Guillaume Tell*, but he himself has asserted that he will do no more than this, and that this opera will be the last to come from his pen."

It is unknown whose idea it was that Bellini should provide the new opera for Parma. The offer was officially made to him on 6 August 1828, when he was preparing to write *La Straniera*. On the same day, he informed Florimo:[3]

> This morning, I have been asked in strict confidence by [Alessandro] Rolla whether or not I would be willing to write for the opening of the theatre at Parma. He told me that, since Rossini can't leave Paris and a Parmesan chamberlain wrote to him asking whether I was free for the spring season, he would like to engage me, provided that the Archduchess – who is at present in Vienna – didn't decide to the contrary. I answered that I was most anxious to have this opportunity, which could do me great credit. My only condition is that I would need the libretto by the beginning of

January, so Rolla will answer me and God will help me for the rest. For the time being, please don't mention anything to anybody, because I fear the plots that others could weave against me. I will be very lucky to get this commission.

Bellini was right to keep it secret, because he had already been questioned on the commission for Parma by the impresario Bartolomeo Merelli, who was known as "the eagle among impresarios" and whom Bellini did not trust. (He had had previous experience of Merelli when he had been engaged to provide Genoa with an opera.) He wrote to Florimo on 14 June 1828:[4]

Here, I've met the impresario Merelli, who, confidentially speaking, is untrustworthy, and he has told me that he has a commission from the Parma impresario to consider me with regard to the opening of the new theatre. Having asked me about my fee, I gave him my answer and we'll see what happens, but I have little faith in this impresario and I believe that he has made me this offer in order to win me over. I told Pollini about this and he promised me that he would find out whether the Parma impresario really has these intentions for me. I asked for 5,000-6,000 francs and therefore, if the offer is genuine, we shall have an answer. The fee that I will ask Barbaja for here will be the same, and if he gives me 5,000 francs (which is equivalent to 1,135 ducats), I will accept. Without this sum, I will not write an opera for either Milan or Naples, because "with my style of writing I would have to vomit blood".

When Merelli realised that Bellini would not be co-operative and had already been officially approached by Parma, he immediately started intriguing with the hope of persuading the Parmesan Court to engage another composer. He wrote to Andrea Bandini, the resident impresario of the Ducale:[5] "I talked to our friend Bellini, who has put on such airs that he now refuses many offers to write, because he expects 6,000 francs for an opera; this is the amount that he is asking from you, too, only that, in order to please me, he would accept 5,000 francs, but not a penny less... How could you consider to engage this upstart, who has only written one opera [*Il pirata*], which, after all, has no real musical value and whose success was only due to Lalande, Rubini and Tamburini? You must know also that his opera failed in Genoa. Would you really like to repeat this failure while there are Pacini, Generali, Coccia and Mercadante around to provide a new opera, all of whom are and will be discreet?"

Merelli was unable to influence Bandini in any way. Even when he tried to commission Francesco Morlacchi instead, with the help of Count Stefano Sanvitale, who was one of Marie Louise's chamberlains and the manager of the Ducale, he failed. According to Merelli, Morlacchi – who had been successful in Parma with *Simoncino*, *Corradino*, *Oreste* and *Tebaldo ed Isolina* – would have been much more agreeable, as his demands were not exorbitant. In the end, Alessandro Rolla, the first violinist and conductor at La Scala, was asked to make the necessary arrangements with Bellini. Several months went by before Bellini's engagement for Parma was confirmed. On 24 September, he wrote to Florimo, informing him that he still had no confirmation from Parma. At last, Bellini signed the contract in mid November. The opera was scheduled to be produced on 12 May 1829.

In the meantime, at the request of the Duchess, the poet Luigi Torrigiani was writing an original libretto entitled *Cesare in Egitto*.[6] Torrigiani, who was born in 1769, was a lawyer by profession but was more interested in the theatre. He had previously written the libretto *Il re Teodoro a Venezia* for the composer Finali. Since the contract provided for the composer to approve the libretto, the Court of Parma asked Torrigiani to go to Milan and discuss the opera with Bellini. When Torrigiani appeared, Bellini was most surprised, as he had taken it for granted that Romani would be providing him with the libretto and had no intention of collaborating with anyone else. Nevertheless, he read Torrigiani's libretto and praised the poet kindly on his efforts but said that he could not accept it, because it did not allow the possibility of expressing deep feelings or sensitive affections, qualities that were necessary for Bellini's kind of music. (There was some truth in this, but Bellini really used it as a pretext.) A few days later, he sent a letter to Florimo, writing that he had refused Torrigiani's work "because its theme is as old as the hills". However, he was aware that he had not yet completely eliminated Torrigiani, who was still officially appointed to provide the libretto, but he also knew that, according to his contract, it was up to him to agree with the subject chosen.

The singers engaged were Lalande, Lablache, Teresa Cecconi and a certain tenor named Carlo Trezzini, who was unknown to Bellini although said by various people to be very good.

Obviously, Torrigiani understood, at least to some extent, that Bellini was trying to get rid of him, for on 14 December, immediately after he had returned to Parma, he lodged his complaint and regret with the Grand Chamberlain:[7]

Your Excellency! I have just returned from Milan and feel that it is my primary duty to report to Your Excellency on my task there. I have repeatedly talked to Maestro Bellini and also with Madame Lalande. She is not displeased to perform the character of Cleopatra, not giving up, however, the possibility of playing the title role of the opera. However, Signor Bellini insisted and still insists on a new libretto supporting Lalande and Lablache, who is the first bass. He repeated that the tenor and the other musical characters need not be of any appreciable importance. As proof, I enclose the original letter that I received from Bellini. I was not wrong in judging the taste of the maestro, who likes Romanticism and exaggeration. He declared that Classicism is cold and boring. He took me to the Vallardi Gallery to show me some lithographs that he thought were wonderful, one of which depicted a father who was having his children slaughtered under his own eyes, and he pointed out this picture as a model of the greatest theatrical effect. He is entranced by unnatural meetings in forests, among graves, tombs and the like. In the end, he gave me back the copy of my drama without noting any comment on the blank sheets that I had provided for this purpose...

I understand, and have no doubt, that everyone in Milan expected this libretto to be written by Romani or Romanelli, both mercenary theatre poets who write at the maestros' and virtuosos' whims. This is the only reason behind Bellini's refusal of my drama, even before he knew anything about it except for the title, which was already known here and which he despised...

Please be kind enough to obtain for me from Her Majesty, our Sovereign, an order to have my work judged by a committee presided over by Your Excellency or by the Minister of the Interior.

Torrigiani's requests were not met, but the Grand Chamberlain decided to send Bandini to Milan in the hope that he would change Bellini's mind about the libretto. The outcome of this visit is described in a long report that Bandini wrote to the Grand Chamberlain on his return to Parma on 14 January 1829.

Bandini understood the situation perfectly and, considering the repercussions that Bellini's refusal to collaborate could have had on his own interests as impresario of the Ducale, he used all his diplomatic skill to find a solution that would comply with the composer's wishes. He wrote:[8]

> Back today in Parma. I report immediately to you about my mission in Milan. I found Maestro Bellini agreeable to set the libretto *Cesare in Egitto* by the lawyer Torrigiani to music. But after all the difficulties the composer raised, I realised that, notwithstanding the excellence of the eminent lawyer's poem, the result would be a very unhappy one and it would be most dangerous under such circumstances to insist on a libretto that would prove unsuccessful. We should instead follow a way by which Bellini would be totally responsible for a possible musical failure, irrespective of the libretto.
>
> Following Her Majesty's intentions, other suggestions instead of *Cesare in Egitto* should now be put forward to Bellini. It would be impossible for Bellini to keep Torrigiani as his librettist, because the latter is engaged on business in Parma and Bellini is busy in Milan until the end of March, and the two of them would need to be together.
>
> Had I strictly followed Your Excellency's instructions, I would have come back to Parma without all the explanations which I can now submit to you. There are only 83 days before the beginning of rehearsals for a performance, the title of which is not yet decided. This short time allows no further delays, and we now need to make a decision very quickly. As with regret we cannot take advantage of Torrigiani's outstanding talents, I thought it best to get information in Milan about the best librettist there. So I discovered that Felice Romani, the librettist of *Il pirata*, is the right person. I talked to him in order to find out whether he would be willing to write the libretto for this occasion. Romani gladly accepted the proposition and suggested the subject *Carlo di Borgogna oppure Giovanni da Procida*[9] as preferable to *Cavaliere Baiardo* (the subject of a new libretto offered by Torrigiani), because it has already failed in Venice and is now being written again in Florence. The poet was inclined to choose *Carlo di Borgogna*, with the approval of Maestro Bellini. He justifies his choice in that it is suitable for modern music, which requires strong situations in somewhat fantastical environments, in this way

offering the possibility of giving every virtuoso a convenient role to play. I made the poet accept the small reward of 700 francs as a result of the document enclosed herewith, which is devoid of any effect until it receives Her Majesty's approval.

Now I look forward to know Your Excellency's decisions on this matter, which has to be settled as soon as possible, due to the lack of time.

All of Bandini's suggestions were fully accepted. The authorities realised that, whatever the merit of Torrigiani's libretto, it was essential for the composer to like the libretto that he would be setting to music. On 9 January 1829, without wasting any more time, Her Majesty officially approved Bandini's action in full. As a way of showing her appreciation of Torrigiani's effort, she sent him a golden box and compensation of 360 new lire for expenses incurred during his trip to Milan.

In the meantime, because of the postponement of *La Straniera* in Milan, Bellini could not begin to think of the new opera for Parma. Romani also left Milan for Venice, promising Bellini that he would soon be sending him verses for the new libretto. It would seem that the idea of *Carlo di Borgogna* was soon dropped as, in a letter to Florimo[10] on 14 March, Bellini mentions a different subject:

By the time you receive this letter, I will already be in Parma, because I'm leaving on Wednesday the 17th of this month. I'm hoping that Romani, who is arriving from Venice today, will come with me. I didn't like the first act of *Il solitario* that you sent me, so I have decided to use Voltaire's tragedy *Zaira*,[11] which again you have suggested that I might consider. I find it very interesting and have already composed some music on the piano. Of course, it all depends on whether Romani will agree to prepare the libretto. I hope to persuade him and to take him with me to Parma, too. It will be better to be in Parma, as neither he nor I have any friends there and so we shall work together much faster.

Romani agreed to write *Zaira*, but on 17 March, when he and Bellini reached Parma, he still had not started the libretto. (The opera was scheduled for production on 12 May, leaving only 56 days in which to compose and rehearse the music.) Two days later, Bellini visited Count Sanvitale in order to tell him that he was definitely writing the music for *Zaira* and not *Carlo di Borgogna*, as previously arranged, and also to ask for a postponement of the first performance on the grounds that some of the singers would arrive in Parma too late and there would be only 14 days in which to rehearse. Bellini's change of libretto was accepted, but his second request for a possible postponement was not.

In order to be constantly in touch with each other, Bellini and Romani stayed at the same lodgings, but they were both dilatory and would not get down to work. There was also a farcical event that took place which also caused delay. According to police regulations then in force in the Parma Ducal states, no foreigner was allowed to wear a moustache after three days' residence. On the third day after his arrival, Romani, sporting a moustache, was challenged by a gentleman to have it removed. The incident occurred while Romani was sitting at a cafe with Bellini, Bandini and other members of the theatre's management, including Count Stefano Sanvitale. Romani immediately stood up, looked at his watch and calmly announced, "I'm still in time. I'll leave right away."

Everybody was shocked at his decision. Bandini and Bellini began to beg him to stay, but Romani was adamant, or so he pretended. After much pleading, Count Sanvitale succeeded in persuading him to postpone his departure for 24 hours. Romani was aware of the importance of his presence in Parma and could afford to be capricious, especially when it was a question of a petty regulation. Sanvitale was obviously quick to see through all this and promptly obtained special permission from the Duchess for "Felice Romani, the poet, to wear a moustache and a beard in her Ducal states for as long as he wishes". Although this concession fully satisfied Romani, he and Bellini went on wasting time.

In his biography of Bellini,[12] Filippo Cicconetti wrote that he was often seen strolling with friends through Parma's streets and was always absent from his lodgings in the evenings. This was certainly true, at least for the first month of Bellini's stay in Parma, when he does not seem to have made any progress with the commission.

On 17 April, Count Sanvitale wrote to Bellini[13] to enquire about the progress of the opera: "Please be so kind as to let me know the reasons why our copyists are kept idle."

Sanvitale must have been given a vague answer, for he immediately wrote back with specific questions: "I'm sorry that you always answer in a way that makes it impossible for me to report to the Court. You are kindly invited to let me know when you will be in a position to give your work to the copyists and the reasons that delay your composition."

The reasons for Bellini's laziness are unknown. No letters to Florimo exist to shed light on his activities. Romani also was not working hard, and possibly Bellini felt that he could not censure the poet whom he had tried so stubbornly to secure as his librettist. In a letter addressed to Carolina Cantù, Giuditta's mother, in Milan,[14] Bellini says very little about *Zaira*: "The day before yesterday, I finished the second piece of the opera and yesterday I would have done something more, had Romani given me more material." (This letter is undated, but as Bellini talks of the "few days since I left Milan" it was most likely written during the end of March, while Giuditta was still recuperating in Milan.) "You certainly deserve many blessings that come straight from the heart for having informed me of dearest Giuditta's present state of health. I have been suffering a great deal because I didn't receive any news of her for a whole week. And once and for all I beg you to inform me regularly about your family, as I feel that this is very necessary for me. When Giuditta is unable to do so herself, perhaps you or Gaetanino [Giuditta's brother] will kindly do this favour for a friend who suffers when he doesn't receive a single letter and who, after all, is used to seeing you and being with you for the greater part of the day…"

As a result of Sanvitale's enquiries and complaints and Bandini's reprimands, Bellini and Romani pulled themselves together and completed *Zaira* on time. However, the opening date was changed from 12 to 16 May because of Lablache's inability to arrive in Parma early enough for the rehearsals.

The opening of the Teatro Ducale was a spectacular event that brought many people to Parma from Milan and other cities. There was also great anticipation over Bellini's new opera. Several inaccurate reports about the outcome of *Zaira* have been published, claiming that the first Parmesan audience wildly disapproved of the opera and hissed at it. (This cannot be correct, as the great majority of those present were important court officials, government members and the nobility from Parma and elsewhere, who surrounded the Duchess. According to the strict etiquette of the time, the audience would hardly have shown its disapproval in such a way.) The report of the theatre's inspector on that night ran, "The performance started at 8.30pm and ended at about 2am. The music wasn't much appreciated, except for the trio in act one. The singers were greatly applauded. The ballet[15] won general approval."

Evidently, the opera failed both with the public – who merely received it coldly – and with the critics. *L'Eco di Milano* commented:

Except for a trio and an aria sung by Lalande, the music of Bellini's new opera was not at all liked. Even Lalande's aria is very similar to one in *La Straniera*, and several other parts of this opera remind one of music from Bellini's other works, even though he had written only three operas before *Zaira*...

There were rumours of a claque who wanted to ruin Bellini's opera. But even if this were true, considering the circumstances under which the opera was given in Parma, this would not have been possible if the music had not been weak. The only consolation that the young maestro might be offered is that many of his distinguished predecessors had been hissed at times, and not only at the beginnings of their careers. "Even good Homer sleeps from time to time."

The *Gazzetta di Parma* was less damning, but only in style:

Romani's libretto was generally liked. As far as Bellini's music is concerned, popular pieces included a duet between Lalande and Cecconi, Lalande's aria and, particularly, the trio with Lalande, Cecconi and Inchindi, after which the singers were given enthusiastic applause. At this point, there was also a call for the maestro. Although the singers were again at various times applauded, there was no more applause for the composer. Nor was there any for that distinguished singer Lablache, who seemed to be miscast, or it could be that the music that Bellini composed for him this time wasn't worthy of the singer's talent.

It is impossible to accuse the Parmesans of wishing to vindicate the local poet Torrigiani, nor Torrigiani himself of organising a conspiracy to ruin the performance of *Zaira*. The casual and irresponsible behaviour of Bellini and Romani during their first month in Parma certainly ensured that people talked about them with mixed feelings, although of course all would have been forgiven if the opera had been successful. But, apart from his music being different from that of Rossini, who in Parma was then very much appreciated,

Bellini had not given the Parmesans anything of consequence that was new or particularly exciting. Many of the situations in *Zaira* are similar to those in *Bianca e Fernando*, and the suicide ending is reminiscent of that in *La Straniera*. Bellini had composed most of the music in a great hurry, without allowing himself time to think about the characters. Moreover, hardly any of the highly promising reforms with which he had experimented in *La Straniera* were developed in *Zaira*. Of course, maybe both composer and, to a great extent, librettist erred on the side of caution when faced with such a great social occasion as the opening of a new theatre.

The failure of *Zaira* did not upset Bellini unduly. He seems to have believed in a large part of the music, which he used to great advantage in subsequent operas, notably *I Capuleti e i Montecchi*. In this respect, Bellini's letter to his uncle Ferlito[16] that he wrote on 16 May, after the dress rehearsal, is of interest: "Last night, we had the dress rehearsal, and I hope that *Zaira* will be as lucky as my other operas. Almost all the scenes were applauded. What the audience appreciated most, however, was Lalande's cavatina, the trio and the duet in the first act and the duet between Lablache and Lalande. Also, Nerestano's rondo, which is sung by a certain Cecconi, who has a wonderful contrasting voice; Lalande's and Lablache's scenes; and the quintet in the finale of act two. All these make me feel hopeful that the public will be quite happy about the whole opera, the music and libretto of which were written in just one month."

Lack of documentary evidence makes it difficult to know exactly when Bellini left Parma, but it could not have been long after the first performance of *Zaira*, as there is no mention of his or Romani's presence at any others, and it is therefore possible that they both left on 17 May. Bellini must have been anxious to return to Milan to find refuge with Giuditta, whom he had not seen for two months.

As if the failure of *Zaira* was not enough, following the performance, insulting leaflets were found scattered around Parma with the inscription, "In case someone finds Bellini's musical talent, he is begged to take it to the office of the impresario Bandini. We shall be very grateful indeed."

Zaira achieved only eight performances and, with the exception of some unsuccessful performances in Florence in 1836, had to wait until 1976 for a revival, at the Teatro Massimo Bellini, Catania. On this occasion, as in the second revival in 1990, it was proved to have considerable merit, despite (or because of) the fact that a great part of its music is familiar from subsequent Bellini operas.

ZAIRA

Opera seria (*tragedia lirica*) in two acts. Libretto by Felice Romani. First performed at the inauguration of the Teatro Ducale (later the Regio), Parma, on 16 May 1829 on a double bill with the ballet *Oreste*, choreographed by Antonio Cortesi to unidentified music.

CHARACTERS AND ORIGINAL CAST

Zaira, Lusignano's daughter, now a slave of the Sultan	Soprano	Enrichetta Méric-Lalande
Orosmane, the Sultan of Jerusalem	Bass	Luigi Lablache
Corasmino, the Sultan's vizier	Tenor	Carlo Trezzini
Nerestano, a French knight, Zaira's brother	Contralto	Teresa Cecconi
Lusignano, a prince once belonging to the line of the kings of Jerusalem, now the Sultan's prisoner	Bass	Giovanni Inchindi
Fatima, a slave of the Sultan	Soprano	Marietta Sacchi
Castiglione, a French knight	Tenor	Francesco Antonio Biscontini
Meledor, an official of the Sultan	Baritone	Pietro Ansiglioni

The action takes place in the court (palace and garden) of the Sultan of Jerusalem at the time of the Crusades, in the Middle Ages.

ACT I

SCENE 1: A magnificent gallery adjacent to the Sultan's harem. In the background, a staircase leads to galleries adorned with flowers and large jars of perfume. Staircases also lead to the *loggias* and other apartments.

The courtiers are happily celebrating with song and dance the imminent wedding of Orosmane, their Sultan, to Zaira, the orphaned Christian slave girl. Only Corasmino, the Sultan's vizier, and a group of officials, all fanatic Muslims, resent the impending marriage, which will enthrone a Christian.

However, as Corasmino cannot openly oppose his Sultan, he vows to find a way of breaking up this sacrilegious union by cunning.

Presently, Zaira tells Fatima, another slave girl in the harem, of her present happiness. All she knows is that she is an orphan. She does not remember her parents. The only trace of memory that has remained to her is that she is a Christian, a fact that she more precisely knows from the little golden crucifix that has always been tied around her neck. In vain, Fatima warns her that soon she will have to deny her own faith in "the arms of a cruel Tartar, an oppressor of your religion". However, Zaira answers that henceforth her only religion will be that of love; she loves and is sincerely loved by the Sultan, who wants to marry her. Presently, the Sultan appears and passionately expresses his deep love for Zaira, who reassures him that their feelings are mutual.

The French knight Nerestano, an ex-slave of the Sultan, arrives from France to bargain for Zaira's ransom and that of ten Crusader knights still held prisoner. Orosmane is perfectly willing to send the knights (who in fact number 100) back to their homeland, with the exception of old Prince Lusignano (whom he has sentenced to death) and Zaira, who will remain in the palace as the Sultan's wife. Hearing this, Zaira promptly persuades the Sultan to reprieve Lusignano from his death sentence.

SCENE 2: A subterranean hall leading to the cells in which the French knights are imprisoned.

Zaira accompanies Nerestano to the prison so that she will see the French knights that have been freed by the Sultan, including Lusignano. Prince Lusignano is deeply moved to see the golden crucifix on Zaira's neck (placed there when she was baptised) and recognises her and Nerestano to be his children, who were lost when he was taken prisoner in the battle with Syria. However, Lusignano's happiness is clouded when he and the liberated knights realise that Zaira, in oriental dress, is about to renounce the Christian faith in order to become the wife of a Muslim; for the old prince, this is a worse torment than his long imprisonment. Her father's grief so disturbs her that Zaira readily promises to do everything she can not to renounce the Christian religion. Meanwhile, the Sultan has asked for her and she hurries to him.

SCENE 3: Interior of the harem.

Orosmane orders that the Frenchmen must leave, disregarding Corasmino's objection that the pitiful condition of the released prisoners in general, and of Lusignano in particular, might easily attract severe criticism in Europe; the Sultan will be blamed for the long martyrdom which he has inflicted on them. The Sultan, however, stands by his decision and also allows Zaira to bid Nerestano a final farewell. Both Zaira and Nerestano are distressed, especially as their father's condition has deteriorated; the weeping Zaira swears that she will never renounce her religion, even at the cost of losing Orosmane's love. Corasmino misconstrues Zaira's behaviour with Nerestano, especially when she asks the Sultan for a short postponement of their wedding. The Sultan furiously warns her that he will kill any man who would dare be his rival.

Act II
Scene 1: Zaira's chambers.

Fatima tries to make Zaira change her mind about marrying the Sultan; she would be betraying her religion and would then lose her family's love, of which she was deprived for so many years. When Orosmane arrives, Zaira, distressed, renews her plea for a day's postponement of the wedding; she will then divulge the reason for her plea. The disappointed Sultan generously agrees to her request.

Scene 2: A remote place near the quarters assigned to the French knights.

The kind Sultan allows the French knights to bury Lusignano, who has just died, with Christian rites and with every honour. Afterwards, the knights are to be escorted as far as the River Jordan, where they will board ship for their homeland. Zaira, however, will be unable to attend the funeral, because her marriage to Orosmane is to be celebrated on the following day. This enrages Nerestano and the knights, especially as in his very last moments Lusignano asked for his daughter to be with him, and they plan to abduct her.

Scene 3: Ground-floor hall in the harem. The mountain slopes are visible through great arches at the back.

Corasmino, who is now certain of Zaira's guilt, produces evidence to the Sultan of the plot that is being hatched against him. A slave secretly carrying a message from Nerestano to Zaira has been intercepted. In the message, Nerestano informs Zaira that he wishes to see her that night in the deserted garden of the mosque. If Zaira fails to do this, he will kill himself by dawn. Convinced of Zaira's treachery, Orosmane agrees to Corasmino's suggestion that they should allow the message to reach Zaira so that she will be trapped. When Zaira receives the message, she is torn between conflicting emotions: her love and duty towards the Sultan and her promises to her father.

Suddenly, a funeral dirge is heard nearby. Zaira runs to the balcony and discovers that it is her father's funeral. Unable to resist her grief, she faints, to the amazement of the slaves and guards, who cannot understand why their mistress, the woman who is about to become Sultana, could be so distressed by the death of a Christian slave.

SCENE 4: A remote part of the harem gardens. In the distance, the minarets of a mosque rise above the trees.

After expressing his unhappiness and humiliation, Orosmane hides with Corasmino to wait for Zaira, who arrives accompanied by Fatima, and soon Nerestano appears. Prompted by her father's death, Zaira has renounced her love for Orosmane and wants now to return to her homeland with her brother. As she is about to go off with Nerestano, Orosmane rushes out and stabs her in a fit of jealousy. The dying Zaira reveals that Nerestano is her brother and not her lover, whereupon Orosmane, in despair, exclaims, "She loved me and I have killed her." He orders everybody to leave as he stabs himself in the heart.

Romani based his libretto on Voltaire's *La Zaïre* (1732). The tragedy of Zaire – the Christian slave brought up in a harem and torn between love and duty to her religion and own people – has a universal appeal in any period and has been used several times as a basis for opera.[17] The librettist avoided philosophical ostentation (appropriate in Voltaire and popular at the time), opting instead for the language of passion so suitable in an opera in which extreme conciseness in the verses is essential.

"*Zaira*," Romani wrote in his preface to the libretto, "is therefore not covered with the ample cloak of Tragedy but wrapped in the tight forms of the Melodrama." As such, he did a good job.

Corasmino's part was expanded – the cold confidant of the Sultan and a fanatic Muslim became a more convincing character when adhering to the strict laws and customs of the harem and also provided an interesting contrast to his exceptionally liberal master, the Sultan. The changes and transformations not only maintained the simplicity of the action but also imbued the drama with considerable oriental colour that was absent in *La Zaïre*. As usual, Romani provides interesting, dramatic situations, although several are similar to those in other libretti that he wrote for Bellini: brother and sister are united with their father, as in *Bianca e Fernando*, and the fatal misunderstanding that Nerestano is Zaira's lover and the suicide at the end are reminiscent of *La Straniera*. Neither poet nor composer seem to have worried about this at the time. They either felt that there was no time to make changes or were confident that they could vary these situations so that they would still be fresh and original. Besides, at that period, opinions were divided as to the literary merits of a libretto; many maintained that familiar subjects and/or situations in opera were, if anything, advantageous.

The collaboration was successful, by and large, except that Romani's verses, good though they are, are not amongst his best. There is too much repetition of words and, even, of concepts. The poet's justification (or, rather, explanation) of this was that he produced the verses as the music was composed and that there was no time for restructuring or revising. The opera was written in a month.

Dispensing with an overture or a prelude, Bellini's opening scene in *Zaira* was most unusual at the time that it was produced. A stately orchestral introduction (an *assai allegro e risoluto* in 32 bars) precedes the raising of the curtain, which is followed by further orchestral music, very quickly setting the oriental atmosphere.

Two contrasting themes from the opera follow: the chorus of the courtiers paying homage to Zaira and the orchestral theme that accompanies the dancing odalisques, further enhancing the scene.[18] Their dance (in march time) is rhythmical, developing into an exciting *crescendo*, the chorus "Gemma, splendor di Solima" ("Splendid jewel of Solima") alternating with the dancing to considerable effect.

Corasmino's *scena* is only partially successful. The recitative "L'odo, ah, l'odo" ("Ah, yes, I hear it") establishes his faithfulness to the Sultan and, to some extent, his own religious fanaticism, and the *larghetto* aria "Perchi mai perchi pugnasti?" ("For whom and what did we fight?") reveals his melancholy, his regret for happier times past. But the weak cabaletta "D'un furor colpevole" ("Anger that betrays guilt") fails to bring the scene to its logical conclusion, somewhat marring the preceding highly expressive music; in reality, it offers little, apart from exhibition of vocal technique.

Zaira's aria is even less successful. In the recitative "Della mia gioia a parte" ("You do not share my happiness"), the composer surprisingly does nothing to enhance the words; the music on its own does not begin to convey the feelings of the love-smitten girl. Moreover, the first part of the aria "Amo ed amata" ("I love and am loved") is lifeless, at best a vehicle for vocal technique and at worst an uninspired *bravura* aria. Only in the second part, "Non, è tormento" ("No, it is not a torment"), also an *allegro*, does Bellini redeem himself and finally convey something of the girl's feelings.

The numbers that follow fail to raise the standard of the work. They are generally weak and affected, even if at times they show that the composer had good intentions. When Lusignano recognises his children, the music does achieve a certain theatrical effect, by means of dramatic simplicity, but obviously the emotions of the characters concerned were not seriously considered. Bellini had done much better in a similar scene in the earlier *Bianca e Fernando*.

The trio "O, me felice!" ("Oh, I am so happy!"), after the recognition scene, is more worthy of the composer, although judging it at face value it is a little difficult to understand its original success. Possibly the physical presence of the three characters contributed greatly to the excitement that was aroused in the hitherto cold and rather hostile Parmesan audience at the premiere.

All three sections of the trio are well constructed, with good, expressive melodies. The first, "Cari oggetti" ("My beloved ones"), conveys the deeply felt emotions of the father towards his new-found children and their reactions to him:

Allegro moderato

A contrast is achieved in the second part, "Qui crudele in questa terra" ("Here in this cruel land"), when Lusignano realises that Zaira is wearing oriental dress. The motif is basically the same as in the first part, but Lusignano is in a different situation; he is now the unhappy, troubled and angry Christian in place of the happy father, and the music is varied accordingly. An ingenious, vibrant cadenza links the first two parts, creating an atmosphere of expectation and thus renewing the interest of the listener. Greater dramatic effect is achieved when Nerestano takes up the same motif in "Deh! ti calma" ("So it will calm you"), but in a different key. In short exclamations that act as embellishments to Nerestano's music, Zaira expresses her distress. Lusignano's voice then joins the other two and finally, with the chorus "A che stai? perdono implora" ("In your situation, implore pardon"), the motif suddenly reverts to its original key. The third part, Zaira's farewell "Ah, perdona... Io qui vivea" ("Ah, forgive me... I have lived here") to her father and brother after the Sultan has asked for her, is the most successful; the subtle mixture of her sorrow and despair is heart-rending and worthy of both the composer's and librettist's best.

Except for the final quartet, the remainder of the act hardly offers anything of consequence. Even though the quartet beginning with Orosmane's "Corsa è l'ora a lei concessa" ("The allotted hour has elapsed") develops from a declaimed passage with asymmetrical notes and rests, it maintains a flowing rhythm, at the same time depicting the state of mind of each character – an auspicious Orosmane, a watchful and sinister Corasmino, an undecided and almost lost Nerestano and a weeping Zaira.

A short prelude for strings precedes the second act. Although Zaira's "Ah, questo di" ("Ah, this day") begins promisingly, conveying her despairing passion well, it lapses into conventionalism after the very expressive phrase of the *andante* "Deh, se tu m'ami" ("Alas, if you love me"). The melody and harmony of this piece is indeed elegant, but somehow it never comes alive. Perhaps it was too mechanically constructed. (Significantly, this part was reworked by Bellini when he transferred it into the powerful trio "Angiol di pace" in *Beatrice di Tenda*.)

In the ensuing chorus, "Più non è" ("Nothing more"), the composer was fully successful. Here, to great advantage, he used music from *Bianca e Fernando*, which is much more suited to the serenely evocative and melancholy outburst of the French knights mourning Lusignano's death than to the conspiracy scene of the earlier opera.

Nerestano's rondo, which follows, was the second piece to be applauded at the first performance. Bellini wrote this *scena* while giving his full consideration to the vocal resources of Cecconi, the creator of the role, who had a beautiful contralto voice and considerable technique. The music, however, is not merely a vocal showpiece but generates a conducive atmosphere of great dramatic intensity. It achieves just as much in Nerestano's recitative "O cavalieri! O amici" ("Oh gentlemen! Oh friends!"), where his state of mind is expressed through music. His aria "O Zaira, in qual momento" ("Oh, Zaira, in that moment"), a beautiful *legato* melody enhances the emotional content of the words with memorable sincerity:

Larghetto

Equally expressive is the cabaletta "Si, mi vedrà la barbara" ("Yes, the barbarian will see me"), an *allegro* with chorus that musically brings Nerestano's scene to a logical conclusion.

Orosmane's duet with Corasmino "E tu saprai, Zaira" ("And you will know, Zaira") is preceded with the reading of Nerestano's message. Because of the importance of the message, the words are read aloud with only a violin tremolo for accompaniment, the violas and cellos taking over briefly at every pause in the reading. In the actual duet, Orosmane at first appears to be astonished. His passionate music is like a monologue with pauses. When Corasmino replies, Orosmane's tone becomes much more vigorous as his astonishment changes to blind rage.

Zaira pours out her lovesick heart in the aria "Che non tentai per vincere?" ("How can I overcome this fatal love?"). It is a tender melody that, with simplicity, touchingly echoes the sighs of a tortured heart while the chorus intones a moving funeral dirge, the kind one hears in some eastern

Mediterranean countries when prayers are intoned over a deceased person. The concluding cabaletta, "Ah! crudeli chiamar" ("Ah! What a cruel call"), is exciting, but here an intensely dramatic one would have been more in keeping with Zaira's despairing anguish.

Undoubtedly, Bellini wanted the final scene of *Zaira* to be the climax of the opera. He gave it to Orosmane, the character for whom he felt the most sympathy, and as the part was sung by Lablache he had every opportunity to make the finale memorable, but it was not to be. There simply was too little time for the composer to give it his undivided consideration.

The orchestral prelude opening the scene – played by full orchestra, contracting to cor anglais solo – does not succeed in establishing the requisite atmosphere. It is the most inferior piece of music of its kind that Bellini wrote. Nevertheless, there are several successful passages in the scene, such as Orosmane's recitative "E' notte alfin" ("Night at last"), which is declamatory in style but also splendidly intermingled with arioso, expressing the character's feelings of humiliation by a love unworthy of him. The orchestra, which restricts itself in this instance to a tremolo on the strings with sporadic intervention from the wind instruments, is merely background music, focusing attention on the voice.

The quintet "Lieto ci mira adesso, o Lusignan" ("Lusignano can smile now") is a well-constructed polyphonic passage:

Andante sostenuto assai

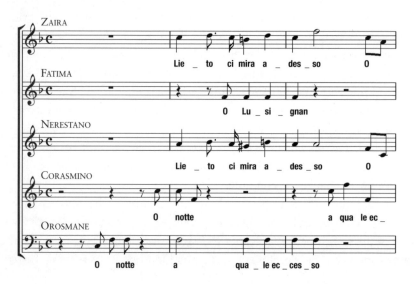

1 (above): Palazzo dei Gravina Gruylas, c1800, the house in Catania where Bellini was born (apartment on first floor). The apartment is today the Museo Civico Belliniano.

2 (right): The alcove in the apartment where Bellini was born. The cembalo on which he practiced belonged to his grandfather. The stool belonged to Bellini and was returned to his family, after his death, by Rossini. "Reconstructed" portrait of Bellini (see No.4)

3 (top left): Oil portrait of Bellini c1831. Painter unknown.

4 (top right): "Reconstructed" portrait of Bellini in his teens, commissioned by Francesco Florimo and painted by Federico Mandarelli.

5 (above left): Oil portrait of Bellini by Giuseppe Patania, Palermo, April 1832.

6 (above right): Nicolò Zingarelli, director of the Naples Conservatorio and Bellini's teacher.

7 (top left): Carlo Pepoli, librettist for Bellini's *I Puritani*.

8 (top right): Felice Romani, Bellini's principal librettist, c1830.

9 (above left): Francesco Florimo, Bellini's intimate lifelong friend, c1840.

10 (above right): Pastel portrait of Giuditta Cantù Turina (Bellini's mistress) by Luigi Bianchi, c1828.

Sanquirico's designs for the premiere of *Bianca e Fernando* at Carlo Felice, Genoa, 1828.

11 (left): Act I, scene 1: Atrium of the palace. In the background, the city and harbour of Agrigento.

12 (left): Act I, scene 2: Filippo's apartment in the castle.

13 (left): Act II, scene 3: The tombs of the Dukes of Agrigento, where Duke Carlo is imprisoned.

The protagonists in the premiere of *Bianca e Fernando*
14 (top left): Tamburini as Filippo.

15 (top middle): Tosi as Bianca

16 (top right): David as Fernando

17 (above): *Bianca e Fernando* at Teatro Margherita, Genoa, 1978. Producer: Sequi.
Designer: Grossi. Act II, Scene 2: Deutekom as Bianca and Piolato as Eloisa – "Sorgi, o padre".

Sanquirico's designs for
the premiere of *Il pirata*
at La Scala, 1827.

18 (left): Act I, scene 3:
An illuminated part of
Caldora Castle's grounds.

19 (left): Act II, scene 1:
A salon leading to
Imogene's apartments.

20 (left): Act II, scene 2:
A terrace before the
castle. Ernesto
(Tamburini) surprises
Imogene (Méric-Lalande)
and Gualtiero (Rubini).

21 (top): Act II, final scene: Ground-floor courtyard of Caldora Castle.

22 (above left): Act I, scene 2: Rubini as Gualtiero in the premiere of *Il pirata* – "Pietosa al padre!"

23 (above right): Act I, scene 2: Rubini as Gualtiero and Comelli-Rubini as Imogene, Vienna, 1828 – "Ah! è mio…è figlio mio… Pietà!"

Il pirata at La Scala, 1958. Producer: Enriquez. Designer: Zuffi. Callas as Imogene.
24 (top): Act I, scene 1: Imogene questions Itulbo (Rumbo) about the shipwrecked.

25 (above left): Act II, scene 2: In vain, Gualtiero (Corelli) pleads with Imogene to flee with him.

26 (above right): Act II, final scene: Out of her mind, Imogene imagines a scaffold for Gualtiero's execution – "La vedete! Il palco funesto, ah!" She entreats the sun to hide her from the horrible sight.

Sanquirico's designs for the premiere of *La Straniera* at La Scala, 1829.

27 (right): Act I, scene 1: Courtyard of Montolino Castle.

28 (right): Act I, scene 3: A remote place outside the Straniera's cottage.

29 (right): Act II, scene 3: Isoletta's apartment at Montolino Castle.

The premiere of *La Straniera* at La Scala.
30 (top left): Tamburini as Valdeburgo – "Bardo al terror…miratema".

31 (top middle): Méric-Lalande as Alaide – "Questo almeno ti renda propizio sacrificio che il core ti fa".

32 (top right): Final scene: Tosi as Alaide – "Or sei pago, o ciel tremendo".

33 (above): *La Straniera* at Teatro Massimo, Palermo, 1969. Producer: Bolognini. Designer: Escoffier. Act II, scene 1: The tribunal. Scotto as Alaide.

Zaira (Parma, 1829) at Teatro Massimo Bellini, Catania, 1976. Producer and designer: Colonello.

34 (left): Act I, scene 2: A Subterranean hall leading to the prisoners' cells. Scotto as Zaira.

35 (below): Act II, scene 4: A remote part of the harem garden. Zaira (Scotto) is mortally stabbed by Orosmane (Roni). On the left are Nerestano (Nave) and Corasmino (Lamberti).

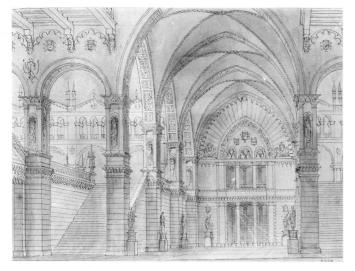

Bagnara's designs for the premiere of *I Capuleti e I Montecchi* at La Fenice, Venice, 1830.

36 (left): Act I, scene 1: A gallery in the Capuleti palace.

37 (left): Act I, scene 3: An internal courtyard of the palace.

38 (left): Act II, scene 3: The Capuleti tombs.

39 (top left): Giuditta Grisi and Amalia Schütz as Romeo and Giulietta in *I Capuleti*, La Scala, 1830.

40 (top right): Malibran as Romeo in *I Capuleti*, Bologna, 1832.

41 (above): *I Capuleti* at La Scala, 1966. Producer: Castellani. Designer: Frigerio. Act I, scene 3 finale: Aragall (Romeo), Scotto (Giulietta), Giacomotti (Lorenzo) and Pavarotti (Tebaldo) – "Soccorso sostegno accordali".

Sanquirico's designs for the premiere of *La sonnambula* at Teatro Carcano, Milan, 1831.

42 (left) Act I, scene 2: Rodolfo's room in the village inn.

43 (left): Act II, scene 1: A wooded valley on the village outskirts.

44 (left): Act II, scene 2: The village green with the water mill. (Originally, Amina sleepwalked on the roof. Later, a bridge was used above the mill wheel.)

45 (top left): Act I, scene 1: The village green. Pasta as Amina in the premiere of
La sonnambula.

46 (top right): Malibran as Amina. Drury Lane, London, 1833.

47 (above left): Patti as Amina sleepwalking in the final scene.

48 (above right): Act I, scene 1: Scotto as Amina and Kraus as Elvino. La Scala, 1960.

La sonnambula at La Scala, 1957. Producer: Visconti. Designer: Tosi. Act II, scene 2: Callas as Amina, Monti as Elvino.
49 (top): Amina sleepwalks on the bridge above the mill.

50 (above left): Amina – "Ah, non credea mirarti si presto estinto, o fiore!"

51 (above right): Amina with Elvino – "Ah, non giunge uman pensiero".

It is self-contained, with all the voices superbly balanced, and it purposefully stops the action. But, even though the ground is well prepared for Orosmane's final cabaletta, "Un grido d'orrore" ("A cry of horror"), this fails to attain the expected dramatic climax. Neither the vocal line nor the accompaniment of *pizzicato* chords rises to the intensity of Orosmane's despair, which is reduced to little more than a final farewell, however heart-rending.

Bellini's statement that "*Zaira* had its revenge in *I Capuleti*" sums up well the merits and defects of the work. The composer pillaged the score and successfully used a great deal of the music that he thought worthy in *I Capuleti e i Montecchi*, the opera that immediately followed *Zaira* and which he again had to write in a hurry. Later, he also used music from *Zaira* in *Beatrice di Tenda* and music that was already parody in *Zaira* (originating in *Bianca e Fernando*) in *Norma*.

This goes a long way to explain why Bellini never revised *Zaira* or even attempted a second staging in another theatre. As Friedrich Lippman pointed out,[19] "Bellini could not easily have restaged *Zaira* after the great success of *I Capuleti* because attitudes to parody were then, around 1830, already changing – a practice that had for centuries been readily accepted was now received with suspicion, if not frowned upon."

Even after Bellini became an international celebrity and his operas were widely performed, attracting the best singers of the day, *Zaira* was revived only once in the 19th century, at the Teatro della Pergola, Florence, in 1836, about nine months after the composer's death. The critic of the *Gazzetta di Firenze* wrote, "The audience – which was obviously not as sensitive as Orosmane – screamed at Zaira and sent her back to the harem... Bellini used *Zaira*'s best ideas to enrich his subsequent operas, which were more successfully produced and became very well known by everyone. Thus *Zaira* is the mother who has transferred her beauties to her daughters already admired by high society. Now it's too late for her to seek admiration for herself. She is strongly advised to go back home."

Writing in the 1960s, Francesco Pastura[20] described *Zaira* as Bellini's only uninspired work: "In *Zaira*, Bellini tried to be a 'professional' operatic composer who could produce music under all circumstances. In this, he failed, and he knew it, because he could only create a work of art when 'by his style he vomited blood'." Having never seen *Zaira* on the stage, Pastura's verdict rests mainly on Bellini's statement and the disappearance of the opera.

Zaira had to wait until 1976 for its second revival, which took place in Catania. It enjoyed considerable success there – mainly because of the renaissance of Bellini's music that began in the 1950s – and appeared an interesting novelty. However, despite Renata Scotto's most accomplished performance of the title role, as well as Luigi Roni's Orosmane, it took 14 years for the opera to be performed again in Catania, this time in 1990 with Katia Ricciarelli as Zaira and, interestingly, with Roni as Lusignano. No other theatre has yet planned to produce it.

8

I Capuleti e i Montecchi in Venice (1830)

By the time Bellini returned to Milan from Parma, Giuditta had recovered from her illness sufficiently to leave for the family country house at Casalbuttano. The Turinas, undoubtedly at Giuditta's initiative, also invited Bellini to Casalbuttano, where he could rest and forget the sad outcome of his opera in Parma.

After about five weeks there, Bellini was back in Milan, where, during the last week of June, the impresarios of the various opera houses usually gathered to commission new operas and engage singers for the carnival season. In Milan, Bellini met impresario Alessandro Lanari, who often worked in association with Crivelli, the impresario of La Fenice, Venice. Lanari would have like to have commissioned Bellini to write a new opera for La Fenice, but it was not possible to do so for the forthcoming carnival season, as two other composers, Giuseppe Persiani[1] and Giovanni Pacini, had already been contracted to provide the new works. However, in the event that Pacini – who was also providing the Teatro Reggio, Turin, with a new opera – dropped out, Lanari promised Bellini that he would definitely be engaged for La Fenice. (Pacini had most likely accepted the commission for Venice before the Turin offer was made.) Romani was to provide both libretti: *Annibale in Torino* for Turin and, for Venice, a libretto as yet to be decided. In the meantime, Lanari made arrangements to present *Il pirata* at La Fenice and thus introduce Bellini to the Venetians.

Sometime in July, Bellini heard the sad news of his grandfather's death in Catania. Vincenzo Tobia had died on 8 June, but it seems that Bellini heard about it as late as a month after this. All the information that exists on this matter comes from the anonymous manuscript in the Museo Belliniano: "Having received the news of his grandfather's death, Vincenzo Bellini couldn't find peace and cried bitterly at his loss. He wrote, 'I am beside myself with grief; my dearest grandfather is dead. It is to him that I owe so much – more than to anyone else – for having kept me for many years in his house, where I learned most of the basic musical principles, and for having demonstrated the greatest affection to me, which was more than any other relative could have done."

The 1829 summer season at La Scala had to be short, and the theatre was closed from 3 July until the end of August for redecoration and stage modernisation. From 16 July to 27 August, the La Scala company put on 24 performances of *Il pirata* at the Teatro della Canobbiana, taking advantage of the availability of Lalande, Rubini and Tamburini. All performances were received enthusiastically. This success, and the tranquillity of Casalbuttano, helped Bellini to get over the failure of *Zaira* in Parma.

Another event of a different nature further lifted Bellini's spirits. Writing on 28 August to his uncle Ferlito[2] in Catania, he describes his exciting encounter in some detail:

After having a great furore with *Guglielmo Tell* [on 3 August 1829] in Paris, the celebrated Rossini is now passing through here on his way to Bologna. Two days ago, when on a visit to the proprietress of this house, he found out from her that I was living here he begged her to bring him to me… You can imagine my surprise; I was trembling with happiness. Not even stopping to put on a jacket, I went out immediately to meet him in my shirtsleeves. When I begged his pardon for the informal manner in which I was presenting myself to him, justified only by the sudden pleasure of meeting so great a genius, he replied that it was of no importance. He then paid me many, many compliments regarding my compositions, which he had come to know in Paris.

He went on, 'I've seen in your operas that you begin where others have stopped.' I answered that such praise, coming from him, would serve to make me immerse myself deeper in the career that I've chosen for myself, and that I considered myself fortunate to have won a compliment from the musician of the century.

He came to hear *Il pirata* that evening and also on the following evening, which was the last performance of the season. And, would you believe it, it didn't take him long to tell all Milan that he found throughout the opera a finish and discipline that is worthy of a mature man, rather than a young one. The work was full of great feeling which, in his view, was carried to such a point of profound reasoning that at times the music lacked brilliance. That is how he felt about my opera, and I shall go on composing in the same way, with common sense as my criterion, as I have already been trying to do in my spontaneous enthusiasm.

Yesterday, I was invited to dinner by the Cantùs [Giuditta Turina's parents], where I met Rossini and his wife. Rossini repeated his compliments to me but without saying anything about feeling and brilliance; but at our first meeting, he did say that he had understood from my music that I must be capable of loving very deeply, because he found great feeling in it.

So in Milan they are now all talking of *Il pirata* and Rossini, of Rossini and *Il pirata*, because each one says what pleases him, and the same thing goes for the singers. Meanwhile, I consider myself fortunate in this incident, which enabled me to make the acquaintance of this great man.

Bellini spent the next three months mainly at Casalbuttano with Giuditta, returning to Milan only to conduct his business affairs. Also, the *Gazzetta Torinese* reported on 3 November that he spent a few days in Turin, where the directors of the Accademia conferred on him an honorary degree. As *Il pirata* was scheduled for production at La Fenice at the beginning of January, Bellini left for Venice on 17 December.

The season at La Fenice opened on 26 December with Persiani's *Costantino in Arles*, cast with Giuditta Grisi, Lorenzo Bonfigli and Giulio Pellegrini, the same singers who were cast in *Il pirata*, which was to follow. *Costantino* was received indifferently, although Bellini liked the singers. "The rehearsals of *Il pirata* seem to be going well and the singers and orchestra are putting their best efforts into it," he wrote[3] to Lamperi.[4] On 16 January, *Il pirata* successfully introduced Bellini to the Venetians.

Several days before the first performance, Bellini was already making tentative arrangements to write a new opera for La Fenice. The original plan was to follow *Il pirata* with Alberto Guillon's *Maria di Brabante*[5] and then with Pacini's new opera, to be staged during the last week in February, as the season lasted only until 20 March. According to his contract, Pacini was expected in Venice not later than 14 January, but Lanari decided to extend his time limit by one week, as the winter was extremely severe that year and made travelling very difficult. In the meantime, Lanari was making provisional arrangements with Bellini for the new opera, as it was doubtful that Pacini would be able to fulfil his obligations in Turin and come to Venice on time. On 5 January, Bellini wrote to Lanari,[6] "If by any chance Pacini doesn't keep his contract for the new opera at La Fenice, I would like to inform you that I will accept your proposal to write the new opera myself, which will be to Romani's libretto on Giulietta Capellio. My fee will be in the region of 325 gold Napoleons. I will also expect to have one and a half months at my disposal from the day the libretto is produced [to write my opera]. This letter will act as a contract until the 14th day of this month, and please believe in my friendship."

A few days later, Bellini informed Giuditta of his plans to stay in Venice, as he was almost certain that he would be writing the new opera. He must have heard from Florimo then, because in his letter to Giuditta he conveys Florimo's greetings to her. Apparently, Florimo had changed his cold attitude towards his friend's love affair; as Bellini commented to Giuditta, "Florimo is now recovering from his ill humour. God wanted it to be so, because these ills are too damaging to one's health and peace of mind, and may God free everyone from such trials."

To Florimo,[7] Bellini wrote about the new opera on 20 January, the day that he signed the contract. It is a relatively short letter, friendly but without the usual endearments:

> I'm telling you that I am obliged to write the opera for this carnival, and this morning I signed the contract which gave me a month and a half to have the work ready for production. You can see that I'm very rushed, and maybe you think that I was wrong in accepting. But the Governor and almost the whole of Venice have been very kind and have persuaded me to accept this dangerous task. In the meantime, all Venice is rejoicing about this, and I only hope to be worthy of their expectations.
>
> If I don't write to you in the near future, or if I write very briefly, don't worry about it, as I'm very hard pressed for time. Here the weather is always bad. *Il pirata* has fared well. Romani, who arrived here yesterday, is writing a libretto for me based on Romeo and Giulietta but with different title, *I Capuleti e i Montecchi*, and with different situations.
>
> Goodbye, my dear Florimo. My health isn't bad, although I have a cold, and if this weather continues I shall never get warm.

It is unknown how Bellini came to consider a libretto based on the tragedy of Romeo and Giulietta, or if this was the same libretto that Romani was preparing for Pacini. A letter that Bellini wrote on 15 January to Gaetano Cantù[8] rather suggests that Pacini's libretto was a different one. After the news that he might have to compose the new opera himself "if that coward Pacini does not come" (a decision to be taken on 20 January), he says, "I don't know whether the libretto that Romani has been writing for Pacini is finished yet, because I've only read the first act and part of the second. I would like to tell you in strict confidence that this libretto is even more insipid than cold Pacini himself."

In *Vita di Vincenzo Bellini*, Cicconetti wrote that Anselmo Del Zio, a contemporary of Bellini at the conservatorio in Naples, had related to him that Bellini wrote *I Capuleti* out of spite for his old teacher Zingarelli, who had himself written *Giulietta e Romeo* (1797). However, there is no documentary evidence for this (Pougin[9] also included the story in his biography of Bellini) and Florimo, in his book, rejects it as misconstrued and imaginary.

Emilia Branca's[10] version of events is also without evidence. She wrote, "Giuditta Grisi, a close friend of Bellini, suggested the subject of *I Capuleti e i Montecchi* and insisted that Bellini should write expressly for her the role of Romeo, which was much more impressive and interesting than the part of Giulietta, which was to be written for the very good singer Rosalbina Carradori. As the subject of the libretto suited Bellini's sensibility, and as, above all, he wanted to please his new friend Giuditta, he accepted it, even though it provided a very unimportant role for the bass and a tiny one for the tenor. Romani was forced to agree with the choice of libretto and, following six weeks of hard work, he was able to finish it."

The most probable reason for the choice of this libretto was the short time that was available to Bellini and Romani. A few years earlier, in 1825, Romani had written a libretto on the same subject for Vaccai. Although the later libretto differed considerably from the earlier one, in some respects it was an easier task than writing an entirely fresh one.

Branca further insinuates that there was something more than just a composer-singer relationship between Bellini and Grisi. This may well have been true, but the friendship failed to develop, as they both went in different directions immediately after the performances of *I Capuleti*. Bellini certainly returned to his other Giuditta.

Giuditta Grisi (born in 1805) was a contralto and six years older than her sister, the celebrated soprano Giulia Grisi, while her cousin Carlotta Grisi was a renowned ballerina. Giuditta studied at the Milan Conservatorio and sang in all the main Italian theatres, as well as those in Paris and Vienna, establishing herself as a distinguished artist. The part of Romeo suited her completely and was her greatest role. Her career was short, however, as she retired from the stage on her marriage in 1834. Six years later, she died.

Once Bellini was officially engaged to write the new opera, he wasted no time. From his letters, it is clear that he was much affected by the bad weather and was feeling ill. He wrote to Giuditta Turina on 26 January,[11] "Only two pieces from the opera are finished and orchestrated. I am slaving from morning till night, and it will be a miracle if I finish without any mishaps. I say this because, with these terrible cold spells, I've caught a cold in my chest, which I cannot get rid of. Thank God, however, that my chest doesn't hurt, although occasionally the coughing troubles me."

On 30 January, Bellini wrote to Lamperi[12] that he was still tired and worried but getting on with the work: "The whole thing makes me suffer terribly. Nevertheless, I've already finished the introduction and nearly the finale of the first act, which drove me crazy."

In spite of Bellini's hard work and his considerable use of music from *Zaira*, the new opera was taking its time to be completed. On 3 March, he wrote to Giuditta,[13] "I'll only write a few letters to you until the opera is in performance, because I still have to complete it. That's to say that I have to write a scene for the second act. This morning, we rehearsed the first act with full orchestra and it looks like it will be impressive. The singers have shown great interest and the music supports them. That's enough. Tuesday is the great day, and who knows whether the opera will be a failure or a success? I have hopes for the latter – first of all because I feel that the music of the first act is very impressive, and secondly because all Venice is on my side."

I Capuleti e i Montecchi was eventually performed (together with the ballet *Chiara di Rosenberg* by Cortesi) on 11 March with great success, but it was performed only eight times because the season finished on 21 March. On 15 March, *L'Eco di Milano* reported:

The new opera *I Capuleti e i Montecchi* was enthusiastically received by everybody in the large theatre. The music is by Bellini. This name brings to mind *Il pirata* and *La Straniera*: but what will you say if I tell you that the first act of this opera has better music than can be found in any of his other operas? Here, Bellini has written very beautiful music that is moving and completely Italian. When Romeo and Giulietta sang "Se ogni speme" at the end of the first act, everyone applauded enthusiastically for a long time. I think that [they] found it impossible to keep silent. The second act made the same impact as the first, an achievement that one would have thought impossible. Actually, the second act was a little cold until the end, when, in the duet that finishes the opera, everyone was so excited that they broke into wild applause and Bellini, together with the singers, was called onto the stage.

Writing to Lamperi[14] on 16 March, Bellini cannot praise his leading singers enough: "With Grisi's beautiful and expansive voice, I've hit on some pleasant chords that create enthusiasm. She is also a great actress. Carradori, in the part of Giulietta, is sublime for her naïve personality and for her spontaneous singing and acting. And the tenor Bonfigli has surpassed himself."

Following the last performance of *I Capuleti*, Bellini remained in Venice for a further week. It is possible that he wanted to relax and see something of the monuments of this unique city. (He could not have seen them earlier because he had been working intensively and the weather had been exceptionally bad.) On 28 March, as was usual after a new opera, he wrote to his uncle Ferlito,[15] "Give my regards to Father, Mother and close family and relatives, whom I believe must already be filled with joy at my new success, which couldn't be more complete. The fact that it was a success at La Fenice has made me considerably important, and this will help me greatly. Now I can say that my style of writing has been accepted with fantastic success by the principal theatres of the world, which were and are the San Carlo, La Scala and La Fenice. Therefore, this encourages me to continue to study and to try and live up to the good opinion that the public has of me, and also [convinces me] of the public's hope to see me create a new musical era."

While Bellini was in Venice, Perotin, the impresario of the Teatro Eretemio at nearby Vicenza, asked him to compose an opera for his theatre, to be performed in the forthcoming summer season. Whether Bellini was not particularly keen on writing for the Eretemio or whether his financial demands could not be met is unknown, but no new opera materialised and

Perotin was content in the end with a production of *Il pirata* which included Rubini in the cast. However, Bellini did make arrangements with the impresario Giuseppe Grivelli for a new opera to be presented at La Fenice during the carnival season of 1830/1. He then left Venice at the beginning of April to spend Easter with the Turinas at Casalbuttano.

Meanwhile, the Catania Council, which had originally awarded the grant enabling Bellini to study in Naples, honoured their illustrious citizen with a medal for his success as an operatic composer – a credit to his country. In return, Bellini dedicated *I Capuleti e i Montecchi* to his compatriots. The score, published later in the summer by Ricordi, bears an excellent engraving made from the portrait of Bellini by Natale Schiavone,[16] together with the dedication, "Vincenzo confidently dedicates this opera, a success on the stage of Venice, in a spirit of kindness and brotherly affection, to the people of Catania, whose fellow citizen he is and who are so generous in their honourable and open appreciation."

I CAPULETI E I MONTECCHI

Opera seria (tragedia lirica) in two acts. Libretto by Felice Romani. First performed at the Teatro La Fenice, Venice, on 11 March 1830 on a double bill with the ballet *Chiara di Rosenberg*, choreographed by Antonio Cortesi. Francesco Bagnara designed the stage sets.

CHARACTERS AND ORIGINAL CAST

Romeo, head of the Montecchi, in love with Giulietta	Mezzo-soprano	Giuditta Grisi
Giulietta, a Capuleti, in love with Romeo	Soprano	Rosalbina Allan-Caradori
Tebaldo, a Capuleti partisan, Giulietta's intended husband	Tenor	Lorenzo Bonfigli
Lorenzo, a physician, friend of Capellio	Bass	Pocchini Cavalieri
Capellio, head of the Capuleti, Giulietta's father	Bass	Gaetano Antoldi

The action takes place in Verona during the 13th century.

ACT I

SCENE 1: A gallery in the palace of the Capuleti. It is very early morning.

Friends and partisans of the Capuleti assemble to discuss with Capellio, their leader, preparations for a possible attack by the Montecchi, their family enemies, with whom they still continue an ancient feud. Tebaldo, an ardent supporter of the Capuleti, pledges his allegiance and tells them that Romeo, the leader of the Montecchi, is a most ferocious criminal. Hearing this, Capellio deplores Romeo's audacity in intending to send an ambassador to broker peace. Only Lorenzo, the Capuleti's family doctor and friend, suggests that they should make peace with the Montecchi and thus end the old feud. But Capellio will not hear of it, for Romeo – whom they now cannot recognise, as he left Verona when a young boy and has since wandered from town to town – slew his son. Only when this death is avenged will Capellio accept any offer of peace.

Tebaldo, who is in love with Capellio's daughter, Giulietta, swears that he will track down Romeo and kill him. On the strength of this, Capellio accepts Tebaldo as a suitable suitor and announces that the wedding between him and Giulietta will take place that very day. Lorenzo tries to delay this wedding on the pretext that Giulietta is unwell, but Capellio dismisses any such argument. While Tebaldo joyfully expresses his feelings of love, Lorenzo laments privately for Giulietta's sake, because the sad secret of her love for Romeo (he has been visiting her clandestinely) will now be discovered.

The sound of a trumpet is heard and Romeo, disguised as his own ambassador, arrives with his men and offers terms of peace which Capellio rejects out of hand, as he cannot trust the Montecchi; when peace was made between them several times in the past, the Montecchi always broke it. The "ambassador" proposes that, if Giulietta becomes Romeo's wife, peace between the two families will be inviolable. Capellio, however, will not consider such a proposal, as there is a barrier between them – the killing of his son – which will always forbid the union of the two houses. Undeterred, the "ambassador" then explains that, since Capellio's son was killed in battle, fate should be blamed, that Romeo still mourns this death and that perhaps Capellio may find another son in him. Finally, when Capellio again scornfully rejects the peace offer and calls for war, adding that he has indeed found another son in Tebaldo, who is to marry his daughter, the "ambassador" swears that Romeo will be avenged – the

Montecchi will fight, but the Capuleti will bear the guilt for the bloodshed. He then departs amidst taunts from the Capuleti that only God shall judge between them.

SCENE 2: A chamber in Giulietta's apartment.

Alone and looking at her wedding dress, Giulietta laments that she is being forced to marry Tebaldo. She would rather die than marry anyone but Romeo. While she is thinking of her plight, Lorenzo unexpectedly appears in order to tell her that Romeo is back in Verona. He then opens a secret door for Romeo to enter through and then departs. The lovers greet each other passionately and Romeo, having failed to obtain Capellio's consent to marry Giulietta, fervently asks her to flee with him. But when he tells her that they can find happiness together only when far away from Verona, she expresses her grief at having to decline; a power greater than love – that of duty, loyalty and honour – stops her from leaving. Romeo is astonished to hear Giulietta speak of honour when she has been taken from him against her will, but Giulietta believes in granting her father his rights.

Suddenly, festive music is heard in the distance, where preparations for Giulietta's wedding are in progress, and she urges Romeo to leave, lest her father finds them together. Once more, he implores her to change her mind, but to no avail. Hurriedly, Romeo then departs alone by the secret door.

SCENE 3: An illuminated courtyard within the palace of the Capuleti. There is a staircase at the back leading to the galleries. The palace rooms can be reached through the wide *loggias*. It is night.

Among the wedding guests, Lorenzo recognises Romeo, who has come disguised as a Capuleti. He urges him to leave before he is discovered, but Romeo refuses; his men are standing by to stop the wedding while he takes Giulietta away. In vain, Lorenzo implores him to leave and let him and Giulietta prevent the marriage in their own way. Just then, however, a loud noise is heard from outside. It is Romeo's men, who have been spotted and are being turned away by the Capuleti. Romeo hastily follows them.

When everyone has gone, Giulietta descends from the gallery. She is thankful that her wedding has not taken place, and as she prays for Romeo's safety, he returns. While he tries to persuade her to elope with him, Capellio comes in with Tebaldo and some armed soldiers, followed by Lorenzo. Tebaldo, still thinking Romeo to be the Montecchi ambassador, orders his arrest, whereupon Giulietta places herself in front of him. Surprised, they ask her for an explanation, but when Romeo is about to answer for her, Giulietta begs him not to disclose his identity. At this moment, Romeo's men return and the Capuleti realise who he is. As Romeo makes another effort to embrace Giulietta, they are both forcibly separated. A fight between the Capuleti and the Montecchi follows.

Act II

Scene 1: An apartment in the palace of the Capuleti, illuminated by ancient torches. It is later that same night.

Giulietta is alone anxiously awaiting news. Sadly, she reflects on her feelings as she does not know the outcome of Romeo's confrontation with her father: should she be mourning for her family or for her lover? Presently, however, she hears from Lorenzo that Romeo has escaped safely to a neighbouring wood. Lorenzo then gives her a drug which produces a sleep that will render her unconscious and make her appear dead; this will prevent her from being taken forcibly to Tebaldo's castle. Instead, she will be believed dead and taken to the Capuleti's ancestral tombs. Then, when she eventually recovers, Lorenzo will be at her side with Romeo. Although Giulietta is terrified that she may never awaken, on realising that she has no alternative, she takes the drug.

Immediately afterwards, Capellio arrives and commands her to prepare for her wedding to Tebaldo, with whom she will leave in the morning. She protests, as she is near death, and begs her father for forgiveness. He is unmoved and she retires to her room supported by Lorenzo. Promptly, Capellio sends for Tebaldo and, his suspicions aroused, orders that Lorenzo is put under house arrest.

Scene 2: A quiet spot in the grounds of the Capuleti palace. At the back of the stage, a gallery leading to the interior of the palace can be seen through a great arch.

While Romeo is looking for Lorenzo, he meets Tebaldo, with whom he has an argument. They are about to fight when they are prevented by a funeral procession which approaches and passes slowly along the palace gallery. On discovering that the procession is for Giulietta's funeral, Romeo throws away his sword and, calling Tebaldo a barbarian, asks him to kill him, but Tebaldo is equally grief-stricken.

SCENE 3: The Capuleti tombs. Giulietta's tomb is at the front of the stage.

Together with his followers, Romeo goes to the cemetery vault in which Giulietta is lying. When they find her tomb, he orders his men to break open the coffin and then leave him alone with his beloved. Sobbing, Romeo embraces Giulietta and expresses his love for her, asking her to receive him in Heaven, where they will find eternal happiness together. He then takes poison and throws down the phial. Almost immediately, Giulietta's voice is heard calling Romeo. She rises from the tomb and the lovers are briefly reunited; they are both surprised that Romeo was not informed by Lorenzo that her death was but a deception. Giulietta is now ready to elope with Romeo, but when she observes the phial, she desperately tries to think of some antidote, but she is too late. Romeo dies in her arms and she stabs herself with his knife.

The Capuleti and the Montecchi arrive to find them both dead. They are all left aghast at the mournful scene before them. Capellio asks, "They are killed – by whom?" Lorenzo and the Montecchi answer, "You, ruthless man."

Romani's libretto for *I Capuleti e i Montecchi* is a revised and simplified version of *Giulietta e Romeo*, a libretto that he had written for Vaccai five years earlier (Teatro della Canobbiana, 1825). *I Capuleti* is based not on Shakespeare's *Romeo and Juliet* but partly on the ninth novella, part two, of Matteo Bandella's *Le novelle* (1550), in which, at one remove, Shakespeare found his source. It is impossible to pinpoint all the sources of Romani's libretti for Vaccai[17] or Bellini.

In both libretti, Romani combined the characters of Tybalt and Paris (which appear in Shakespeare) into one, that of Tebaldo, while Friar Laurence as Lorenzo substitutes also for the Apothecary. Shakespeare's Nurse, Mercutio and Benvolio have no place in Romani's work and the character of Lady Capulet, given some importance in the first libretto, is altogether dispensed with in the second. Possibly because the libretto for Bellini had to be written in a hurry, it is below Romani's best. Also, because of Bellini's rather considerable self-plagiarism (as time was short, he pillaged the score of his previous opera, *Zaira* [1829]) and Romani's own self-plagiarism, the libretto contains much repetition of words, serving to increase the syllables of the verses to fit the borrowed music. Romeo's aria in act two demonstrates this as it runs, "Deh tu, deh tu, bell'anima. Che al ciel, che al ciel, ascendi."

This rehash made the libretto fragmentary, thus robbing it of much of its constructional merit. Its greatest shortcoming, however, is the absence of essential rapture of love, which is in fact the basic difference between Romani and Shakespeare. Furthermore, Romani's hectic dramatic pace, although skilfully and excitingly maintained, cannot escape a degree of monotony in the absence of lyrical reflection and repose; the lovers are not shown falling in love nor experiencing the joy of being in love; only the tragedy of their love is depicted. Nevertheless, it is a logical libretto, concise and effective, in its way, and because Romani succeeded in paring the tragedy down to its essentials, its lyrically expansive five scenes provided Bellini with good dramatic situations (although often in isolation) and much picturesque colour.

The brief overture – in D major, *allegro giusto*, with *crescendo* effects – exhibits considerable Rossinian influence. It is in a single movement and at best can be described as being pleasant, with bright, forceful tunes. After the opening chords, a motif (which recurs in the first finale) is skilfully used to suggest the frequent street brawls and quarrels of the Montecchi and the Capuleti. Instrumentally, the music shows considerable care, and if it fails to leave much of an impression, only partially setting the right atmosphere for what's to follow without suggesting the tragedy, this is because of its brevity. A curtain-raiser, then.

The introductory chorus "Aggiorna appena" ("It is hardly day"), although rather commonplace, at least sets a joyous atmosphere with typical Italian gaiety. It is in Tebaldo's recitative "O di Capellio, generosi amici" ("Generous friends of Capellio") that Bellini comes into his own. The music expresses the meaning of the words well, and the dramatic effect is heightened by the contributions of the chorus and Capellio, while the ensuing aria, "È serbato, è serbato a questo acciaro" ("It is left to this sword") has much heroic blood in it of the kind that Bellini was to perfect later in the role of Pollione in *Norma*. Here, however, the music is further distinguished by a certain sweetness and charm. The ardent cabaletta "L'amo tanto" ("I love her so"), with its strong appoggiaturas – again the kind that Bellini later used to great effect in Orombello's music in *Beatrice di Tenda* – is effective and expresses Tebaldo's determination.

Romeo's scene raises the opera immediately to a more distinguished level. In his recitative "Lieto del dolce incarco" ("I'm glad of this pleasant task"), he is introduced as a peace-seeking, loving young man; Bellini's Romeo (the role is for a mezzo-soprano) is shown to be already in love with Giulietta. His aria "Se Romeo t'uccise un figlio" ("If Romeo has killed your son") has poise and youthfulness expressed in flowing cantilena, and it can be very moving in the hands of the right singer.

Larghetto cantabile

The challenging cabaletta "La tremenda ultrice spada" ("The dreadful sword of vengeance"), with exciting accompaniment for horns in which Romeo swears vengeance, although contrasting with the preceding aria, forms a logical musical conclusion to the scene. This cabaletta, if sung at a moderate pace, skilfully depicts the bolder aspects of Romeo's character; it is not the romantic lover that the music is concerned with here but the warrior, who is romantic nevertheless.

Giulietta's unaccompanied recitative "Eccomi in lieta vesta" ("Look at these joyous garments") conveys with some bitterness the contrast between her superficially happy exterior and her genuinely sad situation. (The role is reminiscent of Rossini's Desdemona and has much in common with Amina in *La sonnambula*.) The introduction to the aria "Oh! quante volte" ("Oh! how often") sets the atmosphere in which Giulietta relives her love for Romeo, knowing only too well that it is a thing of the past. Her allure and vulnerability are vividly evident. This is one of Bellini's loveliest arias, in the sense that it simply and exquisitely portrays the young and tender love of an impassioned soul. The harp accompaniment underlines the whole scene with the nostalgia and melancholy of happier moments gone by; the glow of the sunset is still in the sky – a situation in which music speaks where words would fail.

Bellini borrowed this aria from Nelly's "Dopo l'oscuro nembo" in *Adelson e Salvini* (see page 45 for music example), incorporating slight changes in the accompaniment. Suitable as it is in that work, it really belongs to Giulietta, for it contains all the tenderness of one so young destined to love so much.

In the duet "Sì, fuggire: a noi non resta" ("Yes, run away: we have no alternative") between Romeo and Giulietta, all the passion of the two young lovers is expressed in the melodic writing:

Allegro moderato

This is the music of the very young Bellini, who had already begun to write what Verdi later described as "long, long, long melodies", superbly exploiting every facet of the human voice (excelling in the female voice) with an apparent simplicity that enhances the tenderer emotions. He did more. His ornamented melody, as in the section of the duet that runs "Ah! crudel, d'onor ragioni", is subtly delicate and maintains a rare balance between the declamatory passages of the scene. (This kind of duet was invented by Rossini in *Semiramide* and Bellini perfected it for the soprano and mezzo-soprano or contralto voices.)

The flowing melody of the ensuing cabaletta, "Vieni, ah vieni e in me riposa" ("Come, oh come and place your trust in me") is more florid than in the preceding duet; the *fioriture*, however, are completely integrated into the melody. Dramatically, the scene is even, and the words are always at one with the musical expression. Although for the most part the two singers have the same melody in turn, their different vocal timbres makes the repetitions in the dialogue sound logical, an effect that is further enhanced by the subsequent blending of the two voices.

A short introduction precedes the male chorus "Lieta notte avventurosa" ("A joyful, eventful night", in G major, 3/4 time, *allegro moderato*) with which the next scene opens, gaily showing the other side of the drama.

The composer found one of his finest inspirations in the quintet "Soccorso, sostegno accordagli" ("Give him help and support"), which forms the finale of the first act:

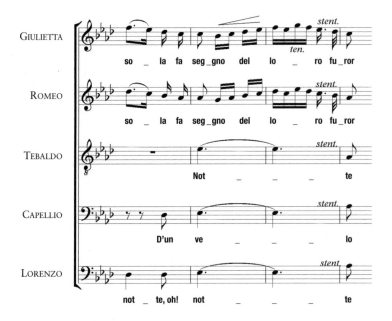

With the slightest of means, or so it sounds, the music of the two lovers (they sing together in tenths while the other voices act like a commenting choral accompaniment) rises above conscious technique to a poetic eloquence. But Berlioz's words can better describe the effect of this music. He saw the opera about a year after its premiere and hated it all, except when, as he wrote in his memoirs, "The lovers, forcibly separated, escape for a moment and rush into each other's arms, singing, 'Soccorso, stegno accordagli'. The setting of these words, which is intense, passionate and full of life and fire, is sung in unison, which, in these special circumstances, intensifies the power of the melody in the most wonderful manner; whether it is owing to the setting of the musical phrase to the unexpected effect of the unison or to the actual beauty of the tune itself, I don't know; but I was completely carried away and applauded frantically."

Although the orchestral introduction (in D major, 4/4 time, *allegro moderato*, with the melody given to the violin) that opens the second act is beautiful and dramatic, it is so short that it does not quite set the right mood. Nor is Giulietta's scene that follows completely successful. Her recitative "Nè alcun ritorna" ("No one is returning") achieves a dramatic and eloquent effect in her exchanges with Lorenzo and characteristically expresses her unhappy state of mind. Also, the first part of her aria "Morte io non temo" ("I never feared death", in A major, 4/4 time, *lento*), with its ecstatic accents, underlines her horror and resignation to a tragic destiny, lest she never reawakens. The music further enhances the meaning of her words, while Lorenzo's incidental utterances increase dramatic interest; but the vocal line is not sustained as well as it could be – the melody has insufficient depth and is not really memorable, descending at times to the level of an ephemeral tune – although it is never vulgar. Haste and a certain superficiality are in evidence here, revealed in the musically superfluous repetition of the rather commonplace part of the aria "Ah! non poss'io partire" ("Ah! I cannot leave").

The opera redeems itself with a duet between Romeo and Tebaldo. A haunting clarinet melody (in E-flat major, 4/4 time, *maestoso*) introduces the scene. Romeo's recitative "Deserta è il lugo" ("The place is deserted") is an expressive arioso that gives way to a characteristically dramatic dialogue with contrasting accents when Tebaldo arrives. Their duet "Stolto! un sol mio grido" ("Fool! I only have to call") has a spark of inner vitality that, in the excitement that it provides, is all the more effective when suddenly interrupted by the funeral chorus "Ahi, sventurata!" ("Alas, unfortunate girl!")

The beautiful melody of the funeral chorus makes it all the more moving, especially with the effect that it has on the now different utterances of Romeo and Tebaldo; faced with their common grief, for a while they are no longer enemies, and this is economically and effectively expressed in their music. In the cabaletta "Svena, ah, Svena un disperato" ("Kill, oh, kill a desperate man"), the harmonic progressions of their voices between major and minor keys achieve a unique abandon.

The finale begins with the chorus "Siam giunti" ("We have arrived") in F major, *andante mosso*, sung by the mourning Montecchi. Romeo's prayer "Deh! tu bell'anima" ("I beg you, fair soul", in G major, *andante sostenuto*) is heart-rending, a mixture of sorrow and despair, dramatically interrupted by the chorus.

A brief final duet, "Ah! qual sospiro" ("Ah! That sigh") between Romeo and Giulietta, although without any special invention, with musical integrity and simplicity manages to be extremely moving. The last scene is creditably constructed: Romeo's death followed by Giulietta's demise, Lorenzo's entrance and the close of the opera all follow hard on each other, and the way in which the composer handles the situations – with expressive recitative, for the most part, and more or less full accompaniment, only finally gathering to a regular duet – achieves an extraordinary dramatic terseness. Also, the orchestra is given a prominent part; the tremolo underlining the chords just before Romeo poisons himself vividly suggests the fatalism of the tragedy. Throughout the scene, the interest is continually sustained without realism. Instead – and this is its greatest merit – the drama has an unbroken, dreamlike quality, as if fancifully recalled like a fairy tale, yet as real as it could be.

For *I Capuleti*, Bellini self-borrowed extensively (to a far greater extent than in other works), mostly from *Zaira*. The second motif of the overture was taken (with a slight change in tempo) from the dance of the odalisques and the courtier's hymn in honour of Zaira. The first part of Tebaldo's aria "È serbato" came from – or, more correctly, was influenced by, so great is the alteration – the music of Corasmino's *larghetto* "Perchi mai" and Romeo's "Deh tu bell'anima" from Zaira's "Non, è tormento". "Soccorso, stegno accordagli", which Berlioz liked so much, came with hardly any change (some words were even left the same) from the last part of the trio "Non si pianga" in act one of *Zaira*. Nerestano's "O Zaira, in qual momento" became Romeo's aria "Se Romeo t'uccise", changed from 3/4 tempo to 9/8, and the opening bars of Zaira's *allegro agitato* "Ah! crudeli chiamar" became Romeo's cabaletta (*allegro marziale*) "La tremenda ultrice", although having undergone a significant transformation from the minor to the major key, as well as some small changes to the melody. Giulietta's "Ah, non poss'io partire" came from Nerestano's "Si, mi vedrala barbara", her phrase "Morte non temo" came from Zaira's "Che non tentai pervincere" and, as already mentioned, her aria "Oh! quante volte" was lifted from *Adelson e Salvini*. The funeral chorus "Ahi sventurata" is taken from the chorus "Poni in fedel" in *Zaira*, which in turn came from a popular Catanian song, and part of the quintet in the finale of the first act is from the finale of the first act of *Bianca e Fernando*.

This extensive borrowing was a risky affair. Bellini worked hard in adapting the old music (some of the plagiarised items underwent major changes) to the new emotional expression and Romani, modifying the new verses, was at times forced to undertake much repetition. But Bellini's task in inventing new melodies was considerably lightened and, as the exercise was successful, the old music sounds fresh and even more appropriate in *I Capuleti*. The composer thus comes through with flying colours in this extensive adaptation.

Notwithstanding its many virtues, *I Capuleti* is not a truly great opera, and the blame for this must rest primarily on the libretto. However, the music is also uneven at times, and although there are several magnificent scenes, with limpid, well-constructed and aptly accompanied melodies (not least the instrumental introductions to the scenes), the work as a whole is not as memorable in its impact as these scenes are when considered by themselves. But when the composer achieved a musical unity* – a remarkable balance between the declamatory and ornamented melodic styles and a successful marriage of pure lyricism and drama – a splendid picture depicting the dreamy, poetic side of mediaeval Italy vividly emerges, and not without that turbulence so characteristic of the period. It is to Bellini's credit that he was able to compensate for the librettist's omission of lyrical repose and thus bring a degree of balance (although not quite of a sufficient amount) to the hectic, dramatic pace.

I Capuleti must be appreciated for its own merit and should not be compared with the composer's later works, such as *La sonnambula*, *Norma* and *I Puritani*, even though in these works the qualities and virtues of the earlier opera are exploited more fully and more ingeniously. It is this

---

* Romeo's "Se Romeo t'uccise" and "Deh! tu, bell'anima". Giulietta's "Oh! quante volte", the quintet "Soccorso, sostegno accordagli", the duet "Stelto! A un sol mio grido" and the final scene are outstanding both musically and dramatically by any standards.

realisation that brought about a renaissance of music that led to the rediscovery of *I Capuleti*.

For some time, even before Bellini's death, the last act of *I Capuleti* was often replaced in performance by the last act of Vaccai's opera on the same subject.[18] This caprice can only be explained by the fact that audiences then preferred Vaccai's beautiful music, which gave the singers greater opportunity to exhibit their vocal accomplishments to greater dramatic achievement which, above all, brings the drama musically to a more natural close. (Bellini's last act was not received as enthusiastically as the rest of the work during its initial season.) This act was eventually restored to its rightful place during the 1895 season in Naples. It may have been that the singers concerned appreciated the merits of the opera and put them above their personal desire to sing "showpieces".

However, it must not be thought that Vaccai's last scene, or indeed his entire opera, is merely a series of beautiful set numbers. True, the work is very much in the Classical style, consisting for the most part of regularly developed pieces, but it does not entirely lack picturesque colour (a quality in which Bellini's opera excels). In contrast to Vaccai, Bellini inclines to a more or less fully accompanied recitative, which often develops into a regular duet, achieving a terse and dramatic climax.

Like Zingarelli and Vaccai before him, Bellini wrote the role of Romeo for a mezzo-soprano voice. Without considering the merits of such casting, modern audiences in particular may not find it agreeable to see a female singer in travesty as Romeo. However, given the right singer, vocally and dramatically accomplished and with a good appearance, the role can be much more successful than with a male singer of comparable standard. Romeo portrays not an individual man but the lover of all ages, in this case presented and expressed in the style of a mediaeval character. Consequently, it is much more difficult, if not impossible, to find a male singer who would look very young and yet be sufficiently poetical. A man might tend to be too individualistic and too realistic to capture the listener's imagination. Furthermore, a woman's voice, with its wider range, can bring to such a role greater brilliance and dash and, at best, make it more credible.

Famous interpreters of this dashing young hero, on whom the task primarily falls to make *I Capuleti* a captivating work, include Giuditta Grisi (the creator of the role), Wilhelmine Schröder-Devrient and Johanna Wagner. All three gave superb, convincing performances. Grisi carried out all Bellini's intentions and left the composer completely satisfied, whereas Schröder-Devrient moved Richard Wagner to write, "I shall never forget the impression that a Bellini opera made on me... Simple and noble song made its appearance again." The effect was mainly due to "the daring, romantic figure of the youthful lover", as he described her. Johanna Wagner, Richard's sister, was also both an excellent singer and a woman of the theatre.

Maria Malibran made a most individual Romeo – romantic, dashing, completely irresistible – but one cannot mention her in quite the same way as other famous interpreters of this role, for she usually substituted for Bellini's last act that of Zingarelli's *Romeo e Giulietta*.

Pauline Viardot-Garcia, Malibran's younger sister, also became a notable Romeo. This was probably her most successful Bellini role, as it was vocally more within her range than Amina or Norma, and she was consequently able to use her dramatic genius to the full.

The role of Giulietta is hardly less demanding. It requires great delicacy and sweetness of tone and considerable vocal security so that the melodic line has the refinement so essential for the character at all times. Rosalbina Allan-Carradori, the first Giulietta, was very affecting, and her performance blended beautifully with Giuditta Grisi's Romeo.

Giulia Grisi, Giuditta's younger sister, was a most creditable successor to the role, which she played to her sister's and to Viardot-Garcia's Romeo. Grisi may not have had creative originality, but she certainly had nobility and even, at times, a tremendous vitality in her most accomplished singing.

In the 1950s, Giulietta Simionato brought to the role of Romeo the vocal brilliance and dramatic credibility – a case of acting with the voice – that the music requires, while in the 1960s Renata Scotto – one of the very few sopranos who sang Bellini's music with style and the correct approach to melodic line – was able to delight and, at times, be very touching as Giulietta.

During this period, the contribution of the tenor Giacomo Aragall in the role of Romeo cannot be considered seriously. Aragall, a good singer, faced the great disadvantage that the transposition of the music from mezzo-soprano to tenor necessarily created. The resulting narrowing of the vocal range and the switching of the chest range to an octave higher, which Bellini so masterly exploited, changed the expressive colour to such an extent that it seriously deformed the music.

I Capuleti e i Montecchi enjoyed several successful modern revivals that established the work in the repertoires of many opera houses. Happily, almost all revivals have been with a mezzo-soprano Romeo, as Bellini intended. The most accomplished contemporary Romeos were Tatiana Troyanos, Agnes Baltsa, Anne Sophie von Otter and Marilyn Horne, whose merit in this role could not be assessed completely, however, because surprisingly she substituted the last act with that from Vaccai's opera. Successful Giuliettas include Katia Ricciarelli, Edita Gruberova and Cecilia Gasdia.

9

La sonnambula at the Carcano (1830-31)

During the beginning of May 1830, a society was founded in Milan by the Duke of Litta and two rich Milanese merchants, Marietti and Sorensi, who wanted to sponsor opera at La Scala. They were great music lovers and wanted to serve art for art's sake. Believing that they could raise the existing standard of the theatre, they engaged most of the famous singers of the time. Donizetti and Bellini, as the two best currently active Italian composers, were each to write an opera with libretti by the most illustrious Felice Romani. It was difficult to engage Bellini, who had already been contracted to Crivelli, but the society did not let this get in its way. In an undated letter written during the beginning of May, Bellini relates these events to his uncle Ferlito:[1]

> They have also tried their utmost to buy from Crivelli my contract, which they finally obtained for the price of 1,500 francs...
>
> As it's not certain that this society will secure a theatre either in Milan or Venice, and as I won't be permitted to write an opera for the carnival season for anywhere else except for the society, I made my demands clear to them before they bought me from Crivelli. I asked for a salary of 1,200 svanzike (which is equivalent to 2,400 ducats) and half of the property of the score once the opera is finished; the total will come to 3,000 ducats in all. They have agreed to all my demands, and therefore I consider myself very lucky, because in this way I shall be making nearly double the amount that Crivelli would have paid me. It seems as if luck is on my side, but I won't abuse this. I shall always continue to study, and I hope that God will help me, if not for my sake then at least for my family's.

While these negotiations were going on, Bellini's health deteriorated rapidly. It is clear that he had never been particularly strong, although several letters that he sent to Florimo reassure his friend of his good health, obviously in answer to enquiries. The breakneck composition of *I Capuleti e i Montecchi*, combined with the exceptionally bad weather in Venice, had tired him out. He wrote to his uncle Ferlito,[2] "I composed *I Capuleti* in 26 days, working ten hours during the day and four in the evening, without a break." The great success of the opera and his subsequent stay of a few days at Casalbuttano made him feel well enough, but when he returned to Milan he lost his appetite and felt worse each day until 21 May, when he had an acute bilious attack with high fever. His doctor, a certain Dr Prina, who was a friend and a great music lover, did not consider the composer's small apartment in Via San Vittore e Quaranta Martiri healthy enough. (Bellini may well have given up his larger apartment in Via Santa Margherita when he went to Venice.) Three days later, the Pollinis moved him into their own house, where they could look after him. Writing to Ferlito,[3] Bellini said, "At the Pollinis' house, I was looked after with so much attention and love that I can't find words to describe it. They have spent quite a lot of money on me, because I only paid for the doctor and for medicines, so you can see how much I am obliged towards this good family, which loves me more than if I were their son."

Bellini's illness lasted until some time in June, when he went to Moltrasio, a delightful village on Lake Como, where he was the guest of the Turinas, who were spending the summer at Villa Passalacqua. Here, the weather was cool and healthier than that in Milan and he was able to recuperate and, conveniently, to be near Giuditta.

Thus far, Bellini may have been artistically successful, but financially he had not made a fortune. Some criticism had already been levelled at him for being mercenary because of his demands for high fees for his operas. His justification for this was, "With my style, I have to vomit blood." A fastidious worker, anxious to give full attention to his work, he wrote on average one opera per year, and however well paid he may have been, he could not earn any more than he needed in order to live reasonably comfortably. The same applied to other composers, even the most successful; at some periods of their lives, Rossini and Donizetti had to write as many as five operas in a year just to make ends meet.

It is difficult to know how extravagant Bellini was, apart from the fact that he always dressed elegantly and expensively, believing this to be necessary for his position as a successful composer.

The family had never been well off. After the death of Vincenzo Tobia, the grandfather, who had always helped them in the best way that he could, the Bellinis found life increasingly difficult. Not for the first time, they were obliged to move to a cheaper house, this time in Via San Berillo. Rosario and Agata's daughter Michela was married in 1827 and their son Francesco in 1829. Rosario still had to support his other two daughters, Giuseppa and Maria, and his youngest son, Mario, who was 20 and studying music. Carmelo, the second son, continued to be an organist in several churches in Catania and also took over many of his grandfather's students.

Sometime in June, when Bellini was ill in Milan, his uncle Ferlito wrote to him, informing him of the family's difficult financial situation and of how Carmelo was making many sacrifices to help his father support them. Bellini, already a celebrity, seemed to them a rich man. Ferlito's letter made a deep impression on him, and on 1 July he wrote to Carmelo[4] from Moltrasio:

> The information that our dear uncle Don Vincenzo [Ferlito] has given me of your virtues has induced me to write to you directly, so as to make you understand my great appreciation for all that you have done for our good family, to whom we owe our physical and moral existence.
>
> Our uncle has probably told you the reasons why I haven't been helping until now. I will now tell you the reasons myself, dear brother, but you must do me a favour and not spread what goes on between us around the town. Moreover, I want the whole family to act accordingly. Do you understand? Well, my plan is to accumulate a capital investment so that I can have at least a definite daily income of six tari[5] for our family and at the same time have enough money for my personal maintenance without having to depend on my profession. Now, this cannot be done unless I save the money.
>
> This is why I have so far withheld from helping our family, and perhaps I may have to continue in this way, if fortune should abandon me. But if fortune remains on my side, I will only require four years to accomplish my plan. I will now send through my uncle 30 onze. If I receive a contract for next February in the next few days, I will send another 30 onze, and I hope that every year I will send the same amount. This will naturally depend on the income that I receive until I am assured of having saved a large enough sum to be secure for every need.
>
> Continue to help the family as you are doing now and I swear on my honour that I, your brother Vincenzo, will never, never let you

down. I will also provide for you if you are ill. I will keep this promise for as long as I have the means of doing so, and as long as you don't abandon our family, of whom you shall continue to be a good and virtuous son. I hope this persuades you. It's better to suffer a little for two or three years and then be assured of a good future forever.

PS: Our uncle will have told you how much help I have received from the good family Pollini during my illness. Had it not been for them, I might have died. Now, thank God, I am regaining my strength and I hope to remain healthy, so as to continue my career with honour.

On 17 July, the *Gazzetta di Milano* officially announced the opera plans of the Marietti and Sorensi Society. Apart from Giuditta Pasta and Rubini, several other singers – Elisa Orlandi, Lina Roser, Eugenia Martinet, Leandro Valencia, Filippo Galli, Luciano Mariani and Giovanni Frezzolini – were engaged. However, the society was unable to rent La Scala, as Crivelli and his associates succeeded in keeping control of both that theatre and La Fenice. Consequently, the society rented the Teatro Carcano[6] in Milan and decided to hold a carnival season of opera there concurrently with that of La Scala.

Donizetti was to provide the first new opera, *Anna Bolena*, which would be followed by Bellini's new work, with a libretto derived from Victor Hugo's *Hernani*, both operas to have Pasta and Rubini as protagonists. In a letter to Cottrau[7] on 15 July from Lake Como, Bellini informed him, "*L'Ernani* pleases me as well as it does Pasta and Romani. I hope to start work at the beginning of September."

Romani was also staying at Lake Como that summer. Almost certainly, he was Pasta's guest at Villa Roda in Blevio, a small place on the other side of the lake from Moltrasio. Bellini had first heard the great Pasta in 1826, when she sang the title role in Mayr's *Medea in Corinto* in Naples, and had met her in Milan in 1828. He immediately appreciated her as the greatest singer of her time and hoped that she would appear in his operas, particularly *Il pirata*, which he felt would suit her. Now Pasta was going to do even more: she was to create her own role in a Bellini opera.

The advent of Pasta (1797-1865)[8] was of the greatest significance to the development of opera as musical drama. With the introduction of the more flexible conventions of *opera buffa* into *opera seria* in the first decades of the 19th century, it was possible to bring a new freshness to this hitherto rather stilted form. The new trend also affected the singers, as a livelier and more immediate kind of drama was in demand and consequently more ordinary mortals appeared as operatic characters. More than any other artist, Pasta introduced this new dramatic development into singing, by combining vocal technique with extraordinary interpretative powers. Thus the art of the singer was brought together with that of the actor.

The way in which this gifted and determined woman achieved her goal, with eventual triumph, was long and laborious. The old Italian saying "Nature has denied her the 99 requisites of the singer" applied in her case, but nature had not denied her the 100th, musical creative genius, and with it she acquired all the other requisites herself. From the beginning, Pasta, who knew that the secret of her talent lay in the intellect and imagination behind the voice, had her own definite ideas about singing. Although she greatly appreciated the famous singers of the time, such as Gertrud Elisabeth Mara, Angelica Catalani and Girolamo Crescentini, she had no intention of becoming like them. She fervently believed in the interpretative powers of singing and, realising that the world was entering a new period of Romanticism, she strove to express "the tears in her voice".

At first, Pasta's shortcomings were serious – her vocal range was limited and her voice was weak, husky at times and lacking in flexibility. However, she was well aware of her shortcomings and subjected herself to a course of severe and incessant study. Some faults were impossible to correct, but she almost always succeeded in investing in them a subtle significance, thus making them an integral part of the music and character that she was portraying. In passages of profound passion, her guttural tones became thrilling, while her uneven lower notes helped to give an unusual depth of expression. Indeed, it was this unevenness in her lower notes, contrasted with the sweetness of her upper register, that unexpectedly caused a kind of musical discordance that was indescribably moving.

In *Vie de Rossini* (1824), Stendhal, a contemporary of Pasta, made a well-informed observation about her vocal technique:

> She can achieve perfect resonance on a note as low as bottom A and can rise as high as C sharp, or even to a slightly sharpened D, and she possesses the rare ability to sing contralto as easily as she can sing soprano… Any composer who writes for her should use the mezzo-soprano range for the thematic material of his music while exploiting, as it were, notes that lie within the more peripheral areas of this

remarkably rich voice. Many of these notes are not only extremely fine in themselves but have the ability to produce a kind of resonant and magnetic vibration which, through some unexplained combination of physical phenomena, exercises an instantaneous and hypnotic effect upon the soul of the listener... Extremely restrained in her use of *fioriture*, she resorts to them only when they have a direct contribution to make to the dramatic expressiveness of the music...

Pasta also had difficulties with her appearance, although she managed a transformation, at least when on stage. In describing her both off and on stage, Chorley[9] is very revealing: "Though her countenance spoke, the features were cast in that coarse mould which is common in Italy. Her arms were fine but her figure was short and clumsy. She walked heavily, almost unequally." Describing a Pasta triumph on stage in Rossini's *Zelmyra*, he wrote, "I remember well the central figure in the blue robe and the Classical diadem adorned with cameos, who stood forth like a sovereign in the midst of her subjects, with a grace and majesty which put many a born Royalty and ambassadress to shame."

Until 1830, when Donizetti and Bellini began to write roles for her, Pasta had established herself as the world's greatest singer by performing in works not expressly written for her, the most famous of which were the title roles in Mayr's *Medea in Corinto*, Rossini's *Tancredi* and Desdemona in Rossini's *Otello*, in which she essentially adapted her vocal ability and dramatic insight to music written for inferior and less imaginative singers. Even in as early as 1823, Stendhal lamented the fact that Rossini had not composed an opera expressly for her talents: "If Rossini were to discover such a world of wonder, who doubts but that the miraculous would happen?"

What Stendhal dreamed of became reality, albeit through other composers.[10] Donizetti was the first to make use of Pasta's extraordinary talents, in *Anna Bolena*. Bellini followed with *La sonnambula*, *Norma* and *Beatrice di Tenda*, which unfolded her vocal and interpretative genius to the maximum. In return, she contributed to Bellini's attainment of his highest development and fame.

With the contract for *Ernani* signed, Bellini was all set to start work on the opera as soon as he had received the verses from Romani. Nothing happened for the moment, however, since Romani was still hard at work on the libretto of *Anna Bolena*, which was scheduled for performance on 26 December 1830.

Meanwhile, in August, Bellini went to Bergamo in order to supervise the production of *La Straniera*. He was anxious that his opera should succeed in Bergamo, Donizetti's birthplace, where Mayr,[11] Donizetti's teacher and the director of the music school there, would no doubt be watching the performance. It was hard work, for Bellini had only just recovered from his illness and the climate in Bergamo in August is hot and humid, but he persevered until the first performance on 17 August, when *La Straniera* was a great success with both the critics and the public. He then joined the Turinas to spend the rest of the summer at Moltrasio and Casalbuttano.

Even though the usually dilatory Romani worked rather rapidly on *Anna Bolena*, as he was apparently particularly captivated with the subject, he delivered the finished libretto to Donizetti on 10 November, leaving him only one month to compose the music. Nevertheless, Donizetti – working closely with Pasta, his protagonist, at Villa Roda – managed to complete the opera in time, and by 10 December he was back in Milan to begin rehearsals.

For Bellini, the situation was more complicated. Although he returned to Milan in November and Romani had completed the libretto of *Anna Bolena*, he was unable to commence the composition of his opera. In a letter to Lamperi[12] on 17 November, he writes that not only had he not yet written a single note for *Ernani* but that Romani had not even begun work on the libretto. Soon, however, Bellini must have received verses from Romani, because between the end of November and most of December he did compose some music for it. Then, on 3 January 1831, Bellini wrote to Giovanni Perucchini,[13] informing him that *Ernani* had been dropped: "You must know that I'm no longer writing *Ernani*, as the story would have had to undergo certain changes, because of the police. Therefore, in order that Romani wouldn't compromise himself, he has given this subject up and is now writing *La sonnambula*. In fact, it was only yesterday that I was able to begin the composition of the introduction to it. You see, once again I have to write this opera in a short space of time, as it has to go on stage on 20 February, at the very latest."

It is unknown whose idea it was to substitute the pastoral *La sonnambula* for the Romantic *Ernani*. A great deal of speculative gossip has been written about the dropping of *Ernani*, mostly deriving from Emilia Branca's book.[14] This has also served to show Bellini in an unfavourable light. With fervid imagination, Branca reported a conversation that was supposed to have taken place between Bellini and Romani shortly after the premiere of *Anna Bolena* (wrongly but conveniently dated 21 rather than 26 December), even to the extent of supplying the dialogue. The alleged conversation is given here because many slanderous impressions formed against Bellini were based on details taken from it or that were ancillary to it.

First, it is necessary to report on the outcome of *Anna Bolena*, as Branca's allegations depend on its reception. The opera scored a great success with the public and most of the critics at the Teatro Carcano on 26 December 1830. The *Gazzetta di Milano* praised the singers more than the work itself in the first act, postulating that much of the music might expire unobserved when sung by artists other than Pasta and Rubini. The second act, however, was praised for its musical merit. "Here," the critic wrote, "the aspect changed and the talent of the composer demonstrated itself with unusual strength... Donizetti has shown himself a worthy and favoured pupil of Mayr."

In his biography of Donizetti,[15] Fraccaroli states that Bellini was present at the premiere of *Anna Bolena*, sitting in a box at the Carcano. (This was based on Branca's story that Bellini was very upset about the opera's success.) In fact, Bellini was not at the Carcano that night but instead at La Scala, where his *I Capuleti e i Montecchi* was having its Milanese premiere. He was certainly upset, but for different reasons, as can be seen in his letter to Perucchini[16] on 3 January 1831:

> I didn't write to you after the first evening because my poor opera couldn't have been more badly performed, so poorly that, even though it had some effect and the public wanted me on the stage, I was so furious that I didn't want to appear... The opera had only half of the effect on me than what I had experienced in Venice. This may be because the theatre here is too large or Rolla's tempi are too broad. It could also be because, in all the ensembles, the voices of the two women,[17] both mezzo-sopranos, do not blend well and Grisi perhaps loses some of her effect in a large theatre. In short, I no longer feel the same for my *Capuleti* as I did in Venice, even though the theatre here is always filled with lots of applause.

According to Branca, Bellini was so sad and in such foul humour after the success of *Anna Bolena* that he desperately tried to force Romani into changing *Ernani*. He used every histrionic trick to have his way because he was afraid to follow *Anna Bolena* with another grand opera, which he felt would be a complete failure and would ruin him. "'I live for glory,' he finally declared. Romani was tired as, apart from having to write four libretti for that carnival season, he was expected to provide another two, *Il disertore Svizzero* and *La neve*, for Pugni and Ricci respectively, both scheduled for performance two months later. However, his affection for Bellini was so great that in the end he capitulated to the composer's infantile whims and wrote *La sonnambula* for him."

Branca's account is the result of her persistently misguided and unnecessary efforts to glorify Romani. Often, she even credits the success of important operas to "Romani's extremely harmonious verses", almost to the exclusion of the music. Moreover, she never misses an opportunity to attribute statements to Bellini (or at best quote them out of context), such as "I live for glory" in the above example. These were later misconstrued by other writers to create a Bellini who was jealous and neurotic to an extreme.

The refutation of Branca's story, however, had to wait until 1957, when Eugenio Gara[18] discovered that the Milanese journals had announced the titles of the new operas, *Anna Bolena* and *La sonnambula*, on 23 December 1830. *Ernani* had obviously already been dropped and *La sonnambula* decided on before *Anna Bolena* had been performed. (The incorrect date of 21 December that Branca supplied for the premiere of *Anna Bolena* thus tied in conveniently with her story.)

Ernani, an adaptation of Victor Hugo's sensational *Hernani*, produced in Paris in the previous February, was a dangerous subject. It depicted Don Carlo of Spain being defied by the outlaw Hernani, and due to the unrest in various parts of Italy caused by revolutionary risings in France, Belgium and Poland in 1830, the opera was sure to run into trouble with the authorities.[19] If anything, it is surprising that Romani and Bellini did not drop the subject earlier, considering the short time that remained to them once they had decided on *La sonnambula*.

From *Ernani*, five scenes are extant: a duet between Ernani and Elvira and a trio between them and Don Carlo from act one; a duet between Don Sancio and Don Carlo from act two; a duet between Don Carlo and Elvira from act four; and a fragment of a concerted piece.[20] The male role of Ernani had been intended for Pasta.

The libretto of *La sonnambula*, the story of a young sleepwalker called

Amina, was based on the scenario for the ballet-pantomime *La Somnambule, ou l'Arrivée d'un Nouveau Seigneur* by Eugene Scribe (Paris Opéra, 1827).

When Bellini returned to Milan in November, he lived as a guest of Contessa Giuseppina Appiani in the Borgo Montforte, remaining there until the end of 1831. This arrangement was almost certainly made through the Cantùs, as Giuditta Turina's mother was related to the Appiani family.

The remarkable Giuseppina Appiani (born *c*1797) was the daughter of the prominent politician Antonio Strigelli and widow of one of the sons (or perhaps a nephew) of the celebrated painter Andrea Appiani. She held a salon that was attended by the artistic bohemians of Milan. Raffaello Barbiera, in his book[21] on the poet Giovanni Prati, describes Appiani as "Prati's most fervent admirer" and a friend of Bellini and Donizetti's,[22] noting, "She passes for one of the loveliest women in Italy and her charms, for which Hayz sighed, will be perfectly preserved, like those of Ninon de l'Enclos, up to her old age." A letter that Appiani wrote to Florimo[23] in 1837, after Bellini's death, shows the affection that she held for him: "I was very fortunate to have had that illustrious person Bellini staying in my home for over a year, besides which I also had the opportunity to help him during the period when he had been ill. It was through me that the divine music of *La sonnambula* was given life. Oh, dear Florimo, how could we not be friends, as we have so many dear and painful recollections in common?"

As there was insufficient time to compose and rehearse *La sonnambula*, which was scheduled to be performed on 20 February, the premiere was extended two weeks, to 6 March.[24] Even so, Bellini had only 61 working days, including rehearsal time, in which to complete the work. Once the new subject was decided, however, and Romani provided verses, Bellini worked rapidly. He began to compose the introduction on 2 January and, as he wrote to Lamperi, managed to finish the first act on around 7 February. Allowing ten days for rehearsals, the second, shorter act was composed in only a fortnight.

Everything went well with the dress rehearsal, except for a small incident mentioned by Branca:[25]

> Just as the orchestra was about to begin the final scene (the famous cabaletta "Ah! non giunge"), Bellini became so agitated that he ran onto the stage in search of Romani. Having finally caught sight of him, Bellini stopped him, embraced him and asked him for the

hundredth time to be so kind as to rewrite the final verses for him, exclaiming, "I would like something that will exalt Pasta and raise her to the skies!"

Already vexed, and taken unawares, Romani finally freed himself from the unwelcome clasp and, muttering a few indistinct words to the young composer, shook his head as he turned his back and hurriedly left the theatre. Bellini, who was sometimes subject to a painful sensitivity, which made the slightest contradiction intolerable to him, abandoned himself to the actions of a peevish child. He was angry for a few moments, but then Giuditta Pasta intervened and, with a few authoritative words, calmed him down. She brought to his notice that the verses which the poet had supplied were most expressive and were sure to be effective.

After this, the capricious Catanese agreed to use the existing verses and asked pardon from Romani for the "unceasing trouble" (these are his own words). The result was that all the arias of the beautiful opera, which were performed in a masterly and impassioned manner, did in fact raise the sublime Pasta to the seventh heaven and transported the enraptured souls of the audience to the celestial spheres.

La sonnambula, performed on 6 March on a customary double bill that also included Louis Henry's ballet *Tutto al contrario*, was an immediate success at the Carcano with both the public, who took it to their hearts, and with the critics, who from the beginning were aware of the music's new qualities. The way in which Bellini reacted to this can be seen in a letter written on 7 March to Lamperi. (The usual post-premiere letter to his uncle Ferlito has not survived, and if Florimo received a letter on this subject, he failed to publish it.) To Lamperi, Bellini wrote,[26] "Here is the happy news of the fantastic success that my opera enjoyed last night at the Teatro Carcano. You'll have to wait until the music is printed to know what it's like, because the critics don't say anything about it. I just want to assure you that Rubini and Pasta are two angels that have aroused the public to the point of madness."

Much later, in a letter to Ricordi[27] written in Paris on 27 September 1934, during the time of the composition of *I Puritani*, Bellini commented, "At the rehearsals, the first act of *Sonnambula* was more appreciated by far than the second act. At the performance, however, the second act proved to be the more effective."

Obviously, Bellini was a little premature when he wrote to Lamperi that the critics said nothing about the music of *La sonnambula*. In fact, the rather extensive reviews that appeared during the next few days are very interesting.

On 7 March, the critic writing for *L'Eco di Milano* reported that so great was the public's enthusiasm at the premiere of *La sonnambula* that even he, who on principle would not allow himself to be seduced easily, on this occasion "simply couldn't help joining in the general frenzy in a theatre deafened by the flood of plaudits and acclamations... Romani's poetry and Bellini's music, no less Pasta's and Rubini's performances, command greater care and calmness on our part and more time to enable us to make good sense of our evaluation."

Two days later, *L'Eco* discussed *La sonnambula* at some length:

The subject of this drama, taken from the French, has affection as its theme and the smooth and flowing poetry of our wonderful maestro, Romani, has rendered it in all its purity.

Is Bellini's music really an original concept, rich in melodious and original cantilenas, or is it a case of very hard work with minute but masterly refinements, like *filigri*, that delight us so?... The question is reduced exactly to this. We shall not decide yet but only say that the more we hear this music, the more we'll like it. Time will be the most honest judge.

In this opera, there are quite a few very pleasant passages, and these will always please. Obviously, the maestro has discontinued – in this work, at least – that style of music called "dramatic" which lies somewhere between recitative and true song [*canto spiegato*]. But we shall say no more about it, confessing very candidly that we have never been able to make a clear distinction of this. It's also said that Bellini has taken great care in dissociating his music from that of Rossini's. We also believe that he has been quite successful in this respect.

According to general opinion, it's impossible to sing better than Pasta and Rubini did here. As for us old folk, since the times of Marchesi, we don't think that we have heard anything better than the singing of Pasta and Rubini. The duet between these two singers seemed to be a challenge of trills [*volate gorgheggi*], but it is a great work of its kind and such a performance will probably never be repeated by other singers. Only those who witness Madame Pasta's performance can really understand and appreciate the spirit of truth, the expressiveness and the...perfect judgement with which she performs her role. She certainly creates an illusion. However, we must frankly say that her figure is a little too well formed for this role...

All the other singers, particularly Mariani [Rodolfo], were very good, but they will forgive us if we don't say more about their merits. Frankly, we did not observe them very much, because when Pasta and Rubini are singing, [everything else] really becomes secondary. An exception to this is the painter Sanquirico, whose perspectives never fail to be noticed. The costumes were [good], too, except for poor Rubini's, a worse one than which I can't remember ever having seen.

On 11 March, *L'Eco* continued its assessment:

The first sleepwalking scene, just before the end of act one, is very well constructed; here, Bellini achieves a wonderful effect by ornamenting his motif with a new and flowing orchestral accompaniment. The ensuing quartet and final section are really exciting and inspired and bring the act to a triumphant close. The second act is greatly enriched by Rubini's aria... Another part that constantly gains in appreciation is the quartet sung by Taccani, Mariani, Rubini and Baillou. The performance ends with a scene in which Pasta sings her masterpiece – a masterpiece of both composition and execution. The beautiful variations that Pasta can build around this song are evidence of what the vocal art can accomplish.

There is nothing more to say about Bellini, except that every opera he has so far written has taken him a step forward to glory.

Other journals[28] also praised *La sonnambula*, above all recognising in the music "a new workmanship, really a new style, with a pastoral colouring in the melody and traces of popular Italian folk song, which basically has the great merit of coherence and/or relevance to its subject and which is always extremely pleasing... The music of *La sonnambula* does not contain reminiscences of Bellini's previous operas or of those by others; its vein is spontaneous, the achievement most fortunate."

The resounding success of *La sonnambula* was not confined to Milan, either; it was soon repeated everywhere in Italy and abroad, establishing Bellini as an international composer, as *Anna Bolena* did for Donizetti. It would be difficult to find a parallel to two operas of such outstanding merit as these, both written and produced during the same season, in the same theatre, having the same librettist and the same singers as protagonists.

This was the third time that Bellini and Donizetti had produced operas for the same season. Henceforth, their names were linked as the outstanding Italian composers after Rossini (who had just gone into retirement, following the production of *Guillaume Tell*, on 3 August 1829). Although their careers overlapped, it was really only after Rossini had retired that Donizetti and Bellini created their best and most important works.

Bellini thought fit to dedicate *La sonnambula* to Francesco Pollini, his friend, adviser and "Milanese father".

LA SONNAMBULA

Melodramma in two acts. Libretto by Felice Romani. First performed at the Teatro Carcano, Milan, on 6 March 1831, on a double bill with the ballet *Tutto al contrario*, choreographed by Louis Henry to music by Giacomo Panizza. Alessandro Sanquirico designed the stage sets.

CHARACTERS AND ORIGINAL CAST

Amina, an orphan, brought up by Teresa	Soprano	Giuditta Pasta
Elvino, a rich young village landowner	Tenor	Giovanni Battista Rubini
Conte Rodolfo, lord of the village	Bass	Luciano Mariani
Lisa, an innkeeper, in love with Elvino	Soprano	Elisa Taccani
Teresa, a mill-owner, Amina's foster-mother	Mezzo-soprano	Felicia Baillou-Hilaret
Alessio, a young peasant, in love with Lisa	Bass	Lorenzo Biondi
A Notary	Tenor	Antonio Crippa

The action takes place in a Swiss village in the early part of the 19th century.

ACT I

SCENE 1: The village green, against a background of gentle hills. At one side and set back stands a water mill and, on the other side, the village inn.

The villagers are making merry over the betrothal of Amina – the young and beautiful orphan raised by Teresa, owner of the local mill – and Elvino, a young and prosperous landowner. Only Lisa, the innkeeper, is unhappy – she was once Elvino's girlfriend and is still in love with him and bitterly jealous. Moreover, she is irritated by the persistent wooing of Alessio, especially as he has recently been turned down by Amina.

Presently, Amina comes out of the mill, accompanied by Teresa, and after thanking everybody for their good wishes, she rapturously expresses her happiness on this day. With the arrival of Elvino, the marriage contract is signed. The wedding is to take place the following day. Elvino then places a ring that his mother used to wear on Amina's finger and, with tender vows, they both declare their love for each other. The betrothal ceremony is concluded to the delight of all but Lisa.

Unexpectedly, a handsome young stranger in an officer's uniform arrives. While everybody is speculating about whom he might be, he falls into a reverie, nostalgically recalling the scenes of his early youth. Then, learning the reason for the present celebration, he compliments Amina on her beauty with extravagant gallantry, much to Elvino's jealous rage.

The stranger is Conte Rodolfo, who left his father's nearby castle when he was very young. Now, on his father's death, he has become lord of the castle, but he does not reveal his true identity to the villagers. Asking the way to the castle, he is told that, as the road is bad and it is almost night, he had better stay in the village. He is also told that it is at about this hour that the strange ghostly woman who haunts the village usually appears. Although Rodolfo takes this lightly, he decides to spend the night at the inn.

The villagers disperse. Only Elvino and Amina remain for a while longer. Still upset by Rodolfo's compliments to Amina, Elvino now picks a quarrel with her, but they are soon reconciled and part happily.

SCENE 2: Rodolfo's room in the inn.

Lisa is flirting with Rodolfo, who is surprised to hear from her that, as the villagers have guessed his identity, they will presently be coming to pay their respects. Their flirtation, however, is interrupted by a noise at the window, whereupon Lisa hastily hides in the cupboard, dropping her scarf, which Rodolfo picks up and places on the bedpost. Turning to the window, he is amazed to see Amina in a white robe entering his room, apparently completely unconscious of her surroundings.

Amina is muttering to herself about the events of the previous day, evidently still worried by Elvino's recent burst of jealousy. Lisa, who has recognised Amina, comes out of the cupboard and leaves unnoticed. Rodolfo feels a momentary attraction towards Amina but, deeply moved by her purity and the sincerity of her love for Elvino, and realising that she is sleepwalking, he decides to leave her alone so that she is not compromised in any way. As he departs, Amina, still asleep, sinks into his bed and almost immediately the villagers arrive.

They see a woman asleep on Rodolfo's bed and are about to leave when Lisa arrives with Elvino and denounces Amina. The noise awakens Amina, who, bewildered by the situation, pathetically protests her innocence while Elvino deplores her perfidy and casts her off. The villagers side with him, as the circumstances are incriminating. Only in Teresa, who has picked up Lisa's scarf from the bedpost, does Amina find some comfort.

ACT II
SCENE 1: A wooded valley on the outskirts of the village, not far from Rodolfo's castle.

The villagers are on their way to the castle to ask Rodolfo if he can clear Amina's name. Amina, following behind, asks Teresa to give her courage as they pass Elvino's house. Just then, he appears and the two men stand aside while he soliloquises on his deep sorrow. Presently, Amina comes forward, but Elvino will not listen to her appeals and bitterly reproaches her. When the villagers return to say that the Count has proclaimed Amina innocent, Elvino becomes even more furious and wrenches her betrothal ring from her finger. Even so, he reflects that, unfaithful though she is, he cannot find it in his heart to hate her.

SCENE 2: The village green, as in act one, scene one. A stream turns the wheel of the mill.

Alessio is still trying in vain to win Lisa's favour, but she is now more than ever set on marrying Elvino. Presently, when she hears from the villagers that he is on his way to propose, Lisa complacently receives their congratulations, despite Alessio's protests. Elvino arrives and, after begging Lisa for her forgiveness for having left her, asks her to marry him immediately. As they are on their way to the church, Rodolfo arrives. He tries to testify to Amina's innocence, but Elvino finds the explanation of somnambulism completely incomprehensible and remains adamant, until Teresa produces Lisa's scarf, which she found in Rodolfo's room at the inn.

"Who can prove it?" cried Elvino. "Look, Amina herself can," answers Rodolfo, for at that moment Amina, who has been sleeping in the mill, is again seen sleepwalking her way through a window in her nightdress, carrying an unlighted lamp. As she crosses a fragile bridge, a plank breaks and her lamp falls into the water below. Still asleep, she approaches the gasping villagers and Elvino, lamenting the loss of her betrothal ring. She also weeps over some flowers that Elvino had given her but have now withered. Finally, she prays that Elvino may yet love her again. Elvino, now convinced of her innocence, replaces the ring on the finger of the sleeping Amina, who awakens in his arms to the rejoicings of the villagers. All that she sees is joy around her and Elvino, ready to lead her to the altar. Ecstatic, she hurries to church for her wedding.

Romani's libretto for *La sonnambula* is based on Scribe's ballet-pantomime scenario *La Somnambule, ou l'Arivée d'un nouveau seigner*, which was choreographed by Jean-Pierre Aumer and set to music by Louis-Joseph-Ferdinand Hérold. The ballet was first performed with great success at the Paris Opéra in 1827. (Scribe's ballet-pantomime scenario was in turn derived from Casimir Delavigne's *comédie-vaudeville La villageoise Somnambule, ou les deux Fiancées*, which was performed at the Théâtre du Vaudeville, Paris, in 1819.) The libretto follows Scribe down to the small details of the action, but the locale is transferred from the French Camargue to early-19th-century Switzerland and the names of the characters altered: Edmond, a rich farmer, becomes Elvino, while Thérèse, his fiancée, is now called Amina; Madame Gertrude, a young widow and innkeeper, is named Lisa; La Mère Michaud becomes Teresa, Amina's foster-mother; M de Saint-Ramert becomes Conte Rodolfo, while his servant Olivier does not appear in the libretto. The librettist, however, introduces another subsidiary character, Alessio, a young peasant, who behaves towards Lisa in the way that the notary did towards Madame Gertrude in the Scribe scenario. The notary is retained, but with a smaller part.

The mainspring of Romani's libretto[29] is the psycho-physical manifestation of somnambulism, which is worked out in a most interesting way, the action proceeding logically, with easily understood dramatic situations and with sharply drawn characters. It is particularly appropriate to quote the librettist himself on how he visualised the heroine:

> The role of Amina in *La sonnambula*, although at first sight seemingly easy to portray, is probably more difficult than many other roles considered more important. It calls for an actress who can be playful, ingenious and innocent and, at the same time, passionate, sensitive and affectionate. Furthermore, she must possess a cry for sorrow as well as a cry for joy and have different timbres in her voice for reproof and pleading. Amina should show in every movement, in every glance, in every sigh that elusive combination of the stylised and the realistic, the kind of element that one detects in certain of Theocritus' idylls and in certain paintings of Albani. Finally, the actual singing must be extremely simple yet full of adornment, spontaneous yet scrupulously controlled, technically perfect yet indicating no sign of study.

Moreover, Romani's verses have unique invention and a felicity that, together with the libretto's theme of affection, perfectly suit Bellini's idyllic and elegiac musical genius.

Bellini agreed with all Romani's ideas, except that of making Amina Rodolfo's illegitimate daughter, as in Scribe and Delavigne's version, in which, having seduced a village girl, Rodolfo had to leave the neighbourhood, with Amina being born after his departure. Although Romani conceded to Bellini's demand, the verses in Rodolfo's cabaletta, addressed to Amina, may be misunderstood to carry traces of the librettist's original idea: "You cannot imagine how those beautiful eyes gently touch my heart, and what an adorable beauty is recalled to my thoughts. She was then, as you are now, in the morning of her life" ("Tu non sai con quei begli occhi come dolce il cor mi tocchi, qual richiami ai pensier miei adorabile beltà. Era dessa, qual tu sei, sul mattino del'età"). As no further explanation follows, this is often considered to be a serious defect in an otherwise very efficient and accomplished libretto.

The criticism, however, is superficial and arises solely because Romani's original but discarded idea is known. Unlike in the original version, where Rodolfo (M de Saint-Ramert) could be taken for a womaniser, here he is presented as a highly sensitive and romantic character who, on his return home, feels quite emotional when he recognises the mill, the stream, the woods. "Oh, lovely scenes, again I see you!" ("Vi ravviso, o luoghi ameni!"), he exclaims. Likewise, Amina's charm and beauty merely and naturally recall to his mind some sweetheart of his youth. The fact that he does not take advantage of Amina when she sleepwalks into his bedroom, even though he is momentarily tempted, implies nothing other than that he respects her innocence. He leaves in order to avoid any possible temptation. This is very much in keeping with his character as drawn in the libretto. His reaction to Lisa's advances is quite different.

What may arguably be considered a defect in the libretto, however, is the improbability that neither the villagers nor anyone in Amina's home know anything of her sleepwalking tendencies or that she is the strange and ghostly woman who is haunting the village. Once this situation is known, the plot of the drama collapses. This may only be justified by the fact that, at the period of the story, somnambulism was to the villagers an unheard-of phenomenon. Also, it may be assumed that Amina's affliction had been recently caused almost certainly by worries and doubts that she may have had before her betrothal. In the opera, after the marriage contract has been signed, Amina sleepwalks twice, both times as a result of strong emotional disturbance – the tiff with her fiancé and after she was cast off by him.

A short, gay prelude (G major, 6/8, *allegro*) of 87 measures in dance-like rhythm concisely establishes the naïvely pastoral character of the opera. Without a break in the music, the villagers' opening chorus, "Viva Amina", is sung behind the scenes. It is a joyous chorus and forms a subtle contrast to Lisa's little aria "Tutto è gioia" ("Everyone is happy", in A-flat major, 4/4 time, *allegro assai moderato*), which follows immediately. The chorus is heard again between the two verses of this aria, clarifying the dramatic situation, and the emphasis on the turn of the words "v'ha contento" poignantly describes Lisa's solitary feelings of discontent.

With the villagers assembled, the cabaletta of their chorus "In Elvezia, non v'ha rosa" ("In Switzerland, there is no better flower") has a folkloric melody in which the same voices at first form an accompaniment to the female ones and then both blend in jubilantly greeting Amina's first charming utterances in the recitative "Care compagne" ("Dear companions"). The ensuing aria, "Come per me sereno" ("How wonderful it is for me") has a beautiful melody with much originality. Its overall effect is that of disarming and deceptive simplicity and piquant naïveté in its expression of perfect happiness, establishing Amina's trusting and lovable nature.

The elaborate embellishments of the cabaletta "Sovra il sen", linked by a chorus, express in turn Amina's affectionate side and passionate sensitivity; the brilliant cascades of chromatic semiquavers her overflowing joy; and the high notes the magical moment when the crest of emotion is reached.

Elvino's recitative "Perdona, o mia diletta" ("Forgive me, my beloved") with its "audible little tears" (especially on phrases such as "prostrato al moarmo") leads into his betrothal duet with Amina, "Prendi l'anel ti dono" ("Take the ring I give you"). Here, pathetic rapture is accomplished with apparent simplicity and with a melody that makes it all the more touching. Amina's *allegretto con brio* part of the duet, "Ah, vorrei trovar parole", further states her characteristic innocence but is underlined with passionate accents.

The short orchestral phrase that announces Rodolfo's carriage,

although not quite in the form of the *leitmotif* that Wagner would establish with such dramatic impact, is nevertheless psychologically effective and Bellini later uses it in various keys, achieving an unmistakable association with the character of Rodolfo. His recitative "Come noiso e lungo" ("How long and tedious"), particularly "Il mulino...il fonte..." ("The mill...the stream..."), concisely and tellingly expresses the words as if it were a true extension of speech. The ensuing aria, "Vi ravviso, o luoghi ameni" ("I see you again, lovely places"), with its sustained *cantabile* line and with the chorus merely marking the beat, has a natural rise and fall with a well-placed climax and a satisfying balance of phrase:

Il mu _ lino.......... il fonte.......... il bosco.......... e vi _ cin la fat _ to _ ri _ a

Andante cantabile

Vi rav _ vi _ so, o luoghia _ me _ _ ni, in cui

lie _ ti, in cui se _ re _ _ ni

The smooth vocal writing is perfectly calculated to show the *basso cantante* in its most affecting range, while the succeeding cabaletta, "Tu non sai" ("You can't know"), adds a further characteristic suavity.

An atmosphere of mystery is created in the brief space of three bars by chromatic wind harmonies, which set the mood for the *sotto voce*, syllabic, E-flat major chorus "A fosco cielo" ("When the sky is dark"), in which the villagers comment on the white phantom. This music paints a wholly dramatic picture by the simple means of parallel thirds and *staccato* word-setting. The scene ends with the duet "Son geloso del zefiro errante" ("I am jealous of the wandering breeze") between Elvino and Amina:

Andante assai sostenuto

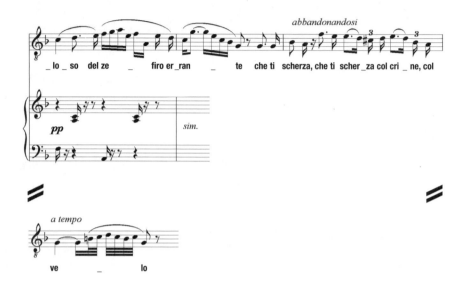

Full of fanciful divisions, this duet is as exquisitely delicate as Dresden china. It has a certain simplicity and ease, although this may not at first be apparent, for it is very difficult to vocalise. Bellini demonstrates his masterly skill in capturing the sense of the words with rhythmic and melodic contours, suggesting at the same time both Elvino's rapture and his shyness in expressing his affection for Amina. The trills in thirds and high arcs of *fioriture*, sung separately and together by the two singers, clearly emanate from a youthful, impassioned love.

Amina's recitative and her duet with Rodolfo "Oh, come lieto è il popolo" ("Oh, how happy the people are"), in the first sleepwalking scene, are well constructed and without a superfluous note. All her innocence and tender love are conveyed through the music, the rhythm of which adds a certain subtlety that creates an atmosphere of somnambulism. Effectively, a snatch of "Son geloso" is heard, and the scene reaches a natural climax when, in "Cielo al mio sposo io giuro" ("By Heaven, I swear my love for my husband"), Amina expresses what she holds most dear – her love for Elvino – while Rodolfo, not trusting himself with her, hesitates momentarily and then flees. Amina's cry of sorrow forms a dramatic contrast when heard in the quintet "D'un pensiero e d'un accento" ("Neither in thought nor in word"), the finale of the first act, after Elvino has cast her off:

Andante sostenuto

This is a particular case in which Bellini not only succeeded in preserving the exact inner emotion of the situation but was also able to build his creation into a faultless melodic line with almost no vocal embellishment. The tenor's expressive phrase "questo pianto del mio cor" ("the tear from my heart"), which follows Amina's cry of sorrow, closes the quintet. It cannot be traced in any dramatic music that preceded it, and in fact it later formed the basis of several ensembles by other composers as well as by Bellini himself. Really a musical landmark.

After the villagers' tranquil chorus "Qui la selva è più folta" ("Here the wood is most dense", in E major, 3/4 time, *allegretto*) opens the second act, Elvino's soliloquy "Tutto è sciolto" ("Everything is over"), a most touching melody, sums up the pathetic situation. His passionate outburst in the cabaletta "Ah, perchè non posso odiarti" ("Oh, why I cannot hate you") further intensifies the scene before the chorus brings it to an affecting close.

Lisa's aria "Dè lieti auguri a voi son grata" ("I am grateful for your wishes"), which follows, has a subtly superficial brilliance in its slightly frivolous embellishments, suggesting her fickle and opportunistic nature. It also provides emotional relief after Elvino's scene and, with its contrasting character, helps to make the ensuing final scene of the opera more moving.

In the closing scene, Bellini brings the work to a climax fully worthy of what has gone before. The second sleepwalking scene of the opera begins with Amina's *andante sostenuto* recitative "Oh! se una volta sola" ("Oh! Just one more time"). It has an eloquence and natural simplicity that raises it to the realm of art that conceals art. Fragments of "Son geloso", "Prendi l'anel" and "Ah! vorrei" are echoed in the orchestra as musical reminiscences rather than fully symbolic *leitmotifs* (the composer remaining closer to the

French School of opera than to Wagner's), achieving dignified thematic transformations. Also, the orchestra no longer acts as mere accompaniment but, with telling effect, partners the vocal line, supplementing the expression of the emotional content of the verses.

Amina's aria is in two contrasting parts. The first, "Ah! non credea mirarti sì presto estinto, o fiore" ("Oh, I never imagined that this flower would have died so soon"), sung while sleepwalking, has a tender, introspective quality:

Andante cantabile

It is heart-rending in its long-drawn notes and extended line, especially where the only accompaniment is a viola. Here, the composer does not follow any traditional architecture in his melody and abolishes repetitions and recapitulations. It is this asymmetry that in some ways paradoxically transforms lyric beauty – already superb, admittedly – into a unique musical realisation. This is one of the most beautiful melodies in all opera and may legitimately be called the true predecessor of the great "Casta Diva" in *Norma*.

The second part of Amina's aria, the rondo finale "Ah! non giunge uman pensiero al contento" ("Nobody can encompass the happiness I feel") is sung when she is awake:

Allegro moderato

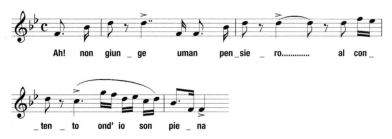

Although this is one of the showpieces of florid singing, it is by no means a mere vocal exhibition. Set for *allegro moderato* (it is a grave mistake for sopranos to polish it off at top speed), its *fioriture* essentially form an integral part of the whole when sung at the correct tempo. The brilliant but highly expressive cascades of embellishment convey the bounding delight of an innocent soul who triumphs over adversity.

With *La sonnambula*, Bellini created a masterpiece of the florid style within the limitations of his material. If it is not the greatest work he wrote (although it is second only to *Norma*), this is because *Norma* provided him with wider scope and range of emotion.

Only a little of the music – the chorus "In Elvezia non v'ha rosa" – was borrowed. This came from the composer's abortive *Ernani*, which he had abandoned in favour of *La sonnambula*. (Five sketches from *Ernani* have survived; three were later used in *Norma*.)

Elvino's music was originally written abnormally high, as it was expressly composed for the tenor Rubini. Some of it was later published in lower keys, and as a rule tenors have sung it in this way ever since. The duet "Prendi l'anel" was in B-flat major (now in A-flat major), the cabaletta "Ah! vorrei trovar parola" was in G minor (now in F minor); the duet "Son geloso" was in G major (now in F major); the aria "Tutto è sciolto" was in B minor (now in A minor); and the cabaletta "Ah, perchè non posso odiarti" was in D major (now in B-flat major).

Remembering what Romani said about the role of Amina, it is obviously one of the most difficult in the Italian repertoire. It requires a soprano who can master the florid style but who is also capable of cantilena and dramatic coloratura – even the final rondo, "Ah! non giunge", is certainly not to be sung solely for vocal display.

Although the composer envisaged Amina to be for a dramatic soprano (capable, of course, of great agility), the role – unlike that of Norma – has also succeeded when sung by lyric-dramatic coloratura sopranos. Both Norma and Amina were written expressly for Giuditta Pasta, yet they are vocally very different. However, at the time, it was not so rare for dramatic sopranos to have tremendous flexibility in their voices (the degree of flexibility that, as a rule, we expect today from light and lyric sopranos), as well as variety of timbre. This last requisite has always been uncommon, but then, Pasta was an exceptional singer. It is because of the character of Amina that a lyric coloratura soprano has a chance of succeeding, whereas she does not as Norma.

Bellini called Pasta an angel who excited the public to an enthusiasm bordering on madness. An equally appealing Amina was Maria Malibran, whom Bellini favoured in this role as much as he did Pasta. Malibran combined the singing and acting of the role to such a high degree that she came close to what could be described as perfection.

Giulia Grisi did not seem to be comfortable with Amina. Bellini thought that the role should have been well within her grasp, but Grisi soon relinquished it after singing it at the King's Theatre, London, in 1834.

It was on Fanny Tachinardi-Persiani, the future creator of the title role in Donizetti's *Lucia di Lammermoor*, that the mantle of Malibran fell. Jenny Lind, Pauline Viardot-Garcia and Henriette Sontag followed, all three of whom were exceptional Aminas, although not quite as outstanding as Pasta or Malibran. Lind, the best of the three, scored on the purely vocal side rather than the dramatic. Her slim, youthful figure was a great asset, but her movements were sometimes wooden. She caused a sensation by performing the final sleepwalking scene carrying a candle and crossing the perilous bridge herself. (The usual practice at the time was for prima donnas to send a "super" across the plank in this scene.) However, it was Lind's singing in this, her greatest Bellinian role, that counted most and that Chopin admired so much when he heard her, in London on 4 May 1848. "Her singing is infallibly pure and true," he wrote to his friend Grzymala "and I admire her *piano* passages above all, the charm of which is indescribable."

Viardot-Garcia was the better dramatic artist. As a contralto, she was forced to transpose the music down but transcended this through her exceptional musicianship. Some even preferred her Amina to Lind's, as they found more humanity and, consequently, more poetry in it. Meanwhile, Sontag, who had all the required flexibility of voice, sang with a tone even sweeter than Lind's, although with less power.

A decade later, other famous Aminas came onto the scene, more lyric coloraturas that were just as brilliant as their predecessors had been. Adelina Patti was the first, followed by Emma Albani,[30] who was succeeded by Marcella Sembrich. They were all successful because of the brilliance and purity of their singing rather than their dramatic expression.

La sonnambula was extremely popular from its first appearance until 1890. For around the next 20 years, it went out of fashion everywhere except in Italy, where it has always remained in the repertoire. In 1909, Luisa Tetrazzini brought it back with great success, for a while. Although her appearance and acting were rather a handicap, Tetrazzini succeeded entirely through her singing, with her impeccable coloratura, which was much more dramatic than is generally apparent from most of her recordings. Maria Barrientos and Amelita Galli-Curci offered their brilliant, undramatic and yet, paradoxically, innately musical coloratura as their greatest asset. Elvira de Hidalgo was a more credible Amina, although she did not sing with quite the same ease as Tetrazzini. In her realistic approach to the role, she was the first to perform the sleepwalking scene barefoot.

The principal Aminas of more recent times have been Toti dal Monte, Lina Pagliughi, Margherita Carosio, Maria Callas, Renata Scotto, Joan Sutherland, Ileana Cotrubas and June Anderson. Dal Monte and Pagliughi offered something of Tetrazzini but without her brilliance or extraordinary flexibility of voice. Their cantilena was also not impeccable, although dal Monte was on occasion very moving through sheer beauty of voice. Carosio attempted to achieve characterisation through her voice, and to a great extent she succeeded in this, but her coloratura singing was not always equal to her well-considered intentions.

Callas[31] was different from all her contemporaries and predecessors, except for Pasta and Malibran. With her dramatic soprano coloratura voice, her impeccable musicianship and her ability to sing cantilena in the true Bellinian style, she was able to combine acting and singing to perfection and thus fulfil both the composer's and the librettist's extraordinary requirements.

Scotto tried along the same lines as Callas, and although she could not quite equal her, she nevertheless achieved a more than creditable interpretation, better than all the others. Meanwhile, Sutherland did not attempt interpretation, relying entirely on the brilliance and remarkable ease of the upper register of her voice, an approach that falls short of the prerequisites of the role.

Where Sutherland fell rather short, however, Cotrubas provided. Her interpretation had sincerity and great feeling for words, and her accomplished technique more than made up for a relative lack of brilliance. Her dramatic approach to the role was on a par with Scotto's, although the Bellinian line sometimes eluded her. Anderson's approach, often reminiscent of (if not similar to) Sutherland's, was with an inferior quality of voice, but often with greater musicianship. Like Sutherland, Anderson was always impressive and at times even exciting, but not moving or convincing.

There have not been many Rubinis since Bellini composed *La sonnambula*, but Mario was quite exceptional. His only drawback was that he did not have access to the very high notes of his predecessor. In more recent years, famous Elvinos have included John McCormack, Jean de Reszke, Alessandro Bonci, Fernando de Lucia, Beniamino Gigli, Tito Schipa, Feruccio Tagliavini, Cesare Valetti, Nicola Monti and Alfredo Kraus. Meanwhile, famous Rodolfos have been Tamburini, Lablache, Charles Santley, Jean-Baptiste Faure, Edouard de Reszke, Ezio Pinza, Cesare Siepi and Nicola Zaccaria.

10

Norma at La Scala (1831)

In the spring of 1830, during the time that Marietti and Sorensi were trying to buy Bellini's contract from Crivelli, the composer was offered another contract to write two operas for La Scala, one for the autumn of 1831 and the other for the carnival season of 1832. After some bargaining over fees, the contract was signed, but no subjects were decided.

As soon as *La sonnambula* was successfully launched, Bellini, who usually suffered from nervous exhaustion after producing a new work, went to Moltrasio to rest with Giuditta Turina's family at Villa Passalacqua. His movements and activities during the next six months are rather difficult to trace, save for the fact that he spent July and August at Moltrasio and part of May and June in Milan, as from there he exchanged letters with the tenor Domenico Donzelli, who was then in Paris.

Born in Bergamo, Donzelli (1790-1873) had a very successful career. With the growing importance of the orchestra, which was becoming larger and more highly pitched – especially in the major opera houses, with their large auditoriums – tenors were required to sing louder in order to be heard. Donzelli had the requisites of this new kind of tenor, who was expected to sing dramatically but with agility in a heroic voice. Rossini's *Otello* was the first such role, and although Donzelli did not create it, he was its finest exponent. Reviewing Donzelli's performance as Otello in 1823, the *Allgemeine Musikalische Zeitung* wrote, "He has a beautiful, mellifluous tenor voice with which he attacks the high A in full chest voice without once resorting to falsetto. Donzelli's acting is thoughtfully conceived, his interpretation well ordered and full of vitality and expression. His declaration is exemplary, particularly in recitatives."

Having been engaged by La Scala to sing in Bellini's autumn new opera, Donzelli[1] wrote to the composer on 3 May describing his vocal ability and limitations: "The range of my voice is nearly two octaves, from low D to top G. My chest voice is to G, and it is in this range that I can declaim with vigour and sustain all the force of the declamation. From G to high G, I can use a falsetto, which provides a means of decoration. I also have a fair amount of agility but find descents much easier than ascents.

Bellini answered Donzelli's[2] letter from Milan on 7 June: "My dear friend, Maestro Mercadante has also told me about the great consideration you give to all the music that you interpret. Therefore, I am only too happy to write my opera for such a worthy artist as yourself, and no doubt you will feel the same about my music. My opera will be centred around you and Pasta, with the other two artists in subordinate roles. I am delighted to have made your acquaintance and I take this opportunity to express my respect for you."

Pasta was the prima donna engaged for Bellini's autumn opera for La Scala. It is surprising that she had not appeared there before, for she had sung in Milan many times. Now, after her unprecedented success in *Anna Bolena* and the very different *La sonnambula* at the Carcano, La Scala at last realised her extraordinary possibilities.

The first mention of the subject for the new opera, scheduled for 26 December, occurs in Bellini's letter to Lamperi on 23 June:[3] "I have already chosen the subject for my new opera, which is called *Norma, ossia l'infanticidio*, the play by Soumet which is now being performed in Paris with tremendous success."

Alexandre Soumet's *Norma* was produced on 25 April 1831 at the Théâtre Royal de L'Odéon, Paris. It is uncertain who thought of using it as the subject for an opera, although Fraccaroli says that Giuditta Turina suggested it after she had read of its success in Paris.[4] In any case, both Bellini and Romani liked it and the libretto was ready by the end of August.

The tragedy of the Druid priestess (Soumet's violent drama was effectively turned into a Classical opera) provided excellent dramatic situations and contrasting characters. Many of Norma's predicaments are similar to those of Medea in *Medea in Corinto*, a role in which Pasta had distinguished herself. Norma's character also has similarities with Giulia in Spontini's *La vestale* and Pacini's *La sacerdotessa d'Irminsul* and Velleda in Chateaubriand's *Les Martyrs*. As presented by Soumet and Romani, Norma is a much more complex character and consequently more demanding. Precisely what it needed was an artist of Pasta's calibre, and her availability was undoubtedly the greatest incentive for Bellini to accept this subject. At first, he disliked the title *Norma*, because the word in Italian means *regular*.

He considered *La serva druidica*, *La druidessa* or *I druidi* instead, but in the end the name of the protagonist, Norma, was used.

On 30 August, Bellini returned to Milan to start work in the quiet seclusion of his room at the Appiani house. Three days later, he wrote to Pasta,[5] who was appearing at the Théâtre Italien in Paris, informing her of the new opera that he was preparing for her:

The other day, I left Borgovigo and your dearest mother, Rachele. Now I must apply myself to work on the opera for which Romani gave me verses only yesterday. I hope that this story will be to your liking. Romani thinks that it's most effective and appropriate to your encyclopaedic character, because this story is that of Norma. He will arrange the situations in such a way that they don't recall others. If necessary, he will modify the characters in order to make them more effective. You will already have read it, and if any ideas should occur to you, write to me about them, and in the meantime try to bring "figurines" of the characters in the Parisian production of the play. If you don't find them to your taste, try to improve them yourself in the way that you think best.

My dear angel, your intelligence and the delicate feelings that flourish in you make it impossible for you not to ascend the steps towards the honourable position that our age accords you. Although these steps are on the ladder of glory that you have already ascended, they have nevertheless decided, from Milan to London, that new thrills are in store for you this year, thrills that are unexpected and great. The temple of such glory has therefore been even more exalted for you.

Excuse this outpouring of my heart, which is full of tender feelings of admiration. I needed to express everything that I felt for you, not forgetting even a feeling of gratitude for that engagement which you undertook in being so good as to have performed my *Sonnambula* in London. I would like to think that *Il pirata* will also be entrusted to you, as I have heard from Marietti that Corelli won't be singing it...

Please try to get Rossini [consultant at the Italien] interested in precise performances of my music. He shouldn't disdain such a plea from one who has called him his master.

Goodbye, dear friend, and may you always be happy.

Although *Norma* deals primarily with the personal relationships of its principal characters, the drama is set at a time of revolution against an oppressive foreign domination. It would not have been surprising for the censor in Milan – which was, after all, a city still under Austrian domination – to have asked for modifications to the libretto, but, perhaps because the drama is set in ancient Gaul during Roman times, he was lenient and asked only for minor changes, such as references to Caesar and "enemy eagles" in the opening chorus, which prays for the downfall of Rome. Apparently, the censor felt that these references were subversive to the house of Hapsburg.

Much has been written and much more has been inferred about Bellini's political awareness. There is no evidence, documentary or otherwise, of his feelings about the nationalistic aspirations of the Italy of his day. Although he could not have been completely unaware of the political tension at the time, he took no active part in politics that we know of, except for the Carbonari incident in 1820, back when he was a student in Naples. The consequences of that episode would have served as a warning against any overt expressions of democratic principles. If Bellini was feeling ardently patriotic, the most plausible way of furthering the cause of Italy would have been through his music.

Some writers believe that this was indeed the case, pointing out distinct political undertones in *Bianca e Fernando*, *Il pirata*, the abortive *Ernani* and, of course, *Norma*. On the other hand, it must also be pointed out that this is not the case in *Zaira*, *I Capuleti e i Montecchi* or *La sonnambula*, and in fact *Ernani* was abandoned for the very reason that it would have had difficulty in getting past the censor. Bellini chose his libretti on their suitability for theatrical effect, and if they contained any political thread – as a great many of the plays and novels of the time did – he tried to present them in an uncontroversial way, rather than using them to further any patriotic cause. Even so, the public often found patriotic sentiment, whether it was intended or not.

As always, Bellini took special care with the preparation of the libretto of *Norma*. It was he who asked for several changes in the verses and the substantial reduction of the libretto's original length,[6] which was longer by about an hour. Once these crucial revisions were made, Bellini proceeded in the composition of *Norma* at comparative leisure, with at least three clear months in which to complete it. On 7 September, he wrote to Giuditta

Turina[7] at Moltrasio, informing her that he had almost finished the overture and the introductory chorus and that "the result does not displease me". However, he was worried by the outbreak of cholera that was fast spreading across Europe. His fears are expressed in his letter to Florimo[8] on 19 September: "I am writing the opera, but it's as if I had no contract, because I'm almost sure that the cholera epidemic will be here and all the theatres will be closed down. As soon as the cholera approaches Milan, I will leave. I am now in Como, but next Wednesday – or probably, at the very latest, on Thursday – I shall return to Milan to continue my work."

It is also evident from this letter that Barbaja had asked Bellini to write an opera for Naples but that they had not yet come to a financial agreement:

> You will see the terms that I expect, should I come to Naples to write an opera. Barbaja hasn't yet agreed. He should be reminded that, when he released Donizetti so that he could come to La Scala, Barbaja demanded 8,000 lire from Crivelli and then Crivelli had to pay Donizetti 4,000 lire on top.
>
> In any case, as far as I'm concerned, I won't accept less than I have already asked for. For *La sonnambula*, I received 3,000 ducats,[9] and I am expecting to make another 800 ducats from the sale of the music to other theatres. Therefore, if Barbaja agrees to pay me 3,000 ducats, I will accept. Otherwise, I won't come…
>
> If I write the new opera for Naples, I should be glad to have Ronzi [Giuseppina Ronzi de Begnis] and Tamburini in the cast, but you understand that a tenor like Donzelli or Rubini will be necessary.
>
> Well, let's hope that everything turns out well, in which case I will come to Naples and we shall be together for some months. My Giuditta isn't too bad and sends you her regards.

With this letter, Bellini also enclosed another, addressed to Prince Ruffano, informing him in a more diplomatic way of his conditions for accepting to write an opera for the San Carlo: "I too share your desire that I should come next year to write an opera for the San Carlo. Your kind invitation gives me great pleasure, for I cherish the occasion of dedicating my time to my home theatre, which first sent me into this difficult arena of the musical world." After detailing how much he is being paid by all the other theatres, Bellini politely but firmly makes it clear that he expects the same treatment from the San Carlo. He also makes sure that his artistic demands are understood: "The libretto is to be written by Felice Romani, the singers are to be chosen from the artists that are included in the *Cartellone* [playbills] and sets and costumes will all be new. Also, one full month of uninterrupted rehearsals will be required. When Barbaja is agreeable to all of these points...I shall be ready to start work and have the opera ready for production at the end of December 1832." However, this project did not reach its conclusion in 1832, and afterwards it was too late for Bellini.

In the meantime, Bellini worked on *Norma*, sometimes at Moltrasio and sometimes in Milan, and perhaps also when he visited the Turinas at Casalbuttano. Everything about the composition continued smoothly and the cholera epidemic did not reach Milan. What seems to have upset Bellini during this period, however, was the piratical publication of his music. He felt very strongly about this, and on 1 December he wrote an open letter of protest to *L'Eco di Milano*:

> It will be only just to advise all the theatre managers, the impresarios and the music-sellers that a theatrical correspondent allowed himself to prepare the orchestration of my opera *La sonnambula* on the basis of the simple reduction of the same for the piano and then sell it as if it were the one written by me for the Teatro Carcano, Milan, during the last Carnival.
>
> I wouldn't have complained if these falsifications were harmful only to a composer's financial interests, but they also damage his reputation, inasmuch as they put into circulation imperfect works that are both monstrous and harmful to those who buy them in good faith, especially with a view to staging them. For this reason, I address myself to the theatre managers, impresarios and music-sellers, asking them to consider as invalid any score of *La sonnambula* that may be offered to them, except those copies that are signed by me or the music publisher Ricordi, who owns the only original.

Norma was completed on 30 November, and full rehearsals began a few days later. "On Monday, I will start rehearsals for *Norma*," Bellini wrote to Mercadante[10] in Turin. "I have also made my will and have thought of leaving you something, should they kill me off. As you are also starting rehearsals,[11] and therefore the same thing may happen to you, I beg you not to forget me. This is the right spirit, I'm sure you'll agree."

The opera received at least three weeks of rehearsals, and considering that Bellini had 90 days (at that period considered leisurely) to compose the music, he thus had the opportunity to work calmly and develop his ideas thoughtfully. Indeed, both composer and librettist gave their full consideration to this work, steering clear of tradition to a degree and introducing innovations that would enhance the drama. This can be seen from the great number of drafts of the music and the libretto that have survived at the Museo Belliniano and the Accademia Musicale Chigiana in Sienna.

Not unexpectedly, when rehearsals began, the management of La Scala asked for changes. They wanted a conventional ensemble finale for act one, whereas Bellini and Romani had provided a trio finale. The management also insisted that the opera should end with a brilliant cabaletta for Pasta, but neither composer nor librettist would hear of it. They both stuck to their ideas and refused to change anything. What Bellini did change many times was Pasta's aria "Casta Diva", in the first act.

Count Barbò,[12] a friend of Bellini's, told Cicconetti, who published his *Vita di Vincenzo Bellini* in 1859, that the composer rewrote this aria eight times before he was satisfied. Even then, Pasta thought that she was unable to sing it; the aria was written in G, and Pasta felt that she could only sing it in F. Bellini suggested that she should sing it every day for a week and then, if she still was not satisfied, he would change it to F. Pasta was unable to sing the aria to her satisfaction, and to show Bellini that she had tried very hard she sent him two unusual gifts accompanied by a charming note addressed simply to "Chez Lui.[13] Allow me to offer you some gifts which have been of great comfort to me amid the fear that constantly assails me when I realise how little suited I am to do justice to your sublime melodies. This lamp at night and these flowers in the daytime have been witnesses to my studies of *Norma* and also my desire always to be worthy of your respect." Bellini rewrote the aria in F, most probably on the morning of the premiere.

It was not only Pasta who had to work extremely hard during the rehearsals. Admittedly, in this role she had to carry most of the opera on her shoulders, but the other singers, too, had difficult roles to perform. Rehearsals extended practically to the last minute (rehearsals for act two continued all morning on the day of the premiere), and yet, as Bellini had reason to say after the first performance, the singers still did not know their parts well enough.

The La Scala *cartellone* officially announced, on 19 December, that *Norma* would be opening the 1831/2 carnival season. Four other operas were also announced. Pacini's *Il corsaro* was to receive its Milanese premiere after *Norma* and a new opera – *La vendetta*, by Cesare Pugni – would be followed by Donizetti's *Anna Bolena*. The last offering of the season was an as-yet-untitled new work by Donizetti.[14]

The premiere of *Norma*, on 26 December (with the two ballets *Merope* and *I pazzi per progetto*[15] also given), was a failure, but the opera began to succeed at subsequent performances until, eventually, it became a triumph for both Bellini and Pasta. The cause of the initial failure is difficult to isolate, as there were several contributory factors. Bellini wrote to Florimo[16] immediately after the first performance (the letter is dated 26 December):

> I'm writing to you with great grief, a grief that I cannot express, and you are the only one who can understand me. The first performance of *Norma* at La Scala was a failure, failure, complete failure. Can you believe it? It's true that the public was severe and looked as if they'd come to judge me – and with some precipitation, I believe. They were determined to give my poor *Norma* the same role and the same end as that of the Druidess. I don't even recognise those dear Milanese who had welcomed me with enthusiasm, joy and exultation of heart at my previous operas, *Il pirata*, *La Straniera* and *La sonnambula*.
>
> In all sincerity, I believed that, with my *Norma*, I was giving them a respectable sister to these operas. Unfortunately, it wasn't like that at all. I made a mistake. My forecast was wrong and my hopes resulted in disappointment. Nevertheless, if passion hasn't jeopardised my judgement, I can tell you from the heart that the introduction, Norma's aria, the duet for the two women with the trio that follows, the war hymn and the finale of the second act are all pieces that delight me musically (with all due modesty!), and I confess that I would be happy if I could again write music as good as this during my artistic life...
>
> We mustn't forget that, in the world of the theatre, the public is the supreme judge. I hope that I can appeal against the sentence that my opera was given, and if the public comes to judge it differently then I

will have won my case, and then I will be able to declare that *Norma* is the best of my operas. If this is not to be, then I shall resign myself to my great sorrow and, as some consolation, say that the Romans also hissed at the divine Pergolesi's *L'Olimpiade.*[17]

As I shall be leaving Milan by mail-coach, I hope to arrive in Naples before this letter. Therefore, either I or this letter will give you the sad news of *Norma*'s failure. Don't get too worried, my dear Florimo. I am young and in my heart I believe that I can make the best of this terrible breakdown. Please show this letter to all my friends, because I'm the kind of person who tells the truth both in good and bad times. In the meantime, receive your Bellini's embraces.

Some writers have disputed the authenticity of this letter, specifically Bellini's declarations of "failure, failure, complete failure" ("fiasco, fiasco, solenne fiasco"), because it is out of style and contradicts the composer's later statements about the outcome of *Norma*. Florimo, the recipient and publisher of the letter, is accused of manufacturing it without ever producing the autograph, yet it is difficult to see Florimo's motives in this case. Besides, human nature – especially that of an artist – can cause hypersensitivity that often magnifies the slightest adversity, as can be seen in Bellini's reaction to the reception of the first performance of *Norma*, which came so soon after the unqualified success of *La sonnambula*. In this case, the hostility was far from slight, largely due to the extreme tiredness of the singers. Bellini's subsequent statements were more positive, as was the success of his great work.

Following the second performance of *Norma*, Bellini wrote to his uncle Ferlito[18] on 28 December. In this letter, not only does he put things in more balanced perspective, but he also gives details about alleged causes for the failure of the premiere:

In spite of the formidable plot against *Norma* engineered by a very rich and powerful person, my opera astounded the public more at the second performance than it did at the first. Yesterday's official *Gazzetta* in Milan announced it a complete failure, because at the first performance the opposing party sat in silence while the well-meaning applauded, and all because this powerful person is in command and can order the newspaper to write whatever she likes. [This is because] this person...is an enemy of Madame Pasta, and as she is also Pacini's mistress she is therefore my enemy. Yet the work was appreciated even more last night, and the theatre was crammed full, a real sign of an opera's success.

On the first night, the introduction and Pollione's and Norma's scenes were applauded loudly. The duet between Pollione and Adalgisa wasn't liked, though, and it never will be, as even I don't like it myself. Then the duet opening the final trio [act one finale] was greatly appreciated, but the trio wasn't sung well because the singers were tired, having been rehearsing the entire second act throughout that same morning, and so there was no applause at the end of this act. In the second act – apart from the chorus, which was liked only fairly well – everything else made such an impact that even my enemies listened in silence. At the end of the performance, I was called onto the stage alone four times and then also with the singers. Last night [the opera's second performance], the singers performed the trio very well and were so successful that perhaps my heretofore persecuted *Norma* will close the carnival season.

Madame Pasta is an angel – the word describes how she sang and acted her role perfectly. Donzelli is very good and sings well but hardly knows his part as yet. Giulietta Grisi, in the role of Adalgisa, does nicely, although she has a rather cold temperament. And the chorus was excellent. The public is cursing the journalists, my friends are jumping for joy and I am completely satisfied, really doubly pleased, because I've discomfited so many of my mean and powerful enemies.

Next week, I will be leaving Milan for Naples. As soon as the season in Naples is over, I will come to see all my family and friends in Sicily. I'll send you some of the parts to *Norma* from Naples the moment they are printed in Milan.

My health is good, although I'm tired. I'll write to you more about the success of *Norma* in the forthcoming performances. Please pass on the news to my family, relatives and friends, but please don't let anyone else read this letter, because it might appear that I'm boasting, and this is not very becoming.

After the third performance, Bellini wrote to two friends, Perucchini[19] in Venice and the singer Rugeri, telling them of the failure of *Norma* on the first night and its subsequent increasing success. He concludes, "If any pieces from this opera should reach you, you should recognise how zealously I wrote it, and at the same time you should understand my assertions."

The "rich and powerful" person whom Bellini mentions as his and Pasta's enemy was the Russian Contessa Giulia Samoyloff.[20] She was certainly Pacini's patroness, if not his mistress, and neither she nor Pacini (whose *Il corsaro* followed *Norma* at La Scala some two weeks later) would have wanted Bellini to score a great success. Contessa Giulia was rich and powerful and could well have paid for a noisy or dead-silent claque to ruin the performance of *Norma*. The inadequacy of the first performance – Bellini himself said as much – obviously aided and abetted such machinations, if indeed they really existed.

Pacini's comments on the outcome of *Norma* were reported by Cicconetti:[21] "I saw Bellini again in Milan at the time that he was producing his masterpiece, *Norma*. I'm sorry to say that the first, second and third performances of this sublime work were not a tremendous success. This afflicted the young composer and brought tears to his eyes."

However, there is strong evidence that contradicts Pacini's ambiguously sly comments. Although *Norma* was a failure at its premiere, on subsequent nights the enthusiasm increased and there was no hostility; certainly the audience showed a different disposition. Furthermore, even if the singers were not as tired as on the first night, they could hardly have been less nervous at the second performance. Moreover, considering that *Norma* contained several innovations (such as in the finale of the first act) and no brilliant cabaletta for Pasta at the end of the opera (which the majority of the audience would have expected), it was too early by the second performance, or even the third, for the public to accept and appreciate the work.

In the history of opera, there are several instances when a work failed disastrously on the first night but succeeded from the second performance onwards. Perhaps the best example is Rossini's *Il barbiere di Siviglia*. At the premiere of this work, there was probably an organised claque ready to ruin the performance, too. On such an occasion, any inadequacy of performance helps organised hostility to succeed. Afterwards, it is difficult to know whether it is the inadequacy of the performance which brought about the audience hostility or vice versa.

Surprisingly, the newspaper reports do not say much about the opposition of the audience, and although they agree with many of Bellini's comments, they do not paint such a dismal picture of the outcome of the opera. They certainly do not appear to have been paid by any "rich and powerful person" to persecute *Norma*, as Bellini claims. As for Pasta, she was no less than fairly received, and Donzelli and Grisi were criticised more severely by Bellini than by any review.

The first review was published in *L'Eco* on 28 December:

In this work, Romani showed all the inspiration that one expects from him, thus proving again that he is a better librettist than any other... From a composer like Bellini and artists like Pasta and Donzelli, one could reasonably expect something extraordinary, but we are compelled to inform our readers, with great surprise, that at the end of the first act there was no applause at all. This was despite the fact that, during this act, the overture, the introduction (which is probably a little too long) and the distinguished singing of Pasta and Donzelli were well appreciated. The audience certainly expected a different, more important ending to the act, and consequently they were disappointed to see the curtain come down after a trio of no great effect.

The second act contains some beautiful pieces of music, and as such we point to the duet between Norma and Adalgisa, another between Norma and Pollione and the finale – which, however, reminded us of the same situation as that in the finale of act one of Spontini's *La vestale*. In this act, Pasta, Donzelli and Grisi, together with the maestro, were clearly satisfied with the reception that they had from the audience, which called them onto the stage at the end [of the opera] several times. Pasta, as usual, was a very distinguished tragic actress and singer.

The *Gazzetta privilegiata di Milano* reviewed *Norma* on 30 December:

It is not impossible that the new opera will please in time, but for the moment one is forced to say, except for a *crescendo* that precedes the finale of act two, the music of our maestro was adjudged rather more sluggish and laboured than not. It was lucky for him that he had renowned singers or who knows what would have been the fate of his *Norma*? Perhaps it would have suffered the fate that the laws of the Druids reserved for perjury.

Donzelli's aria in act one was loudly applauded because it was sung by a splendid artist who has a most expressive method of singing, combined with a powerful, agreeable, extensive and very pleasing voice. But the part was not worthy of such a singer as him. Pasta sang excellently, like a marvel. Applause was often heard during the second act and was most deservedly divided between her and Grisi, who took an honourable place beside the greater star. The choruses are effective but offer very little out of the ordinary. The maestro was also included in the applause at the curtain to act two.

The spectacle was staged with dignity, the scenery is beautiful and the costumes are in character.

The *Gazzetta* published a second article on 3 January, after the fourth performance:

The promise that we made about the progressive appreciation of the new music of Bellini can happily be changed into a much more positive opinion. The piece was appreciated more and more each evening. Impartial justice, our duty and our special satisfaction, impel us strongly to correct – in part, at least – our first hurried and rough notes, which were more of an introduction to the opera than a judgement.

Bellini has a fine talent. He is not a genius, for geniuses are rare and hardly ever is there one to distinguish a century. He is not an innovator, either. Rather, he is a renovator of the old system of melodramatic singing, which the Pesarese [Rossini] alone, a true genius, was able to accomplish and which his successors caused to fall into oblivion – not without meeting obstinate and powerful opposition at the beginning.

Norma's music is declamatory; it fits intelligently to the words, and precisely because this music follows a road that has long been disused, our ears need a longer time to listen to it in order to judge it honestly. For this reason, part of the score didn't please us at the first hearing and met with universal approval only after the passage of time.

Another interesting review appeared in the Paris publication *Revue Musicale*. It was also published in Milan, but much later, after the season had ended:

Bianca, Pirata, Straniera, Capuleti and *Sonnambula* have raised their illustrious composer to a rank from which no less effective or original work can make him descend, but he was destined for a higher place. He was to win our emotions and admiration through power, majesty and tragedy, and he did this through *Norma*...

The music of *Norma* not only has a brilliant effect; it's as vigorous as the plot demands and responds to all the passion that dominates that plot. The music is no unworthy sister of its libretto and is enlivened by an imaginative and truly beautiful instrumentation. Other operas appeared on our stages during the season (I will not mention *Corsaro* and *Vendetta*, which caused the theatre to remain empty), but such as [Rossini's] *Otello* and *Norma* were always in demand, and it was with the latter that the season opened and closed.

Two letters purportedly written by Donizetti further reinforce the polemic about *Norma*. One, published by Florimo,[22] is addressed to the well-known Neapolitan painter and publishers' agent Teodore Ghezzi, a friend of Donizetti's. This letter is dated 27 December 1831, the day after *Norma*'s premiere: "The Milanese neither understood nor judged *Norma* fairly. For my part, I would have been honoured to have composed it myself. The introduction and the finale of the second act are enough to establish the greatest musical reputation, and I think that before long the Milanese will realise how foolish they were to misjudge so hastily the merits of this opera."

The other letter, published by Vincenzo Ricca[23] in 1932, is headed "Milan, 31 December 1811" and addressed to a Maestro Rebotti of Pesaro:

I'm extremely happy at the marvellous reception that *Norma* had after its opening on the 26th of this month. It was a brilliant and festive reception that was repeated at subsequent performances. This is a very significant result, especially when you consider that *Norma* had a somewhat chilly – even, to be frank, hostile – greeting from some of the audience on its first performance. After four performances, however, a huge crowd filled the boxes, the galleries, the balconies and every other part of the large theatre, applauding every piece with tremendous enthusiasm.

Everybody is praising the music of my friend – or, rather, my brother – Bellini to the skies. They are all greatly impressed by his supreme genius and are finding in his opera undreamed-of beauty and sublime harmony... The duet "In mia man alfin tu sei" is a superb example of dramatic melody. (Verdi is of the same opinion.)

The authenticity of these letters is contested by some writers on the grounds that the autographs have never been produced. Also, at the time, Donizetti was in Naples, rehearsing his *Fausta* (produced on 12 January 1832), and he would hardly have wanted to make the long journey to Milan, where according to the letters he stayed at least five days, unless he had to finalise his contract with La Scala for the opera that he was expected to write for the spring, *Ugo, conte di Parigi*. Indeed, no documentary evidence exists for this. Moreover, the remark about Verdi's opinion is absurd. This parenthesis can only be justified if the publisher of the letter inserted it under the assumption that it would be more informative to his readers. Verdi was unknown and only 18 years old at the time, and it is unlikely that Donizetti would have considered his opinion, let alone quoted him. However, Verdi did make this remark about *Norma* in a letter dated 2 May 1898, addressed to Camille Bellaigue: "What truth and power in declamation there is in the duet between Pollione and Norma, for example! And what nobility of thought in the first phrase of the introduction."

In essence, both letters serve to confirm that *Norma* is a good opera and that it failed on its first performance because of hostility and ignorance from part of the audience. But if these letters are forgeries, by the time that they were published (1882 and 1932 respectively) it was too late for concern over *Norma*'s reputation; the opera was already established as one of the most important in the Italian repertoire.

Notwithstanding its tempestuous start, *Norma* achieved 40 performances during its first season. Soon it was performed all over Europe, bringing Bellini great fame. He considered it to be his greatest work. Also, Pasta overcame her initial difficulties and continued to sing a role that offered her the widest scope for her extraordinary dramatic and vocal powers. Eventually, the role became very much her own and swept her to the pinnacle of her already outstanding career, where she remained unrivalled for some time to come.

NORMA

Opera seria (*tragedia lirica*) in two acts. Libretto by Felice Romani. First performed at La Scala, Milan, on 26 December 1831 on a triple bill with the ballets *Merope* and *I pazzi per progetto*, choreographed by Antonio Cortesi, the first to music by Luigi Viviani and Giacomo Panizza, the second to music by an unknown composer. Alessandro Sanquirico designed the stage sets.

CHARACTERS AND ORIGINAL CAST

Norma, High Priestess of the Druids, Oroveso's daughter	Soprano	Giuditta Pasta
Pollione, Roman Proconsul in Gaul	Tenor	Domenico Donzelli
Adalgisa, a virgin in the Temple of Irminsul	Mezzo-soprano or soprano	Giulia Grisi
Oroveso, chief Druid Priest, Norma's father	Bass	Vincenzo Negrini
Clotilde, Norma's confidante	Soprano	Marietta Sacchi
Flavio, a centurion, friend of Pollione	Tenor	Lorenzo Lombardi

The action takes place in Gaul during the Roman occupation at an unspecified pre-Christian date, usually set at around 50 BC.

ACT I

SCENE 1: The sacred grove of the Druids. There is a clearing in the centre with the oak of Irminsul standing in it. At the foot of the tree stands the Druidic stone, which serves as an altar. There are wooded hills in the distance with fires seen through the trees. It is night.

The Druids, followers of the ancient cult of Irminsul, enter their sacred grove. Oroveso, the chief Druid, bids his people make their way to the hill, where, with the rising of the moon, Norma, his daughter and High Priestess of the Druids, will come to advise them when they should rebel against their cruel Roman oppressors. The Druids then implore the gods to rouse their priestess to war.

As they depart, Pollione, the Roman Proconsul, and his friend Flavio enter cautiously. Pollione reveals to his friend that he no longer loves Norma, the mother of his two sons. (Norma has long ago broken her vows of chastity, with Pollione, but none of her people suspect that she is not the virgin priestess that her cult demands.) For some time now, Pollione has been in love with Adalgisa, a young and beautiful novice of the Temple of Irminsul. He tells Flavio of a dream he has had in which he heard Norma swearing vengeance on him, as he and Adalgisa were about to be married before the altar of Venus in Rome. Suddenly, the two Romans are interrupted by the striking of the sacred shield, signalling that Norma is coming to perform her rites, and the voices of the returning Druids are heard announcing the rising of the moon. "Barbarians," exclaims Pollione and, on leaving, threatens to destroy the blasphemous temples of the Druids in order to win Adalgisa.

Presently, the Druids reassemble and, while waiting for Norma, express their implicit trust in her, revering her as a goddess with prophetic powers. Norma enters with her attendants and ascends the steps of the altar. She wears a wreath of vervain on her head and she carries a golden sickle. She rebukes the Druids for their impatient demand to wage war against the Romans, an act that is contradictory to her own oracular prophecy – that Rome will fall through its own decadence and not at the hands of the Druids. After performing the rite of cutting the mistletoe with her sickle, Norma prays to the chaste goddess of the moon for peace. Although the faithful Druids respond with their pledge to strike only at Norma's command, they continue their threat to kill the Proconsul, their hated enemy. Norma agrees but almost immediately realises what this would mean to her, and she reflects to herself that she will avert the danger from Pollione when the time comes. She then secretly and nostalgically proclaims her love for Pollione, praying that he will soon come back to her.

The rite ended, they all depart, except for Adalgisa, who stays behind to pray for strength so that she might resist the illicit love that she feels for a Roman. Her prayer is interrupted by this Roman, who is in reality Pollione. In vain, Adalgisa entreats him to leave. Pollione tells her that he is about to return to Rome and begs her to flee with him. After considerable hesitation, Adalgisa helplessly consents and promises to meet him the following day.

SCENE 2: Outside Norma's forest dwelling, where she lives with her two children and her confidante, Clotilde.

Because of Pollione's recent attitude – he has not visited Norma for some time – and his imminent departure for Rome, Norma is greatly disturbed. She has now developed a love/hate relationship with their children; but for them, she would follow him to Rome.

Someone is heard approaching and Norma bids Clotilde hide the children. It is Adalgisa who, tortured by her conscience, comes to her superior and friend to confess her sacrilegious love and at the same time ask to be released from her vows. Thinking of her own similar circumstances when she first fell in love, Norma is very understanding. "But tell me, who is this man you love?" she asks. "A Roman," Adalgisa answers. "There he is," she says, for at that very moment Pollione comes in to see his children prior to his departure. At once, Norma grasps the situation and furiously reproaches him. Adalgisa, at a complete loss, spurns him and declares that she would never elope with the betrayer of the High Priestess while Pollione entreats Norma to vent her anger on him alone. Norma then warns Adalgisa that she is only another victim of the faithless Pollione, who protests vigorously and is still determined to elope with the young priestess, even though her happiness is shattered by the knowledge of his secret. As the sound of the sacred shield calls Norma to her rites, she repels Pollione and orders him to leave alone.

ACT II

SCENE 1: Inside Norma's dwelling, later during the same evening. Norma's two children are asleep on a Roman couch covered with bear skins.

Torn between love and hatred for her children, Norma contemplates killing them while they are asleep. Unable to do the actual deed, her desperate cry awakens them. She embraces them lovingly and sends Clotilde to bring Adalgisa to her. Eventually, Norma begs Adalgisa to take the children, marry Pollione and bring them up as her own. Still loyal, Adalgisa agrees to go to Pollione, but only to persuade him to return to Norma and their children. Norma will hear none of it. Nevertheless, when Adalgisa expresses her devotion for her friend and attempts to placate her and arouse her motherly feelings, Norma relents and the two women are reconciled. Together they prepare to face their problems. Adalgisa then leaves for the Roman camp.

SCENE 2: A secluded place near the sacred grove of the Druids, surrounded by caves and rocks. A lake with a stone bridge can be seen in the distance.

The Druids secretly assemble in a council of war, again anxiously demanding that they rise against the Romans. Although Oroveso confirms that Pollione is to be succeeded by an even more cruel Proconsul, he exhorts them to keep their hatred of the enemy alive but, for the moment, to demonstrate patience and apparent docility.

SCENE 3: The temple of Irminsul. On one side stands the altar of the Druids.

Clotilde informs Norma that Adalgisa, having failed in her mission to Pollione, has now returned to the temple. Meanwhile, Pollione has sworn to carry off Adalgisa by force. This news infuriates Norma, who swears that human blood will flow in torrents and strikes the sacred shield. When the Druids arrive, she jubilantly declares war on the Romans and announces that the war-god will have a sacrificial victim. At this moment, a Roman who was captured while trying to break into the temple is brought before Norma for judgement. It is Pollione. Not knowing who he is, the Druids demand that he should be their sacrificial victim, whereupon Norma takes the dagger from Oroveso to kill the Roman, but she falters and asks for time to interrogate the prisoner privately.

Left alone with Pollione, Norma offers to save his life if he leaves Gaul alone. When he refuses, she threatens that, with him, not only will his children and thousands of Romans perish but so, too, will Adalgisa. Pollione begs Norma to kill him alone, whereupon she summons the Druids and announces that the sacrificial victim will be a faithless priestess who has betrayed her god and her people. The Druids demand her name. "It is I," Norma reveals simply and orders the sacrificial pyre to be prepared. Turning to Pollione, she tells him that, in spite of everything, she still loves him, even to her death. Pollione recognises her greatness and, finding his love rekindled, asks for forgiveness. In vain, Oroveso and the Druids implore Norma to retract this self-accusation and rescind her judgement. Instead, Norma confesses all to her father, asking his pardon and begging that her children be spared. As Norma mounts the funeral pyre, Pollione joins her, both accepting their punishment for the sacrilege committed.

Romani's libretto for Norma is loosely based on the tragic play in verse *La Norma, ou l'infanticide* by Alexandre Soumet[24] (with Jules Lefèvre's limited collaboration), first performed at the Théâtre Royal de l'Odéon, Paris, on 25 April 1831. The five-act play scored a great popular success (the celebrated actress Mlle Georges achieved total identification with the title role) rather than a critical one. Even though the critics appreciated several moving and highly accomplished scenes, their enthusiasm was somewhat dampened by the many longueurs and the amalgamation of very familiar situations frequently found in other works.

Dramatically one of the most distinguished libretti of all time, *Norma* is inarguably Romani's best, a shade superior to that of *Anna Bolena*, which he had provided for Donizetti less than a year earlier. It is extremely well constructed and in poetic, flowing verse. The action is transplanted from very early Roman times to Gaul at around 50 BC, when the Druids[25] – the leading class and religious aristocracy of the Gauls – were about to revolt against their Roman oppressors. Bellini and Romani added the opening scene – the Druid assembly – but omitted the fifth act, in which Norma goes mad and, after murdering one of her children, jumps over a cliff with the other to their deaths. Thus, by substituting infanticide and suicide with renunciation followed by reconciliation and voluntary death, the protagonists became more human, more dignified. Furthermore, the new structure broke the hitherto rather stereotyped finale of the opera, where a brilliant coloratura aria was usually expected of the prima donna. They also incorporated the play's Gallic warriors Sigismar and Ségeste into the more moderate Oroveso, who became Norma's father, thereby intensifying the final scene.

Other changes in the libretto concern Norma's sons Clodomis and Agenor, who now have mute parts; the scene in the play in which they relate to their mother the dream that they shared of a sumptuous wedding in Rome is given to Pollione, who recounts his dream to Flavio. Also, as the action of the opera was transplanted to a pre-Christian period, the religious theme – which particularly concerns the Christian Clotilde and the two children – is discarded; Clotilde is now given a *comprimario* role. The most fundamental change, however, is the simplification of the motives behind the relationships between Norma, Pollione and Adalgisa. In order to make the libretto work and enable the composer to concentrate on the heightened emotions, Romani reduced the principals' relationships to physical love. But even though all the other characters in both opera and play are ancillary to the three principals, it is around Norma that inevitably everyone revolves.

Norma's predicament concerns her love for a man of a hostile race, for whom she has sacrificed everything without enduring returns, including her duty to her country. Her characterisation constitutes one of the greatest portraits in the history of opera.

It is to Romani's credit that he did not neglect the other characters. The faithless Pollione is not made into an utterly dishonourable person and Adalgisa, Norma's rival, does not behave in the superficially obvious way of a scheming minx. The Druids are presented as noble savages, which is historically true, as they were a barbarous people only at times during the Roman occupation. Moreover, Romani did not create the conventional hate-oriented world usually found in the *melodramma* of the period. Instead, and to great advantage, a world of understanding and forgiveness is brought to life – a violent drama is turned into a Classical tragedy. The ritual ceremonies and the declaration of war in the last scene are authentically captured in the opera. Soumet's play contains only a hint of Druid ceremony.

Schopenhauer declared that the libretto of *Norma* was unsurpassed in the dramatic handling of a tragic theme. The successful opera, it may be added, killed the play.

The opera begins with an overture (commencing in G minor, 4/4 time, *allegro maestoso e deciso*) in the nature of a dramatic orchestral prelude that succeeds in setting a martial atmosphere and that of tender, personal emotion. The first chords majestically create a mood of solemnity and proceed, intermingled with chromatic phrases, to suggest subtly the Druidic landscape. Norma's theme, melancholic yet somewhat gay, describes her love while other, subordinate themes intermittently represent her heroism, vindictiveness and defiance. The cellos and violas (divided), together with the horns, further suggest the rustle of leaves and the moonlight that falls on the Grove of Irminsul. The overture presents a foretaste rather than a description of the drama. Its purpose is not merely to evoke the appropriate atmosphere but to place the listener in the right frame of mind and thus in harmony with the personages of the drama, as well as in unison with the spirit of the *milieu* in which the action will take place – where bellicosity is at odds with the transcendental, religious world that is the cornerstone of the work. Even so, the overture can be performed separately from the opera without losing its significance.

Three explanatory arias introduce Oroveso, Pollione and Norma. Each aria is conventionally divided into two parts – one *legato* and expressive preceded by recitative, the other faster and exciting – and punctuated by choral utterances. Although this structure might appear to be somewhat cumbersome, it succeeds in differentiating the characters fully by putting into deliverance their interior lives (primarily through differences in recitative style) and also serving to build considerable dramatic tension.

Oroveso's solemn and authoritative invocation "Ite sul colle, o druidi" ("Hasten to the hills, oh Druids"), the first voice heard, is a semi-recitative type of cantilena, where vocal and instrumental melodies are practically the same, and this develops into an inflammatory address of grave dignity, "Dell'aura tua profetica" ("With your prophetic spirit"), which is given unalterable firmness by the chorus of priests swearing vengeance on the Romans.

There is notable suppleness and musical colour quite distinct from that of the Druids in the Roman Pollione's accompanied recitative "Svanir le voci" ("Their voices have ceased", in G minor, 4/4 time), in which he is given to trumpeting with arpeggio figures, telling Flavio of his past love for Norma. With rare naturalness, the recitative leads into Pollione's cavatina "Meco all'altar di Venere" ("Before the altar of Venus"), which, with a quick modulation from C major to E minor, is a magnificent example of the heroic cavatina, although it must be acknowledged that its great intensity is largely derived from Romani's words. Distant sounds of the approaching Druids build up the tension for the ensuing cabaletta, but here the composer descends into a banal tune with trite harmony. However, this vulgarity becomes a redeeming factor, as this is one aspect of Pollione's nature.

At first, even Bellini himself disliked the cabaletta, as well as the Pollione-Adalgisa duet, because the original singers were cold and inexpressive. However, he changed his opinion when, before long, he heard other singers perform the piece, particularly the tenor Domenico Reina, who sang the cabaletta with "so much fire…as if I had written a different one".

After a menacing orchestral introduction that ranges from *fortissimo* to *pianissimo*, the stage band joins the chorus intermittently in the march "Norma viene!" ("Norma is coming!"). The march (specifically the stage band) that also ends the scene is one of few moments in the opera that, to contemporary ears, sounds rather incongruously weak in its tinniness. This is a superficial assessment, however, as adverse opinions are biased by military music initiated by the French Revolution. In Bellini's time, this type of criticism would not have been voiced. What was valid then (and should be now) within the period of the drama is that, with awe-inspiring chords, the march admirably sets the Druidic atmosphere and builds anticipation for Norma's arrival.

Norma's unaccompanied recitative "Sediziose voci" ("Seditious voices") has authority and grandeur. With full accompaniment, Oroveso takes part and the chorus also interjects, thereby enhancing Norma's stature. Norma then replies, and hers is a more pertinent dramatic recitative – characteristic of an incendiary-like disposition – than those of Oroveso and Pollione. The whole is a successful example of Bellini's method of composition by capturing the correct atmosphere after declaiming his verses, resulting in a happy marriage between words and music.

Following a mere three measures of an enchanting, arpeggiated introduction, a solo *pianissimo* flute gives the melody of Norma's invocation to the moon, "Casta Diva". At once, one is transported into an atmosphere that represents the kingdom of the moon-goddess. (During this introduction, Norma cuts the sacred mistletoe with the sickle. The moon shines forth with all its light and, arms extending towards heaven, Norma begins.) This is one of the most beautiful melodies, perhaps the most beautiful, in all opera:

Andante sostenuto assai

The aria, with its oriental mysticism and great elegance, possesses a vigour and variety all its own, an uncanny combination of chastity and eroticism that aptly represents the person of Norma. Bellini's technique in composing for the voice is here fully employed as the means to the highest artistic end. The result is that "Casta Diva" contains nothing of an exhibitionistic nature but is a musical poem, complete in its dramatic justification and utterly memorable. The melody, with pleading eloquence (comprising a basically simple but heavily ornamented line), is given solely to the voice while the orchestra discreetly and subtly, but not inefficiently, accompanies Oroveso, and the chorus, echoing her prayer in *sotto voce*, adds further accompaniment, contributing another dimension to the character of Norma, whose florid vocalises at the end of the first verse float above the choral background, expressing in an almost wordless ecstasy the mystery of her divine nature.

The second verse, beginning "Tempra o Diva, de' cori ardenti" ("Oh goddess, restrain burning hearts") is slower but embellished, and the rite is concluded with a cadenza. Basically, the unusually long melody extends to 15 bars, achieving a climax near the end that intensifies the Romanticism of the music – a principle that cannot be traced before Bellini.

In "Casta Diva", Norma is the leader of her people, and in the ensuing cabaletta she is the highly troubled woman in love who is isolated from her people.[26] The composer then shifts from the entrancing F (or higher version G) *allegro* to the more earthly E-flat major, the stage band recommences the march and Norma orders the Druids to leave, promising them that the Romans will be killed, at the appropriate time. When the Druids demand that Proconsul Pollione must die first, Norma's feminine emotions are awakened in her soliloquy "Cadrà!... Punirlo io posso... Il cor non sa" ("He will fall!... I can punish him... My heart cannot").

The *allegro* in F (or G) is reinstated in Norma's cabaletta "Ah! bello a me ritorna" ("When will my beloved return"), which, if sung with insufficient dramatic expression – merely as a great vocal display – can sound rather banal and superficial and thus impair the unique effect of the preceding "Casta Diva". What the composer really intends here is a dramatic climax in which Norma expresses to herself alone her true inner feelings about her lover (the agitated descending chromatic runs convey her anxiety and yearning) as a counterpoint to the angry sentiment of the chorus, which is at the same moment demanding his death.

Adalgisa is introduced with a most impressive explanatory recitative "Sgombra è la sacra selva" ("The sacred wood is empty"), in B-flat major, suggesting the character's terrified anxiety. She comes alive in her invocation "Proteggimi o Dio!...perduta io son!" ("Protect me, oh God...for I am lost!"). In her duet with Pollione "Va, crudele" ("Go, cruel woman"), the force of the Roman's seduction is vividly conveyed in a semiquaver figure with restless appoggiaturas that is constantly reiterated by the orchestra. The duet moves through several well-contrasted phrases before reaching a triumphant conclusion in which Adalgisa swears to follow Pollione.

The scene then changes to Norma's dwelling. The orchestral introduction (in A minor, 4/4 time, *allegro agitato*) evokes the atmosphere of earlier times, before the Druids had been displaced by their Roman conquerors. The drama unfolds in a series of extremely well-constructed duets between Norma and Adalgisa and a trio with Pollione. In the touching melody "O, rimembranza" ("Oh, I remember"), Norma simply and nostalgically relives the emotions of being loved by Pollione, emotions that are aroused on hearing Adalgisa express her own new-found love. The dialogue is an almost unaccompanied conversational recitative, with the orchestra merely maintaining pitch. The cantilena "Io fui così rapita" ("I was thus transported") is taken up in turn by both women, each interrupting the other, thus stressing the irony of their discussion; neither as yet realises that they are describing the same lover.

The finale of the first act is a masterpiece of dramatic presentation. Norma's "Tremi tu?" ("Do you tremble?") is terrifying and full of contempt and despair, both attitudes accentuated by the florid nature of the music – cascades of brilliant dramatic declamation express her emotional vehemence. In the trio "O! di qual sei tu vittima" ("Oh, what a victim you are"), one of Bellini's most moving creations, musical originality is evident in the way in which it combines breathlessness and continuity with interspersed rests. The phrases pour forth scornfully like an organised hurricane, reaching a great climax in the frenetic unison cabaletta that brings the act to a close.

The orchestral introduction (in D minor, 4/4 time, *allegro assai moderato*) that opens the second act establishes Norma's hesitation and agony in melancholy chromatic phrases. Then the clear melody of "Dormono entrambi" ("They are both peacefully asleep"), at times a lament, exploits a wide range of emotions as Norma changes from extreme fury to tenderness, culminating in a most shattering climax with "Feriam... Ah, no! son miei figli" ("Strike... Ah, no! They are my sons").

The duet that concludes the scene is known by its middle section, "Mira, o Norma" ("You see Norma"):

Andante sostenuto assai

Mi _ ra, o Nor _ ma,   a' tuoi gi _ no _ chi ques _ ti

ca _ ri.............. tuoi par _ go _ let _ ti

This duet is one of the finest in all opera, its style controlled by an inner vitality that never falters, and like "Casta Diva" it has come to be a touchstone of the *bel canto* method of singing. Unusually beginning with the cabaletta "Deh! con te li prendi" ("For pity's sake, take them with you"), in the slow middle section the two voices at first alternate with the main melody and then continue to repeat it, in sixths and thirds, developing it to a striking double cadenza. The concluding *allegro* "Si fino all'ore estreme" ("For the rest of my life"), which also begins in sixths and thirds, finds the voices in canon ("Teco del fato") but then combining again in brilliant *staccato* scales to bring this memorable scene to a natural conclusion, when impending tragedy changes to hope. Throughout this duet, the accompaniment is largely restricted to a supporting role.

"Mira, o Norma", perfect in form, owes much of its construction and idea (although not its melody) to Rossini's duet "Ebben a te ferísci" in *Semiramide*. There is also a similarity in the emotions involved in each: reconciliation – of Norma and Adalgisa in one and of mother and son in the other. In both cases, the characters, finally united, pledge to face adversity together.

In the secret political meeting of the warrior Druids, the short chorus "Non parti" ("He has not left"), in F major, 4/4 time, *allegro maestoso*, accompanied by *pizzicato* strings, expresses somewhat sentimentally their grief at having to delay taking vengeance on the Romans. In the lyrical aria "Ah! del Tebro al giogo indegno" ("Ah! I too suffer under the Roman yoke"), which has ferocious undertones, Oroveso tries to hold back his warriors for just a little longer. (Historically, this aria forms a link between Rossini's *Mosè in Egitto* and Verdi's *Nabucco*.)

Bellini's melodic inspiration achieves the full weight of tragedy, akin to a lyrical *crescendo* of power, in the last scenes of the opera. The rousing *allegro feroce* chorus "Guerra! Le galliche selve" ("War! The forests of Gaul", *fortissimo e marcatissimo*), in which the Druids declare war on the Romans, has an electrifying quality that is accentuated by the constant drone of the bass. With its strongly pagan flavour, the music adds a Druidic touch of its own.

The drama then gathers momentum for the two climactic duets between Norma and Pollione, when they inevitably have to face each other. In the first, "In mia man" ("At last, you are in my hands"), they are alone together, whereupon all Norma's fury, anguish and vindictiveness, underlined with despair, find outlet in her condemnation of Pollione.

Andante sostenuto assai

The *diminuendo* on "Son io" ("It is I"), at Norma's confession that she is the guilty priestess, diminishes from the greatest intensity to the least and personifies in a single stroke the complete collapse of a human being who knows that death is the only absolution.

The second duet, "Qual cor tradisti" ("The heart that you have betrayed"), in G major, *largo*, takes place before the assembled Druids. With choral support, the music expresses Norma's submissiveness to and eventual ecstatic reunion with Pollione. It is the little sob on *fuggire* in "Da me fuggire" ("You would have run away from me") that touches the listener's heart.

Suddenly, Norma remembers her children first as hers and then, looking at Pollione, as "ours", while the Druids and Oroveso demand that she vindicate herself. This finale finds the composer rising, with sublime inspiration and absolute control of all the dramatic elements, to achieve the only acceptable solution without slackening the tension; he succeeds in making Norma's immolation scene more human and consequently more moving than Brünnhilde's in *Götterdämmerung*. Norma's pathetic plea to her father to spare the lives of her children, "Deh! non volerli vittime" ("Oh, do not make them victims"), leads into an ensemble in which Pollione and Oroveso express their contrasting reactions while the chorus implacably demands the inevitable sacrifice.

Norma's vocal line then reaches a transcendence that holds the scene together, her despair reflecting the realisation of her complete purification, her final phrases – "Padre, ah, Padre!" – rising to divine heights of eloquent poetry.

With *Norma*, the most ambitious of his operas, Bellini created a work of extraordinary lyrical and dramatic beauty. Through melody of a kind that had not been written before or has been since, the structure of the music expresses a tragedy that is virtually of epic scale. *Norma*'s merit, however, does not lie in the way in which it provides the singers with merely lyric arias of original melody and brilliant *fioriture*; in this work, there is a classic tranquillity of purpose, together with a profundity of dramatic power, and the *fioriture* are an integral part of the whole.

Bellini gave *Norma* his greatest attention and consideration. As the autograph score shows, it is full of revision. The published scores do not agree faithfully with the autograph. For instance, "Casta Diva" has been published in F major, yet the autograph is in G major, the transposition to F being made by Bellini for Pasta. The same applies to the two Norma-Adalgisa duets, which are transposed from F major to E major.

In the composition of *Norma*, Bellini employed considerable self-borrowing. The trio "Oh! di qual sei tu vittima", the final part of "Mira, o Norma" ("Si fino all'ore") and Oroveso's "Ah! del Tebro" all came from sketches that Bellini had composed earlier for the abortive *Ernani*. Meanwhile, the cabaletta 'Ah! bello a me ritorna" and the chorus "Non parti" were derived from the revised version of *Bianca e Fernando*, the first being an elaborated version of "Contenta appien quest'alma". The second part, "Sol promessa", of the Pollione-Adalgisa duet came from a section of Bellini's song "Bella Nice".

The role of Norma is generally considered to be the most difficult in the repertoire. Of course, there are others that are extremely difficult in their own ways, such as Leonora (*Il trovatore*), Fiordiligi (*Così fan tutte*), Lady Macbeth (*Macbeth*) and Santuzza (*Cavalleria rusticana*). The difference, however, is that, whereas the operas to which these heroines belong survive and even retain adequate integrity without a great interpreter, a protagonist who can fully meet the extraordinary demands of the role, *Norma* disintegrates in such a situation. The role – a prototype – calls for essentially a dramatic soprano with tremendous agility (and nature rarely produces such a voice), who possesses singing technique of the highest order. She must be able to sing cantilena without distorting Bellini's highly personal melodic line ("Casta Diva" is otherwise impossible). After managing the technical difficulties of the work, a suitable Norma must further have enough in reserve for sheer dramatic impact, and this must necessarily be accomplished through both the medium of her voice and her physical presence.

Lilli Lehmann, one of the great Normas of the past, always considered this role more demanding than the three Brünnhildes in *Der ring des Nibelungen* and also claimed that "Norma is ten times as exacting as Leonore [*Fidelio*]". It is therefore not surprising that, in the opera's 171 years, there have been very few truly great Normas.

Nor are the other proles in the opera easy. Adalgisa, although a shorter part and not as dramatically demanding as Norma, is technically just as exacting. It requires a dramatic coloratura mezzo-soprano but also a high register. Although the original Adalgisa (Giulia Grisi) was a soprano who later became a great Norma, she obviously had a wide range. (The distinction between soprano and mezzo as we know it today did not exist then.) A soprano Adalgisa without a mezzo range and quality (the *tessitura* of Adalgisa's music is not as high as Norma's) would be unable to provide the contrast in her many exchanges of identical phrases with Norma. Furthermore – and this is important for the credibility of the drama – Adalgisa must appear younger in character, rather inexperienced and passive, as opposed to the mature and positive Norma. Some of Grisi's successors as great Adalgisas include Marion Telva, Irini Minghini-Cattaneo, Ebe Stignani, Giulietta Simionato, Fedora Barbieri and Marilyn Horne.

The role of Pollione contains great difficulties, too. Heroic tenors with flexibility of voice and ability to sing cantilena are never plentiful. Donzelli's worthy successors have been few: Mario, Enrico Tamberlick and Giovanni Martinelli and, in more recent years, Mario Del Monaco, Franco

Corelli and Placido Domingo. Only Oroveso's bass role is somewhat easier to cast; a sumptuous voice able to invest the music with dignity and authority is more easily found amongst basses. Lablache, Ezio Pinza, Giulio Neri, Cesare Siepi and Nicola Zaccaria have been some of the accomplished exponents of this role.

The first great Normas were Giuditta Pasta (the creator of the role), Giulia Grisi (who gave up Adalgisa in favour of Norma) and Maria Malibran. Pasta had genius and the ability to transform natural faults into the rarest beauty. Grisi modelled her Norma on Pasta's, and although she did not have Pasta's genius, according to Chorley she was the better vocalist. With Pasta's virtual retirement in the late 1830s and Malibran's very early death in 1836, Grisi became the Norma of her day, even though discussion on her assumption of the role will always remain controversial; whereas Bellini thought her tame and of the wrong temperament, Chorley declared that there was a great deal of animal passion in her. Malibran, meanwhile, played the role in her own individual way. On one occasion, when some of Pasta's admirers said that Malibran was unable to play the role like their idol, she proved them wrong. On the following evening, she introduced into her performance much of Pasta's Classicism, but in subsequent performances her portrayal combined qualities of both of her previous interpretations, and she was acclaimed for this feat of versatility.

There then followed Teresa Tietjens and Lilli Lehmann. Tietjens gave the role great truth and intensity and Lehmann, who learned it from her mother (who herself had learned it from Wagner), sang and acted with fanatical dedication and artistic reverence. Writing of Lehmann's Norma in Vienna, Eduard Hanslick praised almost every aspect of her vocal art, from exquisite *portamento* to the finest intonation. He further described her pure and fluent coloratura as always "remaining noble, serious and an integral part of the whole". Lehmann is the only singer to have sung, on separate occasions, all three female roles in the opera: Clotilde, Adalgisa and Norma.

The greatest Normas of the 1920s and 1950s were Rosa Ponselle and Maria Callas, respectively. Ponselle gave the music Classicism through the splendour of her voice, and what she did not quite achieve in dramatic coloratura (her singing often lacked dramatic urgency) and *bravura* delivery she made up, to a degree, with beautiful cantilena. Callas, with her genius, her ability to give unique dramatic expression to the music and her versatility in improvising in her characterisation and even making use of vocal flaws (a particular case of interpreting beyond the technical demands of the music), like Pasta and Malibran, has been acclaimed as the last great Norma. Throughout the 17 years during which she sang this role, between 1948 and 1965, Maria Callas was indisputably the reigning Norma, an achievement not yet surpassed.

In spite of (or rather because of) its great difficulties, the role has had a constant appeal and remains a great temptation to many singers. The majority of them have failed, although some were very good singers indeed. The list is long, but mention must be made of some of those who, although having failed to win the crown of Norma, nevertheless came very close.

Pauline Viardot-Garcia, the highly talented younger sister of Maria Malibran, knew herself that somehow the part was beyond her. Jenny Lind, a light lyric soprano, was sadly miscast; when a German critic praised her characterisation as "maidenly", Chorley commented that this was "praise original, to say the least of it, when the well-known story of Norma is remembered". Rosa Raisa was defeated only by her indulgence in over-exhibiting the flexibility of her voice (although she gave spectacular performances), while Claudia Muzio failed through insufficient *bravura* delivery. Gina Cigna and Zinka Milanov were unreliable and unpredictable singers, and even at their best Norma eluded them. Despite Cigna's often exciting singing, she all but lacked Bellini's highly personal style, while Milanov seemed particularly unconcerned with the all-important recitatives.

In more recent times, and after Callas, several well-known and accomplished singers have tackled this formidable role. All of them tried to model their interpretation, more or less, on Callas's, but as yet none have succeeded. Notwithstanding Leyla Gencer's vocal competence and exciting temperament, with a touch of animal passion, her Norma bordered perilously on caricature of Callas's grand conception of the role. Meanwhile, Joan Sutherland's vocal brilliance stood her in good stead in this role, although this was not enough; she could not vocalise Bellini's music with consistent clarity, brightness or virtuosity in the way that she did for Donizetti's Lucia, for example. Moreover, her shortcoming in dramatic declamation (an essential requisite in *Norma*) proved too much of a handicap in an otherwise painstaking effort. Elena Souliotis's shortcomings, however, were different. She could be excitingly ferocious and always commanded attention, but she was often vocally undisciplined, despite possessing great natural musical talent. Her greatest sin, however, was that she sang Bellini's Classical/Romantic music as if it were *verismo* and Norma became more of a Santuzza.

Neither Christina Deutekom nor Beverly Sills, both light lyric sopranos, had enough voice for the role. Of the two, Sills was the more accomplished vocalist and the greater artist, with a highly developed coloratura technique, and yet, despite her involvement in the role, her performance remained a lightweight affair without grandeur. Meanwhile, both Grace Bumbry and Shirley Verrett sang Adalgisa first, and then, when they changed from mezzo-soprano to soprano, they also attempted Norma. Their characterisations were no more than promising, and their singing on the whole was only fairly accomplished, with Verrett weaker in coloratura and Bumbry in cantilena.

Montserrat Caballé, with a marvellous portamento and secure intonation, is the most accomplished *bel canto* singer since Callas. At best, her interpretation of Norma was refined and subtle but inconsistently so – admirable passages are followed by ordinary, inexpressive phrases. Consequently, complete success has eluded her, even though she is by and large the best Norma of her generation.

Meanwhile, one of the most important singers of her time, Renata Scotto – at first a lyric soprano, later lirico-spinto – has not yet found success as Norma, despite commendable effort, musical intelligence and considerable vocal technique; Norma, a larger-than-life character, is not within her scope.

Sylvia Sass, a gifted lirico-spinto, is the youngest of the considered contestants. An exciting singer with sensuous warmth and radiance and with respectable coloratura technique, she can also illuminate certain phrases memorably. However, her singing is inconsistent, too, and can become unruly and careless.

At best, the present-day Normas' contributions have served as little more than a means of keeping the opera in the repertoire.

11

Homeland Revisited (1832)

With *Norma* launched, Bellini then began a long holiday that was to take him to Naples and then to Sicily. He left Milan by coach on 5 January and, after a brief stop in Rome, arrived in Naples on the eleventh. Giuditta Turina also arrived on the same day, almost certainly accompanied by her brother, Gaetano. They may even have joined Bellini in Rome for the remainder of the journey.

It is unsurprising that Giuditta followed Bellini to Naples, as she loved him and wanted to be with him, but she also wanted to meet his friends there, as they were part of an important area of his life that was virtually unknown to her. Above all, she wanted to meet Florimo. We can only speculate about the explanation that she gave her husband for the journey; whether she said that it was that her health would improve in the warmer climate of southern Italy, or that she wanted to visit friends and see that part of the country, it really did not matter. As long as there was a plausible reason, the indifferent Ferdinando Turina would not stop his wife from going wherever she chose.

Florimo, who surprisingly reported little about this visit, said only that Bellini lodged at the conservatorio, in the same room in which he had lived while he was a student there, but he does not say whether or not this was from the day of arrival. Fraccaroli,[1] on the other hand, wrote that Bellini stayed with Giuditta in a hotel, where they occupied adjoining rooms, and that, when they arrived in Naples they were met by Florimo, Marsigli and two *maestrini* from the conservatorio.

Nothing is known of what Florimo and Giuditta felt on their first meeting. Their subsequent friendship, which was expressed after Giuditta had fallen out with Bellini and which blossomed after Bellini's death, suggests that they liked each other; only their rivalry for Bellini's love had been a barrier between them.

Bellini was very happy to be back in Naples with his friends from the conservatorio, and especially Florimo, with whom his relationship was again in perfect harmony; whatever coolness there had been in the past between them because of Giuditta was now forgotten in the joy of reunion.

Much had happened in the four years since Bellini had left Naples. Not only had he established himself as an operatic composer but he had also become a celebrity. However, he conducted himself with humility and showed no conceit. At the conservatorio, he was greeted enthusiastically by both teachers and students, to whom he talked endlessly on his operas. He also paid special homage to Zingarelli, visiting him at the conservatorio twice a day, and it was to him, his dear teacher, that he dedicated his greatest work, *Norma*. Zingarelli was deeply moved by this gesture from one of his most beloved students. Their cordial relationship is well described by Florimo.[2]

"I am no longer under any obligations whatsoever towards you, my dear maestro," Bellini jokingly said to Zingarelli, "and for nothing except for your severities and, allow me to say, for the crusty way in which you treated me. And I remember well that unhappy day when you told me that I wasn't born for music! Well," Bellini said, becoming serious, "I ask your pardon if the unruliness of my youthful nature prevented me from showing my gratitude for so much kind attention on your part, but believe me, my gratitude towards you will be everlasting. I acknowledge you as being responsible for what little I know. Moreover, I'm sure that the fact of having been your pupil has been more helpful to me amongst foreigners than my slight talent and my scant worth."

Zingarelli, moved by what Bellini said and at a total loss for words, got up and embraced him affectionately.

The students of the conservatorio paid their homage to Bellini in a different way, as both Florimo and Fraccaroli describe. On one evening when Bellini was at the conservatorio, talking lengthily after supper, he decided to spend the night there as it was rather late – no doubt at the insistence of Florimo and his other friends – and slept in Florimo's room. In the morning, when the students found out, they decorated the door with flowers. In the middle of these, a large ribbon displayed the words, "Love, honour, virtue, glory – all are to be found in Bellini."

According to a letter written on 18 January by a certain Giovanni[3] to his uncle in Catania, Bellini could well have continued to stay at the conservatorio. This charming letter tells us something of Bellini's disposition during his stay in Naples:

> I cannot refrain from telling you of two meetings – one with Bellini and one with Walter Scott – as you understand and appreciate well-earned merit...
>
> The Sicilian or, rather, the Catanese Swan is staying at a college of music. This fact, seemingly of small importance, reveals a man who, after acquiring such fame in Europe, disdains any self-importance or display and goes to live in that very place which saw the birth of that brilliant career that he has pursued in so short a time. He is familiar with his old friends and respectful towards his masters. Also, he prefers to be the object of everyone's affection rather than an object of respect and veneration...
>
> Vincenzo didn't truly recognise me when I was paying my compliments, but as soon as he realised who I was, he threw himself into my arms, hugged me tight and kissed me several times, saying, "My dear Giovanni, is it really you?" I was both surprised and delighted, dear uncle, at so much friendliness and affection, which is uncommon in men whose merits have raised them so high. We spent a couple of very happy hours together. From our long conversation, it was apparent how much gratitude this divine genius still retains for his homeland, which he will see again in March or April at the latest...
>
> But the letter is finished and Walter Scott hasn't come into it. Of this famous novelist and historian, I will only say that he arrived in Naples on 1 January and has allowed himself to be seen only once, at the Teatro dei Fiorentini. Your nephew will describe everything for you later, dear uncle.

The promised letter about Sir Walter Scott is not extant, although it is known that Scott did visit Naples during this time and was enthusiastically received. Bellini may well have met him.

There is very little information about Giuditta's stay in Naples. Fraccaroli says that she was very upset on the night that Bellini slept at the conservatorio and waited up for him long into the night. However, she accompanied him to the San Carlo on 5 February, when a performance of *I*

Capuleti e i Montecchi took place in the presence of Ferdinand II (who had succeeded Francesco I in 1830) and his brother, the Prince of Capua. The performance was a success and the *Giornale delle Due Sicilie* described the occasion two days later: "The performance was even more interesting due to the knowledge that the famous composer of this music, Signor Bellini, was in Naples and that in fact he too was in the audience. The aria by Signora De Begnis (Romeo) and the first duet of the same singer with Signorina Boccabadati (Giulietta) was honoured by receiving the applause of the maestro, which was echoed by that of the public. During the performance, the opera so occupied everyone's attention that the composer's presence was almost forgotten. But as soon as the performance was over, the attention and enthusiasm was directed towards him."

On this occasion, Bellini sat in a box with Giuditta and Florimo. There is no doubt that he tried hard to convince Florimo that his affair with Giuditta was in no way diminishing their friendship. It seems that, of the three of them, it was Florimo who needed the most reassurance, and Bellini possibly neglected Giuditta somewhat because of this. He may have also quarrelled with her. In a later letter to Florimo from Paris,[4] dated 30 November 1834, Bellini recalls his annoyance at what he considered Giuditta's coquettish behaviour in Naples with an elderly gentleman. This was obviously no more than a lovers' tiff, and Giuditta may well have flirted in order to attract more attention from Bellini.

Giuditta had also been ill with her usual gynaecological complaint, which began towards the end of January, as she had to make a special effort to attend the performance of *I Capuleti* on 5 February. "Poor Giuditta," Bellini wrote to Giuditta Pasta[5] on 21 February, "has been in bed for more than 20 days, owing to pains she has suffered, but for two days now she has been able to go out a little in a carriage."

Her illness may have been – in part, at least – the cause of Bellini's delay in departing for Sicily, although when he wrote to his uncle Ferlito[6] on 3 February he gave his impending audience with the royal family as the reason for the delay. In fact, he was received in private audience with the Queen Mother, Isabella of Spain, on 25 February, by which time Giuditta had largely recovered. However, she did not accompany him to Sicily, as it would have been unwise for him to take his mistress, a married woman, to see his parents in Catania. Consequently, Giuditta accepted the decision and resigned herself to wait for his return.

It was different for Florimo. Whatever the difficulties in leaving the archives of the conservatorio, he allowed himself to be persuaded, and on 25 February he left with Bellini for Messina. They arrived on the morning of 27 February and were greeted by Bellini's father and other members of the family.

On the evening of Bellini's arrival in Messina, *Il pirata* was performed at the local theatre, the Munizione. Musicians young and old wanted to talk to the celebrated composer of *La sonnambula* and *Norma*. In an article included in *Omaggio a Bellini*, published in 1901, on the occasion of the 100th anniversary of Bellini's birth, Arenaprimo writes much about the visit. (This account is particularly interesting, as most other records of this period were destroyed during the 1908 earthquake.) He writes, "These Romantic artists were also followers of Bellini, admirers of that new school inspired by grief and sustained by that feeling which alone is capable of kindling hope, of strengthening faith in great measure and of reviving fearlessness. Well, those young men of talent, who were so patriotic, have embraced it ever since our theatre was shaken by the notes of *Il pirata*, that giant of musical reform and expression of Italy's grief."

The coach journey to Catania took almost three days. The road was poor and the weather stormy. One night was spent *en route* at Acireale. Here, it was already known that Bellini was on his way to Catania and a reception was arranged. Most of the population turned up to greet him and an orchestra serenaded him with pieces from his operas. His arrival in Catania on 3 March was announced by a band playing his music, and among the huge crowd that welcomed him at the Porta d'Aci[7] were members of the council that had given him the grant to study in Naples, university professors and most of the distinguished citizens of Catania.

Among the various celebrations given in Bellini's honour was a memorable evening at the Teatro Comunale. The correspondent of the Neapolitan *Giornale delle Due Sicilie* wrote:

> Bellini is in Catania, among his fellow citizens and in the bosom of his family. It's easy to imagine the effect of the return to the town of a man who is now so different from the one who left it, a man who, apart from being one of the seven wonders of the world of his time, has in such a short time achieved, if not eclipsed, the fame of the early masters or the delectable art that he practises... Catania, too, became celebrated because of Bellini's fame and, in order to show its affection for him, had cast a medal in his honour...

On the following evening, when some excerpts from *Il pirata* and *La Straniera* were performed, the enthusiasm of the Catanese knew no bounds and they embarrassed Bellini by making him take a curtain call amidst deafening applause. Furthermore, a shower of pamphlets praising him were scattered throughout the theatre.

After a very happy month in Catania, Bellini and Florimo left for Palermo on 5 April, planning to stay there until the 18th, when they would sail for Naples in time for Easter. The only reason for Bellini wanting to spend Easter there and not with his family, was that Giuditta had been alone for a long time.

Palermo, too, gave Bellini a royal welcome. On 11 April, he was honoured by a special performance of *I Capuleti e i Montecchi* at the Teatro Carolino and, on the 15th, a banquet that Florimo described in a letter to Angelica Giuffrida[8] in Catania: "The people of Palermo can't do enough to honour Bellini. The Accademia Filarmonica staged an excellent evening performance at which a great deal of his music[9] was played, as well as a cantata that was expressly written to celebrate the visit of the young Catanese maestro… Indeed, Bellini deserves all the homage that is paid to him… Sicily gave him evident proof of its affection and the esteem that it has for his true and splendid talent."

Due to bad weather, Bellini and Florimo had to postpone their journey to Naples for a few days, which they spent happily in Palermo. There Bellini made several new friends, in particular Filippo Santocanale, a young Palermian lawyer, who was introduced to him by Giuffrida. Santocanale, probably the last great friend that Bellini made, was extremely hospitable to him and Florimo during their stay.

While at Palermo, Bellini also visited a childhood friend, the charming Marietta Politi, for whom it has been supposed he wrote the song "La farfalletta" many years earlier in Catania. Marietta came to live in Palermo when she married. Agostino Gallo,[10] writing in 1846 about Bellini's visit to Palermo, mentions this meeting: "When Bellini reached Palermo in 1832, he wanted to see Marietta again, after so many years. He accompanied her on the piano in several pieces that she chose from his scores and he corrected some errors that had crept into them. 'I keep these sheets of music,' Marietta later said, 'for they are a precious and eternal memory of that angel of music whose beloved likeness is always before my eyes in my room.'"

Before Bellini left Palermo, his portrait was painted by Giuseppe Patania[11] and his bust sculpted by Giuseppe Pollet, one of the painter's students.

The journey on to Naples was a pleasant one, as the weather had improved, and Bellini and Florimo arrived there on 25 April. It is most unlikely that Giuditta had left Naples during Bellini's absence – she had no expectation that his stay would be so long in Sicily and would no doubt have rather stayed in a warm climate to recuperate from her recent illness and wait for the man she loved, however lonely she may have been.

The few days that Bellini spent in Naples on his return were with Giuditta. He may have showed her around the city, something he could hardly have found time to do when they had first arrived. They were still in Naples on 28 April, when Bellini wrote two letters. One was to his new friend Santocanale,[12] in Palermo, thanking him for his hospitality and friendship and announcing that he had been offered a contract to write an opera for Pasta to be performed during the carnival season in Venice. In his other letter, to Pasta's husband,[13] Bellini elaborated on this:

Lanari has handed to me the contract for an opera for the carnival season in Venice. He also gave me a short letter from you in which you tell me that, as Lanari had offered me what I expected, you were sure that I would accept the contract without any problem. Rest assured that I will accept the commission. I've already written to Lanari telling him so and telling him that we'll make all the necessary adjustments in accordance with what the splendid Giuditta [Pasta] requires, but for the other singers I won't change a single note.

When I return to Milan, at the end of May at the latest, we shall have further and longer discussions. I also think that I'll spend a few months by Lake Como with Giuditta Turina... Therefore, as I will be very near you, we can then talk and arrange everything, and I hope to be able to begin my work there, too. I'm up to date with all the theatrical news of Milan. My *Norma* couldn't fail to meet with success there, as it is being interpreted by the encyclopaedic angel [Pasta]. That's enough for now; when I start talking about that divine woman, I can't find suitable words enough to express what my heart feels. Give her my deepest regards, and also mother Rachele, Clelia [Pasta's daughter] and all my friends.

Please accept my best wishes and my...sincere thanks for your efforts in arranging this contract, which is so much to my liking, as I shall have to write for...Giuditta. In a word, I am content. Goodbye.

The visit to Sicily and Naples was a most satisfying experience for Bellini. His happiness in seeing his family and friends again and being reunited with Florimo was so great that it often moved him to tears. Henceforth, letters to Florimo reappear, or perhaps Florimo no longer withheld them. To be precise, these letters became very frequent from the time that Bellini went to London and his affair with Giuditta was over.

Only one person in Naples seems to have been forgotten by Bellini during his visit: Maddalena Fumaroli. A few years later, after her premature death, Fraccaroli claimed (without any evidence) that, while Bellini was in Naples, Florimo suggested several times that he should pay a visit to Maddalena. Apparently, Bellini kept putting off such a visit on the grounds that it would have been unfair to Giuditta. Neither Florimo nor Bellini ever wrote anything about this.

On 30 April, Bellini and Giuditta arrived in Rome on their way back to Milan. Very little is known about Bellini's stay in Rome, apart from the fact that he attended a performance of *La Straniera* on 1 May and that he received a cross[14] from Pope Gregory XVI.

Another event is also supposed to have taken place in Rome. It has been claimed that Bellini composed an opera with the title of *Il fu ed il sara* (*The past and the present*), which was supposedly performed privately in Rome. However, there is no reference to such a work in any of his letters or any letters concerning him. *Il fu ed il sara* is mentioned by Hugo Riemann in *Der Geschichte der Musik seit Beethoven (1800-1900)* (Berlin-Stuttgart, 1901) and by Guido Adler in *Handbuch der Musikgeschichte* (Berlin, 1930). The opera is also mentioned in the fifth edition (1954) of Grove's *Dictionary of Music and Musicians* (but omitted from the sixth edition [1981]) and in a few other publications that transfer the information from Grove, whose source was Riemann. All these publications merely attribute *Il fu ed il sara* to Bellini, stating that the librettist is unknown and that it was only privately performed in Rome in 1832. Almost certainly, this information came from Alberto Cametti's *Bellini a Roma*, published in 1900, in which the author also mentions the librettist:

Among the manuscripts of the Roman operatic poet Jacopo Ferretti, there is preserved a one-act opera, which is undated and is called *Il fu ed il sara*, to be performed to the music of Maestro Vincenzo Bellini at the propitious marriage of Signor Camillo Giuliani, member of the Arcadian Academy in Rome, to Signora Carolina Persiani.

The characters of the opera are described as follows: the ghost of the past – Collini, a leading tenor; Plenty – Teresa Ferretti, leading lady; chorus of ancestors; and chorus of descendants. The work is dedicated to Vincenzo de Liberi, member of the Arcadian Academy and a Tiberian, his "old friend and master", concerning whom he says, "I dedicate this hastily written opera to you, who taught me how to write operas."

No music for this opera exists. Furthermore, the wedding of Giuliani and Persiani, for which occasion the opera was supposedly written, took place on 18 February 1832. (Bellini did, indeed, pass through Rome on his way to Naples but could hardly have stayed there more than a day, as he left Milan by coach on 5 January and arrived in Naples on the eleventh.) Although the alleged opera – described as "a one-act cantata scenica" – is short, it is beyond any reasonable assumption that Bellini, after the fatiguing experience of composing *Norma*, would have composed anything during his very brief stop in Rome. He would have had time for a very short work during his 21-day stay in Rome on his way back, but that was in May and the wedding had already taken place some three months earlier.

The possibility of a hoax on Ferretti's part cannot be entirely ruled out. He may also have hoped that Bellini would write the opera, as he was at the time the most celebrated composer in Italy. What may have happened – and this is also the opinion of Pastura, who, after extensive research, has not been able to trace anything on *Il fu ed il sara* – is that existing Bellini music was set to Ferretti's libretto without the consent or even the knowledge of the composer.

Bellini left Rome for Florence on around 20 May, and his name does not appear in any passenger manifest to or from Florence, a fact that would indicate that Giuditta Turina was still with him and that they travelled by private coach. On 23 May, he attended a performance of *La sonnambula* at the Teatro della Pergola. It was not a success, according to the review that appeared in the *Giornale di Commercio*, the only paper in Florence at the time that dealt with musical criticism. The reviewer found the plot of the opera naïve and improbable and the composer a sentimentalist. He even considered much of the music to be cold and trivial, in spite of the good performances of the singers. Bellini did not like the performance that he attended (a different one from the one reviewed), although for other reasons. On 24 May, he wrote to Ricordi,[15] "Yesterday evening, I heard *La sonnambula* performed and it was quite unrecognisable. Everything was taken at breakneck speed; Carradori was colder than ice itself; the chorus screeched as though possessed by devils; the tenor Duprez performed the aria in act two very well, as did Carradori, partly, in the cavatina of act one, but the rest was frightful! The courteous Florentine audience wanted to…honour me with its applause, as they knew that I was in the theatre, so I was obliged to show myself at least twice from the box in which I was sitting in order to thank them."

A few days later, Bellini reached Milan but soon went to Moltrasio for most of June. On 1 July, he wrote to Santocanale in Palermo,[16] "I'm in Milan for the moment…trying to find a good subject for my new opera for Venice. In August, I shall go to Bergamo for the production of my *Norma* with Pasta, but I won't be leaving Milan for about a fortnight. I have no other news to tell you."

Even though *Norma* had eventually been successful in Milan, Bellini felt that it was in Bergamo that it was truly understood and appreciated. Writing to Romani[17] on 2 August, he expressed his great joy at *Norma*'s overwhelming success:

> Everyone wants to know me and congratulate me, and yet we're in Donizetti's home town. Our *Norma* is decidedly a great success. If you heard how it's performed in Bergamo, you'd almost think that it was a new work. It seems like another opera even to me and it has a marvellous effect upon me… Giuditta Pasta is in good form and voice and declaims and sings in such a way that everyone is moved. She even moves me. In fact, I wept [with] the emotions I felt in my soul. I wanted you near me so that I could share these emotions with you, my good adviser and collaborator, because you alone understand me. My glory is intrinsic to yours.
>
> The verses were appreciated so much that if you'd been here [the audience] would have called you up onto the stage. They found the poetry tragic and sublime. Knowing you, you wouldn't have wanted

to appear, but they would have dragged you on to the stage by force...
You would have been satisfied with our *Norma* and your Bellini, who
owes you so much gratitude and thanks you with great affection in
return. PS: Mayr sends you his affectionate greetings. He has
embraced and kissed me...and to think we're in Bergamo!

The *Gazzetta privilegiata di Milano* also praised *Norma*, on 5 September in
an article written by the same critic who had been quite unfavourably
disposed towards the opera and Bellini at the time of the Milan performances:

> According to what's being said generally and some of the Milan
> newspapers, we know enough to declare that *Norma* [at Bergamo]
> has given the greatest pleasure, in the same way that it has given
> increasing pleasure to us; to the intelligent, this opera seems extremely
> logical. There were even those who wrote that *Norma* is our splendid
> maestro's masterpiece.
>
> As for Pasta, who plays the leading part, there's nothing left to add
> to what has already been said and repeated from the lands of fiery
> heat to the icy Triones! She is the greatest of all singing artists. Taccani
> [Adalgisa] and Reina [Pollione] are also applauded at the side of the
> greater star...
>
> In any event, remaining faithful to our creed of impartiality, we are
> under the obligation of announcing the new triumph of a musical
> work the true worth of which, unfortunately for us, we have been
> unable to appraise fully before.

Giuditta Turina, who had stayed at Bergamo for only a short time, returned
shortly to Casalbuttano, where Bellini joined her sometime around 10
September. A week later, he returned to Milan, anxious to decide with
Romani on the libretto for his forthcoming opera, which was scheduled for
production at La Fenice on 20 February 1833.

12

Venetian Recriminations – *Beatrice di Tenda* and the breach with Felice Romani (1832-33)

After signing the contract with Lanari to provide a new opera for La Fenice, Bellini tried for almost two months to decide with Romani on a subject for the libretto. Romani was the leading Italian librettist and in great demand, despite a reputation of often failing to deliver libretti on time. For the 1833 season, he was engaged to write the libretti of *Caterina di Guisa* (La Scala, 14 February) for Carlo Coccia, of *Il segreto* (Teatro Ducale, Parma, 26 February) for Luigi Masocchi, of *Il conte di Essex* (La Scala, 10 March) for Mercadante and of *Parisina* (Teatro della Pergola, Florence, 17 March) for Donizetti.

In view of their long collaboration and close friendship, Bellini expected preferential treatment from Romani, and so far he had more or less got it. At times, it had been hectic – for example, the composition of *Zaira* at Parma, with its disastrous results – so on this occasion he tried hard to settle the matter in good time. And yet, when Bellini returned to Milan in September, they could not reach a decision; Romani was expecting dramas to reach him from Paris, so they had to wait. One thing was decided, however: the story chosen would have to be built around Pasta, allowing her the opportunity to express her particular talents to the greatest advantage.

By 24 September, the dramas from Paris had arrived and the choice fell on Alexandre Dumas' play *Christine, ou Stockholm, Fontainebleau et Rome*, a typical Romantic play that had been successfully produced at the Théâtre de l'Odéon, Paris, on 30 March 1830, with Mlle George in the title role. The subject of this rather long play – in five acts, with a prologue and an epilogue and a cast of 22 – was Queen Christina of Sweden. Romani faced a laborious problem of condensation, but once they had agreed on the subject, he promised to get on with the libretto, half of which he would give to Bellini in October and the remainder in November.

Perhaps Bellini's feelings towards the play were somewhat lukewarm, but he did approve it. Writing to Santocanale[1] on 6 October, he announced the title of his new opera as *Cristina, regina di Svezia*. "It seems interesting to me," Bellini said, "and I hope good will come of it, as it is in the hands of Romani, my fine and splendid poet. On Monday, I hope to write the first note of my new opera."

However, Romani failed to deliver the first act of *Cristina* in October as agreed, and by the beginning of November the subject had been dropped in favour of another.

On 15 September in the previous year, La Scala had inaugurated its autumn season with the first performance in Milan of Mercadante's *Caritea, regina di Spagna*, while the ballet *Beatrice di Tenda*, choreographed by Antonio Monticini, was also performed on the same evening. The scenario of the ballet (with certain choreographic licence) was based on the tragedy of the historical Beatrice di Lascari (1370-1418) and it was such a great success that it was performed with every other opera that followed during the next six weeks.

One evening, shortly after 6 October, Bellini and Giuditta Pasta saw the ballet, which was then performed with Mercadante's *Ismalia, ossia morte ed amore*. They were both greatly impressed and Bellini saw in the ballet the kind of subject that could really inspire him. Its fast action and emotional impact were superior to those in *Cristina*. Pasta was also taken by what the principal character offered. She was reminded of Carlo Coccia's *Maria Stuarda* and Donizetti's *Anna Bolena*, in which she had been so successful, and their closing scenes resembled that of the ballet.

Encouraged by Pasta's enthusiasm, Bellini embarked on the task of persuading Romani to change the subject of their libretto to that of *Beatrice*. At first, Romani disagreed and, in fact, used the very same arguments against the change. For artistic reasons, he pointed out (because the final scene of *Beatrice* was similar to that of *Anna Bolena* and would be sung, again, by Pasta), it could form a dangerous parallel that could dull public appeal. Bellini, however, was not convinced. Even Romani's hint that there would be comparisons between Bellini and Donizetti (and Donizetti had, after all, done it first) could not dissuade him. Once his imagination was fired, he would let nothing stand in his way, and he certainly knew how to persuade Romani, who had more than once in their fruitful collaboration given in to the "irresistible Sicilian", as he had called him. This time, too, he concurred, as Bellini assured him, "I'm confident that a man of your great abilities will be able to change the final scene so that it doesn't appear to be similar to that of *Anna Bolena*."

By 3 November, the matter was settled and Bellini wrote to Pasta[2] of his final arrangements:

> You'll be amazed [and] say I'm mad, but it's now a fact and I hope that you'll be happy with the result: the story has been changed and we will now write *Beatrice di Tenda*. I had some difficulty in persuading Romani but I succeeded, and for well-founded reasons.
>
> Knowing that the story pleases you (as you told me that evening when we saw the ballet version of it) and finding out that the final scene is so congenial to you, on account of the scope that it offers to an artist of your calibre, and the fact that the whole story is so interesting makes me very happy. Romani will arrange it so that no situation recalls *Anna Bolena*. He shows goodwill, but I want him to show it even more positively by finishing the first act quickly.

Romani may have capitulated, but he did so reluctantly, for he did nothing about preparing the libretto for *Beatrice di Tenda*. The fact that Bellini practically forced him to change the subject gave him sufficient excuse for other more pressing undertakings to take precedence. Also, the idea that he would have to discard any verses that he had already written for *Cristina di Svezia*[3] did not exactly incite him to work on the new subject.

The season at La Fenice was to begin with *Norma*, and Bellini left for Venice with Pasta about 5 December in time to start rehearsals on 10 December. The other singers – Anna Del Serre, Alberico Curioni and Federico Crespi – were the same ones for whom Bellini was writing his new opera. However, these singers proved to be as inferior as Bellini had feared, and the fact that Romani had not yet produced any verses for *Beatrice* completely unnerved him. In desperation, Bellini went to Lanari, who immediately lodged a protest against Romani with the Governor of Venice. The protest was then passed on to the Governor of Milan, with the result that Romani was summoned to the police headquarters there. The proud Romani, a free citizen of Piedmont, tolerated the affront of being sent for by the ruling Austrian authorities, but only with difficulty. He defended himself, arguing that Bellini had changed the subject at the eleventh hour and that he himself had additional obligations to the Milanese and other Italian theatres.

Enraged after this humiliation, Romani arrived in Venice at the beginning of January and immediately demanded an explanation from Bellini, who now was keeping a low profile, trying together with Lanari to be very friendly while evading any justification of their action. In the end, Bellini's affectionate nature succeeded in pacifying Romani. The matter was settled and the poet promised to write the expected libretto. However, he did not stay in Bellini's lodgings, as he always had done in the past whenever they had had to work together away from Milan. Moreover, he was so slow in his work that, by 11 January, he had produced verses only for Beatrice's cavatina and a duet between Agnese and Orombello. On 27 January, Bellini wrote to Ricordi[4] of his disconsolate hope…

> …to begin the finale of act one tomorrow, if Romani gives it to me; but how my opera will be able to go on, God only knows. What a frightful company! In the meantime, Romani has given me some fine verses. I'm now engaged at my usual task of composing. If the music isn't intrinsically bad, it could take on a positive nature with another company. Of course, all my hopes rest with Pasta, who is still safe in the midst of this shipwreck. In act one, there is a romance, a cavatina, a great duet with a bass and a finale for her, and all these depend on her. In act two, there is the judgement scene and her great final scene. It has these pieces, and if I don't do them too badly, I hope I shall be saved when they appear on the stage.

The finale of the first act *was* delivered, although long after the composer had hoped. Consequently, Bellini was unable to finish the first act until 17 February, thus forcing the management of La Fenice to postpone the premiere from 20 February to 6 March and hope for the best. The tension brought Bellini close to breaking point. More than ever before, the failure of *Zaira* (which had, after all, been caused by less serious circumstances) must have been preying on his mind. Furthermore, he was hurt by Romani's behaviour, which was causing their hitherto excellent relationship to deteriorate badly.

In a letter to Santocanale[5] dated 17 February, Bellini's morale is very low: "I'm glad that your health is good and that of your friends. Mine is good, too, but my spirits are greatly afflicted because that lazy poet of mine has put me in such a difficult situation that I despair of finishing the new opera. There are only 15 days left before it goes onstage, and I still have the entire second act to do! Oh, what a disaster I foresee!"

As if all these troubles weren't enough, an additional turmoil of a

personal nature was playing havoc with Bellini's nerves at this time. A burst
of jealous fury directed against Giuditta Turina made him almost irrational
in his demands of her. Giuditta related this to Florimo[6] later, on 17 February
1834, when Bellini was in Paris, by which time her affair with him was over:

> Last year, when Bellini was in Venice, there was a zealot, such as one
> always finds, who told him that a certain man was paying court to me
> and that he had once stayed in my house until two in the morning. I
> assured Bellini that [this allegation] was false, and I have 1,000
> witnesses able to attest to this. He treated me very badly when I
> reached Venice, but it wasn't long before we were on very good terms
> again. You must know that last year my husband received an
> anonymous letter telling him of our relationship and he didn't want
> me to go to Venice. Bellini wanted it, though, and so I insisted until I
> wrested permission from my husband. That was a bad move and the
> beginning, perhaps, of the storm that burst in May. But what I
> wouldn't do for Bellini!

It was Bellini's acute anxiety over *Beatrice* that made him insist on having
Giuditta near him; she could understand and sympathise with him at a time
when he was under great stress. He probably did accept Giuditta's
explanations but used his alleged jealousy to insist, unwisely and
unreasonably, on her presence in Venice, despite the difficulties that she had
with her husband.

Beatrice was eventually finished at the end of February or the beginning of
March. According to Branca,[7] Bellini discarded several verses of the libretto,
mainly from the second act, including much from a scene between Beatrice
and Agnese, as well as a solo for Beatrice. The exhausted Romani, who was
obviously trying hard to finish the libretto, acquiesced. On the last page,
however, he expressed his feelings in a note that appeared after the final verse:
"Here is the finale for you. It took a Bellini to go on swearing until the end
and then to laugh. Gather together all the writings you have and send them
to me early tomorrow morning, because the copyist is coming at ten o'clock."

There was a further complication when rehearsals began. The bass
Federico Crespi was completely inadequate in the important role of Filippo.
Bellini had just about tolerated him in the role of Oroveso in *Norma* that
season at La Fenice, but now it was clear that he would do so no longer. The

Venetian audience had had enough of Crespi's deficiencies, and the risk of him singing in *Beatrice di Tenda* was too great. A few days before the premiere, at Bellini's insistence, Orazio Cartagenova was substituted, and this had further repercussions. As it was necessary for Bellini to adapt at least three pieces in the opera to suit Cartagenova's voice and technique, once again the management of the theatre was forced to postpone the premiere, this time to 16 March. The Venetians' patience was wearing thin. The current season had begun with *Norma* and continued with Rossini's *Otello* and Persiani's *Eufemio da Messina*, which failed after only one performance. Rossini's *Tancredi* replaced *Beatrice* in the February postponement, but circumstances necessitated more performances of *Norma*, *Otello* and *Tancredi* without anything new being offered. The redeeming factor was the presence of Pasta, who gave an enormous number of performances in all three operas. To cover the latest postponement of *Beatrice*, Donizetti's *L'elisir d'amore* was staged, but it met with an unfavourable reception.

The season would end on 24 March, and as the new opera was to have its premiere on as late as 16 March, grumbles began to be heard against the management of La Fenice and against Bellini. The press also launched an attack. On 13 March, the *Gazzetta privilegiata di Venezia* published an article in the form of a letter dated 6 March, the date of the second postponement of *Beatrice*. This letter was fictitiously signed "AB, a subscriber from Fonzaso", a remote little village, but it was actually written by Locatelli, the editor of the paper, who also published his answer in the same issue. The subscriber enquired with naïve trepidation about the new Bellini opera: "A new opera is required at La Fenice every year, written by a celebrity. This is taken for granted. The carnival, however, is to start and end with alternate performances of some old operas. These will be good rather than very good, which is no laughing matter in Venice. But, good God, when will the new opera be heard? It's at this point that my mind clouds over. We're in Lent – the first and second weeks have gone by, the third is beginning and still the new opera hasn't appeared! We complain, grumble and make a fuss, but we're up against a brick wall. The new opera isn't yet being sung and won't be performed until the last few days of the season."

In answering his own letter, Locatelli pretended to take Lanari's and Bellini's side. With assumed excessive politeness, he recalled delays of new operas during previous seasons and pointed out the few performances that these operas had received when they eventually reached the stage. *I Capuleti* in 1830 had been given five or six times, *Benjowski* in 1831 four or five and *Ivanhoe* in 1832 three or four.[8] He concluded:

> Delays aren't really unusual but, judging by the law of reduction in past performances, *Beatrice* will probably be given two or three times. Of course, one can never be sure about everything. *Beatrice* may be postponed until next year so that Bellini will have time to polish it. After all, one year isn't too long a period in which to compose an opera like *Beatrice*, which certainly is unlike any other opera. Besides, Bellini has promised to take *Beatrice* to London. What is more natural, therefore, than that the composer should wish his opera to be as perfect as possible when it crosses the English Channel? Here, it will merely be given a *bon voyage* or, we could say, a passport.

These publications, appearing just three days before the premiere of *Beatrice*, could only incite public hostility. Moreover, a rumour that Bellini had had the audacity to criticise Rossini's music during the rehearsals of *Tancredi* – hastily put on when *Beatrice* was postponed – turned public opinion decidedly against him.

On the evening of 16 March, the Venetians crowded La Fenice to capacity. They were already in a bad mood, and those who had purchased the libretto were brought up even sharper by the last lines of Romani's preface, which insinuated that faults in the libretto were not his: "Fragments of the present opera are based on that story which can be found in the works of Bigli, Redusio Ripamonti and various writers of those times and others. I say 'fragments' because unavoidable circumstances have changed their order, background and characters. All these contingencies call for the indulgence of the reader."

The librettist's qualifying words provided the fuel for the Venetians' rage. When Bellini appeared in his customary seat in the orchestra pit, wearing a rather too colourful jacket, he was greeted with whistles and laughter and ironic kisses were blown to him, insinuating that he was too precious and fragile. During the overture and the first scene, laughter, chatter and occasional hisses made it almost impossible for the music to be properly heard. Bellini tried to effect an outward composure, but his occasional stares at the audience were completely ineffective. Only when Pasta at last appeared did a stony silence fall abruptly. Usually, her first entrance was enthusiastically applauded, but this time not a single handclap was heard. No sooner had she begun her aria than cries of "*Norma! Norma!*" broke out, implying that she was singing a parody of music from that opera. Pasta, not at all perturbed, varied the repetition in the cabaletta with great musicianship and skill, as if playing for time to control the audience. She waited for the opportunity until her duet "Duolo d'un cor piagato" with Filippo, her husband in the opera, when she turned from him to the audience and with great force delivered her lines to them instead: "Se amar non puo, rispettami" ("I know you cannot love me, but at least respect me"). The audience was stunned and responded by remaining silent and giving Pasta an ovation at the end of the scene. Some order was restored, but for the remainder of the performance occasional shouts were heard against Bellini, who refused to appear on the stage at the end of his opera.

The theatre had put on a splendid production, and after Pasta had managed to break the tension, the audience could blame only Bellini. Even when they were comparatively quiet in the second half they still did not (or were not prepared to) like the music. Apart from the quintet, the rest of the opera fell quite flat.

On 18 March, Locatelli reviewed *Beatrice* in the form of another ironic letter to "AB of Fonzaso". Having indirectly absolved the management of the theatre, Locatelli puts the entire blame for the delay of the opera on Bellini:

> You see, I'm giving you perhaps more than you have asked of me. If certain things at certain times aren't done at leisure, you must therefore be content with the little I can do. I'll tell you the facts and the essentials: the truth is that *Beatrice* had no luck. The public didn't give it their approval and the maestro could be seen sitting between the cello and the violin, ignored. Indeed, some of his admirers tried to stir up some enthusiasm for him, and here and there his name was heard, but what could you expect? These were pious desires, no applause resulted, and in the end these admirers were silenced themselves. Now I must tell you of the danger of too much repetition. Here in Venice, we all know *Norma* by heart... I wonder if the maestro has his head full of it, too? It would seem that he did, to the extent that he transferred the accompaniment of one opera to the other. In *Beatrice*, not only [were there] some analogies but also some equalities. The public noticed this and loudly shouted, "*Norma! Norma!*" Other words followed, too.

For the rest [of the opera], Pasta was much applauded, because Pasta always sings as few people on Earth sing (in a manner of speaking). The new bass, Cartagenova, was also pleasing for his acting and for the colour in his singing. Curioni and Del Serre gave of their best.

Up until now, I promise you that I've been a faithful historian, because certain things that are said about the faithfulness of newspaper reporting shouldn't be believed. With the exception of a certain article that we said has been sent to us, you can believe us implicitly. If you were to ask me for my personal opinion with the liberty of not offering an assessment, since I have now a certain authority, I would tell you that in act one there is a fine introduction for a graceful theme that is developed in several ways and always returns to the same melody. There is also a beautiful duet between Pasta and Cartagenova and a finale of splendid workmanship. The two choruses could have been considered beautiful, if only they were more relevant. But I can't use the word beautiful here; I mean to say that they would have been splendid in *opera buffa*.

The beauties of act two are restricted to the last part of a quintet and the middle section of a bass aria with new and graceful accompaniment to the second part, although the first part of this aria calls to mind those evenings when Madame Pasta used to sing "Qual cor tradisti" [*Norma*].

The great aria with which Pasta ends the opera had very little effect on me. (As it's always good to get things correct, I want to make it clear that by this I don't mean the performance as a whole.)

And now I'm going to risk sharing a confidence with you that I wouldn't mention to the public for the whole world. I believe that the audience expected something other than what they got. And, indeed, they had a right to something better than this work, which seemed to be so dishonest. However, the spectacle was staged magnificently.

Now what will they say at Fonzaso? Please take our side there, and since it was you, with your first letter, who removed all scholasticism from my mind, repeat to them at Fonzaso that "the bow which menaces does not always wound".

Two days later, *L'Eco di Milano* also reported on *Beatrice*:

The plot of this lyric tragedy…as treated by our Romani presents interesting situations and abounds in fine poetry, such as that which always occurs in all his dramas…

The overture, the introduction, the short song sung by Del Serre [Agnese] and the duet between the latter and Curioni didn't have any effect on the public, although it seems to me that this last piece merited applause. Pasta's opening aria aroused hostile feelings, as it was too similar to the aria in *Norma*, but Pasta sang with so much power, mastery and expression that she won clamorous applause. The following duet, between her and Cartagenova [Filippo], was pleasing, but not so the cabaletta, which lacked vitality. The finale to the act languished from beginning to end.

The second act opens with a fine chorus, followed by a concert piece, and this would have also been engaging if the public hadn't found in it repetitions of some strains from the final scene in *Norma* and the famous ending to the finale of the first act of *I Capuleti*, "Se ogni speme". Cartagenova's aria was not applauded, but the following short trio between Pasta, Del Serre and Curioni was most warmly received. In this, Curioni sang behind the scenes. I assure you that this [piece] contains a very sweet melody, the voices are splendidly blended and it is quite new and beautiful. Pasta's last aria, with which the opera ends, was found to be somewhat trivial, and this time she wasn't accorded the applause that she is accustomed to receiving for her solo pieces.

Beatrice's reception in subsequent performances improved, however, and the theatre was always well attended. And yet, although the opera grew in favour and the public no longer whistled at Bellini, the applause was for Pasta, not for the music. The performances came to an end with the closing of the season, on 24 March.

The outcome of *Beatrice* hurt Bellini deeply. He believed that his work did not deserve such a reception and was infuriated by the failure. To refute the imputation that he had copied his own *Norma*, he sent to the newspaper copies of "Ma la sola" from *Beatrice* and "In mia man" from *Norma* for comparison.

Undoubtedly, other factors having nothing directly to do with the merit of the opera played a part in its failure. But had *Beatrice* been as good an opera as *Norma* or *La sonnambula*, it would in all probability have overcome its initial difficulties and eventually triumphed. *Norma* had its share of trouble, perhaps even more, but it was not long before it was acclaimed. This is not to say that *Beatrice* is worthless. Far from it. There are wonderful scenes in it, but because Bellini had to compose the music in a very short time – something contrary to his nature – it remains an uneven work; its various pieces do not always coalesce.

On 25 March, Bellini wrote to Santocanale at Palermo:[9]

My delay in writing to you was because I was expecting some newspapers to come out so that, whatever opinion was voiced, you would be able to have news of the outcome of my new opera, which, owing to a series of unfortunate circumstances, has been as unsuccessful as *I Capuleti* was successful.

I'm being blamed for having delayed the opera until the 16th of this month, whereas it was entirely the poet's fault. And the party that was adverse to Pasta, which is a powerful one (more so than rumour has it), joined forces with the one that is against me, and so on the first night there was such an uproar and such shouting, hissing, laughing, etc, that I thought I was in a bazaar. All my Sicilian haughtiness took hold of me and my bold appearance impressed some and enraged others so that, when I was called for by the audience after four or five pieces which had great effect, I remained as though glued to my seat. Five or six pieces were applauded at the other two performances, too, and the audience was so large that the management sold almost twice the number of tickets as had been sold for the first performance. If the theatre box-office is the [barometer] of appreciation, as they say, then my opera has been a resounding success. I can only add that *I Capuleti* made amends for *Zaira*, which failed at Parma; that *Norma*, which was partially disapproved of during the early performances in Milan, made amends for itself; and that I hope *Beatrice*, which I rate as not being unworthy of its two sister-pieces, will also make up for its inauspicious beginning...

Tomorrow I will go to Milan, whence I go to London on around 10 April, where I am to conduct my new opera. Accept my embraces and believe me to be your affectionate Bellini.

Later, on 11 April 1834, when *Beatrice* was performed at Palermo, Bellini wrote from Paris to Santocanale:[10] "So my *Beatrice* has been a success? I'm glad to hear it. From the Neapolitan papers, I see that the people of Palermo have applauded this unfortunate opera of mine, which I myself didn't believe merited the fate that it had met in Venice. I was convinced that causes extraneous to the merits of my opera induced the Venetian public to disapprove of it."

On the day that Bellini left Venice, an anonymous friend of his – and one who obviously knew in detail what had gone on between the composer and Romani during the preparation of the libretto – wrote a long letter to the *Gazzetta di Venezia*. Bellini was completely exonerated therein and the blame was laid on Romani. Readers were also informed of the action taken through the authorities and, as proof of this episode, one of the relevant documents was cited by its official number. It was not long before Romani saw the letter and, losing no time, answered the *Gazzetta* at great length. He also wrote a rejoinder, stronger and more detailed, which he sent to *L'Eco di Milano*:

I will now state the facts of this affair, alone and without the help of anonymous friends.

It's entirely true, as my unnamed friend has written, that I was supposed to deliver a *melodramma* to maestro Bellini (and not a libretto, as he calls it), half of which I should have given him in October, the other half in November. It's also true (and this was certainly not mentioned by Bellini's friend) that the composer reserved the right to choose the subject of the *melodramma*.

Whether because Minerva was cruel to him or another goddess had taken the place of Minerva, July passed, August passed, September went and October came, and finally November arrived and that blessed subject still wasn't found. In addition, Bellini had disappeared. The new Rinaldo was idling on Armida's isle. When Heaven desired it, he came forth, but the time had passed and previous engagements that I couldn't neglect forced me to refuse him my co-operation. Nevertheless, since he constantly implored me, and as I was used to making sacrifices for him, I finally accepted and began to write a lyric tragedy called *Cristina di Svezia*.

One fine morning, however, Bellini's Minerva abandoned her severity and suggested the subject of *Beatrice di Tenda* to him, and on another fine morning my affection for Bellini and my respect for his Minerva again forced me to the sacrifice of accepting it.

While I was busy in Milan with *Beatrice*, Bellini left for Venice and, as a sign of gratitude for the sacrifice I made for him, he now indicates that the responsibility for the delay rests with me. I was far away, and those who are far away aren't always successful in protecting themselves from blame. The impresario, who knew nothing at all about the story, went to the authorities, and to the shame of both the impresario and the maestro I was summoned by the police in Milan. Although I didn't make excuses for myself, I protested, but Bellini's defender has given his own version of my position. So I decided to go to Venice myself and demand an explanation for these proceedings, but all I got for my effort was that the maestro blamed the impresario and the impresario the maestro. In the end, with sweet words from one and sweet words and affection from the other, my rage was calmed down and I started again writing and rewriting my *melodramma*, changing and putting it together in 1,000 different ways. This continued until the day before it went on the stage, when my poem finally became a libretto.

Now, what is it exactly that Bellini or someone else is trying to prove? Doesn't the time that elapsed apply to both of us, or did the months that were lost affect only him? Should I have been a slave to him completely in every respect and left all my other work aside? Were the 12,000 francs that he was going to obtain to come to my own pocket? If his prestige and self-respect are so important to him, he can't expect to preserve them at my expense. If he had to write in a hurry, I too have had to write in a hurry, with the additional burden of being tormented every day by his whimsical ideas. In fact, I was more harassed than Orombello, because Bellini had already established the music in his mind before I wrote the verses. The fact that his music didn't achieve the success for which he had hoped doesn't give him the right to blame me for it.

Is it really very important that one of his operas was unsuccessful? It happened to the great Rossini, too, but he didn't make excuses or blame anyone... There's no fear that a fully-grown tree will fall down after one stroke. What is it that this misadventure deprives Bellini? Money? No. He received 12,000 francs. Glory? Well, the "milords" of the Thames are still awaiting him. Reputation? He doesn't lack friends. But I will stop here – to thank my own good fortune, which kept me in Venice for a few more days than I expected so that I could have the opportunity of rectifying in person this controversy that was thrown on the public.

Bellini, who had in the meantime returned to Milan, did not answer Romani. Obviously very hurt by the outcome of both his opera and his friendship with Romani, he sought consolation with friends such as Mercadante and prepared for his forthcoming journey to London. Even after his departure, however, the controversy over *Beatrice* continued in the Milanese press.

A certain Pietro Marinetti (almost certainly the pen-name of one of Bellini's friends) answered Romani in the *Barbiere di Siviglia*. Marinetti lectured Romani on the principles of conduct that were becoming of a gentleman while the editor deplored the washing of two artists' dirty linen in public and in a manner that was beneath that of "feminine gossip".

Determined to have the last word, Romani wrote yet another letter cruelly accusing Bellini of being a coward who had run away from the scene of the crime. It was a sad affair – the friendship and collaboration of two great artists, who had given the world six operas, was well and truly over.

Since 1830, Bellini had been living at Appiani's house when in Milan. On his return from Sicily and Naples during the previous summer, however, he had bought furniture and set up his own home in an apartment in the Contrada dei Tre Monasteri. He had hardly moved in there when he went to Venice for *Beatrice*. Now, before his departure for London, he consigned his apartment, furniture and some of his savings to Giuditta Turina's care, while he forwarded his portraits to Florimo in Naples. On around 10 April, he set out with Pasta and her husband for London, where he was to supervise productions of his operas at the King's Theatre.

Beatrice Di Tenda

Opera seria (tragedia lirica) in two acts. Libretto by Felice Romani. First performed at Teatro La Fenice, Venice, on 16 March 1833 on a double bill with the ballet *L'ultimo giorno di Missolungi*, choreographed by Antonio Cortesi to music by Luigi Viviani. Francesco Bagnara designed the stage sets.

Characters and Original Cast

Beatrice, Filippo Maria Visconti's wife	Soprano	Giuditta Pasta

Orombello, Lord of Ventimiglia, secretly in love with Beatrice	Tenor	Alberico Curioni
Filippo Maria Visconti, Duke of Milan, in love with Agnese	Baritone	Orazio Cartagenova
Agnese Del Maino, loved by Filippo, secretly in love with Orombello	Mezzo-soprano	Anna Del Serre
Anichino, ex-minister of Beatrice's late first husband, friend of Orombello	Tenor	Alessandro Giacchini
Rizzardo Del Maino, Agnese's brother, confidant of Filippo	Bass	Unknown

The action takes place at Binasco Castle, near Milan, in AD 1418.

Giovanni Maria Visconti, Duke and feudal Lord of Milan, was assassinated on 16 May 1412 by conspirators. When Facino Cane, a powerful leader of warlike troops, also died at about the same time, his widow, Beatrice de' Lascari (1370-1418), Contessa di Tenda, married Filippo Maria Visconti, the assassinated Duke's brother. Beatrice's huge dowry, which included Binasco Castle and her late husband's troops, provided the foundation of Filippo's power to reconquer the Duchy of Milan. Six years later, Filippo, a tyrant and a libertine and rather bored with the rather elderly Beatrice, fell in love with the young and beautiful Agnese Del Maino, Beatrice's lady-in-waiting. Henceforth, he determined to rid himself of his wife. (These events and personalities are true historic fact.) At this point, the opera begins.

ACT I

SCENE 1: An inner courtyard of Binasco Castle. The façade of the palace is brightly illuminated. A fête is in progress.

Courtiers attendant upon Filippo are surprised to see him leave the fête so soon. He tells them that he can no longer tolerate his wife, who is apparently more respected than he is, a fact that humiliates him and constantly reminds him that, in actuality, Beatrice is still the ruler. While the courtiers sycophantically flatter him and encourage him to free himself from the yoke of matrimony, Agnese's voice is heard from within the palace singing a sweet song about the power of true love. Filippo applies the words of her song to himself and, fired by it, determines to rid himself of his wife. He then expresses the love that he cherishes for Agnese.

SCENE 2: Agnese's apartments. She is sitting, agitated, at a table on which a lute lies. It is almost daybreak.

Agnese has sent an anonymous invitation to Orombello, the young Lord of Ventimiglia, with whom she is enamoured. Orombello, however, imagines the invitation to have come from Beatrice, with whom he is secretly in love. When he hears the lute playing, he goes where the sound of music guides him but is most surprised to find Agnese, not Beatrice. Nevertheless, Agnese detains him, telling him that someone is secretly in love with him; this someone is apparently loved by the Duke, yet she loves only Orombello.

Again, Orombello takes this to be a reference to Beatrice. Agnese then informs him that she also knows that he is in love, having watched him closely at court. Orombello, now convinced that Agnese knows everything, in a moment of confusion lets slip his love for the "divine Beatrice".

Feeling humiliated at this revelation, Agnese swears vengeance while Orombello implores her not to bring ruin on Beatrice. In the end, Agnese angrily dismisses him.

SCENE 3: A solitary grove in the ducal garden. Day has dawned.

Beatrice is depressed and tells her ladies-in-waiting of her husband's neglect and ingratitude. She weeps for her suffering and laments that she has allowed her people to fall under Filippo's tyrannical domination. Finally, she places her trust and hope in Heaven's mercy.

As her ladies leave, Filippo appears. Having heard of Orombello's love for Beatrice from Agnese, he seizes on this as justification for suspecting his wife of infidelity. At first, he reproaches her on the pretext that she has been avoiding him. Her reason for avoiding him, Beatrice readily replies, is because of the jealousy that she feels, as it is common knowledge that he loves someone else. Filippo then produces some documents – stolen for him by Agnese – of petitions from Orombello and others who are discontented with his rule. These documents, he maintains, are evidence that Beatrice is in love with Orombello and that she is also aiding Filippo's rebellious subjects. Beatrice indignantly rejects all these accusations and reminds him that it was she who gave him the power that she is now accused of trying to take away. She then tearfully entreats him not to bring dishonour on her. Finally, when Filippo refuses to return her papers, Beatrice vows her faith in the justice of the world.

SCENE 4: A remote corner of the castle. The statue of Duke Facino Cane stands at the side.

A troop of knights discuss their orders to spy on Orombello, whom they feel will soon be driven by his love to betray himself. As they depart, Beatrice enters. Feeling abandoned by everyone, she prays before her late husband's statue for compassion and guidance.

Orombello has entered unobserved and, overhearing Beatrice's last words that she is abandoned by all, exclaims that he is always ready to offer his support. Moreover, he has gathered forces at Tortona who only await Beatrice's word to come to her aid against Filippo. He then tries to persuade her to flee with him, but she will not because, if they do, they will be accused of being lovers, and she is determined to preserve her name and honour at any price. Unable to restrain himself, Orombello confesses that he is in love with her, but Beatrice is so shocked that she orders him to leave. While Orombello begs on his knees for her forgiveness, Agnese and Filippo appear on the scene, together with the entire court. Filippo openly accuses Beatrice of infidelity; Beatrice regrets her marriage to him; Agnese flagrantly rejoices; Orombello laments the horrible situation that he has dragged Beatrice into; and the surprised courtiers condemn and pity in turn. Finally, Orombello tries to protest that Beatrice is guilty of nothing, but Filippo tells him that it would be wiser if he thought of his own defence. When Beatrice asks if anyone present has enough courage to defend her honour, Filippo promptly orders the guards to arrest her and Orombello. They are both swiftly removed to imprisonment.

ACT II

SCENE 1: The great hall of the castle, arranged as a tribunal court. Guards are posted at the doors.

Beatrice's maids of honour are protesting at such a disgraceful trial when they hear from the courtiers that Orombello, who at first bore the torture inflicted on him bravely, has eventually confessed his guilt and implicated Beatrice. Horrified, they all bemoan Beatrice's inevitable fate. Anichino, a friend of Orombello and a former minister, pleads for Beatrice, whose subjects have become restless and are on her side, but Filippo responds by ordering the gates of the city to be guarded so that no one is admitted.

The council assembles and, after Filippo has addressed the judges, Beatrice is brought in. She does not accept her judges, however, who are all her subjects, and again implores her husband not to dishonour her. Filippo accuses her once more, and when Beatrice denies the charges, she is informed that Orombello has already confessed, implicating her. Orombello is then fetched, but when he is confronted by Beatrice, he repudiates his confession and declares her innocent. She forgives him.

While Beatrice and Orombello stand firm in their defence, Filippo expresses his ruthlessness, Agnese her remorse and the rest their confusion and pity. The judges, however, demand a new trial after further interrogation of the prisoners by torture has been made. The court withdraws and the two prisoners are led away.

In vain, Agnese pleads with Filippo to pardon the prisoners, and when she subsequently confesses that it was she who defamed them, he sends her away, disturbed by her change of heart. At the same time, Beatrice's groans are heard as she is led from the torture chamber to her cell; even though she did not confess, both she and Orombello are condemned to death. However, when Anichino brings the death warrant for signature, Filippo is so overcome that he relents as he recalls what Beatrice has done for him and cries, "Let her live!" But when presently courtiers announce that Beatrice's subjects are armed and demanding her freedom, Filippo's feelings of clemency are obliterated and he signs the warrant. He then declares that Beatrice is condemned by her own audacity and wickedness and by that of others, and that the gap between them can never be bridged.

SCENE 2: A hall leading to the castle prison. There are guards on all sides.

Beatrice's ladies and friends, who have been visiting her in her cell, mourn for her and pray that she may meet her death with fortitude. Presently, Beatrice comes from the prison on the way to her execution, plainly dressed and with her hair falling about her shoulders. Proudly, she says that she has been able to triumph over torture. She affirms her innocence and calls for vengeance on Filippo and even more so on the unknown informer who has falsely accused her. At these words, Agnese, distraught, rushes in and confesses her guilt – her love for Orombello led her to steal the letters from Beatrice's room. Beatrice is enraged but tells her to say no more, as she will not curse her in the hour of death. When Orombello's voice is heard from a distant tower forgiving his enemies, Beatrice is so moved that she forgives Agnese, too.

The sounds of a funeral march bring a group of officials to escort Beatrice to the block. She begs everybody not to weep for her and asks the women to decorate her tomb with flowers and to pray for Filippo, not for her. As they all continue to lament, Beatrice embraces Agnese, and after welcoming her executioners with courage and dignity she is led away by the guards.

Romani's libretto for *Beatrice di Tenda* is directly based on the ballet of the same title by Antonio Monticini. The scenario of the ballet that deals with the tragedy of Beatrice de' Lascari was derived from the histories of Andrea Biglia (*Rerum Mediolanensium Historiee*, after 1431) and Giuseppe Ripamonti (*Historiarium Patriae in continuatianem Tristani Calchi*, 17th century) and the 1825 tragedy *Beatrice di Tenda* by Tebaldi Fores. It is also possible that the novel *Il castello di Binasco* (1819) by Diodata Saluzzo-Roero also served as a remote source.

Although Romani keeps to historical facts as well as personalities, he makes three relevant omissions: Beatrice was 22 years Filippo's senior and unable of giving him an heir; moreover, she *did* succumb to torture, admitting all allegations of her illicit relationship with Orombello, but then, after her conviction, she retracted her confession, first privately and then publicly, on her way to the scaffold. (Both Beatrice and Orombello were beheaded at Binasco Castle during the night of 13/14 September 1418.)

To a contemporary public that favours historical accuracy, it may appear rather surprising that Romani opted to leave out these details, as the balance of his plot would have been strengthened had they been included. But in the early 1830s, the period in which the libretto was written, the public's emotional participation was particularly solicited. In turn, in both Romantic theatre and literature, the public eagerly expected the depiction of intrigues, treason and all other crimes – especially those committed by mediaeval, historic figures – and thus experience horror and pity at the grave injustice done to innocent victims. It was therefore an astute choice for Romani to present a sublimated protagonist, a heroine, as well as to accentuate Filippo's notorious villainy.

Even though the libretto is skilfully written, inasmuch as it contains many felicitous verses, considerable grace and interesting (if not exciting) confrontation scenes, its characters remain dull. Only Agnese is multidimensional, but she is reduced to a minor, almost inconsequential role in the development of the tragedy.

The libretto has also many resemblances to that of *Anna Bolena*, written by Romani for Donizetti three years earlier. In *Beatrice*, there is the fabricated charge of adultery, the trial scene, and Agnese, like Seymour in the earlier opera, expresses her remorse to the unforgiving husband too late. (This goes some way to explain why the roles of Agnese and Orombello were curtailed so that their resemblance to similar characters – Seymour and Percy in *Anna Bolena*, respectively – would be diminished.) Yet, at the time, the libretto was not criticised because of these resemblances, as they were not as evident as they would be to present-day audiences, even on first hearing. Romantic opera was then in its infancy; *Il pirata* (1827), the prototype of this genre, was only five years old and had not yet captured fully the imagination of a public still fascinated by Rossini's canon. What seems to have been more important at the time was the absence of the traditional element of sensual love between the protagonists, Beatrice and Orombello.

Three themes that recur during the opera, all in the same key, make up the prelude that begins the work. The rather extensive use of brass in the prelude evokes a majestically solemn atmosphere.

The first theme, of Rossinian cast, is associated with pleading for mercy:

Allegro

The second is in turn courtly and powerful:

Allegro

The third is in the form of a prayer:

Filippo's first scene, beginning with "M'e importuna" ("It bores me"), in which he complains vituperatively of his wife, is musically rather commonplace – the libretto characterises him, with hardly any subtlety, as an unmitigated villain. However, the chorus of courtiers (tenors and basses) "Se più soffri" ("If you continue to suffer"), who sycophantically appear to be against Beatrice, is dramatically effective to some degree by means of its repetition, something that Verdi was later to perfect in his choruses. Agnese's song "Ah! non pensar" ("Oh! Do not believe", *andante sostenuto assai* with lute accompaniment), on the power of true love, has a certain romantic sweetness and is more effective by being heard from within the palace. (Amelia's "Come in quest'ora bruna" in Verdi's *Simon Boccanegra* is strongly reminiscent of this melody.) It also serves to make Filippo's ensuing "Come t'adoro" ("How I adore you") more lively, more impassioned, and with the courtiers' interjections encouraging him to dump Beatrice, a respectable enough finale to the first scene (the only one in the opera that is not oppressive) is thereby achieved.

The next scene is entirely dominated by Agnese and Orombello. In their duet "Si, rivale" ("Yes, rival") she discovers where his affections lie. Here, like Donizetti, Bellini employs musical dialogue in which the keys change as the tempers of the two characters rise. In the second part, "E la mia spietato?" ("And what about my life, you hard-hearted man?"), again after the style of a Donizetti cabaletta, as in *Anna Bolena*, Bellini achieves some dramatic exchanges – Agnese condemning and swearing vengeance, Orombello pleading for forgiveness.

Beatrice is introduced in the recitative "Respiro io qui" ("Here I can breathe"). Expressive though this may be, her solitariness manifested in *fioriture*, it is the felicitous chorus "Come, ah, come ogni cosa il suo sorriso allegra" ("How, oh, how its smile brightens everything") – the second theme of the prelude – that musically raises the scene to a higher level, the highest so far in the opera. While Beatrice's aria "Ma la sola, ahimè!" ("But I am the only one, alas!") shows Bellini's usual command of the extended phrase, the frequent use of appoggiaturas tends to distort the basic simplicity of the line. In the intensely emotional cabaletta "Ah! la pena in lor piombò" ("Alas, the pain has fallen upon them"), a *sostenuto* passage (an unusual and expressive device) at the close of each verse adds an element of faith and hope to Beatrice's suffering.

Beatrice's duet with Filippo "Duolo d'un cor' piagato" ("The suffering of a wounded heart"), *allegro moderato*, depicts musically the emotions involved, but the ensuing cabaletta "Ah, il mondo che imploro" ("Oh, I implore the world"), which begins with a lively and beautiful melody *con tutta forza e passione*, soon relapses into a meaningless sequence. Only the orchestration – specifically an oboe melody in thirds that underlines the duet with a rhythmic pattern – maintains a degree of excitement.

The composer redeems himself considerably in the closing scene of the act. The chorus "Lo vedeste?" ("Have you seen him?") is interesting, convincing and reminiscent of *Norma* (Adalgisa's music before Norma's "Tremi tu?" in act one). Beatrice's recitative "Il mio dolore" ("My grief") leads with touching sincerity into her aria "Deh! se mi amasti" ("Oh! If you loved me"), the third theme of the prelude. This prayer, with its elegiac music, truly soars to Heaven – an authentic Bellinian cantilena.

When Filippo accuses Beatrice of infidelity, there is adequate dramatic tension, although not as much as in the equivalent scene in *Anna Bolena*. But the ensemble finale, "Oh! vil rampogna!" ('Oh, vile reproof!"), which begins with a *largo* after Rossini's style, maintains a sustained grandeur and ends majestically with a flowing melodic line. Despite Filippo's unbending arrogance, the composer never neglects the character's aristocratic authority.

The trial scene in the second act is modelled on a similar scene in *Anna Bolena*, which it manages to rival with recurrent melodic and rhythmic motifs (the first theme of the prelude). The introductory chorus "Lassa! e può il ciel permettere" ("Alas! And can Heaven allow"), very solemnly accented, first relates Orombello's confession under torture and then, after a dramatic pause, comments on Beatrice's "Orombello! Oh, sciagurato!" ("Orombello! Oh, unhappy man!"). Orombello, weakened by torture, is then brought in. The recitative in his exchange with Beatrice is both melodic and dramatic and on the level of the best in *Norma* – she reproaches him and he repudiates his forced confession – but it is in the phrase "Io soffrii...soffrii tortura cui pensiero ah non comprende" ("I suffered...suffered torture the likes of which the mind cannot conceive") that Bellini reaches his greatest heights in this opera:

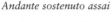

The breaks and accents here are so apt that they do not produce the sluggish effect sometimes evident elsewhere but rather give powerful expression and an abstract dimension to the words. Also, the ingenious use of the orchestra in accompaniment, continually repeating the first theme of the prelude, builds to a rhetorical and impressive climax.

In the following scene, the simple eloquence of Agnese's pleading increases the interest in Filippo's recitative and aria "Rimorso in lei?... Qui m'accorse oppresso" ("Is she remorseful?... She welcomed me here when I was down"), the only scene in which Bellini shows him some sympathy. Here, regret and tenderness are interweaved in a notable balance between the declamatory recitative and the aria's flowing melody, further enhanced by the orchestral accompaniment to achieve a musically moving entity.

The noteworthy chorus "Ah! no, non sia la misera" ("Ah! No, leave the unhappy woman") opens the final scene, but in Beatrice's ensuing recitative "Nulla io dissi" ("I said nothing") Bellini's obviously high intentions fall short of his best, most probably through insufficient variation. The same applies to the next scene, in which Agnese remorsefully asks Beatrice for forgiveness. Expressive though the music may be, it does not add another dimension to Romani's verses, as it should. Nevertheless, the composer rises to the occasion in the trio "Angiol di pace" ("Angel of peace") – borrowed from the duet between Zaira and Orosmane in act two of *Zaira* – for Beatrice, Agnese and Orombello, whose voice blends ecstatically with that of the two women. This is touching, if not ultimately moving:

Beatrice's final aria, "Ah! se un'urna" ("Oh! If I am given a tomb"), in which she asks that her tomb is not bare of flowers and that prayers are offered for Filippo, is intensely and nobly profound:

However, the dramatic effect of the aria is all but seriously damaged by the ensuing cabaletta, "Ah! la morte a cui m'appresso è trionfo e non è pena" ("Oh, the approaching death is a triumph, not a punishment"), which fails to reinforce the assertion of Beatrice's character exemplified by the words.

This cabaletta was lifted from *Bianca e Fernando*, where the *allegro* finale "Alla gioia e piacer" (in turn traced to Rossini's *Otello*) was within the conception of the work. Also, the composer's career at that stage accommodated readily and unquestionably Rossinian coloratura, as it were. But by the time of *Beatrice* (preceded by *La sonnambula* and *Norma*), it was expected that Bellini integrated his coloratura thematically, and this he failed to do.

The relative failure of *Beatrice di Tenda* was due to the libretto, which was written in a hurry, but also because the turbulence around Bellini at the time seriously impaired his concentration. He had to compose the music in a very short time and, in his haste, cut an extended duet between Beatrice and Agnese at the end of the opera so drastically that he compromised the dramatic effect. Romani may have provided good poetry suitable for Bellini's musical style, but the characters failed to capture his imagination in the way that others had in previous works. Beatrice, as portrayed by Romani, is dull. She seems to be constantly suffering nobly, with Orombello inspiring merely her gratitude. Bellini also found the character of Filippo quite repulsive. "I confess that the subject is horrible," he said, "but I tried to modify and minimise the disgust that the character of Filippo arouses with my music."

The work has wonderful moments and effective scenes, such as the great trial, but it also has long stretches of music that either begin well only to collapse into banality or fail to rise above the level of mediocrity. Above all, *Beatrice* is uneven; the various pieces do not fit together. It is a transitional work, and although the steps that Bellini took in a new direction after *Norma* were not huge, they at least matured to a certain extent in his next opera, *I Puritani*. In *Beatrice*, the dramatic ensemble (used especially in the magnificent finale in *Norma*) was developed further and employed more often. Strangely, at this stage in his career, after *La sonnambula* and *Norma*, Bellini tried to imitate Donizetti's style in an effort to balance the lyric and dramatic elements in both vocal and instrumental parts. What *Beatrice* needs, however, is revision. This was, in fact, the composer's intention, but he did not live long enough to carry it through.

The role of Beatrice is not an easy one. But then, neither are those of

Bellini's other soprano or tenor parts. Like Amina and Norma, Beatrice was written for Giuditta Pasta, who had extraordinary talents that are seldom found elsewhere. The failure of the opera at its first presentation was not at all due to Pasta, although the other singers in the cast were very much her inferiors. In addition to the technical difficulties, the role of Beatrice boasts little variety of utterance and, consequently, too much is expected of the singer if she is to bring it to life.

There are no great interpreters to mention in the few revivals of the opera, although Mario was an exceptional Orombello. In any case, apart from performances in Rome in the 1860s and 1870s, *Beatrice di Tenda* disappeared from the opera houses. Although revivals in recent times have, in themselves, been quite successful, the opera has failed to establish itself. The more notable of these productions were those in Catania in 1935 (the centenary of Bellini's death), with Giannina Arangi Lombardi as Beatrice; at La Scala in 1961, with Joan Sutherland and Giuseppe Campora; at La Fenice in 1964, with Leyla Gencer and Juan Oncina; in Bologna in 1976, with Mirella Freni and Renzo Casellato; and at La Scala in 1993, with Cecilia Gasdia and Vincenzo La Scola.

The Beatrices of these performances were all accomplished singers who coped well with the vocal technicalities of the role. Dramatically, however, they left something to be desired. All in all, Lombardi distinguished herself inasmuch as she was able to combine vocal and dramatic resources in fair measure. Gencer's considerable vocal technique was marred only by a passion to imitate Callas to the extent that her otherwise respectable acting became caricature. From a purely vocal point of view, Sutherland scored over her contemporaries in the role. Her stumbling block was an inability to apply her great technique (facility is a better word) in the realisation of the character, and the already dull Beatrice failed to come to life. Freni scored where Sutherland had failed, although brilliant virtuosity, particularly in the final cabaletta, was beyond her vocal resources. The best all-round performance was given by Gasdia. She was the noble victim, who projected her rather modest voice with impeccable artistry.

The four tenors of these revivals were never less than competent, except for Oncina, who, like Gasdia, used his rather small voice with considerable dramatic expression.

It is unfortunate that neither Maria Callas nor Montserrat Caballé have shown any interest in Beatrice, a role that would have greatly benefited from their talent in this kind of music.

13

The Journey to London (1833-34)

The earliest proposals that Bellini should visit London had been made in the autumn of 1828, when Lalande's husband tried to arrange a presentation of *Il pirata* with Pierre-François Laporte, the impresario of the King's Theatre. Donzelli and Lablache were booked to appear with Lalande, and Bellini, who was to direct and supervise the production, was also expected to provide a new work for the spring of 1830. However, in a letter to Florimo[1] on 22 November 1828, Bellini explains his failure to reach agreement with Laporte:

> The negotiations for the London engagement have collapsed, probably because Pacini has offered his services for half the fee I demanded. The impresario expected me to give *Il pirata* (of which he had bought the score) and to write a new opera, and that I was expected to pay for the libretto. Moreover, I was expected to be in London from the middle of March until the end of May 1830. Consequently, I asked for 20,000 francs, but he offered me 15,000. I then came down to 18,000, but he stuck to his figure.
>
> The day before yesterday, I received a message from [Giuseppe] Pasta advising me not to give up the rights of the score but to keep no less than half of it for myself. Even if the opera is only moderately successful, the score will still sell for at least 25,000 francs. After I heard this, I went to Lalande's husband and proposed to him that I would accept 12,000 francs, provided I kept half the rights of the score. The matter was referred to the impresario, but he didn't agree. Therefore, my dear Florimo, it seems that I cannot accept less than I have asked for, because I shall have to pay for the trip there and back to Italy. As I shall also have to find board and lodgings for almost three months, there will be very little money left. But what can I do, if Pacini will accept only 10,000 francs?
>
> In one way, I'm sorry not to have come to an agreement, but then

I feel that perhaps it's better not to go to London in the first year that Lalande and Lablache are going, as they will have rather a lot of engagements. They are definitely booked to sing in *Pompei* and *Arabi ed Amazilia*... I myself don't think that I'll be very successful, because I can't have Rubini and *Il pirata* won't go down well with Donzelli. It'll be better for me if Pacini goes to London in 1830 and I go in 1831, when perhaps I will go with operas written in Italy, and then, if they're already successful, I can go over there with more prestige. In such circumstances, it might be easier for me to go to Paris, which I prefer to London, anyway. But enough – let's not push fate too much and instead wait and see what happens.

Four years later, Bellini did accept a proposal to go to London. It is quite possible that the new negotiations with the King's Theatre were carried through Giuditta Pasta's husband. By 25 March, all arrangements had been made, for on that date Bellini informed Santocanale that he would be leaving on around 10 April for London, where he would direct the production of his opera. (He must have meant *Norma*, which had not yet been produced there. He also wrote to his uncle Ferlito,[2] informing him that in London he would direct *Norma*, *La sonnambula*, *Il pirata* and *I Capuleti e i Montecchi*, all with Giuditta Pasta as prima donna.

The contract required Bellini to be in London by 1 May, when Laporte would pay him an advance of £100 on arrival and £300 later. This was a very high fee, with which Bellini hoped to save a considerable amount. *En route*, he made a brief stop in Paris, where he met Dr Louis Véron, the director of the Paris Opéra. In an extant fragment of a letter dated 23 April, probably addressed to Santocanale,[3] Bellini writes, "I'll tell you a secret that I won't tell anyone else. The director of the Académie Française – that is, of the Théâtre de l'Opéra, Paris – begged me strongly to write an opera in French for the Grand Theatre, offering me a salary, besides author's rights. It's probably wise to reserve my reply for a month or two, or until I return to Paris at the end of July. To write an opera for that theatre will really boost my ego."

Bellini arrived in London with the Pastas towards the end of April, as on the 27th he was reported to have been in the audience for a performance of Rossini's *Cenerentola* at the King's Theatre. Pasta, Maria Malibran, Rubini, Paganini, the violinist Charles de Bériot, Vaccai, Hummel, Mendelssohn and Henry Herz were also present. On the same day, the directors of the

Philharmonic Society presented Bellini with a free pass to all their concerts. One concert that Bellini certainly attended was that staged on 13 May, when Mendelssohn conducted the first performance in England of his symphony in A minor, "the Italian". Bellini and Mendelssohn definitely met, though possibly only briefly; in his book *Mendelssohn and his friends in Kensington*, RB Gotch mentions that, for one Sophy Horsley, Mendelssohn collected autographs of Pasta and Malibran and a bar of *Il pirata* in Bellini's handwriting.

Shortly after his arrival in London, Bellini took up lodgings at 3 Old Burlington Street. Giuditta Pasta and her husband, Lablache and Tamburini also stayed at this address. In an undated fragment from two letters sent to Florimo[4] at this time, Bellini described his impressions: "London looked like a big light. I was so taken by such a wealth of light and colour that I wanted to walk alone in the big streets, along the banks of the foggy River Thames and in the parks, which are so beautiful and so full of flowers in the spring. The impression that mysterious London has made on me – trying to conquer even the fog with so much light – is unforgettable."

On 16 May, he wrote to Lamperi[5] about London, telling him, "It would be superfluous to talk to you about this city. It's enough to tell you that it's number one in the world, peerless except for wealthy Tyre of ancient times."

Then, to Santocanale,[6] he wrote, "I'm enjoying myself hugely in this magnificent city, the finest in the world. The architecture of the houses is superb and the huge carriages, equipped with all sorts of luxuries, are beautiful. Then there is also the conversation. Every night, there are two or three parties, brilliant enough to amuse even the most depressed person in the world. Too bad that London is so far from Italy. If it hadn't been for this, I would come back frequently, because the people are very kind and the women possess an enchanting beauty. In one word, I would say that life here is blissful."

But even in the midst of such pleasure, Bellini still thought of Sicily. He added, "I'll never be as happy as I was in Sicily during those two short months. Unfortunately, I don't as yet see me going back there in the immediate future, although I'm determined to come back to my country before very long."

As far as we know, from a letter that he wrote to Florimo, Bellini did not speak any English. However, a number of Italian expatriates were living in London at the time and, together with the considerable number of Italian artists, they formed a fairly large colony. One member of the Italian community was Michael Costa (1808-84), who was in fact musical director of the King's Theatre. Costa had not only been a pupil of Bellini's at the Naples Conservatorio but he was also a friend. He had been settled in England since 1829, when he had directed an opera by Zingarelli in Birmingham, where he became one of the most famous conductors of his time.

The first Bellini opera to be heard in London was *Il pirata*, at His Majesty's Theatre on 17 April 1830, with Lalande, Donzelli and Santini in the principal roles. The opera was not favourably received, however, although Lalande and Donzelli were successful. It was repeated in the following year with Comelli and Santini and Rubini, who scored a sensational triumph. In this season, *La Straniera* and *La sonnambula* were also heard, with Giuditta Grisi and Pasta in the leading roles respectively. Neither can be said to have been very successful. Chorley,[7] the most notable music critic of the time, summed up the initial reaction to Bellini's music in England:

> Although the predominance of the composer of *Il barbiere* had as yet given way in no respect, there were other modern Italian composers whose works were worth trying... With the temporary mitigation of that master's popularity, they were sure to perish forever, since their life amounted to his forms reproduced second-hand. It is not so with *Il pirata*. Weak as that opera is, an individuality exists in Bellini's music. Whenever individuality is not mere eccentricity, there is always interest in it – there is always a chance of that interest becoming a charm. But until Rubini adopted "Tu vedrai", the charm was not recognised in this country and the young Sicilian composer was treated with unanimous contempt.

Lord Mount Edgecumbe[8] had better things to say, although after 1828 his main interest was rather with the singers and he seldom went to the opera. About the period between 1829 and 1834, he wrote, "There have been fewer operas and with less merit in the last five years than in any other similar period. *Il pirata* and *La sonnambula* by Bellini are the only good ones, and he is the best of present composers."

The controversy in London about Bellini was such that the majority of the public was divided into two camps – strong adversaries on one side and warm, enthusiastic admirers on the other. At the time of his arrival there, the people were crowding the Theatre Royal, in Drury Lane, where they were acclaiming the incomparable Maria Malibran[9] as the heroine in *La sonnambula*.

Perhaps no one has described Malibran better than Rossini. In 1858, when asked whom he considered to have been the greatest female singer of his early years, he replied, "The greatest was Colbran, who became my first wife, but Malibran was unique. Ah, that marvellous creature! She surpassed all her imitators with her truly uncanny musical genius and all the women I have ever known with the superiority of her intelligence, the variety of her knowledge and her flashing temperament, of which it's impossible to give you any idea."

This great singer belonged to an extraordinary Spanish family[10] of musicians who are without parallel in the history of music, particularly opera. They had a power, genius and originality that left a permanent impression on the technique of vocal art and, especially, on the art of ornamentation in singing.

Chorley, who heard Malibran in London on her official debut in 1825 and then followed her career closely, was impressed from the beginning:[11] "From the first hour when she appeared on the stage – first in *Il barbiere* and subsequently in *Il crociato* – it was evident that a new artist, as original as extraordinary, was come – one of nature fairly endowed, not merely with physical powers but also with that inventive, energetic, rapid genius before which obstacles become as nothing and, by aid of the sharpest contradictions, can be reconciled. She may not have been beautiful, but she was better than beautiful – inasmuch as a Spanish-speaking human countenance by Murillo is ten times more fascinating than many a faultless angel-face such as Guido could paint…"

Later, after hearing her in a variety of roles, Chorley wrote of her vocal powers:

Her voice was not naturally a voice of first-rate quality. It was of a mezzo-soprano timbre, extended upwards and downwards by that hardy and tremendous exercise, the introduction of which has been ascribed to the appearance of her father, in singing and tuition… As it was, the girl was early put into possession of an instrument two octaves and a half in compass, if not more, weakest in the tones between F and F – a weakness audaciously and incomparably disguised by the forms of execution, modification and ornamentation that she selected. Her topmost and deepest notes were perpetually used in connected contrast... On the stage, her flight and sallies told with electric effect. There was much of her restless and impassioned southern nature in them – as much of a musical invention and skill, which required no master to prompt or to regulate her cadences; but there was something, too, of an instinctive eagerness on her part to evade display in the portion or her voice to which display would have been the least becoming.

Like many singers of Italian opera, Malibran performed mainly in Paris and London. In March 1832, however, she decided that it was time for her to appear in Italy and sang in Rome, Naples, Bologna and other Italian cities and took her audiences by storm. In these performances, she repeated her old successes (mainly her Rossinian roles) and appeared for the first time in *La sonnambula* and *I Capuleti e i Montecchi*. While she was singing *La sonnambula* in Naples, Bellini was busy producing *Beatrice di Tenda* in Venice. As it happened, they met soon afterwards, on the stage of the Theatre Royal, Drury Lane, London. Bellini described what happened in a letter to Florimo:[12]

> The day after my arrival in this great city of grey skies, which have been called with much truth "leaden skies", I read in the theatrical announcements (which here are carried about the streets) that *La sonnambula* was being performed here in English with Maria Malibran in the title role. It was more because of my interest in hearing and admiring the diva – who occupies such a position in the musical world, and whom I knew by reputation alone – than to hear my opera that I went to the theatre, where I'd been invited by one of the greatest ladies in the highest English aristocracy, the Duchess of Hamilton (who apparently sings exquisitely, having been a pupil of our Crescentini – he who gave me a letter of introduction to her, as you know).
>
> Dear Florimo, I can't find words to tell you how my poor music was murdered and hacked about or, as the Neapolitans would say, flayed alive [*scorticata*] by these[13]...Englishmen, the more because it was sung in the language that, with reason, was called the language of birds, particularly parrots (I don't remember by whom), and of which I still

don't know even a single syllable. But it was only when Malibran sang that I recognised *La sonnambula*. And in the *allegro* of the last scene, especially at the words "Ah m'abbraccia!", she put so much emphasis and expressed the words with such veracity that I was startled at first and then felt such great pleasure that, without thinking that I was in an English theatre and forgetting social customs and my obligation to the lady on whose right I was seated in her second-tier box, and putting aside modesty (which every author preserves, even if he doesn't feel it), I was the first to start clapping and crying out loud, "Viva! Viva! Brava! Brava!" This southern and rather volcanic outburst was a novelty in the chilly, calculating, impassive country and surprised and aroused the curiosity of the fair sons of Albion, who began asking one another who the outrageous fellow was. But after a few minutes, they discovered (I don't know how) that I was the composer of *La sonnambula*. They then gave me such an ovation that I refrain from describing it, even to you. Not content to applaud me frantically – I couldn't tell you for how long – while I thanked them from my box, they wanted me on stage at all costs, and I was almost dragged there by a crowd of young noblemen who spoke enthusiastically of my music and whom I didn't even have the honour of knowing...

First to greet me was Malibran, who threw her arms around my neck and, with indescribable delight, sang my four notes in "Ah, m'abraccia" ["Embrace me"] and said nothing more. I was at the peak of excitement; I thought I was in paradise. Unable to speak, I just stood there, stupefied. I remember nothing more. The renewed stamping and clapping of the English audience, who become very excited once they warm up, called us before the footlights, and we stood there hand in hand. You can imagine the rest... All I can say is that I don't know if I shall ever again experience a greater emotion. From this moment on, I became an intimate friend of Malibran's. She told me of the admiration that she had for my music and I, in turn, realised that I brought out the best in her immense talent. I promised to write an opera for her on a subject to her liking. It's a thought that already electrifies me, my dear Florimo. Goodbye.

La sonnambula, which was conducted by Henry Bishop and which had John Templeton as the leading tenor, continued to fill the Theatre Royal at Drury

Lane. These performances, with an English translation by Samuel Beazley, were arranged by Bishop and T Cooke. We have no idea what this "arrangement" was like, but it was no improvement on Bellini's opera. The popular success of *La sonnambula* was clearly due to Malibran, even though some critics did not approve of her unreservedly. Chorley still remembered Pasta's performance in this opera, which was quite the opposite of Malibran's, and he certainly preferred it. There was no exaggeration in Pasta's pure Italianate style of singing, which was the perfect model of the Classical School, while in Chorley's view Malibran employed "a vehemence too nearly trenched in frenzy to be true".

Whatever the case, Malibran captured the imagination of the public, which found her dramatic temperament irresistible. On 10 May, *The Times* was unreserved in its praise of her artistic achievement:

> Her performance of this part Amina in *La sonnambula* is too well known to require any detailed criticism; but it would be unjust to pass it by without characterising it as one of the most perfect and exquisite specimens of scenic art of which the stage can boast...
>
> The purity of her voice, the accuracy and facility of her execution, the profusion of gracefulness and the intensity of feeling which she displays give charm to the whole representation, which seems to react as nearly as human genius can reach the highest point of excellence; of all the parts she has yet played in England, this of *La sonnambula* is her *capo d'opera*.

It is difficult to reconstruct Bellini's movements in London in detail. Apart from the performances of his operas, he led a busy social life, attending balls, dinners and musical evenings. The concert on 5 May at the Marchioness of Landsdowne's house must have been a memorable occasion; Pasta, Malibran, Rubini, Tamburini and Galli were among the artists taking part. With typical modesty, Pasta mentioned it in a letter to her mother:[14] "Bellini, who was there as a spectator, very kindly accompanied me in the 'Casta Diva', which they liked well enough."

There was also Lady Morgan's salon, where many artists gathered. Lady Morgan, born Sydney Owenson in Ireland, was herself an accomplished poet and writer. She greatly appreciated music, particularly singing, and Pasta often visited her. For Bellini, there was probably another interest – Lady

Morgan had a young niece, Josephine Clarke, called José, with whom he flirted. All that is known of Bellini's association with Lady Morgan consists of a few entries in her diary:[15]

24 June 1833: Today had a visit from Madame Pasta... Bellini came in, and Pasta, Bellini and José went through one act of his *Norma*. Bellini was charmed with José's voice...

1 July 1833: Pasta and Bellini jumped out of a hackney coach at our door today with a roll of music in their hands – it was the score of *Norma*. They came, Pasta said, from the second rehearsal. Bellini scolded his great pupil like a *petite pensionnaire*.

4 August 1833: Yesterday, Bellini and Gabussi[16] came and sang and played like angels.

15 August 1833: Yesterday was curious and interesting; people coming in to take leave of us. We had at the same moment Thomas Moore, Madame Pasta, Bellini, Gabussi...

José, who later became Lady Geale, wrote from Dublin to Florimo[17] in 1886: "To my aunt's [Lady Morgan's] memories I add my own impressions of that unique genius. I shall never forget his noble and charming figure or that fair and curling hair and those eyes of his. Oh, what eyes the divine Bellini had! They were blue and with an absolutely incomparable serenity of expression. One could describe them by our expression 'sleepy blue eyes'. The general picture of the great artist gave the impression of a handsome English type. I shall never forget the strange expression of his face when, seated at our piano, he struck a few notes which made the first and greatest musical impressions of my life palpitate in my young girl's heart."

In London, Bellini also became friendly with Henry William Greville (1801-72), a young diplomat then being posted to the British Embassy in Paris, where Bellini later saw more of him. In his entry for 23 June 1833, Greville mentioned in his diary:[18]

I have seen a great deal of Bellini, who is very attractive, very "fin", and at the same time very unsophisticated and natural...

Calais, Wednesday 26 June: My last three days were passed in hurrying after commissions and taking leave of friends. On Tuesday, I dined at the Wharncliffes and went for the last time to see *Norma*, and probably to see Pasta for the last time. Also, I went between the acts with Bellini to her dressing room, when she invited me very cordially to visit her at her villa at Como... Afterwards, Bellini and I strolled about the streets for a long while, talking over all sorts of musical subjects. I hope to see him again, for he is original and agreeable.

Writing to Lamperi[19] on 16 May, Bellini gives an account of his artistic and social activities in London:

Now that the weather is beautiful here, no one is talking about influenza... I developed a terrible cough during the trip on the boat from Calais to London, but now I'm almost completely recovered and the doctor didn't call it influenza, because I had no fever.

At Drury Lane, they performed my *Sonnambula* in English with Malibran as the star... Pasta has so far sung *Anna Bolena* and *Medea* [*in Corinto*] and in both operas she was celebrated incredibly. London has found her stronger and younger in voice. When we next meet, I will tell you in confidence what my feelings are about Malibran and Pasta. For the time being, I will only say that the latter is inimitable, especially in sublime tragedy.

In 15 days from today, *Il pirata* will be performed with Pasta, Rubini and Tamburini, and the performance is to be for Rubini's benefit. *Norma* will be performed at the beginning of July for Pasta's benefit.

Now I must tell you that I'm enjoying myself here very much, attending many balls, dinners, theatres, concerts, country houses, etc... I know everyone in London and they all invite me [over], and I'm so busy that I'm almost smothered by all these entertainments... So you see I naturally find myself in the middle of a world of beauties, really divine beauties; but one finds only superficial sentiment here, because it's not enough for someone who's leaving the country in two months, so I shall rely more on friendship than on love and not run the risk of landing myself with a wife...

There is no evidence that Bellini's appreciation of Malibran was mere infatuation. He did not like her better as a singer than Pasta, as has sometimes been said, or vice versa; he simply appreciated both singers in their own ways. A conversation with Carlo Botta in 1834 – related in a letter[20] by Botta to Signora Teofila Billotti-Colla[21] of Paris – expresses his views:

"Malibran's genius has nothing to do with Pasta's, who is unique in herself," Bellini said.

"You weren't able to hear the great Marchesi because you were too young," Botta replied, "but I heard her and I swear and must protest to you, maestro, that no man or woman except Mme Pasta has inherited Mme Marchesi's manner. I mean that kind of singing and gesture which is high, noble, grand, moving and which could lift the mind to the highest plane and raise them above this ugly, wretched world. Only someone who has heard Mme Pasta in all her roles, or Mme Marchesi in all of hers, especially in Cherubini's *Achille in Sciro*, knows what singing of the tragic and dramatic kind is."

"I agree completely with everything you say about Mme Pasta," Bellini answered and then added, "but Malibran also has very great merit."

Florimo, who had heard Malibran in *La sonnambula* at the Teatro del Fondo, Naples, a few months earlier, described in some detail the impression that she made on him:[22]

Maria Malibran was the most sublime interpreter of *La sonnambula*. She could easily claim that she had created the role for a second time… The eminent Crescentini, after hearing and admiring Malibran in this opera, said that singers of the old school – Farinelli, Gizziele, Caffarelli, Marchesi, Velluti and others, with himself not included – would have been able to sing the *andante* of this opera, "Ah! non credea mirarti", on a par with Malibran, but better than her? Never. However, Crescentini continued, no one would have sung the *allegro* – not even one of the past celebrities would have stressed it – with such feeling and such powerful passion, especially in that phrase "Ah m'abbraccia", where Malibran became incomparable and carried the public to the highest level of enthusiasm.

Interestingly, on 25 July, *The Observer* also commented on the two distinguished singers: "Pasta and Malibran present a vivid contrast between genius and talent. There is something regarding talent which cannot be attributed to Malibran; but she will always remain far from the sublimity of Pasta. Malibran amuses herself by 'showing off' her voice; she is a delightful singer, without the delicate perfection of La Cinti [Laure Cinti-Damoreau] but with more strength and variety."

Much has been written, and more implied, about Bellini's alleged love affair with Malibran. Documentary evidence reveals nothing concrete, but the indications are strong that, apart from admiring her as a superb artist, he found her quite irresistible as a woman. She too liked Bellini very much but did not fall in love with him. At the time of their meeting, Malibran was already separated from her husband, Louis Malibran, and the Belgian violinist Charles de Bériot (by whom she had had a son only three months earlier) was her lover. Malibran and Bellini became very good friends, and for as long as both remained in London they saw a great deal of each other. She even painted a portrait of him. According to Bellini,[23] Pasta often teased him about Malibran: "She already realises that I've lost my mind over this extraordinary Spaniard and is always saying to me, 'Bellini, you won't leave London without having to fight a duel with M Bériot.' And when I try to calm her down by telling her that I'm neither in love nor infatuated with Malibran, Pasta – who is a woman and, like all women, sees far in these matters – replies to me, 'Your love can be seen in your eyes.'"

Had circumstances been different, and had Bellini and Malibran stayed together for longer, it is possible that a real love could have developed between them. Time, however, proved short. They met only once more, two years later at a friend's house in Paris, and although Bellini kept his promise to write an opera for her, events took a different course.

On 31 May, *Il pirata* was performed at the King's Theatre and was a great success with the public, although the press, while praising Pasta and Rubini, were hostile towards the music. *Norma*, the novelty of the season, was then staged on 20 June with Pasta, Joséphine de Méric as Adalgisa, Donzelli as Pollione and Galli as Oroveso. It was a sensational success with the public, but the press was divided about both *Norma* and the singers. On 24 June, *The Morning Chronicle* dismissed Bellini as an imitator who would not have been a composer had it not been for Rossini. The writer of

Calignani's Messenger was even more dismissive: "We were not prepared to expect much from Bellini, and therefore the outcome did not disappoint us. The scene is set in Gaul, but the music in the opera is everything but Gallic… Pasta sang and acted in her accustomed manner. We have often had occasion to speak of her very false intonation, but never, either from her or from any other well-known singer, have we heard this grave imperfection carried to greater excess. It would not be exaggerated to say that not a single phrase of the entire opera was sung on the correct pitch."

The Times saw things differently, however. Reporting on the second performance, it praised the singers and continued, "Bellini rose, with his style, to a genre of composition more elevated than anything else he has done up to now and succeeded in obtaining an effect full of nobility and beauty. His music moves along sublimely and with grandiosity and could sustain comparison with various operas of Rossini in their passionate, well-coloured combinations. In any case, he excels Donizetti in the vigour and character of his music and seduces the listener's mind with superior talents and feelings that Donizetti would not know how to master."

Only from the little that Bellini wrote to Santocanale[24] on 26 June do we know what he thought of these performances: "*Norma* was performed in this theatre [the King's Theatre] and no one can remember a similar occasion in English theatre. Pasta is and always has been great. Donzelli sings very well indeed and the chorus isn't too bad."

Giuseppe Pasta's letter to Rachele Negri[25] also confirms Bellini's opinion, in greater detail: "Neither *Medea* [*in Corinto*] nor *Anna Bolena* can boast a greater success than the first performance in London of *Norma*. With the orchestra and chorus under Bellini's direction, it was a performance the like of which had never before been seen at London's Italian Theatre [King's Theatre]. In fact, it surpassed Giuditta's expectations and Bellini's hopes. The applause was extraordinary and the tears flowed in the second act. Giuditta appeared to have been overcome with her character and gave a performance in which she used the force of her every fibre."

I Capuleti e i Montecchi followed, eliciting a similar enthusiastic reaction from the public – particularly for Pasta and Donzelli – and hostility from the press. On 18 July, *The Examiner* wrote, "A dull affair Bellini found it, and a dull affair he left it. No genius, indeed, could make much of such a *caput mortuum* as the drama is reduced to in the Italian version, but Bellini has made less of it than either Zingarelli or Vaccai."

Bellini stayed in London for about two months. His movements there can be traced up to 3 August, when he visited Lady Morgan, and it is likely that he left the capital at some point during the following week.

14

The Break with Giuditta Turina

While Bellini was in London, Giuditta's marriage to Ferdinando Turina finally foundered and they obtained a legal separation. An anonymous letter had informed Ferdinando of his wife's relationship with Bellini before the Venice production of *Beatrice di Tenda* and Romani had alluded to Giuditta in the newspaper article that he later published in answer to accusations about the *Beatrice* affair. Before long, in May 1833, Bellini also sent compromising letters to Giuditta from London which fell into Ferdinando's hands, giving him the evidence that he needed.

It is difficult if not impossible to believe that Ferdinando was unaware of his wife's liaison with Bellini for all those years. Perhaps not at the beginning, but certainly later, the fact that Bellini spent so much time with Giuditta in Milan, Moltrasio and Casalbuttano, culminating in their long stay in Naples, must have been enough for the scales to fall from his eyes.

Ferdinando and Giuditta can hardly be said to have lived as husband and wife; they both led their own lives, not often together, and as far as is known they were indifferent to each other. He seems to have been a complaisant observer as long as his wife was discreet, allowing her to go anywhere she chose without him. However, the moment that he received the anonymous letter, which he considered a sign that other people knew, he became difficult and severe, if only for the sake of his ego. Even so, Giuditta was able to convince him that the anonymous letter was the malicious act of someone unknown and that her friendship with Bellini was purely spiritual. Romani's allusions – "another goddess has taken Minerva's place" and "the new Rinaldo was idling on Armida's isle" – ensured that all Milan knew that Giuditta was Bellini's mistress, and the scandal forced Ferdinando to take action.

What is perplexing is Bellini's behaviour towards Giuditta before and after her separation from her husband. Her reactions to this can be seen in a long letter that she wrote to Florimo[1] on 17 February 1834 which also refers to several others that she had received from Bellini after his departure for London:

My dear Florimo, I have only just received a letter from you... I don't need to read the letters you wrote to Bellini to be convinced of our friendship. I have had ample proof not to doubt this for a moment.

It's a fact that everything alluding to Bellini hurts me in a way that I can't describe. Of all the misfortunes and losses that I've suffered, I feel only the loss of Bellini's affection and – woe is me! – I still think only of him...

He now writes to me that his love for me cooled 18 months ago. Why, then, when I begged him never to write anything that might compromise me, did he write those letters that fell into the hands of my husband? Afterwards, Bellini put the blame for this on his great love, which couldn't be content with simple, indifferent phrases. Why, instead of waiting until September [1833, in Paris] to speak of the decline in his affection, did he not tell me about it when he learned of my trouble with my husband? Then, possibly, things could have been very different. Instead, at the time, he wrote that he hoped that I wouldn't forsake him if my husband abandoned me. And what did I do? I dismissed my own interests, reputation, everything, and considered only Bellini, whom I always loved more than anyone else. And when he asked my forgiveness for the troubles he had brought on me, what did I reply? That only the loss of his affection could make me unhappy. In the end, he deprived me of his love at a time when it was my only support! And his reasons – what were they? The Venetian jealousies and other [items of] gossip in Paris, one about a letter which I can prove false. I didn't reply to Bellini about these accusations, as I felt that I would be degrading myself. When all my friends saw the state that I was reduced to, both physically and morally, they wrote to Bellini about it, but would you believe it, dear Florimo? He replied to them all, denigrating my reputation in order to make excuses for his own conduct, not concerning himself in the least about my situation. Bellini should know me well enough not to believe idle gossip. I'm sure that, in the depths of his heart, he doesn't believe them but [acts as if he does] only because it apparently suits his purpose. He says, his career *avant tout*. How can he say this to a woman who has sacrificed everything for him, to a woman who for five years has loved him with the same ardour and purity with which the angels adore the Divinity? And who, despite his cruel and indelicate conduct, still loves him? In these five years, have I ever harmed his career in any way? On the contrary, it seems to me that everything prospered for him. I never asked him to forgo what Paris offered him. No one could have participated more in his triumphs than I. I've always wanted him to glorify his name through his music rather than degrade it by his conduct, for I assure you that all the admiration that they had for Bellini in Milan has turned to contempt, and this distresses me very much. I only wish that he could justify himself in the eyes of the public. For him to be the cause of my separation and then abandon me is really a painful and cruel thing. If he thought that, as an independent woman, I might go to Paris (something that he wouldn't have liked), it would have indicated that he thought me very affectionate... He's all the more wrong to treat me like this. I *did* rejoice in my independence, but only in order to dedicate it entirely to him, and I had every intention of behaving exactly in the way that he would have wished me to... But enough – it was fate that it should be so. Bellini can't be without remorse. He will, no doubt, find women in Paris more beautiful than I, but will they love him with the intensity with which I still do? Never. Never.

Forgive me, dear Florimo, for this long and tiresome letter, but I couldn't help opening my heart to the friend of the man who treats me with such cruelty and injustice... Write to me from time to time and believe that I am always the same affectionate friend.

We also know from Bellini's letter to Florimo[2] on 11 March 1834 that Giuditta's friends in Milan informed him that she was going to Paris in search of him: "They still threaten me from Milan that Giuditta is coming to Paris, but I haven't yet received a reply to my letters to the Contessa Martini, which I think will have some effect. If not, I will leave Paris, because I don't want to recommence a relationship that has caused me great displeasure."

Bellini's "great displeasure" was rather absurd; the displeasure was surely caused to Giuditta, whom he still made use of as his financial agent. She wrote to Florimo[3] on 17 April 1834, telling him, "Bellini entrusts me to pay in Naples 5,000 Austrian lire, which you will collect from the banker Falconet. He will have written to you about what you're to do with it, and I beg you to acknowledge receipt."

In a later letter, written after she had posted a portrait of Bellini to

Florimo,[4] she expresses a kind of love/hatred: "That the portrait you wanted so much has been sent off, and you might have received it before this letter reaches you. Admire and kiss the effigy of the man who was so dear to me. I wish that I'd felt nothing more than friendship for him, for perhaps then I wouldn't have reached the point of despising him."

On the same day, Giuditta wrote to Bellini in an effort to win him back. Then, on 24 July, Bellini wrote back to Florimo,[5] who had passed the content of Giuditta's letters onto him:

> While she wrote to you of her contempt for me, Giuditta tells me in a letter dated the ninth of this month that she can't change the love that she still feels for me into friendship... "Accept this and I guarantee that I won't annoy you and I will resign myself to receive nothing but cool friendship from you," etc.
>
> Her whole letter is most affectionate, and if it weren't for my career I would resolve to renew the relationship that tied me to her; but with so many engagements in different countries, such a relationship would be fatal, since it would rob me of time and, more importantly, tranquillity. So I shall reply evasively, without upsetting her, if possible.

From the above correspondence, it can be concluded that Giuditta genuinely loved Bellini and that it was never in her mind to use him as a pretext to obtain a separation from her husband. Furthermore, she went on loving Bellini after their affair had ended. On the other hand, whatever Bellini's reasons for breaking off the affair, his behaviour towards her was disgraceful and cruel. He wrote compromising letters to her when he had been expressly asked not to do so and, by his own admission, inexplicably waited 18 months after his love for her had cooled (when they were together in Naples, during the winter of 1832) to tell her that he was quite finished with her, by which time she had been separated from her husband for a good three months.

What was nearer the truth behind Bellini's break with Giuditta can be found in his letter to Florimo[6] on 4 August: "I have no further news from Giuditta. I swear to you that I think of her regretfully and that I haven't forgotten her at all, but the very idea of tying myself down again frightens me... I've found in Paris a companion who is beautiful, amiable, undemanding and very docile. I'm not in love with her, but I see her sometimes. I make love and then I think about my opera."

When Giuditta separated from her husband and was consequently free to live with Bellini on a permanent basis, he simply shied away. In the past, he had done the same with Maddalena Fumaroli when there had been no obstacle to their marriage. Rumours that he was about to marry a rich girl in London or Paris remained just rumours, nothing more. He had hardly left Milan for London with the Pastas when it was said that he was going to marry Clelia, Pasta's rich daughter. There was also an English girl whom Giuditta Turina mentioned in a postscript to Florimo: "Bellini is making love to an English girl whom he perhaps hopes to marry. Much good it may do him." One wonders whether this was Josephine (José) Clarke.

Later, in Paris, Bellini seems to have had just two ideas in mind: to become a celebrity as an operatic composer in Paris and to become rich – by marriage, if necessary. He was not quite as keen on marrying for money, as it is evident that he was trying to convince himself. His demands were almost impossible to satisfy. He wanted someone very rich, young and beautiful who would love him. What he was offering in return, if anything, was vague.

Another English girl, also unnamed, offered a dowry of 150,000 francs, but this was not enough for Bellini, considering that she could only offer him friendship and esteem without love. Moreover, she was over 25 years old and it might well have been difficult to mould her after his own fashion. Bellini also tried to revive the possibility of marrying Pasta's daughter. "I wrote to Pasta," he informed Florimo[7] in a letter dated 13 October 1834, "and from her answer I shall know whether I can renew my former ideas, and hers, about her daughter;[8] but the whole matter must be treated extremely delicately. Is that clear?" Nothing materialised from this, however. In a letter to Florimo[9] on 30 November 1834, Bellini writes, "[Pasta] had her husband answer me (because she never answers herself) and the husband, would you believe it, addressed me as his right honourable friend. In one word, it was a very formal but also a very cold letter and left me very far from having any hope that they were considering such a marriage project at all."

In the same letter, Bellini mentions an old Baronessa Selliere, who wished him to marry a very pretty and wealthy girl "who is at present in Rome with her parents, her father being the famous painter Horace Vernet". Apparently, Henry Greville had given him an excellent report of her and advised him to marry this girl, provided that her dowry was not less than 200,000 francs.

Again, nothing came of this, but in a letter to Florimo[10] a few months later, in February 1835, Bellini continues to be preoccupied with the question of marriage or, more correctly, with a marriage of convenience. However, the marriage market was still difficult. A girl of 18 with enough money was "diabolical and imperious" in character; also, Baronessa Selliere, now herself in love with him, wanted him to marry her young but penniless niece.

There are no extant letters between Bellini and Giuditta Turina or concerning her during this period. On 7 April 1835, however, after he had triumphantly produced *I Puritani* in Paris, Bellini wrote to Contessa Martini.[11] The letter, although calm and with the air of having been written during a period of repose, is not without thinly veiled references to his already finished affair with Giuditta. After describing how the genuine success of *I Puritani* had silenced his enemies, Bellini gets to the point: "I have a great desire to apply myself more and more, especially now, when I have no amorous relationships, and may God preserve me from such for the rest of my life! You can't imagine how happy and peaceful I am now. I don't want to say anything against women, but I think it's difficult for a man to be happy if he loves a woman who isn't his own and whom he cannot possess as he would want to. I might be in love with the woman who becomes my wife, but I believe that I would never find her as I imagine her to be. For the rest, I'm amusing myself here and meet with only friendship. Therefore I feel no jealousy and have no worries."

Bellini then enquires about his furniture, which he had left in Milan in the care of Giuditta, who was to sell it for him. He also alludes ironically to Giuditta's alleged German lover, of whom he had heard: "No one mentions my furniture any more, so I suppose that it's abandoned. I should like to ask the Duke of Cannizzaro to take an interest in the matter himself; perhaps he'll be able to sell it for me? I need money, as I'm earning little at the moment in this country while I'm spending a lot. So, if you see Giuditta, give her my kind regards and ask her to get a move on, if she can spare a moment from 'Germany' for the 'isolated islander' and arrange for the furniture to be sold."

Whether or not Giuditta did take a German or Austrian lover is uncertain. Florimo, who had all this time been friendly towards Giuditta (although he maintained a neutral position on the breaking of her affair with Bellini), does not appear to have believed in the existence of this new lover. He heard about the German from Bellini, to whom he wrote on 18 July:[12]

"Giuditta doesn't write to me any more, but I know that she's very badly off, financially. At least, so they tell me, writing from Milan. They don't confirm that she is really making love with that German, as you say. Perhaps it isn't true. I sincerely hope so."

In his reply to Florimo, Bellini infers that he rather believed in the existence of the German lover but not Giuditta's financial difficulties: "All Milan knows that Giuditta has a German lover; if this isn't so, then all the better for her, because such conduct has harmed her a great deal in public esteem. She doesn't write to me any more and has asked Pasta's husband to write to me about my affairs. I hear that she's spending enormous sums of money and is trying to get an increase in the annual alimony that her husband has assigned her. That's all I know. She has about 6,000 francs of my money and all my furniture, which she will sell at the next public auction."

This letter,[13] dated 13 August 1835, is the last one extant in which Bellini mentions Giuditta. On 23 September, he died. Almost two months after his death, Giuditta resumed her correspondence with Florimo,[14] to whom she transferred some of her affection and who was her only link with the memory of Bellini. She wrote:

> I've been meaning to write to you for over a month now, but how could I have found the courage then, if even now tears still stream from my eyes? I can't express the sorrow I felt when they told me of the terrible tragedy for you and his poor family. You were my first thought. Oh, why did he ever turn his back on Italy? If he'd been here, or at Naples, you or I, we would have saved him... But enough. Providence has been too unjust in cutting short a life so precious...
>
> As you know, I was entrusted by poor Bellini with the sale of his furniture. I've sold some things and I have the money here. I also owed him 5,523 Milanese lire, on which I've been paying five per cent interest. Please write to his family on my behalf, offer them my services and tell them that I beg them to make use of me in any way that they see fit.
>
> You should come to Milan for a little diversion. I would welcome you with the greatest pleasure...

Florimo was very friendly towards Giuditta after Bellini's death. He tried to comfort her by assuring her that Bellini had never forgotten her and that he had never really cared for another woman. These letters were helpful to Giuditta and through them Florimo no doubt found comfort himself. The death of Bellini was a mutual loss and Florimo needed Giuditta as much as she needed him.

For several years, Giuditta had a lot of trouble, not only with the Turina family but also with the Bellinis, and she was on bad terms with Francesco Pollini, Bellini's friend in Milan, who at that time was acting for his family. She paid the balance of the money from the sale of his furniture, but as she had been unable to get back her original receipt for the 5,000 lire paid at Bellini's request in 1834, Pollini expected her to pay over the whole original sum that had been deposited with her. She wrote to Florimo[15] on 14 February 1837: "Sometimes I despair... I'm still quarrelling with the Turinas. I long for...the moment when my troubles with them are over. Really, these affairs keep me tied like a dog on a chain. Don't believe that because of this I nurse any hatred for poor Bellini, however. God forbid. At the time of his death, I forgot all the harm that he'd done to me and remembered only our tender affection. I swear to you that I would have done or given anything, if only he still lived!"

Over the years, Giuditta became sadder and lonelier. Her friend Contessa Martini died, as did her father. Her health, which had never been very good, deteriorated further, and she even contracted cholera, although she survived. She continued to correspond with Florimo for many years and he visited her in Milan at least once, in 1858.

It has been reported that Giuditta went into deep mourning when Ferdinando Turina died, although this is based only on gossip.[16] The same source also names a Doctor Tarchiani-Bonfanti as Giuditta's lover after Bellini's death. Perhaps this is true, perhaps not. She died on 1 December 1871. The inscription on her tombstone in Milan pays tribute to her: "To Giuditta Cantù, the widow of Turina, a shrewd and cultivated woman of singular kindness and sweetness, gentle in appearance, with charming and polished manners, constant in affection. She bore suffering with firm dignity; her own afflictions were many. She comforted those of others, intelligent and refined, until her last breath on 1 December 1871 in the 68th year of her life."

15

The Making of the Musician

The mainstream of opera during the first 200 years of its existence was primarily Italian. During this time, Italian opera became fashionable all over Europe, its audiences mainly confined to the upper classes. After the French Revolution, however, the tastes of the new social order changed completely and Rousseau's call for a return to nature found sympathy everywhere. This change was reflected in opera, as well as in all other forms of art and entertainment, and each country began to develop its own style. Henceforth, Italian opera began to lose its international monopoly. Napoleon's empire attracted the most talented Italian composers to Paris, which became the European capital of music. Paisiello (1740-1816), Zingarelli (1754-1837), Spontini (1774-1851), Cherubini[1] (1760-1842) and Salieri (1750-1825) along with the Frenchmen Mêhul (1763-1817) and Lesueur (1760-l837) and others all wrote operas for Paris in the Italian tradition but adapted to French tastes.

   In the second half of the 18th century in Italy, the leading Italian composers – the successors of Pergolesi[2] (1710-36) – were Domenico Cimarosa[3] (1749-1801) and Giovanni Paisiello[4] (1740-1816). While neither can be said to have created a new style, they summed up and perfected the intentions and aims of Pergolesi and the other Italian composers of his school. What they accomplished in their music – with its flowing melodies, variety and imagination – was beyond anything that their Italian predecessors had achieved. They also had a lot in common with Mozart's style, although they were never able to write with his unaffected naturalness and simplicity. Cimarosa wrote excellent overtures, was the first to place concert pieces in the midst of dramatic action and, like Paisiello, gave greater importance to orchestration. He also abandoned the practice of having *ritornelli* before or after a song, as it held up the action. These composers' style of writing was in striking contrast to that of Alessandro Scarlatti (1660-1725). The long, flowing, richly embellished melodic curves and formal rhythms now gave way to clear-cut lines, fast and vivacious rhythms and a well-defined harmonic outlook. Both Cimarosa and Paisiello were successful in *opera buffa* and *opera seria*.

At the end of the 18th century, the so-called Classical period of Italian opera had come to a close. Paisiello had already retired by 1800 and Cimarosa died in 1801. Italy, so long preoccupied with producing and exporting its own operas and singers, had paid no attention to new musical ideas in other countries, notably in Germany and Austria. In Italy, there had been a tendency towards musical inbreeding, and even musical instruction deteriorated because many students, anxious to turn out quickly the kind of music that was in demand, did not complete their studies.

It is therefore unsurprising that a hiatus is perceived in the history of Italian opera during the first decade of the 19th century. Of course, a number of minor composers,[5] such as Fioravanti, Tritto, Niccolini, Mayr, Päer and others, were active during this period. However, despite the scholarship and achievement of Mayr[6] (1763-1845), a Bavarian priest who settled in Italy in 1788, and to a lesser extent Ferdinando Päer[7] (1771-1839) – the more important composers of their period – the others merely filled a gap at the end of the 18th century, in effect linking the reign of Cimarosa with that of Rossini.

The greatest change to occur in opera in the 19th century, when the new period began, was the relationship of the composer to his music. Whereas in the previous century the composer, however inspired, remained in his attitude to his art a craftsman, dealing with well-ordered themes in a style that was to be later called "Classical", the 19th-century composer, the "Romantic", became more personally involved with his music, projecting his feelings and ideas through his somewhat uncontrolled imagination. Consequently, this led to a different demand from the listener, who had to place himself in sympathy with the composer in order to comprehend this music that appealed more to his emotions than to his intellect.

The assimilation of music became decisive in Rossini's operas. Hitherto, there had been only hints of assimilation, as for example in the operas of Mayr, who produced his first work, *Saffo*, in 1794 but who was later eclipsed by the young Rossini. Before *Tancredi* in 1813, his first great success, Gioachino Rossini (1792-1868) had written eight operas which were more or less in the tradition of Pergolesi and Cimarosa. Some of them enjoyed short-lived success and nothing more. His more important works include *L'Italiana in Algeri* (1813), *Il Turco in Italia* (1814), *Elisabetta, regina d'Inghilterra* (1815), *Il barbiere di Siviglia* (1816), *Otello* (1816), *Cenerentola* (1817), *Armida* (1817), *Mosè in Egitto* (1818), *Semiramide* (1823), *Le comte Ory* (1828) and *Guillaume Tell* (1829), his last opera.[8]

Although there exists today some doubt about Rossini being a truly revolutionary musician, his Italian contemporaries thought differently. There was hardly anything in his more important reforms that Mozart (1756-91) and Gluck (1714-87) had not already done, but it was new to the Italians. His remarkable memory made it possible for him to absorb the works of his great predecessors and also enabled him to compose music for any situation and under any circumstances. Furthermore, he used what he borrowed from others – even in his more mature works, including *Il barbiere* – in such an admirable way and with such sparkling and stimulating effect that his own individuality was never sacrificed. Moreover, neither Mozart nor Cimarosa were in any sense his rivals; Cimarosa was no longer food for Italian musical passion after about 1810 and it would take Mozart many years to become accepted in Italy.

Above all, Rossini cared about the human voice, and although he may never have acquired the mastery that he ought to have, few other composers were to equal him in the invention of abundant and vital melodies, which were usually short and demanded no high vocal range. His employment of basses and mezzo-sopranos in leading roles was a novelty in Italy at the time, although Mozart had already made two of his principal characters basses. Similarly, the *crescendo* form of composition that became such a characteristic feature in almost all of Rossini's music had been used before by Paisiello in *Re Teodoro* (1784), yet Rossini would make this innovation very much his own, so much so that later in Paris he was satirically known as "Signor Crescendo".

Even more revolutionary for the Italians was Rossini's introduction of the more flexible conventions of *opera buffa* into *opera seria*. He wrote concert pieces and maintained dramatic action (previously, the practice had been to use monotonous *recitativo secco*) and began to give the chorus a dramatic function. The result brought new freshness to *opera seria*, hitherto a rather stilted form. Conversely, he created comedy in *opera buffa* that was beyond the level of rather unvaried farce, on occasion even introducing an element of sentiment. Thus, by being less serious in *opera seria* and less grotesque in *opera buffa*, he succeeded in rendering such styles in a more natural, more realistic and, consequently, more dramatic way than his Italian predecessors had done. Also, the resourcefulness of his orchestral writing, again new for the Italians, was a definite advance, as was his orchestral accompaniment to recitatives, an effect that he used for the first time in *Elisabetta*.

Undoubtedly, comic opera was Rossini's true medium. At his best in *opera buffa*, he possessed and expressed resourceful wit, irresistible vivacity and excitement through his music in incomparably greater measure than even Mozart. However, great feeling or intellect was never his strength; there is little portrayal of tender love in his operas and a distinct lack of passion and melancholy. Also, possibly because of his rather inadequate education, he paid little attention as an operatic composer to literary values; several of his operas failed because of poor libretti. The success of *Il barbiere* owed much to Sterbini, who so expertly adapted the libretto from Beaumarchaís.

Eventually, Rossini's achievement impressed his contemporaries and successors, and it became imperative for them to emulate his qualities in the best way that they could. A statement made by Pacini in his memoirs puts the advent of Rossini in sharp perspective: "Everyone followed the same school, the same fashions, and as a result they were all imitating the great luminary Rossini. But in God's name, what else could one do? There was simply no other way for a composer to make a living. If I followed the great Pesarese Rossini, so did everyone else."

Nevertheless, those who imitated Rossini superficially failed to reproduce either his virtues or produce their own. Those who fully appreciated him learned a freedom of dramatic expression that did not exist in pre-Rossinian music.

Julian Budden summed up Rossini's position in the *primo ottocènto* (in Italian, music referring to the first half of the 19th century) most aptly:[9] "This was the Romantic age, and Rossini was certainly no Romantic. His own talent was for comedy, as he was always ready to admit. The world of serious lyric drama he had inherited by default. His phenomenal success in this field was due to the sheer strength of his musical personality and also to the robustly Italianate quality of his style... He retired from the operatic scene in 1829, at the age of 37, having defined the form and language of early Italian Romantic opera once and for all. He had created the master plan, leaving Donizetti and Verdi to fill it out each in his own way."

To these composers, Mercadante (1795-1870) and Pacini (1796-1867) may be added, although their contribution was influential only to a much lesser extent. After the first half of the 19th century, Verdi, one of operatic music's geniuses, and later Puccini (1858-1924) dominated Italian opera and continue to do so to the present day. In 1801, when Bellini was born, Rossini was nine years old and Donizetti two. Verdi, born in 1813, lived to the age of 88, whereas the lives of the other operatic composers were comparatively short.

Bellini was primarily an operatic composer. His other music, which includes many songs as well as sacred and secular instrumental pieces, is merely a side-product with no direct bearing of any importance on his reputation as a composer. Eight of his operas – *Bianca e Fernando* (two versions), *Il pirata*, *La Straniera*, *Zaira*, *I Capuleti e i Montecchi*, *Norma*, *Beatrice di Tenda* and *I Puritani* – are *serie*. *Adelson e Salvini* and *La sonnambula* are *semi-serie*, although only the former contains explicit comic scenes. All have often been called "singers' operas" and have sometimes been dismissed as such. It is true that, with the exception of *Adelson e Salvini*, which was composed for and performed by Bellini's fellow students at the Naples Conservatorio, they were expressly written for outstanding singers, but what is not true is the inference that he merely provided singers with opportunities to display their brilliance and technique. Bellini's music, which depends so much on the quality of performance, is mostly full of dramatic effect achieved by beautiful melody, brilliant but well-integrated *fioritura* and good taste; dramatic expression is almost never abandoned. He could never have set a laundry list to music, as Rossini once boasted of being able to do, nor could he improvise as fluently as Donizetti, who obviously possessed a readier flow of melodic inspiration.[10] Instead, Bellini was content (or only able) to write one opera a year, on average, giving each work the most careful consideration and refusing to accept inadequate libretti, as Rossini and Donizetti often did.

Basically, it is his individual spirit that gives life to Bellini's music, which is profoundly Latin but without the enormous exuberance or vitality that animates the music of Cimarosa, Rossini or Verdi. However, it possesses something else; it is as if Bellini united oriental music with his Latin temperament and transformed it into the most elegant melody. Even his most celebrated melody, "Casta Diva", has greater affinity with oriental music than with anything else. (See page 237 for a music example.) In spite of the enormous refinement that the composer brought to it, the flowing melodic line and mysticism of the opening phrase still contains the sensations and voluptuousness of orientalism. It is the tempo, the clearly defined phrase structure and the harmonic basis, together with its Latin spirit, that make it so acceptable to our Western ears.

The folk music of Sicily, where songs have always been a part of people's lives, must also be considered a significant part of Bellini's formative musical background, especially as it owes more than a little to Arabic influences and, through this, to the oriental style – a fact not fully recognised in Western countries. However, it is usually difficult to be certain of the origins of folk music, doubly so in Bellini's case, as Sicilian folk music had, long before his time, not only influenced art music but it is also possible that his own melodies permeated and modified the traditional songs of his country. Nevertheless, although it is difficult to define any direct influence of Sicilian folk song in Bellini's music, the composer frequently employed 12/8, 9/8 and 6/8 rhythms, which are so typical of 18th-century Sicilian folk music, with which he was well acquainted. As a young man in Catania, he had collected Sicilian folk songs, which undoubtedly remained in his musical consciousness. (Also, Florimo said to Scherillo[11] that, while at the Naples Conservatorio, Bellini often set Sicilian poems to music.) Nor could he have been deaf to the characteristic qualities of Neapolitan folk song when he later studied at the conservatorio; the strong Spanish-oriental elements in this music are part of its compelling fascination. These features are echoed to a degree in the contours and vocal style of some of Bellini's most characteristic melodies. If the harmony and the metrical rhythm are removed from his music, one is left with a cantilena that is essentially Sicilian and, by extension and through Arabic influence, oriental in inspiration.

Also, while at the Naples Conservatorio Bellini copied out the scores of quartets by Haydn and quintets by Mozart,[12] but by the time he had become a professional composer it was too late for their music to be imitated. Besides, from the Italian point of view, neither Haydn nor Mozart were true melodists, and nor was writing for the voice their strength. Their operas were not performed in Italy, although they commanded great admiration as composers of symphonic music. Yet one can still trace their influence in Bellini's music, albeit only in the invention of melody. The Druid's march in act one of *Norma* could hardly be imagined without "Non più andrai" from *Le nozze di Figaro*, and the first phrase of Mozart's symphony in G minor (K550) provided the motif for Bianca's cabaletta "Godrà l'alma dolce calma" in *Bianca e Gernando*. (See page 52.)

To Beethoven, Bellini owed more. The chorus "Qui non visti qui segreti" in *La Straniera* was derived from his fourth symphony, while Fernando's aria "All'udir del padre afflitto" in *Bianca e Fernando* (which also provided the movement used in the chorus "Non parti" in *Norma*) can be traced to the opening of Beethoven's sonata in C-sharp minor ("the Moonlight"). There is also a fleeting resemblance between "Deh! non volerli vittime", from the last act of *Norma*, and the music in the last scenes of *Fidelio*. It must be stressed, however, that it was not so much that Bellini imitated or copied other people's melodies as that he was influenced by them. He undoubtedly studied the Classical composers, and no matter how individualistic he may have been, he could not have gone through life without allowing the music he liked to leave a trace on his own, consciously or not. In the same way, Bellini adored the music of Pergolesi, especially the *Stabat Mater* (1736) and *La serva padrona* (1733), and Paisiello's *Nina* (1789).

Nevertheless, the immediate influences at the beginning of Bellini's career as an composer of opera derive from two conflicting sources. At the conservatorio, his teacher, Zingarelli, fervently preached that melody, conceived in the simplest way possible, should be the basic element of music. Consequently, he strongly disapproved of modern music, which at that time was the music of Rossini, a style that had a vitality and exuberance in its melodies and rhythms and relative excessive use of coloratura, all characteristics totally antipathetic to simplicity.

Even though Bellini identified with this melodic simplicity, which indeed became central to his development as a composer, Zingarelli's uncompromising aversion to modern music not only failed to prevent but may well have heightened the young composer's natural curiosity of modern trends. This normal reaction to a rather dogmatic teacher (and in many ways the highly eminent Zingarelli was said to be very severe) also applied to other students at the conservatorio, particularly to the more gifted. Thus the performances of Rossini's *Semiramide* (Venice, 1823) in Naples in 1824 made such a tremendous impact on Bellini that he fell under the spell of this type of music. Henceforth, Rossini became his idol.

This decisive musical experience, the influence of which was, unlike the melodic "simplicity", to be transitory, is at its most evident in Bellini's first opera, the student work *Adelson e Salvini* (1825). There is Rossinian influence in several scenes in this *semi-seria* opera, particularly in the part of Bonifacio and also in orchestral passages such as the introduction. Here, interestingly, Zingarelli's melodic "simplicity" is juxtaposed alongside the Rossinian passages, but of more importance is the relatively brief presence of the composer's own individuality.

As with most cases of individuality, it is always difficult, if not impossible, to define it, especially in its initial undeveloped stages, and in Bellini's case it was overshadowed by no less than Rossini's canon, which was then at its peak and universally popular. Nevertheless, considering Bellini's subsequent development and the breaking away from Rossini's influence, it can be deduced that the nucleus of Bellini's individuality comprised a Romantic feeling for sound (basically conveyed by major-minor shifts) fully integrated with the dashing vigour of his melodies. Such musical style was quite original in opera and cannot be traced to the traditions or principles of the preceding Neapolitan School, which Bellini liked so much. If anything – and this is to stretch the point – the individuality of Bellini's musical lyricism had something akin to that of Rossini but with that almost indefinable, abstract element of Romanticism, which created another form of musical expression.

As Bellini's melody owed very little to his predecessors but gave a great deal to the important composers who followed him and became influential in their own right, his contribution to the evolution of modern music has been of great significance. A parallel may be drawn between Bellini as father of modern melody and Weber (1786-1826) as father of modern orchestration, who revolutionised German opera – purely colouristic qualities gave a significant independence to instrumental conception. Similarly, Chopin (1810-49) can be described as the father of modern harmony.

Given that Bellini's melodic individuality somewhat increased in his next, first professional opera, *Bianca e Gernando*, in 1826 (the second *Bianca* was a much improved revision), it was not sufficiently evident to stand comparison with either Rossini or any of the better Italian composers of the time. It was in *Il pirata* (1827) that his individuality finally took over, the opera becoming a more fully integrated work.

In his subsequent operas, Bellini was to show a definite reaction against Rossinian *fioritura*, coming nearer to succeeding in *La Straniera* (1829), where coloratura in general is drastically reduced to a minimum. When he later returned to coloratura, he was able to integrate it thematically (with the exception of the final scene in *Beatrice di Tenda*). "Sovra il sen", "Son geloso" and "Ah! non giunge" in *La sonnambula* (1831) and "Casta Diva" and "Oh! non tremare" in *Norma* (1831) are perfect examples of this thematic integration. The celebrated duet "Mira, o Norma", which owes its construction and idea – although not its melody – to Rossini's "Ebben a te ferisci" in *Semiramide*, is more of an integral part of the whole in the Bellini work. In his last opera, *I Puritani* (1835), the Rossinian influence is confined to the orchestration. Strangely this influence is not great, considering that Rossini took a genuine interest in its composition.

Before the form and style of Bellini's music is discussed, the relationship between music and words in his operas must be considered, as it is of paramount importance in the composer's conception. Wagner told Florimo in 1880 that "Bellini's music comes from the heart and it is intimately bound up with the libretto." More significant were Felice Romani's views on this issue. Romani, the greatest librettist of his time and Bellini's collaborator in practically all his operas, declared that "few composers, other than Italian, understood as well as Bellini the necessity for a close union of music with poetry, dramatic truth, the language of emotions and the proof of expression."

For his part, when he was at his best, as in *Norma* and *La sonnambula*, Romani was able to write libretti with skilfully drawn outlines and which were suitably adapted for musical colouring. Also, the dramatic situations that he created were practical and the words in the recitatives were exceptionally well selected. Above all, however, apart from the basic structure of the libretto, Romani's greatest achievement was his instinct for the essential compromise between stage action and song. When Bellini composed *I Puritani* to Pepoli's clumsy libretto, after the quarrel with Romani, the opera that could have been his best suffered considerably. Considering Bellini's method of work, as described by himself in a letter,[13] his acceptance of this libretto was primarily forced by circumstances at the time:

> Since I have determined to write few works, not more than one a year, I bring to bear on them my utmost powers of invention. Believing as I do that a great part of the success of a work depends on the choice of an interesting subject with strong contrast of passions and harmonious and deeply felt verses, and not merely dramatic situations, my first object is to obtain a perfect drama from a good writer; Romani, a very gifted talent, particularly in musical drama, has been my preference. Once the work of the poet has been completed, I study closely the disposition of the characters, the passions that sway them and the sentiments that they express. Possessed by the feelings of each of them, I imagine myself for the moment to have become the one who is speaking and make an effort

to feel like him and express myself in his manner. Knowing that music results from the employment of a variety of sounds, and that the passions of mankind manifest themselves by means of the utterance of diverse tone, I have reproduced the language of passion in my art through incessant observation. Then, in the seclusion of my study, I begin to declaim the parts of the different characters in the drama with the utmost warmth, observing in the meanwhile the inflexions of my voice, the degree of haste or languor in their delivery – the accent, in short – and the tone of expression that nature gives to the man who is in the throes of emotion, and I find in this way the musical motifs and tempi best adapted to their communication to others through the medium of sounds. I transfer the result to paper, try it over on the piano and, if I feel in it the corresponding emotion, I consider myself to have succeeded. If I don't, then I try again.

This is one of Bellini's most quoted letters. Its authenticity has also been for some time the favourite point of dispute between biographers and chroniclers. The eminent musicologist Friedrich Lippmann[14] does not fully accept its provenance, feeling that "Bellini was far too good a musician to have been able to follow the principle of composition expounded in this 'letter', according to which the composer works through the following stages: study of the characters; declamation of the verses and attention to their 'speech melody'; trying out on the piano. In fact, Bellini's melodies arose in the most varied ways: often, certainly as the 'letter' has it, through the inspiration of a specific text; but equally frequently in daily exercises." The contents may be considered authentic, if not the actual document itself, as they legitimately describe one of the two methods of composition that Bellini employed. The fact that he may not have written the letter himself but that possibly Gallo, the purported recipient of the letter, distorted remarks made by reporting them only in part, need not be the main issue.

Evocative verses and a good libretto were necessary to capture Bellini's imagination. Even in as late as 1834,[15] in a letter to Pepoli, Bellini wrote, "Opera, through singing, must make one weep, shudder, die," and to Florimo on 4 August 1834[16] he wrote that he expected the libretto to be "with numerous thrilling situations and verses designed to portray the passions in the liveliest manner". His great sensitivity to the text also accounts for his ability to compose recitative that is superior, musically and dramatically, to that of his contemporaries and capable of rising to an unusual intensity of expression, as in Norma's "Dormono entrambi", to quote but one example.

The composer's other method can be confirmed by sketches preserved at the Museo Belliniano. He often drafted melodies (daily exercises) with a rough scene in mind or, occasionally, at random. These stock sketches were then sometimes used as the basis of scenes in his operas.

Whichever method Bellini used, he expected too much from himself, and occasionally his ingenuity proved insufficient. Perhaps his technical knowledge of music was deficient in some respects. This was the opinion of several musicians, including Verdi, who once said, "Bellini knows all that the conservatorio cannot teach him but does not know all that the conservatorio can." His work did not stop when he had found the right declamation to express the inner emotion of the words, for he would then try to build this element into a flawless melodic line. To accomplish both intentions simultaneously was a very difficult task, and it is unsurprising that he did not always succeed. But when he did, as in "Casta Diva", "D'un pensiero" (*La sonnambula*), "Quì la voce" (*I Puritani*) and elsewhere, the result was an extraordinary and immensely rewarding fusion of lyricism with drama.

(Operatic composers from the Camerata to Debussy and Schönberg have, of course, sought to achieve perfect declamation and emotional interpretation of the words. In most cases, their musical styles did not lead them in the direction of the flawless Bellinian melodic line but, rather, to a form of recitative somewhat lacking in vividness and intensity.)

However, the universal appreciation of Bellini's exceptional ability to express elegiac emotions in a most intimate way, as in "Ah non credea" and "Casta Diva" – two perfect examples – has led many to label him a marvellous but fundamentally restricted composer. One need only cite Norma's fury and vengeance in "Oh! non tremare" and "I Romani a cento", the war cries of "Guerra! Guerra!" (*Norma*) and Amina's bounding joy in "Ah! non giunge" (*La sonnambula*) to demonstrate that Bellini also excelled in expressing a wide variety of human emotions. These qualities were appreciated in their time, but with changing tastes, influenced to a high degree by the passion that Verdi brought to scenes of violent emotions, Bellini's corresponding scenes were made to appear subordinate to his delicately elegiac ones.

Opera buffa does not appear to have been within Bellini's scope. Only the *semi-seria Adelson e Salvini* contains comedy, which is provided by Bonifacio, a *basso buffo* character in the true Neapolitan tradition. Even though this comic part was successful to a degree, Bellini never wrote, nor attempted, comic opera. Only rarely did he express great joy in his works, most of his music having a melancholy disposition.

The majority of Bellini's melodies, in which multiple expressive elements unite, demand singers who can offer an enormous variety of colour, brilliantly adapted to a coherent dramatic realisation. Singers only succeed in doing justice to Bellini's music when they are capable of singing, with impeccable phrasing, the cantilenas that so often alternate with cabalettas, demanding extraordinary flexibility and coloratura. Furthermore, the *fioriture* must never be sung for exhibition but must form an integral part of the dramatic whole.

Because of these maxims, many people – perhaps the majority – have misguidedly labelled Bellini's works as *bel canto* operas. Although *bel canto* literally means "beautiful song", it is a grossly misleading term. Others translate it as "beautiful voice", which is even more wrong. *Bel canto* is the most efficient musical training method (the word *beautiful* here is irrelevant) that prepares a singer to surmount all the complexities of operatic music and, through these complexities, express human emotions with profundity.[17] Flexibility of voice – and, consequently, coloratura – that is superficially usually considered the main and, by inference, only requirement, apart from a "sweet" lyric voice, is in fact necessary for all singers, whether they use it in performance or not. Without this training, the singer will remain limited, even lame. It is the same if an athlete – a runner, say – trains only the muscles in his legs. And in addition to the numerous vocal complexities, the singer must also acquire good taste. *Bel canto* is the complete vocal schooling without which one cannot sing any opera really well, not even the most modern pieces. It is therefore incorrect to refer to some works – such as those of Rossini, Bellini and Donizetti – as specific *bel canto* operas. In reality, there are no such works.

This rather superficial differentiation was in all probability invented when, towards the end of the 19th century, the *bel canto* method began to be neglected or, more precisely, taught less thoroughly. As the new music, *verismo*, no longer relied on actual coloratura or other embellishments (which the *bel canto* method essentially teaches) to express the drama, many singers left the classroom prematurely for the stage in order to become rich and famous quickly. This was ill advised, because these singers still required a full training. Instead, some teachers concocted dangerously abridged singing courses with the inevitable repercussions; in *verismo* works – for example, those of Puccini – singers may survive, albeit to a very limited extent, but in the earlier operas (those inaccurately labelled *bel canto* operas) they cannot – that is, if their integrity is to be maintained, and it must be. Make-believe can only be achieved with the utmost sincerity on the performer's part.

The forms employed in Bellini's operas were standard in Italian operatic composition at the time and comprised overtures, preludes, arias, duets, ensembles, the *scena* and fully accompanied recitative. Four of his eleven operas (including the two *Bianca*s) have preludes: *La Straniera*, *La sonnambula*, *Beatrice di Tenda* and *I Puritani*. These preludes are fairly long (over 40 bars), but only one – to *Beatrice* – contains tunes that are actually sung in the opera. The others merely serve to set the atmosphere of each individual work. All the other operas have independent overtures frequently constructed from melodies heard later in each opera. This may perhaps suggest a mere pot-pourri of tunes, but Bellini knew how to juxtapose them to create a well-integrated whole. In the best examples, such as in *Norma* and *Il pirata*, he created an atmosphere that was relevant to the drama that followed.[18]

All Bellini's operas, as in others of the period, open with an introductory chorus and *scena*, generally for male voices. To create a sense of anticipation, the entrance of the prima donna is usually delayed until the second scene, as in *Il pirata*, *La sonnambula*, *Norma*, *Beatrice di Tenda* and *I Puritani*. This delay also gave (in the past, as it is no longer applicable today) more time to the latecomers in the audience. The placing of the prima donna's music was partly her prerogative, and in *Il pirata*, *La sonnambula* and *Norma*, Bellini gives her an entrance *scena*. This normally begins with a dramatic recitative with simple orchestral punctuation and is then followed by the aria proper, which has an extended orchestral introduction – a practical addition that allows the singer time to disengage from the preceding recitative and exploit the opportunity for physical stage action. A further characteristic feature of this type of orchestral introduction, later also adopted by Verdi, is the interruption of the melody just before the cadence, after which the prevailing accompaniment pattern is re-established and the singer begins.

Handel and Scarlatti also used this kind of false beginning, but in their case it was to provide a proclaimed title and thus attract the audience's attention. Bellini's (as well as Donizetti's) purpose went further than this; he employed the false beginning as a seductive appeal to whet the appetite, as well as to attract the audience's attention.

Generally, Bellini's most successful arias are slow cantilenas, a form of composition of which he was a master. They are true florid melodies, not melodies with superficial florid decorations. Lippmann[19] identified Bellini's commonest aria form as A1/A2/B/A1 + coda (lines one and two of the first verse, lines three and four of the first verse, lines one and two of the second verse, lines three and four of the second verse). "Ah per sempre" (*I Puritani*) is a typical example of this. Also, if appropriate, the chorus accompanies and comments, thus enhancing the dramatic atmosphere. At the point of climax, the singer's lines overflow into a cadenza which brings this section to a close. A dramatic linking passage follows, declamatory in style but treated in an arioso fashion. This leads directly into the orchestral introduction to the cabaletta, a section in quick time using all kinds of coloratura, which dramatically intensifies the feelings developed during the aria. Later scenes for all the principal characters follow this general outline, while much the same development is found in duets, trios and other ensembles, which normally open with an extended recitative and continue with an expressive cantilena for the voices separately and together, concluding with music in a faster tempo.

In his duets, which are usually in three sections, Bellini excelled when he wrote for women, and in *Norma* he surpassed himself. Those between Norma and Adalgisa are generally considered to be the finest duets for female voices in the whole of Italian opera from whatever point of view, dramatic or melodic. However, like Rossini and Donizetti and the early Verdi, occasionally here Bellini relies too much on repeated unison lines. This is particularly true in "Suoni la tromba" (*I Puritani*), and the same also occurs at times in ensembles. No doubt the object was to create an overwhelming vocal effect, despite a comparatively small chorus and orchestra, which were so often the only resources available to the composer.

Only four of his operas provided the prima donna with the customary concluding aria and rondo finale. Although this custom often blunted the natural working-out of the plot, in *Bianca e Fernando*, *La sonnambula* and *La Straniera* Bellini was able to express through his music the mood of the situation and thus bring a logical conclusion to the drama. In *Beatrice di Tenda*, however, he used the formula unsuccessfully, and in *Norma* he refused the request of the management of La Scala to provide Giuditta Pasta, the protagonist, with a final cabaletta.

The way in which Bellini used the chorus extends well beyond the normal practice of the time, which dictated that the opening scene of an opera should have a chorus. This is conspicuous not only in *I Puritani*, where the composer was adapting himself to Parisian requirements of grand opera, but also in *Norma* and, even more so, in *La sonnambula*, where the chorus also acts in the manner of a Greek Chorus by providing a commentary on the characters and situation. Donizetti first used the chorus in the same fashion in *Anna Bolena*, which was produced a few months before *La sonnambula*.

There is little doubt that Bellini understood the human voice as few other composers have done. He wrote for particular voices and, as it happened, these were the greatest voices of the time and probably some of the best of all time. This has posed a difficult task for those who followed, and less than first-rate singers do not have much chance in maintaining the integrity of his music; many melodies that may look banal on paper become extraordinarily eloquent when sung by one who understands the style and tradition of his music.

By the time that Bellini began to write his operas, the excessive power of the singer over the music had greatly diminished. Whereas in the 17th, 18th and very early 19th centuries the singer performed music very much in the way that he wanted, in the Romantic period the composer himself had gained enough power to demand that his art should be respected to the full. In fact, during the period 1820-50, not only was contemporary music expected to be performed largely as written but this also applied to the music of the 17th and 18th centuries. This practice was, of course, often wrong, because the earlier composers usually wrote a sketch of the vocal line and expected the singers to insert the appoggiaturas and improvise all sorts of vocal embellishments that were considered to be important factors in the singer's interpretation of the music. Consequently, even if very little music of the 18th century was really popular in the 19th (Mozart's *Don Giovanni*, Handel's *Messiah* and Haydn's *Die Schöpfung* being the principal works performed), the traditions and the true method of performing this music had been lost during this period.

Rossini was one of the first composers who tried to write out his own embellishments and thus leave as little latitude as possible to singers who might otherwise distort his music.[20] He believed that in this way he would ensure more balanced results, especially where less sensitive singers were concerned.

It is quite evident that, as a rule, Bellini did not want singers to introduce embellishments into his music; he expected them to sing what he wrote. Even as early as *Il pirata*, when he could hardly be described as a powerful composer, he succeeded in persuading his singers – all of whom were more famous than he was at the time – to sing in the way that he wanted. An even more striking example of the absence of elaborate embellishments in his

Sanquirico's designs for the premiere of *Norma* at La Scala, 1831.

52 (right): Act I, scene 1: The sacred grove of the Druids.

53 (right): Act II, scene 2: A secluded place near the sacred grove.

54 (right): Act II, scene 3: The Temple of Irminsul. Norma (Pasta) begs Oroveso (Negrini), her father, for forgiveness before she dies with Pollione (Donzelli) – "Deh, non volerli vittime".

55 (top left): Act I, scene 2: Norma's dwelling. Pollione (Donzelli), Adalgisa (Grisi) and Norma (Pasta) in the premiere – "Trema per te, fellon!"

56 (top right): Pasta as Norma in the premiere – "Casta Diva"

57 (above left): Grisi as Norma – "e il sacro vischio io mieto".

58 (above right): Malibran as Norma, La Scala, 1834.

Norma at La Scala, 1955. Producer: Wallman. Designers: Benois and Fiume. Callas as Norma.
59 (top left): Act II, scene 1: Norma is contemplating to kill her children – "Dormono entrambi!".

60 (top right): Norma confronts Pollione (Del Monaco) – "In mia man alfin tu sei".

61 (above): Act II, scene 3: Norma declares war on the Romans.

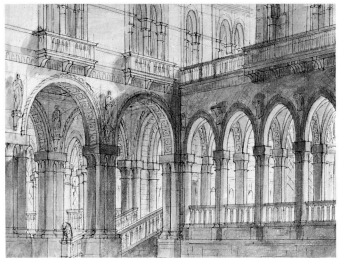

Bagnara's designs for the premiere of *Beatrice di Tenda* at La Fenice, 1833.

62 (left): Act I, scene 1: Internal courtyard of Binasco Castle. Façade of the illuminated palace.

63 (left): Act I, scene 3: A solitary grove in the ducal gardens.

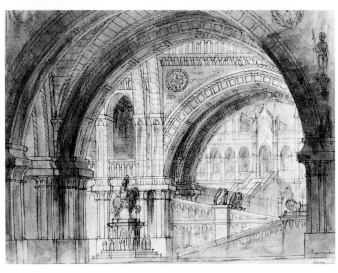

64 (left): Act I, scene 4: A remote part of the castle. At one side, the statue of Duke Facino Cane.

Beatrice di Tenda at La Scala, 1961. Producer: Enriquez. Designer: Colonello.

65 (above): Act II, scene 2: A hall leading to the prisons of the castle – courtiers moan and pray for the imprisoned Duchess Beatrice.

66 (right): Act I, scene 4: Joan Sutherland as Beatrice prays before her late husband's (Duke Facino Cane) statue for compassion.

67 (above): *I Puritani*: Part I, scene 3: The great hall of arms of the castle. Verarde's design for the premiere at the Théâtre-Italien, Paris, 1835.

68 (left): The "second" *Puritani* quartet at Her Majesty's, London, 1844. Mario (Arturo), Grisi (Elvira), Lablache (Giorgio) and Fornasari (Ricardo).

69 (top left): *I Puritani* at La Fenice, 1949. Part I, scene 2: Christoff as Giorgio, Callas as Elvira – "O amato zio".

70 (top right): Rubini as Arturo in the premiere of *I Puritani*.

71 (above): *I Puritani* at the Comunale, Florence, 1952. Part III, scene 1: Callas as Elvira, Conley as Arturo – "Vieni fra queste braccia".

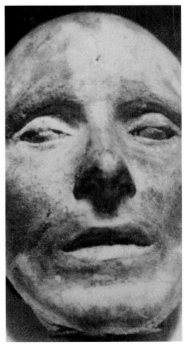

72 (above left): Levys' villa at Puteaux, where Bellini died on 23 September 1835.

73 (above right): Death-mask of Bellini taken at Puteaux on 24 September 1835.

74 (left): Bellini's tomb in the Cathedral of Sant' Agata, Catania. The inscription on the white marble and bronze tomb – *"Ah, non credea mirarti si presto estinto, o fiore!"* ("Ah! I never imagined that this flower would have died to soon!"), words and music from Amina's aria in *La sonnambula* – was chosen by his compatriots.

music, and of course his insistence that the singers not introduce any, was shown when he quarrelled with Adelaide Tosi during the rehearsals of *Bianca e Fernando* in Genoa. Tosi described the music, with its lack of embellishments, as suitable for boys and threatened to substitute for her aria another piece, a *"pezzi di baule"*.[21] Bellini, however, was in no way intimidated, and not only did Tosi sing his music as he wanted it but she also realised that this was the correct way and asked the composer for his forgiveness. Clearly, Bellini's music is complete as written and does not allow for additional ornamentation – a case of embellished melody as opposed to melody with embellishments. Two particularly apt examples are "Casta Diva" (*Norma*) and the cabaletta "O sole di vela" (*Il pirata*).[22]

On this matter, Bellini was not absolutely inflexible, however. He would deal differently with exceptional singers, such as Pasta and Malibran, who had creative musical genius. But even with these artists he preferred to supply any variations himself, thus taking advantage of each particular singer's special accomplishments and also concealing their weaker points.

The question of appoggiaturas, as distinct from all other optional embellishments, is a different matter. Singers can and should sing appoggiaturas, particularly in recitatives. Even so, Bellini was almost always careful to write out most of them, especially from *I Capuleti* onwards. In *Norma*, for example, there are some 500.

The merits and defects of Bellini as a composer will always remain, of necessity, a matter of opinion. Although few would deny the richness of feeling and the individual, often disarming melancholy or the exciting and passionate expression of fury of his vocal lines, the main criticism levelled against him in about the last 70 years concerns the poverty and bareness of his harmony and orchestration. His orchestra has been described as a "big guitar", a term referring to the practice of early-19th-century opera composers who occasionally provided a merely arpeggiated accompaniment to an aria (*arpeggiando cavatina*). These accusations certainly have considerable justification. Nevertheless, a strong case in favour of the composer can also be made. Whereas Bellini's harmonies are sometimes thought to be bare and even banal when considered superficially and out of context, these same harmonies are nearly always the best that can be found for his melodies.

The simplification of harmony and the spare use of counterpoint may often confine the orchestra to an apparently elementary accompaniment. However, in Bellini's case, it does not detract from the effect of the all-important vocal core of the music and indeed has the positive virtue of enhancing it. When counter-melodies are given either to the voice or to the orchestra, the effect is of great intensification and a gain in effectiveness results from its sparing use. Like folk song, Bellini's vocal line instinctively rejects harmonic elaboration, in general, as foreign to its nature. What it requires is a certain degree of accompaniment that must never become so obtrusive as to distract the listener's attention from the melody. This was exactly what Bizet discovered when he was commissioned to re-orchestrate *Norma*. He gave up the task in despair, declaring, "For these melodies, the appropriate accompaniment is that given to them by Bellini." Cherubini also came to the same conclusion: "It would be impossible to place any other accompaniments underneath these melodies." Were Bellini's music to be provided with elaborate orchestration and the harmonies enriched, it would become insufferable, as demonstrated when Felix Mottle re-orchestrated *Norma*.

Ultimately, it is a question of whether one likes Bellini's melodies or not, and on a matter like this there is hardly any argument. One considers a melody to be either good or bad. Likewise, appropriate harmony in itself will not necessarily make the result a masterpiece. Whereas elaborate orchestration complements and gives a marvellous new dimension to the operas of Richard Strauss, Wagner and others, in Bellini's works it seriously upsets the musical balance.

Therefore, like all innovators in music, Bellini must be judged by what he set out to do and accomplished rather than by what we think he ought to have done. Also, it must not be thought that, because he often used the orchestra like a "big guitar", he was incapable of providing more subtle, complex orchestration. Even though the broken-chord patterns preponderate as accompaniment textures, adapted in various ways to suit the melody in question, Bellini was far from mechanically applying a stereotyped pattern, in the manner of an Alberti bass. On the contrary, the placing of the notes is a matter of extreme care and subtlety, designed to achieve the best possible blend with the voice and, at times, to convey a peculiarly melancholic quality or to heighten the tension, with the simplest means. The composer was acutely sensitive to details of colour – chords link phrases and inner voices with the greatest discretion and often with telling effect. A typical example is "Ah non credea" (*La sonnambula*), in which the use of the viola d'amore solo towards the end, accompanying the voice in parallel sixths, adds with its individual colour a new intensity and poignancy to the final cry of sorrow:

It must be pointed out that Bellini does not always use this type of accompaniment. The orchestra's contribution can be of equal importance to the vocal line; *ostinato* figures of varying complexity are used to heighten the emotional content of the verses, as can be seen in this example from *Norma*:

Allegro moderato

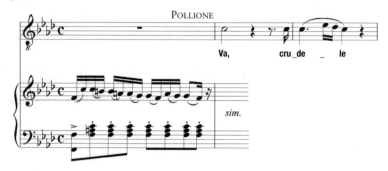

Also, in some instances, individual colour intensifies the impact of a phrase or a word. As L Orrey observed in *Bellini* (London, 1969), "Deh! non volerli vittime" (*Norma*) is a brilliant example: "The harmony is simple and austere, with something of the reserve and dignity of a Bach prelude; the single touch of horn colour, off the beat, imbues the passage with a quiet and noble grief."

There are several other instances, including purely instrumental passages, where resourceful orchestration strongly suggests the appropriate mood of the drama. A striking example occurs in the introduction to "In mia man" (*Norma*), in which the opening phrases of the melody are anticipated by the cellos, playing in their tenor register. This gives a marvellous intensity to the colour, which is then taken up in the lower register of the soprano voice when it enters with the same music. By such economical yet perfectly judged means, the scene is set as with one or two masterly brushstrokes on a canvas.

The prelude to the final scene in *Il pirata* (see page 89 for music example) demonstrates Bellini's command of the orchestra – a feat of instrumentally dark and sombre colouring achieved by the intensely emotional use of solo cor anglais and its accompaniment. Orrey interestingly commented that this introduction is on a par with the best of Rossini's early-19th-century orchestration during the composition of *I Puritani*, Bellini's last work.

It was Bellini's occasionally excessive fondness for the big drum and cymbals in orchestral passages – as in the overture to *Il pirata* – that caused his contemporaries, particularly in England, to accuse him of composing music that was noisy. This accusation, however, is not valid, because it ignores the fact that the composer reserved great effects for appropriate climaxes and always maintained a good balance between the orchestra and the vocal line.

He knew only too well what his music needed. At the time of the first performance of *Norma*, Florimo asked him to re-orchestrate it, but Bellini refused, not because he was incapable but because he knew and believed that, for his method of musical expression, "orchestral complexities would destroy the dramatic effect" ("gli artifizi musicali ammazzano l'effetto delle situazioni").[23] That he was capable of more complex workmanship is proved to a great extent, for example, by the sextet "Parlati ancor per poco" from the first-act finale of *Il pirata* (see page 87 for music example, "Ti scosta, o Dio"). This was Bellini's third operatic work, but however successful and impressive it may have been, one would hardly consider the composer to have been sure or even conscious of his own ideals and of the direction in which he was going.

The real shortcomings of Bellini's operas lie elsewhere. Scenes are not always connected psychologically, although they are in themselves logical, with the intellectual content musically interpreted. More serious is the composer's inability to discern musically between various types of characters. The good-hearted express their emotions using the same types of melody as the cruel and unscrupulous. Musically, there is hardly any difference between Filippo (*Beatrice di Tenda*), Riccardo (*I Puritani*) and Ernesto (*Il pirata*), all of whom are baritones, although their characters are diametrically opposite. They all express their feelings within the same *cantabile* style. And, as Lippmann observed, "A love aria is a love aria, no matter who sings it." (This flaw was a common shortcoming in Italian opera between 1820 and 1850. It was left to Verdi to accomplish real musical characterisation, first with *Rigoletto* [1851].) This lack of musical characterisation extends with significant consequences to the chorus; the absence of appropriate musical colour from the Puritans and the Cavaliers is as serious a cause of the limited success of *I Puritani* as any deficiencies of its libretto.

Undoubtedly, Bellini reached his greatest achievement in *La sonnambula* and *Norma*. The reasons why his last opera, *I Puritani*, is not his best have already been mentioned – the music certainly does not show an arrested development, in any sense. Yet it is difficult to imagine what he could have achieved, had he lived to produce subsequent works.

It seems more likely that Bellini would have purified his style rather than altered it drastically, until he reached those heights where melody and harmony become one. Unlike Mozart, who also died young, Bellini did not reach full musical maturity. Rossini expressed as much in a letter to Florimo:[24]

"Bellini still had much to learn; he died too young to learn all the secrets of his art. Had he lived two or three years longer, he would have learned all that he needed. He was gifted by nature and determined to rise above his rivals. They, on the other hand, could never hope to acquire the qualities that were his. Bellinis are born, not made." This is why Bellini's influence on both his contemporaries and successors was of the greatest importance in the evolution of music; his new type of melodic writing is one of the most specific qualities that differentiate the music of the 19th century from that of the 18th.

Chopin had a great regard for Bellini's operas, especially *La sonnambula*. The melodic inspiration of these two composers shows such affinity that, while listening to a typical cantilena of Bellini, one could easily imagine it to have come from the pen of Chopin. Nor is the indebtedness all on one side; if Chopin owed much to Bellini's melody, Bellini was not deaf to the other's harmony. This is particularly noticeable in *I Puritani*, in the remarkable chain of diminished sevenths in the duet "Vieni fra questa braccia" (part three) and in the mad scene (part two), shown below:

Andante

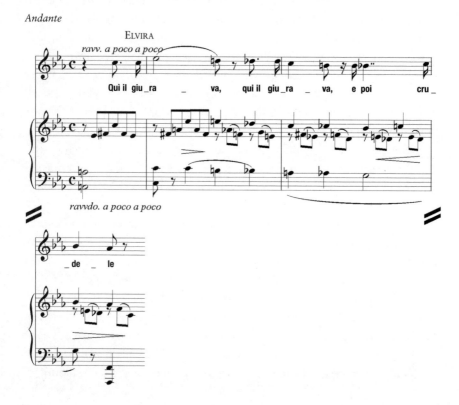

The most obvious influence on Chopin may be found in the nocturnes, which often move at a tempo almost identical to that of many of Bellini's characteristic arias. These works likewise support an expressive *cantabile* melody with the simplest possible broken-chord harmonies, transformed by Chopin into an essentially pianistic texture:

Moderato

The melodic outline of the above example from the first act of *La sonnambula* could be the matrix for many of Chopin's melodies. Played on the piano at a slower tempo, it can readily be transformed into a Chopinesque nocturne. The same applies to Giulietta's aria "Oh! quante volte" (*I Capuleti e i Montecchi*), to "Casta Diva" and to several other pieces. Also, in the second movement, the *larghetto*, of Chopin's piano concerto in F minor, one hears Bellinian cantilena throughout. The middle section of the *Fantaisie Impromptu* in C-sharp minor, opus 66,[25] and the *Allegro de Concert*, opus 46, may also be cited.

But it must be stressed that careful examination of these respective scores does not reveal Chopin to be an imitator of Bellini or indeed of Italian opera in general, which was the greatest proportion of the music heard in Warsaw during Chopin's youth. Chopin was simply a very successful stylist in Italian music, as it is vividly demonstrated in the *Barcarolle* in F-sharp major (1645-6), in which the swaying parallel thirds of Bellini's vocal *fioriture* are transformed into the pianistic equivalent of the sensation of floating on water. These compositions, however much they owe to Bellini's melody, differ mainly in that Chopin gave them his own individual harmonisation, which is absolutely inseparable from the melody.

Even though the music speaks for itself, Bellini's influence on Chopin has been often summarily refuted by many since Arthur Hedley wrote in *Chopin* (London, 1947/1963), "A comparison between the *dates* and *places* of the production of Bellini's works, the times when Chopin could have become acquainted with them (or extracts from them) and the chronology of the composition in which Bellini's influence is said to be discoverable, soon establishes the fact that, although Chopin's debt to Italian opera in general was enormous, he owed nothing to Bellini specifically."

Hedley's statistical theory rests entirely on the claim that Chopin could not have heard any of Bellini's music, or even of Bellini himself, before he left Warsaw in 1831. (In Warsaw, Bellini's operas were first performed in 1841.) Moreover, he points out that, although the *Allegro de Concert* was published in 1841, it was actually composed in 1832. However, Hedley accepts that, "from 1833 to 1835, a warm friendship existed between Chopin and Bellini". These statements are of course correct, but they give a distorted picture. In fact, the weight of evidence, when historical facts are taken into account, is to the contrary. Between July 1829 and January 1833, Chopin could well have been acquainted with *Il pirata*, *La Straniera*, *La sonnambula* and *I Capuleti e i Montecchi*.[26] Bellini arrived in Paris in April 1833, and the two musicians not only became friends but also played their compositions on the piano to each other. (See page 340-1.)

Considering the dates of composition of Chopin's nocturnes, only the opus 72 nocturne in E minor (1827) was written before he could have heard any opera. Apart from the opus 9 nocturnes (B-flat minor, E-flat major, B major) and the opus 15 (F major, F-sharp major) of 1830-1, all the others were composed after Chopin had definitely become acquainted with Bellini's music. The composition of the piano concerto in F minor was begun in July

1829 but completed sometime during the first months of 1830, after Chopin's visit to Vienna. The piano concerto in E minor was composed in September 1830.

Liszt also owed much to Bellini, in his suave and voluptuous cantilenas. The theme of "A te, o cara" from *I Puritani* (see page 376 for music example) is the type of melody that Liszt wrote in his *Liebesträume*, particularly number three.

In the *Hexameron* (1837), Chopin and Liszt[27] collaborated with various other composers on a set of variations upon the march "Suoni la tromba" from *I Puritani*. Liszt had also made transcriptions of *La sonnambula* and *Norma* by 1841. But in 1854, when Liszt conducted *I Capuleti* in Weimar, he called the opera a stale product of an old-fashioned school: "It needed the indolent fancy, the slack indifference of an agreeable young 'gentleman', this fair-haired, weak, womanish, poor-spirited Bellini, with the seeds of consumption[28] in him, with his elegant *laissez faire*, with the melancholy grace of his whole mental and bodily outfit, to induce us, for mere entertainment's sake, to make use of Italian opera without ever asking whether it accorded in any degree with our demands for dramatic truth or, at any rate, dramatic probability!"

In the finale of *Tristan und Isolde* (1857-9), Wagner re-echoed the powerful melodic shape of the finale of *Norma*. But in as early as 1834, when he had only composed one opera, *Die feen*, he wrote, "I shall never forget the impression that a Bellini opera[29] only recently made upon me, when I was thoroughly satiated with the eternal symbolic tumult of the orchestra and once again encountered the noble simplicity of song."

During the 1835/6 season, Wagner conducted *Norma* and *I Capuleti* at Magdeburg. He also conducted Rossini's *Otello* and *Il barbiere di Siviglia* and Paisiello's *La molinara*. Moreover, in the following year, he chose *Norma* for his benefit night at Riga.[30] In his article "Bellini, win Wort zu seiner Zeit", published in the Riga *Zuschauer* before the performance, he wrote, "It is with pure melody and simple nobility and beauty of song that Bellini enchants; this is certainly no sin. On the contrary, it may be a good thing if one prayed to Heaven that German composers would also write such melodies. Song, song, always song. Oh, Germans! Men can only communicate with one another through song; this type of language must also be made and kept as arbitrary as any other cultivated language should be."

Later, however, in "Mein Leben", Wagner wrote harshly of Italian operatic composers, including Bellini. But then, with the exception of Weber and Beethoven, he disparaged most of his contemporaries and immediate predecessors, especially those from whom he borrowed. In a letter to Theodor Apel dated 27 October 1835, Wagner wrote, "I'm rehearsing [Spohr's] *Jessonda*, and how I shy away again from those reactionary ideas! The opera fills me once more with utter disgust; the soft Bellini is a veritable Hercules compared with this lengthy, pedantic, sentimental Spohr. A little while ago, it occurred to me to compose an overture to *Romeo and Juliet*. I was thinking out a rough plan when – would you believe it? – Bellini's stale, insipid [*I Capuleti*] overture, with its battlefield of a *crescendo*, turned up of itself in my sketch!"

It was much later, in 1880, during the last years of his life, that Wagner, on a visit to the Naples Conservatorio, again showed the warmest affection for Bellini in a strangely moving statement to Florimo:[31] "People believe that I hate the Italian School of music and, especially, Bellini. No, no, 1,000 times no! Bellini is one of my predilections because his music is strongly felt and intimately bound up with the words. The music which I abhor, on the contrary, is that vague, indeterminate music that mocks libretto and situations."

Berlioz had only contempt to show for Bellini, whom he called "a grinning puppet". Yet he remembered him when he tried to express passion and ardour in the love scene of his *Romeo et Juliette*.

Richard Strauss's melodies, too, short though they may be in *Salome* and *Elektra*, have their seed in Bellini's longer-spun examples. Bellini's influence can also be felt in Bizet's *Les pêcheurs de perles* and in Mascagni's *Cavalleria rusticana*.

Donizetti often imitated Bellini, consciously or not. In *Il furioso all'isola di San Domingo*, one can hear more than a trace of Rodolfo's "Vi ravviso" (*La sonnambula*), composed less than two years earlier. Meanwhile, Lucia's "Regnava nell silenzio" (*Lucia di Lammermoor*) is reminiscent of Norma's "Teneri figli", as is the sextet "Chi mi frena" of "Suoni la tromba" from *I Puritani*.

Even in as late as 1898, Verdi wrote bluntly to his friend, the critic Camille Bellaigue,[32] "True, Bellini was poor in orchestration and harmony...but rich in feeling and in an individual melancholy that was all his own! Even in his less familiar operas, *La Straniera* or *Il pirata*, there are long, long, long melodies such as no one ever wrote before his day. And what truth and power of expression – for instance, in the duet between Pollione and Norma! And what loftiness of thought in the opening phrase of the overture to *Norma*... Badly orchestrated, but nobody ever wrote a lovelier or more celestial passage of the kind."

Verdi had already paid his tribute to Bellini. The great love-duet in *Un ballo in maschera* was modelled on Pollione's "Meco all'altar di venere" (*Norma*). The rousing chorus "Guerra! Guerra!" (*Norma*) is re-echoed in the first scene of *Aïda*, and Rodolfo's musical characterisation on his entry in *La sonnambula* is clearly heard in the overture of *La forza del destino*. The polacca "Vergin vezzosa" (*I Puritani*) became the bolero "Merce diletti amici" (*I vespri Siciliani*) and the quintet from *Beatrice di Tenda* was used twice by Verdi, first in the quartet of *Nabucco* and then in *Macbeth*. A more striking example is the way in which Verdi adapted "D'un pensiero" (*La sonnambula*) in his ensemble "Alfredo, di questo core" in *La traviata*.

Others unreservedly paid tribute to Bellini: "I would give all my music for 'Casta Diva'," declared Halévy, while Pizzetti (1880-1968) described Bellini thus: "Bellini's lyricism expressed itself in a song that gushes forth with the essence of an emotion that springs from the drama, that gushes forth especially at moments that bring the drama to a resolution, similar to a fire that is ignited after it emits hot sparks. And this song, gushing forth, becomes a stream, a river, finally an ocean that rolls away to the distance towards the immense horizon... Here was one who spoke with the voice of God."

The vain Gabriele d'Annunzio (1863-1938) uttered humbly at Bellini's shrine, "His melodies soar beyond the eloquence of words." More interestingly, Igor Stravinsky (1882-1971) said that Bellini was not only far ahead of his own time but so far in advance of our own that it will yet be many years before the music world fully appreciates his genius.

The severe criticism and eulogies specifically directed at Bellini, notwithstanding Wagner's contradictions already mentioned, simply amount to a superficial charge that the Italians did not adopt the philosophical German theories that purport to consider all fine art as subordinate to music, which of course is not true. The difference is that Italians never felt the need to devote time to the building of philosophical theories but rather employed a more practical, more spontaneous approach to music. Both sides have experienced success and failure, but the debate must continue without defeating itself at its own purpose. In the final analysis, it is superfluous to condemn Bellini solely on standards achieved in another land for music of a different nature and outlook. The same applies to Wagner, to cite but one example.

While essentially Italian, Bellini's music also has universal appeal. Most of his works were successful from the beginning and were performed as long as there were singers capable of conveying the music's extremely delicate emotional impact – the basic characteristic of enabling the appropriate impact to reach the listener. It is in this respect that Bellini is significantly different from Verdi or Puccini as well as non-Italians such as Wagner, Mozart and most of the 20th-century composers.

By the end of the 19th century, Bellini's operas gradually began to disappear from the world stage (although in Italy *Norma*, *La sonnambula* and *I Puritani* never disappeared completely); his art slipped out of fashion, mainly through crucially frustrating and risky casting problems. It was a period when singers were increasingly sacrificing dramatic expression for vocal display, and Bellini's operas need both great vocal technique *and* dramatic expression.

With the exception of *Norma*, Bellini's music was more or less forgotten between the two world wars. In the early 1950s, with the advent of Maria Callas, a true successor of Pasta and Malibran, who understood Bellini's scores, a renaissance of his operas began. Other singers also contributed to the resurgence, including the sopranos Renata Scotto, Joan Sutherland, Montserrat Caballé, Beverly Sills, Edita Gruberova and June Anderson; the mezzo-sopranos Ebe Stignani, Fedora Barbieri, Giulietta Simionato and Marilyn Horne; the tenors Mirto Picchi, Mario Del Monaco, Franco Corelli and Cesare Valletti; and the basses Nicola Rossi-Lemeni, Cesare Siepi, Nicola Zaccaria and Samuel Ramey.

Today, *Norma*, *La sonnambula* and *I Puritani* are in the international standard repertoire, while *I Capuleti e i Montecchi* is on the fringe and *Il pirata*, *La Straniera* and *Beatrice di Tenda* are occasionally performed. Both *Bianca e Fernando* and *Zaira*, which disappeared from the opera house after 1837 and 1836 respectively, have enjoyed revivals in the last two decades, thus making it possible for the world to hear Bellini again as a totality.

NON-OPERATIC COMPOSITIONS

Rossini, Bellini and Donizetti, although always referred to as strictly operatic composers, also wrote other music, both instrumental and vocal. Apart from a few minor compositions, Rossini wrote his songs and sacred music (*Stabat Mater*, *Petite messe solenelle*, etc) after he had given up writing operas. Donizetti, in addition to over 70 operas, wrote an incredible amount of non-operatic music, including two oratorios, 28 cantatas, 120 religious pieces, 20 instrumental pieces for orchestra, 19 string quartets, about 200 songs and a miscellany of other compositions. Bellini's output, in a career that lasted only ten years, was much smaller. Even so, he produced a comparatively appreciable amount of non-operatic music which, with the exception of most of the songs and two canons, he composed before he wrote his first professional opera.

Considering their extraordinary understanding of the technical and expressive potentialities of the human voice, it is not surprising that, between them, these three composers left a considerable legacy of songs. In their instrumental works, too, they frequently treated musical instruments as if they were human voices.

Generally, Bellini's songs are in the style characteristic of his operatic music: the long, flowing line is extremely refined, depending for its effect on melody alone and tinged with Bellinian melancholy. Musically, they transfer early-19th-century Italian opera to the drawing-room piano, albeit in a simplified manner. Consequently they cannot be compared with the genre of Lieder, which at its best shows a perfect combination of vocal melody, quasi-dramatic expression and profound harmony coupled with a significant piano part that is often as expressive and important as the voice. However, it does not necessarily follow that Bellini's songs are of inferior quality, even though in musical complexity Lieder such as Schubert's reign supreme. Yet Bellini's songs can be just as expressive in their simplicity, bareness of accompaniment and harmony. They, too, create a variety of moods, but the singer, as in the *arie antiche* of the previous centuries, has to achieve everything through the vocal line alone, with little help from the piano. In fact, the simplicity of these songs is deceptive, as they fully exploit the voice. Unlike the Germans, the Italians did not take up the challenge of the newly developed pianoforte, and there was no equivalent flowering of Romantic poetry. Some of the texts of the Italian songs are yet more settings of Metastasio, who supplies the elegant formalism for this essentially Classical style.

The *Composizioni da camera*, which includes Bellini's 15 best-known published songs, comprises nine separate songs and six ariette. The earliest song is "La farfalletta" (attributed to Bellini), a slight but attractive (if somewhat repetitive) essay that Bellini composed at the age of twelve. The rhythmic style interestingly suggests the polonaise-like features that so often propel Bellini's later music when a sense of flowing energy is needed. Of the others, two fully developed arias stand out from the rest. "Quando incise su quel marmo" is in fact labelled "scena ed aria"; its piano accompaniment suggests the orchestra and it is complete with recitative, *larghetto affettuoso*, *allegro* link and a final *allegro moderato*, occasionally florid with lively, dotted rhythms, in the manner of a cabaletta. "Torna, vezzosa Fillide", although entitled a "romanza", is in fact a long aria in several sections. After an important piano introduction, a graceful first section in A major leads to a change of mood and metre, *un poco meno mosso* (in A major again), and the line becomes more expressively embellished. The final section, *agitato*, is in the minor key. The intense Rossinian motif, first played on the piano alone, is later combined with the voice part to make an effective climax.

These two songs are exceptions, however. The majority are relatively short with elementary broken-chord accompaniments. They are rarely through-composed (with the exception of "Malinconia, ninfa gentile" and "Ma rendi pur contendo"), the most usual form being A/B/A, sometimes with a varied reprise, as in "L'abbandono" and "Vanne, o rosa fortunata", or with the last two sections repeated, as in "L'allegro marinaio", and sometimes with a codetta, as in "Vaga luna che inargenti", where the whole process is repeated, and "Per pietà bel idol mio", which has a more extended coda.

A more elaborate structure (although in miniature) is found in "Bella Nice", in which a basic A/A/B/A organisation is repeated with varied harmony and some melodic variation and extension and even followed by an extended variant of A, which develops into a coda. (Some of its most expressive phrases are also heard in the duet between Adalgisa and Pollione in *Norma*.) However, this type of internal organisation is not typical of the songs in general, which normally rely on simple statements and counter-statements with basic modulations to related keys. The only simple strophic form (with one varied strain) is found in "Sogno d'infanzia", which is feeble and over-extended, with a sentimental style and weak use of chromatic harmony and ninth chords.

Apart from the two arias already mentioned, perhaps the best music is found in "L'abbandono", where the harmonic colour truly supports the vocal line and the accompaniment texture is sufficiently varied, while in the hands of a fine artist, "Dolente immagine di fille mia" achieves considerable expressive power with minimum means.

Bellini's extant instrumental music consists mainly of seven sinfonie and an oboe concerto. With two exceptions (one composed in 1817-18 and the other sometime earlier), the sinfonie were composed during 1821-4 and the oboe concerto in *c*1823. These sinfonie are in the 18th-century Italian tradition of one-movement works, corresponding to operatic overtures, cast in a rudimentary sonata form – normally an *allegro* with a slow introduction. The ideas are presented simply, with little elaboration of detail or complexity of thematic development. The scoring is for Classical orchestra, with occasional use of trombones, although the early sinfonia in D is scored for strings with horns and clarinets only. (This choice of instruments was probably dictated by the personnel available for student performance.) In any case, the sinfonia in D is comparatively rudimentary. The essentially melodic themes of the *allegro*, which alternate between clarinets and violins, show little contrast in character and the themes are not developed. The texture is chiefly accompanied melody, pleasant but undistinguished.

In contrast, the sinfonia in E flat, for orchestra with trombones, is a fluent work. Beginning with a *largo* that contains some stirring modulations, it moves into a Rossinian *allegro vivace*. While the lively triplet figures of the first subject are taken largely by the first violins, there are moments of effective scoring for wind and brass and the jaunty second subject is cheerfully passed from flute to clarinet and back before being taken up by the strings. There is some lively development of the dotted-rhythm motif, although the key remains firmly anchored to the dominant before the themes are recapitulated. The Rossinian coda is also based on the dotted rhythms and ends *più mosso*.

Although Bellini adapted most of the characteristics of the Italian instrumental concerto – especially as composed by Cimarosa, Salieri and others, in which euphony and virtuosic brilliance were the main features – he confined the interest of the work to the solo line, employing the orchestra chiefly as accompaniment. Nevertheless, he was able to infuse his work with his own individual charm of melody and style. The concerto for oboe in E-flat major is in three sections: a short opening *maestoso* for orchestra alone, in the somewhat unexpected key of G major; a *larghetto cantabile* in E flat, based on a very vocal theme; and a final *allegro* in polonaise style, which brings the work to a brilliant conclusion. These sections clearly correspond to the traditional sections of an operatic *scena*, in which the oboe is the singer displaying both the *cantabile* style and *agilità* in the manner of the voice.

Church music occupied Bellini only during his early years and his student apprenticeship. His style was influenced by the music of his grandfather,

Vincenzo Tobia Bellini, his first teacher and an organist and composer of some repute. The boy thus grew up in the provincial environment of Sicilian church music and absorbed its language.

Ecclesiastical music was interwoven with secular trends, and much that seems naïve today was then taken for granted. As with Mozart and Haydn, the dividing line between sacred and secular conventions was not clearly drawn, but once accepted on its own terms, the music at its best radiates simple reverence and sincerity; at its worst, it need not detain us.

Typical of the religious works are the *Salve regina* in A major (*c*1818), the *Tecum principium* (1819) and the *Mass* in A minor (*c*1821). The first two works are typical products of a talented student, no better and no worse than hundreds of pieces composed yearly for church use, then and now. Their weaknesses lie in shortness and squareness of phrase and conventional harmonic and melodic progressions, with little interest in the texture or originality of melody.

The *Salve regina*, composed under the guidance of Bellini's grandfather at Catania, is for four-part chorus with orchestral accompaniment. There is little attempt at counterpoint, apart from occasional imitative entries in the voices. The music is divided into three unrelated sections in the keys of A major/minor, C major and A major. The final *larghetto* is barely long enough to balance the preceding sections. Chromatic chords occasionally appear, such as Italian sixths, but their introduction seems self-conscious.

The *Tecum principium* for soprano solo with orchestra was composed during Bellini's student days in Naples. It is a short movement (part of section three of his *Dixit Dominus*) in binary form, in a simple diatonic idiom, with perhaps a hint of Bellini's later mastery in the easy flow of the vocal line, although there is as yet little original thought.

The *Mass* in A minor for four solo voices, chorus and orchestra shows some of Bellini's more mature ability, but it is a curious mixture of the naïve and the sophisticated. Many of the choral sections are foursquare and conventional, but the solo voices are treated in ensemble with considerably increased skill and the vocal lines begin to have an expansive quality with greater range and freedom of rhythm. At times, the music maintains a certain elevation of style, but there are some painful lapses into banality, especially at the opening of the *Gloria*, which indulges in the rum-ti-tum town-band style of which Bellini would never rid himself entirely and which sometimes mars his operatic choruses.

The *Laudamus te* is an unashamed operatic duet for soprano and tenor in a lilting 6/8, with flutes and clarinets in thirds, leading to a rousing *allegro* cabaletta in 2/4 at the words "gratias agimus".

The *Domine Deus* is set as an extended bass solo, with a slow middle section in pastorale style, with flute obbligato. The writing for quartet and chorus in *Qui tollis* suggests some of Bellini's best operatic ensembles, while *Qui sedes* is an extended movement for soprano and tenor solos with chorus and with some concerto-like moments for solo clarinet, including a cadenza. The writing is fluent and again operatic.

The brief *Cum sancto spirito* introduces an extended double-figure setting of the *Amen*, which is vigorous in style and clearly meant to evoke a more "sacred" atmosphere than the preceding movements. The step from theatre to cathedral is but a small one in Italy; however, taken as a whole, the stylistic dichotomy in this mass can be disturbing to some modern ears.

The style of all Bellini's sacred music is by and large operatic, even though he composed it before *Adelson e Salvini* and therefore couldn't have transferred to it themes from his operas. However, the basic shortcoming lies elsewhere. The very young Bellini may have been quite exceptional, but by this time he had not yet developed his musical expression and originality; at best, his sacred works are a simple musical expression of the religious emotion that was completely bound up with the aesthetic climate of the time and place of its origin.

Therefore, despite the naïveté of his non-operatic output in general and of his sacred in particular, his music should be appreciated for what it is rather than condemned for what it is not; it must perforce be judged on its ability to render the character of a situation and reflect the meaning of particular phrases, albeit in the composer's terms.

16

I Puritani at the Italien, Paris (1834-35)

Bellini arrived in Paris on 20 August 1833, anxious to pursue the contract for the Paris Opéra that Levron had promised him when he had briefly stopped there on his way to London a few months earlier. However, he soon realised that the Opéra was not as easily accessible, especially to foreigners, as had appeared on his first encounter with this exclusive institution, the French lyric stage *par excellence*. "Indeed, after five months, I returned to Paris and, on talking things over again with the aforementioned director, it was impossible to settle anything, owing to the clash of interests," he would write later, on 1 April 1835, to his uncle Ferlito.[1] Bellini then turned to the Théâtre-Italien, but without giving up the idea of writing for the Opéra too, the latter being the goal on which he had set his heart. Life in Paris was very pleasant, and as it quickly became clear that negotiations for a new opera for either the Italien or the Opéra would be slow, he decided to stay indefinitely.

Some of Bellini's operas were already known in Paris – *La sonnambula* had been performed at the Italien in 1831, *Il pirata* was to be revived and *I Capuleti e i Montecchi* was also to be performed. As in London, Bellini soon met a number of Italian expatriates in Paris, whose social life revolved around Princess Cristina Belgioiso's salon. (He had met her in Milan in October 1827, following the success of *Il pirata*.) After several years of great difficulties, during which Princess Belgioiso was separated from her husband and exiled from Italy, losing her fortune in the process, she established herself once again as a great hostess in Rue Montparnasse. There, her salon attracted most of the Parisian intellectuals. George Sand, Alexandre Dumas, Victor Hugo, Heinrich Heine, Alfred de Musset, Count Carlo Pepoli, Chopin, Liszt, Ferdinand von Hiller and many others enjoyed her hospitality, protection and encouragement. Bellini would meet them all and become friendly with a few, including Chopin and Pepoli, the latter of whom would later provide the libretto for *I Puritani*.

Some of these people later wrote descriptions of Bellini. Usually, these are of the man rather than the artist, and if in some cases they seem a little superficial (they consider Bellini at leisure rather than in moments of seriousness) then they at least serve to tell us of the type of man that he was, his disposition and his general behaviour. These are the only detached descriptions of Bellini that have survived, and they are all the more interesting because they originate from first-hand testimony.

The poet Heinrich Heine had left Germany after the 1830 revolution and settled in Paris. In Germany, he was held to be a traitor and his works were banned. His love/hate relationship with Bellini is present in his maliciously witty description of the composer.[2] When asked the question, "Was he handsome?" Heine replied:

He was not ugly. You see, one cannot answer in the affirmative when one is asked such a question about one's own sex. He had a tall, slender figure, which moved in an elegant, I might say a coquettish manner, always *à quatre épingles*; a long, regular face with a pale rosiness; very fair, almost golden hair set in small curls; a very high brow; a straight nose; pale blue eyes; a beautifully chiselled mouth; a round chin. His features had something vague and characterless, something milky, and in this milk-face often mingled a sour-sweet expression of sorrow. This expression of sorrow compensated for the want of soul, but it was a sorrow without depth; it glistened in the eyes without poetry; it played passionless about his lips... Bellini's face, like his whole appearance, had that physical freshness, that bloom of flesh, that rosiness that makes a disagreeable impression on me – on me because I like much more what is deathlike and marble.

His clothes sat so languidly about his frail body and he carried his little Spanish cane in such an idyllic way that he always reminded me of the affected young shepherds with their beribboned sticks and brightly coloured jackets and pantaloons that we meet in our pastorales. And his gait was so young-ladylike, so elegiac, so ethereal. The whole man looked like a sigh *en escarpins*...

Later on, when I had known him a long time, I felt some liking for Bellini. This arose after I observed that his character was thoroughly noble and good. His soul was certainly pure and unspotted by any hateful contagion. And he was not wanting in that good-natured childlike quality that we never miss in men of genius, even if they don't wear it as an outward show.

While the inhibited, rather homophobic Heine saw Bellini to be a weak and effeminate young man, the German pianist and composer Ferdinand Hiller[3] perceived him in a different light:

Bellini's appearance was like his melodies – graceful, pleasing and charming. A perfectly proportioned figure, a head whose brow might have belonged to the most profound thinker, while his fine, fair curls, clear and frank regard, pointed nose and full lips capable of all expressions gave him an aspect more charming than that which any handsome person could desire. In no way did his appearance correspond with the usual idea one has of a Sicilian. One saw in him, rather, a descendant of one of those sons of the North who had accepted asylum in his native island and who had willingly exchanged the pine forests for the orange groves...

Gifted persons don't shine only on account of their talents; their imperfections can also be most fascinating. Bellini, as a true Sicilian, didn't speak Italian well and wasn't very advanced in French, not even as regards pronunciation, but his thinking was shrewd and he listened attentively, and his speech, therefore, although somewhat confused through the arrangement and vigour of its content, commanded an attention that a better-equipped speaker often fails to attract.

During the all-too-short winters that the maestro spent in Paris, I often had the pleasure of seeing him. A new musical world was opening up before him and a large number of phenomena affected him profoundly. Jos Dessauer, one of the best Viennese composers of Lieder,[4] had already introduced him to the marvels of instrumental music in Milan, and Bellini profited therefrom greatly. But what was this in comparison with the visions that opened out before him on hearing Beethoven's symphonies at the "Concerts du Conservatoire"? "It's as beautiful as nature!" he exclaimed when we met in the foyer after hearing the Pastoral symphony, and his eyes sparkled as though he himself had achieved something remarkable...

He also took much interest in music for the piano, even though he might not be a Chopin himself as a pianist. I shall never forget the evenings I spent in the most intimate of circles with him and Chopin at Signora Freppa's[5]... Chopin and Signora Freppa used to take their places at the piano alternately. I also used to do my best. Bellini made observations and used to accompany one or other of the airs, more by way or illustration of what he wished to demonstrate than to have it heard through. He could sing better than any German composer I have ever met, with a voice which was more full of feeling than it was resonant. His piano playing scarcely sufficed for his orchestral rehearsals and, truth to tell, this did not amount to much. But he knew exactly what he wanted and was very far from being a sort of natural poet, as some people have perhaps portrayed him. Thus I recall that, when dealing with a "song without words" in which the harmonic aspect was being stressed at the expense of the melody itself, Bellini explained with great assurance the rules under which it would be regarded, were it music for the theatre. In order to make his point, he once sang that most charming phrase in F minor, "Ah! vorrei trovar parola" from *La sonnambula*, in which for two half-bars the combination is attained with little alteration of the chords. In opera, and particularly in important arias, he wanted both delicacy of expression and technical accuracy.

Another description of Bellini, from an entirely different point of view, was given by Madame Jaubert,[6] who was closely connected with many of Bellini's friends and acquaintances. She obviously loved Bellini like a son, and in her house he found hospitality and warm friendship. She wrote:

The *simpatico* composer Bellini was another of Heine's victims, upon whom he persistently directed his mischievousness. Unfortunately for him, Bellini had frankly confessed that he was superstitious...

"You are a genius," Heine said to Bellini, "but you will pay for your great gift with a premature death. All great geniuses die young. Raphael and Mozart are good examples."

"For the love of God, don't talk like that!" Bellini promptly interrupted him. But Heine continued, "Let's hope, my friend, that the world is wrong and you are not a genius. I shouldn't worry about it. After all, the good fairies granted you the face of a cherub, the sweetness of a boy and the stomach of a stork. We can always hope that the evil fairy didn't spoil it all by giving you genius..." Bellini was not amused by this macabre wit...

The young maestro was often mischievous and naughty in his ways, and when he reached the height of his fame, he was worshipped and adored by the most beautiful women in Paris. In a word, he was the rage of the time. One could describe him with the same verses that describe [André de] Chénier's *Jeune Captive*: "You could see in his eyes how much he loved life." He appeared to be a nice young man without vanity or pretensions.

Surprisingly, in his extant letters, Bellini hardly mentions the friends that he made in Paris. The letters of this period that Florimo published, although numerous, long and detailed, mostly confine themselves to information about contracts and financial affairs. Apart from his rupture with Giuditta Turina, which was nothing new, either these letters omit any substantial information about his personal life or Florimo decided to conceal it.

Of Bellini's friendship with Chopin, there is only a single reference in their extant correspondence. In a note[7] written in Paris on 30 December 1834, in which Bellini answers in French to Madame Coltiau, he makes his excuses for being unable to accept her invitation and adds, "If I see M Chopin, I will let him know what you said." It is only through other people that knowledge of their friendship has survived.[8] Further to Hiller's references, Frederick Niecks writes in his *Life of Chopin* that Chopin met Bellini here and there in the salons of the aristocracy, and Robert Schumann, writing in 1841, says that the two composers played their music to each other, with consequent mutual artistic influence.[9]

In Paris, Bellini took up rooms in the Bains Chinoix in the Boulevard des Italiens so that he could be near the Théâtre-Italien. There was, however, another attraction – Rossini had offices at the Italien, and although he was no longer a director there, he was an artistic consultant to the directors Robert and Severini. Moreover, Rossini was still very influential in the artistic life of Paris.

The young composer Bellini, who had met Rossini four years earlier in Milan, when he attended performances of *Il pirata* at La Scala, was now anxious to renew his acquaintanceship with the great master. Apparently, during this time in Paris, Bellini considered Rossini to be against him. He explains this in a letter to his uncle Ferlito, dated 1 April 1835:[10]

I accepted the offer of the management of the Théâtre-Italien to write a new opera because it suited me in many ways. Firstly, they paid me better than I had so far been accustomed to in Italy, although admittedly not much more; secondly, it was because of the magnificent company; and finally, so that I could remain in Paris at other people's expense.

But, at that time, Rossini was my worst enemy, only of course on professional grounds, etc. As it's unusual to commission composers to write expressly for the Italien, Rossini – who truly has tremendous influence in Paris, especially with the newspapers – had the idea of commissioning an opera from Donizetti so that, brought into competition with me in this way, he would crush me... And indeed, when I heard that Donizetti had been commissioned, I became ill with fever for three days, because I realised what a trap was being laid for me. At the time, an acquaintance of mine told me that I couldn't possibly hope for much success in Paris, for if anyone was going to have any success, it would be Donizetti, who had Rossini's patronage.

However, after I recovered from this initial shock...I told myself firmly that the first thing to be done was to study my new situation more closely and then to pay court to Rossini and approach him so that I might tell him how much I admired his immense talent, etc. Also, to draw near to his ladyfriend[11] and see them both more often, to put myself almost in an intimate relationship with them, so that they themselves would resolve to protect me rather than to persecute me. All this, of course, didn't require any great effort on my part, because I've always adored Rossini, and I succeeded, while in the meantime I went on working as hard as I could. At the time, I was staying at the country house of a close English friend of mine, Mr Lewis.

Having won Rossini's friendship, I said to myself that now Donizetti was very welcome. As a matter of fact, this was the third time that I found myself writing for the same theatre as Donizetti; in 1831, I think he wrote *Anna Bolena* for the Carcano in Milan and I responded with *La sonnambula*; in the following year, he wrote *Ugo, conte di Parigi* for La Scala (it was a fiasco) and I gave them *Norma* [actually, *Ugo* followed *Norma*]; and now here I was with him again. Once I was able to overcome Rossini's dislike of me, I had no more fears, and with redoubled courage I finished *I Puritani*, the work that was to bring me so much honour, as Rossini foretold three months before the first performance.

There is no precise evidence concerning Bellini's allegations about Rossini. In fact, Rossini's subsequent behaviour towards Bellini belies them. Not only was Rossini ready to help, advising him so that his compositions would have a better chance of succeeding with the French public, but he also spoke affectionately of Bellini after his death, praising him as both artist and man.

When in the past Bellini had been engaged to write new operas for the same theatres as Donizetti – during the same seasons and, at times, for the same singers – he had been prey to rivalry. His hypersensitive nature intensified his jealousy and, immediately a rival achieved a reputation or received support, Bellini would be convinced that he was being persecuted by his enemies – a phobia often suffered by composers in similar situations. In Paris, Bellini simply could not understand why Rossini would want another composer, and especially Donizetti, when he himself was available and willing. However, it is also possible that Rossini had made remarks about Bellini's music, in his usual humorous way, that sounded maliciously critical by the time they reached Bellini.

It is not known the extent to which Rossini helped in getting Bellini the contract for the Italien, if any. Nor is it known whether Bellini asked for the commission directly or through other people, or if the management of the Italien simply invited him to write a new opera. Rossini certainly did not present any opposition, and he must have been consulted.

The contract with the Italien was signed, in all probability, sometime during January 1834. In a letter to Ferlito[12] on 22 December 1833, Bellini says nothing about it: "I've been ill in bed with a high fever for a week and I haven't yet rid myself of it completely... The only news I have is that *Il pirata* and *I Capuleti* have been performed successfully, except for Unger, who pleased very little. The other evening, Donizetti's *Gianna di Calais* was performed, but it was a failure."

The success of both *Il pirata* and *I Capuleti* may have finally motivated the management of the Italien to engage Bellini. But it is only on 12 February 1834, in a letter to Lamperi,[13] that Bellini first mentions the contract to write an *opera seria* for the Italien, scheduled to be produced towards the end of December.

At about the same time that Bellini signed the contract, he received another offer to write an opera for Naples, to be performed at the San Carlo during the autumn/winter season of 1834/5. The project was sponsored by an industrial society, and most likely it was Florimo who engineered it in an attempt to bring his friend to Naples. (Because of the Turina scandal, it would have been very difficult – for a while, at least – to lure Bellini back to Milan.) However, Bellini politely refused on the grounds that he would have to compose the opera for Paris first and, as it was expected to be performed towards the end of 1834, he would not have enough time to write another opera for production in Naples before the end of May 1835. Finally, he expressed the hope that he would be asked again at a later date.

Nevertheless, Florimo refused to give up so easily. At this time, Malibran was enjoying a triumph in *Norma* at the San Carlo, and the industrial society persuaded the theatre to engage her for January 1835, when they wanted Bellini to produce the new opera for them. However, as exciting as this idea may have been, Bellini simply could not undertake to write two operas virtually simultaneously. Writing to Florimo[14] on 11 March 1834, Bellini explains his reasons for having to refuse such a tantalising proposition:

> The great success of Malibran in *Norma* that you describe makes me very happy. I can sense your motive that, with Malibran under contract for the Festival, I should agree to write the opera for Naples in January instead of later. But, my dear Florimo, how can I find suitable libretti? I'm just about going out of my mind trying to find a subject for the opera I'm to compose for Paris. So it's impossible for me to take the risk of accepting two engagements, especially as both are for very important theatres, where a lot will be expected of me. You're right that having Malibran is already a great incentive, but do you realise that, if I write for a later date [May], it may be possible to have Rubini, Tamburini and Ronzi [De Begnis] in the company? Since their London engagement is by no means certain, because the theatre there may go bankrupt at the end of August, I would have these two and Ronzi, or some other first-rate singer. In this way, I would have time to choose suitable subjects and write music. I think you can see my point of view. And then, dear friend, there is the possibility of finding myself under contract for the Paris Opéra and, what's more, of having great difficulty in finding yet another suitable subject. You may tell Galeota that I've been given the offer to write

the opera for January but that I've replied to you about it as I have explained above.

Once the Paris contract had been signed, Bellini's immediate concern was to decide on the subject for the opera and find a suitable librettist, and this time there was no Romani. Instead, the choice fell on Count Carlo Pepoli (1796-1881), whom Bellini had already met at Princess Belgioiso's house. It is possible that Rossini suggested him, as at the time he was the only Italian librettist of any substance in Paris.

Pepoli had already enjoyed considerable fame as poet and patriot. He was another of the Italian expatriates who had been imprisoned for his political activities, after serving in a provisional revolutionary government in 1831. When he was later banished from Italy, he came to live in Paris.[15]

The usual agonised search for a suitable subject followed. "I'm looking for a subject," Bellini wrote to Barbò[16] on 12 March 1834, "and hope to find one soon, or at least choose one from the three or four that have been proposed to me. Count Pepoli will provide the verses. He is well known in Italy, as you are aware, so it all looks promising."

The subjects considered for the libretto are unknown, as again there is a gap in the extant Bellini correspondence. The choice finally fell on *Têtes rondes et Cavaliers*, a drama by François Ançelot and Xavier Boniface Saintines, later called *I Puritani*. On 11 April 1834, Bellini informed Ferlito[17] that the subject for the new opera for Paris dealt with the times of Cromwell after he had had King Charles I of England executed. After outlining the plot, Bellini pointed out that the main interest of the story would begin when the heroine lost her reason: "Giulia Grisi will play the girl, Rubini the bridegroom, Tamburini a rival of lofty feelings and Lablache a relative of the girl... I'm enthusiastic about this story and find it...inspirational. Hopefully, I shall start to compose on Tuesday at the latest, if the poet (Count Carlo Pepoli of Bologna) gives me the verses for it."

A year had passed since Bellini's rift with Romani. Although for some time he believed that he was in the right and that Romani had behaved unfairly towards him, he no longer felt any grievance; all the bitterness was gone and the wounds had healed. Apart from the affection that existed between them, Bellini also missed Romani as collaborator. When Pepoli was appointed librettist for *I Puritani*, he realised that loss more than ever. "I'll try to make peace with Romani," he wrote to Florimo[18] on 26 May, "as I have great need of doing so. If I still want to write for Italy, no one could satisfy me after him. And so, without humbling myself, I'll do my best to make peace."

The first step was taken through a man called Bordese, a mutual friend of Bellini and the estranged librettist. Acting as an intermediary, Bordese, who was in Paris at the time, wrote to Romani in Milan:[19]

> Everything to do with human feelings must be resolved. May the coldness that has unhappily sprung up between two most talented men (who do so great an honour to letters and music), two gifted men whom everyone says are born for each other, also end.
>
> Last night, I was expressing again my due respects to our friend Bellini, who spoke to me as follows: "I desire it [reconciliation with Romani] very much, more than you, my good friend... Dear Romani has allowed himself to get too angry. It pains me greatly that this has happened. May the peace that I desire, which has been called for so loudly, finally come. He would then favour me again with the fire of his genius and would reawaken mine."
>
> That fine young man left me then, repeating that Romani is the king of poets and similar things that have already been confirmed.

Although Romani was amicably disposed and was willing to make peace, he implied to Bordese that first he would have liked some explanation as to why Bellini had called the police to intervene when the libretto of *Beatrice* was delayed. This attitude prompted Bellini to write directly to Romani:[20]

> After what Signor Bordese told me of the conversation he had with you in Milan, and after your letter addressed to Bordese...I can see that you still nourish some affection for me, as I do for you. It wasn't I who did you harm. I was protesting my innocence to the public of Venice, which accused me of a secret pact with the impresario for the purpose of giving the opera *Beatrice di Tenda* at the end of the season. What proof could I deduce from the newspapers but that you were the main cause? Such a statement did you no harm, because everyone knew that the large number of libretti for which you were commissioned during that year made it very difficult for you to satisfy the composers and the theatre managers, myself included, but did you not hurl that ferocious article against me, your friend?

You say in your letter to Bordese, "Nevertheless, I haven't stopped loving him [Bellini], because I know that the fault wasn't all his, that he was encouraged by improvident friends and that he was deceived by more than one person, whose intention it was to separate us." But doesn't your conscience prick you about all the falsehoods that you asserted and wrote against me in the newspapers with such bitterness? Wasn't I at your door for all July, up until 10 August? Didn't I go to Bergamo for 20 days to stage *Norma*, and then wasn't I in Milan until 7 December? As to the choice of subject, didn't you assure me that you were waiting for plays to come from Paris? And didn't you add needless insults to what you called your "defence"? Oh, my dear Romani, you have never loved me, never! You've always attacked me, and I can prove it to you at each stage. Pappadopoli[21] can bear witness that, during that ill-starred time when I met you in Venice, when my heart was torn and my soul was in torment, I said to myself, "Can I abandon the man who has brought such glory to my career, the man who is the friend of my heart and who shares my most tender thoughts?" However, the last lines in your preface to the libretto of *Beatrice* impelled me to defend myself against the Venetians, the biggest gossips and pettiest public in the world.

But let's draw a veil over so many unhappy events and, if possible, put them right by mutual repentance, and let's return to being what I believe we've always been: mutual friends. What I proposed to Bordese, and what I now propose to you (and it's a matter of primary necessity), is that you should write an article in the papers of Venice, Milan, Genoa and Turin and say in it that Signor Romani and Signor Bellini, after repairing their mutual friendship in order that they may continue their work, have agreed to consider what appeared in the newspapers as unsaid, since these were the result of momentary irritation, etc etc. I'm just giving you the general idea, and you can express it with your knowledge in such a way that the dignity of us both will be preserved and we shall be able without shame to resume the collaboration that began with my career and that I hope will last as long as I live.

On 4 August, Bellini wrote to Florimo[22] that "Romani has never replied to my letter. This shows that he doesn't much like my frank way of expressing myself. And so I'm awaiting the return of my friend Bordese from London in order to start negotiations again."

Romani may have needed time to forgive and forget. At some point during the beginning of October, he at last wrote to Bellini, telling him that everything was all right between them. Bellini replied on or about 7 October:[23]

It is with great pleasure that I see our old and happy friendship reborn, and I thank you for it. Frankly, it seemed to me that I couldn't exist without you. I approve of your proposals, and as I won't write any more Italian operas with any poet other than you, you will thus have Bellini at your side. Tell me, therefore, if you're fixing your domicile in Turin or if you are dividing your time between Turin and Milan. If you are domiciled in Turin and I have to compose for Naples or Milan or even for Paris (as I no longer have any amorous relationships with any woman), I will come to Turin to write the operas, or I will go wherever you will be. I like to think that now, as you are a royal employee,[24] you won't have to load yourself down with so many engagements for the writing of libretti for Turin or for some other place; write for me alone, only for me, your Bellini!

Ask double what you've received per page up to now. You will thus earn more money, have more time to produce a libretto to your liking, and as your work will be more exceptional, not only will you be better paid but you will also furnish more theatrical masterpieces...

Let me know how many libretti you will write during this festival and where and for whom. Also, let me know the subjects that you'll be dealing with. I've prepared three or four such subjects, which will cause a sensation if written by you. They are subjects of an altogether new type. I hope that singing actors (good ones, I mean) won't be lacking...

I almost signed a contract with the manager of the French [Paris] Opéra, but it didn't come to a successful conclusion, owing to the amount of time that they were allowing me, which was too short, etc. Perhaps I shall write for Naples, perhaps for Milan, perhaps even for Paris – you see how many offers have been made to me at this time! I propose to accept those offers that are most favourable to us in every way. Now that I've found you again, my dear Romani, my splendid collaborator and protector, I feel at peace and am content.

Write to me soon, and I say to you again, just forget, as I will, our disagreements of the past, which should never have taken place. I shall never be able to forget your kindnesses and the fame that I owe to you. Now let's begin a new, more beautiful and glorious life together. I know that you've been made a "*cavaliere*" by your King. I will say nothing about your new position or about the decoration that you've received; you deserve it and it does honour to you, as it also does honour to your King, who conferred it on you. Goodbye, my dear friend. Believe in the affection of your ever-grateful Bellini.

PS: Write to me at once and tell me where you are, whether in Milan or Turin, so that we can meet soon. I can't wait to embrace you.

The meeting with Romani that Bellini was so anxious to arrange was not to be; he would never return to Italy, nor would ever live to see Romani again.

Although Bellini began composing his new opera on 15 April, by the end of the month he had stopped, because he found Paris too distracting. He wrote to Florimo,[25] "I hear that you met Greville, who wrote and told me of the conversation that he had with you about my laziness. My good friend was right, and I confess that I feel great regret for all the time that has been lost, but if you consider that a young man in my position who is in London and Paris for the first time cannot but amuse himself immensely, you will sympathise with me. I am now, with great difficulty, able to get used to studying music and writing a few notes, after a year of sheer inactivity. So let's speak no more of the harm that's been done, while I seek to put it right by applying myself seriously."

Sometime in May, Bellini moved to Puteaux, a suburb west of Paris and just beyond the Pont de Neuilly, where he stayed at the country house of Mr Levys,[26] "a close English friend", as Bellini described him.

Not much is known about Samuele Levys, who was to play such a strange part in Bellini's last illness and in whose house the composer was given hospitality for several months. Bellini gives no more information about him. Levys was a young, rich, Jewish banker who had a villa at Puteaux and a house in Paris. He liked to mix with society people and it is possible that he met Bellini in one of the Parisian salons. During this period, he lived with a woman whom he introduced as his wife, but some writers, particularly Baron Aymè d'Aquino, have recorded that Levys was not married and that the lady in question was a Miss Olivier, apparently beautiful but lacking in personality.

At Puteaux, Bellini was given a comfortable room overlooking the Pont de Neuilly and a garden by the River Seine. On 26 May, he wrote to Florimo,[27] "I'm now living in the country house of an English friend; it's near Paris – only half an hour away on foot. Here I can write without anyone disturbing me, so I hope to finish the opera without any more interruptions. As I wrote to you before, the introduction and Tamburini's entrance are already planned. Pepoli is working, although keeping him moving ahead is quite tiring."

The congenial location of the English friend's house encouraged Bellini to stay at Puteaux until the autumn, with only occasional visits to Paris. He began writing in earnest but soon discovered that, although Pepoli was a good poet, he lacked experience in adapting his verses to the demands of music drama. This situation created problems for Bellini, who found it necessary to constantly guide the preparation of the libretto. In an undated letter (obviously written in the spring of 1834), he wrote to Pepoli:[28]

Don't forget to bring the piece I've already sketched out with you, so that we can settle the matter of the first act; provided that you fortify yourself with a good dose of moral patience, you'll find that the poetry will turn out magnificent and gripping and absolutely right for the music, in spite of yourself and all your absurd rules, which are fine but futile and can never convince anyone who has known how to move people to tears by means of song.

If my music turns out to be good and the opera pleases, you may write a million letters protesting against the injuries inflicted on poets, etc, without being able to prove anything. Facts are what count, not rhetorical prattle, however polished it may be, otherwise you have nothing but long and tiresome discourses. Carve in your head in indelible letters, "In opera, it is the singing that moves one to tears, that causes horror, that inspires death." Simplicity is the keynote. Musical artifice is what destroys the effectiveness of situations, but poetic artifice is even worse; naturalness and nothing more is what is required. Poetry and music can only be effective when they are true to nature, and that is all. Anyone who forgets this is lost and will only produce a dull, heavy work which will please only pedants. It will never appeal to the heart. But if the heart is moved, then one can't go wrong, in spite of a flood of words that can prove nothing at all.

Will you at last understand this or not? I beg you to understand it before you start writing the libretto, and I'll tell you why: because good drama has nothing to do with good sense. It's because I know only too well what intractable animals the literati are, and also how ridiculous they can be, with their general rules of good sense. What I say has been proved by the facts in the world of art, for almost the majority of your famous men have gone astray in this respect. And so be at peace. Carluccio and Vincenzillo have a command to become honourable together, and if you don't believe it, I would require it with all my strength. I'm certain that I can prove it to you, provided that inspiration and your obedience don't leave me.

Goodbye, with a hug from your incorrigible Vincenzillo.

When the subject for *I Puritani* was decided, Bellini prepared a rough scenario for the libretto.[29] Pepoli later wrote on it his personal comments concerning their collaboration: "Maestro Vincenzo Bellini had melody in his soul and considered it paramount. An excellent man with goodness in him, he was sometimes eccentric by nature. At certain times, he called me angel, brother, saviour. However, to my observation about the difficulty and impossibility of changing the composition of the drama or the verses – when he wanted to alter the melodies of his music for the third and fourth time – he would fly into a rage, calling me a heartless man without feeling or friendship. Afterwards, we would become better friends than we were before."

Nonetheless, the collaboration of composer and librettist was progressing. On 24 July, Bellini wrote to Florimo,[30] "I've finished the first act, except for the finale, which is, however, already thought out. As it is, the opera seems endless. Therefore, I've asked Pepoli to reduce the two remaining acts to one. There are nine pieces of music in the first act – imagine, then, what fun!"

Writing to Pepoli[31] on 8 September, Bellini comments on the verses and gives further detailed instructions:

The trio is just right as you've arranged it. When I came to the chorus that opens the second part, however, I realised straight away that it was too short; therefore, try to extend it to eight lines and make a chorus worthy of the lines Giorgio has to sing. Consider it carefully first, my dear fellow!

Another little thing. In the chorus "Qual novella? Giorgio", instead of launching into "Cinta di rose", etc, I would like Giorgio to be able to reply "Ah! si, ognor" (for instance). Then the chorus "Senza tregua?", to which Giorgio answers, "Accostatevi, ascaltare", or something like that, etc. This makes a preparation for the scene and the audience will listen more eagerly to the beginning of the story.

When you have something ready, come here. Even if you run into difficulties of any kind, come just the same to see your tormentor, who loves you in spite of your pig-headedness.

The hard-pressed librettist persevered, and before the end of September Bellini had composed most of the music. He wrote to Santocanale on 21 September,[32] "My opera is in its concluding stages. I have worked and am working on it with diligence. We must always remember that the public is a monster, especially the Parisian public, because it is a blend of various nationalities. My opera will be called *I Puritani* and it's to go on stage at the end of December... I saw Rossini yesterday and he asked about you, etc. He told me that Casarano had proposed, or had already commissioned you, that you should guarantee a credit, etc. I told Rossini many bad things about you, as you hate me so deeply, don't you? He will write to you... Goodbye, dear friend."

In the meantime, Bellini, who had been so anxious to cultivate a friendship with Rossini, had achieved little more than some brief social meetings. When the season at the Italien closed in June 1834, Rossini left for Italy to recuperate at Castenaso. He had been feeling weak and his physician had urged him "to breathe the air of his native land".

Rossini travelled to Italy in the company of Robert and Severini, who went there for the purpose of finding new operas and new singers. Late in August, he returned to Paris, his health so much improved that he again began to lead a social life. Early in September, Bellini took Rossini some of the music that he had composed for *I Puritani*. His main purpose was to make a good impression and thus try to win Rossini over as friend and protector. Writing to Florimo[33] from Puteaux on 4 September, Bellini describes the meeting:

Rossini has returned to Paris. He received me very well. I think he's very pleased with me, and I also hear that he speaks very well of me. He is now much more affectionate towards me and has told Pepoli that my frank nature pleases him and that my music tells him that I must have deep feelings. Pepoli answered, "Bellini's greatest gift is to speak well of all musicians, without exception." (And I, since leaving Italy, have been careful not to make the slightest remarks about the works of other composers.)

Then I asked Rossini to advise me (we were alone) as a brother and begged him to love me well. "But I do love you well," he answered.

"Yes, you love me well," I added, "but you must love me better." He laughed and embraced me. But let's wait and see whether Rossini is genuine about his feelings for me or not.

Following this successful meeting, Bellini tried in every possible way to secure and maintain Rossini's interest. Writing to Santocanale[34] on 24 November, he strives to do Rossini a good turn: "I hope I succeed on this occasion in imploring you to attend to Rossini's affairs.[35] Please interest yourself greatly in this matter, as he wants once and for all to see his affairs taken care of, so that he doesn't merit the bad humour of his wife, who is the owner of the property. Rossini is always polite to me, now. He protects me and wishes me well, and I can repay him at this moment only by giving you this plea, about which he knows nothing, understand? If his protection becomes stronger, my glory will profit greatly, as in Paris he is the 'musical oracle'."

Henceforth, Bellini's meetings with Rossini became more frequent, and to some extent he entered the elder composer's circle of friends. His aim was to become Rossini's favourite before Donizetti arrived in Paris to produce his opera for the Italien.

Meanwhile, *I Puritani* was nearing completion and Bellini, who had not composed an opera for a year and a half, was rather pleased with himself. He wrote to Florimo[36] on 21 September, "As yet in Paris, I'm considered the best after Rossini, and I hope – if I'm not deceiving myself – to strengthen this idea with my new opera, which appears to me to be turning out very well. I've orchestrated it with indescribable accuracy so that, as I look at each piece I complete, I feel the greatest satisfaction. The first act is completely orchestrated, apart from two pieces; for the second act, I've orchestrated everything I've set to paper."

After listing in detail the sections of the opera still to be written, he continues:

Rossini is very satisfied with everything he's seen and is always telling me that they were wrong, very wrong, to describe me as tardy and lazy…

If we wish to count the pieces, they come in fact to 14, but my dear Florimo they are in accordance with my custom, short and ardent, and the action develops well during them. Pepoli is showing true friendship towards me, and there's nothing wrong with anything that he's done with respect to myself. He's better than anyone else, but he is no Romani, and Romani is not easily found... I've not yet orchestrated the duet between Lablache and Grisi, because Lablache arrived only the day before yesterday and neither Grisi nor Rubini are yet in Paris and I need them to rehearse it first... I hope to have everything finished in October.

Giulia Grisi[37] was the best soprano that the Italien could produce at this time. Rossini had heard her sing in his operas in Italy a few years before and he appreciated her greatly, and in 1832 he assisted her engagement at the Italien. In her first season there, she sang Semiramide and Donna Anna, but as her success was only moderate, she withdrew from the stage for a period to rest and study. When she reappeared at the Italien as Giulietta in the first presentation in Paris of *I Capuleti e i Montecchi*, in the following year, her success was so complete that it established her as a star. This led to her London debut in 1834 as Ninetta in Rossini's *La gazza ladra*. Chorley[38] has left a vivid description of her impact:

> Never has so beautiful a woman as Mme Grisi been so little coquettish on the stage... And what a soprano voice was hers! Rich, sweet, equal throughout its compass of two octaves (from C to C) without a break or a note which had to be managed... In 1834, she commanded an exactness of execution not always kept up by her during the [successive] years of her reign. Her shake was clear and rapid; her scales were certain; every interval was taken without hesitation... Nor has any woman ever more thoroughly commanded every gradation of force than she – in those early days, especially... In the singing of certain slow movements *pianissimo* – such as the girl's prayer on the road to execution in *La gazza* or as the *cantabile* in the last scene of *Anna Bolena* (which we know as "Home sweet home") – the clear penetrating beauty of her reduced tones was so unique as to reconcile the ear to a certain shallowness of expression in her rendering of the words and the situation...

I have never tired of Mme Grisi, during five and 20 years. But I have never been, in her case, under one of those spells of intense enjoyment and sensation which make an epoch in life, and which leave a print on memory never to be cancelled by any later attraction – never to be forgotten so long as life and power to receive shall endure.

Bellini did not think particularly highly of Grisi's artistic capabilities at the time that she created the role of Adalgisa in 1831.[39] Even though she had improved greatly by 1834 and was then the only rival of Pasta[40] and Malibran to speak of, as well as becoming a celebrity after *I Puritani*, Bellini's opinion of her, expressed in a letter to Florimo[41] dated 1 July 1835, still carried serious reservations:

There is also news that *Norma* has been [performed] in London with Grisi playing the leading part and that it was a very great failure. The newspapers say that she sang and acted worse than in any other opera, and they recall Pasta, regretting greatly that she didn't take part in this performance. Oh, dear Florimo, you can't imagine how pleased I was that Grisi has had this failure in London rather than in Paris. My dear friend, you have no idea of the harm that I would suffer if *Norma* failed here... On the other hand, a successful performance will give me good press, which will further enhance my fame in France.

I had heard Grisi sing the cavatina ["Casta Diva"] extremely badly, and this was enough for me to judge her incapable of the remainder by having seen her in *Anna Bolena*, which, apart from the tenor, was unbearable anyway, especially as regards the tragic side. For *La sonnambula*, *I Puritani*, *La gazza ladra* and 1,000 works of a simple and ingenious nature, I'm sure that Grisi would be second to none, but for more elevated characters she neither understands nor feels them, as she doesn't have the genius or the education to sustain such parts with the nobility and style that they require. It's therefore my feeling that, as Norma, she would amount to nothing, and in this opera only the part of Adalgisa is suited to her character. I hope that the London result will persuade her not to appear in *Norma* in Paris – Malibran should perform Norma and bring pleasure to the French.

An episode[42] at the end of September 1834 provided the opportunity for Rossini to hear some of the music of *I Puritani* with the result that, from then on, his interest in Bellini became more constructive. When Giulia Grisi arrived in Paris, Bellini went to her house to show her and Lablache some of the music that he had composed for them. They tried out the prayer "La luna, il sol, le stelle", which is inserted into the introduction of the opera, and Lablache proposed to repeat it so that Rossini, who had just come in, should hear it. "Rossini complimented me," Bellini later wrote to Florimo, "and then I asked him (in order to flatter him and also because I believe he is capable of giving excellent advice) if he would be so kind as to look at my opera. He told me that he would."

In another letter, Bellini informed Florimo of the aftermath of this meeting:

> A few days later, I sent a mutual friend around in order to urge Rossini not to forget the favour that I asked of him. Rossini replied tactfully that he felt happy with the pieces that he'd already seen (he alluded to the prayer) and from which he'd gathered that I was still working on the score... He believed that he could advise me about instrumentation when he had the complete score... As I've orchestrated [here] better than ever before, I hope he will find (to his surprise) that I have advanced equally in that direction...
>
> If I really had Rossini's patronage, I would have broken the back of the work. Soon, I will show him a few items and then I'll tell you everything he says. I'll go to him with the greatest pleasure, as I believe that I'll benefit by his advice or praise; his advice will be useful and his praise will give me courage.

Not long afterwards, Bellini won Rossini's interest and affection by a calculated strategy. His meeting with Olympe Pélissier[43] is described in a letter to Florimo[44] on 24 October 1834: "Among other things, the other day I met Madame Pélissier, Rossini's *inamorata*, in the management office. I acted as if I were enchanted by her and asked her permission to call on her at home. Yesterday evening, I saw that my attention had produced the desired effect, as both she and those who were in her box applauded enthusiastically."

Almost certainly, Bellini was referring to a performance of *La sonnambula* at the Italien with Giulia Grisi and Tamburini in the lead roles.

Undoubtedly, Rossini did take an interest in Bellini and his music. Precisely what advice he gave, or whether he did any "touching up" of the score of *I Puritani*, is difficult to know. In a letter to Florimo[45] on 18 November 1834, Bellini again mentions Rossini's interest.

> The best news that I can give you is that Rossini loves me very, very, very much. (Don't tell anyone about this.) Two days ago, he began to look at the score of my introduction and found it magnificent (and there *are* some wonderful things in it), so much so that he's given orders that I am to have an organ on the stage to accompany the prayer quartet in a particular passage, etc. He said that I'd orchestrated in a way that he would never have believed me capable. He found Tamburini's cavatina graceful, the duet between Lablache and Mme Grisi very beautiful and the chorus just before Rubini's entrance orchestrated with great taste. So Rossini is enchanted; he is praising me to everybody, and several people have already told me about it. Also, he talked to me in such a way that I'm quite sure, this time, that he is absolutely genuine. He told me the day before yesterday, after looking at the introduction, that he would see that I remained in Paris. In any case, if this opera was a success, the directors of all the theatres would make handsome offers, and therefore I ought to stay on in Paris and think no more about Italy.

Albert Soubies, in his *Le Théâtre-Italien de 1801 à 1813*, also mentions Rossini's interest in Bellini, but again nothing particular is specified: "It may thus be seen that Rossini has no scruples when it comes to touching up the works of his young rivals – even the most accomplished one, *I Puritani*, for example."

Rossini's own comment on *I Puritani*, made after the opera was performed, appears in a letter that he wrote to Santocanale:[46] "The score shows a notable advance in instrumentation. I have been constantly urging Bellini not to allow himself to be beguiled by Germanic harmony and to rely all the time on his own felicitous ability for inventing melodies both simple and sure in their effect."

Throughout his time in Paris, Bellini was constantly engaged in negotiations for new operas. The Opéra had not actually made an offer, although it had seemed hopeful that they would. Bellini did not bother with the Opéra-Comique when he realised that they were not going to pay him what he asked. There were also long negotiations with Naples, where Florimo was faithfully looking after his interests, and he missed no opportunity to further his friend's welfare. On 24 July 1834, when writing to Florimo[47] from Puteaux, Bellini enclosed a copy of a letter to Lanari so that Florimo would be fully aware of his negotiations. (Naples was then negotiating for three operas.) The letter to Lanari ran:

It is already an established fact that, before concluding a contract, at least 100 letters must be written first. However, in the end, we do reach an agreement, and it's my good fortune that I always finish by being in the right. This is what happened respecting *Norma*, *I Capuleti* and *Beatrice*. I fervently wish to write for my country, but why do I find such reluctance among the rich gentlemen who conduct the enterprise with so much splendour, and reluctance only as regards my contract, a contract which I, they and the public wish to be drawn up? Well, I will make a final acceptable proposal, whereby the company will undertake the same engagement as that when I wrote for the San Carlo. The fact is that I cannot and will not suffer uneasiness about ownership of the score. You yourself know what fraudulence is committed regarding musical scores, which are sold before they are even performed. All this being admitted, and as I have asked, through Cav. Galeota, for 4,000 ducats for a single opera, without right of ownership, now that the contract is no longer for one but three operas, I restrict my claims to 10,000 ducats for all three. I mean 2,000 ducats less than if calculated according to my first request. The effort I shall have to make in order to supply you with the first opera by this winter must also be borne in mind, and the society must take this into consideration...

Let's move on to the conditions that the contract is to contain, assuming that you don't come up with any other objections (to which I would no longer know how to answer).

(1) I will stage my first opera in the early part of February 1835. It will be written for Malibran, [Gilbert-Louis] Duprez, [Carlo] Porto and for all the singers engaged by the royal theatres, as the libretto requires. I wouldn't be able to deliver the opera earlier, owing to the time needed for writing the opera and the time needed for the journey. Furthermore, the management here may need me to be in Paris. But

as I've finished the first act of the opera I'm writing [*I Puritani*], I hope to finish the work completely by mid September so that I can immediately apply myself to the opera for Naples, and should the management decide to stage it in November, I will come to Naples as soon as I'm required. Otherwise, it will have to be in February, but not in a gala performance, for such occasions are worse than cholera itself, as regards musical values.

(2) If the society can secure the theatre, I will supply the second opera in January 1836 and the third in January 1837, but should the contract of the society with the government terminate with the festival of 1836, then I shall supply the second opera in July 1835 and the third in January 1836. The contract is thus concluded for three operas. (I could and should have earned more for all this work.)

(3) I shall be in Naples for a month before staging the first opera and I will help with the rehearsals for about a month and a half.

(4) I will undertake responsibility for the libretti. The management will pay 1,000 francs for each libretto. This is the price that Romani demands and which the Théâtre-Italien has agreed to pay Pepoli...

(5) Ownership of the three operas shall be assigned by me to the management.

These are the main conditions. I hope that they suit you. I await either the contract for my signature or else a refusal, so that I can make my arrangements, as I still have other answers to give. Have you understood, my dear Lanari? Think it over carefully and remember that Mazarin tells us to "think things over first so as not to regret them later".

To Florimo, Bellini wrote:

Be assured, and assure Cottrau, that the opera for Paris will be finished in 50 days. At least, I will do everything possible to make it so. Therefore, when Rossini arrives, he will find the score ready and this will be before the date (30 October) by which I am obliged to deliver it... In accordance with the letter addressed to Lanari, it transpires that I am obliged, despite possible extenuating circumstances, to supply an opera for Naples in February. You do see that I shall have to finish the one for Paris before I begin the other. You told me that you might see that an exceptional clause is inserted in the contract to the effect that, in case of my inability to finish the new opera, the one written for Paris (but with Malibran) might be used instead. This could not be done. First, because this opera is written for two leading basses, both with interesting parts; second, because the society must guarantee a new opera to the season-ticket holders and therefore could not accept the "said condition" without engaging another composer who, should I not supply the new opera, would fulfil the conditions of the contract. By giving my assurance now that I will certainly write the opera, it transpires that it will be easier for the society to pay what I ask, thus saving the cost of engaging another composer. Have you understood?

On 21 September, Bellini informed Florimo[48] of the results of his negotiations:

I have delayed in answering your letter of 25 August in view of my dealings with the management of the Opéra-Comique, with whom I have finally broken altogether because, dear friend, it's a difficult thing to conclude advantageous contracts with the Jews, and in this case it was rather a question of money, as far as I was concerned, rather than of personal prestige.

Having now received a negative reply from Naples, I told the managing director of the Opéra-Comique that I was freed from any engagement and that we could renegotiate. We then talked about the cast, payment and time available. The next day, I received the draft of the contract, whereby I was placed under the obligation of delivering the completed opera six months after the libretto had been accepted by me. I replied that such a clause was outside our agreement... Consequently, I have abandoned them...

I hope you haven't forgotten that the manager of the Grand Opéra [Paris Opéra] as good as invited me to write an opera for him, and that after I asked a price, as Rossini had done, apart from the author's dues, the matter [fell through]. Perhaps they will ask Donizetti now; he will accept it, but I've refused it. You may well think, dear friend, that now that the Grand Opéra is in the hands of a director (what we call an impresario, they call a director here) it is easier for an opera or a maestro not approved by the French Institute to be admitted to the

Great Theatre. This is exactly so. Can you imagine that a certain Monsieur [Jacques] Halévy,[49] who failed at the Italien and at the Opéra-Comique and who is now chorusmaster at the Opéra, is to give an opera there within three months – in the same theatre where *La vestale, Guillaume Tell* and *Robert le Diable* were first performed?

In spite of Bellini's disagreements with Naples, negotiations still continued. When it became clear to him that he would never be able to write the first of his three operas for Naples in time, he agreed instead to arrange *I Puritani* for Malibran and Pedrazzi and other singers of the San Carlo company. On 20 November 1834, the contract was at last sent for Bellini's signature. On the following day, he informed Florimo[50] of his definite plans for Naples:

Yesterday, I finally received the documents, accompanied by the most friendly letter from Prince Ottajano. You know how much I want to please these gentlemen, especially the Prince, so I am inclined to agree to the contract. But as you know from my letter of the 18th, I'm not certain that I can come to Naples, for two important reasons. One is because of a contract with the French Opéra (although I haven't yet signed anything, I've promised on my word of honour) and the other, more important reason is that I will be needed for the staging of *I Puritani* here. Suppose they decide to stage *I Puritani* at a later date. What would I do then? I wouldn't be able to oblige them without jeopardising my opera. Even if one performer of the four should fall ill, what could any of us do about it? I emphasise this point because I want you to go to Prince Ottajano and express my regret to him for this alteration and tell him that I fully intend to ensure that my opera will be staged for him shortly before the end of Madame Malibran's contract...

And so tomorrow I will begin the necessary arrangements that the opera requires: I will transpose the part of Tamburini for Pedrazzi; I will instruct Pepoli to produce the verses for Malibran's cavatina. In a word, I shall make certain of despatching the whole score "cut and dried" (so that it won't be subject to excisions) on 1 January to the person Prince Ottajano instructs me to, should I be unable to come myself. I will also send you libretti or plays which you will read to Prince Ottajano, but in secret, because I don't want other composers to use them before me... *Gustav III*[51] is interesting, spectacular and historical, and I believe that the [censors would allow it]. Perhaps it would be best not to have Gustav killed, should they so desire it, but the situations are fine and novel. Then there is *Un duel sous Richelieu*,[52] which is dramatic and highly effective. I'd like to set them both to music. Do you think the Minister of Police could be persuaded to approve, as he has fewer prejudices, all in all?

You can imagine how eagerly I await your answers... I hope to apply myself as much to the two [new] operas for Naples as I did for the opera in Paris and that, if inspiration isn't hard to find, I will prove to [Prince Ottajano] how much my heart has been touched by his generosity in this matter, which for more than a year couldn't be concluded either by Galeota or Lanari or anyone else.

Goodbye, dear Florimo... I will send the libretto when it's completed, in a few days. I hope there will be no trouble about it, as neither religion, illicit love nor politics enter into it. If the title *I Puritani* should prove prejudicial, let it be called *Elvira* instead. *Le teste rotonde ed i cavalieri* is too long, and we have chosen the former because it is famous through Walter Scott's *The Puritans*.

The day after Bellini wrote the above letter, a new obstacle loomed large: the presentation of *I Puritani* at the Italien was postponed until 21 January. This meant that it would be impossible for Bellini to be in Naples to prepare the performances there, which were scheduled for the beginning of February. He wrote to Florimo[53] on 30 November:

I am working like Hercules, but I'm happy, delighted, because everything I do is turning out well and pleases me: the libretto is full of feeling, as you guessed; it isn't tragic, not high-flown, but tender and passionate, and I think I've hit on the right music; if my tunes suit the taste of the French public, the opera will cause an unprecedented furore because of its suavity, with most delicate and original accompaniments, with harmonies that are tasteful and limpid, like some of those in *Norma* and *La sonnambula* and which lend interest to a piece without disturbing the melody. Anyhow, I hope that my labours will be crowned with success...

You can see how right I was to fear that I couldn't be in Naples in time to stage *I Puritani* myself. It was impossible to fix the date for the first rehearsal before 15 December. I therefore won't get my opera staged until 15 January, at the earliest, as long as no one is sick. When will I get to Naples? When will I get the rehearsals over? You may say, "This is because he made no provision [for something like this]," but, dear friend, you need a month to get a reply from Naples, and these difficulties hadn't yet arisen when I wrote. Therefore, if the gentlemen of the society will allow me to come to Naples to stage one of my old operas instead of the January one, the matter can be settled. Otherwise, I don't know what to rely on, but I'm almost certain that Ottajano won't object to what I have asked and that this contract will be concluded, especially after I read in your letter of yesterday that this nobleman is a great patron of [Ronzi] De Begnis and it will therefore please him if I write an opera for her. With Versace, I have revised *Un duel sous Richelieu*, so that the female part can be adapted for De Begnis. I see no problem of it being suppressed by the censor, and therefore Romani could prepare a good libretto out of it for me...

I await letters from Romani every day. I think that he still causes despair to those poor maestri who are dependent upon him. I mean to go to Turin and stay with him during the period I need to compose the two operas. He was very foolish not to accept my invitation to stay with me at my house in Paris. If I accept other engagements with these French theatres, I may have to remain here, in which case I would be very glad to have Romani with me. But in any event, unless he refuses, he alone can satisfy my requirements, and I would want him to provide all the libretti for the operas that I hope to compose for Italy.

I Puritani was completed during the second week of December and Bellini presented it to Rossini for his inspection with the words, "Here is my 'humble' work, all finished, and which I present to you, my great master. Make what you will of it: cut, add or change it completely, if you think it's necessary, and in this way my music will benefit greatly!"

Again, what Rossini modified, if anything, is unclear. One piece of advice that he gave, and which Bellini adopted, was to break the opera into three acts instead of two, the second act to end after "Suoni la tromba", the cabaletta for the two basses. This change was made only after the dress rehearsal on 20 January 1835. (Rehearsals for the opera had begun in around the middle of

December, but because of Tamburini's indisposition the premiere of the opera was postponed to 24 January.) What went on at the dress rehearsal is best described by Bellini, who wrote about it to Florimo[54] on 21 January:

> I don't want to waste a moment to tell you the great news about yesterday's dress rehearsal. There were as many people there as at a first night, and my music was considered absolutely splendid! I've never been so happy in my life. All [of high] society, all the great musicians and all the most cultured people in Paris were at the theatre. They were very enthusiastic about the music and everyone embraced me, even my dearest Rossini, who now really loves me as a son...
>
> I received your letter about the *Puritani* score, which should have reached you today. Tell Prince Ottajano to write to me as soon as possible to say if they are satisfied with the subject of the *Duel de Richelieu*. I have to start work on it immediately, because I'm bound to have some tempting propositions from the Opéra here, and then I will have to stay in Paris for as long as my career demands.
>
> Oh, my dear Florimo, I so wish you were in Paris, but one can't have everything in life. Goodbye, my Florimo. Give my greetings to all and love your Bellini.

I Puritani was a triumph in Paris, which was then the operatic showcase of the world, and Bellini was reaffirmed without reservation as being the Italian operatic composer of the day. (Rossini was still considered to be the great master, even though *Guillaume Tell*, written in 1829, proved to be his last work for the stage.) Bellini's opera was magnificently staged by Domenico Ferri, another Italian exile in Paris. Giulia Grisi, Rubini, Tamburini and Lablache, who sang the principal roles, surpassed themselves and from that point on were known as "the famous *Puritani* quartet".

Rossini's opinion of *I Puritani* has survived in a letter that he wrote on 27 January 1835 to Santocanale:[55] "I'm delighted to be in a position to tell you that Bellini's opera *I Puritani*, composed expressly for Paris, has just achieved a brilliant success. The composer and the singers were called on the stage twice, and I must tell you that such demonstrations are rare in Paris and only happen if they are truly deserved. My prophecies, as you can see, are fulfilled, even to the extent that they are beyond what I had hoped for..."

"Please convey the news of Bellini's success to my good Cesarrano and tell him that *I Puritani* is the most accomplished score that Bellini has yet composed."

The composer's reactions to the success of *I Puritani* are described in a letter to Florimo,[56] almost certainly written on 26 January:

I cannot find words to describe to you how I feel. On Saturday, my opera finally went onto the stage, and the effect, although [similar to] that of the dress rehearsal, surprised even me. After the introduction, Tamburini's cavatina was charming and was applauded, Rubini's entry was most effective, the *duettino* gave great pleasure, the polonaise quartet was frenziedly applauded, as were the trio and Rubini's solo. The finale brought the house down. In act two (we have divided the opera into three acts, putting Grisi's aria before the duet for the two basses which concludes the second act with very great effect), the chorus was very much appreciated, and so was Lablache's romanza. Grisi's recitative and aria were a huge success, especially the entire first movement, when she goes mad and passes from one thought to another. Besides, Grisi sang and acted the part like an angel. Everyone was in tears. Her entry in 6/8 time, when she thinks she is going to her wedding and to the ball, was especially moving.

The effect that the two basses made was incredible. The Frenchmen went out of their minds, and there was so much noise and shouting that they were astonished to be so transported... In short, dear Florimo, it was an unparalleled occasion, and since Saturday night Paris has been talking of it with amazement... Lablache had to drag me tottering from behind the scenes, so to speak, and present me to the public, who yelled like a lot of madmen. All the women waved their handkerchiefs and the men waved their hats...

The curtain rose for act three and the public was still in a state of frenzy. Rubini's romanza was loudly applauded but was found rather long, because of the repetition and the long recitative; thereafter, the duet (particularly the part where the recognition is made) was very effective, even though half of the *largo* had been cut out at the last rehearsal because it was too long. The cabaletta was also very effective, but the finale brought the house down. The audience called loudly for [me] and the singers, so we were obliged to appear a second time.

The second performance takes place tomorrow, Tuesday. I've made some other cuts, because if the two pieces are to be repeated, as at the first performance, the opera will finish at midnight, and here they aren't accustomed to, nor do they like, staying in the theatre late. So yesterday I cut out pieces of little importance and have thus shortened the opera by 35 to 40 minutes.

Oh, dear Florimo, what an effect the orchestral part made... How happy I am! What a challenge we've faced, and with what a marvellous result! I'm still trembling from the effect that this success has had on my moral and physical condition. At the present moment, I am like a blockhead, so great was the impression on me.

The Court wishes to perform the choruses from *Norma* and I will do my best to ensure that it goes splendidly for them. Also, last Wednesday they wanted pieces from *I Puritani* to be played at the Court concert, but it wasn't possible because there wasn't enough time to rehearse the orchestra. The Queen has had a letter sent to me saying that she will attend the second performance tomorrow. I plan to offer the dedication to her (and – silence!).

Notwithstanding some reservations about the music and the shortcomings of the libretto, the French press generally agreed that *I Puritani* was a resounding success. *Le Temps* reported:

Bellini's music is tender, sweet and expressive, like its composer... Bellini has reached that point in his artistic life at which he needs to consolidate his fortune and fame with a grand opera, in which the public is right in demanding great things from him. But does he satisfy that condition for his existence with his opera *I Puritani* or has he still to realise it? I wouldn't dare express my opinion.

The poem was originally announced with great excitement. There aren't many so versed in Italian poetry that they can admire the verses of Count Pepoli, which appear to be written with passion, but then, so might those of Ariosto or Tasso have been. It would therefore be preferable to consider only the dramatic situations. Now, these situations, taken from Ançelot's vaudeville, appeared to be rather more feeble and confused than otherwise.

A similar criticism was made by a writer in the *Journal de Paris* and also by Gaglignani in the *Gazzetta Piedmontese*, who added that the character of Elvira, the heroine of whom it was wished to make another *Anne Boleyn*, runs contrary to the dramatic effect. Elvira goes mad, but with a madness that approximates imbecility more than raving. This can only be made tolerable on the stage by stretching the imagination too far. *Le Temps* continued:

For these scarcely novel situations, Bellini has created a great variety of pleasing numbers. The introduction, which was excellently put together by the poet, could nevertheless have been more originally constructed. From the beginning of the act, the audience understandably applauded the most beautiful singing – the duet between Grisi and Lablache, particularly his aria "Piangi, o figlia!". Lablache was also acclaimed in the quintet with the chorus, in which his powerful voice dominated all the others. This music was conceived with great skill and originality, and although it aroused the greatest enthusiasm, by force of good taste I have some reservation about it.

At present, however, scarcely anything else is being talked about in Parisian society, and they also speak of the famous unison duet between Lablache and Tamburini and of that inimitable song "Chi pur la patria adora", which was encored and applauded to excess and after which it was necessary for Bellini to appear on the stage between the two singers who had given voice to this sublime conception. But amongst the intoxicated public, in that audience thrown into confusion by the thunder of bravos, there were perhaps five people who didn't deceive themselves as to the true value of such a song.

I have too much esteem for Bellini not to include myself among these five persons. He knows and should know that the song is composed with talent and written with charm, but he equally knows that it's setting back the beautiful art of music to make use of two such sublime voices as those of Lablache and Tamburini to make them sing in unison and, moreover, as loudly as possible an aria full of vigour and fervour, which in this form is no more than a drinking song.

The *Gazette de France* praised Bellini with few reservations:

Signor Bellini has great qualities as a composer. If he doesn't combine them all, like Rossini, he has the most precious of them, those that relate to the spirit and to feeling. In his operas, there abound those songs that the Italians call cantilena (smooth, melodious writing), and there is a smoothness, charm and a truly singular purity in them. If there is some lack of variety in invention, and even in ideas (insofar as such an expression can be applied to music), there can always be found in his writing a rich spring of emotion, something of a penetrating nature, and if this doesn't make a lively or unexpected impression, it is novel, emotional and rouses tender feelings. Bellini addresses himself more to the heart than to the imagination.

For this reason, the new opera is a most distinguished one, and the first performance was enough to allow one to think that it will take its place among the finest productions of musical art. The sung sections, in particular, had the approval of all intelligent people and forced some to ignore the accompaniment and general uniformity of the orchestra. The composer has accentuated the effects of the instrumentation but has abused this expedient perhaps a little too much and hasn't stressed the contrasts sufficiently. Great capital has been made of the effect of a prayer sung by Puritan soldiers with organ accompaniment. The prayer is beautiful in its simplicity. It recalls the most beautiful masterpieces and true treasures of melody that church music has created in Italy. But the organ accompaniment produced no effect, as nothing can which is out of place[57]... All in all, Bellini has achieved greatness in this opera, but not as much as certain enthusiasts would have wished him.

The second performance of *I Puritani* was honoured with the presence of Queen Marie-Amélie, to whom Bellini dedicated the score, and a few days later, on 31 January, Bellini was informed that King Louis Philippe had created him a Chevalier de la Légion d'Honneur. Florimo said that the decree and the ribbon were presented by Secretary General Marshal Saintmarc at a ceremony that took place in the theatre at the third performance of *I Puritani*, on 3 February.

On 5 February, Bellini was granted an audience by the Queen, but it was not until 27 February that he informed Florimo,[58] who, like most Neapolitans, seems to have resented the idea of his dedicating *I Puritani* to the French Queen:

It is necessary, my dear friend, to understand the customs of a nation before criticising certain actions. It has always been the precedent here that a musical score, an opera that has been greatly acclaimed, should be dedicated to an individual person. Spontini dedicated his *Vestale* to the Empress Joséphine and Rossini his *Guillaume Tell* to Louis XVIII, and I could do no less than dedicate my opera to the person I have. The problem was how to make the offer of such dedication. After I had received the official notification and the order of the Legion d'Honneur (official despatch dated 31 January), I asked Butera to arrange for me to have an audience with the Queen in order to thank her and ask her to express my gratitude to His Majesty the King for the kindness he had shown creating me a chevalier. I asked her furthermore to accept the dedication of the opera in token of my immense gratitude and thus to set the seal on the patronage that she has been so good as to bestow upon me. And if our enemies should express a different version of the matter, it is of little importance. The fact is that, the day after the second performance (28 January), the Minister of the Interior issued an order, the King signed a decree on the matter on 31 January and the Queen was unaware of it until the King himself told her. I owe this great honour directly to the Minister, who is inclined to encourage talent.

I PURITANI

Opera seria (*melodramma serio*) in three parts. Libretto by Carlo Pepoli. First performed (premiere as *I Puritani e i cavalieri*) at the Théâtre-Italien, Paris, on 24 January 1835. Domenico Ferri designed the stage sets.

CHARACTERS AND ORIGINAL CAST

Elvira, Gualtiero Valton's daughter	Soprano	Giulia Grisi
Arturo (Lord Arthur Talbot), Cavalier, Stuart partisan	Tenor	Giovanni Battista Rubini

Riccardo (Sir Richard Forth), Puritan colonel	Baritone	Antonio Tamburini
Giorgio (Sir George Walton), Elvira's uncle, a Puritan	Bass	Luigi Lablache
Gualtiero Valton (Lord Walter Walton), Elvira's father, a Puritan	Bass	M Profeti
Enrichetta (Henrietta Maria of France), widow of Charles I, King of England	Mezzo-soprano	Mlle Amigo
Sir Bruno Roberton, a Puritan officer	Tenor	M Magliano

The action takes place at a castle and its park near Plymouth, England, held by Puritans (Roundheads), followers of Oliver Cromwell, during the English Civil War in the 1650s, shortly after the execution of King Charles I.

PART I

SCENE 1: A large courtyard of the castle. Wall turrets, drawbridges and other fortifications are visible. On the ramparts, sentinels stand guard. The rising sun gradually illuminates first the mountains in the distance and then the changing of the guard.

The Puritan soldiers on the ramparts are preparing themselves for the day's duties, confident of victory over the Stuarts (Cavaliers). As strains of a morning hymn are heard from the castle chapel, the retainers of the stronghold sing their praises for the forthcoming marriage of Elvira. While the retainers are dispersing, Riccardo, a Puritan colonel, appears in the courtyard. He is grief-stricken at the unexpected news that Elvira, who was betrothed to him, is now in love with Arturo, a Stuart partisan and her political enemy, and is about to marry him, with her father's consent. Bruno, a Puritan commander and Riccardo's friend, tries in vain to persuade him to forget Elvira and to concentrate upon a life of heroic deeds in the wars, but Riccardo dwells on his loss with thoughts of both love and rage.

SCENE 2: Elvira's apartment in the castle. The fortifications of the castle are visible through the open Gothic windows.

When Giorgio tells his niece Elvira, whom he looks upon as a daughter, to prepare for her wedding, she is horrified, as she thinks that she will have to marry Riccardo. Touchingly, she vows that she would rather die of remorse, whereupon Giorgio happily explains that her father now agrees that she should marry Arturo, the man she loves. In fact, Arturo, for whom a safe contact to the fortress has already been granted, is on his way. Just then, bugles and voices welcoming Arturo are heard and Elvira jubilantly goes to meet him, accompanied by her uncle.

SCENE 3: The castle's great hall of arms. Between the columns at the back, fortifications can be seen.

After the wedding guests have welcomed the bridal pair, Arturo addresses Elvira most lovingly. The rejoicing, however, is interrupted when an important female prisoner is brought in. She is supposed to be a Stuart spy whom Gualtiero has to deliver to trial by Parliament in London, and consequently he now cannot attend his daughter's wedding. He places Elvira under her uncle's care and gives a safe conduct to Arturo so that he will be able to leave the castle with his bride.

When Elvira and the others leave the hall to dress for the wedding, the prisoner finds her chance and secretly reveals to Arturo that she is Enrichetta, widow of King Charles I. As it is expected that Parliament will condemn her to death, Arturo's loyalty is aroused and he decides there and then to help her escape. At this point, Elvira reappears in her bridal dress but carrying the wedding veil that Arturo has given her. In her happiness, she playfully asks the prisoner to try on her veil. Seeing this, Arturo, struck by an idea, secretly urges Enrichetta to retain the veil when Elvira is recalled to her chamber for the final preparations of her wedding.

As soon as Arturo is alone with Enrichetta, he covers her head with the veil so that she can escape with him. On their way out, they are intercepted by Riccardo, who draws his sword on Arturo before realising that the woman is not Elvira but the prisoner. As it suits him to have his rival out of the way, he allows the two Stuarts to pass, promising not to reveal their flight until they have reached safety. While sounds of rejoicing are heard from inside, signalling the commencement of the wedding festivities, Arturo once more expresses his love for Elvira before riding away.

Presently, Elvira enters with her family and the courtiers. The escape is discovered and Elvira, believing herself betrayed and deserted at the altar for another woman, loses her reason from grief. She then imagines Arturo to be present and, promising that she will love him always, tries to hurry him off to church. Finally, she again realises her true situation and wishes only to die. The others curse the faithless Arturo and call out for vengeance.

Part II

Scene 1: A large salon in the castle. Through a large window, fortifications and, on the distant plain, the camp of the Stuart forces can be seen.

Elvira's madness has cast a dark shadow on the whole fortress. Anxious inhabitants and officials who have assembled at the castle learn from Giorgio how Elvira is suffering, how unsure she is of her own identity and how for a moment her reason returns, only to disappear once more as she sinks again into oblivion. Meanwhile, Riccardo comes in and announces that Parliament has decreed that Arturo shall perish on the scaffold on his capture but that Gualtiero has been pardoned for his carelessness in letting the prisoner escape.

Everyone goes off to search for Arturo, save Riccardo and Giorgio. Just then, Elvira's voice is heard from without, lamenting. Eventually, she enters, her dishevelled hair and her behaviour demonstrating madness. Pathetically, she recalls at one moment her betrayal and at another comforts herself by imagining that Arturo is with her. Taking Giorgio to be her father, she asks him to weep no more, for he is to escort her to her wedding. Elvira then perceives that Riccardo is in tears and touchingly asks him whether he is weeping for love. Imagining herself to be with Arturo again, she reassures him that her father will consent to their marriage and that she will make him happy. She continues to call on Arturo to return to her, his first love, without delay, until, overcome by her delirium, she is taken to her rooms.

After hinting at his suspicion of Riccardo's involvement in the escape, Giorgio tries to turn his thoughts from vengeance; only sudden joy will restore Elvira's sanity, whereas Arturo's death will almost certainly mean hers as well, and this would be an unbearable burden on Riccardo's conscience. Finally, they pledge themselves to save Arturo's life for Elvira's sake; henceforth, they will direct their vengeance in fighting for their country against the Stuarts.

Part III

Scene: A terrace in the castle grounds near Elvira's apartment. Through the wooded garden, the doors and windows of the building are visible, as are fortifications in the distance. It is early evening three months later.

Arturo, wrapped in a cloak and having so far eluded his pursuers, appears from the shrubbery and reflects how sweet it is for an exile to be back in his native land and again near to his beloved Elvira. His soliloquy is suddenly broken by Elvira's singing of the same love song with which he used to serenade her. He responds by singing a verse himself but with different words, now expressing regret and desolation.

After a brief interruption, when the sound of soldiers' footsteps forces him to hide, his resumed song brings out Elvira. She calls for him and he kneels before her, assuring her of his love and begging for her forgiveness. The sudden joy of seeing him, and his explanation that the other woman was really the Queen, whom he had to save from certain death, restore Elvira's sanity. The lovers fall into each other's arms ecstatically, but a sudden drum roll and the voices of soldiers searching for Arturo disturb Elvira's mental balance again. She denounces the "other woman" as being her rival and describes how she destroyed her bridal attire when Arturo deserted her. Realising that her mind is wandering, Arturo tries to persuade her to flee with him, but she is convinced that he is going to abandon her once more and calls for help. Her cries bring the search party of Giorgio, Bruno and Riccardo and Arturo is captured. But when Riccardo pronounces the death sentence that Parliament has decreed on Arturo, Elvira is so shaken that her reason is fully restored.

Everybody realises the sudden change in Elvira, and Arturo, now fully aware of her dangerously erratic state of mind, explains that she thought that he had abandoned her, whereas in fact it was fate that brought about this situation. Arturo pleads that Elvira should be given full consideration. As for himself, he is willing to die at her side. Giorgio and Riccardo, who is now remorseful and does not wish Arturo's death, both try to restrain the more uncompromising of the Puritans in their anxiety to see the prisoner dead. Arturo joins Elvira in a last farewell and then appeals to his would-be executioners to show mercy for her sake, as she is almost at the point of death.

Just as the soldiers are about to tear Arturo from Elvira's side, a fanfare is heard and a messenger brings the news that the Stuarts have been routed, the wars are at an end and Cromwell has granted amnesty to all political prisoners. With great rejoicing, the happy couple are united.

Pepoli drew the libretto of *I Puritani* from the play *Têtes rondes et Cavaliers* (Théâtre National du Vaudeville, Paris, 1833) by François Ançelot[59] and Xavier Boniface Saintine. Bellini chose the title *I Puritani* because at the time it was popular and taken from Sir Walter Scott's novel *Old Mortality*, known in its Italian translation as *I Puritani di Scozia*. Beyond its title, the plot of the libretto, which takes place entirely in Plymouth, England, during the Civil War, has nothing to do with the novel.

Although Pepoli's verses are in themselves for the most part felicitous, the ineptly constructed stage action occasionally makes the libretto seem rather clumsy. It is also a theatrical miscalculation that Arturo is excluded from the crucial part two, which is also static, providing no development in his character or of the themes in the plot, and neither Giorgio nor Riccardo have any lines in part three. This defect arose, or became more pronounced, when Bellini changed his opera from two parts to three before its first performance. Furthermore, Arturo's conflict between love and duty is resolved so quickly that it is difficult for anyone to appreciate it. Moreover, the fact that Elvira – who practically dominates the score – spends much time bereft of her senses, or more accurately loses and regains her reason several times, and not always with sufficient justification, has often been considered the work's serious defect. Superficially, this is true, but when it is understood that Elvira is exceedingly vulnerable and lives on a precipice between fantasy and reality, between insanity and reason, it becomes superfluous to justify each change in her mental balance. Consequently, when a singer conveys this mental instability, the way Elvira's mind teeters on the brink of sanity (achievable only through dramatic coloratura), the character becomes perfectly credible, even assuming Pirandellian stature; in fact, a parallel may be drawn between Elvira and Zara in Pirandello's play *As you desire me*.

The prelude establishes the atmosphere of a soldiers' camp, mainly by means of variation on the sound of the bugle, whereupon the rousing chorus "Quando la tromba squilla" ("When the trumpet shrills") is heard. This is in distinct contrast to the prayer "La luna, il sol, le stelle" ("The moon, the sun, the stars") that can be heard from within the castle. Elvira's voice soars above the others, and as she is not seen, this makes her delayed first entrance more anxiously anticipated.

The first principal number, Riccardo's cavatina "Ah! per sempre io ti perdei" ("Ah! I have lost her forever") is preceded by a touching arioso recitative in which he laments his love of Elvira. The cavatina bears a subtle resemblance to Arturo's entrance aria, "A te, o cara" ("To you, my dear"), yet the music is characteristic of two different situations: Arturo is the winner and Riccardo the loser of the same woman. The former's music is appropriately written in the (very high) tenor key, while the latter's lies within the normal baritone range.

"A te, o cara" has an unparalleled transparency, a clarity of form and an original melody. The piece finishes in an ensemble, during which are heard Elvira's high sustained notes, Giorgio's and Gualtiero's comments in thirds and the effective contribution of the chorus in detached chords:

There is a suavity and sensuality in this long melody that, when sung with style, make it a memorable experience. It is the tenor's answer to "Casta Diva", and one may again cite Verdi's words about Bellini writing "long, long, long melodies that no one before him had written". Most striking is the way in which these melodies establish the situation and the characters involved – lover, rival and woman in between.

Elvira appears, and in the duet with Giorgio "O, amato zio" ("Oh, beloved uncle"), she emerges as innocent, over-sensitive and passionate. The orchestral accompaniment here is relatively simple and unobtrusive.

In an uninteresting scene between Arturo and Enrichetta, including her aria "Figlia a Enrico" ("Henry's daughter"), both the music and the verses suffer a relapse. There is an indifference about the whole scene (made more evident by the composer's cuts before the premiere) that creates appreciable unevenness in the opera. Only Elvira's sudden entry in her brilliant cavatina

"Son vergin vezzosa" ("I am a happy maiden") revives the musical interest, but not soon enough:

Allegro moderato

ver _ gin vez _ zo _ sa, in ve _ sta di spo _ sa

bian _ ca ed u _ mi _ le, qual gi _ _ glio d'a _ pril

Written in the style of a light-hearted polonaise, the song's many florid passages (which can be somewhat too long, if not sung dramatically) express Elvira's gaiety and naïveté, yet not without introducing undertones – especially in the first notes – of the tragedy to come, as if underneath the happiness there is a moment of concealed anxiety. The scene evolves into a quartet with Enrichetta, Arturo and Giorgio commenting on Elvira's virtues while she repeats parts of her song.

With admirable eloquence, Elvira's recitative "Arturo, tu ritorni?" ("Arturo, will you return?"), as she imagines she sees Arturo, prepares the way for the first mad scene, "Ah, vieni al tempio" ("Oh, come to church"). Bellini comes very much into his own in this scene, in which the sudden disappearance of all Elvira's light-heartedness is expressed in lyrically mournful music, convincingly portraying her loss of reason. The chorus, in a concerted finale, comments on the situation in tragic accents.

Part II opens with a short prelude, followed by the five-part chorus "Ah! dolor! Ah! terror!" ("Alas, what grief! How fearful!"), in which the courtiers mourn and comment on Elvira's derangement in the manner of a Greek Chorus. Giorgio's ensuing aria, "Cinta di fiori" ("Wreaths of flowers"), with choral punctuations, is one of the composer's noblest inspirations. Its flowing melody, with steady repetitions, gives it a memorably dignified solemnity and prepares the atmosphere for Elvira's second mad scene, the climax of the opera.

This is one of the loveliest mad scenes in the history of opera, and certainly the most purely musical. By means of superb and reminiscent themes of wide-ranging melody, the composer was able to evoke Elvira's earlier happiness, blurred recollections and refocusings of mind. The prayer-like recitative "O rendetemi la speme o lasciatemi morir" ("Either restore my faith or let me die") is sung offstage to *pianissimo* quivers in the orchestra, creating a suspension of disbelief, and hearing Elvira before she is seen gives the impression that she is wandering aimlessly, lamenting over and over again.

The aria "Quì la voce sua soave" ("It was here that his voice was so sweet"), sung on stage, is a cantilena of unusual beauty, with its melancholy and pathos – as well as some appealing sensuousness – delicately creating an almost unbearable tension:

On the surface, it may appear that Elvira's aria is not as psychologically ingenious as, for example, that in Lucia's mad scene in *Lucia di Lammermoor*, but it must be pointed out that Elvira's madness is a very fragile, non-violent derangement, quite different from Lucia's homicidal insanity. In fact, Elvira's broadly arching and meditative melody suggests more subtly the horror of the tragedy. Furthermore, Giorgio's and Riccardo's comments evoke a marvellous atmosphere which enhances Elvira's music and makes the simplicity of her "Egli piange… Forse amò?" ("He is crying… Is it for love?") doubly moving. She repeats the melody of "O rendetemi la speme" with different words, but this time the sadness is underlined with despair.

Preceded by a long, evocative silence, the cabaletta "Vien, diletto" ("Come, my beloved"), which ends the mad scene, has a breathtaking brilliance, a certain bittersweetness, making it sound insanely joyous. Its descending scales are not designed merely for vocal exhibition but, when sung observantly (the composer's detailed markings range from "con estasi", "con abbandono", "con slancio", "sotto voce", etc), are completely integrated into the drama, signifying the fragility of the heroine's mental state, the dislocation of a suffering soul:

Allegro moderato

Vien di _ let _ to, è in ciel la lu _ na, tut _ to

ta _ ce in _ tor _ no in _ tor _ no

Part II ends with the duet "Suoni la tromba" ("Let the trumpet sound") between Giorgio and Riccardo. Composed as a march, it is a sonorous proclamation of martial ardour and patriotic feeling, forming another climax. However, the duet is crude, with short mechanical phrases and trite harmony. It is also very long (or so it seems), with the two voices endlessly singing in unison. The original singers, Lablache and Tamburini, were possessors of extraordinary voices and reportedly able to produce an electrifying effect. In view of this, it is perhaps unfortunate that the composer failed to make even better use of these singers' special vocal qualities.

Part III belongs mostly to Arturo, for whom Bellini surpassed himself in creating superb melodies. "Corre a valle, corre a monte" ("Through valleys and over mountains") may not be as exciting as "A te, o cara", but it has a melancholy all its own and is more of a love song. Elvira's voice, heard from within, first employs the same melody to the words "a una fonte, afflitto e solo" ("by a fountain, lamenting and alone"), an invocation heightening the dramatic tension when repeated by Arturo* on stage. Their reunion forms an extended scene with a variety of emotions. A wonderful moment occurs when Elvira sings the melody of "A te, o cara", followed by a rapturous recitative. Arturo expresses his love in "Nel mirarti" ("Seeing you"), which also has something of the ardour and earnestness of "A te, o cara". The scene culminates in the ecstatic love duet "Vieni, fra queste bracia" ("Come, let me embrace you").

The ensuing ensemble, "Credeasi misera" ("Unhappy girl"), dominated by Arturo, requires him to sing high – an unprecedented top F. This note, as with the high Ds in the preceding duet, is artistically integrated and produces a thrilling effect at that magic moment when the crest of emotion is reached:

Largo maestoso

Breadth of phrasing, clarity of form and melancholic profundity combine to make this melody supreme of its period. Its lyric beauty is further enhanced by Elvira and the chorus, who act as accompaniment.

In *I Puritani*, even though several long scenes are full of the loveliest melodies, they are not consistently well connected or integrated into the drama because of a certain lack of direction. Above all, the greatest weakness of the work is the absence of period character in the music. This is due partly to the poor libretto but more to the composer's failure to represent the Puritans and their opposing Stuarts in musical terms, and no singing actors

---

* Verdi may have well got the idea for the "miserere" duet in *Il trovatore* from this scene.

can rectify this. Moreover, although many of Bellini's intentions in *Beatrice di Tenda* almost find fulfilment in *I Puritani*, where the harmonies are richer, the feeling for tone quality more intense and several innovations such as the horn, trumpets and drums are used in choral passages, the later opera remains, to an appreciable extent, a "transitional" work.

Nevertheless, and notwithstanding these weaknesses, *I Puritani* stands on the strength of its music. The composer's inspiration was generally involved to a high level, also indicating that there was in him considerable reserve of creative talent, which he would have almost certainly developed, given a longer life. But *I Puritani* was Bellini's last work, his swan song; he died eight months later. In the final analysis, it can be said that, whereas *La sonnambula* inspired Bellini primarily by its idyllic qualities and *Norma* by its Classicism, *I Puritani* inspired him no less by its Romanticism.

Three scores of the opera exist. The Paris version, which is traditionally performed, differs from the original unperformed score because of the cuts that Bellini made, mostly at rehearsals. These cuts include the Enrichetta-Arturo-Riccardo trio (beginning with Arturo's "Se il destino", which preceded the first finale and followed Arturo's "Addio, o Elvira"), the middle section (*largo*) of the Elvira-Arturo duet in the finale of the opera and parts of little importance from various pieces.

The third version, the one that Bellini prepared for Naples, was intended to be performed by different singers from those in Paris: Malibran (Elvira), Duprez (Arturo), Porto (Giorgio) and Pedrazzi (Riccardo), now cast as a tenor instead of a baritone. This version is in two parts (as the Paris version was, originally) and includes a small amount of transposition in the roles of Elvira and Arturo. Because of Malibran's exceptional vocal range (basically described a mezzo-soprano), only the second mad scene was taken down a minor third, and the whole of Part III was lowered a tone, as in the Paris version. "Son vergin vezzosa", which had in fact been written expressly for Malibran in the first instance, was also included in the Paris version, where Bellini originally intended a "little" quartet. The Naples score contains the Enrichetta-Arturo-Riccardo trio, the *largo* of the Elvira-Arturo duet and the final cabaletta, a rondo to the words "Ah, sento, o mio bell'angelo", which were cut in the Paris rehearsals, but Elvira now sings the greater part of "Credeasi misera". In effect, in the Naples *I Puritani*, Elvira is more explicitly the protagonist than Arturo.

Bellini borrowed the music for "Ah! vieni al tempio" (with some variation) from "D'un pensiero" in *La sonnambula* and Elvira's "Quì la voce" has a (perhaps coincidental) momentary resemblance to the Scottish song "Annie Laurie". For the Enrichetta-Arturo-Riccardo trio, retained in the Naples score, he used the melody "Ah, riedi ancor", which he had at one time intended to follow "Casta Diva" in *Norma*.

Nearly all the principal roles in *I Puritani* are vocally and dramatically difficult, and Elvira's and Arturo's are exceptionally so. The work was expressly composed for "the famous *Puritani* quartet" of Rubini, Grisi, Tamburini and Lablache, who performed it often and in many theatres with enormous success. Rubini seems to have been the only tenor of his time who could sing the music well, because of its exceptionally high keys. The opera, however, was very successful, even after Rubini was replaced by Mario (completing the second "*Puritani* quartet"), who compensated with better appearance and more dramatic expression, if not with matching vocal command. Nevertheless, Mario's honeyed tone and extensive vocal range, combined with a strong feeling for the stage, made him an ideal Arturo; undoubtedly, he was the prototype Romantic tenor.

Elvira was Grisi's most successful Bellini role. Her illustrious successors have included Angiolina Bosio, Giuseppina Strepponi (Verdi's future wife) and Rosina Penco, all of whom met the challenge vocally, as well as dramatically, to a high degree. Then came Ilona di Murska, Adelina Patti and Emma Albani, who were successful in a brilliant rather than dramatic way, as were most of the Elviras that followed, such as Marcella Sembrich, Etelka Gerster, Luisa Tetrazzini and Maria Barrientos. The extraordinary flexibility of their voices tempted them to indulge at times in excessive embroidery, thereby depriving the vocal line of its all-important meaningfulness. All astounded with the cadenzas they sang, although Patti's lyric qualities put her performance on a higher level. Tetrazzini, on the other hand, could not adapt her amazing voice to advantage in this role and is mentioned only because she was the more accomplished artist amongst her contemporaries, capable of deeper dramatic expression.

Towards the end of the century, after years of great popularity, the opera disappeared, first from England and, before the First World War, from America; with the coming of *verismo* operas, there were no longer many suitable singers, male or female, to perform this kind of music. In Italy, until the end of the 1940s, as with *Norma* and *La sonnambula*, *I Puritani* was performed only rarely and usually unsatisfactorily.

The principal Elviras of this period were Mercedes Capsir, Margherita Carosio and Lina Pagliughi, all of whom were good singers, although none succeeded in reinstating *I Puritani*'s former popularity. Capsir was the more dramatically exciting, regardless of the relative lightness of her timbre and rather less than perfect coloratura technique. Despite Carosio's affecting manner and exceptional musical intelligence, she was surprisingly miscast, the simplicity of the role eluding her, while Pagliughi, an artist who was less gifted but who possessed a lovely, lyric, limpid voice with efficient coloratura technique, could be touching, if not quite convincing.

At the beginning of 1949, Maria Callas, a dramatic coloratura soprano with vocal technique and interpretative powers amounting to genius, succeeded in reinstating *I Puritani* as an important work, under the guidance of the stylistic conductor Tullio Serafin. The circumstances under which this was accomplished were fortuitous. Callas was singing Brünnhilde (*Die Walküre*) under Serafin's direction at La Fenice, Venice, when Margherita Carosio, who was to sing Elvira in *I Puritani* (also to be conducted by Serafin), fell ill and withdrew nine days before the premiere. As a substitute was extremely difficult to find, the management of the theatre were seriously considering cancelling the performances when Serafin proposed a solution. To his accompaniment, Callas sang "Quì la voce", the only aria from *I Puritani* that she knew, and was given the role, which she then had to learn in one week, during which time she still had two performances of *Die Walküre* to fulfil. Coached by Serafin, Callas did learn the role in time and scored a resounding success as Elvira. Musical Italy enthused about the event, which eventually proved to be of the utmost significance in the renaissance of early-19th-century Italian opera. With time, other good singers were encouraged to sing in *I Puritani*, and once again the opera entered the repertoire.

The most notable Elviras following Callas were Virginia Zeani, Joan Sutherland, Gianna D'Angelo, Beverly Sills and Katia Ricciarelli. They all met with sufficient success and kept the general interest in the opera alive. Sutherland, with a stupendous high register and agility, was very impressive and at times exciting but seldom moving or convincing because of her inability to apply her vocal technique dramatically. D'Angelo's appreciable technique and special brand of charm pulled her through, meanwhile, always enabling her to give an enjoyable if not memorable performance. Sills, a light lyric coloratura soprano of impeccable technique and great dramatic sense, was only denied complete success by the thinness and occasional blandness of her timbre, as well as by her occasional indulgence in impressive *fioriture* which rather destroyed the simplicity of the drama. Both Zeani's and Ricciarelli's lack of warmth and certain detachment from the role, in otherwise highly accomplished performances, proved stumbling blocks in their efforts to identify with the heroine and win the full sympathy of the audience.

More recently, Editta Gruberova's all-round successful Elvira was only partially marred by inefficient Italian diction and occasional tendency to flaunt rather than apply coloratura in the service of expression. Another notable Elvira, June Anderson, endowed with a pleasing flexible lyric voice and proficient coloratura technique, showed great potential for this role, which, however, failed to materialise.

The outstanding Arturo who followed Rubini and Mario was Napoleone Moriani. According to Chorley, Moriani, the leading Arturo for several years, used his superb and strong voice most dramatically, except when "he was either led away by bad taste or fashion into drawling and bawling". However, he often aroused the most fanatical enthusiasm in the audience.

After Moriani, in the mid 1870s, Julian Gayarré, possibly the supreme tenor of his time, made Arturo his own. With his unique powers of expressive singing, he exerted a rare fascination on the public.

About a quarter of a century later, Alessandro Bonci claimed Arturo's crown. His voice was rather small but exquisitely modulated and he sang the music in the original key with a refined elegance, perfect diction and subtlety that none of his contemporaries could rival.

Hipólito Lazaro, the next important Arturo, was not as distinguished. Nevertheless, amongst so much that was exhibitionistic to a degree, the magic of his magnificent voice, the exciting high notes and, above all, his artistry would unexpectedly appear to carry the listener away.

In more recent times, notable Arturos have been Giacomo Lauri-Volpi, Giuseppe di Stefano, Nicolai Gedda, Alfredo Kraus and Luciano Pavarotti. Lauri-Volpi, a lyric-dramatic tenor with brilliant top notes and sensual tone, made an ideal Arturo when he was not indulging in vocal display *per se*. Not as thrilling as Lauri-Volpi but more ardent and charming, di Stefano sang the music as written, with a warmth and velvety tone that appealed to the soul and heart. Although neither singer had the elegance and style of some of their predecessors, at their best they gave very exciting performances.

Nicolai Gedda used his even and agile lyric voice, of enormous range, with musical intelligence and dramatic insight. His cautious approach, however, robbed his portrayal of much of its ardency. Similarly, Pavarotti's golden Italianate timbre, phenomenal high register and winsome exuberance (he was not always fat) could not compensate for his lack of appropriate style, specifically the individuality of the Bellinian cantilena. It was Kraus who scored in this role; his elegance and style in every phrase, accompanied with stimulating dramatic expression, as well as fidelity to the score, made him the ideal Arturo. His mantle in *I Puritani* fell on Chris Merritt, whose extensive range, outstanding technique and rare feeling for the style of early-19th-century music places him in a category of his own. Meanwhile, the lyric tenor Giuseppe Sabbatini, who made his operatic debut in 1986, has shown great promise, both vocally and stylistically, for this type of music. He came to *I Puritani* with good credentials but has not made the role his own.

17

Phantom Projects – Finale (1835)

After *I Puritani*'s launch in Paris, Bellini turned his full attention to his obligations in Naples. He had already sent the first act of *I Puritani* there but, because of the cholera outbreak, it had not arrived, being delayed in Marseilles, where it had been sent by coach to be despatched, by sea, to Naples. For this reason, on 5 January, Bellini sent the second and third acts by mail-coach all the way to Naples. These arrived on 29 January.

The society that managed the San Carlo stipulated in their contract with Bellini that the score of *I Puritani* should be in Naples by 20 January 1835. As none of the score had reached there by this date (one part arrived as late as 11 February), the society exercised their right to withdraw the contract and refused to have the opera performed. Despite the endeavours of Florimo, Cottrau and, more importantly, Malibran to have the opera staged, the decision of the San Carlo authorities was irrevocable.

Malibran's contract expired on 3 February, yet she was willing to prolong her stay in order to sing in *I Puritani*, in a concert version if necessary. However, all efforts came to nothing. In a letter to Florimo[1] on 18 February, Bellini expresses his great disappointment: "I've just heard of all the accidents that have prevented my *Puritani* from being performed and of all the efforts our dear Mme Malibran has made to have it staged. If one thing irritates me more than anything else in this contrary world, it's that this angel hasn't been able to sing in *I Puritani* to the Neapolitans."

On 27 February, Bellini also wrote a rapturous letter to Malibran:[2]

> My good and dear friend, I cannot restrain myself from thanking you personally and directly for the affectionate treatment you accorded me in the recent affair over the score of my *Puritani*. Florimo writes that not even a lover could have shown me more favour, and I believe him and shall always believe that you love me. I adore you and have always adored you – your miraculous talent, your graceful and lively

figure, and your "three souls" besides (for you must have three, not just one, like all other women). From now on, I want to write to you from time to time, I want you to reply to me and I want our friendship to be fraternal and filled with mutual advantage. I want us to love each other and tell each other so. Thus our friendship, founded upon true regard, will become a precious thing. And so, henceforward, what Malibran desires, Bellini will carry out!…

Farewell, dear angel. I hope that, in Milan, you and no one else will perform in *I Puritani*,[3] and I hope that great miser, the Duke of Visconti, will give me plenty of money so that I may write an opera especially for you. Goodbye, goodbye, and may your Carlo [Charles de Bériot] allow me to send you a kiss of gratitude.

It is impossible to know the true motives of the San Carlo management in refusing to concede a few days for the production of *I Puritani*. Certainly, they were able, contractually, to cancel the performances, but *I Puritani* had just scored a resounding triumph in Paris, and furthermore, in Naples, Malibran was ready, in fact desperate, to appear in this opera, even if the score arrived after her contract had expired. One would think that, under such circumstances, an enterprising opera management could have made it possible for the work to be performed, especially as there was every indication of it being a great success, considering the presence of Malibran. True, the opera is very difficult to produce in a short time, but it could have been given in concert form, as was the intention at one stage. Later, when only one part of the opera arrived, the prospective concert was also cancelled.

Perhaps the management disapproved of Bellini's dedication of the opera to the Queen of France. Of course, this must have been a minor point in the argument, if any argument existed, but it is the only one, apart from the management's correct, if inflexible and unusual policy. Florimo also expressed great displeasure at Bellini's gesture to the French Queen, but he never gave any indication as to his reasons; Bellini had explained his action as a matter of course, something that he considered was expected of him.

The Paris performances of *I Puritani* continued until 31 March, the end of the season, with great success and always to a full theatre. "On the last night," Bellini wrote to Ferlito[4] on 1 April, "it was impossible for me to show my face in the stalls without the audience applauding me, and so many people turned around to look at me that I had to remain in hiding."

Also, during this performance, an event that Bellini described as "extravagant and unparalleled" took place. While Rubini was singing alone on the stage, a note was thrown to him and the audience shouted, "Read it! Read it!" The orchestra stopped and Rubini, turning to the audience, said, "With great pleasure, gentlemen." The note was from the many habitués of the theatre, begging Rubini to sing, between acts, the aria from *Il pirata* that he had sung so superbly a month earlier, on his benefit night. "When Rubini sang the aria," Bellini continued, "I just can't tell you what the effect was like! The applause was tremendous and it was also showered upon the other singers. The whole stage was flooded with bouquets and garlands of flowers."

It was as if fate had organised a special celebration because, as it turned out, this was the last time that Bellini would hear his music in an opera house. On this last occasion, he was applauded simultaneously for *Il pirata*, his first great success, and *I Puritani*, his last.

In the same letter to Ferlito, Bellini sums up the end of the season at the Théâtre-Italien and basks in his own glory:

> Last night, *I Puritani* gave such pleasure that Donizetti's party was persuaded to send *Marino* [*Faliero*] to the grave, for it had died between Sunday 12 and 31 March. *Marino* had five performances and *I Puritani* 14, plus Tamburini's benefit and the last two nights of the theatre season, making 17 performances in all between 25 January and 31 March. This is unheard of in Paris, where the public – volatile by nature – won't usually submit to seeing the same opera more than about six times in the season, which lasts six months… In short, last night was a real fiesta, an evening that will stand out in the annals of the Théâtre-Italien. *I Puritani* has now put me in the position that was my due – that is, the first after Rossini. I say this because Rossini had at first so convinced everyone that Donizetti had more talent (because he had nothing to fear from him) than myself, but now Italy, Germany and France grant me the position I have worked so hard to attain and which I hope ever to enhance.

Piqued by the alleged support that Donizetti had received from Rossini ("the good things that Rossini has said about Donizetti have greatly influenced the newspapers"), Bellini was now far too carried away by his own success. Continuing his mean-spirited account, he writes:

At the first performance, the hall – or the pit, as they call it here – was filled with the claque, but as the Teatro Italiano [Italien] was full, very full of subscribers, the claque was unable to impress anyone and the reception of *Marino Faliero* was mediocre. At the second performance, it was judged more harshly; at the third, everyone deemed it a positive funeral, so much so that the management, having wanted to support it and present it at Lablache's benefit, has lost 3,200 francs... What an opera he wrote! It's an incredible thing – he who in *Anna Bolena* showed talent... And Rossini, who patronised him, eventually said that Donizetti couldn't have written more trivial music if he'd tried.

Writing to his friend Dolci in Bergamo four days after *Marino Faliero*'s premiere, Donizetti presents a different picture.[5] He is generous to Bellini, but the inference that his opera enjoyed practically the same success as *I Puritani* is a gross exaggeration: "I wanted to send you only the article from the *Messager*, but I think I'll tell you a word or two about the second and third performances, too, which were brilliant... The reception Bellini had with *I Puritani* made me tremble more than a little, but the character of our work is so different that we've both achieved a fine success without displeasing the public."

With the season at the Italien ending, many of the singers, including the four principals of *I Puritani*, went to London to fulfil engagements at the King's Theatre. On 21 May, *I Puritani* was performed with the same cast as it was in Paris, with overwhelming success.

As soon as Bellini was informed of *I Puritani*'s success in London, he wrote to Florimo[6] on 25 May: "You must know that the opera, in spite of some uncertainty on the part of the chorus, met with such a triumph, such enthusiasm and such enormous success that no London theatre before had resounded to such applause... It's also said that Princess Victoria (heiress presumptive to the English throne) was seen to clap after the great duet for two basses and was the first to call for an encore. *The Times* and *The Post* (English newspapers) have published articles in my honour."

Chorley, in his *30 Years' Musical Recollections*, mentions the London reception of both operas:

The production of these two new operas in London was the event of the season. On such occasions, there is always a success and a failure. The public will not endure two favourites...

London was steeped in the music of *I Puritani*; organs ground it, adventurous amateurs dared it, the singers themselves sang it to such satiety as to lose all consciousness of what they were engaged in and, when once launched, to go on mechanically. I must have heard Mlle Grisi's polacca that year alone if once, 100 times, to speak without exaggeration. In short, Bellini had "the luck". Donizetti's turn of triumph[7] was to come later – and, to my judgement, in a work very inferior to his *Marino Faliero*.

This, then, is the year for attempting some character of the composer who displaced for a while Signor Rossini – seeing that it was the year of his last opera.

Once the possibility of producing *I Puritani* in Naples had vanished, Bellini decided to remain in Paris, because he hoped for a contract from the Opéra. In the meantime, the Opéra-Comique made a new move to re-open negotiations with him, but he did not pursue this. He wrote to Florimo[8] on 18 May: "I no longer have any fears about Rossini's friendship. He will be favourable to me under any circumstances. I have allied myself to him with the closest affection. He gives me correct advice about everything (but I am no fool), and thanks to him I have avoided accepting new arrangements with the Opéra-Comique. Rossini wants me to write a grand opera for the Opéra, and after that I will do as I please!"

However, nothing definite happened, as financial difficulties at the Opéra resulted in an administrative crisis, and until this was resolved no formal offer could be made to Bellini or to any other composer.

Between 10 and 14 May, Bellini moved to Puteaux to stay at M Levys' villa. Although he transferred many of his belongings there, he did not give up his apartment in Paris. It was clear that he intended to keep a permanent residence in Paris, even if he would be writing operas for Italy. "I like Paris, and I hope you won't blame me for this," he wrote to Santocanale.[9] "While promising you that I will come to visit my beloved Sicily from time to time, I find it best to live in the place where music needs me most!" On 13 May, almost certainly at the villa, Bellini began work on the motifs[10] for new melodies to use in his next opera.

During the first week in June, Bellini received from Florimo the sad news of Maddalena Fumaroli's death. She had, in fact, died on 15 June 1834, when Bellini had been deeply involved with the composition of *I Puritani*, and the ever-thoughtful Florimo decided to say nothing of it until a year later. It is unknown whether Florimo remained a friend of the Fumarolis after Bellini had refused to marry Maddalena, but there is little doubt that he was aware of the deterioration in her health which finally led to her premature death. He wrote,[11] "I couldn't remain a cold observer of such a disaster. Moreover, irresistible forces moved me to render a feeble tribute to her in tears; few women, indeed, deserved it as much as she did. I therefore begged Merelli, who was both Bellini's and Maddalena's friend and himself in deep grief over such a misfortune, to write some appropriate verses. He was very kind to do so. I then set them to music in the form of a romance, which I dedicated and sent to Bellini."

In these verses, entitled "Le due speranze", Merelli presents Maddalena as a girl who is first loved and then abandoned. Her love and grief remain constant, despite the indifference shown by her lover. In the end, when the girl is dying, she has one hope left: that her lover should come to intone a hymn over her tomb.

On 7 June 1835, Bellini gave vent to his feelings in a letter to Florimo:[12]

The news of the death of poor Maddalenina afflicted me tremendously. The conduct of Giuditta had set my heart against renunciation, but on receiving such sad news, and on reading the verses that you had put to music, I wept bitterly and found that my heart was still susceptible to grief. That is enough; let us speak no more of it. Have some verses written for me by the author of "Le due speranze", extolling the virtues and sweetness of Maddalenina, so that I can set them to music, and thus I will gladly obey the desire of someone who wants a song of mine dedicated to her memory. May it be a reply to "Le due speranze", tender, and may it be as though I were speaking to her dear soul!

Later, Florimo also claimed (although without reliable evidence) that Bellini said that he felt that he would soon follow Maddalena to the grave. However much Florimo embroidered his friend's sorrow, the fact remains that Bellini was indeed moved to tears by the poetry expressing Maddalena's love and suffering. But he was unable to express his own sorrow in the way that he knew best; the poem that he wanted to set to music did not reach him in time.

On 1 September, Bellini was unwell with the usual diarrhoea and fever from which he had suffered often in the past. After three days in bed, he wrote to Florimo, informing him that he was much improved and thought that the illness had passed. Feeling well enough, he spent the following day in Paris, as he was still anxious to obtain a commission to write for the Opéra and was trying to speed things up, and he hoped that influence might be brought to bear on the director of the Opéra through an acquaintance who was a friend of the Minister of the Interior.

Bellini had hardly returned to Puteaux when he was again confined to bed with diarrhoea. It is unlikely that he received any medical treatment during the early stages of his illness. However, when he failed to appear at Princess Belgioioso's, she asked Doctor Montallegri,[13] an Italian expatriate, to go to Puteaux and investigate. Montallegri visited Bellini on 9 September and on his return to Paris assured the composer's friends that his condition was not serious. To Princess Belgioioso, however, he may have indicated that he suspected that Bellini was suffering from cholera, an illness then a recurrent risk every summer. This would explain Levys' decision to keep the patient in strict quarantine. Henry Greville and several others tried to visit him at Puteaux, but without success. After Bellini's death, Greville wrote in his diary on 26 September 1835 of his efforts to visit his sick friend:

> Poor Bellini is dead after an illness of three weeks! The last time I saw him was at the Barriere de l'Etoile, where Lady Hunlock, with whom I had been dining, brought us. He came into town from Puteaux to make an arrangement about our opera box, but I missed him. We were to have dined together at Madame Graham's, on a day that he was to fix, and I had written to him at her request. Receiving no answer, I wrote again and had a note in reply from a Mr Levys, at whose house Bellini was staying, saying that he was ill and unable to write. I wrote again and Levys answered that he was still ill. I went to enquire, but they assured me that there was no danger. However, I wasn't permitted to go up [and see him], as he was forbidden to see anyone. I then wrote again to Levys to enquire about him, and he answered that, having been better the previous day, his night had not been good and he was less well, but that he hoped to send me better news shortly. At the moment that I received this letter, [Bellini] had ceased to live. It was from the Thursday's newspaper that I learned that, at four o'clock [*sic*] on the preceding day, [Bellini] had expired.

Poor fellow! Those Levyses have much to answer for, as they not only kept away – and in ignorance! – all of his best friends but, in addition, they neglected to call in fresh medical advice.

Levys may have been acting prudently in keeping Bellini under quarantine. It was not very difficult to mistake dysentery for cholera at that time, and the symptoms of Bellini's illness indicated something of the kind. Nevertheless, whatever the case from the evidence available, Levys cannot be entirely absolved from blame. If he had thought that Bellini had been suffering from dysentery – an illness of which Bellini had had attacks previously – then why was he made inaccessible to his friends? Also, if Levys and Montallegri thought that Bellini had had cholera – a most likely assumption, in view of the fact that Bellini was kept under such strict quarantine – then why was no further medical advice sought when his state of health deteriorated? There is no explanation for this neglect, unless Levys and Montallegri, being absolutely certain that it was a hopeless case, left the patient to die.

At first, the whole case had to be kept strictly secret, or the authorities would have removed Bellini to an isolated cholera camp, and this would certainly not have been desirable. What Levys did, however, was to go to Paris, leaving Bellini alone in the villa at Puteaux. Only a gardener remained to guard the sick man, equipped with instructions to refuse admission to everybody except Doctor Montallegri.

Baron Augusto Aymé d'Aquino, Michele Carafa's nephew and an official of the Paris Embassy of the Kingdom of the Two Sicilies, recorded in his diary[14] his efforts to see the sick Bellini:

11 September: The news has been circulated that Bellini is ill at Puteaux, where I saw him a few days ago. I found him in bed. He told me that he had slight dysentery, but that he will soon be back in Paris. At that moment, in came Mme Levys, whom I used to know when she was Mlle Olivier. She scolded the invalid severely, telling him that he needed complete rest. It was evident that she was scolding me for visiting him. I told my uncle Carafa and all my friends about my visit.

12 September: I return to Puteaux. I'm not allowed in by that monster the gardener who is at the gate and will not allow anyone in.

13 September: I return with Mercadante. We're not allowed in.

14 September: Carafa goes and poses as a doctor. He found Bellini in bed.

22 September: During these days, with no one having been able to see Bellini, the discontent of his friends erupted this evening at Lablache's house. There was even talk of having the King's procurator intervene.

Although there is nothing in the diary about Bellini's condition, after Carafa's visit, Montallegri changed his attitude somewhat and began to issue bulletins that were addressed to Robert and Severini at the Italien. Between 15 and 20 September, the first bulletin ran, "There is still no noticeable improvement in our Bellini's condition, which continues to give cause for alarm. Tonight, he discharged mucus and blood at least six times but did get a little sleep. The blister ointment seems as though it may work, and I expect it to bring on a beneficial crisis."

On 21 September, Bellini's condition deteriorated further. Montallegri's bulletin is more alarming but still no fresh advice is sought: "The blister ointment has begun to bring about a crisis of sweating. Last night, our Bellini became less restless and uneasy. As the discharges have been fewer in number, he has been able to get sufficient sleep."

On the following day, Montallegri followed up his bulletin with, "The discharge of matter has greatly decreased and its quality has changed. I hope that tomorrow I shall be able to declare him out of danger."

No other information was given, and as Bellini continued to be kept under strict quarantine nobody was able to see him, despite the constant efforts of some of his friends, and there was not enough time for anyone to intervene.

On 23 September, Montallegri's bulletin, anxiously awaited in Paris, announced gravely,[15] "The 13th day has started and is alarming, Bellini having passed a most restless night because the sweating crisis was not produced, as on the two previous days. I'm staying beside him for the whole day and night in order to see in the 14th day. I shall write something more detailed to you tomorrow."

Even so, Bellini spent a relatively calm morning on 23 September, but after lunch he had high fever and was in a state of delirium. Either Montallegri or the gardener – the only other person who was at the villa –

stayed in Bellini's room all the time. During these moments of delirium, Bellini imagined that his family were with him. "Can't you see all my family have arrived?" he said and then began to name each one of them, starting with his father and mother. (Florimo said that Bellini was also asking for him.) Presently, Montallegri was convinced that Bellini's end was very near and sent a note to Severini announcing that "a convulsion has rendered him unconscious and he may not live until tomorrow".

In fact, Bellini died that afternoon at 5pm. Whether or not Montallegri was with him is unknown, but he was not there ten minutes afterwards, when d'Aquino arrived. The entry in d'Aquino's diary on 23 September reads:

> As I was going to spend the day with my sister-in-law at Rueil, I left on horseback at an early hour. At the bridge at Courbevoie, I stopped at Puteaux. The gardener's attitude was the same. During the day, a terrible storm broke out, and at about ten past five, soaked to the skin, I knocked at Mr Levys' door. No answer. I pushed the gate and it gave way. After tying up my horse, I went into the house, which appeared to be completely deserted. I found Bellini on the bed as if asleep, but his hand was icy. I couldn't believe the horrible truth. The gardener then came in and told me that Mr Bellini passed away at 5 o'clock and, as Mr and Mrs Levys were in Paris, he had to go out to call for help and get some candles. Out of my mind with sorrow, I went quickly to Lablache in the Rue des Trois Frères, whence the fatal news was circulated throughout Paris.

By the morning of 24 September, all Paris knew of Bellini's death and immediately all kinds of rumours began to spread, as not many people would readily accept that young Bellini had died a natural death. Dysentery could be fatal, of course, but the speed with which it killed him (he had been seen in Paris only 15 days earlier and apparently looking well) seemed incredible. Added to this, the manner in which Bellini was kept in strict quarantine, with none of his many friends being permitted access, and the strange behaviour of the Levyses, who left him alone in the house, gave rise to wild suspicion. Before long, gossip had it that Bellini had been poisoned. This rumour was directed at Mrs Levys (supposedly Bellini's mistress), who had allegedly poisoned him out of jealousy. Needless to say, no evidence exists to indicate that she had at any time been Bellini's mistress. That neither she – nor anyone else, for that matter – poisoned him is proved beyond any doubt by the evidence of the autopsy.

At the instigation of many of Bellini's friends, headed by Rossini, a Professor Dalmas performed the autopsy on Bellini. Dalmas reported:[16]

On 25 September 1835, I carried out the autopsy and the embalmment of the body of Bellini, who had died 36 hours earlier, at the house of Mr Levys, at Puteaux, near Paris. The organs contained in the head and the chest were intact and perfectly healthy, but I found the organs of the abdomen greatly changed and in the following state:

All the large intestine, from the anal extremity of the rectum up to the ileac-coecal valve, was covered with innumerable ulcers about the size of freckles, with a greyish foundation formed by a layer of pus of a purulent detritus that could easily be squeezed out. These ulcerations had very thin edges, which were slightly loose and floated in water. No part of the mucous membrane was thickened or hardened but, on the contrary, was generally soft and came away in the form of pulp, where it was not ulcerated. Where it was ulcerated, the ulcers went right through it and affected part and sometimes the whole of the muscular layer, but no part of the serous membrane was eroded, so there was no perforation.

The right lobe of the liver contained within it an abscess the size of a fist, full of thick, yellow, homogenous pus. The abscess walls were formed of the same substance as the liver, but slightly softer and with no sign of cysts or new tissue of any kind. No other abscess existed in the liver or anywhere else. The hepatic blood vessels were free and in a normal state. The bile of the vesicle was slight, black and viscous, but the orifices and passages passing through this liquid were not affected by any contraction, and the bile flowed easily up to the duodenum. There had not been, nor was there, any jaundice.

All the other viscera, organs and parts of the system were in the most satisfactory condition. It is clear that Bellini died from acute inflammation of the colon, complicated by an abscess of the liver. The inflammation of the intestine had given rise to violent symptoms of dysentery, which had been recurrent during his life. Owing to its position, the abscess had not yet produced any adverse effect, but as it was near the convex surface of the liver it might at any time have burst into the abdomen and given rise to a fatal discharge. There was no adhesion between the abdominal wall and the liver, so such an ending was most probable.

Since Bellini's death, several medical studies have been made of both the autopsy and the symptoms as far as they are known. There was then no remedy for what we understand Bellini's illness to have been today – acute amoebic dysentery with amoebic liver abscess and ulcerative colitis – and he would have died no matter what medical attention he might have received.[17] However, this does not absolve the Levyses or, for that matter, Montallegri, who never called for fresh advice or even a second opinion. Bellini deserved the beneficial attention of consulting physicians, which he never received. Furthermore, he was left to die alone.

The news of Bellini's death reached Sicily from a letter that Rossini wrote to Santocanale on 27 September:[18]

It is with grief that I have to announce to you the death of our mutual friend, Bellini. The poor man died on Wednesday 23 [September]... I am inconsolable, owing to the loss of my friend, and am also inconsolable when I think of the sorrow this letter of mine will bring you and of the grief that will be visited upon his parents. All Paris mourns him, and if there is any compensation in tragedies of this kind, which are irreparable, it lies surely in the fact that the manifestations of grief by an educated and civilised people like the Parisians must greatly comfort our sorrow. I loved and helped him during his life, and I shall tell you what I have done on his death so that you can tell his family, without delay, what happened.

Although it was only a few hours after the death of our friend when I returned from the country, where I had spent the summer, the magistrate had already put his seal on all effects belonging to the deceased. Bellini's body was embalmed and I had the heart set aside, similarly embalmed, so that, should his relations or native town desire his body or his heart, both will be preserved. The report on the autopsy has been made and I am enclosing it herewith so that you should learn what illness he suffered from.

A committee was immediately formed from the leading artists of the three royal theatres in Paris, of which I am the chairman, in order to have a mass performed at Les Invalides with all the pomp suitable for honouring our friend. The members of the committee are Cherubini, Päer, Carafa, Halévy, Habeneck, Panserun, Nourrit, Rubini, etc.

Circulars have already been ordered for the opening of a subscription to raise a statue to Bellini, whereby (once the costs of the embalming and the obsequies have been paid off) we shall be able to honour him and thus avoid the expense falling on his relations. I cannot, at the moment, tell you how much Bellini's estate comes to, because it hasn't been possible to examine his letters, which, as I said, are under seal, but I believe, from what he has told me several times, that his property amounts to 40,000 francs – ie 10,000 in the hands of the Englishman Mr Levys (in whose country house he died, and where he received unparalleled help) and another 20,000 in Spanish dividend coupons. There must also exist 10,000 or 12,000 francs at the Turina house in Milan, and I have written to them for information. But I must repeat to you that this is all approximate, because I haven't been able to examine anything. This will be done when his relations send the power of attorney, of which I hope to send you the draft copy tomorrow, so that no difficulties may arise respecting French legal formalities. Pay my respects to his family and, unless some preference has been made in the power of attorney, please ask them to grant some latitude to the person appointed, that he may give some small object belonging to the deceased to the persons who were held highest in Bellini's affection.

You can see that I'm doing all I can to arrange matters with all pomp, yet without prejudice to the family. I believe that the ceremony will take place on Friday 2 October. When sending you the copy of the power of attorney, I will include a programme of everything that is to take place. For the present, I can tell you that I have at my disposal all the singers of the Opéra, the Italien and the Opéra-Comique, and I tell you frankly that they all feel it an honour and a duty to take part in this solemn and sad ceremony. I don't know if my emotional state makes my letter easy to read. Please be indulgent towards me and tell relatives and friends that the sole comfort remaining to me is that of consecrating my efforts to honour my friend, compatriot and distinguished colleague. I arranged some excellent business for Bellini at the Opéra. This was his good fortune, and now death has cut everything short.

Bellini was buried in Père Lachaise Cemetery, Paris, on 2 October. (On the previous evening, the Théâtre-Italien began its season with *I Puritani*, sung by the original cast. It was a memorable occasion, the whole performance being the most appropriate requiem in homage to the dead composer. From time to time, both the musicians and the audience broke into sobs.) Rossini, Cherubini, Päer and Carafa were in charge of the funeral. Habeneck, the director of orchestral music at the Académie Royale, was in charge of the music at the funeral ceremony. Bellini's body was taken privately from Puteaux to the Église des Invalides, where the proceedings began at 11.30am with a solemn requiem by Cherubini. It was sung softly and in the Gregorian style. The rest of the mass was sung by a choir of about 200 that included Rubini, Tamburini, Lablache and Ivanoff, who were the soloists in the *Lacrymosa*. The Latin text of this was adapted by Auguste Panseron to the music of "Credeasi misera", the tenor aria in the last act of *I Puritani*. The cortège then proceeded to the cemetery, headed by a band of 120 performers. Rossini, Cherubini, Päer and Carafa were pall-bearers.

There were several funeral orations. Professor Orioli spoke on behalf of the Italians, Päer on behalf of all the artists and Doctor Furnari, a young Sicilian living in Paris, bade the last farewell on behalf of Sicilian youth. Furnari, in tears, concluded, "Bellini, goodbye. While there are tender and sensitive hearts in the world, altars will be set up to your memory and your music will be a powerful provoker of tears. You will live in *Pirata* and *Puritani* and, most of all, in that moving work *Norma*, which represents the sweet gentleness of your soul. Goodbye, dear Bellini. Accept this tribute of the grief and lamentation of Sicilian youth, on whose behalf I speak, and as a layer of earth is about to be sprinkled over you, I can but address to you those words which you clothed in the sweetest notes: Peace to your sweet soul!"

The coffin was finally lowered into the grave.[19] Cherubini, sobbing, threw upon it the first handful of earth. The others followed. The following day, Rossini described the event in some detail to Santocanale:[20]

I have the sad, sad satisfaction of telling you that the exiquies of our deceased friend were carried out with universal love, with extraordinary solicitude on the part of all the artists and with honour that would have been fit for a king. Two hundred voices performed the funeral mass, the leading artists of this capital city joined in singing the choruses. After the mass, they all walked to the cemetery (where poor Bellini's body will rest until other arrangements are made). A military band of 120 musicians escorted the cortège. Every ten minutes, a blow on the tam-tam resounded, and I assure you that the huge crowd of people and the sorrow that one saw reflected on all their faces produced an inexpressible effect. I can't tell you how great the affection is that this poor friend of ours has inspired.

Now I'm in bed, half dead, for I won't hide from you the fact that I wanted to be present when the last word was pronounced over Bellini's grave. The weather was atrocious, raining all day, but that didn't discourage anyone, not even me, although I had been unwell for several days. My having stayed for three hours in the mud and getting drenched with water has been bad for me.

Rossini's interest in Bellini, which really started with the composition of *I Puritani*, lasted after his death. He devoted considerable time and effort to help settle Bellini's estate in Paris. Rosario Bellini, who knew of Rossini's affection for his son, wrote a most touching letter to him.[21] After expressing his grief and despair over the loss of his son, Rosario wrote, "You always encouraged my son in his work; you took him under your protection, you neglected nothing that could increase his glory and his welfare... I'm overcome with gratitude for your great kindness, as well as for that of a number of distinguished artists, which I shall also never forget. Pray, sir, be my spokesman and tell these artists that Bellini's father and family, as well as our compatriots in Catania, will cherish an imperishable recollection of this generous conduct."

Rosario Bellini also wrote to Levys on 25 October 1835:[22]

If the immense loss that I have suffered in my dear son Vincenzo has marked the peak of my desolation and has made an unhappy mother inconsolable and has brought the deepest sorrow into both of our lives, I still retain a feeling of gratitude and recognition for your respected person who, after receiving my son into the bosom of your kind family, showed him the most loving care during his illness in the last period of his life. Gossip, which is carrying the unhappy news of

Bellini's death everywhere, is not silent and will not be silenced on the subject of the name of Levys, in whose mansion the late lamented was cared for and breathed his last.

What fatal disease killed him? This is what I long to know in order to give respite to the grief that troubles me because of the very many distressing rumours... You know everything and can tell me everything. You're keeping the body of my son while his homeland is thinking about claiming it for itself. The property and letters belonging to him couldn't be entrusted to better hands than those into which he confided them while he was still alive. Michele Chiarandà, Baron of Triddini, has been given power of attorney by me to collect everything, and my most afflicted family and I derive comfort and consolation from this fact. With tears of gratitude, I pray to God to repay you for all that you did for my distinguished son while promising to do whatever an unhappy father and afflicted family can do in return.

It not only took Levys over a month to reply[23] but even then he failed to tell Rosario Bellini what he wanted to know. On 15 December, he wrote:

I was deeply moved by your kind letter of 25 October. The anguish that I felt for the grievous loss of your dear Vincenzo allowed me to understand fully what you must have felt, as I considered him a brother and a member of my family.

His last illness was diarrhoea, an ailment from which he had often suffered in Milan. It would take up too much space to give you all the details, but if you should absolutely desire them, I would be pleased to supply them for you.

It is necessary for me to reveal my heart fully to the father of my dear Bellini in letting him know the sorrow I feel in not having some small souvenir of my dear friend and brother that could keep his memory more alive for me. I've already made such a request to Signor Rossini, but he replied that he couldn't remove anything without being authorised by you.

However plausible this reply is, it is odd and inconsistent, to say the least. Of course, Levys may have avoided answering Rosario's query "What fatal disease killed him?", thinking that, by giving him all the details revealed in the autopsy, he would have tortured him further. But surely under the circumstances, when so many rumours had already circulated about Bellini's death (and had even reached Bellini's father himself), the obvious line to take was to give the facts precisely. Instead, he gave a vague promise to obtain the details of the autopsy, should Rosario Bellini "absolutely desire them"; Rosario could hardly have made his request more strongly, so receiving this kind of answer could have made him feel that there might have been some truth in the rumours that he had heard. In addition, Rosario's other stronger request, "you know everything and can tell me everything", was completely evaded.

Levys obviously had not spent much time, if any at all, at Bellini's deathbed. He had actually made it impossible for any of Bellini's friends even to see him. Therefore, he knew nothing – from first hand, at least – of what Bellini had said or what his actions were, if any, during the last days of his life. It would have been dishonest to report anything that he had not heard personally; however, it would have been more open of him if he had told the grieving father the truth. Instead, he answered Rosario's heartfelt questionings with a request of his own: that he should be given "some small souvenir of my dear friend and brother".

Florimo heard of Bellini's death by letter from Mercadante,[24] who on 3 October, after describing the funeral ceremony, wrote:

> None of us remained dry-eyed. We were all in tears. All our emotions were swayed, and we all experienced feelings of love and respect for the deceased. A subscription has been opened to raise a monument to him, which, along with the fame that he deservedly enjoyed, will bequeath his eternal memory to posterity. A bust will be placed in the Italien; a vast amount has been published in his praise... The managements of the Italien and the Opéra rivalled each other in their expressions of enthusiasm to make him immortal. His *I Puritani* charmed and delighted the public and *La sonnambula* and *Norma* are being rehearsed.
>
> Let us resign ourselves, dear Florimo, to a fate stronger than we are and let us always keep alive in our hearts the memory of such a fine and excellent friend.
>
> PS: Rossini has all your correspondence with Bellini and has told me that he has taken from it what you advised, in not just a friendly way but in a fatherly way, and for this he is loud in your praise.

Romani's tribute to his friend is of particular interest. It was published in the *Gazzetta Piemontese*, Turin, on 1 October 1835:

> The 24 September [*sic*], the last day of an illustrious Italian, ended at Puteaux, near Paris. [After] a short life of 33 years which was full of hope and shining brightly with glory, Vincenzo Bellini is no more... A tear falls on these words, but I cannot erase them.
>
> Catania, where he was born; Naples, where he studied; Milan, where the beautiful wreath adorned his youth; Paris, where he was generously given hospitality and glory – in short, everywhere where the light of the arts, the flame of talent and the love of the beautiful penetrate – will lament this untimely extinguished light and weep for the loss of the sublime young man, as for a common loss. But perhaps no one as much as I will be able to feel the emptiness that he leaves, because no one as much as I penetrated into the most remote recesses of that noble intellect and perceived the source of his inspiration.
>
> I was his companion, collaborator and friend; I was his guide, adviser and support; I was more than a brother to him. When he arrived in Milan from Naples – where he had already made his mark with his first efforts but was inexperienced and not yet freed from the conventions that restricted him in his first work for the theatre, *Bianca e Fernando* – I alone read in that poetic soul, in that passionate heart, in that wonderful mind anxious to fly beyond the sphere in which he was restricted by the school regulations and the servility of imitation; I perceived that a different *dramma* was right for him, different poetry than that which was created by the bad taste of the times, the demands of the singers and the ignorance of the theatrical poets and still more from the naïveté of the composers. It was then that I wrote *Il pirata* for Bellini, a subject that I thought suitable and capable of touching the depths of his art, and I wasn't wrong.
>
> From that day, we understood each other and together we fought the spitefulness of the musical theatre little by little with courage, perseverance and love. From that union of ideas and intentions, we produced *La Straniera*, *I Capuleti e i Montecchi*, *Norma* and *La sonnambula*; when that union was for a while a little less close, less successful operas, *Zaira* and *Beatrice di Tenda*, were born. That made it quite clear that from then on in Italy music could not be separated

from poetry. This period of temporary discord between us is one of which we were both ashamed.

Those, who are in some respects more educated than I will no doubt analyse Bellini's works, his style, his methods, his resources; they will investigate the path that he opened after the great Pesarese [Rossini], where the latter stopped and where the former took a forward step...

In Bellini, death took away more than a composer; it stopped plans that may never be carried out. I knew all these plans completely. Undoubtedly, biographers, masters of art and critics will be paying their tribute to this generous young man, for whom I will always weep. Then it will be my turn to rectify some opinions, to inspect some judgements, to recall the past and look into the future; only then shall I publish our projects,[25] our discussions and the hopes that we both shared, despite the distance that separated us.

Alas, perhaps those hopes are dead. It took me 15 years to find Bellini, yet a single day took him from me. The spirit that responded to mine is silent.

After reading these words, if anyone wishes to accuse me of vainglory or to misconstrue my intentions in any way, obviously such a person does not deserve to understand my sorrow.

At the time of Bellini's death, Maria Malibran was enjoying unprecedented triumph in *Norma* at La Scala. On hearing of the sad news, she was reported to have been stunned and then to have burst into tears. Afterwards, falling into great melancholy, she put her hand on her forehead and exclaimed, "I feel I shall soon follow him."[26] On the following day, she wrote to Florimo,[27] and the postscript of her letter expresses the vacuum that she felt: "This black day, 23 September, will be a day of ill omen in the annals of the Italian stage."

The finale of the act of homage to Bellini took place 41 years later. On 15 September 1876, Bellini's remains were at last transferred to their final resting place at the Cathedral of Sant' Agata in Catania. The 76-year-old Florimo was present in both ceremonies: at Père Lachaise and at the cathedral in Catania, on 23 September 1876. Also present at the reburial service in Catania were Bellini's brothers and sisters – Carmelo was 73, Francesco 72, Michela 70, Giuseppa 69, Mario 66 and Maria 63 – as well as the septuagenarian Santocanale.

Of all the tributes paid to Bellini, perhaps the most appropriate is the inscription on his white marble and bronze tomb: "Ah, non credea mirarti si presto estinto, o fiore!" ("Oh, I never imagined that this flower would have died so soon!"), words and music from Amina's aria in *La sonnambula*, chosen by his compatriots.[28] For his part, Bellini left his music as a legacy to the entire world. As long as his music is heard, the tragedy of his premature death is diminished.

Notes on the Text

The following abbreviations are employed to denote the sources most frequently cited:

BML   *Bellini: Memorie e Lettere*, edited by Francesco Florimo, (Florence, 1882);

CSMN Francesco Florimo: *Cenno Storico sull Scuola Musicale di Napoli* (Naples, 1869-71, in two volumes);

SMN   Francesco Florimo: *La Scuola Musicale di Napoli* (Naples, 1881-2, in four volumes);

BSS   Francesco Pastura: *Bellini Secondo la Storia* (Parma, 1959);

EP   *Epistolario*, edited by Luisa Cambi (Milan, 1943);

CN   Conservatorio San Pietro a Miella, Naples;

MB   Museo Belliniano, Catania.

Chapter 1

1. Filippo Cicconetti: *Vita di Vincenzo Bellini* (Prato, 1859); Michele Scherillo: *Belliniana: Nuove Note* (Milan, 1885) and *Vincenzo Bellini: Note Aneddotiche e Critiche* (Ancona, 1882); Giuseppe Coco Zanghi: *Memorie e Lacrime de la Patria sul Sepolcro di Vincenzo Bellini* (Catania, 1876).

2. F Verlengia: "Gli Antenati abruzzesi di V.B." in *Riv Abruzzese* (Chieti, 1952).

3. Cotumacci had been a student of Alessandro Scarlatti and Dol of both Scarlatti and Francesco Durante.

4. Scherillo: *Belliniana* (Milan, 1885). Only the libretto of this oratorio was published.

5. Ercole Fischetti: *Catania nell' Ottocento* (Catania, 1934). Although Sicily was nominally an independent kingdom, successively under the sovereignty of Piedmont, Austria and Naples, it was isolated from the mainland during the Napoleonic Wars (1798-9 and 1805-15). The island remained virtually remote even after the fall of Napoleon, when the old Italian monarchies were reinstated but under Austrian control.

6. In 1795, Michela died and Vincenzo Tobia remarried in 1796, when he was 52. His 26-year-old new wife, Mattea Cognat, came from the province of Agrigento. There were no children from this marriage.

7. 26 works are listed: eight *Tantum ergo*, six *Salve regina*, three masses, four symphonies (sacred music), two *Compieta*, one *Qui sedes*, one *Te deum* and one *Magnificat*.

8. Policastro wrote of Rosario's disability (without documentary evidence) in *Vincenzo Bellini (1801-19)* (Catania, 1935).

9. When Francesco Florimo, Vincenzo Bellini's bosom friend, met Agata Bellini in Catania in 1832, he described her (in *SMN*, volume three, p177) as "intelligent and good-looking". She was 53 years old at the time.

10. Bellini, who was always affectionately attached to his parents and all his relations, came to feel closest to his paternal grandfather during his childhood and later to his uncle Vincenzo Ferlito.

11. Of the 75 operas that Valentino Fioravanti (1764-1837) wrote, all of which were popular in their time, only *Le Cantatrici villane* (first performed sometime between 1795 and 1801, with libretto by Giovanni Palomba, later adapted for a shortened one-act version by Giuseppe Maria Foppa) is at all remembered today. His other operas include *Robinson nella isola deserta* (Naples, 1825) and *Adelson e Salvini* (1815, with libretto by Andrea Leone Tottola, a libretto that Bellini also used in 1825 for his student work *Adelson e Salvini*.)

12. The Bellinis had seven children. After Vincenzo (1801-35), the only one to die young, there followed Carmelo (1802-84), Francesco (1804-84), Michela (1806-83), Giuseppa (1807-79), Mario (1810-85) and Maria (1813-84).

13. The priest Neri does not appear in the local records and is only mentioned in the anonymous manuscript.

14. A purported copy of Bellini's first musical composition is preserved in the Biblioteca Comunale Ursino, Catania.

15. Coco Zanghi (*Memorie e Lagrime Ecc*, Catania, 1876) wrote of one *Tantum ergo* which was performed on Christmas Eve and repeated on 30 December at the two churches mentioned respectively.

16. "Le tre ore di agonia", in *Rivista de Comune di Catania* (Catania, 1953). Francesco Pastura had, until his death in 1969, been the director of MB.

17. Filippo Cicconetti: *Vita di Vincenzo Bellini* (Prato, 1859).

18. Antonino Amore: *Vincenzo Bellini: Vita* (Catania, 1894).

19. It was to Gallo that Bellini wrote this most famous letter, though its authenticity is dubious. (See page 314-15 for the text of the letter.) Bellini met Gallo in Palermo in 1832.

20. In *L'Olivuzza* (Palermo, 1846). Gallo published the song under the heading "'La farfaletta [*sic*]', canzoncina, musica inedita, composta all'età di dodici anni dal Maestro Cav Vincenzo Bellini di Catania". The song was reprinted in Guglielmo Policastro's *Vincenzo Bellini (1801-19)* (Catania, 1935) with the comment, "The motif was adapted only to the first two stanzas and then was repeated for the other, which had not survived. But Gallo completed the whole part from memory."

21. Herbert Weinstock: *Vincenzo Bellini: His Life and his Operas* (New York, 1971), p10.

22. See page 289-90 for the text of the letter.

23. *BSS* p17.

24. *BSS* pp30-1.

25. Filippo Cicconetti: *Vita di Vincenzo Bellini* (Prato, 1859).

26. Catania's first public theatre, the Comunale, was inaugurated in 1821 with Rossini's *Aureliano in Palmira*. This theatre endured until 1890 but was used only intermittently.

27. The minutes of this meeting are preserved in MB.

28. *BSS* p40.

29. Autograph in MB. First published in *EP*, p18.

30. 36 onze are approximately £300 in 2002 purchasing value.

31. The autographs of these compositions are in the library of the Naples Conservatorio: 1) *Tantum ergo* for two sopranos with *Genitori* for four voices and orchestra; 2) *Tantum ergo* for soprano with *Genitori* for four voices and orchestra; 3) *Tantum ergo* for chorus with *Genitori* for four voices and orchestra; 4) *Gratias agimus* for four voices and orchestra; 5) *Scena ed aria di Cerere* (a *cantata da camera*) for soprano and orchestra; 6) *Prima messa* for four voices (two sopranos, tenor and bass) and orchestra; 7) *Seconda messa* for four voices (two sopranos, tenor and bass); 8) "Si, per te, Gran Nume eterno", a cavatina for soprano and orchestra; 9) "E nello stringerti a questo core", an *allegro a guisa di cabaletta* for soprano and orchestra; 10) "*Sinfonia a più strumenti* in *re maggiore*".

CHAPTER 2

1. Autograph originally in the Succi collection, Bologna. Now lost. First published by Antonino Amore in *Vincenzo Bellini: Vita* (Catania, 1894), p293. Also in *EP*, p20.

2. Florimo recounted this event in 1882 to Michele Scherillo, who used it in his *Vincenzo Bellini: note aneddotiche e critiche* (Ancona, 1882).

3. Conti (1797-1868) was described by Rossini as "the best Italian contrapuntalist of his day".

4. Tritto (1733-1824) had at first been an operatic composer, with little success. He later taught counterpoint.

5. Donizetti was born in Bergamo on 29 November 1797. Inspired by the music of Rossini, he realised at an early age that his vocation lay in the opera house. At first, he studied with Simone Mayr at the Lezione Caritevole, Bergamo, and later, when he was 17 years old, with Padre Mattei at the Bologna Liceo. One of the most important early-19th-century opera composers, he wrote some 74 works for the stage and a great number of other works, including religious, piano, vocal and instrumental music. By the time he was 48, the first signs of spinal syphilis showed themselves. Mental derangement and general paralysis followed. He died in Bergamo on 8 April 1848.

6. In *BML*, p129. Florimo has often been criticised on the authenticity of his detailed reproduction of conversations that had taken place such a long time before. This is reasonable, unless of course he had kept a diary. Whatever the case, the general reliability of the content of these conversations need neither be rejected nor diminished.

7. Zingarelli's most successful opera was *Giulietta e Romeo* (Milan, 1796). His *opera buffa Il mercato di Monfregoso* (Milan, 1792) was fairly successful.

8. In *CSMN*, volume one, p486.

9. In *BML*, p6.

10 Pergolesi (1710-36) was 26 years old when he died. Bellini lived for just less than 34 years.

11. In *CSMN*, volume two, p716.

12. In *SMN*, volume three, p154.

13. Bellini recalled this incident in a letter to Florimo on 4 August 1834. Autograph in CN. First published in *BML*, p427. Also in *EP*, p423.

14. This libretto had already been used by Valentino Fioravanti (1764-1837), Tottola's father. The opera was performed in 1815 in Lisbon and in 1816 at the Teatro dei Fiorentini, Naples. On 4 January 1839, another *Adelson e Salvini*, by Luigi Savj, was performed at the Teatro della Pergola, Florence.

15. Girolamo Crescentini (1762-1846), the celebrated castrato, was at this time teaching singing at the Naples Conservatorio. The great singer Isabella Colbran had been one of his students. Bellini only studied theory of singing under him.

16. Outstanding students usually had their operas performed at the conservatorio. Zingarelli's student work *I quattro pazzi* (1768) was produced at the Conservatorio di Santa Maria di Loreto; Conti's *Le Truppe in Franconia* (1819), Nicola Fornasini's *Il marmo* (1822), Luigi Ricci's *L'impresario in angustie* (1823) and Francesco Stabile's *La spòsa al lotto* (1826) were all produced at the Conservatorio di San Sebastiano.

17. In *BSS*, p78

18. In *SMN*, volume three, p249.

19. The plays of the French pre-Romantic writer Arnaud provided the sources for several opera libretti: his *Les amans malheureux, ou Le Comte de Comminge* (1764) was used by Donizetti (but only for the final scene, at the monastery) for *La favorite* (1840); by Nicolas Dalrayrac for *Raoul, Sire de Créqui* (1793); and by Ferdinando Päer for *Sargino* (1803).

CHAPTER 3

1. In *EP*, p167.

2. *Otto mesi in due ore* (1827), *Il borgomastro di Saardam* (1827), *L'esule di Roma* (1828), *Gianni di Calais* (1828), *Il giovedì grasso* (1828), *Il paria* (1829), *I pazzi per progetto* (1830), *Il diluvio universale* (1830), *Francesca di Foix* (1831), *La romanziera e l'uomo Nero* (1831) and *Fausta* (1832).

3. The theme was certainly popular, for very soon after Bellini had produced his *Bianca*, Capiuti's *Bianca e Fernando* followed in Venice in 1827, Francesco Berio's at Treviso in 1827 and Vaccai's *Bianca di Messina* in Turin in 1828.

4. Roti (1781?-after 1854), a Venetian actor, won his first success as a playwright in 1820 with *Bianca e Fernando*.

5. *Belliniana: Nuove Note* (Milan, 1885). Bellini did not use this cabaletta in the second version of *Bianca*.

6. Guido Zavadini: *Donizetti: Vita – Musiche – Epistolario* (Bergamo, 1948).

7. In *BML*, p14.

8. Pacini: *Le Mie Memorie Artistiche* (Florence, 1875 edition), p53.

9. In *BML*, p103.

10. Autograph in possession of antiquarian collector Leonardo Lapiccerella. Published in *BSS*, p97.

11. From 1826 onwards, Barbaja was only a director, though he was still very influential on the group Giuseppe Crivelli e Compagni, which managed both La Scala and the Teatro della Canobbiana in Milan.

12. Rossini wrote *Elisabetta, regina d'Inghilterra* (San Carlo, 1815), *La gazzetta* (Teatro dei Fiorentini, Naples, 1816), *Otello* (Teatro del Fondo, Naples, 1816) and, for the Teatro San Carlo, *Armida* (1817), *Mosè in Egitto* (1818), *Ricciardo e Zoraide* (1818), *Ermione* (1819), *La donna del lago* (1819), *Maometto II* (1820) and *Zelmyra* (1822).

   Donizetti wrote *La zingara* (Nuovo, 1822), *La lettera anonima* (Fondo, 1822), *Alfredo il Grande* (San Carlo, 1823), *Il fortunato inganno* (Nuovo, 1823), *Emilia di Liverpool* (Nuovo, 1824), *Elvida* (San Carlo, 1826), *Otto mesi in due ore* (Nuovo, 1827), *Il borgomastro di Saardam* (Nuovo, 1827), *Le convenienze ed inconvenienze teatrali* (Nuovo, 1827), *L'esule di Roma* (San Carlo, 1827), *Il castello di Kenilworth* (San Carlo, 1829), *I pazzi per progetto* (Fondo, 1830), *Il diluvio universale* (San Carlo, 1830) and *Sancia di Castiglia* (San Carlo, 1832).

   Carl Maria von Weber wrote *Der Freischütz* (Berlin, 1821) and *Euryanthe* (Vienna, 1823).

13. In *SMN*, volume three, p358.

CHAPTER 4

1. From his arrival in Milan until the premiere of *Il pirata*, just over seven months later, Bellini could also have heard at La Scala Rossini's *La donna del lago*, *L'inganno felice*, *Il barbiere di Siviglia* and *Mosè in Egitto*; Felice Frasi's *La selva d'Hermanstadt*; Pacini's *L'ultimo giorno di Pompei*; and *Il trionfo della musica*, a *pasticcio* by several composers.

2. Pollini composed the operas *La casetta nei boschi* (Teatro Canobbiana, 1798) and *L'orfana Svizzera* (posthumous, Milan Conservatorio, 1856), the cantata *Il trionfo della pace* (La Scala, 1801), a *Stabat Mater* and many pieces for the piano.

3. Ferretti, who was a part-time librettist while at the same time working for the papal government in Rome, provided Rossini with *La Cenerentola* (1817, which, incidentally, was based on Romani's *Agatina* [1814]) and *Matilde di Shabran* (1821) and Donizetti with *L'ajo nell' imbarazzo* (1824), *Olivo e Pasquale* (1827), *Il furioso all'isola di San Domingo* (1833) and *Torquato Tasso* (1833).

4. Romani's first libretto was an adaptation of René-Charles-Guilbert de Pixerécourt's play of the same title.

5. Some of the other libretti that Romani provided include *Gli Illinesi* (1819) for Francesco Basily; *I due Figaro* (1820), *Il sonnambulo* (1824) and *Adele di Lusignano* (1837) for Michele Carafa; *Caterina di Guisa* (1833) and *La solitaria delle Asturie* (1838) for Carlo Coccia; *Il finto Stanislao* (1818) for Adalbert Gyrowetz, the libretto of which was later used as *Il giorno di regno* (1840) by Verdi; *Gli avventurieri* (1825) for Giacomo Cordella; *Amleto* (1822), *Francesca da Rimini* (1828), *Zaira* (1831), *I Normanni a Parigi* (1832), *Ismailia* (1832) and *Medea in Corinto* (1851) for Mercadante; *Il barone di Dolsheim* (1818), *Il falegname di Livonia* (1819) and *La sacerdotessa d'Irminsul* (1820) for Pacini; *Margharita d'Anjou* (1820) and *L'esule di Granata* (1822) for Meyerbeer; *Il Turco in Italia* (1814) and *Bianca e Faliero* (1819) for Rossini; *Chiara e Serafina* (1822), *Alina, regina di Golconda* (1828), *Anna Bolena* (1830), *Ugo, conte di Parigi* (1832), *L'elisir d'amore* (1832), *Parisina* (1833), *Lucrezia Borgia* (1833), *Rosmunda d'Inghilterra* (1834), *Gianni di Parigi* (1939) and *Adelia* (1841) for Donizetti; *Giulietta e Romeo* (1825) for Vaccai; *Maometto* (1817) for Peter von Winter; *Francesca da Rimini* (1823) for Feliciano Strepponi; and *La voce mysteriosa* (1821) for Mosca. Romani's last libretto was *Cristina di Svezia* (1855) for the pianist/composer Sigismond Thalberg.

6. Autograph in CN (unpublished).

7. *Felice Romani ed i più riputati maestri di musica sel suo tempo* (Turin, 1882).

8. See page 240 on hard copy

9. Rubini was born at Romano de Lombardia, a small town near Bergamo, on 7 April 1795. It was here that he retired, in 1845, and where he died, on 2 March 1854. The details of his early life are obscure. The tenor whose vocal technique and style were to be considered matchless was self-taught. As a child, he made his debut at the age of twelve in one of the theatres at Bergamo, in a female part. Later, he played the violin in the orchestra between acts of comedies and sang in the chorus during the opera season. It was only accidentally that Rubini attracted attention when he offered to sing a very difficult aria that no one else in the company could. After this, he was given minor parts instead of being confined to the chorus. Before long, he was engaged in several touring companies as a second tenor, but during this time he continued his private studies.

    In 1816, Barbaja engaged him for his theatres in Naples, but when Rubini first began to sing leading parts, he did not make a great impact, as he was overshadowed by the Rossinian tenors Giovanni David, Manuel Garcia and Andrea Nozzari. However, by the mid 1820s, he had made a great impression, mainly through perfect vocalisation in several Rossinian roles, but his glory really began not so much with his first Bellinian role (that of Gernando in *Bianca e Gernando* [1826]) but with Gualtiero in *Il pirata* (1827).

    Up until 1831, Rubini sang mainly in Italy. From 1831 to 1842, he sang in Paris and London and, in 1843, St Petersburg. The comments of Anton Rubinstein and Franz Liszt

– that they formed their ideas of noble and eloquent phrasing from the example of the great tenor Rubini – reveal his real magic.

He created a great number of roles. Apart from those that Bellini wrote for him – Gernando, Gualtiero, Elvino (*La sonnambula*) and Arturo (*I Puritani*), Donizetti composed expressly for him Filinto (*La lettera anonima*, 1822), Alfonso (*Elvida*, 1826), Settirmio (*L'esule di Roma*, 1828), Seide (*Alina*, 1828), Gianni (*Gianni di Calais*, 1828), Ernesto (*Il giovedì grasso*, 1828), Idamore (*Il paria*, 1829), Percy (*Anna Bolena*, 1830), Fernando (*Marino Faliero*, 1838) and Gianni (a role he never sang) in *Gianni di Parigi* (1839). Pacini also composed a few roles for Rubini.

10. *Thirty Years' Musical Recollections* (London, 1830-60).

11. In *Biographie universelle des musiciens et bibliographie générale de la musique* (Paris, 1833-44).

12. In *BML*, p17. Also quoted by Cicconetti in *Vita di Vincenzo Bellini* (Prato, 1859), p24.

13. Choreography by Salvatore Taglioni. Composer unknown.

14. Choreography by Antonio Cortesi. Various composers.

15. Autograph owned by Cicconetti now lost. A copy exists in MB. Published in *EP*, p25.

16. Autograph in CN. First published in *BML*, p293. Also in *EP*, p39.

17. The French-born Adèle Chaumel studied singing at the Paris Conservatoire. After she married Rubini in 1819, she Italianised her name to Adelaide Comelli and was often billed as Comelli-Rubini. On 3 December 1820, she created the role of Calbo in Rossini's *Maometto II* at the San Carlo. She had a big voice of large range, but it was uneven and often inaccurate. However, Comelli possessed great vitality and her vocal colourations could be exciting. She never became a singer of the first rank.

18. Pastura, who copied it before the autograph was lost, published it in *BSS*, p21.

19. Autograph in CN. Published in *BML*, p291. Also in *EP*, pp35 and 38.

20. Autograph in CN. Published in *BML*, p296. Also in *EP*, p42.

21. Autograph in CN. Published in *BML*, p288. Also in *EP*, p31.

22. Carolina Unger (1803-77), Hungarian soprano. She later created the role of Isoletta in Bellini's *La Straniera*.

23. Autograph in CN. Published in *BSS*, p48.

24. Autograph in CN. Published in *BML*, p291. Also in *EP*, p36.

25. Autograph in CN. Published in *BML*, p293. Also in *EP*, p41.

26. Bartolomeo Merelli (1793-1879), a childhood friend and fellow student of Donizetti at Bergamo, later became one of the most influential impresarios of his time. At various times, he was an impresario in all the major European opera houses and in several Italian cities. In addition, he wrote libretti for Donizetti, Mayr, Morlacchi and Vaccai and played an important part in the commissioning of Rossini's *Guillaume Tell*, Donizetti's *Lucia di Lammermoor*, Pacini's *Saffo* and Verdi's *Oberto, conte di San Bonifacio, Un giorno di regno, Nabucco, I Lombardi* and *Giovanna d'Arco*. It was Merelli who persuaded Verdi to compose again (*Nabucco*, 1842) after the failure of *Un giorno di regno*.

27. Autograph in CN. Published in *BML*, p298. Also in *EP*, p48.

28. Autograph in CN. Published in *BML*, p1104. Also in *EP*, p58.

29. Autograph in CN. Published in *BML*, p293. Also in *EP*, p39.

30. Autograph in CN. Published in *BML*, p334. Also in *EP*, p95.

31. Autograph in CN. Published in *BML*, p340. Also in *EP*, p104.

32. Florimo also wrote about Bellini in *CSMN*, in *SMN* and in *Traslazione delle ceneri di Vincenzo Bellini* (Naples, 1877).

33. Autograph in CN. Letter dated 27 September 1828, Milan. Published in *BML*, p374. Also in *EP*, p161.

34. Daniele Napoletano, who knew Florimo, told Pastura that many of the more intimate letters from Bellini were burned by Florimo in his old age, before he presented his papers to the library of the Conservatorio di San Pietro a Maiella, Naples.

35. See page 343.

36. Published in *Vincenzo Bellini* (Catania, 1959), p395.

37. Andrew Porter pointed this out in his article for the EMI recording of *Il pirata*. He wrote that, "unless we assume that something of the kind happened... it doesn't really make sense. There is a loose end in Romani's otherwise tidy work."

38. The final scenes, which were not set to music but published in the libretto for the premiere of *Il pirata*:

Scena 9: Gualtiero e coro di Cavalieri, indi coro di pirati ed Itulbo

Cavalieri: La tua sentenza udisti, Il tuo destin t'è noto
        Ma noi possiam d'un voto
        Farti contento ancor.
        Parla. Che vuoi?

Gualtiero: Null'altro fuorchè spedita morte.
        Incontro alla sua sorte
        Vola ansioso il cor.

Cavalieri: Pago sarai. Guidatelo
        Tosto a morir... Quai grida!... (*s'odono delle grida nell'interno*)

Coro di Pirati: Viva Gualtier!
(*di dentro*)

Cavalieri: Ci assalgono I fidi suoi (*si precipitano da varie parti I Pirati*)
        Si uccida.

Itulbo, Pirati voi, soli, voi morrete.

Cavalieri: Ebben, il difendete.
(*combattono fra di loro*)

Scena Ultima: Imogene, Adele, coro di damigelle e detti.

Imogene: Lasciatemi! Lasciatemi!
        Io vo' saper chi muor.
        (*Gualtiero attraversa il ponte seguito dai suoi*)

Gualtiero: Scostatevi!
    (*ai Pirati*)
    L'impone il vostro duce.
    Un' abborrita luce
    Fuggo cosi
    (*s'uccide*)

Tutti: Che orror!
    (*Imogene sviene nelle braccia delle damigelle quandro di terrore*)

    FINE

39. At the time that the opera was written, this chorus was not considered to have been trivial and Bellini himself thought very highly of it, although it is unknown for precisely which reasons.

40. "Vivi tu" in Donizetti's *Anna Bolena*, an aria similar in construction to "Tu vedrai" and expressly written for Rubini, also suffers the same shortcomings in performance.

CHAPTER 5

1. Autograph in CN. First published in *BML*, p319. Also in *EP*, p73.

2. Donizetti's opera *Alina, regina di Golconda* did not follow *Bianca e Fernando* immediately, as Bellini says in his letter, but five weeks later and after Rossini's *Il barbiere di Siviglia* and *Otello* were performed. *Alina*, however, was the next new opera to be performed after *Bianca*.

    The cabaletta "Contenta appien quest'alma", which Tosi wanted changed, eventually became "A bello, a me ritorna", the cabaletta following "Casta Diva" in *Norma*.

3. This *Inno reale* was a hymn with chorus. Letizia Cortesi, Antonio Tamburini and Giovanni Battista Verger were the soloists.

4. Autograph in CN. Published in *BML*, p329. Also in *EP*, p79.

5. Autograph in CN. Published in *BML*, p326. Also in *EP*, p83.

6. Autograph in CN. Published in *BML*, p87. Also in *EP*, p88.

7. Autograph in CN. Published in *BML*, p322. Also in *EP*, p75.

8. Autograph in CN. Published in *BML*, p328. Also in *EP*, p85.

9. 4,000 lire are approximately £2,200 in 2002 purchasing value.

10. Roti's play was published in *L'Ape-teatrale, ossia Nuova Raccolta di drammi, commedie e tragedie, II* (Naples, 1825).

11. Another operatic *Bianca e Fernando*, composed by Giovanni Belio in 1806-18?, was first performed at the Accademia Filarmonica, Treviso, on 31 March 1827. Also, at about the same time that *Bianca e Gernando* was first performed (spring 1826), another *Bianca e Fernando* with libretto by Martino Cuccetti and music by Pietro Capiuti (date of composition unknown) was presented at the Teatro San Benedetto, Venice.

12. At Bellini's request, Romani included in the revised libretto Filippo's attempt to save himself by threatening to stab Bianca's son, as in Carlo Roti's play, a scene that was omitted in Gilardoni's version.

Friedrich Lippmann pointed out (*Quellenkundliche Anmerkungen*, op cit, p135, ft14) that Bellini needed the scene "not for pure theatrical effect, but rather for Bianca to sing the touching 'Deh, non ferir'".

13. In *EP*, pp58-9.

CHAPTER 6

1. In *Note aneddotiche e critiche* (Ancona, 1882) and in *Nuove Note* (Milan, 1885).

2. Autograph in CN. Published in *BML*, p356. Also in *EP*, p124.

3. Autograph in CN. Published in *BML*, p373. Also in *EP*, p161.

4. Autograph in CN. Published in *BML*, p374. Also in *EP*, p162.

5. Autograph in CN. Published in *BML*, p343. Also in *EP*, p106.

6. Autograph in CN. Published in *BML*, p346. Also in *EP*, p112.

7. Autograph in CN. Published in *BML*, p350. Also in *EP*, p115.

8. Domenico Reina of Lugano (1797-1843) was reported to have had a beautiful tenor voice that he used with considerable force, intelligence and agility. He made his debut at La Scala on 12 January 1829 as Ilo in Rossini's *Zelmyra*. He was to create the role of Arturo in *La Straniera* and Tamas in Donizetti's *Gemma di Vergy*.

9. Grisi refers to the mezzo-soprano Giuditta (1805-40), sister of the more celebrated soprano, Giulia Grisi.

10. Autograph in CN. Published in *BML*, p374. Also in *EP*, p161.

11. Autograph in CN. Published in *EP*, p146. Undated but almost certainly written on 5 August 1828.

12. Autograph in CN. Published in *BML*, p364. Also in *EP*, p148.

13. Autograph in CN. Published in *BML*, p367. Also in *EP*, p151.

14. Autograph in CN. Published in *BML*, p154. Also in *EP*, p154.

15. Autograph in CN. Published in *BML*, p378. Also in *EP*, p156.

16. Gaetano Rossi (1780-1855?), an official librettist at La Scala, was technically very competent but lacked creative imagination. He provided Rossini with *La cambiale di matrimonio*, *Tancredi* and *Semiramide* and Donizetti with *Maria Padilla* and *Linda di Chamounix*. He also wrote libretti for Mayr and Meyerbeer.

17. Autograph (undated) in CN. Published in *BML*, p371. Also in *EP*, p158.

18. Published in *BSS*, p150.

19. Autograph in CN. Published by Pastura in *Le Lettere di Bellini* (Catania, 1935), p274.

20. Autograph in CN. First published in *BML*, p383. Also in *EP*, p176.

21. Autograph in CN. First published in *BML*, p386. Also in *EP*, p180.

22. Autograph (undated) in CN. First published in *BSS*, p279. Florimo, who published a small excerpt, dated it 4 March 1829.

23. Autograph in CN. First published in *BML*, p387. Also in *EP*, p186.

24. This anecdote was first published in the *Gazzetta Musicale di Napoli* on 20 October 1855 by Raffaele Colucci.

25. It has often been stated that Bellini had the inspiration and in fact composed *La Straniera* at Villa Galoni in Moltrasio, a village on Lake Como. A commemorative plate exists at the villa, but documented evidence disproves the connection. The misunderstanding arose from a letter that Doctor Tarchiani-Bonfanti wrote to Florimo in as late as 1882. Doctor Bonfanti, who had been Giuditta Turina's physician at Moltrasio, had in his possession 15 letters from Bellini: 13 to Giuditta, one to her mother and one to her brother. In 1882, after Giuditta's death, he sent the letters to Florimo and in an accompanying letter mentioned that at Villa Galoni, where he was then living, Bellini had composed a great part of an (unnamed) opera in the autumn of 1829 and had also written *La sonnambula* there. It is true that Giuditta Turina had lived in the villa, but only during the last years of her life. Furthermore, in the autumn of 1829, Bellini did not compose any operas. Both *La Straniera* and *La sonnambula* were composed in Milan in 1828 and 1830 respectively. (See note 24, chapter 9.)

26. Published both in facsimile and textually by Franco Abbiati in *La Scala – Rivista dell'Opera* number five, 15 March 1950.

27. Autograph owned by Euplio Reina, Catania. First published in facsimile in *Illustrazione Italiana* (Milan, 6 December 1931). Also in *EP*, p182.

28. Copy of autograph in MB. Published in *BSS*, p159.

29. Bellini was enthusiastic about the *mis-en-scène* of this scene and the three different voices of the chorus.

CHAPTER 7

1. Marie-Louise was Napoleon's ex-empress. The duchy of Parma was given her as consolation after her divorce.

2. The operas were *Le comte Ory* (20 August 1828) and *Guillaume Tell* (3 August 1829).

3. Autograph in CN. First published in *BML*, p364. Also in *EP*, p149.

4. Autograph in CN. First published in *BML*, p346. Also in *EP*, p109.

5. Published by Cesare Alcari, "La Zaira fu veramente fischiata?" in *Musica d'Oggi* (July 1935), p262. Alcari of Biblioteca Maria Luisa, Parma, quoted many letters and other documents.

6. The subject of this libretto, however, was not original, as several other poets had previously written scripts based on it. Giacomo Francesco Busani's libretto of *Cesare in Egitto* was set to music by both Antonio Sartorio (Venice, 1667) and Geminiano Giacomelli (Teatro Regio Ducal, Milan, 1735). Jomelli (1751), Piccinni (1770), Tritto (1805) and Pacini (1821) also wrote operas on the same subject.

7. Published by Alcari (see note 4 above), p263.

8. Published by Alcari (see note 4 above), p264.

9. Giovanni da Procida (1210-98), a historical character, appears in a leading role in Verdi's *Les Vêpres Siciliènnes* (1855), libretto by Scribe and Charles Duveyrier.

10. Autograph in CN. First published in *BML*, p387. Also in *EP*, p186.

11. Refers to Voltaire's *Zaïre* (1732).

12. *Vita di Vincenzo Bellini* (Prato, 1859).

13. Published by Alcari (see note 4 above), p266.

14. Autograph in CN. Published in *BSS*, p101. Also in *EP*, p211.

15. *Oreste*, choreographed by Antonio Cortesi, was the customary ballet given with *Zaira*.

16. Autograph lost. Copy in MB. Published in *Numero Unico Vincenzo Bellini – Rivista del Comune di Catania* (1935), p3. Also in *EP*, p213.

17. By Sebastiano Nasolini (1797), Marcos Antonio Portogallo (1802), Francesco Federici (1803), Peter von Winter (1805), Duke Ernst of Saxe-Coburg-Gotha (1846) and Paul Véronge de la Nux (1890). Romani's libretto was also used by Alessandro Gandini (1829), Saverio Mercadante (1831) and Antonio Manni (1845).

18. Although the score calls for oriental instruments, these are not specified. As there are no particular notes assigned to them, it is obvious that they are meant to be light percussion instruments (of the *banda Turca* of Mozart and Beethoven) such as the triangle, cymbal, tambourine and possibly drums.

19. *Vincenzo Bellini und die italienische Opera Seria seiner zeit* (Cologne/Vienna, 1969), pp380-1.

20. In *BSS*, p213.

Chapter 8

1. Persiani (1805-69) won considerable fame with *Eufemio di Messina* (Lucca, 1829) and *Il fantasma* (Théâtre-Italien, Paris, 1843), both operas to libretti by Romani, and *Ines di Castro* (San Carlo, Naples, 1835) to a libretto by Salvatore Cammarano. In 1830 he married Fanny Tacchinardi, the creator of the title role in Donizetti's *Lucia di Lammermoor* (1835).

2. Photocopy of autograph (owned by Professore Antonio Caldarella of the Archivio di Stato, Palermo) in MB. Published in *BSS*, p220.

3. Autograph in the Federico Patetta collection, Turin. First published by Alessandro Luzio in *Atti della Reale Accademia delle Scienze di Torino*, vol LXVII, 1932. Also in *EP*, p223.

4. Bellini almost certainly met Lamperi in Turin through a mutual friend, Grosson, who was a member of the Accademia Filarmonica, Turin. Lamperi was at the time Under-Secretary of State in the Ministry of Foreign Affairs of the Kingdom of Sardinia and Piedmont.

5. A new opera with libretto by Rossi.

6. Autograph in the Biblioteca del Conservatorio di Musica "Cherubini", Florence. Published in *BSS*, p229.

7. Autograph owned by Conte Treccani. Published in *EP*, p232.

8. Autograph in CN. First published in *BML*, p388. Also in *EP*, p231.

9. *Bellini: Sa Vie, ses oeuvres* (Paris, 1868).

10. In *Felice Romani ed i più riputati maestri di musica del suo tempo* (Turin, 1882).

11. Autograph in CN. Published in *BSS*, p286. Also in *EP*, p238.

12. Published by Alessandro Luzio (see note 3 above).

13. Autograph in CN. First published in *BML*, p389. Also in *EP*, p239.

14. Published by Alessandro Luzio. (See note 3 above.)

15. Fragment of autograph in MB. Published in *EP*, p251.

16. In 1892, this portrait was presented to Verdi. It is now in the collection of the Carrara-Verdi family at the Villa Sant' Agata, Busetto.

17. For the Vaccai libretto, Romani had borrowed from Giuseppe Foppa's earlier version of *Giulietta e Romeo*, set to music by Zingarelli in 1796. Foppa found his source mainly in Girolamo della Corte's *Storie di Verona*. (See F Cella's "Indagini sulle fonti francesi dei libretti di Vincenzo Bellini" in *Contributi dell' instituto di filologia moderna, Serie francese*, V, Milan, 1968, p451.) There were also many dramatic versions of the story, such as Luigi da Porto's *Istoria novellamente ritrovata di due nobili amanti* (*c*1530), Girolamo della Corte's *Dell' Istorie della citta di Verona* (1594-96) and Luigi Scevola's *Giulietta e Romeo* (1818).

18. Operas based on the tragedy of *Romeo and Juliet* include Georg Benda's *Romeo und Julia* (1776), Daniel Steibelt's *Romeo et Juliette* (1793), Zingarelli's *Giulietta e Romeo* (1796), Guglielmini's *Romeo e Giulietta* (1810), Nicolò Vaccai's *Giulietta e Romeo* (1865), Gounod's *Romeo et Juliette* (1867), Richard d'Ivry's *Les amants de Verone* (1878), LW Barksworth's *Romeo and Juliet* (1920) and Riccardo Zandonai's *Giulietta e Romeo* (1922).

CHAPTER 9

1. Autograph in MB. Published in *Numero Unico Vincenzo Bellini della Rivista del Comune di Catania* (1935), p6. Also in *EP*, p251.

2. Autograph in MB. Published in facsimile by G Delogu, "La Casa di Bellini", in *Emporium* (March 1931), p169. Also in *EP*, p252.

3. As in note 2 above. Also in *EP*, p253.

4. Autograph owned by F Chiarenza Ascot of Catania. First published by A Amore in *Vincenzo Bellini: Arte* (Catania, 1892), p13. Also in *EP*, p254.

5. Four tari are approximately £3 and 30 onze are £226 in 2002 purchasing value.

6. This Teatro Carcano had been inaugurated on 3 September 1803 with Francesco Federici's *Zaira*.

7. Autograph lost. First published in *BML*, p390. Also in *EP*, p256.

8. Pasta, the daughter of a Jewish father, Antonio Negri, and Rachele Ferranti of Como, was christened (date of birth unknown) a Catholic at Saronno near Milan on 28 October 1797. She was named Maria Costanza Giuditta and was brought up by her maternal grandmother at Como.

   Giuditta Negri grew up in a happy and musical environment, having lessons for the organ as well as singing with Bartolomeo Lotti at Como. At the age of 15, she moved with her maternal uncle to Milan, where she studied singing with Scappa. Three years later, she made her professional stage debut in her teacher's *semi-seria* operetta *Le tre Eleonore* at the Teatro degli Filodrammatici, Milan. Her achievement there aroused the interest of Päer, who procured an engagement for her at the Théâtre-Italien, Paris. Giuditta married Giuseppe

Pasta, a Milanese lawyer by profession but a singer by choice, who sang the leading tenor role in *Le tre Eleonore*, and went to Paris, where she made her debut in Päer's *Il principe di Taranto*. She followed this with Donna Elvira (*Don Giovanni*) and Giulietta (in Zingarelli's *Giulietta e Romeo*), but she was not a success, only managing to please the critics in the last act of *Giulietta*, when "her voice ceased to be veiled".

After Paris, both Giuditta and her husband were engaged by Ayrton of the King's Theatre, London. In January 1817, she sang the travesty role of Telemaco in Cimarosa's *Penelope* and followed this with Cherubino, Servilia (*La clemenza di Tito*) and the Shrew in Ferrari's *Il sbaglio fortunato*. The indifference with which Pasta was received in all these roles aroused in her a strong, searching introspection, and as she was also pregnant she did not sing for the next 13 months, though she went on studying to improve her vocal technique.

In September 1818, six months after her daughter, Clelia, was born, Pasta returned to the stage, scoring her first real success in Pacini's *Adelaide e Comingio* at the Teatro San Benedetto, Venice. Several other engagements followed, confirming her unusually great potential. Some of her more successful appearances in the next three years included the title roles in Rossini's *La Cenerentola* and Nicolini's *Giulio Cesare delle Gallie*, and particularly Desdemona in Rossini's *Otello*, in which role she returned to the Italien in 1821. From then on, her fame grew constantly. During the 1820s, Pasta distinguished herself in a great variety of roles, the most outstanding being the title roles in Rossini's *Tancredi* and Mayr's *Medea in Corinto*.

Before she created the title role in *Anna Bolena* and Amina in *La sonnambula*, in 1830-1, Pasta's repertoire included operas by Rossini (*Aureliano in Palmira, Odoardo e Cristina, Elisabetta, regina d'Inghilterra, Mosè in Egitto, Zelmyra, Semiramide* and *Il viaggio a Reims*); Pacini (*Il barone di Dolsheim, Califfo di Bagdad* and *Niobe*), Päer (*Camilla, Sargine* and *Agnese*), Mayr (*La rosa rossa e la rosa bianca* and *Le Danaidi*), Nasolini (*Cleopatra*), Vaccai (*Giulietta e Romeo*), Coccia (*Maria Stuarda*), Paisiello (*Nina*), and Carafa (*Gabriella di Vergy*). She also sang Donna Anna in Mozart's *Don Giovanni*, Romeo in Zingarelli's *Giulietta e Romeo*, Armando in Meyerbeer's *Il crociato in Egitto* and the title role in Rossini's *Otello*.

9. *Thirty Years' Musical Recollections* (London, 1830-60).

10. In fact, Pasta created the role of Corinna in Rossini's *Il viaggio a Reims*, written for the occasion of the coronation of Charles X at Reims in 1825. After five performances, Rossini withdrew the score, a great deal of which he reused in *Le comte Ory* (1828).

11. The Bavarian priest Johann Simon Mayr (1763-1845) came to Italy in 1788 to complete his musical education. As Giovanni Simone Mayr, he made his mark as a composer of oratorios and later of opera in Venice. In 1805, he became the director of the newly founded music school *Lezioni Caritevoli* at Bergamo, where he later taught Donizetti.

12. Published in full by Franco Schlitzer: "Nell' Intimità di Vincenzo Bellini: Lettere inedite sparse o disparse" in *Il Mattino d'Italia* (Naples, 8 June 1951).

13. Published by Salvioli in 1884. Also in *EP*, p264. Autograph lost.

14. *Felice Romani ed i più riputati maestri di musica del suo tempo* (Turin, 1882).

15. *Donizetti* by Arnaldo Fraccaroli (Milan, 1945?), a biography in the form of a novel.

16. Published by Salvioli in 1884. Also in *EP*, p264. Giovanni Battista Perucchini, born in Bergamo in 1784, lived mainly in Venice, where Bellini met him during the time *I Capuleti* was produced. Perucchini, an amateur musician, was a friend of Rossini.

17. Born in Italy as Amalia Oldosi. Performed under the stage name Mme Schütz, the Giulietta.

18. Gara wrote this in his article "La seconda moglie di Re Barbablu", published in the programme of the 1957 revival of *Anna Bolena* at La Scala.

19. In 1844, Verdi composed *Ernani* to Piave's libretto, experiencing considerable trouble with the censor. Operas on the same subject by Gabussi (1834), Mazzucato (1844), Laudamo (1849) and Hirschman (1908?) achieved only local interest.

20. Bellini used some of this music later in *Norma* and a little of it in *La sonnambula*.

21. *Il Salotto della contessa Maffei* (Milan, 1895).

22. Appiani also became a great friend of Verdi. In 1841-2, Donizetti composed *Linda di Chamounix* and completed *Maria Padilla* in her home.

23. Autograph in CN. Published in *BSS*, p278.

24. There has been a great deal of speculation and confusion concerning whether or not Bellini actually composed *La sonnambula* at Moltrasio, the idyllic village by Lake Como. Although Bellini did stay with the Turinas at Moltrasio (in Villa Salterio), he certainly composed at least most of *La sonnambula* in Milan. Nevertheless, it is also almost certain that Bellini was inspired by the natural surroundings of Villa Passalacqua, where he had been a guest. When I visited the locale in the early 1990s, a villager guided me to the hill by the lakeshore at the south end of Moltrasio, where Villa Passalacqua is situated. There, I discovered the setting of *La sonnambula* – the mill, the stream (now dried), the woods, the nearby farm that Rodolfo so vividly describes in the opera ("Il mulino...il fonte...il bosco! E vicin la fattoria!"). Bellini's and Romani's village of their opera, designed by Sanquirico, is all there, at least traces of it.

25. As in note 14 above.

26. Autograph in Federico Patetta collection, Turin. Published by Alessandro Luzio in *Atti della Reale Accademia delle Scienze di Torino,* vol LXVII (January 1932). Also in *EP*, p268.

27. Autograph in CN. Published in *BML*, p441. Also in *EP*, p440.

28. Quoted by Pastura in *BSS*, p282. Source not specified.

29. Romani wrote libretti on the same subject set to music as *Amina* by Giuseppe Rastrelli (1824) and Antonio D'Antoni (1825) and as *Il sonnambulo* by Carlo Valentini (1834). Also, Luigi Piccinni wrote *Il sonnambulo* (1797) to an anonymous libretto and Päer wrote *La sonnambula* (1800) to Giuseppe Maria Foppa's libretto.

30. Albani recounted in her autobiography that the Sicilians sympathised so warmly with her interpretation of Amina that they called her "Bellini's daughter", while the Florentines called her the Sonnambula herself.

31. Callas, like her teacher Elvira de Hidalgo, played the final sleepwalking scene in bare feet but did not wear the nightcap, as Malibran did.

CHAPTER 10

1. Autograph owned by Donzelli's great-nephews. First published by Adelmo Damerini in *Corriere Emiliano* (*Gazzetta di Parma*), number seven (9 January 1932). Also in *BSS*, p286.

2. As in note 1 above.

3. Autograph owned by Prince of Torre e Tasso. Published in *Tribuna* (Rome, 1936). Also in *EP*, p275.

4. The principal roles in Soumet's *tragédie La Norma* were taken by Mlle George (Norma), Lockroi (Pollion), Alexandrine Noblet (Adalgise) and Eric-Bernard (Orovése).

5. First published in Maria Ferranti Giulini's *Giuditta Pasta e i suoi tempi* (Milan, 1935), p139. Also in *EP*, p278.

6. Franco Schlitzer observed this in the original libretto, which is in the Accademia musicale chigiana.

7. Autograph in CN. First published in *EP*, p280. Also in *BSS*, p294.

8. Autograph in CN. First published in *BML*, p293. Also in *EP*, p283.

9. 3,000 ducats are approximately £7,000 in 2002 purchasing value.

10. Mercadante mentioned this in a letter to Florimo on 12 December: "…and I think it will interest you to read a paragraph from Bellini's letter that made me laugh very much…" Autograph of Mercadante's letter in CN. Published in *BML*.

11. Mercadante's new opera was *I Normanni a Parigi*, which, however, had its premiere later, on 7 February 1832, at the Teatro Reggio, Turin.

12. Barbò was the author of *Cenni Illustrativi alla Nuova Opera La Straniera* (Milan, 1829).

13. Autograph and objects acquired by MB from the Martinez family of Catania.

14. This materialised on 13 March 1832 as *Ugo, conte di Parigi* with libretto by Felice Romani.

15. Both ballets were choreographed by Cortesi; *Merope* was set to music by Luigi Viviani and Giacomo Panizza; the composer of the music of *I pazzi per progetto* is unknown.

16. Autograph never produced. First published in French translation by Arthur Pougin in *Bellini: Sa Vie, ses oeuvres* (Paris, 1868), p112. A note reveals that the letter had been communicated to Pougin by Florimo. It was also published in Italian (1882) in *BML*, pp31 and 397 – two versions differing slightly in orthography. Also in *EP*, p290.

    Florimo stated that he had given the autograph as a gift to Cavaliere Temple, brother of Lord Palmerston, who was then Minister of Her Britannic Majesty in Naples.

17. *L'Olimpiade* (Teatro Tordinona, Rome, 1735), a complete failure at its premiere, later became popular. Today, it is considered Pergolesi's best *opera seria*. The libretto is by Metastasio.

18. Autograph owned by Euplio Reina, Catania. Published in facsimile in *Illustrazione Italiana*, (Milan), December 1931. Also in *EP*, p291.

19. Published by Salvioli in 1884. Also in *EP*, p296.

20. Born as Countess Pahlen (1803-75) in Russia. She died in Paris.

21. *Vita di Vincenzo Bellini* (Prato, 1859).

22. Autograph never produced. Published in *CSMN*, p819.

23. It must be stated, however, that Ricca's book has been shown to contain several forgeries concerning its hitherto unpublished material. The strongest point against the authenticity of this letter is that Ricca asserted that he had found it in a book published in Genoa in 1854 by a certain Carlo Nava. This book has never been found by any of several scholars who have persistently searched for it.

24. Alexandre Soumet (1788-1845) combined successfully the beautiful simplicity of Classicism with the mercurial complexities of Romanticism, thus bridging the rapidly widening gap between the two genres. He is chiefly remembered today as the creator of the source of *Norma*, for which he most probably drew on Chateaubriand's *Les martyrs* and on Euripides' *Medea*, and as collaborator with Luigi Balochi of the French text for Rossini's *Le Siège de Corinthe* (1826). His plays, which were almost always based on history or mythology, include the prize-winning (Academie Française) *Découverte de la Vaccine* (1815), *Clytemnestra* (1822), *Cleopâtre* (1824), *Jeanne d'Arc* (1825), *Le Gladiateur* (1841) and others.

25. The word Druid itself means "holy man of the oak". According to the writings of Pliny, "the Druids held nothing more sacred than the mistletoe and the tree that bears it, always supposing that the tree be oak". Neither the oak nor the mistletoe were considered to be the gods themselves; instead, the gods lived in them. This is why the Druids worshipped in groves of trees, believing mistletoe to be the seed duct of the oak tree. Consequently, they used its berries to impart fecundity to barren women. The mistletoe was ceremoniously cut from the oak with a golden sickle, followed by the slaughtering of two young white bulls, whose blood was taken up by the oak. (Omitting the bovine ritual slaughter, this ceremony is performed during the introduction to "Casta Diva".) The Druids often slaughtered human beings as sacrifice to their gods, thus giving the Romans some reason (or excuse) to dominate Gaul and civilise its gods.

When Druidism spread to Celtic and Saxon lands, places in which there were no groves of trees, the Druids erected dolmens and megaliths, as at Carnac, in Brittany, thus producing artificial sacred groves. This does not apply to Stonehenge, in England, which, although possibly used by ancient Druids (as it is used by modern English Druids), definitely pre-dates the earliest mention of Druidism by about 2000 years.

Since 58 BC, when Caesar invaded Gaul, rebellion was perpetually in the air. In 52 BC, the Gallic warrior Vercingetorix almost routed the Romans from the Auvergne but surrendered after the Siege of Alesia. After this defeat, the Romans forced their governors on Gaul, such as Pollione.

The most likely geographical setting of *Norma* must have been the site of Chartres Cathedral in modern-day France, where, according to Julius Caesar in his *Gallic Wars*, the Druids at a certain time of year conducted their rites at Carnutes, the centre of all Gaul. However, Lewis Spence, a modern authority on Druidism, says that at the time that *Norma* is supposed to take place, the chief Druid deity was a black virgin and not the chaste moon goddess, who, as Norma says in "Casta Diva", "bathes the ancient grove in a silvery light". The Druids did worship a moon goddess, but this was long after the Roman occupation. It is more difficult to explain the god Irminsul, who in mythology was referred to as a "giant column". (*Norma* was at one stage subtitled *La foresta d'Irminsul*.)

26. Maria Callas, a great exponent of this role, believed that Norma is more of a frantic woman and mother of the children of her Roman lover, playing for time (trying very hard to dominate and keep the ferocious Druids, who want war against the Romans, quiet), than the prophetic demi-goddess that she is trying to be. When Norma finally convinces them that she foresees Rome's destruction, the Druids are appeased. Then "Casta Diva" follows as a prayer for peace.

CHAPTER 11

1. Arnaldo Fraccaroli: *Bellini* (Milan, 1942).

2. In *SMN*, volume three, p204.

3. Autograph in MB. Published in *BSS*, p312. This Catanese Giovanni is otherwise unidentified, but Pastura, who first published this letter, has identified the uncle to whom the letter was addressed as Ignazio Giuffrida-Moschetti, apparently one of Bellini's friends.

4. Autograph in CN. First published in *BML*, p466. Also in *EP*, p483.

5. Published in facsimile by M Ferranti Giulini in *Giuditta Pasta e i suoi tempi* (Milan, 1935). Also in *EP*, p303.

6. Published by A Amore in *Vincenzo Bellini: Vita* (Catania, 1894), p317. Also in *EP*, p300

7. Today it is the Piazza Stesicoro.

8. Presumably Angelica, the daughter of Giuffrida and cousin of Giovanni, who wrote of his meeting with Bellini in Naples. Autograph held in the Biblioteca Nazionale di Firenze. Published in *EP*, p307.

9. The programme included several duets from *La Straniera*, *Bianca e Gernando* and duets and finales from *I Capuleti e i Montecchi* and *Il pirata*. The cantata was by Luigi Somma. Also included were piano concerti by Moscheles and Hummel.

10. In *L'Olivuzza* (Palermo, 1846). (See also note 20, chapter 1.)

11. The painting is in the Public Library, Palermo, and the bust is in the Conservatorio di Musica di Palermo.

12. Autograph held in Biblioteca Comunale di Palermo. Published by Francesco Guardiere in *Omaggio a Bellini* (Catania, 1901), p132.

13. Autograph held in the Paris Conservatoire. Published by Della Corte e Pannain in *Vincenzo Bellini* (Paravia, 1935), p59. Also in *EP*, p312.

14. Amore confirms this in *Belliniana*.

15. Autograph now lost. First published in *BML*, p398. Also in *EP*, p314.

16. Autograph held in the Biblioteca Comunale di Palermo. First published by Francesco Guardione in *Omaggio a Bellini* (Catania, 1901), p133. Also in *EP*, p316.

17. Autograph now lost. First published in *BML*, p400. Also in *EP*, p319.

CHAPTER 12

1. Autograph held in Biblioteca Comunale di Palermo. Published by F Polazzolo-Drago in *Archivio Storico Siciliano*, number one, XVIII.

2. Published by M Ferranti Giulini in *Giuditta Pasta e i suoi tempi* (Milan, 1935), p151. Also in *EP*, p326.

3. Romani wrote *Cristina di Svezia* in 1853 as his last libretto for the pianist/composer Sigismond Thalberg (Kärntnertortheater, Vienna, 1855).

4. Autograph held in Museo Teatrale alla Scala, Milan. Published in part in *SMN*, p404. Also in *EP* in full, p332.

5. No autograph survives. Published in *SMN*, p405. Also in *EP*, p335.

6. Autograph in CN (in the collection "Lettere al Florimo: Signore"). Published in *BSS*, p676.

7. Branca: *Felice Romani ed i più riputati maestri di musica del suo tempo* (Turin, 1882).

8. Pietro Generali's *Benjowski* and Pacini's *Ivanhoe* were first performed at La Fenice on 17 March 1831 and on 19 March 1832, respectively.

9. Autograph held in Biblioteca Comunale di Palermo. First published by A Amore in *Corriere di Catania* (9 June 1882). Also in *EP*, p345.

10. Autograph in Biblioteca Comunale di Palermo. Published in *SMN*, p411. Also in *EP*, p345.

CHAPTER 13

1. Autograph held in CN. First published in *SMN*, p380. Also in *EP*, p173.

2. Autograph has not survived. Published by A Amore in *Vincenzo Bellini: Vita* (Catania, 1894), p319. Also in *EP*, p334.

3. Autograph has not survived. First published by Cicconetti in *Vita di Vincenzo Bellini* (Prato, 1859). Also in *EP*, p362.

4. Autograph has not survived. Published in *SMN* (letter undated and incomplete). Also in *EP*, p363.

5. Autograph in Federico Patetta collection, Turin. First published by Alessandro Luzio in *Atti della Reale Accademia delle Scienze di Torino* (1932), volume LXVII. Also in *EP*, p368.

6. Autograph has not survived. Published by G Vallanti in Palermo, who copied it from the autograph then in Biblioteca Comunale di Palermo (letter dated 26 June 1833). Also in *EP*, p371.

7. *Thirty Years' Musical Recollections* (London, 1830-60).

8. *Musical Reminiscences* (London, 1834).

9. Maria Felicia Malibran was born in Paris on 24 March 1808 of Spanish parents. Her first years, however, were spent in Spain and Italy, where her parents sang. A vivacious and intelligent child, she made her stage debut in Naples when only five years old, in Päer's *Agnese* – she merely had to hand over a letter. But at one performance, when the prima donna was suddenly taken ill, Maria promptly sang the duet herself with the tenor, who was her father, Manuel Garcia.

At the age of seven, she received her first formal lessons in music, studying theory with Auguste Panseron and the piano with Ferdinand Hérold. She was about 15 when her father began to train her voice. In 1824, she sang in a private performance of a Rossini cantata at a musical club which Garcia had formed in Paris. Her operatic debut took place on 11 June 1825 as Rosina (*Il barbiere di Siviglia*) to her father's Almaviva at the King's Theatre, London. She followed this with Felicia in *Il crociato in Egitto*, and at the end of the season, after making a few appearances in the provinces, she left for New York with her father and his company, which included his entire family. During a nine-month season in America, her repertoire included Rosina, Desdemona (*Otello*), Elena (*La donna del lago*), the title roles in *La Cenerentola*, *Semiramide* and *Tancredi*, Donna Fiorilla (*Il Turco in Italia*), Zerlina (*Don Giovanni*), Giulietta (Zingarelli's *Giulietta e Romeo*) and the leading soprano role in *L'amante astato*, which was composed by Garcia for his daughter.

While in New York, Maria, dazzled by a supposed fortune and almost certainly subconsciously wanting to get away from her father's brutality, married a middle-aged

Franco-spanish banker named François Eugène Malibran (she was 18, he 45), who was soon afterwards rendered bankrupt and may have been briefly imprisoned for debt. In an effort to help pay her husband's debts, Maria went back to the stage (she sang ballad operas, including Braham's *The Devil's bridge* and Arne's *Love in a village* at the Bowery Theater, New York, and in concerts), but in November 1827 she returned to Paris alone, singing in several private concerts, and appearing in the title role in *Semiramide* at the Paris Opéra. Despite success there, no other engagement followed at the Opéra, but she was then engaged at the Théâtre-Italien, where her appearances as Semiramide, Rosina, Cenerentola and Giulietta established her as a star. At the end of the season there, she created the title role in Halévy's *Clari*. Later, she also created the title roles in Donizetti's *Maria Stuarda* (La Scala, 1835) and Balfe's *The maid of Artois* (Drury Lane, London, 1836).

During the next four years, Malibran alternated appearances mainly between Paris and London, adding new roles to her repertoire, namely Ninetta (*La gazza ladra*), Romeo (*Giulietta e Romeo*) and the title role in *Otello*.

At a concert in Brussels in 1829, Malibran met the Belgian violinist Charles de Bériot, who was also one of the participating artists. After her first marriage was annulled in 1835, she married Bériot in March 1836. She died six months later, on 23 September.

10. Malibran's father, Manuel del Popolo Garcia (1775-1832), a uniquely versatile musician, was the composer of 71 Spanish, 19 Italian and seven French light operas, as well as a singer, actor and conductor. His fame, however, has survived as an outstanding Rossinian tenor. He created Almaviva in *Il barbiere di Siviglia*, a role written expressly for him.

    Malibran's brother, Manuel (1805-1906), a good singer, was the most celebrated singing teacher of the 19th century. Amongst his pupils were Jenny Lind and Sir Charles Santley. Malibran's sister, Pauline Viardot-Garcia (1821-1910), younger than her by 14 years, became one of the greatest (and certainly one of the most intelligent) singers of her time.

11. *Thirty Years' Musical Recollections* (London, 1830-60).

12. This letter has been published by Florimo in *BML* (p137), *SMN* (p256) and *CSMN* (p824). It is undated and fragmented and no autograph survives. The doubt that has been expressed about this letter concerns not so much its authenticity as the accuracy of Florimo's presentation. Also in *EP*, p364.

    The fact that Bellini did not mention this episode to Lamperi and Santocanale when he subsequently wrote to them has, in the author's opinion, been wrongly used to cast doubt on the accuracy of the letter.

13. This deletion appears in all three of Florimo's publications of this letter.

14. Published by M Ferranti Giulini in *Giuditta Pasta e i suoi tempi* (Milan, 1935), p158.

15. *Lady Morgan's Memoirs: Autobiography, Diaries and Correspondence* (London, 1863).

16. Vincenzo Gabussi (1800-46) of Bologna was a composer who lived in London. He knew Rossini well.

17. Lady Geale wrote to Florimo on the occasion when he and Michele Scherillo were preparing the *Album-Bellini*, which was published in 1886, at the time of the unveiling of a monument to Bellini in Naples.

18. *Leaves From the Diary of Henry Greville*, edited by the Viscountess Enfield (London, 1883).

19. Autograph held in the Federico Patetta collection, Turin. First published by Alessandro

Luzio in *Atti della Reale Accademia delle Scienze di Torino* (1932), vol LXVII. Also in *EP*, p367.

20. Published by M Ferranti Giulini in *Giuditta Pasta e i suoi tempi* (Milan, 1935), p166.

21. A friend of Bellini. She almost certainly met him through Lamperi.

22. In *SMN*, volume two, p826.

23. As in note 12 above.

24. Autograph held in Biblioteca Comunale di Palermo. Published by G Vallanti (Palermo). Also in *EP*, p371.

25. Published by M Ferranti Giulini in *Giuditta Pasta e i suoi tempi* (Milan, 1935), p159.

CHAPTER 14

1. Autograph in CN. First published in English translation by Frank Walker in an article entitled "Giuditta Turina and Bellini" in *Music and Letters* (London, January 1959). Also in *BSS*, p675.

2. Autograph in CN. First published in *BML*, p408. Also in *EP*, p389.

3. Autograph in CN. Published in *BSS*, p678.

4. Autograph in CN. First published by Frank Walker (see note 1 above).

5. Autograph in CN. Published in *EP*, p418.

6. Autograph in CN. Published in *EP*, p420.

7. Autograph in CN. Published in *EP*, p460.

8. Clelia, Pasta's only child, was at this time 16 years old. Later, according to Bellini (in a letter to Florimo dated 13 August 1835, published in *EP*, p582), rumour had it that Clelia was to marry her first cousin. Bellini called the young man in question a "stupid beast".

9. Autograph in CN. Published in *EP*, p483.

10. Autograph in CN. First published in *BML*, p462. The letter is undated, but internal evidence places it very soon after 18 February 1835. Also published in *EP*, p522.

11. Autograph in CN. Published by Barbiera in *Grandi e piccole memorie* (Florence, 1910), p484. Also in *BSS*, p470. Contessa Virginia Martini Giorgio della Torre (1778-1836) was Giuditta Turina's closest female friend.

12. Pastura, *Le lettere di Bellini*, p309. Autograph in CN.

13. Autograph in CN. First published by A Amore in *Vincenzo Bellini: Vita* (Catania, 1894), p377. Also in *EP*, p580.

14. Autograph in CN. First published by Frank Walker (see note 1 above). Also in *BSS*, p701.

15. Autograph in CN. First published by Frank Walker (see note 1 above). Also in *BSS*, p705.

16. Barbiera published this in his *Il salotto della contessa Maffei* (Milan, 1895).

CHAPTER 15

1. Luigi Cherubini was perhaps the most important composer of this period. A father figure of French Grand Opera and, to a lesser general extent, Romantic Opera, Cherubini's *Les deux journées* (1800) influenced, to a degree, the style of Beethoven, in particular *Fidelio* (1805).

2. Giovanni Battista Pergolesi, in *La serva padrona* (1733), was the first composer to establish (though not to invent) the principles and traditions on which *opera buffa* was to be modelled for over 100 years. Whereas Pergolesi found most complete expression in *opera buffa* and the intermezzi, he was also accomplished in *opera seria*, for which his melodies were distinguished with considerable sensitivity to the libretto. His best *opere serie* were *Salustria* (1732) and *L'Olimpiade* (1735).

3. Cimarosa's *opera buffa Il matrimonio segreto* (1792) is his most important work.

4. Paisiello's greatest works are *Nina, ossia La pazza per amore* (1789), an opera *semi-seria*, and *Il barbiere di Siviglia* (1792), an *opera buffa*.

5. Modern research is, however, revealing interest and charm in their music, which may well be worth reviving.

6. Mayr provided the most notable operas in Italy during the first decade of the 19th century, although his fame as an opera composer was to last for only a few years. *Lodoiska* (1800), *La rosa rossa e la rosa bianca* (1813) and *Medea in Corinto* (1813) are his most accomplished operas. Today, Mayr is famous more as the teacher of Donizetti than as a composer in his own right.

7. Päer's main works include *Camilla* (1779), *Sargine* (1803) and *Agnese di Fitz-Henry* (1819). He, like Mayr, was also eclipsed by the young Rossini.

8. After *Guillaume Tell*, the works Rossini composed during his 40-year period of retirement (which were mainly religious) added little to the reputation that he had won in his early career. He died in Paris on 13 November 1868.

9. *The Operas of Verdi*, volume I (London, 1973).

10. When Bellini died, at the age of almost 34, he had written eleven operas (including *Adelson e Salvini* and two versions of *Bianca*). At the same age, Rossini had written 34 and Donizetti 35.

11. *Belliniana: Nuove Note* (Milan, 1885).

12. Also, a copy of Mozart's *Davidde penitente* in Bellini's hand is in the library of Stanford University.

13. The authenticity of this letter is doubtful, for various reasons. No autograph has ever been produced. It is incomplete, undated and is claimed to have been addressed to Agostino Gallo (indeed the only extant letter addressed to Gallo), whom, as far as we know, Bellini met for the first time in Palermo in 1832. In 1843, Gallo published this letter, assigning it to 1828, in the pamphlet "Sull' Estetica di Vincenzo Bellini, notizie comunicate da lui stesso sl Gallo".

    Furthermore, the style of the letter is completely different from anything else of Bellini's that is extant, and Bellini was not the kind of person who normally liked to speak about his own method of working. Nevertheless, in the final analysis, all opposing arguments can be invalid.

14. F Lippmann: *Analecta Musicologica VI: Vincenzo Bellini und die italienische Opera Seria seiner zeit* (Cologne, 1969) and *The New Grove Dictionary of Music & Musicians* (London, 1980).

15. Letter to Count Pepoli dated sometime between May and October 1834. Published in *EP*, p400.

16. In *BML*, p424. Also in *EP*, p422.

17. I had the opportunity to discuss the meaning and aim of the term *bel canto* with Maria Callas, the singer and teacher Elvira de Hidalgo, the conductor Tullio Serafin and the critic Eugenio Gara.

18. For more detailed discussion of overtures and preludes, see individual operas.

19. F Lippmann: *The New Grove Dictionary of Music & Musicians* (London, 1980).

20. In *Aureliano in Palmira* (1814), Rossini wrote a role for Velluti, the greatest castrato of his time, who showed no respect whatever for Rossini's music and who elaborated and affectedly adorned the music to an inordinate extent. Although Velluti impressed the public greatly with his exhibitionistic displays, the opera itself failed. However, it was not really Rossini's music that the public had heard, so much was it changed. Rossini never again wrote for castrati.

21. *Pezzi di baule* ("suitcase pieces") were arias with scope for vocal exhibition. They were carried and often used by singers (when the composer was absent) in stock operatic situations.

22. A perfect example of embellished melody is Rossini's "Bel raggio lusinghier" in *Semiramide*.

23. Published in *Omnibus di Napoli* and in A Amore's *Vincenzo Bellini: Arte* (Catania, 1892).

24. Autograph in MB. Published in *SMN*, volume IV.

25. It was composed in 1834 and published in 1835 by Fontana, who gave it the rather superfluous title of *Fantaisie*.

26. On 24 September 1828, Chopin visited Berlin, where he heard Spontini's *Riccardo Cortez* and other operas. He also frequented Schlezinger's Music Shop, where the latest publications were available. *Il pirata* was performed in Vienna on 25 February 1828 and was then published. *La Straniera* was performed in Dresden during Chopin's visit there, between 11 and 19 November 1830.

   Chopin arrived in Paris in mid September, 1830. *La sonnambula* and *I Capuleti e i Montecchi* were performed at the Italien in October 1831 and January 1833 respectively.

27. Liszt wrote the introduction, the connecting links and the finale. Chopin wrote a *larghetto* in E major.

28. In 1854, Liszt, too, believed the erroneous rumour that Bellini had been consumptive. As the autopsy and documentary evidence has shown, the rumour was without foundation.

29. The opera was *I Capuleti e i Montecchi* at Leipzig with Wilhelmine Schröder-Devrient as Romeo.

30. Wagner also composed an aria with chorus for Oroveso to insert in *Norma*. Later, in 1840, in Paris, Wagner, in an effort to win over the great bass Lablache, composed another aria (or adapted the first) for him in the part of Oroveso as a virtuosic alternative but a skilful imitation of Bellini's style for "Ah! del Tebro". Lablache did not sing it. Eventually, the aria was published in 1914 in volume XV of Wagner's collected works *Einlage zu Vincenzo Bellinis Oper* Norma, *von Richard Wagner/Arie (mit Männerchor)*, as "'Norma il predesse

o Druidi...' des Orovisto". As far as is known, this aria was first sung in 1971 in Sarah Caldwell's production of *Norma* in Boston.

31. In *SMN*, volume III.

32. In *I copialettere di Giuseppe Verdi* (Milan, 1913) by A Luzio and G Cerari.

Chapter 16

1. Autograph in MB. First published by A Amore in *Strenna del Corriere di Catania* (1882). Also in *EP*, p536.

2. This description appeared in Heine's *Sämtlichewerke, Vol I (Prosadichtungen. Florentinische Nachte: "Erste Nacht")* (Insel Verlag, Leipzig) several years after Bellini's death. Also in Heine's *Reisebilder*.

3. Ferdinand Hiller (1811-85) wrote about Bellini in *Deutsche Rundschau* (Berlin, April-June 1878). He gave the first performance of Beethoven's piano concerto in E-flat major in Paris and was a close friend of Felix Mendelssohn.

4. Dessauer (1798-1876) was born in Bohemia. He also wrote operas, his best known being *Ein Besuch in Saint-Cyr* (Dresden, 1838).

5. Signora Lina Freppa, born in Naples of French parents, later settled in Paris (in the suburb of St Germain) with her mother. There, she gave singing lessons, mainly to members of the aristocracy. She is the dedicatee of Chopin's four mazurkas (B-flat major, E minor, A-flat major and A minor), Opus 17.

6. Published in *Souvenirs* (Paris, 1881).

7. In the Charavay collection, Paris. The note is in French.

8. On 15 October 1849, Countess Delphine Potocka visited Chopin on his deathbed. He is reputed to have said, "Bury me by the side of my dear Bellini." (Chopin died on 17 October.) This is without documentary evidence and may have been one of the many stories told, years afterwards, by Chopin's friends and acquaintances. Whatever the case, it goes some way to show that a close friendship between Chopin and Bellini existed.

9. See page 340-41.

10. Autograph in MB (see note 1 above). Also in *EP*, p536.

11. This refers to Olympe Pélissier. (See note 43 below.)

12. Published in facsimile in *Omaggio a Bellini* (1901), p270.

13. Autograph in Federico Patetta collection, Turin. First published by A Luzio in *Atti della Reale Accademia delle Scienze di Torino* (January 1932), vol LXVII. Also in *EP*, p382.

14. Autograph in CN. First published in *BML*, p408. Also in *EP*, p536.

15. In 1835, Pepoli (1796-1881) went to London, where he became professor of Italian literature at the University of London. In 1863, he married the eminent Italian contralto Marietta Alboni (1823-94).

16. Autograph supposedly in CN but cannot be traced. First published by A Amore in *Vincenzo Bellini: Arte* (Catania, 1892), p203. Also in *EP*, p393.

17. Autograph in Auteri family collection, Catania. Published in *BML*, p411.

18. Published by Florimo in *BML*, p413. Also in *EP*, p401.

19. Published in Branca's *Felice Romani ed i più riputati maestri di musica del suo tempo* (Turin, 1882), p181.

20. Published by A Amore in *Vincenzo Bellini: Arte* (Catania, 1892). Also in *EP*, p413. It is undated but almost certainly written in July 1834.

21. A Venetian friend (probably Greek) of Bellini.

22. Published by Florimo in *BML*, p424. Also in *EP*, p422.

23. Autograph supposedly in CN but cannot be traced. Published in *BML*, p504. Also in *EP*, p447. It is undated but almost certainly written on 7 October 1834, as on that day Bellini also wrote to Lamperi and mentions that he had written to Romani.

24. Romani became editor of the official *Piedmontese Gazzetta* and also continued to write libretti. In 1849, he gave up this post and wrote libretti only sporadically afterwards. In the latter part of his life, he became blind and was pensioned by the government. He spent his last years with his family at Moneglia, where he died on 28 January 1865.

25. Autograph in CN. Published in *EP*, p391.

26. This name has also at times been spelled as Lewis or Levy, but in a letter addressed to Bellini's father, after Bellini's death, the person in question spelled his name as Levys. His house at Puteaux, Rampe de Neuilly, 19 bis, has long been demolished. In its place stands a modern block of flats bearing a large marble plaque commemorating Bellini's stay and death there.

27. Published in *BML*, p413. Also in *EP*, p401.

28. Published in *Corrispondenze Epistolari del conte Carlo Pepoli* (Bologna, 1881). H Weinstock wrote in *Bellini* that, in 1966, he saw a copy of the autograph, which was then owned by Paul C Richards of Brookline, Massachusetts. Also in *EP*, p399.

29. Autograph owned by Maestro Natale Gallini. Two pages from this scenario are reproduced in T D'Amico's *Come si ascolta l'opera* (Milan). Also cited in *BSS*, p418.

30. Autograph in CN. First published in *BML*, p418. Also in *EP*, p416.

31. Published in *BML*, p413. Also in *EP*, p404.

32. Autograph in Biblioteca dell' Università di Palermo. First published in *Rivista Europea* (March, 1874). Also in *EP*, p434.

33. Autograph in CN. First published in *BML*, p431. Also in *EP*, p429.

34. Published in *BML*, p465. Also in *EP*, p479.

35. These affairs referred to Isabella Colbran's (Rossini's wife) estate in Sicily. Isabella was living in Bologna during this period.

36. Autograph in CN. Published in *BML*, p436. Also in *EP*, p437.

37. Giulia Grisi was born in Milan on 28 July 1811. Her father was an Italian officer in the service of Napoleon. She was brought up in a very musical environment – one of her mother's sisters was the once-celebrated contralto Josephina Grassini (1773-1850); her older sister, Giuditta, was an excellent singer, for whom Bellini had written the part of Romeo; and her cousin Carlotta Grisi was one of the most famous ballet dancers of her time. Her musical education began when she was a child, first with piano and then with singing lessons from her sister. Before long, however, Giulia entered the Milan Conservatorio, where she studied singing with the composer Marliani, and from 1825-8

also with her aunt in Bologna and Giacomo Guglielmi, the son of the composer.

Her stage debut in 1828 was in the small role of Emma in Rossini's *Zelmyra* in Bologna. She made such a good impression that in the following season she sang Rosina (*Il barbiere di Siviglia*) and Dorliska (*Torvaldo e Dorliska*). Her success led to other engagements in Pisa and Florence, where the impresario Lanari deceived her into signing a six-year contract on extremely low terms.

During this early period, under Lanari's management, she sang Giulietta to her sister Giuditta's Romeo in *I Capuleti e i Montecchi* and Giulietta in Vaccai's *Giulietta e Romeo*. As her fame spread rapidly, Lanari's profits exceeded his expectations, especially as in 1830 he sub-contracted her at a high commission to Crivelli, the director of La Scala. Grisi's appearance in Coccia's new opera *Enrico di Montfort* in 1831 at La Scala led to her creating the role of Adalgisa. After the advent of *Norma*, she appeared in several other leading roles, such as Semiramide, Elena (*La donna del lago*), Desdemona (*Otello*), Giovanna Seymour (*Anna Bolena*) and Donna Anna (*Don Giovanni*). Her successful reception in these roles made her realise her true worth, and when Lanari refused to revise her contract in 1832 she ran away to Paris, where she was engaged at the Théâtre-Italien.

In the spring of 1834, she made her debut in London as Ninetta (*La gazza ladra*), impressing Chorley and winning the English public; in 1835, she created Elvira (*I Puritani*) and in 1843 Norina (*Don Pasquale*), both operas first performed at the Italien. Grisi had many triumphs in her career in a variety of roles.

Her repertoire also included the title roles in *Norma* and *Lucrezia Borgia*, the Queen (*Les Huguenots*) and others. By 1844, she formed a liaison with the famous tenor Mario. Henceforth, they sang together everywhere, visiting St Petersburg in 1851 and going on an extensive tour of the United States in 1854.

Even though her vocal powers deteriorated alarmingly after her American tour, Grisi continued to sing in Europe, occasionally with disastrous results. In 1861, in an effort to stop Grisi from making a fool of herself, Gye, the impresario of the King's Theatre, London, signed a contract with her not to sing on the stage for five years. Grisi honoured her contractual obligations, but when the five years had expired she again appeared in *Lucrezia Borgia* in 1866. It was her biggest failure and the last one she made. She died from inflammation of the lungs during a visit to Berlin on 29 November 1869.

38. *Thirty Years' Musical Recollections* (London, 1830-60).

39. In his *Memoirs* (translated from the Russian by Richard B Mudge, 1963), Mikhail Glinka, who was present at a performance of *Norma* (with Pasta, Donzelli and Grisi) during its initial season at La Scala in 1832, had harsh words for Grisi: "Just beginning her career, she wasn't as fat as she was later in Paris and consequently she looked remarkably well, but she sang in a sort of caterwauling manner – that is, wishing to soften or modify a given musical phrase, she more or less miaowed in her nose."

40. Pasta continued to sing in Italy, Paris and London as long as she was able to compensate for her vocal decline (particularly in respect of intonation) by utilising dramatic revelation. She retired in 1838 but made a comeback in 1840, singing in Berlin and St Petersburg. These were splendid dramatic performances, even if her voice was almost gone.

After 1841, Pasta retired from the stage, spending her winters in Milan, where she taught singing. Nine years later, she sang at a concert (excerpts from *Anna Bolena*) in London given for the benefit of the Italian cause. It proved to be altogether a painfully disastrous occasion. The comments of other artists present, some of whom were in fact hearing her for the first time, could not have been a more memorable requiem for one of the greatest singers that the world has ever known.

The famous actress Rachel enjoyed the humiliation of decayed grandeur and sarcastically commented that Pasta's reputation had obviously been exaggerated. The great singer Pauline Viardot-Garcia (Malibran's younger sister) responded differently. "You're right!" she exclaimed to a friend by her side, while her eyes streamed with tears, "You're right! Her voice is like Leonardo da Vinci's 'Last Supper' in Milan – a wreck of a picture, but the picture is the greatest in the world!" Pasta never again sang in public. She died in 1865.

41. Autograph in CN. Published in *BML*, p507.

42. Bellini related this episode to Florimo in a letter dated 4 October 1834. Autograph in CN. First published in *BML*, p422. Also in *EP*, p442.

43. Olympe Pélissier had been Rossini's mistress since about October 1832, five years before he became legally separated from his wife, Isabella Colbran, in September 1837. Rossini married Olympe in August 1846, ten months after Isabella had died.

44. Published in *BML*, p451. Also in *EP*, p463.

45. Autograph in CN. First published in *BML*, p459. Also in *EP*, p474.

46. Published in *Omnibus di Napoli*. Also by Florimo in *BML* and by A Amore in *Vincenzo Bellini: Arte* (Catania, 1892).

47. Autograph in CN. First published in *BML*, p418. Also in *EP*, p414.

48. Autograph in CN. First published in *BML*, p436. Also in *EP*, p435.

49. Refers to Jacques François Halévy (1799-1862), the composer of *La Juive* (Paris Opéra, 1835).

50. Autograph in CN. First published in *BML*, p463. Also in *EP*, p476.

51. Had Bellini composed this opera, Verdi might not have written *Un ballo in maschera* in 1859, which is based on the same subject.

52. No music that Bellini may have composed for this opera has survived. *Un duel sous le cardinal de Richelieu*, a drama in three acts by Lockroi and Edmond Badon, was successfully produced at the Théâtre National du Vaudeville, Paris, on 9 April 1832. Operas based on this drama were written by Federico Ricci (*Un duello sotto Richelieu*, La Scala, 1839), Giuseppe Lillo (*Il conte di Chalais*, San Carlo, 1839) and by Donizetti (*Maria di Rohan*, Vienna, 1843).

53. Autograph in CN. First Published in *BML*, p466. Also in *EP*, p480.

54. Autograph in CN. Published in *BSS*, p447.

55. Published in *Omnibus di Napoli* (see note 46 above).

56. Autograph in CN. The letter is undated but the postmark is 26 January. First published in *BML*, p488. Also in *EP*, p501.

57. The Puritans detested the organ, and it was therefore out of place in the opera, a fact of which neither Bellini nor Rossini seem to have been aware.

58. Autograph in CN. First published in *BML*, p498. Also in *EP*, p529.

59. The libretti of Donizetti's *Roberto Devereux* and *Maria Padilla* were also drawn from plays by Ançelot.

CHAPTER 17

1. Autograph in CN. First published in *BML*, p496. Also in *EP*, p519.

2. Autograph in Brussels Conservatoire. First published in French translation in *Le Soir Illustré* (Brussels). In original Italian in *EP*, p526.

3. In fact, arrangements were made for Malibran to sing in the first performance of *I Puritani*, at La Scala on 26 December 1835. She fell ill, however, and was unable to appear. Her place was taken by Sofia dell'Oca-Schoberlechner, while Antonio Poggi was the tenor. Although Malibran recovered sufficiently to sing in Donizetti's *Maria Stuarda* on 30 December (she was described as "voiceless" on the first night), she did not sing in any performances of *I Puritani*. In fact, she never sang in this opera, as she had died by the following September.

4. Autograph owned by Bellini's descendants in Catania. First published by A Amore in *Strenna del Corriere di Catania* (1882). Also in *EP*, p538.

5. Published by Zavatini in *Donizetti: Vita – Musiche – Epistolario* (Bergamo, 1948), p158.

6. Autograph in MB. First published by A Amore in *Vincenzo Bellini: Vita* (Catania, 1894), p364. Also in *EP*, p557.

7. The triumph refers to *Lucia di Lammermoor*, first produced on 26 September 1835 at the San Carlo, Naples.

8. Autograph in CN. First published in *BML*, p501. Also in *EP*, p552.

9. Autograph in Biblioteca Comunale di Palermo. Published by Francesco Guardione in *Omaggio a Bellini* (Catania, 1901), p135.

10. One of these motifs has survived and is now at the MB.

11. In *BML*, p108.

12. Autograph in CN. First published in BML in two parts, p503 and p107. Also in EP, p561.

13. According to Francesco Giugni in *L'Immatura fine di Vincenzo Bellini alla luce di nuove circonstanze* (Lugo, 1938) and *La Malattia e la Morte di Vincenzo Bellini* (Faenza, 1931), Montallegri, born in Faenza, had served as a doctor with the Napoleonic Army in Italy. A liberal patriot, he was imprisoned in Venice and then exiled to France. He was a close friend of Pepoli.

14. The quotations from d'Aquino's diaries comprised part of a letter from d'Aquino to Florimo, which is in MB. Florimo published it in *BML*, p61. Also in *EP*, p593.

15. Autograph of Montallegri's notes in MB. Published by Pastura in *Vincenzo Bellini*, p427.

16. Copy of the original French document in MB. First published by A Amore in *Vincenzo Bellini: Vita* (Catania, 1894), p204. Also in *EP*, p598.

17. At my request, the distinguished British doctor Sir Ronald Bodley Scott most generously examined Professor Dalmas's autopsy on Bellini. His verdict was that, beyond any doubt, Bellini had died from acute amoebic dysentery. Had Bellini lived today, he could have had some chance of being cured. It is only in relatively recent years, however, that medical science has been able to provide such treatment.

It was also the authoritative opinion of Dr Victor de Sabata (Milan, 1969), after studying Professor Dalmas's autopsy, that Bellini quite obviously died from chronic amoebiasis.

Manson's Tropical Diseases: A Manual of the Diseases of Warm Climates, by Sir Philip H

Manson-Bahr (London, 1966, 16th edition), says, "Definition: *Amoebiasis* denotes infection with the protozoan *Entamoeba histolytica*. When confined to the intestinal canal, it produces amoebic dysentery, or primary intestinal amoebiasis. Insidious in its onset, chronic in its course. Metastatic lesions may be produced in the liver and elsewhere."

It is therefore surprising that Bellini's death is still considered by some as mysterious – that he was tuberculous and, above all, that he was poisoned – when conclusive evidence exists to the contrary. And yet, in 2000 (the bicentenary of Bellini's birth was in 2001), some of his compatriots decided to have his DNA examined to determine if he had in fact been poisoned – a rather futile exercise.

18. Autograph in MB. First published (in mutilated text) by A Amore in *Vincenzo Bellini: Vita* (Catania, 1894), p233. Also in *EP*, p601.

19. Bellini's grave in Père Lachaise Cemetery is between those of Grétry and Boieldieu. A monument by Carlo Marochetti was erected.

20. Autograph in Biblioteca Comunale di Palermo. First published by Mazzantini-Manis in *Lettere di G Rossini* (Florence, 1902), p62.

21. Published by Giuseppe Radiciotti in *Gioacchino Rossini* (1928, volume II), p181.

22. Copy of autograph in MB. Published in *BSS*, p539.

23. Autograph in MB. Published in *BSS*, p539.

24. Published in *EP*, p603.

25. Although Romani lived for another 30 years after Bellini's death and had in the meantime seen publications about Bellini, he unfortunately never published any of the material mentioned.

26. Little did she know how true her words were. One year later, on 23 September 1836, Malibran died at the age of 28 following an accident when she was thrown off her horse in Hyde Park, London. Rejecting medical attention, she later went to sing in Manchester, where, after much suffering, she died almost certainly from a cerebral haemorrhage. Until recently, Malibran's date of death was given as 24 September, the day of her funeral, whereas documentary evidence in Manchester shows that she was, in fact, pronounced dead by Dr Belluomini at 11.40pm on 23 September – to the day, exactly a year after Bellini's death.

27. In *CSMN*, volume two, p826.

28. The principal public park and garden in Catania now bears Bellini's name, and the house in which he was born has become the Museo Belliniano. On 31 May 1890, the long-awaited theatre in Catania was at last completed (work was officially begun in 1860) and was named Teatro Massimo Bellini. It was inaugurated with a performance of *Norma*, with Virginia Damerini in the title role, Olympia Boronat as Adalgisa, Francesco Gianni as Pollione and Giuseppe Rossi as Oroveso. (There had been a previous, inadequate Teatro Bellini, built in 1864, which burned down in 1869.)

Appendices

The following abbreviations are employed to denote the sources most frequently cited:

MB   Museo Belliniano, Catania;

CN   Conservatorio San Pietro a Miella, Naples;

CGV   Conservatorio Giuseppe Verdi, Milan.

i
List of Works

CHURCH MUSIC

Gallus cantavit – MS copy (or autograph) in Biblioteca Riunite Civica e Antonio Ursino Recupero, Catania — 1807

Tantum ergo – lost — 1808

Compieta with *Salve* – lost (Giuseppe Coco Zanghy mentions this in *Memorie e Lagrime*) — 1808-13

Tre Salve regina – lost — 1808-14

Mass – lost — 1810

Mass – lost — 1814

Versetti da cantarsi il Venerdi Santo: eight verses for two tenors and organ – autograph in collection of Signora Marusia Manzella, Rome — 1815

Gratias agimus for four voices with orchestra – lost — 1817-18

Gratias agimus in C major for soprano with orchestra – autograph in CN; published by Boccaccini e Spada, Rome — 1817-18

Litanie pastorale in onore della Beata Vergine for two sopranos with organ – autograph fragments in MB — 1817-18

Pange lingual (for the procession on Monday) for two voices with organ – autograph in MB — 1817-18

Tantum ergo with *Genitori* in B-flat major for soprano with orchestra – autograph in CN — 1817?

Tantum ergo with *Genitori* in E-flat major for soprano with orchestra – autograph in CN; published by Ricordi (Milan, 1901, "Revisione di FP Frontini") — 1815-19

Tantum ergo with *Genitori* in F major for two sopranos, four voices for Genitori, with orchestra – autograph in CN? — 1817?

Tantum ergo with *Genitori* in G major for four-voice chorus with orchestra – autograph in CN — 1815-19?

Tantum ergo in F for soprano – autograph in CN; published by Ricordi (Milan, 1901, "Revisione di FP Frontini") — 1810-19?

Mass (*Kyrie* and *Gloria*) in D major for two sopranos, tenor and bass with — 1818 orchestra – autograph in CN

Mass (*Kyrie* and *Gloria*) in G major for two sopranos, tenor and bass with   1818
orchestra – autograph (in fragments) in CN

Tantum ergo in F major for soprano and orchestra – published by Ricordi   1815-19
(Milan, 1901, "Revisione di FP Frontini")

Tantum ergo with *Genitori* in E-flat major for soprano with orchestra –   1815-19
published by Ricordi (Milan, 1901, "Revisione di FP Frontini")

Salve regina in A major for four-voice chorus with orchestra – published by Ricordi   ?
(Milan) in *Composizioni giovanili inedite*

Salve regina in F minor/major for bass with organ – published by Ricordi (Milan,   1818
March 1862)

Magnificat for four-voice mixed chorus with orchestra – autograph fragments in   1818-20
Bibliothèque Nationale, Paris

Tecum principium (see *Dixit Dominus* below)

Mass in A minor for soprano, contralto, tenor and bass with orchestra –   *c*1821
incomplete autograph and complete MS copy in MB; published in full score and
with alternative organ accompaniment by Ricordi (Milan, October, 1843)

Quattro Tantum ergo – autograph in CN, published by Ricordi (Milan, 1862):   1823
1) *Tantum ergo* in G for soprano and orchestra, 2) *Tantum ergo* in E for four-voice
chorus with orchestra, 3) *Tantum ergo* in F for two voices and full orchestra,
4) *Tantum ergo* in D for bass and orchestra

Credo in C major for four-voice chorus and orchestra – lost   1824

Mass in G major for two sopranos, tenor, bass and orchestra – autograph fragment   1824
and incomplete MS copy in MB; vocal and instrumental parts in CN; mass
reconstructed by Pastura; unpublished

Dixit Dominus: psalm for soloists, four-voice chorus and orchestra – autograph in   1824
CN; only *Tecum principium* (part of section three) is in full score in facsimile; published
by Boccaccini e Spada (Rome, 1961) and by Camus-Verlag (Stuttgart, 1981)

Te deum in E-flat major for four-voice chorus and orchestra   1819-26

Te deum in C major for four-voice chorus and orchestra   1824

Cor mundum crea (motetto) for two voices, *Miserere* verse with organ –   before 1825
autograph in the collection of Filippo Cicconetti; published in *Pubblicazione
Periodica di Musica sacra sotto gli auspici della SC di Propaganda Fide*, 11/2
(Rome, 1879); also in *Cronache musicali*, 1 (Rome, 1901)

Cum sanctis – autograph in CN   before 1825

De Torrente – autograph in CN   before 1825

Domine Deus – autograph in CN   before 1825

Juravit – autograph in CN   before 1825

Kyrie – autograph in CN   before 1825

Laudamus te – autograph in CN   before 1825

Qui sedes – autograph in CN   before 1825

Qui tollis – autograph in CN   before 1825

Quoniam with *Cum sanctis* – autograph in CN

Quoniam – autograph in CN. Also 14-page autograph of *Quoniam* for tenor, chorus and orchestra in Bibliothèque Nationale, Paris

Virgam virtutis – autograph in CN

SECULAR MUSIC

INSTRUMENTAL MUSIC

Sinfonia in C minor for large orchestra – published by Ricordi (Milan, April 1941, ?"Revisione di Maffeo Zanon")

Sinfonia in D major (*andante maestoso allegro*) for small orchestra – autograph   1817-18
in CN; published by Ricordi (Milan, April 1941) in *Composizioni giovanili inedite*;[1] by Zanibon (Padua, 1953), edited by Ettore Bonelli; and (1959), edited by Santi di Stefano

Sinfonia in E-flat major (*largo assai, allegro vivace*) for small orchestra –   1821-24
autograph in MB; published by Ricordi (Milan, April 1941) in *Composizioni giovanili inedite*;[1] also published by Boccaccini e Spada (Rome)

Sinfonia in B-flat major (*larghetto espressivo, allegro*); autograph in MB;   1821-24
unpublished

Sinfonia in C minor (*lento, in tempo ordinario, allegro tempo*), for small orchestra   1822?

Sinfonia in D minor (*andante maestoso, allegro con spirito*) for small   1821-24
orchestra – autograph in MB; unpublished

Sinfonia in E-flat major (*larghetto maestoso, allegro moderato*) for small   1821-24
orchestra – published by Ricordi (Milan, 1941, "Revisione di Maffeo Zanon")

Concerto for oboe and string orchestra in E-flat major (*maestoso e deciso,*   *c*1823
larghetto cantabile, allegro "alla polonese") – autograph in CN and in Library of
Congress, Washington, DC; published by Ricordi (Milan, February 1961,
"Revisione e rielaborazione di Terenzio Gargiulo"); also included in *Composizioni
giovanili inedite*[1]

Polacca for four hands and piano   *c*1823

Sonata for four hands and piano – autograph in CN   ?

Sonata for organ in G major – autograph in the Pierpont Morgan Library, New York   ?

Allegretto for piano (eleven-measure albumleaf) – autograph in Biblioteca Nazionale   ?
Florence

Theme for piano in F minor – autograph in Bibliothèque Nationale, Paris   ?

Clarinet, flute, oboe and violin pieces – Florimo wrote in *Memorie e Lettere*   1819-27
that Bellini composed these pieces in Naples

---

[1] *Composizioni Giovanili Inedite* is a facsimile edition of *Salve regina*, *Sinfonia* in D major ("*Revisione di Maffeo Zanon*"), *Tecum principium* (*Dixit Dominus*), concerto for oboe and strings in E-flat major and *Sinfonia* in E-flat major, with an introduction by Francesco Cilea, Reale Accademia d'Italia (Rome, 1941). Published by Ricordi (Milan, April 1941).

VOCAL MUSIC

"La farfalletta", canzonetta for mezzo-soprano and piano – published in 1813
L'Olivuzza (Palermo, 1846); included in *Composizioni da camera*[2]

"Si per te, Gran Nume eterno", cavatina for soprano and orchestra – autograph in 1818
CN; published by Boccaccini e Spada (Rome)

Scena e Aria di Cerere for soprano and orchestra – autograph in CN; 1817-18
published by Boccaccini e Spada (Rome)

"E nello stringerti", *allegro a guisa di cabaletta* for soprano and orchestra – 1817-18
autograph in CN; published by Boccaccini e Spada (Rome)

Ombre pacifiche, trio for soprano and two tenors with orchestra – incomplete 1817-18
autograph in Pierpont Morgan Library, New York, and MS copy in MB; publisher
unknown ("Rielaborazione di FP Frontini")

"So che un sogno è la speranza", aria for soprano – only a sketch of vocal line 1819-26
survives

"Dolente immagine di Fille mia", aria for mezzo-soprano and piano in B-flat 1821
major – autographs in CN and Biblioteca Nazionale, Florence; autograph copy titled
"La tomba di Fille" in Bibliothèque Nationale, Paris; published by Ricordi
(Milan, 1824/ October 1837), by Girard (later Cottrau, Naples, 1825) and by
Pacini (Paris); included in *Composizioni da camera*[2]

"Ismene", cantata for a wedding for three solo voices, chorus and orchestra – 1824
lost, but could be an autograph in MB for soprano, tenor and bass

"Torna vezzosa fillide", romanza for soprano and piano – autograph in CGV 1826
(Noseda collection); published by Ricordi (Milan, February 1933); included in
Composizioni da camera[2]

"Se il mio nome", arietta – included in *Tre ariette* 1820-26

"Fu che al pianger", arietta – published by Girard (Naples) 1820-26?

"La malinconia", arietta for mezzo-soprano and piano – published by Girard 1829
(Naples); included in *Sei ariette per camera*[3] and in *Composizioni
da camera*

"Vanne, o rosa fortunata", arietta for mezzo-soprano and piano – published by 1829?
Girard (Naples); included in *Sei ariette per camera*[3] and in *Composizioni da camera*[2]

"Bella Nice", arietta for mezzo-soprano and piano – published by Girard 1827-33
(Naples); included in *Sei ariette per camera*[3] and in *Composizioni da camera*[2]

"Almen se non poss'io", arietta for mezzo-soprano and piano – published by 1827-33
Girard (Naples); included in *Sei ariette per camera*[3] and in *Composizioni da camera*[2]

"Per pietà, bel idol mio", arietta for mezzo-soprano and piano – published by 1829?
Girard (Naples); included in *Sei ariette per camera*[3] and in *Composizioni da camera*[2]

"Mi rendi pur contendo", arietta for mezzo-soprano and piano – published in 1832?
Sei ariette per camera[3] and in *Composizioni da camera*[2]

"A palpitar d'affani", arietta *c*1827-33

"Numi, se giusti siete", arietta – lost *c*1827-33

439

"La Mammoletta", arietta – lost	*c*1830
"Ah! non pensai", arietta – lost	*c*1827-33
"L'abbandono", romanza for mezzo-soprano and piano – autograph in CN and in Accademia di Santa Cecilia, Rome; published by Ricordi (Milan, February 1831, in French and Italian) and by Girard (Naples)	1835?
"Il fervido desiderio", arietta for mezzo-soprano and piano – autograph in Libreria Gaspare Casella, Naples; published by Ricordi (Milan, October 1837); included in *Composizioni da camera*³ and in *Tre ariette per camera*⁴	1827-33
"Vaga luna che inargenti", arietta for mezzo-soprano with piano – published by Ricordi (Milan, January 1838), by Girard (Naples) and by Schott's Söhne (Mainz); included in *Composizioni da camera*² and in *Tre ariette per camera*⁴	1827-35
"Era Felice un di", arietta for mezzo-soprano and piano – unpublished	1827-33
"L'allegro marinaro", ballata for mezzo-soprano and piano – published by Ricordi (Milan, October 1844); included in *Composizioni da camera*²	1827-33
"Cavatina" for Duchesa Litta's album – lost	1827-35
"Piccola arietta" for Lady Cristina Dudley Stuart – lost	1833
"O Souvenirs", albumleaf – published by Ricordi (Milan, 1901)	?
"Il sogno d'infanzia", romanza – included in *Composizioni da camera*²	1835
"Alla luna (Ode Saffica)" – lost	1834?
Quattro Sonetti (Verses by Pepoli): "Amore" (lost); "La malinconia" (lost); "Ricordanza" (autograph dated 15 April 1834 in the Library of Congress, Washington, DC); "Speranza" (lost)	*c*1834
Canon in B-flat major (for Cherubini's album) for two voices and piano – published by Sonzogno (1883) in *La Musica Popolare*, volume II, number 37	1835
Canon in F major (for Zimmerman's album) for four voices – published in facsimile in Pougin's *Bellini: Sa Vie, ses oeuvres*	1835

---

² *Composizioni da camera per canto e pianoforte* was published by Ricordi (Milan, 1935/1948): 1) "La farfalletta"; 2) "Quando inciso su quel marmo"; 3) "Sogno d'infanzia"; 4) "L'Abbandono"; 5) "L'Allegro marinaro"; 6) "Torna, vezzosa fillide"; 7) "Fervido desiderio"; 8) "Dolente immagine di Fille mia"; 9) "Vaga luna che inargenti"; 10) "Malinconia, ninfa gentile"; 11) "Vanne, o rosa fortunata"; 12) "Bella nice"; 13) "Almen se non poss'io"; 14) "Per pietà, bell' idol mio"; 15) "Mi rendi pur contendo".

³ *Sei ariette per camera* was published by Ricordi (Milan, 1829, dedicated to Marianna Pollini) and by Girard (Naples): 1) "Malinconia, ninfa gentile"; 2) "Vanne, o rosa fortunata"; 3) "Bella Nice"; 4) "Per pietà, bell' idol mio"; 5) "Almen se non poss'io"; 6) "Mi rendi pur contento".

⁴ *Tre ariette per camera* was published by Ricordi (Milan): 1) "Il fervido desiderio"; 2) "Dolente immagine di Fille mia"; 3) "Vaga luna che inargenti".

OPERAS

ADELSON E SALVINI

First version, 1825 – incomplete autograph score in MB. Autograph sketches, autograph pages and MS copies in MB, CN and in the archives of Accademia Filarmonica, Bologna. Some pages of autograph full score in Bibliothèque Nationale, Paris. Unpublished.

Second version, 1827-29? – no complete autograph score survives. MS copy in full score and two in piano-vocal score, and some autograph pages (second-act finale) in CN; MS copy in full score in the British Museum, London. Published in piano-vocal score (without recitatives) by Schonenberger (Paris, 1843/1875); published by Ricordi (Milan, January 1903) in piano-vocal score

BIANCA E GERNANDO (1826)

Incomplete autograph score, autograph in piano-vocal score of the "Gran Scena ed Aria Finale" and incomplete MS copy (dated San Carlo, Naples, 30 May 1826) in CN; MS copy without all recitatives, two copies of piano-vocal transcription by Florimo and some autograph sketches in MB. Published in incomplete piano-vocal score by the Calcografia e Copisteria de' Reali Teatri (later Girard) (Naples, 1826); reprinted in 1828 with some numbers from the revised *Bianca e Fernando*.

IL PIRATA (1827)

Autograph score in CN. MS copy in the archives (with autograph annotations) of La Fenice, Venice, and in CGV. Published in piano-vocal score by Ricordi (Milan, January 1828/December 1903); in full score by Garland Publishing (New York, 1977).

BIANCA E FERNANDO (1828)

No complete autograph score survives. Autograph of Bianca's final aria, "Deh, non ferir", in CN. Published in piano-vocal score by Ricordi (Milan, 20 March 1837/4 July 1903).

LA STRANIERA (1829)

Autograph score owned by Ricordi (Milan); MS copies in CN and in CGV (with autograph interpolations and passages); MS copy (with autograph fragment of four pages from Alaide's "Or sei pago") in Bibliothèque Nationale, Paris. Published in piano-vocal score by Ricordi (Milan, 1829/April 1864/23 June 1902); in full score by Garland Publishing (New York, 1977).

ZAIRA (1829)

Autographed score in CN. Never published, except for *scena* and duetto "Io troverò nell asia" and trio "Cari oggetti in seno a voi", which were published in piano-vocal score by Ricordi (Milan, 1829/1894) and by Girard (later Cottrau) (Naples, 1829).

I CAPULETI E I MONTECCHI (1830)

Autograph score in MB; two MS copies in CN, one in CGV and one in the archives of La Fenice, Venice; MS copy in the Archivio Ricordi, Milan, is with autograph interpolations, mainly in the adaptation of the soprano role of Giulietta to the mezzo-soprano register. There is also an autograph insertion of an *allegro agitato* piece, "Morir dovessi ancora", into Giulietta's aria "Morte io non temo, il sai". Published in piano-vocal score by Ricordi (Milan, 24 February 1831/11 November 1870); by Girard (later Cottrau) (Naples); and by Pacini (Paris). Claudio Abbado's edition, arranging the mezzo-soprano role of Romeo to a tenor, was published by Ricordi (Milan, c1962 – special edition, not for sale). Also published in full score by Garland Publishing (New York, 1977).

LA SONNAMBULA (1831)

Autograph score owned by Ricordi, Milan. Two MS copies in CN, one in CGV and two in Accademia di Santa Cecilia, Rome. Some autograph sketches of the score in MB and some autograph sketches of the libretto in Accademia Musicale Chigiana, Sienna. (Only the autograph score gives the music, particularly Elvino's, in the high key in which Bellini wrote it.) Published in full score by Cottrau-Ricordi (Naples/Milan, 1851); in piano-vocal score by Ricordi (Milan, 15 June 1858/2 December 1869).

NORMA (1831)

Autograph score (chorus "Guerra! Guerra!" non-autograph) and a MS copy in Accademia di Santa Cecilia, Rome. Four MS copies at CN and two in CGV. Published in full score by Ricordi (Milan, 1895/1915); in piano-vocal score by Ricordi (Milan, 1832/1859/1869); by Girard (later Cottrau) (Naples); by Pacini (Paris). A facsimile of the autograph full score was issued by the Reale Accademia d'Italia (Rome, 1935). Also published in full score by Garland Publishing (New York, 1977).

BEATRICE DI TENDA (1833)

Autograph score (with ten pages in non-autograph) and MS copies in Accademia di Santa Cecilia, Rome. MS copy in the archives of La Fenice, Venice, and some autograph and copyist's sketches in MB. Published in full score by Pietro Pittarelli e Co (Rome, c1833); in piano-vocal score by Ricordi (Milan, 1833/1863/1877); by Girard (later Cottrau) (Naples); by both Pacini and Lanner (Paris); in full score by Garland Publishing (New York, 1977).

I PURITANI

Autograph score at Biblioteca Comunale di Palermo. MS copy (with autograph annotations) in the Archivio Ricordi, Milan, and two MS copies in CN. Some pages of MS copy (with autograph annotations) in MB. Published in full score by Cottrau-Ricordi (Milan/Naples, c1895); in piano-vocal score by Ricordi (Milan/Florence, 1836); twice by Pacini (Paris); by Mills (London, 1870), Schott's Söhne (Mainz/Antwerp, 1870), Girard (later Cottrau) (Naples, 1870), Clausetti (Naples, 1870) and Ricordi (Naples, 1870); in full score by Garland Publishing (New York, 1977).

I PURITANI (1835, "Naples" or "Malibran" version)

Autograph of the different numbers from the first version of *I Puritani* in MB.

Autograph fragments of *Ernani*, composed in 1830 but abandoned, are at MB. There is also a scene for Ifigenia, Clitennestra, Achille, Agamennone and Patroclo from *Ifigenia in Aulide*.

ii

Discography

Bellini's music on compact disc. Includes studio commercial and "live" performance recordings as well as transfers from 78rpm and microgroove LPs.

The list cannot be complete; new and old recordings are constantly issued and a number of recording companies (some of which are obscure) have a temporary existence.

Reissues are usually given new catalogue numbers. In order to avoid inevitable confusion, the present discography omits numbers (redundant in tracing a recording) but includes recording companies.

ABBREVIATIONS USED IN THE DISCOGRAPHY

tn – tenor
sop – soprano
m-sop – mezzo-soprano
br – baritone
bs – bass
p – pianist
cond – conductor
rec – recorded
Chor – Chorus
Orch – Orchestra
Op – Opera
Met – Metropolitan
WNO – Welsh National Opera
ROH – Royal Opera House,
   Covent Garden
NY – New York
MMF – Maggio Musicale Fiorentino
SO – Symphony Orchestra
CO – Chamber Orchestra
RO – Radio Orchestra

PO – Philharmonic Orchestra
ECO – English Chamber Orchestra
ECCO – European Community
   Chamber Orchestra
BPO – Berlin Philharmonic
   Orchestra
LPO – London Philharmonic
   Orchestra
LSC – London Symphony Chorus
LSO – London Symphony Orchestra
NPO – National Philharmonic
   Orchestra
Philh – Philharmonia Orchestra
PSO – Philharmonic Symphony
   Orchestra
ROHO – Royal Opera House
   Orchestra
RPO – Royal Philharmonic
   Orchestra
RSO – Radio Symphony Orchestra

ORCHESTRAL MUSIC

Concerto for Oboe and String Orchestra in E-flat major (c1823)

Solo: H Schellenberg, BPO, cond J Levine (rec 1991)	DG – Polygram
Solo: R Lord, Academy of St Martin's in the Fields, cond N Marriner (rec 1964)	DECCA
Solo: H Holliger, Frankfurt RSO, cond E Inbal	PHIL – Philips
Solo: M André, Zurich CO, cond E de Stoutz (rec 1991)	EMI
Solo: B Glaetzner, Leipzig Radio CO, cond W-D Hauschild	LASE – Laserlight
Solo: J van den Haawe, I Fiamminghi, cond R Werthen (rec 1998)	SCHW – Koch Schwann
Solo: R Smedvig, Scottish CO, cond J Ling (rec 1990)	TELD – Telarc
Solo: A Gamden, CLS, cond N Ward (rec 1995)	NAXOS
Solo: S Verzari, cond A Sacchetti (rec 1995)	BONG – Bongiovanni
Solo: S Trubasnik, Radio Luxembourg, cond K Redel	FORL – Forlane
Solo: Peterborough String Orchestra, cond N Daniel	HYPE – Hyperion

Sinfonia in C minor (1822?); Sinfonia in D major (1817-18); Sinfonia in E-flat major (1821-24)

Warmia National Orchestra, cond S Frontalini

Organ Sonata in G major

R Saorgin (rec 1979)	HARM – Harmonia Mundi
F Haselböck	SCHW – Koch Schwann

CHURCH MUSIC

Mass in A minor (c1821)

L Bersiani, V di Cola, S Salvati, JA Campo, C Lapore, Czech Radio Chor, Prague SO, cond E Brizio (rec 1994)	STUD – Studio

Mass in D major (1818); Mass in G minor (1824)

P Cigna, AM Chiuri, A Bastian, R Emili, Orch Teatro del Giglio di Lucca, Choir Capella S Cecilia della Cattedrale di Lucca, cond G Cosmi (rec 2001)	BONG – Bongiovanni

Salve regina in A major(?)

Czech Radio Chor, Prague SO, cond E Brizio (rec 1994)	STUD – Studio

Cappella S Cecilia della Cattedrale di Lucca, cond G Cosmi   BONG – Bongiovanni
   (rec 2001)

Gratius agimus in C major (1817-18)

J Omilian, Warmia National Orchestra, cond S Frontalini   BONG – Bongiovanni

Tecum principium (part of section three of Dixit Dominus) (1824)

J Omilian, Warmia National Orchestra, cond S Frontalini   BONG – Bongiovanni

SONGS

L'Abbandono – romanza

M Caballé (sop), M Zanetti (p)   FORL – Forlane

D O'Neill (tn), I Surgenor (p) (rec 1997)   COLL – Collins Classics

C Bartoli (m-sop), J Levine (p) (rec 1996)   DECCA

L'Allegro marinaro – ballata

M Caballé (sop), M Zanetti (p)   FORL – Forlane

D O'Neill (tn), I Surgenor (p) (rec 1997)   COLL – Collins Classics

Almen se non possio – arietta da camera

D O'Neill (tn), I Surgenor (p) (rec 1997)   COLL – Collins Classics

Bella Nice, che d'amore – arietta da camera

N Gedda (tn), J Eyron (p)   BLUE – Bluebell

L Pavarotti (tn), R Bonynge (cond), Orch Teatro Comunale   DECCA
   Bologna

L Pavarotti (tn), L Maggiera (p)   DECCA

D O'Neill (tn), I Surgenor (p) (rec 1997)   COLL – Collins Classics

Malinconia, ninfa gentile – arietta da camera

L Pavarotti (tn), R Bonynge (cond), Orch Teatro Comunale   DECCA
   Bologna

L Pavarotti (tn), L Maggiera (p)   DECCA

R Tebaldi (sop), R Bonynge (p)   DECCA

M Caballé (sop), M Zanetti (p)	FOR – Forlane
S Jo (sop), V Scallera (p) (rec 1997)	ERAT – Erato
J Carreras (tn), M Katz (p)	SONY
C Bartoli (m-sop), J-Y Thibaudet (p) (rec 1998)	DECCA
C Bartoli (m-sop), J Levine (p) (rec 1996)	DECCA
D O'Neill (tn), I Surgenor (p) (rec 1997)	COLL – Collins Classics
O Pasiecznik, K Borucinska (p) (rec 1999)	OLIV – Oliverius

Vanne o rosa fortunata – arietta da camera

R Tebaldi (sop), G Favaretto (p) (rec 1956)	DECCA
N Gedda (tn), J Eyron (p)	BLUE – Bluebell
C Bartoli (m-sop), J Levine (p) (rec 1996)	DECCA
L Pavarotti (tn), R Bonynge (cond), Orch Teatro Comunale Bologna	DECCA
D O'Neill (tn), I Surgenor (p) (rec 1997)	COLL – Collins Classics

Per pietà, bell'idol mio – arietta da camera

R Tebaldi (sop), G Favaretto (p) (rec 1957)	DECCA
E Mei (m-sop), F Bidini (p) (rec 1994)	RCA
J Carreras (tn), M Katz (p)	SONY
S Jo (sop), V Scalera (p) (rec 1997)	ERAT – Erato
C Bartoli (m-sop), J Levine (p) (rec 1996)	DECCA
D O'Neill (tn), I Surgenor (p) (rec 1997)	COLL – Collins Classics
O Pasiecznik, K Borucinska (p) (rec 1999)	O111

Ma rendi pur contento – arietta da camera

L Pavarotti (tn), R Bonynge (cond), Orch Teatro Comunale Bologna	DECCA
L Pavarotti (tn), L Maggiera (p)	DECCA
M Caballé (sop), M Zanetti (p)	FORL – Forlane
D Cohen-Licht, M Wiesenberg (p)	OLYM – Olympia
E Mei (sop), F Bindini (p) (rec 1994)	RCA
V La Scola (tn), P Molinari (p) (rec 1994)	BONG – Bongiovanni
D O'Neill (tn), I Surgenor (p) (rec 1997)	COLL – Collins Classics
C Bartoli (m-sop), J-Y Thibaudet (p) (rec 1998)	DECCA

Sei ariette da camera

1) "Malinconia ninfa gentile"; 2) "Vanne o rosa fortunata"; 3) "Bella Nice che d'amore"; 4) "Almen se non poss'io"; 5) "Per pietà bell'idol mio"; 6) "Ma rendi pur contento"

R Evans (tn), M Pollock (p) (rec 1996)	EMI

Dolente immagine di Fille mia – arietta

L Pavarotti (tn), R Bonynge (cond), Orch Teatro Comunale Bologna	DECCA
L Pavarotti (tn), L Maggiera (p)	DECCA
J Carreras (tn), M Katz (p)	SONY
R Tebaldi (sop), G Favaretto (p) (rec 1956)	DECCA
G di Stefano (tn), R Bibl (p) (rec 1968)	SCHW – Koch Schwann
J Sutherland (sop), R Bonynge (p)	BLV – Bella Voce
C Bartoli (m-sop), J Levine (p) (rec 1996)	DECCA
D O'Neill (tn), I Surgenor (p) (rec 1997)	COLL – Collins Classics

La farfalletta – canzoncina

C Bartoli (m-sop), J Levine (p) (rec 1996)	DECCA
D O'Neill (tn), I Surgenor (p) (rec 1997)	COLL – Collins Classics

Il fervido desiderio – arietta da camera

J Carreras (tn), M Katz (p)	SONY
C Bartoli (m-sop), J Levine (p) (rec 1996)	DECCA
D O'Neill (tn), I Surgenor (p) (rec 1997)	COLL – Collins Classics

E nello stringerti a questo – concert aria

J Drivala (sop), N Walker (p) (rec 1994)	SOMM – Somm Recordings
J Omilian (sop), S Frontalini (cond), Warmia National Orch	BONG – Bongiovanni

Vaga luna che inargenti – arietta da camera

L Pavarotti (tn), P Gamba (p)	DECCA
M Caballé (sop), M Zanetti (p)	FORL – Forlane
D Cohen-Licht (tn), M Wiesenberg (p)	OLYM – Olympia
E Mei (sop), F Bidini (p) (rec 1994)	RCA

J Carreras (tn), M Katz (p)	SONY
R Tebaldi (sop), G Favaretto (p) (rec 1957)	DECCA
V La Scuola (tn), P Molinari (p) (rec 1994)	BONG – Bongiovanni
G di Stefano (tn), R Bibl (p) (rec 1968)	SCHW – Koch Schwann
C Bartoli (m-sop), J Levine (p) (rec 1996)	DECCA
D O'Neill (tn), I Surgenor (p) (rec 1997)	COLL – Collins Classics

Sogno d'infanzia – romanza

D O'Neill (tn), I Surgenor (p) (rec 1997)	COLL – Collins Classics

Torna, vezzosa fillide – romanza

C Bartoli (m-sop), J Levine (p) (rec 1996)	DECCA
D O'Neill (tn), I Surgenor (p) (rec 1997)	COLL – Collins Classics

L Ricordanza – song

J Carreras (tn), M Katz (p)	SONY
D O'Neill (tn), I Surgenor (p) (rec 1997)	COLL – Collins Classics

Quando incise sul quel marmo – scena ed aria

D O'Neill (tn), I Surgenor (p) (rec 1997)	COLL – Collins Classics
J Omilian (sop), S Frontalini (cond), Warmia National Orch	BONG – Bongiovanni

Feneste che lucive – song (attrib Bellini)

F Corelli (tn), F Ferraris (orch cond) (rec 1961)	EMI
G di Stefano (tn), D Oliveri (orch cond) (rec 1956)	TEST – Testament
S Franchi (tn), W Stott (orch cond) (rec 1962)	RCA

Sí per te Gran Nume eterno

J Omilian (sop), S Frontalini (cond), Warmia National Orch	BONG – Bongiovanni

Gioite, amiche contrade

J Omilian (sop), S Frontalini (cond), Warmia National Orch	BONG – Bongiovanni

Operas

Adelson e Salvini (opera in three acts – Naples Conservatorio, 1825)

Order of principal characters in complete recordings of *Adelson e Salvini*: Lord Adelson, Salvini, Nelly, Bonifacio, Fanny, Madama Rivers, Struley, Geronio

F Previati, B Williams, A Nafé, A Tomicich, L Rizzi, E Jankovic,   NUOV – Nuova Era
R Coviello, G Tosi, EAR Bellini Theatre Chor & Orch,
cond A Licata (rec 1992, live)

Excerpts

Dopo l'oscuro nembo

N Focile, Philh, cond D Parry	OPRA – Opera Rara
E Mei, Munich RO, cond J Kovács	RCA
M Caballé, Teatro Liceo (Barcelona) Orch, cond D Gimenez (rec 1995)	RCA

Ecco signor, la sposa

J Carreras, LSO, cond J López-Cobos (rec 1976)	PHIL – Philips

---

Bianca e Fernando (opera in two acts – Teatro Carlo Felice, Genoa, 1828)

Order of principal characters in complete recordings of *Bianca e Fernando*: Bianca, Fernando, Filippo, Eloisa

Young OK Shin, G Kunde, H Fu, E Manhart, Teatro Massimo   NUOV – Nuova Era
Bellini (Catania) Chor & Orch, cond A Licata (rec 1991, live)

Excerpts

A tanto duol

J Pruett, RTBF SO, cond R Zollman (rec 1990, live)	PRES – President

Ove son?... Sorgi, o padre

M Freni, R Scotto, NPO, cond L Magiera (1978)	DECCA

Sorgi, o padre

C Muzio, Orch (rec 1922)	ROMO – Romophone

Sogi, o padre, e la figlia rimira

J Eaglen, A-M Owens, OAE, cond M Elder (rec 1955/6)	SONY

IL PIRATA *(opera in two acts – La Scala, 1827)*

Order of principal characters in complete recordings of *Il pirata*: Imogene, Gualtiero, Ernesto, Goffredo

M Callas, P Ferraro, C Ego, C Watson, NY American Opera Society, cond N Rescigno (rec 1959, live)	EMI, DIVA, VERONA
M Caballé, B Marti, P Cappuccilli, Rome RAI SO & Chor, cond G Gavazzeni (rec 1970)	EMI

EXCERPTS

Sorgete è in me dover. Lo sognai ferito

M Callas, M Sinclair, A Young, Philh, cond A Tonini (rec 1961)	EMI

Sì vincemmo, e il preggio io sento

D Hvorostovsky, Philh, cond I Marin (rec 1992, live)	PHIL – Philips

Tu vedrai la sventura

G Morino, Warmia NPO, cond B Amaducci (rec 1990, live)	NUOV – Nuova Era

Oh! s'io potessi... Col sorriso d'innocenza

M Callas, Philh, cond N Rescigno (rec 1958)	EMI
M Callas, SO Norddeutschen Rundfunks (Hamburg), cond N Rescigno (rec 1959, live)	GALA
M Callas, Concertgebouw, cond N Rescigno (rec 1959, live)	EMI, RODOLPHE
M Caballé, F Raffanelli, F Baratti, B Marti, RAI Rome Chor & Orch, cond G Gavazzeni	EMI
M Caballé, Chor & Orch cond CF Cillario (rec 1965)	RCA
M Caballé, F Rafanelli, MMF Chor & Orch, cond F Capuana (rec 1967, live)	VERONA
E Gruberova, M Schmidt, Bavarian Radio Chor, Munich RO, cond F Luisi (rec 1994)	NIGH – Nightingale Classics

Col sorriso d'innocenza

M Caballé, Rome RAI Orch, cond G Gavazzeni (rec 1970)	EMI
L Aliberti, Munich RO, cond L Gardelli	ORFE – Orfeo
M Dragoni, cond C Visco	NUOV – Nuova Era

LA STRANIERA (opera in two acts – La Scala, 1829)

Order of principal characters in complete recordings of *La Straniera*: Alaide, Valdeburgo, Arturo

M Caballé, V Sardinero, A Zambon, NY Opera Society,   GALA
    cond A Guadagno (rec 1969, live)

EXCERPTS
Un ritratto?... Sventurato il cor che fida

J Sutherland, R Conrad, LSO, cond R Bonynge (rec 1963)   DECCA

Ciel pietoso, in sì crudo momento

K Ricciarelli, M Katz (p) – Liberty, Kansas, and Miami, Florida   GALA

ZAIRA (opera in two acts – Ducale, Parma, 1829)

Order of principal characters in complete recordings of *Zaira*: Zaira, Orosmane, Corasmino, Nerestano

R Scotto, L Roni, GC Lamberti, ML Nave, Teatro Massimo   MCD – Myto
    Bellini (Catania) Chor & Orch, cond D Belardinelli (rec 1976, live)

K Ricciarelli, S Alaimo, R Vargas, A Papadjiakou, Teatro   NUOV – Nuova Era
    Massimo Bellini (Catania) Chor & Orch, cond P Olmi (rec 1990)

EXCERPT
Amo ed amata in sono

Y Kenny, L Daniels, G Mitchell, Phil, cond D Parry (rec 1995)   OPRA – Opera Rara

---

I CAPULETI E I MONTECCHI (opera in two acts – La Fenice, Venice, 1830)

Order of principal characters in complete recordings of *I Capuleti e i Montecchi*: Giulietta, Romeo, Tebaldo, Capellio, Lorenzo

R Scotto, G Aragall, L Pavarotti, M Petri, A Giacomotti, with   GALA, Butt – Butterfly
    tenor as Romeo, La Scala Chor & Orch, cond C Abbado
    (rec 1967, live)

K Ricciarelli, D Montague, D Raffanti, M Lippi, A Salvadori,   NUOV – Nuova Era
    La Fenice Chor & Orch, cond B Campanella (rec 1992, live)

E Gruberova, A Baltsa, D Raffanti, G Howell, J Tomlinson,   EMI
    ROH Chor & Orch, cond R Muti (rec 1984, live)

E Mei, V Kasarova, R Vargas, U Chiummo, S Alberghini,   RCA
   Munich Radio Chor & Orch, cond R Abbado (rec 1997, live)

HK Hong, J Larmore, P Groves, R Aceto, R Lloyd,   TELD – Teldec
   Scottish Chor & CO, cond D Runnicles (rec 1998, live)

EXCERPTS

Overture

Philh, cond D Atlas (rec 1992)   CARL

E' serbata a questa acciaro. L'amo, ah, l'amo e mi e più cara

L Pavarotti, Teatro Comunale Bologna, Hague Residential Orch, GLOB – Globe
   cond C Abbado (rec 1966)

Se Romeo t'uccise un figlio

G Fabbri, cond S Cottone (rec 1903)   SYMP – Symposium

B Fassbaender, Stuttgart RSO, cond H Graf   ORFE – Orfeo

Se Romeo t'uccise un figlio. La tremenda ultrice spada

V Kasarova, A Shulist, L Savitzky, Bavarian Radio Chor,   RCA
   Munich RO, cond F Haider (rec 1996)

La tremenda ultrice spada

J Larmore, WNO, cond C Rizzi (rec 1995)   TELD – Teldec

Eccomi in lieta vesta...Oh! quante volte

G Sciutti, R Berger, VPO, cond A Quadri (rec 1960)   BELA

R Streich, Berlin Deutsche Op Orch, cond R Peters (rec 1965)   DG – Polygram

M Devia, Svizzera Italiana Orch, cond M Rota (rec 1992)   BONG – Bongiovanni

B Sills, Vienna St Op Orch, cond J Jalas (rec 1968)   NNMC – Millennium
    Classics

A Gheorghiou, Turin Teatro Regio Orch, cond J Mauceri (rec 1995) DECCA

S Jo, ECO, cond G Carella (rec 1996)   DECCA

K Battle, LPO, cond B Campanella (rec 1991)   DG – Polygram

Oh! quante volte

L Orgonasova, Bratislava RSO, cond W Humburg   NAXOS

R A Swenson, LSO, cond J Rudel (rec 1998)	EMI

Deh! tu deh! tu bell'anima

G Simionato, Santa Cecilia Academy Orch, Rome, cond F Ghione (rec 1954)	DECCA

LA SONNAMBULA (opera in two acts – Teatro Carcano, Milan, 1831)

Order of principal characters in complete recordings of La sonnambula: Amina, Elvino, Rodolfo, Lisa

M Callas, N Monti, N Zaccaria, E Ratti, La Scala Chor & Orch, cond A Votto (rec 1957)	EMI
M Callas, N Monti, N Zaccaria, M Angioletti, La Scala Chor & Orch in Cologne, cond A Votto (rec July 1957, live)	DIVA
M Callas, N Monti, N Zaccaria, E Martelli (La Scala Chor & Orch at Edinburgh Festival, cond A Votto (rec August 1957, live)	VIRTUOSO
M Callas, C Valletti, G Modesti, E Ratti, La Scala Chor & Orch, cond L Bernstein (rec March 1955, live)	MCD – Myto
J Sutherland, N Monti, F Corena, S Stahlman, MMF Chor & Orch, cond R Bonynge	DECCA
J Sutherland, L Pavarotti, N Ghiaurov, I Buchanan, NPO & London Opera Chor, cond R Bonynge	DECCA
J Sutherland, R Cioni, E Flagello, Kölner Rundfunks Chor & Orch, cond J Keilberth (rec 1961, live)	GALA
R Scotto, A Kraus, I Vinco (excerpts), La Fenice (Venice) Chor & Orch, cond N Santi (rec May 1961, live)	GALA
R Scotto, A Kraus, I Vinco (excerpts), La Fenice (Venice) Chor & Orch, cond N Santi (rec May 1961, live)	GALA
M Devia, L Canonici, A Venducci, E Battaglia, Piacenda SO & Como City Chor, cond M Viotti (rec 1988)	NUOV – Nuova Era
L Orgonasova, R Giménez, FE d'Artegna, Netherlands Radio Chor & Orch, cond A Zedda (rec 1992, live)	NAXOS
E Lind, W Matteuzzi, P Salomaa, Nationale Reisopera Chor, Eastern Netherlands Orch, cond G Bellini (rec 1991)	ARTS – Art Music

EXCERPTS

ACT 1: 1) "Viva Amina!"; 2) "Tutto e gioia"; 3) "In Elvezia non v'ha rosa"; 4a) "Care compagne"; 4b) A te diletta tenera madre"; 4c) "Come per me sereno"; 4d) "Sovra il sen"; 5) "Io più di tutti o Amina"; 6a) "Ah! vorrei trovar parole"; 6b) "Elvino che rechi?"; 6c) "Prendi 'lane ti dono"; 7a) "Qual rumore"; 7b) "Il mulino"; 7c) "Vi ravviso, o luoghi ameni"; 7d) "Tu non sai con quel begli occhi"; 8a) "Contezza del paese avete voi Signor"; 8b) "A fosco cielo, a notte bruna"; 8c) "Basta così"; 9a) "Elvino! E me tu lasci"; 9b) "Son geloso del zefiro errante"; 10) "Davver, non mi dispiace"; 11) "Che veggo?"; 12) "Osservate! L'uscio è aperto"; 13) "È menzogna"; 14a) "D'un pensiero e d'un accento"; 14b) "Non più nozze"

ACT 2: 15) "Qui la selva è più folta"; 16a) "Reggimi, o buono madre"; 16b) "Tutto è sciolto"; 16c) "Pasci il guardo e appaga l'alma"; 17a) "Viva il Conte!"; 17b) "Ah! perchè non posso odiarti"; 18a) "Lasciami: avercompreso"; 18b) "De'lieti auguri a voi son grata"; 19a) "Signor Conte, agli occhi miei"; 19b) "V'han certuni che dormendo"; 19c) "Piano, amici, non gridate"; 20) "Lisa mendace anch'essa!"; 21a) "Signor, che creder deggio?"; 21b) "Chi? Mira...ella stessa"; 22a) "Oh! se una volta sola"; 22b) "Ah! non credea mirarti"; 22c) "Ah! non giunge"

4a: J Sutherland, NY Op Society Orch, cond N Rescigno (rec 1961)	BLV – Bella Voce
4a, 4b, 4c, 4d: M Callas, La Scala Chor & Orch, cond A Votto (rec 1957)	EMI
4a, 4b, 4c, 4d: M Devia, Svizzera Italiana Orch, cond M Rota (rec 1992)	BONG – Bongiovanni
4a, 6c, 7c, 9b, 13, 14a, 14b, 17b, 22a-c: M Devia, L Canonici, A Verducci, Como City Chor, Piacenza Orch, cond M Viotti	NUOV – Nuova Era
4a-c: Dilbér, Estonia Op Orch, cond T Serafin (rec 1995)	EMI
4a-c, 22a-c: M Callas, La Scala Chor & Orch, cond T Serafin (rec 1955)	EMI
4a-d: M Callas, La Scala Chor & Orch, cond A Votto (rec 1957)	EMI
J Sutherland, ROH Orch, cond F Molinari-Pradelli (rec 1960)	DECCA
B Sills, Vienna Academy Chor & Orch, cond J Jalas (rec 1968)	NNMC – Millennium Classics
M Callas, La Scala Orch, cond T Serafin (rec 1955)	EMI
RA Swenson, LPO, cond N Rescigno (rec 1993)	EMI
4c: L Orgonasova, Bratislava RSO, cond W Humburg	NAXOS
O Boronat, Orch (rec 1908)	MARS – Marston
G Sciutti, Lamoureux Concerts Orch, cond P Dervaux (rec 1953)	PHIL – Philips
A Galli-Curci, Orch, cond J Pasternack (rec 1920)	ROMO – Romophone
4c, 22b: M Carosio, Orch (rec c1930)	VINT – Vintage Music Co
4c, 22b, 22c: M Callas, La Scala Orch, cond T Serafin (rec 1955)	EMI

4c, 4d: L Pagliughi, EIAR Orch, cond U Tansini (rec 1934)	PREI – Preiser
M Barrientos, Anon (rec 1906)	ARIR
L Tetrazzini, Orch (rec 1912)	PEAR – Pearl
4c, 4d, 22b: A Galli-Curci, Orch (rec 1917-20)	PEAR – Pearl
4c, 4d, 22b, 22c: M Robin, LPO, cond A Fistoulari (rec 1955)	LOND – London
4d: A Galli-Curci, Orch, cond R Bourdon (rec 1919)	NIMB – Nimbus
A Galli-Curci, Orch, cond J Pasternack (rec 1919)	ROMO – Romophone
6b: T Dal Monte, T Schipa, La Scala Chor & Orch, cond F Ghione (rec 1993)	EMI
J Sutherland, L Pavarotti, NPO, cond R Bonynge (rec 1976)	DECCA
6c: F Tagliavini, EIAR Orch, cond U Tansini (rec 1940)	CENT – Centaur
J Zoon, H de Vries, London Studio SO, cond Vrijens	PHIL – Philips
F Wunderlich, E Köth, Munich RO, cond K Eichhorn (Germany)	DG – Polygram
T Dal Monte, T Schipa, Orch, cond F Ghione (rec 1993)	MMOI – Memoir Classics; PREI – Preiser
D Borgioli, Orch (rec c1921)	PEAR – Pearl
E de Muro Lomanto, Orch (rec 1927)	TEST – Testament
A Giorgini, Orch (rec 1905)	RECO – Record Collector
6c, 17b: F De Lucia, M Galvany, anon (rec 1908)	BONG – Bongiovanni
6c, 9b: F De Lucia, M Galvany, anon (rec 1908)	SYMP – Symposium
7b, 7c: P Plançon, anon (rec 1903)	NIMB – Nimbus; PEAR – Pearl
B Christoff, Rome Op Chor & Orch, cond V Gui (rec 1955)	EMI
7c: M Journet, anon (rec 1905)	SONY
A de Segurola, Orch (rec 1906)	PREI – Preiser
A Scotti, Orch (rec 1906)	PEAR – Pearl
F Chaliapin, La Scala Orch, cond C Sabajno (rec 1912)	PREI – Preiser
L Sibiriakov, Orch (rec 1911)	PEAR – Pearl
T Pasero, Rome Teatro Reale Orch, cond L Ricci (rec 1943)	PREI – Preiser
C Siepi, Orch (rec 1947)	PREI – Preiser
S Ramey, Philh, cond D Renzetti (rec 1986)	PHIL – Philips
7c, 7d: S Ramey, Ambrosian Op Chor, Philh, cond D Renzetti (rec 1987)	PHIL – Philips
7d: T Pasero, Orch, cond L Molajoli (rec 1928)	PREI – Preiser

9b: T Schipa, A Galli-Curci, Orch, cond R Bourdon (rec 1923)   RCA; ROMO – Romophone

14a: D Borgioli, M Gentile, G Pedroni, I Mannarini,   PEAR – Pearl
La Scala Chor & Orch, cond L Molajoli (rec 1927)

G Pareto, G Manurita, Chor & Orch, cond C Sabajno (rec 1924) PEAR – Pearl

14a, 22b: T Dal Monte, A Sinnone, Vienna St Op Chor &   SCHW – Koch Schwann
Orch, cond G del Campo (rec 1935)

17b: F De Lucia, anon (rec 1908)   SYMP – Symposium

L Pavarotti, NPO, cond R Bonynge (rec 1986)   DECCA

22: RA Swenson, LSO, cond J Rudel (rec 1998)   EMI

22a, 22b: J Sutherland, NY Op Society Orch, cond N Rescigno   BLV – Bella Voce
(rec 1961)

R Tebaldi, Monte Carlo NOP Orch, cond F Cleva (rec 1968) DECCA

22a, 22b, 22c: Y Huang, LSO, cond J Conlon (rec 1996)   SONY

22a-c: E Mei, Munich RO, cond J Kovács (rec 1996)   RCA

K Battle, R Stene, R Croft, MS Doss, LPO,   RCA
cond B Campanella (rec 1991)

22b: A Patti, A Barilli (rec 1906)   EMI

A Pendachanska, Sofia SO, cond M Angelov (rec 1994)   CAPR – Capriccio

A Galli-Curci, Orch (rec 1917)   CONI – Conifer

C Muzio, Orch, cond L Molajoli (rec 1935)   NIMB – Nimbus

T Dal Monte, La Scala Orch, cond C Sabajno (rec 1929)   PREI – Preiser

L Tetrazzini, Orch, cond P Pitt (rec 1909)   PEAR – Pearl

A Gluck, Victor Orch (rec 1911)   MRS – Marston

C Muzio, Orch, cond L Molajoli (rec 1939)   ROMO – Romophone

L Pagliughi, EIAR Orch, cond U Tansini (rec 1936)   PREI – Preiser

B Sayäo, Columbia SO, cond F Cleva (rec 1945)   SONY

M Dobbs, Philh, cond A Galliera (rec 1953)   TEST – Testament

E Gruberova, Munich RO, cond L Gardelli   ORFE – Orfeo

22b, 22c: L Tetrazzini, Victor Orch, cond J Pasternack (rec 1911) ROMO – Romophone

G Pareto, Orch (rec 1907)   PEAR – Pearl

S Kurz, Orch (rec 1924)   PREI – Preiser

L Pons, Columbia SO, cond A Kostelanetz   SONY

M Callas, F Cossotto, N Monti, N Zaccaria, La Scala   EMI
Chor & Orch, cond A Votto (rec 1957)

J Sutherland, N Monti, F Corena, MMF Chor & Orch, cond R Bonynge (rec 1962)	DECCA
S Jo, Monte Carlo PO, cond P Olmi (rec 1994)	ERAT – Erato
L Aliberti, Munich RO, cond L Gardelli	ORFE – Orfeo
M Dragoni, cond C Visco	NUOV – Nuova Era
22c: M Sembrich (rec 1904)	ROMO – Romophone
M Sembrich (rec 1908)	NIMB – Nimbus
L Tetrazzini, cond C Campanini (rec 1904)	ROMO – Romophone
L Tetrazzini, Orch (rec 1911)	NIMB – Nimbus
A Galli-Curci, Orch, cond R Bourdon (rec 1924)	ROMO – Romophone

---

NORMA *(opera in two acts – La Scala, 1831)*

Order of principal characters in complete recordings of *Norma*: Norma, Pollione, Adalgisa, Oroveso

M Callas, M Filippeschi, E Stignani, N Rossi-Lemeni, La Scala Chor & Orch, cond T Serafin (rec 1954)	EMI
M Callas, F Corelli, C Ludwig, N Zaccaria, La Scala Chor & Orch, cond T Serafin (rec 1960)	EMI
M Callas, K Baum, G Simionato, N Moscona, Palacio de Bellas Artes, (Mexico City) Chor & Orch, cond G Picco (rec 1950, live)	MCD – Myto
M Callas, M Picchi, E Stignani, G Vaghi, ROH (London) Chor & Orch, cond A Votto (rec 1955, live)	GALA
J Sutherland, J Alexander, M Horne, R Cross, LSO & Chor, cond R Bonynge	DECCA
J Sutherland, L Pavarotti, M Caballé, S Ramey, WNO Chor & Orch, cond R Bonynge (rec 1988)	DECCA
J Sutherland, J Alexander, H Turangeau, C Grant, San Francisco Op Chor & Orch, cond R Bonynge (rec 1972, live)	GALA
M Caballé, P Domingo, F Cossotto, R Raimondi, LPO & Ambrosian Op Chor, cond CF Cillario	RCA
M Caballé, G Raimondi, F Cossotto, I Vinco, La Scala Chor & Orch, cond G Gavazzeni (rec 1972, live)	MCD – Myto
R Scotto, G Giacomini, T Troyanos, P Plishka, NPO & Ambrosian Op Chor, cond J Levine (rec 1978)	SONY
L Gencer, G Limarilli, F Cossotto, I Vinco, Lausanne Op Chor & Orch, cond O de Fabritiis (rec 1966, live)	MCD – Myto
S Verrett, N Todisco, A Milchewa, C Grant, San Francisco Op Chor & Orch, cond P Peloso (rec 1978, live)	GALA

C Deutekom, R Merolla, T Troyanos, C Grant, San Francisco Op Chor & Orch, cond CF Cillario (rec 1975, live)	GALA
E Ross, M Del Monaco, F Cossotto, I Vinco, La Fenice (Venice) Chor & Orch, cond G Gavazzeni (rec 1968, live)	BLV – Bella Voce
G Cigna, G Breviario, E Stignani, T Pasero, EIAR Chor & Orch, cond V Gui (rec 1936)	PEAR – Pearl
G Cigna, G Martinelli, B Castagna, E Pinza, NY Met Op Chor & Orch, cond E Panizza (rec 1937, live)	GA – Golden Age
J Eaglen, V La Scola, E Mei, D Kavrakos, MMF Chor & Orch, cond R Muti (rec 1994)	EMI

EXCERPTS

1) Overture

ACT 1: 2) "Ite sul colle, O Druidi"; 3a) "Svanir le voci!"; 3b) "Meco all'altar di Venere"; 3c) "Me protegge"; 4a) "Norma viene"; 4b) "Sediziose voci"; 4c) "Casta Diva"; 4d) "Fine al rito"; 4e) "Ah! bello a me ritorna"; 5) "Sgombra è la sacra"; 6a) "Eccola! Va, mi lascia"; 6b) "Va crudele"; 7a) "Vanne, e li cela entrambi"; 7b) "Oh, rimembranza!"; 7c) "Sola, furtiva al tempio"; 7d) "Ah sì, fa core, abbracciami"; 8a) "Tremi tu? E per chi?... Oh, non tremare"; 8b) "Oh! Di qual sei tu vittima"; 8c) "Perfido!... Or basti"

ACT 2: 9) "Dormono entrambi"; 10a) "Me chiami, o Norma"; 10b) "Mira, o Norma"; 10c) "Cedi! Deh, cedi!"; 10d) "Si, fino all'ore estreme"; 11a) "Non parti!"; 11b) "Guerrieri"; 11c) "Ah! del Tebro"; 12) "Ei tornerà"; 13) "Guerra!"; 14a) "In mia man"; 14b) "Ah! Crudele"; 15a) "All'ira vostra"; 15b) "Qual cor tradisti"; 15c) "Deh! Non volerli vittime"

1: South West German RSO, cond K Arp (rec 1994)	PIER
2: F Chaliapin, La Scala Orch, cond C Sabajno (rec 1912)	PREI – Preiser
T Pasero, Orch, cond L Molajoli (rec 1927)	PREI – Preiser
T Pasero, Orch, cond A Albergoni (rec 1927)	PREI – Preiser
E Pinza, NY Met Op Chor & Orch, cond G Setti (rec 1927)	NIMB – Nimbus; PREI – Preiser; MMOI – Memoir Classics
E Pinza, NY Met Op Chor & Orch, cond F Cleva (rec 1946)	PREI – Preiser
B Christoff, Rome Op Chor & Orch, cond V Gui (rec 1955)	EMI
2, 11b, 11c: S Ramey, WNO Chor & Orch, cond R Bonynge (rec 1984)	DECCA
3a-c: M Del Monaco, A Cesarini, Rome RAI Orch, cond T Serafin (rec 1955)	NUOV – Nuova Era
P Domingo, P Domingo Jnr, NPO & Ambrosian Op Chor, cond E Kohn	EMI

3b: G Lauri-Volpi, Orch, cond R Bourdon (rec 1928)

RCA
SYMP – Symposium
NIMB – Nimbus
PREI – Preiser

M Gilion, Orch (rec c1909)

BONG – Bongiovanni

F Merli, Orch, cond L Molajoli (rec 1935)

PREI – Preiser

L Pavarotti, K Begley, WNO Chor & Orch, cond R Bonynge
(rec 1988)

DECCA

3b, 3c: F Corelli, La Scala Orch & Chor, cond T Serafin (rec 1960)

EMI

4b, 4c: R Ponselle, NY Met Op Chor & Orch, cond G Setti
(rec 1928/9)

NIMB – Nimbus

M Callas, La Scala Chor & Orch, cond T Serafin (rec 1954)

EMI

R Tebaldi, Turin Lyric Chor & Monte Carlo National Op,
cond F Cleva (rec 1968)

DECCA

4b-d: J Sutherland, R Cross, LSO & Chor, cond R Bonynge
(rec 1964)

DECCA

M Callas, Paris Opera Chor & Orch, cond G Sebastian
(rec 1958)

GALA

L Price, B Martinovich, Ambrosian Op Chor, Philh,
cond H Lewis (rec 1979)

RCA

4b-d, 7b, 8a, 10a-d, 13, 15, 15c: J Sutherland, M Horne,
J Alexander, R Cross, LSO & Chor, cond R Bonynge

DECCA

4b-e: J Sutherland, ROH Chor & Orch, cond F Molinari-Pratelli
(rec 1960)

DECCA

R Ponselle, NY Met Op Chor & Orc, cond G Setti
(rec 1928/9)

ROMO – Romophone
NIMB – Nimbus

4b-e, 10b-d: R Ponselle, M Telva, NY Met Op Chor & Orch,
cond G Setti (rec 1928/9)

PEAR – Pearl

4c: C Muzio, Orch, cond L Molajoli (rec 1935)

ROMO – Romophone

T Dal Monte, Orch (rec 1933)

PREI – Preiser

M Foley, Orch (rec 1949-53)

ODE – Ode Record Co

G Cigna, Orch, cond L Molajoli (rec 1932)

PREI – Preiser
LYRO

M André, Toulouse Capitol Chor & Orch, cond M Plasson

EMI

R Ponselle, Orch (rec 1919)

PEAR – Pearl

T Arkel, Orch, cond C Sabajno (rec 1905)

EMI

D Giannini, La Scala Chor & Orch, cond C Sabajno (rec 1931)

PREI – Preiser

L Lehmann, Orch, cond F Kark (rec 1907)

PEAR – Pearl

A Patti, cond A Barili (rec 1906)	PEAR – Pearl
E Calvé, Orch (rec 1920)	MARS – Marston
R Raisa, Orch (rec 1920)	MARS – Marston
M Callas, La Scala Chor & Orch, cond T Serafin (rec 1954)	EMI
M Callas, La Scala Chor & Orch, cond T Serafin (rec 1960)	EMI
M Callas, Turin Radio Symphony Orch, cond A Basile (rec 1949)	RODOLPHE – Harmonia Mundi
I Galante, LPO	EMI
R Scotto, NPO, cond J Levine (rec 1979)	SONY
G Simionato, Santa Cecilia (rec ome) Academy Chor & Orch, cond A Paoletti (rec 1961)	DECCA
4c: E Urbanova, Prague SO, cond J Belohlávek (rec 1993)	SUPR – Suprafon
R Fleming, London Voices BBC Orch, cond C Mackerras (rec 1999)	DECCA
L Garrett, London Voices BBC Orch, cond P Robinson	RCA
N Kirsch, Orch, cond B James	BMGC
J Harjanne, Norwegian Radio Orch, cond A Rasilainen (rec 1999)	FIN
J Huguet, Orch	DIVR – Diverdi
F Giordano, London Session Orch, cond C Valli (rec 1999)	ERAT – Erato
C Makris, Oulu SO, cond A Volmer (rec 1988)	ALB
A Cerquetti, MMF Chor & Orch, cond G Gavazzeni (rec 1956)	DECCA
4c, 10b: G Arangi-Lombardi, E Stignani, Orch, cond L Molajoli (rec 1927/9)	NAXOS
4c, 15b, 15c: E Burzio, Orch (rec 1912/16)	MARS – Marston
4c, 15c: I Pacetti, Orch, cond L Molajoli (rec 1928)	PREI – Preiser
4c-e: M Callas, La Scala Chor & Orch, cond T Serafin (rec 1954)	EMI – Electrola Gmb
M Callas, Rome RAI, cond T Serafin (rec 1955)	RODOLPHE – Harmonia Mundi
4c, 4e: R Raisa, Orch (rec 1917)	MARS – Marston
M Sembrich, Victor Orch (rec 1907)	ROMO – Romophone NIMB – Nimbus
D Giannini, La Scala Chor & Orch, cond C Sabajno (rec 1931)	DANT
M Caballé, Orch, cond CF Cillario (rec 1965)	RCA
N Ermolenko-Yuzhina, Moscow Imperial Op Chor & Orch, cond Russ (rec 1909)	PEAR – Pearl

R Scotto, NPO, cond J Levine   SONY

J Eaglen, New Company, OAE, cond M Elder (rec 1995/6)   SONY

M Callas, Turin RSO, cond A Basile (rec 1949)   WFC

5: I Minghini-Cattaneo, La Scala Orch, cond C Sabajno (rec 1929)   PREI – Preiser

5, 10b: G Cigna, E Stignani, EIAR Orch, cond V Gui (rec 1937)   PREI – Preiser

5, 6a, 6b: M Caballé, L Pavarotti, P Maag, cond R Bonynge   DECCA
(rec 1984)

7b-d, 8a-c: J Sutherland, M Horne, L Pavarotti,   DECCA
NY City Op Orch, cond R Bonynge (rec 1981)

7c: G Russ, V Guerrini, Orch (rec 1913)   EMI

L Lehmann, H Helbig, Orch (rec 1907)   PEAR – Pearl

8b-c: J Sutherland, M Caballé, L Pavarotti, WNO Chor & Orch,   DECCA
cond R Bonynge (rec 1984)

10a-d: L Price, M Horne, NY Met Op Orch, cond J Levine (1982)   RCA

J Sutherland, M Caballé, WNO Orch & Chor, cond R Bonynge   DECCA
(rec 1984)

10b: G Groves, J Watson, cond J Partridge (rec 1994)   ASV

R Ponselle, M Telva, NY Met Op Orch, cond G Setti   NIMB – Nimbus
(rec 1929)

M Caballé, S Verrett, New Philh, cond A Guadagno   RCA

A Gluck, L Homer, Orch (rec 1916)   PEAR – Pearl

J Zoon, H de Vries, London Studio SO   PHIL – Philips

M Siems, G Forstel, anon (rec 1906 – Germany)   RECO – Record Collector

10b-d: M Caballé, S Verrett, New Philh, cond A Guadagno   RCA

H-K Hong, J Larmore, Munich RO, cond J Lopez-Cobos   TELD – Teldec
(rec 1998)

J Sutherland, M Horne, LSO, cond R Bonynge (rec 1964)   DECCA

R Ponselle, M Telva, NY Met Op Orch, cond G Setti   ASV
(rec 1928)

M Caballé, F Cossotto, LPO, cond CF Cillario (rec 1972)   RCA

11a: E Pinza, NY Met Op Chor & Orch, cond G Setti (rec 1929)   RCA

11c: E Pinza, NY Met Op Chor & Orch, cond C Sabajno   PEAR – Pearl
(rec 1923)

11c, 15c: E Pinza, T Pol-Randaccio, Orch, cond C Sabajno   PREI – Preiser
(rec 1923)

13: J Sutherland, S Ramey, WNO Chor & Orch, cond R Bonynge

(rec 1984)

14a: G Zenatello, E Mazzoleni, Orch (rec 1911)   PEAR – Pearl

    M Callas, M Del Monaco, Orch Sinfonica Rome RAI,
    cond T Serafin (rec 1955)

14a, 14b, 15a-c: M Callas, M Filippeschi, N Rossi-Lemeni,   EMI
    La Scala Chor & Orch, cond T Serafin (rec 1954)

BEATRICE DI TENDA *(opera in two acts – La Fenice, Venice, 1833)*

Order of principal characters in complete recordings of *Beatrice di Tenda*: Beatrice, Orombello,
    Filippo, Agnese

J Sutherland, L Pavarotti, C Opthof, J Veasy, LSO &   DECCA
    Ambrosian Singers, cond R Bonynge (rec 1966)

J Sutherland, R Cassily, E Sordello, M Horne,   BLV – Bella Voce
    NY Opera Society Chor & Orch, cond N Rescigno
    (rec 1961, live)

M Nicolesco, V La Scola, P Cappuccilli, S Toczyska, Prague   SONY
    Philcher, Monte Carlo National Orch, cond A Zedda (rec 1986)

E Gruberová, D Bernardini, I Morozov, V Kassarova, Vienna   NIGH – Nightingale
    Jeunesse Chor, Austrian RSO, cond P Steinberg (rec 1992)   Classics

EXCERPTS

*Nulla io dissi; Angiol di pace; Chi giunge?; Ah! se un urna; Ah! la morte a cu
    m'appreso*

J Sutherland, G Campora, R Kabaivanska, La Scala Chor   BLV – Bella Voce
    & Orch, cond A Votto (rec 1961)

Angiol di pace

J Sutherland, R Conrad, M Horne, LSO, cond R Bonynge   DECCA
    (rec 1963, live)

J Sutherland, L Pavarotti, M Horne, NY City Orch,   DECCA
    cond R Bonynge (rec 1981, live)

I PURITANI *(opera in three parts – Théâtre-Italien, Paris, 1835)*

Order of principal characters in complete recordings of *I Puritani*: Elvira, Arturo, Giorgio,
    Riccardo

M Callas, G di Stefano, N Rossi-Lemeni, R Panerai, La Scala Chor & Orch, cond T Serafin (rec 1953)	EMI
M Callas, G di Stefano, R Silva, P Campolonghi, Palacio de Bellas Artes (Mexico City) Chor & Orch, cond G Picco (rec 1952, live)	DIVA
J Sutherland, P Duval, E Flagello, R Capecchi, MMF Chor & Orch, cond R Bonynge (rec 1963)	DECCA
J Sutherland, L Pavarotti, N Ghiaurov, R Cappuccilli, ROH Chor, LSO, cond R Bonynge (rec 1973)	DECCA
B Sills, N Gedda, P Plishka, L Quilico, LPO & Ambrosian Op Chor, cond J Rudel (rec 1973)	NNMC – Millennium Classics MCD – Myto
J Sutherland, G Raimondi, F Mazzoli, M Zanasi, Teatro Massimo Bellini (Palermo) Chor & Orch, cond T Serafin (rec 1961, live)	BLV – Bella Voce NUOV – Nuova Era
M Caballé, A Kraus, A Ferrin, M Managuerra, Philh Orch & Ambrosian Op Chor, cond R Muti (rec 1980)	EMI
M Freni, L Pavarotti, B Gaiaotti, S Bruscantini, Rome RAI Chor & Orch, cond R Muti (rec 1969, live)	NUOV – Nuova Era
M Devia, W Matteuzzi, P Washington, C Robertson, Teatro Massimi Bellini (Catania) Chor & Orch, cond R Bonynge (rec 1989)	
E Gruberova, J Lavender, FE d'Artega, E Kimm, Bavarian Radio Chor, Munich RO, cond F Luisi (rec 1993)	

EXCERPTS

1a) Sinfonia

PART 1: 1b) "Al'erta"; 2) "O di Cromvel guerrieri"; 3) "A festa!"; 4a) "Or dove fuggo"; 4b) "Ah! per sempre"; 4c) "Bel sogno beato"; 5a) "O amato zio"; 5b) "O ciel! E fia vero"; 6) "Ad Arturo onore"; 7) "A te, o cara"; 8) "Il rito augusto"; 9) "Son virgin vezzosa"; 10a) "Sulla verginea"; 10b) "Ferma invan"; 11) "Arturo! Tu ritorni"; 12) "Ma tu già mi fuggi"

PART 2: 13) "Ah! dolor"; 14) "Cinta di fiori"; 15) "E di morte"; 16a) "O rendetemi la speme"; 16b) "Qui la voce"; 16c) "Vien diletto"; 17a) "Il rival salvar"; 17b) "Suoni la tromba"

PART 3: 18a) "Son salvo"; 18b) "A una fonte"; 19a) "Son già lontani"; 19b) "Finì! Me lassa!"; 19c) "Nel mirarti un solo istante"; 20) "Vieni, fra queste braccia"; 21a) "Ascolta ancora"; 21b) "Credeasi, misera"

4a: C Tagliabue, La Scala Orch, cond U Berretoni (rec 1946)	PHOG
4a, 4b: G Taddei, San Carlo (Naples) Op Orch, cond U Rapalo	PREI – Preiser
G De Luca, Orch (rec 1922)	PEAR – Pearl
P Domingo, T Hampson, Philh, cond E Kohn (rec 1995)	EMI

S Milnes, LPO, cond S Varviso (rec 1972)	DECCA
4b: D Hvorostovsky, Philh, cond I Marin (rec 1992)	PHIL – Philips
M Battistini, Orch, cond C Sabajno (rec 1911)	PEAR – Pearl ROMO – Romophone
C Alvarez, Basque NO, cond M Venzago (rec 1999)	CLAV – Claves
M Ancona, Victor Orch, cond WB Rogers (rec 1907)	ROMO – Romophone
7: A Bonci, anon (rec 1905)	EMI
A Giorgini, Orch (rec 1905)	RECO – Record Collector
G Lauri-Volpi, Orch (rec 1930)	PEAR – Pearl
G Lauri-Volpi, Orch, cond R Bourdon (rec 1928)	NIMB – Nimbus
M Fleta, Orch (rec 1923)	PREI – Preiser
A Pertile, La Scala Chor & Orch, cond C Sabajno (rec 1930)	PREI – Preiser
G di Stefano, M Callas, N Rossi-Lemeni, C Fort, La Scala Chor & Orch, cond T Serafin (rec 1953)	EMI
L Pavarotti, J Sutherland, N Ghiaurov, G Luccardi, ROH Chor & Orch, cond R Bonynge	DECCA
F Burger, A Auger, H Lackner, Vienna Op Orch, cond N Rescigno (rec 1969)	DECCA
G Sabbatini, Berlin RSO, cond R Paternostro	CAPR – Capriccio
G Monno, Warmia NPO, cond B Amaducci	NUOV – Nuova Era
A Kraus, M Caballé, A Ferrin, S Elenkov, Ambrosian Chor & Philh, cond R Muti (rec 1979)	EMI
A Bocelli, MMF Orch, cond G Noseda (1997)	PHIL – Philips
7, 18a, 18b, 20, 21b: M Devia, W Matteuzzi, C Robertson, P Washington, Teatro Massimo Bellini Chor & Orch, cond R Bonynge (rec 1989)	NUOV – Nuova Era
7, 20: H Lazaro, Orch (rec 1916)	CLAM – Tima
9: F Toresella, anon (rec 1900)	SYMP – Symposium
A Galli-Curci, Orch (rec 1923)	PEAR – Pearl NIMB – Nimbus
L Pons, Columbia SO, cond A Kostelanetz (rec 1949)	SONY
J Sutherland, ROH Chor & Orch, cond F Molinari-Pratelli (rec 1960)	DECCA
M Caballé, A Kraus, J Hamar, A Ferrin, S Elenkov, Ambrosian Op Chor, Philh, cond R Muti (rec 1979)	EMI
E Gruberova, V Walterova, LM Vodička, P Horacek, Smetana Theatre Chor, Czech PO, cond F Haider	SONY

L Aliberti, Berlin RSO, cond R Paternostro	CAPR – Capriccio
Dilber, Estonia Op Orch, cond E Klas	ONDI – Ondine
J Sutherland, Groot Omroeporkest (Amsterdam), cond F Venizzi (rec 1962)	GALA
9, 16a-c: J Sutherland, ROH Orch, cond F Molinari-Pratelli (rec 1960)	DECCA
J Sutherland, M Elkins, P Duval, R Capecchi, E Flagello, MMF Chor & Orch, cond R Bonynge (rec 1963)	DECCA
9, 16b: S Jo, ECO, cond G Carella (rec 1996)	ERAT – Erato
9, 16b, 16c: M Robin, LPO, cond A Fistoulari (rec 1955)	LOND – London
S Jo, St Luke's Orch, cond R Bonynge (rec 1996)	ERAT – Erato
11, 12: M Callas, RAI Milan Chor & Orch, cond A Simonetto (rec 1956)	RODOLPHE – Harmonia Mundi
14: E Pinza, Orch, cond C Sabajno (rec 1924)	PREI – Preiser NIMB – Nimbus
14, 17a: M Pertusi, C Alvarez, Bulgarian National Chor, Sofia PO, cond E Tabakov (rec 1994)	CAPR – Capriccio
16a: E Mosuc, Hungarian St Orch, cond J Schultsz (rec 1999)	ARTN
16a, 16b: O Boronat, anon (rec 1904)	MARS – Marston
V Zeani, A Mongelli, A Protti, Trieste Teatro Verdi Orch, cond F Molinari-Pratelli (rec 1957)	BONG – Bongiovanni
M Callas, Turin Radio Symphony Orch, cond A Basile (rec 1949)	NIMB – Nimbus RODOLPHE – Harmonia Mundi
16a-c: M Callas, R Panerai, N Rossi-Lemeni, La Scala Chor & Orch, cond T Serafin (rec 1953)	EMI EMI Electrola GmbH (Cologne)
J Sutherland, LSC, cond F Molinari-Pratelli (rec 1960)	DECCA
M Caballé, M Manuguerra, A Ferrin, Philh, cond R Muti (rec 1988)	EMI
R Tebaldi, Monte Carlo National Op Orch, cond F Cleva (rec 1968)	DECCA
M Freni, Rome Op Orch, cond F Ferrara	EMI
E Gruberova, E Kim, FE d'Artagna, Munich RO, cond F Luisi (rec 1993)	NIGH – Nightingale Classics
RA Swenson, LPO, cond N Rescigno (rec 1993)	EMI
E Mei, Munich RO, cond J Kovács (rec 1996)	RCA
16b: A Galli-Curci, Orch, cond R Bourdon (rec 1917)	NIMB – Nimbus PEAR – Pearl
M Sembrich, Orch (rec 1907)	NIMB – Nimbus

L Orgonasova, Bratislava RSO, cond W Humburg   NAXOS

A Nezhdanova, Bratislava RSO, cond W Humburg   NIMB – Nimbus

G Sciutti, Lamoureux Concerts Orch, cond P Dervaux (rec 1953) PHIL – Philips

M Carosio, Orch (rec c1930)   VINT – Vintage Music Co

M Carosio, Orch, cond A Erede (rec c1948)   EMI

A Case, Orch (rec 1920)   CLAR – Claremont

L Aliberti, Munich RO, cond L Cardelli   ORFE – Orfeo

M Capsir, La Scala Orch, cond L Molajoli (rec 1926)   NAXOS – Historical

16b, 16c: M Capsir, La Scala Orch, cond L Molajoli (rec 1933)   PREI – Preiser

M Devia, Svizzera Italiana Orch, cond M Rota (rec 1922)   BONG – Bongiovanni

A Galli-Curci, Orch, cond J Pasternack (rec 1920)   ROMO – Romophone

A Galli-Curci, Orch, cond J Pasternack (rec 1917)   ROMO – Romophone

M Sembrich, Victor Orch (rec 1907)   ROMO – Romophone

H Lawrence, NPO, cond R Stapleton (rec 1979)   BEUL – Beulah

16c: L Tetrazzini, Orch (rec 1912)   PEAR – Pearl

17a: M Biscotti, A Silvestrelli, Berlin RSO, cond R Buckley   SCHW – Koch Schwann

17a, 17b: N Ghiaurov, P Cappuccilli, LSO, cond R Buckley   SCHW – Koch Schwann

T Pasero, G Vanelli, Orch, cond L Molajoli (rec 1928)   PREI – Preiser

T Hampson, S Ramey, Munich RO,
cond MA Gomez-Martinez (rec 1997)   TELD – Teldec

A Miles, Philh, cond D Parry (rec 1999, England)   CHAN – Chandos

17b: T Ruffo, A de Segurola, Orch, cond C Sabajno (rec 1907)   PEAR – Pearl
PREI – Preiser

M Ancona, M Journet, Victor Orch, cond WB Rogers (rec 1907)   ROMO – Romophone

M Journet, P Amato, Orch (rec 1912)   NIMB – Nimbus
PEAR – Pearl

L Neroni, G Monachini, Orch (rec 1939)   PREI – Preiser

18a, 18b, 19a: Y Huang, M Alvarez, WNO Orch, cond C Rizzi (rec 1998)   SONY

18b: A Giorgini, Orch (rec 1908)   RECO – Record Collector

19a: L Pavarotti, Teatro Massimo Bellini (Catania) Orch, cond A Quadri (rec 1968)   RCA

20: F Marconi, M Galvany, Orch (rec 1908)   SYMP – Symposium

21a: C Gonzales, E Ferretti, M Biscotti, A Silvestrelli, Erst-Senff, Berlin RSO Chor, cond R Buckley   SCHW – Koch Schwann

iii

Bibliography

ADAMO, MR, and LIPPMANN, F: *Vincenzo Bellini* (Turin, 1981)

AMORE, A: *Vincenzo Bellini: Vita Studi e ricerche* (Catania, 1894)

AMORE, A: *Vincenzo Bellini: Arte Studi e ricerche* (Catania, 1902)

AMORE, A: *Belliniana* (Catania, 1902)

BRANCA, Emilia: *Felice Romani ed i più riputati maestri di musica del suo tempo* (Turin, 1882)

BRUNEL, P: *Vincenzo Bellini* (Paris, 1981)

CAMBI, Luisa: *Bellini: La Vita* (Milan, 1934)

CAMBI, Luisa (editor): *Vincenzo Bellini: Epistolario* (Milan, 1943)

CAMETTI, A: *Bellini a Roma: brevi appunti storici* (Rome, 1900)

CAVAZZUTI, P: *Bellini a Londra* (Florence, 1945)

CHORLEY, HF: *Thirty Years' Musical Recollections* (London, 1830-60)

CICCONETTI, F: *Vita di Vincenzo Bellini* (Prato, 1859)

CICCONETTI, F: *Lettere inedite di uomini illustri* (Rome, 1886)

CORTE, Andrea della and PANNAIN, Guido: *V Bellini: Il carattere morale, i caratteri artistici* (Turin, 1935)

COLOMBANI, A: *L'Opera italiana nel secolo XIX* (Milan, 1900)

COTTRAU, Guglielmo: *Lettres d'un Mélomane pour servir de document à l'histoire musicale de Naples de 1829 à 1847* (Naples, 1885)

DE ANGELIS, Giuseppe Tito: *Vincenzo Bellini: La vita, l'uomo, l'artista* (Brescia, 1935)

EDWARDS, Henry Sutherland: *The Prima Donna: Her history and surroundings from the seventeenth to the nineteenth century*, in two volumes (London, 1888)

EINSTEIN, A: "Vincenzo Bellini", in *Music and Letters* XVI (1935)

Enciclopedia dello spettacolo, in ten volumes, with supplement (Rome, 1954-66)

ESCUDIER, Léon: *Mes Souvenirs* (Paris, 1863)

FARINELLI, Arturo: *Vincenzo Bellini* (Rome, 1935)

FERRANTI (Nob. Giulini), Maria: *Giuditta Pasta e i suoi tempi* (Milan, 1935)

FERRIS, George T: *Great Singers, First and Second Series* (New York, 1893)

FLORIMO, Francesco: *Cenno storico sulla Scuola musicale di Napoli*, in four volumes (Naples, 1882)

FLORIMO, Francesco: *Bellini: Memorie e lettere* (Florence, 1882)

FLORIMO, Francesco: *La Scuola musicale di Napoli*, in four volumes (Naples, 1882)

FLORIMO, Francesco: *Translazione delle ceneri di Vincenzo Bellini* (Naples, 1887)

FRACCAROLI, Arnaldo: *Bellini* (Milan, 1942)

GATTI, Carlo: *Il Teatro alla Scala nella storia e nell'arti* (1778-1963, in two volumes, with *Cronologia completa degli spettacoli e dei concerti a cura di Giampiero Tintori* [Milan, 1964])

GERARDI, Filippo: *Biografia di Vincenzo Bellini* (Rome, 1835)

GIUGNI, Francesco: *L'immature fine di Vincenzo Bellini alla luce di nuove circostanze* (Lugo, 1938)

GREVILLE, Henry: *Leaves from the Diary of Henry Greville*, edited by Viscountess Enfield, (London, 1883)

GUI, Vittorio: "Beatrice di Tenda", *Musica d'oggi*, new series ii (1969)

HEINE, Heinrich: *Florentinische Nächte: "Erste Nacht"* (vol VI of *Sämtliche Werke* [Leipzig, 1912])

HILLER, Ferdinand: *Künstlerleben* (Cologne, 1880)

HOGARTH, George: *Memoirs of the Musical Drama* (London, 1838)

KIMBELL, David: *Vincenzo Bellini: Norma* (Cambridge, 1998)

LIANOVOSANT, Luigi (Giovanni Salvioli): *Saggio bibliografico relativo ai melodrammi di Felice Romani* (Milan, 1878)

LIPPMANN, Friedrich: *Vincenzo Bellini und die italienische Opera seria seiner Zeit Analecta Musicologica 6*, (Cologne, 1969)

LIPPMANN, Friedrich: *Belliniana, nuovi documenti* (Turin, 1977)

LOCATELLI, Agostino: *Cenni biografici sulla straordinaria carriera teatrale percorsa da Giovanni Battista Rubini* (Milan, 1884)

LOEWENBERG, Alfred: *Annals of Opera 1597-1940*, second edition, in two volumes (Geneva, 1955)

MALVEZZI, Aldobrandino: *Cristina di Belgiojoso*, in three volumes (Milan, 1936-37)

MEGALI, del Giudice, G: *Francesco Florimo, l'amico di Vincenzo Bellini* (Naples, 1901)

MOCENIGO (M Nani-Mocenigo): *Il Teatro la Fenice* (Venice, 1926)

MORGAN, Lady (Sidney Owenson): *Lady Morgan's Memoirs*, in two volumes (London, 1862)

MOUNT EDGCUMBE, Earl of: *Musical Reminiscences* (London, 1834)

OEHLMANN, W: *Vincenzo Bellini* (Zurich, 1974)

Omaggio a Bellini nel Primo Centenario dalla sua nascita (Catania, 1901)

L'OPERA: *Teatro Massimo Bellini, Catania* (Anno VN 16/17), with articles on Bellini and his operas by Niny Genguzza, Don Giosuè Chisari, Domenico Tempio, Benedetto Gondorelli, "Gani" and Vittorio Consoli (Milan, 1970)

ORREY, Leslie: *Bellini* (London, 1969)

PANNAIN, Guido: "*Norma*: cento anni" *Ottocento musicale Italiano* (Milan, 1952)

PANNAIN, Guido: *L'Opera e le opere* (Milan, 1958)

PASTURA, Francesco (editor): *Le Lettere di Bellini 1819-35* (Catania, 1935)

PASTURA, Francesco: *Bellini secondo la storia* (Parma, 1959)

PERSIANO, Filippo: *La Sonnambula di Felice Romani* (Florence, 1903)

PETROBELLI, P: *Bellini e Paisiello* (Turin, 1977)

PIZZETTI, Ildebrando: *La Musica di Vincenzo Bellini* (Milan, 1916)

PIZZETTI, Ildebrando (editor): *Vincenzo Bellini: L'uomo, le sue opere, la sua fama* (essays by Luisa Gambi, Andrea Della Corte, Gianandrea Gavazzeni, Carl Holl, Edward J Dent, Jean Chantavoine, Adelmo Damerini) (Milan, 1936)

PIZZETTI, Ildebrando: *Bellini: Studi di vari autori a cura di IP* (Milan, 1940)

POLICASTRO, Guglielmo: *Vincenzo Bellini (1801-19)* (Catania, 1935)

PORTER, Andrew: "*Norma*" *Opera on Record* (London, 1979)

POUGIN, Arthur: *Bellini: Sa Vie, ses oeuvres* (Paris, 1868)

PUGLIATTI, Salvatore: *Chopin e Bellini* (Messina, 1952)

REINA, Calcedonio: *Il Cigno Catanese: Bellini – La Vita e le Opere* (Catania, 1935)

RINALDI, Mario: *Felice Romani: Dal melodramma classico al melodramma romantico* (Rome, 1965)

ROSSELLI, John: *The life of Bellini* (Cambridge, 1996)

SAUSSINE, H De: "L'harmonie bellinienne" *Rivista musicale Italiana* xxvii (1920)

SCAGLIONE, N: *Vincenzo Bellini a Messina* (Messina, 1934)

SCHERILLO, Michele: *Vincenzo Bellini: Note aneddotiche e critiche* (Ancona, 1882)

SCHERILLO, Michele: *Belliniana: Nuove Note* (Milan, 1885)

SCHLITZER, Franco: *Cimelli Belliniani* (Sienna, 1952)

SCHLITZER, Franco: "Vincenzo Bellini" *Mondo teatrale dell'ottocento* (Naples, 1954)

SOUBIES, Albert: *Le Théâtre-Italien de 1801 à 1913* (Paris, 1913)

STENDHAL (Henri Beyle): *Life of Rossini*, translated by Richard N Coe (London, 1956)

TIBY, Ottavio: *Vincenzo Bellini* (Turin, 1938)

TIBY, Ottavio: *Il Real Teatro Carolino e L'Ottocento musicale Palermitano* (Florence, 1957)

WALKER, Frank: "Amore e amori nelle lettere di Giuditta, Bellini e Florimo" *La Scala*, No.112, p13, (1959); English translation as "Giuditta Turina and Bellini", *Music and Letters*, ML, xl, p19, (1959)

WEINSTOCK, H: *Vincenzo Bellini: his Life and his Operas* (New York, 1971)

Picture Acknowledgements

Museo Civico Belliniano, Catania: 1, 2, 4, 9, 10, 72, 74

Museo Teatrale alla Scala (and Biblioteca Livia Simoni): 3, 8, 11-16, 18-23, 39, 40, 42-46, 52-58, 67, 68, 70

Teatro alla Scala/Erio Piccagliani: 24-32, 41, 48-51, 59-61, 65, 66

Museo Correr, Venice: 36-38, 62-64

Courtesy Conservatorio di Musica, Naples: Frontispiece, 6, 73

Courtesy Teatro Carlo Felice, Genoa: 17

Courtesy Biblioteca Comunale, Palermo: 5

Collection Dr R L Copeman: 7

Victoria and Albert Theatre Museum: 47

Courtesy Teatro Massimo, Palermo: 33

Courtesy Teatro Massimo Bellini, Catania/Consoli: 34, 35

Courtesy Teatro Comunale, Florence/Locchi: 71

Teatro La Fenice, Venice/Giacomelli: 69

Index